BY CORNELIUS RYAN

THE LAST BATTLE—1966
THE LONGEST DAY—1959

Cornelius Ryan

THE LAST BATTLE

A TOUCHSTONE BOOK
Published by Simon & Schuster
New York   London   Toronto   Sydney   Tokyo   Singapore

TOUCHSTONE
Rockefeller Center
1230 Avenue of the Americas
New York, NY 10020

First Touchstone Edition 1995

TOUCHSTONE and colophon are registered trademarks
of Simon & Schuster Inc.

Manufactured in the United States of America

1   3   5   7   9   10   8   6   4   2

Library of Congress Catalog Card Number: 65-18654
ISBN 0-684-80329-1

THIS BOOK IS FOR THE MEMORY OF A BOY
WHO WAS BORN IN BERLIN DURING THE
LAST MONTHS OF THE WAR. HIS NAME
WAS PETER FECHTER. IN 1962 HE WAS
MACHINE-GUNNED BY HIS OWN PEOPLE
AND LEFT TO BLEED TO DEATH BY THE
SIDE OF THE MOST TRAGIC MEMORIAL TO
THE ALLIED VICTORY—THE BERLIN WALL.

CONTENTS

❖

"Of the events of war, I have not ventured to speak from any chance information, nor according to any notion of my own; I have described nothing but what I saw myself, or learned from others of whom I made the most careful and particular inquiry. The task was a laborious one because eyewitnesses of the same occurrence gave different accounts of them as they remembered, or were interested in the actions of one side or the other. And very likely the strictly historical character of my narrative may be disappointing to the ear. But if he who desires to have before his eyes a true picture of the events which have happened . . . shall pronounce what I have written to be useful, then I shall be satisfied."

—THUCYDIDES, *Peloponnesian War*, Volume 1, 400 B.C.

FOREWORD

A-Day, Monday, April 16, 1945

The battle for Berlin, the last offensive against Hitler's Third Reich, began at precisely 4 A.M., Monday, April 16, 1945—or A-Day as it was called by the Western Allies. At that moment, less than thirty-eight miles east of the capital, red flares burst in the night skies above the swollen river Oder, triggering a stupefying artillery barrage and the opening of the Russian assault on the city.

At about that same time, elements of the U.S. Ninth Army were turning away from Berlin—heading back to the west to take up new positions along the river Elbe between Tangermünde and Barby. On April 14 General Eisenhower had decided to halt the Anglo-American drive across Germany. "Berlin," he said, "is no longer a military objective." When U.S. troops got the word, Berlin, for some of them, was only forty-five miles away.

As the attack began, Berliners waited in the bombed rubble of their city, numb and terrified, clinging to the only politics that now counted—the politics of survival. To eat had become more important than to love, to burrow more dignified than to fight, to endure more militarily correct than to win.

What follows is the story of the last battle—the assault and capture of Berlin. Although this book includes accounts of the fighting, it is not a military report. Rather, it is the story of ordinary people, both soldiers and civilians, who were caught up in the despair, frustration, terror and rape of the defeat and the victory.

Part One

THE CITY

<h1 style="text-align:center">✤ 1 ✤</h1>

IN THE NORTHERN LATITUDES the dawn comes early. Even as the bombers were turning away from the city, the first rays of light were coming up in the east. In the stillness of the morning, great pillars of black smoke towered over the districts of Pankow, Weissensee and Lichtenberg. On the low clouds it was difficult to separate the soft glow of daylight from the reflections of the fires that blazed in bomb-battered Berlin.

As the smoke drifted slowly across the ruins, Germany's most bombed city stood out in stark, macabre splendor. It was blackened by soot, pockmarked by thousands of craters and laced by the twisted girders of ruined buildings. Whole blocks of apartment houses were gone, and in the very heart of the capital entire neighborhoods had vanished. In these wastelands what had once been broad roads and streets were now pitted trails that snaked through mountains of rubble. Everywhere, covering acre after acre, gutted, windowless, roofless buildings gaped up at the sky.

In the aftermath of the raid, a fine residue of soot and ash rained down, powdering the wreckage, and in the great canyons of smashed brick and tortured steel nothing moved but the eddying dust. It swirled along the broad expanse of the Unter den Linden, the famous trees bare now, the leaf buds seared on the branches. Few of the banks, libraries and elegant shops lining the renowned boulevard were undamaged. But at the western end of the avenue, Berlin's most famous landmark, the eight-story-high Brandenburg Gate, though gashed and chipped, still straddled the *via triumphalis* on its twelve massive Doric columns.

On the nearby Wilhelmstrasse, lined by government buildings and former palaces, shards of glass from thousands of windows glittered in the debris. At No. 73, the beautiful little palace that had been the official residence of German presidents in the days before the Third Reich had been gutted by a raging fire. Once it had been described as a miniature Versailles; now sea nymphs from the ornate fountain in the forecourt lay shattered against the colonnaded front entrance, and along the roof line, chipped and gouged by flying fragments, the twin statues of Rhine maidens leaned headless over the littered courtyard.

A block away, No. 77 was scarred but intact. Piles of rubble lay all around the three-story, L-shaped building. Its yellowish-brown exterior was scabrous, and the garish golden eagles above each entrance, garlanded swastikas in their claws, were pitted and deeply scored. Jutting out above was the imposing balcony from which the world had been harangued with many a frenzied speech. The Reichskanzlei, Chancellery of Adolf Hitler, still remained.

At the top of the battered Kurfürstendamm, Berlin's Fifth Avenue, bulked the deformed skeleton of the once fashionable Kaiser-Wilhelm Memorial Church. The hands on the charred clock face were stopped at exactly 7:30; they had been that way since 1943 when bombs wiped out one thousand acres of the city on a single November evening.

One hundred yards away was the jungle of wreckage that had been the internationally famed Berlin Zoo. The aquarium was completely destroyed. The reptile, hippopotamus, kangaroo, tiger and elephant houses, along with scores of other buildings, were severely damaged. The surrounding Tiergarten, the renowned 630-acre park, was a no man's land of room-sized craters, rubble-filled lakes and partly demolished embassy buildings. Once the park had been a natural forest of luxuriant trees. Now most of them were burned and ugly stumps.

14

In the northeast corner of the Tiergarten stood Berlin's most spectacular ruin, destroyed not by Allied bombs but by German politics. The huge Reichstag, seat of parliament, had been deliberately set ablaze by the Nazis in 1933—and the fire had been blamed on the Communists, thus providing Hitler with an excuse to seize full dictatorial power. On the crumbling portico above its six-columned entrance, overlooking the sea of wreckage that almost engulfed the building, were the chiseled, blackened words, "DEM DEUTSCHEN VOLKE"—To the German People.

A complex of statuary had once stood before the Reichstag. All had been destroyed except one piece—a 200-foot-high, dark red granite-and-bronze column on a massive colonnaded base. After the 1933 burning Hitler had ordered it moved. Now it stood a mile away on the Charlottenburger Chaussée, close to the center of the East-West Axis—the series of linked highways running across the city roughly from the river Havel on the west to the end of the Unter den Linden on the east. As the sun rose on this March morning its rays caught the golden figure at the top of the column: a winged statue bearing a laurel wreath in one hand, a standard adorned with the Iron Cross in the other. Rising up out of the wasteland, untouched by the bombing, was Berlin's slender, graceful memorial—the Victory Column.

Across the tormented city sirens began wailing the All Clear. The 314th Allied raid on Berlin was over. In the first years of the war the attacks had been sporadic, but now the capital was under almost continuous bombardment—the Americans bombed by day, the R.A.F. by night. The statistics of destruction had increased almost hourly; by now they were staggering. Explosives had laid waste more than ten square miles of built-up districts—ten times the area destroyed in London by the Luftwaffe. Three billion cubic feet of debris lay in the streets—enough rubble for a mountain more than a thousand feet high. Almost half of Berlin's

1,562,000 dwellings had sustained some kind of damage, and every third house was either completely destroyed or uninhabitable. Casualties were so high that a true accounting would never be possible, but at least 52,000 were dead and twice that number seriously injured—five times the number killed and seriously injured in the bombing of London. Berlin had become a second Carthage—and the final agony was still to come.

In this wilderness of devastation it was remarkable that people could survive at all—but life went on with a kind of lunatic normality amid the ruins. Twelve thousand policemen were still on duty. Postmen delivered the mail; newspapers came out daily; telephone and telegraphic services continued. Garbage was collected. Some cinemas, theaters and even a part of the wrecked zoo were open. The Berlin Philharmonic was finishing its season. Department stores ran special sales. Food and bakery shops opened each morning, and laundries, dry-cleaning establishments and beauty salons did a brisk business. The underground and elevated railways functioned; the few fashionable bars and restaurants still intact drew capacity crowds. And on almost every street the strident calls of Berlin's famous flower vendors echoed as in the days of peace.

Perhaps most remarkable, more than 65 per cent of Berlin's great factories were in some kind of working condition. Almost 600,000 people had jobs—but getting to them now was a major problem. It often took hours. Traffic was clogged, there were detours, slowdowns and breakdowns. As a consequence, Berliners had taken to rising early. Everyone wanted to get to work on time because the Americans, early risers themselves, were often at work over the city by 9 A.M.

On this bright morning in the city's sprawling twenty districts, Berliners came forth like neolithic cave dwellers. They emerged from the bowels of subways, from shelters beneath public buildings, from the cellars and basements of their shattered homes. Whatever their hopes or fears, whatever their loyalties or political beliefs, this much Berliners had in common: those who had survived another night were determined to live another day.

The same could be said for the nation itself. In this sixth year of World War II, Hitler's Germany was fighting desperately for survival. The Reich that was to last a millennium had been invaded from west and east. The Anglo-American forces were sweeping down on the great river Rhine, had breached it at Remagen, and were racing for Berlin. They were only three hundred miles to the west. On the eastern banks of the Oder a far more urgent, and infinitely more fearful, threat had materialized. There stood the Russian armies, less than fifty miles away.

It was Wednesday, March 21, 1945—the first day of spring. On radios all over the city this morning, Berliners heard the latest hit tune: "This Will Be a Spring Without End."

✤ 2 ✤

To THE DANGERS that threatened them, Berliners reacted each in his own way. Some stubbornly disregarded the peril, hoping it would go away. Some courted it. Others reacted with anger or fear—and some, with the grim logic of those whose backs are to the wall, prepared bravely to meet their fate head on.

In the southwestern district of Zehlendorf, milkman Richard Poganowska was, as usual, up with the dawn. In years past his daily routine had often seemed monotonous. Now he was grateful for it. He worked for the 300-year-old Domäne Dahlem farm in Zehlendorf's fashionable suburb of Dahlem, only a few miles from the center of the huge capital. In any other city the dairy's location would have been considered an oddity, but not in Berlin. One fifth of the city's total area lay in parks and woodlands, along lakes, canals and streams. Still, Poganowska, like many other Domäne employees, wished the farm were somewhere else—far outside the city, away from the danger and the constant bombing.

Poganowska, his wife Lisbeth and their three children had spent the night once again in the cellar of the main building on the Königin-Luise Strasse. Sleep had been almost impossible because of the hammering of anti-aircraft guns and the bursting of bombs. Like everyone else in Berlin, the big 39-year-old milkman was constantly tired these days.

He had no idea where bombs had dropped during the night, but he knew none had fallen near the Domäne's big cow barns. The precious milk herd was safe. Nothing seemed to bother those two hundred cows. Amid the explosion of bombs and the thunder of anti-aircraft fire, they stood patiently, placidly chewing their cuds, and in some miraculous way they continued to produce milk. It never ceased to amaze Poganowska.

Sleepily, he loaded the ancient brown milk wagon and its trailer, hitched up his two horses, the fox-colored Lisa and Hans, and, with his gray spitz dog Poldi on the seat beside him, set out on his rounds. Rattling across the courtyard cobblestones he turned right on Pacelli Allee and headed north in the direction of Schmargendorf. It was 6 A.M. It would be nine at night before he finished.

Worn out, aching for sleep, Poganowska still had not lost his cheerfully gruff manner. He had become a kind of morale-builder for his 1,200 customers. His route lay on the fringes of three major districts: Zehlendorf, Schöneberg and Wilmersdorf. All three had been badly bombed; Schöneberg and Wilmersdorf, lying closest to the center of the city, were almost obliterated. In Wilmersdorf alone, more than 36,000 dwellings were destroyed, and almost half of the 340,000 people in the two districts had been left homeless. Under the circumstances, a cheerful face was a rare and welcome sight.

Even at this early hour, Poganowska found people waiting for him at each intersection. There were queues everywhere these days—for the butcher, the baker, even for water when the mains were hit. Despite the lines of customers, Poganowska rang a large cowbell, announcing his arrival. He had begun the practice early in the year when the increase in daylight raids made it impossible for him to deliver door-to-door. To his customers the bell, like Poganowska himself, had become something of a symbol.

This morning was no different. Poganowska greeted his customers and doled out their rationed quantities of milk and dairy products. He had been acquainted with some of these people for nearly a decade and they knew he could be counted on for a little extra now and then. By juggling the ration cards, Poganowska could usually produce a little more milk or cream for special occasions like christenings or weddings. To be sure, it was illegal and therefore risky—but all Berliners had to face risks these days.

More and more, Poganowska's customers seemed tired, tense and preoccupied. Few people talked about the war any more. Nobody knew what was going on, and nobody could have done anything about it in any case. Besides, there were enough armchair generals. Poganowska did not invite discussions of the news. By submerging himself in his fifteen-hour daily routine and refusing to think about the war, he, like thousands of other Berliners, had almost immunized himself against it.

Each day now Poganowska watched for certain signs that helped keep him from losing heart. For one thing the roads were still open. There were no roadblocks or tank traps on the main streets, no artillery pieces or dug-in tanks, no soldiers manning key positions. There was nothing to indicate that the authorities feared a Russian attack, or that Berlin was threatened with siege.

There was one other small but significant clue. Every morning as Poganowska drove through the sub-district of Friedenau, where some of his more prominent customers lived, he glanced at the home of a well-known Nazi, an important official in the Berlin postal department. Through the open living-room windows he could see the big portrait in its massive frame. The garish painting of Adolf Hitler, features boldly arrogant, was still there. Poganowska knew the ways of the Third Reich's bureaucrats; if the situation were really critical, that shrine to the Führer would have disappeared by now.

He clucked softly to the horses and continued on his route. Despite everything he could see no real reason to be unduly alarmed.

No part of the city had been completely spared from the bombing, but Spandau, Berlin's second largest and most western district had escaped the kind of attack everyone feared most: saturation bombing. Night after night the inhabitants expected the blow. They were amazed that it had not come, for Spandau was the center of Berlin's vast armament industry.

In contrast to districts in the very heart of the city that had suffered 50 to 75 per cent destruction, Spandau had lost only 10 per cent of its buildings. Although this meant that more than one thousand houses were either destroyed or unusable, by the standards of raid-toughened Berliners that was a mere flea bite. A caustic remark was current in the bomb-blackened wastelands of the central districts: *"Die Spandauer Zwerge kommen zuletzt in die Särge,"*—The little Spandauites are last to reach their coffins.

On Spandau's westernmost fringe, in the quiet, pastoral subdistrict of Staaken, Robert and Ingeborg Kolb were more than grateful to live in a kind of backwater. The only bombs that had fallen even close were those that missed the nearby airfield—and the damage was slight. Their two-story orange and brown stucco home, with its glass-enclosed veranda and its surrounding lawn and garden, remained unharmed. Life went on almost normally —except that Robert, the 54-year-old technical director of a printing plant, was finding the daily trip to his job in the city's center increasingly arduous. It meant running the gamut of the daylight raids. It was a constant worry to Ingeborg.

This evening the Kolbs planned, as usual, to listen to the German-language broadcasts of the BBC, although it was a practice long forbidden. Step by step they had followed the Allied advances from east and west. Now the Red Army was only a bus ride from the city's eastern outskirts. Yet, lulled by the rural atmosphere of their surroundings, they found the imminent threat to the city unthinkable, the war remote and unreal. Robert Kolb was convinced they were quite safe and Ingeborg was convinced that Robert was always right. After all, he was a veteran of World War I. "The war," Robert had assured her, "will pass us by."

Quite certain that no matter what happened they would not be involved, the Kolbs calmly looked to the future. Now that spring was here, Robert was trying to decide where to hang the hammocks in the garden. Ingeborg had chores of her own to do: she planned to plant spinach, parsley, lettuce and early potatoes. There was one major problem: should she sow the early potatoes in the first part of April or wait until the more settled spring days of May?

* * *

At his headquarters in a gray stucco, three-story house on the outskirts of Landsberg, twenty-five miles from the Oder, Marshal of the Soviet Union Georgi K. Zhukov sat at his desk pondering some plans of his own. On one wall, a large map of Berlin showed in detail Zhukov's proposed offensive to capture the city. On his desk were three field phones. One was for general use; another linked him to his colleagues: Marshals Konstantin Rokossovskii and Ivan Stepanovich Koniev, commanders of the huge army groups on his northern and southern flanks. The third phone was a direct line to Moscow and the Supreme Commander, Josef Stalin. The barrel-chested 49-year-old commander of the First Belorussian Front spoke to Stalin each night at eleven, reporting the day's advances. Now Zhukov wondered how soon Stalin would give the command to take Berlin. He hoped he still had some time. At a pinch Zhukov thought he could take the city immediately, but he was not quite ready. Tentatively, he had planned the attack for around the end of April. With luck, he thought he could reach Berlin and reduce all resistance within ten or twelve days. The Germans would contest him for every inch—that he expected. Probably they would fight hardest on the western edge of the city. There, as far as he could see, lay the only clear-cut escape route for the German defenders. But he planned to hit them from both sides as they tried to get out. By the first week of May he anticipated wholesale slaughter in the district of Spandau.

* * *

In his second-floor Wilmersdorf apartment, Carl Johann Wiberg pushed open the shuttered French windows of his living room, stepped out onto the little balcony and took stock of the weather. With him were his constant companions, Uncle Otto and Aunt Effie, two waddling, liver-colored dachshunds. They looked up at him expectantly, waiting for their morning walk.

Walking was about all Wiberg did to pass the time these days. Everyone in the neighborhood liked the 49-year-old Swedish businessman. They considered him a "good Berliner" first, a Swede second: he had not left the city like so many other foreigners when the bombing began. Moreover, although Wiberg never complained about his troubles, his neighbors knew that he had lost almost everything. His wife had died in 1939. His glue factories had been bombed out of business. After thirty years as a small businessman in Berlin, he had little left now but his dogs and the apartment. In the opinion of some of his neighbors he was a better man than many a true German.

Wiberg looked down at Uncle Otto and Aunt Effie. "Time to go out," he said. He closed the windows and walked across the living room to the little foyer. He put on his beautifully tailored Chesterfield and settled his carefully brushed Homburg on his head. Opening the drawer of a polished mahogany hall table, he took out a pair of suede gloves and for a moment stood looking at a framed lithograph lying inside the drawer.

The print, sketched in flamboyant colors, showed a fully armored knight mounted on a rampaging white stallion. Attached to the knight's lance was a streaming banner. Through the helmet's open visor the knight gazed fiercely out. A lock of hair fell over his forehead; he had piercing eyes and a small black moustache. Across the waving banner were the words, *"Der Bannerträger"*— The Standard Bearer.

Wiberg slowly closed the drawer. He kept the lithograph hidden because the derisive lampoon of Hitler was banned throughout Germany. But Wiberg did not want to get rid of it; the caricature was too amusing to throw away.

Snapping leashes on the dogs, he locked the front door carefully behind him, and went down the two flights of stairs and into the rubble of the street. Near the apartment house he doffed his hat to some neighbors and, with the dogs leading, made his way down the street, stepping carefully around the potholes. He wondered where *Der Bannerträger* was now that the end seemed near. In Munich? At his Eagle's Nest in the mountains at Berchtesgaden? Or, here, in Berlin? No one seemed to know—although that was not surprising. Hitler's whereabouts was always a big secret.

This morning Wiberg decided to drop in at his favorite bar, Harry Rosse's at 7 Nestorstrasse—one of the few left open in the district. It had a varied clientele: Nazi bigwigs, German officers, and a smattering of businessmen. There was always good conversation and one could catch up on the latest news—where last night's bombs had fallen, which factories had been hit, how Berlin was standing up under it all. Wiberg liked meeting his old friends in this convivial atmosphere and he was interested in just about every aspect of the war, especially the effects of the bombings and the morale of the German people. In particular he wanted to know where Hitler was. As he crossed the street he once again tipped his hat to an old acquaintance. Despite all the questions that crowded his mind, Wiberg knew a few things that would have surprised his neighbors. For this Swede who was more German than the Germans was also a member of America's top-secret Office of Strategic Services. He was an Allied spy.

In his ground-floor apartment in Kreuzberg, Dr. Arthur Leckscheidt, Evangelical pastor of the Melanchthon Church, was beset
by grief and despair. His twin-spired Gothic church was destroyed
and his flock dissipated. Through the windows he could see the remains of his church. A few weeks before it had received a direct
hit and, minutes later, incendiaries had set it ablaze. The sorrow
he felt each time he looked at it had not yet abated. At the height
of the raid, oblivious of his own safety, Pastor Leckscheidt had
rushed into the blazing church. The back of the edifice and its
magnificent organ were still intact. Running swiftly up the narrow
steps to the organ loft, Leckscheidt had but one thought: to bid
farewell to his beloved organ and to the church. Singing softly to
himself, eyes filled with tears, Dr. Leckscheidt played his farewell.
As bombs burst all over Kreuzberg, incredulous patients in the
nearby Urban Hospital and people sheltering in adjacent cellars
heard the Melanchthon organ pealing out the ancient hymn,
"From Deepest Need I Cry to Thee."

Now he was saying a different kind of good-bye. On his desk
was the draft of a round-robin letter he would send to those many
parishioners who had left the city or were in the armed forces.
"Even though fighting in the east and west is keeping us in tension," he wrote, "the German capital is constantly the center of air
raids . . . you can imagine, dear friends, that death is reaping a
rich harvest. Coffins have become a scarcity. A woman told me
that she had offered twenty pounds of honey for one in which to
lay her deceased husband."

Dr. Leckscheidt was also angered. "We ministers are not always
called to burials of air raid victims," he wrote. "Often the Party
takes over the funerals without a minister . . . without God's
word." And again and again throughout his letter, he referred to
the devastation of the city. "You cannot imagine what Berlin looks
like now. The loveliest buildings have crumbled into ruins. . . .

Often we have no gas, light or water. God keep us from a famine! Terrific prices are asked for black-market commodities." And he ended on a note of bitter pessimism: "This is probably the last letter for a long time. Perhaps we shall soon be cut off from all communication. Shall we see each other again? It all rests in God's hands."

Cycling purposefully through the littered streets of Dahlem, another clergyman, Father Bernhard Happich, had decided to take matters into his own hands. A delicate problem had worried him for weeks. Night after night he had prayed for guidance and meditated on the course he should take. Now he had reached a decision.

The services of all clergymen were in great demand, but this was particularly true of Father Happich. The 55-year-old priest, who carried the words "Jesuit: not fit for military service" stamped across his identity card (a Nazi imprint like that reserved for Jews and other dangerous undesirables), was also a highly skilled doctor of medicine. Among his many other duties he was the Father Provincial of Haus Dahlem, the orphanage, maternity hospital and foundling home run by the Mission Sisters of the Sacred Heart. It was Mother Superior Cunegundes and her flock who had brought about his problem, and his decision.

Father Happich had no illusions about the Nazis or how the war must surely end. He had long ago decided that Hitler and his brutal new order were destined for disaster. Now the crisis was fast approaching. Berlin was trapped—the tarnished chalice in the conqueror's eye. What would happen to Haus Dahlem and its good, but less than worldly, Sisters?

His face serious, Father Happich pulled up outside the home. The building had suffered only superficial damage and the Sisters were convinced that their prayers were being heard. Father Happich did not disagree with them, but being a practical man he thought that luck and bad marksmanship might have had something to do with it.

As he passed through the entrance hall he looked up at the great statue, garbed in blue and gold, sword held high—Saint Michael, "God's fighting knight against all evil." The Sisters' faith in Saint Michael was well founded, but just the same Father Happich was glad he had made his decision. Like everyone else he had heard from refugees who had fled before the advancing Russians of the horrors that had taken place in eastern Germany. Many of the accounts were exaggerated, he was sure, but some he knew to be true. Father Happich had decided to warn the Sisters. Now he had to choose the right moment to tell them, and above all he had to find the right words. Father Happich worried about that. How do you tell sixty nuns and lay sisters that they are in danger of being raped?

✣ 3 ✣

THE FEAR OF SEXUAL ATTACK lay over the city like a pall, for Berlin, after nearly six years of war, was now primarily a city of women.

At the beginning, in 1939, there were 4,321,000 inhabitants of the capital. But huge war casualties, the call-up of both men and women and the voluntary evacuation of one million citizens to the safer countryside in 1943-44 had cut that figure by more than one third. By now the only males left in any appreciable number were children under eighteen and men over sixty. The 18-to-30 male age group totaled barely 100,000 and most of them were exempt from military service or wounded. In January, 1945, the city's population had been estimated at 2,900,000 but now, in mid-March, that figure was certainly too high. After eighty-five raids in less than eleven weeks and with the threat of siege hanging over the city, thousands more had fled. Military authorities estimated that Berlin's civil population was now about 2,700,000, of whom more than 2,000,000 were women—and even that was only an informed guess.

Complicating efforts to obtain a true population figure was the vast exodus of refugees from the Soviet-occupied eastern provinces. Some put the refugee figure as high as 500,000. Uprooted, carrying their belongings on their backs or in horse-drawn wagons or pushcarts, often driving farm animals before them, fleeing civilians had clogged the roads into Berlin for months. Most did not remain in the city, but continued west. But in their wake they left a repository of nightmarish stories; these accounts of their experiences had spread like an epidemic through Berlin, infecting many citizens with terror.

The refugees told of a vengeful, violent and rapacious conqueror. People who had trekked from as far away as Poland, or from the captured parts of East Prussia, Pomerania and Silesia, gave bitter testimony of an enemy who offered no quarter. In fact, the refugees declared, Russian propaganda was urging the Red Army to spare no one. They told of a manifesto, said to have been written by the Soviet Union's top propagandist, Ilya Ehrenburg, which was both broadcast and distributed in leaflet form to the Red troops. "Kill! Kill!" went the manifesto. "In the German race there is nothing but evil! . . . Follow the precepts of Comrade Stalin. Stamp out the fascist beast once and for all in its lair! Use force and break the racial pride of these Germanic women. Take them as your lawful booty. Kill! As you storm onward, kill! You gallant soldiers of the Red Army." *

* I have not seen the Ehrenburg leaflet. But many of those I interviewed did. Furthermore, it is mentioned repeatedly in official German papers, war diaries and in numerous histories, the most complete version appearing in Admiral Doenitz' *Memoirs*, page 179. That the leaflet existed I have no doubt. But I question the above version, for German translations from Russian were notoriously inaccu-

The refugees reported that advancing front-line troops were well disciplined and well behaved, but that the secondary units that followed were a disorganized rabble. In wild, drunken orgies these Red Army men had murdered, looted and raped. Many Russian commanders, the refugees claimed, appeared to condone the actions of their men. At least they made no effort to stop them. From peasants to gentry the accounts were the same, and everywhere in the flood of refugees there were women who told chilling stories of brutal assault—of being forced at gunpoint to strip and then submit to repeated rapings.

How much was fantasy, how much fact? Berliners were not sure. Those who knew of the atrocities and mass murders committed by German SS troops in Russia—and there were thousands who knew—feared that the stories were true. Those who were aware of what was happening to the Jews in concentration camps —a new and horrible aspect of National Socialism of which the free world was yet to learn—believed the refugees, too. These more knowledgeable Berliners could well believe that the oppressor was becoming the oppressed, that the wheel of retribution was swinging full circle. Many who knew the extent of the horrors perpetrated by the Third Reich were taking no chances. Highly placed bureaucrats and top-ranking Nazi officials had quietly

---

rate. Still Ehrenburg wrote other pamphlets which were as bad, as anyone can see from his writings, particularly those officially published in English during the war by the Soviets themselves, in *Soviet War News*, 1941-45, Vols. 1-8. His "Kill the Germans" theme was repeated over and over—and apparently with the full approval of Stalin. On April 14, 1945, in an unprecedented editorial in the Soviet military newspaper *Red Star*, he was officially reprimanded by the propaganda chief, Alexandrov, who wrote: "Comrade Ehrenburg is exaggerating . . . we are not fighting against the German people, only against the Hitlers of the world." The reproof would have been disastrous for any other Soviet writer, but not for Ehrenburg. He continued his "Kill the Germans" propaganda as though nothing had happened—and Stalin closed his eyes to it. In the fifth volume of his memoirs, *People, Years and Life*, published in Moscow, 1963, Ehrenburg has conveniently forgotten what he wrote during the war. On page 126 he writes: "In scores of essays I emphasized that we must not, indeed we cannot, hunt down the people —that we are, after all, Soviet people and not Fascists." But this much has to be said: no matter what Ehrenburg wrote, it was no worse than what was being issued by the Nazi propaganda chief, Goebbels—a fact that many Germans have conveniently forgotten, too.

moved their families out of Berlin or were in the process of doing so.

Fanatics still remained, and the average Berliners, less privy to information and ignorant of the true situation, were also staying. They could not or would not leave. "Oh Germany, Germany, my Fatherland," wrote Erna Saenger, a 65-year-old housewife and mother of six children, in her diary, "Trust brings disappointment. To believe faithfully means to be stupid and blind . . . but . . . we'll stay in Berlin. If everyone left like the neighbors the enemy would have what he wants. No—we don't want that kind of defeat."

Yet few Berliners could claim to be unaware of the nature of the danger. Almost everyone had heard the stories. One couple, Hugo and Edith Neumann, living in Kreuzberg, actually had been informed by telephone. Some relatives living in the Russian-occupied zone had risked their lives, shortly before all communications ceased, to warn the Neumanns that the conquerors were raping, killing and looting without restraint. Yet the Neumanns stayed. Hugo's electrical business had been bombed, but to abandon it now was unthinkable.

Others chose to dismiss the stories because propaganda, whether spread by refugees or inspired by the government, had little or no meaning for them any longer. From the moment Hitler ordered the unprovoked invasion of Russia in 1941, all Germans had been subjected to a relentless barrage of hate propaganda. The Soviet people were painted as uncivilized and subhuman. When the tide turned and German troops were forced back on all fronts in Russia, Dr. Joseph Goebbels, the Reich's club-footed propaganda chief, intensified his efforts—particularly in Berlin.

Goebbels' assistant, Dr. Werner Naumann, privately admitted that "our propaganda as to what the Russians are like, as to what the population can expect from them in Berlin, has been so successful that we have reduced the Berliners to a state of sheer terror." By the end of 1944 Naumann felt that "we have overdone it—our propaganda has ricocheted against us."

Now the tone of the propaganda had changed. As Hitler's empire was sheared off piece by piece, as Berlin was demolished, block by block, Goebbels had begun to switch from terror-mongering to reassurance; now the people were told that victory was just around the corner. About all Goebbels succeeded in doing was to generate among cosmopolitan Berliners a grotesque, macabre kind of humor. It took the form of a large, collective raspberry which the population derisively directed at themselves, their leaders and the world. Berliners quickly changed Goebbels' motto, "The Führer Commands, We Follow," to "The Führer Commands, We Bear What Follows." As for the propaganda chief's promises of ultimate victory, the irreverent solemnly urged all to "Enjoy the war, the peace will be terrible."

In the atmosphere of near-panic created by the refugees' reports, facts and reason became distorted as rumor took over. All sorts of atrocity stories spread throughout the city. Russians were described as slant-eyed Mongols who butchered women and children on sight. Clergymen were said to have been burned to death with flamethrowers; the stories told of nuns raped and then forced to walk naked through the streets; of how women were made camp followers and all males marched off to servitude in Siberia. There was even a radio report that the Russians had nailed victims' tongues to tables. The less impressionable found the tales too fantastic to believe.

Others were grimly aware of what was to come. In her private clinic in Schöneberg, Dr. Anne-Marie Durand-Wever, a graduate of the University of Chicago and one of Europe's most famous gynecologists, knew the truth. The 55-year-old doctor, well known for her anti-Nazi views (she was the author of many books championing women's rights, equality of the sexes and birth control—all banned by the Nazis), was urging her patients to leave Berlin. She had examined numerous refugee women and had reached the conclusion that, if anything, the accounts of assault understated the facts.

Dr. Durand-Wever intended to remain in Berlin herself but

now she carried a small, fast-acting cyanide capsule everywhere she went. After all her years as a doctor, she was not sure that she would be able to commit suicide. But she kept the pill in her bag —for if the Russians took Berlin she thought that every female from eight to eighty could expect to be raped.

Dr. Margot Sauerbruch also expected the worst. She worked with her husband, Professor Ferdinand Sauerbruch, Germany's most eminent surgeon, in Berlin's oldest and largest hospital, the Charité, in the Mitte district. Because of its size and location close by the main railway station, the hospital had received the worst of the refugee cases. From her examination of the victims, Dr. Sauerbruch had no illusions about the ferocity of the Red Army when it ran amok. The rapes, she knew for certain, were not propaganda.

Margot Sauerbruch was appalled by the number of refugees who had attempted suicide—including scores of women who had not been molested or violated. Terrified by what they had witnessed or heard, many had slashed their wrists. Some had even tried to kill their children. How many had actually succeeded in ending their lives nobody knew—Dr. Sauerbruch saw only those who had failed—but it seemed clear that a wave of suicides would take place in Berlin if the Russians captured the city.

Most other doctors apparently concurred with this view. In Wilmersdorf, Surgeon Günther Lamprecht noted in his diary that "the major topic—even among doctors—is the technique of suicide. Conversations of this sort have become unbearable."

It was much more than mere conversation. The death plans were already under way. In every district, doctors were besieged by patients and friends seeking information about speedy suicide and begging for poison prescriptions. When physicians refused to help, people turned to their druggists. Caught up in a wave of fear, distraught Berliners by the thousands had decided to die by any means rather than submit to the Red Army.

"The first pair of Russian boots I see, I'm going to commit suicide," 20-year-old Christa Meunier confided to her friend, Juliane

31

Bochnik. Christa had already secured poison. So had Juliane's friend Rosie Hoffman and her parents. The Hoffmans were utterly despondent and expected no mercy from the Russians. Although Juliane did not know it at the time, the Hoffmans were related to Reichsführer Heinrich Himmler, head of the Gestapo and the SS, the man responsible for the mass murder of millions in the concentration camps.

Poison—particularly cyanide—was the preferred method of self-destruction. One type of capsule, known as a "KCB" pill, was in especially great demand. This concentrated hydrocyanic compound was so powerful that death was almost instantaneous— even the fumes could kill. With Germanic forethought some government agency had laid down vast quantities of it in Berlin.

Nazi officials, senior officers, government department heads and even lesser functionaries were able to get supplies of poison for themselves, their families and friends with little difficulty. Doctors, druggists, dentists and laboratory workers also had access to pills or capsules. Some even improved on the tablets' potency. Dr. Rudolf Hückel, professor of pathology at the University of Berlin and the best-known cancer pathologist in the city, had added acetic acid to cyanide capsules for himself and his wife. If they needed them, he assured her, the acetic acid would make the poison work even faster.

Some Berliners, unable to get the quick-acting cyanide, were hoarding barbiturates or cyanide derivatives. Comedian Heinz Rühmann, often called the "Danny Kaye of Germany," was so fearful of the future for his beautiful actress wife Hertha Feiler and their young son that he had hidden a can of rat poison in a flowerpot, just in case. The former Nazi ambassador to Spain, retired Lieutenant General Wilhelm Faupel, planned to poison himself and his wife with an overdose of medicine. The General had a weak heart. When he suffered attacks he took a stimulant containing digitalis. Faupel knew that an overdose would cause cardiac arrest and end matters quickly. He had even saved enough for some of his friends.

For others a fast bullet seemed the best and bravest end. But an astonishing number of women, mostly middle-aged, had chosen the bloodiest way of all—the razor. In the Ketzler family in Charlottenburg, Gertrud, forty-two, normally a cheerful woman, now carried a razor blade in her purse—as did her sister and mother-in-law. Gertrud's friend, Inge Rühling, had a razor blade too, and the two women anxiously discussed which was the most effective way to ensure death—a slash across the wrists or a lengthwise slit up the arteries.

There was always the chance that such drastic measures might not have to be taken. For most Berliners there still remained one last hope. In terror of the Red Army, the vast majority of the population, particularly the women, now desperately wanted the Anglo-American forces to capture Berlin.

❂   ❂   ❂

It was almost noon. Back of the Russian lines, in the city of Bromberg, Captain Sergei Ivanovich Golbov gazed bleary-eyed about the large living room of the luxurious third-floor apartment he and two other Red Army correspondents had just "liberated." Golbov and his friends were happily drunk. Every day they drove from the headquarters in Bromberg to the front ninety miles away to get the news, but at the moment everything was quiet; there would not be much to report until the Berlin offensive began. In the meantime, after months of front-line reporting, the good-looking, 25-year-old Golbov was enjoying himself.

Bottle in hand, he stood looking at the rich furnishings. He had never seen anything quite like them. Heavy paintings in ornate gold frames adorned the walls. The windows had satin-lined drapings. The furniture was upholstered in rich brocaded materials. Thick Turkish carpets covered the floors, and massive chandeliers hung in the living room and the adjoining dining room. Golbov was quite sure that an important Nazi must have owned this apartment.

33

There was a small door ajar at one end of the living room. Golbov pushed it open and discovered a bathroom. At the end of a rope hanging from a hook on the wall was the body of a Nazi official in full uniform. Golbov stared briefly at the body. He had seen thousands of dead Germans but this hanging body looked silly. Golbov called out to his friends, but they were having too much fun in the dining room to respond. They were throwing German and Venetian crystal at the chandelier—and at each other.

Golbov walked back into the living room, intending to sit down on a long sofa he had noticed there—but now he discovered that it was already occupied. Lying on it at full length, in a long Grecian-like gown with a tasseled cord at the waist, was a dead woman. She was quite young and she had prepared for death carefully. Her hair was braided and hung over each shoulder. Her hands were folded across her breasts. Nursing his bottle, Golbov sat down in an armchair and looked at her. Behind him, the laughter and the smashing of glassware in the dining room continued. The girl was probably in her early twenties, and from the bluish marks on her lips Golbov thought she had probably taken poison.

Back of the sofa on which the dead woman lay was a table with silver framed photographs—smiling children with a young couple, presumably their parents, and an elderly couple. Golbov thought of his family. During the siege of Leningrad his mother and father, half-starved, had tried to make a soup out of a kind of industrial oil. It had killed them both. One brother had been killed in the first days of the war. The other, 34-year-old Mikhail, a partisan leader, had been caught by the SS, tied to a stake and burned alive. This girl lying on the sofa had died quite peacefully, Golbov thought. He took a long swig at the bottle, stepped over to the sofa and picked up the dead girl. He walked over to the closed windows. Behind him, amid shouts of laughter, the chandelier in the dining room smashed to the ground with a loud crash. Golbov broke quite a lot of glass himself as he threw the dead girl's body straight through the window.

✤4✤

BERLINERS, who almost daily shook their fists at the bombers, who, as often as not, sorrowed for family, relatives or friends lost in air raids or in the armed forces, now fervently spoke of the British and Americans not as conquerors but as "liberators." It was an extraordinary reversal of attitude and this state of mind produced curious results.

Charlottenburger Maria Köckler refused to believe the Americans and British would let Berlin fall into Russian hands. She was even determined to help the Western Allies. The gray-haired, 45-year-old housewife told friends she was "ready to go out and fight to hold back the Reds until the 'Amis' get here."

Many Berliners fought down their fears by listening to BBC broadcasts and noting each phase of the battles being fought on the crumbling western front—almost as though they were following the course of a victorious German Army rushing to the relief of Berlin. In between raids Margarete Schwarz, an accountant, spent night after night with her neighbors, meticulously plotting the Anglo-American drive across Western Germany. Each mile gained seemed to her almost like another step toward liberation. It seemed that way to Liese-Lotte Ravené, too. Her time was spent in her book-lined apartment in Tempelhof, where she carefully penciled in the latest American advances on a big map and feverishly willed the Amis on. Frau Ravené did not like to think of what might happen if the Russians came in first. She was a semi-invalid—with steel braces around her hips and running down her right leg.

35

Thousands were quite certain the Amis would get to Berlin first. Their faith was almost childlike—vague and unclear. Frau Annemaria Hückel, whose husband was a doctor, began tearing up old Nazi flags to use as bandages for the great battle she was expecting on the day the Americans arrived. Charlottenburger Brigitte Weber, 20-year-old bride of three months, was sure the Americans were coming and she thought she knew where they intended to live. Brigitte had heard that Americans enjoyed a high standard of living and liked the finer things of life. She was ready to bet they had carefully chosen the wealthy residential district of Nikolassee. Hardly a bomb had fallen there.

Others, while hoping for the best, prepared for the worst. Sober-minded Pia van Hoeven and her friends Ruby and Eberhard Borgmann reluctantly reached the conclusion that only a miracle could keep the Russians from getting to Berlin first. So they jumped at the invitation of their good friend, the jovial, fat-cheeked Heinrich Schelle, to join him and his family when the battle for the city began. Schelle managed Gruban-Souchay, one of the most famous wine shops and restaurants in Berlin, situated on the ground floor below the Borgmanns. He had turned one of his cellars into a resplendent shelter, complete with Oriental rugs, draperies and provisions to withstand the siege. There was little food except for potatoes and canned tuna fish, but there were ample supplies of the rarest and most delicate of German and French wines in the adjacent wine cellar—plus Hennessy cognac and case after case of champagne. "While we wait for God knows what," he told them, "we might as well live comfortably." Then he added: "If we run out of water—there's always the champagne."

Biddy Jungmittag, 41-year-old mother of two young daughters, thought that all the talk about the Americans and British coming was—in her own words—"just so much tripe." The British-born wife of a German, she knew the Nazis only too well. Her husband, suspected of belonging to a German resistance group, had been executed five months before. The Nazis, she thought, would fight as fiercely against the Western Allies as against the Russians, and a glance at the map showed that the odds were against the Anglo-Americans getting to Berlin first. But the Red Army's impending arrival did not unduly alarm Biddy. They would not dare touch her. In her sensible English way, Biddy intended to show the first Russians she met her old British passport.

There were some who felt no need for documents to protect them. They not only expected the Russians, they longed to welcome them. That moment would be the fulfillment of a dream for which small groups of Germans had worked and schemed most of their lives. Hunted and harassed at every turn by the Gestapo and the criminal police, a few hardened cells had somehow survived. The German Communists and their sympathizers waited eagerly for the saviors from the east.

Although totally dedicated to the overthrow of Hitlerism, the Communists of Berlin had been so scattered that their effectiveness—to the Western Allies, at any rate—was minimal. A loose-knit Communist underground did exist, but it took its orders solely from Moscow and worked exclusively as a Soviet espionage network.

Hildegard Radusch, who had been a Communist deputy to the Berlin House of Assembly from 1927 to 1932, was getting by almost on faith alone. She was half-starved, half-frozen and in hiding, along with a few other Communists near the village of Prieros, on the southeastern fringe of Berlin. With her girl friend Else ("Eddy") Kloptsch, she lived in a large wooden machinery crate measuring ten feet by eight and set in concrete. It had no gas, electricity, water or toilet facilities, but to the burly 42-year-old Hildegard (who described herself as "the man around the house") it was the perfect refuge.

Hildegard and Eddy had lived together since 1939. They had existed underground in Prieros for almost ten months. Hildegard was on the Nazi "wanted" list, but she had outwitted the Gestapo again and again. Her greatest problem, like that of the other Communists in the area, was food. To apply for ration cards would have meant instant disclosure and arrest. Luckily Eddy, though a sympathizer, was not wanted as a Communist and had weekly rations. But the meager allowance was hardly enough for one. (The official Nazi newspaper, the *Völkischer Beobachter,* had printed the week's adult allowance as four and a quarter pounds of bread; two pounds meat and sausage; five ounces fat; five ounces sugar; and every three weeks two and a quarter ounces of cheese and three and a half ounces of ersatz coffee.) Occasionally the two women were able to supplement their diet by cautious buying on the black market, but prices were exorbitant—coffee alone cost from $100 to $200 per pound.

Hildegard was preoccupied with two thoughts constantly: food, and liberation by the Red Army. But waiting was hard, and simply surviving was growing more difficult month by month—as she methodically recorded in her diary.

On February 13, 1945 she wrote: "It is high time the Russians got here . . . the dogs haven't got me yet."

February 18: "No report since the seventh from Zhukov about the Berlin front and we are so desperately awaiting their arrival. Come, Tovarishti, the quicker you are here, the quicker the war will end."

February 24: "To Berlin today. Coffee from thermos; one piece of dry bread. Three men looked at me suspiciously during the trip. So comforting to know that Eddy is beside me. Didn't get anything to eat anywhere. Eddy really took the trip to get cigarettes on the ration card she bought on the black market—ten cigarettes were due on that. None in the store, so she took five cigars. She had hoped to barter a silk dress and two pairs of stockings for something edible. Nothing doing. No black market bread either."

February 25: "Three cigars are gone. Still no communiqués from Zhukov. None from Koniev either."

February 27: "I'm getting nervous from all this waiting. It is catastrophic for someone anxious to work to be cooped up here."

March 19: "Wonderful meal at noon—potatoes with salt. In the evening potato pancakes fried in cod-liver oil. Taste isn't so hot."

Now, on this first day of spring, Hildegard was still waiting and, her diary noted, "almost crazy for something to eat." There were no reports from the Russian front. All she could find to write down was that "winds are sweeping winter from field and meadow. Snowdrops are blooming. The sun is shining and the air is warm. The usual air raids . . . judging by the detonations the planes are coming closer to us." And later, noting that the Western Allies were on the Rhine and could, by her reckoning, "be in Berlin in twenty days," she bitterly recorded that Berliners "would rather have the men from the capitalistic countries." She hoped that the Russians would arrive quickly, that Zhukov would attack by Easter.

About twenty-five miles due north of Prieros, at Neuenhagen on the eastern fringes of Berlin, another Communist cell grimly waited. Its members, too, lived in constant fear of arrest and death, but they were more militant and better organized than their comrades in Prieros and they were luckier, too: they were barely thirty-five miles from the Oder and expected that theirs would be one of the first outlying districts captured.

Members of this group had worked night after night under the very noses of the Gestapo preparing a master plan for the day of liberation. They knew the names and whereabouts of every local Nazi, SS and Gestapo official. They knew who would cooperate and who would not. Some were marked for immediate arrest, others for liquidation. So well organized was the group that it had even made detailed plans for the future administration of the township.

All members of this cell waited anxiously for the Russians to come, sure that their recommendations would be accepted. But none waited more anxiously than Bruno Zarzycki. He suffered so badly from ulcers that he could hardly eat, but he kept saying that the day the Red Army arrived his ulcers would disappear; he knew it.

Incredibly, all over Berlin, in tiny cubicles and closets, in damp cellars and airless attics, a few of the most hated and persecuted of all Nazi victims hung grimly to life and waited for the day when they could emerge from hiding. They did not care who arrived first, so long as somebody came, and quickly. Some lived in twos and threes, some as families, some even in small colonies. Most of their friends thought them dead—and in a sense they were. Some had not seen the sun in years, or walked in a Berlin street. They could not afford to be sick for that would mean getting a doctor, immediate questions and possible disclosure. Even during the worst bombings they stayed in their hiding places, for in air raid shelters they would have been spotted immediately. They preserved an iron calm, for they had learned long ago never to panic. They owed their very lives to their ability to quell nearly every emotion. They were resourceful and tenacious and, after six years of war and nearly thirteen years of fear and harassment in the very capital of Hitler's Reich, almost three thousand of them still survived. That they did was a testimonial to the courage of a large segment of the city's Christians, none of whom were ever to receive adequate recognition of the fact that they protected the despised scapegoats of the new order—the Jews. *

Siegmund and Margarete Weltlinger, both in their late fifties, were hiding in a small, ground-floor apartment in Pankow. A family of Christian Scientists, the Möhrings, risking their own lives,

* The estimated figure of Jewish survivors comes from Berlin Senate statistics prepared by Dr. Wolfgang Scheffler of Berlin's Free University. They are disputed by some Jewish experts—among them Siegmund Weltlinger, who was Chairman for Jewish Affairs in the post-war government. He places the number who survived at only 1,400. Besides those underground, Dr. Scheffler states that at least another 5,100 Jews who had married Christians were living in the city under so-called legal conditions. But at best that was a nightmarish limbo, for those Jews never knew when they would be arrested. Today 6,000 Jews live in Berlin—a mere fraction of the 160,564 Jewish population of 1933, the year Hitler came to power. Of that figure no one knows for certain how many Jewish Berliners left the city, emigrated out of Germany, or were deported and exterminated in concentration camps.

had taken them in. It was crowded. The Möhrings, their two daughters and the Weltlingers all lived together in a two-room flat. But the Möhrings shared their rations and everything else with the Weltlingers and had never complained. Only once in many months had the Weltlingers dared venture out: an aching tooth prompted them to take the chance and the dentist who extracted it accepted Margarete's explanation that she was "a visiting cousin."

They had been lucky up to 1943. Although Siegmund was expelled from the stock exchange in 1938, he was asked soon afterward to take over special tasks with the Jewish Community Bureau in Berlin. In those days the bureau, under the leadership of Heinrich Stahl, registered the wealth and properties of Jews; later it tried to negotiate with the Nazis to alleviate the sufferings of Jews in concentration camps. Stahl and Weltlinger knew that it was only a question of time before the bureau was closed—but they bravely continued their work. Then, on February 28, 1943, the Gestapo closed down the bureau. Stahl disappeared into the Theresienstadt concentration camp and the Weltlingers were ordered to move to a sixty-family "Jews' house" in Reinickendorf. The Weltlingers stayed in the Reinickendorf house until dark. Then they removed the Star of David from their coats and slipped out into the night. Since then they had lived with the Möhrings.

For two years the outside world for them had been only a patch of sky framed by buildings—plus a single tree which grew in the dismal courtyard facing the apartment's kitchen window. The tree had become a kind of calendar of their imprisonment. "Twice we've seen our chestnut tree decked out with snow," Margarete told her husband. "Twice the leaves have turned brown, and now it's blooming again." She was in despair. Would they have to spend yet another year in hiding? "Maybe," Margarete told her husband, "God has forsaken us."

Siegmund comforted her. They had a lot to live for, he told her: their two children—a daughter, seventeen, and a son, fifteen— were in England. The Weltlingers had not seen them since Siegmund had arranged to get them out of Germany in 1938. Opening a Bible he turned to the Ninety-first Psalm and slowly read: "A thousand shall fall at thy side, and ten thousand at thy right hand; *but* it shall not come nigh thee." All they could do was to wait. "God is with us," he told his wife. "Believe me, the day of liberation is at hand."

In the previous year, more than four thousand Jews had been arrested by the Gestapo in the streets of Berlin. Many of these Jews had risked detection because they were unable to stand confinement any longer.

Hans Rosenthal, twenty, was still hiding in Lichtenberg, and was determined to hold out. He had spent twenty-six months in a cubicle barely six feet long and five feet wide. It was actually a kind of small tool shed attached to the back of a house owned by an old friend of Hans's mother. Rosenthal's existence up to now had been perilous. His parents were dead and at sixteen he was put into a labor camp. In March of 1943 he escaped and, without papers, took a train to Berlin and refuge with his mother's friend. There was no water and no light in his cell-like hiding place and the only toilet facility available was an old-fashioned chamber pot. He emptied that at night during the air raids, the only time he dared leave his hiding place. Except for a narrow couch, the cubicle was bare. But Hans did have a Bible, a small radio and, on the wall, a carefully marked map. Much as he hoped for the Western Allies, it seemed to him that the Russians would capture Berlin. And that worried him, even though it would mean his release. But he reassured himself by saying over and over, "I am a Jew. I have survived the Nazis and I'll survive Stalin, too."

In the same district, in a cellar in Karlshorst, Joachim Lipschitz lived under the protection of Otto Krüger. On the whole it was quiet in the Krüger cellar but sometimes Joachim thought he heard the distant boom of Russian guns. The sound was soft and muttering, like a bored audience applauding with gloved hands. He put it down to imagination—the Russians were much too far away. Still he was familiar with Russian cannonading. The son of a Jewish doctor and a Gentile mother, he had been inducted into the Wehrmacht. In 1941 on the eastern front, he had lost an arm on the battlefield. But service to Germany had not saved him from the crime of being a half-Jew. In April, 1944, he had been marked for internment in a concentration camp. From that moment on, he had been in hiding.

The 27-year-old Joachim wondered what would happen now as the climax approached. Every night the Krügers' eldest daughter, Eleanore, came down to the basement to discuss the outlook. They had been sweethearts since 1942 and Eleanore, making no secret of their friendship, had been disqualified from attending a university because of her association with an "unworthy" person. Now they longed for the day when they could marry. Eleanore was convinced that the Nazis were militarily bankrupt and that the collapse would come soon. Joachim believed otherwise: the Germans would fight to the bitter end and Berlin was sure to become a battlefield—perhaps another Verdun. They also disagreed about who would capture the city. Joachim expected the Russians, Eleanore the British and Americans. But Joachim thought they should be prepared for any eventuality. So Eleanore was studying English—and Joachim was mastering Russian.

None waited in more anguish for Berlin to fall than Leo Sternfeld, his wife Agnes and their 23-year-old daughter Annemarie. The Sternfelds were not in hiding, for the family was Protestant. But Leo's mother was Jewish, so he was categorized by the Nazis as a half-Jew. As a result, Leo and his family had lived in a torment of suspense all through the war; the Gestapo had toyed with them as a cat with a mouse. They had been allowed to live where they wished, but hanging over them always was the threat of arrest.

The danger had grown greater as the war had come nearer, and Leo had struggled to keep up the women's spirits. The night before, a bomb had demolished the post office nearby, but Leo was still able to joke about it. "You won't have to go far for the mail any more," he told his wife. "The post office is lying on the steps."

As he left their home in Tempelhof on this March morning, Leo Sternfeld, the former businessman now drafted by the Gestapo to work as a garbage collector, knew that he had put off making his plans until too late. They could not leave Berlin, and there was no time to go into hiding. If Berlin was not captured within the next few weeks they were doomed. Leo had been tipped off that the Gestapo planned to round up all those with even a drop of Jewish blood on May 19.

❖　　❖　　❖

Far to the west, in the headquarters of the British Second Army at Walbeck, near the Dutch border, the senior medical officer, Brigadier Hugh Glyn Hughes, tried to anticipate some of the health problems he might encounter within the coming weeks—especially when they reached Berlin. Secretly he feared outbreaks of typhus.

Already a few refugees were passing through the front lines, and his assistants had reported that they carried a variety of contagious diseases. Like every other doctor along the Allied front, Brigadier Hughes was watching developments very carefully; a serious epidemic could be disastrous. Tugging at his moustache, he wondered how he would cope with the refugees when the trickle became a flood. There would also be thousands of Allied prisoners of war. And God only knew what they would find when Berlin was reached.

The Brigadier was also concerned about another related problem: the concentration and labor camps. There had been some information about them via neutral countries, but no one knew how they were run, how many people they contained or what conditions were like. Now it looked as if the British Second would be the first army to overrun a concentration camp. On his desk was a report that one lay directly in the path of their advance, in the area north of Hanover. There was almost no further information about it. Brigadier Hughes wondered what they would find. He hoped the Germans had shown their usual thoroughness in medical matters, and had the health situation under control. He had never heard of the place before. It was called Belsen.

✢5✢

Captain Helmuth Cords, a 25-year-old veteran of the Russian front, was a holder of the Iron Cross for bravery. He was also a prisoner in Berlin—and he probably would not live to see the end of the war. Captain Cords was a member of an elite group—the small band of survivors of the seven thousand Germans who had been arrested in connection with the attempted assassination of Hitler eight months before, on July 20, 1944.

Hitler had wreaked his vengeance in a barbaric orgy; almost five thousand alleged participants had been executed, the innocent and the guilty alike. Whole families had been wiped out. Anyone even remotely connected with the plotters had been arrested and, as often as not, summarily executed. They had been put to death in a manner prescribed by Hitler himself. "They must all be hanged like cattle," he had ordered. The principals were hanged in exactly that fashion—from meat hooks. Instead of rope most of them were strung up with piano wire.

Now, in Wing B of the star-shaped Lehrterstrasse Prison, the last group of the alleged plotters waited. They were both conservatives and Communists; they were army officers, doctors, clergymen, university professors, writers, former political figures, ordinary workingmen and peasants. Some had no idea why they were imprisoned; they had never been formally charged. A few had been tried, and were awaiting retrial. Some had actually been proved innocent, but were still being held. Others had been given sham trials, had been hurriedly sentenced, and were now awaiting execution. No one knew exactly how many prisoners there were in Wing B—some thought two hundred, others fewer than one hundred. There was no way of keeping count. Each day prisoners were taken out, never to be seen again. It all depended on the whims of one man: the Gestapo chief, SS Grüppenführer Heinrich Müller. The incarcerated expected little mercy from him. Even if the Allies were at the very prison gates, they believed Müller would continue the butchery.

Cords was one of the innocent. In July, 1944, he had been stationed at Bendlerstrasse as a junior officer on the staff of the Chief of Staff of the Reserve Army, Colonel Claus Graf von Stauffenberg. There was, as it turned out, just one thing wrong with that assignment: the distinguished-looking, 36-year-old Von Stauffenberg—he had only one arm and wore a black patch over his left eye—was the key figure in the July 20 plot, the man who had volunteered to kill Hitler.

At the Führer's headquarters in Rastenburg, East Prussia, during one of Hitler's lengthy military conferences, Von Stauffenberg had placed a briefcase containing a time bomb beneath the long map table near where Hitler stood. Minutes after Von Stauffenberg had slipped out of the room to start back to Berlin, the bomb exploded. Miraculously, Hitler had survived the blast. Hours later in Berlin, Von Stauffenberg, without benefit of a formal trial, was shot to death in the courtyard of the Bendlerstrasse headquarters along with three other key military figures in the plot. Everyone even remotely associated with him was arrested—including Helmuth Cords.

Cords's fiancée, Jutta Sorge, granddaughter of the former German Chancellor and Foreign Minister Gustav Stresemann, had also been arrested and imprisoned. So had her mother and father. All of them, including Helmuth Cords, had been held without trial ever since.

Corporal Herbert Kosney, imprisoned in the same building,

knew even less about the July 20 plot than Cords. But Kosney had been implicated unwittingly. He was part of a Communist resistance group, and his participation in the assassination attempt had consisted of transporting an unknown man from Lichterfelde to Wannsee.

Although not a Communist, Herbert had been on the fringes of various Red underground groups since 1940. In November, 1942, while he was on military leave in Berlin, his elder brother Kurt, a member of the Communist Party since 1931, had violently dissuaded Herbert from returning to the front: he broke Herbert's arm with a rifle, took him to a military hospital and explained that he had found the injured soldier lying in a ditch.

The trick worked. Herbert never returned to the front. He was stationed with a reserve battalion in Berlin and every three months got a new medical certificate from Dr. Albert Olbertz which kept him on "light duty." Dr. Olbertz happened to be a member of a Communist resistance group, too.

It was Olbertz who brought about Herbert's imprisonment. A few days after the attempt on Hitler's life, Olbertz told Herbert to come with him on an urgent transportation job. Taking a military ambulance, they picked up a man unknown to Herbert—a senior officer in the Gestapo, General Artur Nebe, Chief of the Criminal Police, who was wanted for questioning. Some time later Nebe was captured; so were Olbertz and Herbert. Olbertz committed suicide; Nebe was executed; Herbert was tried and condemned to death by a civilian court. But because he was still in the army a retrial by a military court was necessary. Herbert knew it was a mere formality—and formalities meant little to Gestapo Chief Müller. As he looked out his cell window, Herbert Kosney wondered how soon he would be executed.

Not very far away another man sat wondering what the future had in store for him—Herbert's brother, Kurt Kosney. He had been interrogated again and again by the Gestapo, but so far he had told them nothing about his Communist activities. Certainly he had not revealed anything to incriminate his younger brother. He worried about Herbert. What had happened to him? Where had he been taken? Only a few cells separated the two brothers. But neither Kurt nor Herbert knew that they were in the same prison.

Although they were not in jail, another group of prisoners was living in Berlin. Uprooted from their families, forcibly removed from their homelands, they had but one desire—like so many others—and that was for speedy deliverance, by anybody. These were the slave laborers—the men and women from almost every country that the Nazis had overrun. There were Poles, Czechs, Norwegians, Danes, Dutch, Belgians, Luxembourgers, French, Yugoslavs and Russians.

In all, the Nazis had forcibly imported nearly seven million people—the equivalent of almost the entire population of New York City—to work in German homes and businesses. Some countries were bled almost white: 500,000 people were shipped out of diminutive Holland (population 10,956,000) and 6,000 from tiny Luxembourg (population 296,000). More than 100,000 foreign workers—mostly French and Russian—worked in Berlin alone.

The foreign laborers were engaged in every conceivable type of work. Many top Nazis acquired Russian girls as domestic servants. Architects engaged in war work staffed their offices with young foreign draftsmen. Heavy industry filled its quotas of electricians, steelworkers, diemakers, mechanics and unskilled laborers with these captive peoples. Gas, water and transportation utility companies "employed" extra thousands—with virtually no pay. Even German military headquarters on Bendlerstrasse had its allotment of foreign workers. One Frenchman, Raymond Legathière, was employed there full time replacing window panes as fast as the bomb blasts blew them out.

The manpower situation in Berlin had become so critical that the Nazis openly flouted the Geneva Convention, using prisoners of war as well as foreign workers for essential war work. Because

Russia was not a signatory to the Convention, Red Army prisoners were used in any manner that the Germans saw fit. There was now, in fact, little distinction between prisoners of war and foreign workers. As conditions deteriorated day by day, prisoners were being used to build air raid bunkers, to help rebuild bombed military quarters and even to shovel coal in industrial power plants. Now, the only difference between the two groups was that the foreign workers had greater freedom—and even that depended on the area and the type of work.

Foreign nationals lived in "cities" of wooden barracks-like buildings near to, or located on, factory premises; they ate in community mess halls and wore identifying badges. Some concerns closed their eyes to regulations and allowed their foreign workers to live outside the compounds, in Berlin itself. Many were free to move about the city, go to movies or other places of entertainment, provided they observed the strict curfew.*

Some guards, seeing the writing on the wall, were relaxing their attitude. Many foreign workers—and sometimes even the prisoners of war—found they could occasionally dodge a day's work. One guard, in charge of twenty-five Frenchmen who journeyed to work in the city by subway every day, was now so amenable that he no longer bothered to count the prisoners getting off the train. He did not care how many got "lost" on the trip—so long as everyone was at the Potsdamer Platz subway station by 6 P.M. for the journey back to camp.

Not all the foreign workers were so lucky. Thousands were closely restricted, with virtually no freedom at all. This was particularly true in municipal or government plants. Frenchmen working for the gas utility company in Marienfelde in South Berlin had few privileges and were poorly fed in comparison with

---

* There was another category of laborer—the voluntary foreign worker. Thousands of Europeans—some were ardent Nazi sympathizers, some believed they were helping to fight Bolshevism, while the great majority were cynical opportunists—had answered German newspaper advertisements offering highly paid jobs in the Reich. These were allowed to live quite freely near their places of employment.

workers at private plants. Still, they were better off than their Russian counterparts. One Frenchman, André Bourdeau, wrote in his diary that the chief guard, Fesler, "never sends anybody to a concentration camp," and on a Sunday, to supplement the rations, "allows us to go into the fields to pick a potato or two." Bourdeau was glad he was not from the east: the Russian compound, he wrote, was "terribly overcrowded, with men, women and children all jammed together . . . their food, most of the time, inedible." Elsewhere, in some privately run plants, Russian workers fared as well as those from the west.

Curiously, western workers all over Berlin noted a change in the Russians, almost with each passing day. In the Schering chemical plant in Charlottenburg, the Russians, who might be expected to be elated at the course of events, were, on the contrary, greatly depressed. The Ukrainian and Belorussian women, in particular, seemed uneasy about the possible capture of the city by their compatriots.

On their arrival, two and three years before, the women had been dressed in simple peasant style. Gradually they had changed, becoming more sophisticated in dress and manner. Many had begun using cosmetics for the first time. Hair and dress styles had altered noticeably: the Russian girls copied the French or German women around them. Now others noticed that the Russian girls almost overnight had reverted to peasant dress again. Many workers thought that they anticipated some sort of reprisals from the Red Army—even though they had been shipped out of Russia against their will. Apparently the women expected to be punished because they had become too western.

Among the western workers morale was high all over Berlin. At the Alkett plant in Ruhleben, where 2,500 French, Belgian, Polish and Dutch nationals worked on the production of tanks, everyone except the German guards was planning for the future. The French workers, in particular, were elated. They spent their evenings talking about the enormous meals they would have the moment they set foot in France, and singing popular songs: Maurice

Chevalier's "Ma Pomme" and "Prospère" were among the favorites.

Jean Boutin, 20-year-old machinist from Paris, felt especially cheerful; he knew he was playing some part in the Germans' downfall. Boutin and some Dutch workers had been sabotaging tank parts for years. The German foreman had repeatedly threatened to ship saboteurs off to concentration camps, but he never did—and there was a very good reason: the manpower shortage was so acute that the plant was almost totally dependent on the foreign workers. Jean thought the situation was pretty amusing. Each ball-bearing part he worked on was supposed to be finished in fifty-four minutes. He tried never to turn in a finished machined piece in under twenty-four hours—and that was usually defective. At Alkett the forced laborers had one simple rule: every unusable part they could sneak by the foreman brought victory and the capture of Berlin another step closer. So far no one had ever been caught.

✧6✧

INEVITABLY, despite the constant bombing, despite the specter of the Red Army on the Oder, despite the very shrinking of Germany itself as the Allies pressed in from east and west, there were those who doggedly refused even to consider the possibilities of catastrophe. They were the fanatical Nazis. Most of them seemed to accept the hardships they were undergoing as a kind of purgatory—as a tempering and refining of their devotion to Nazism and its aims. Once they had demonstrated their loyalty, everything would surely be all right; they were convinced not only that Berlin would never fall, but that victory for the Third Reich was certain.

The Nazis occupied a peculiar place in the life of the city. Berliners had never fully accepted Hitler or his evangelism. They had always been both too sophisticated and too international in outlook. In fact, the Berliner's caustic humor, political cynicism and almost complete lack of enthusiasm for the Führer and his new order had long plagued the Nazi Party. Whenever torchlight parades or other Nazi demonstrations to impress the world were held in Berlin, thousands of storm troopers had to be shipped in from Munich to beef up the crowds of marchers. "They look better in the newsreels than we do," wisecracked the Berliners, "and they also have bigger feet!"

Try as he might, Hitler was never able to capture the hearts of the Berliners. Long before the city was demolished by Allied bombs, a frustrated and angry Hitler was already planning to rebuild Berlin and shape it to the Nazi image. He even intended to change its name to Germania, for he had never forgotten that in every free election in the thirties Berliners had rejected him. In the critical balloting of 1932 when Hitler was sure he would unseat Hindenburg, Berlin gave him its lowest vote of all—only 23 per cent. Now, the fanatics among the citizenry were determined to make Berlin, the least Nazi city in Germany, the last *Festung* (fortress) of Nazism. Although they were in the minority, they were still in control.

Thousands of the fanatics were teen-agers and, like most of their generation, they knew only one god—Hitler. From childhood on they had been saturated with the aims and ideology of National Socialism. Many more had also been trained to defend and perpetuate the cause, using an array of weapons ranging from rifles to bazooka-like tank destroyers, called *Panzerfäuste*. Klaus Küster was typical of the teen-age group. A member of the Hitler Youth (there were more than one thousand of them in Berlin), his specialty was knocking out tanks at a range of less than sixty yards. Klaus was not yet sixteen.

The most dedicated military automatons of all were the members of the SS. They were so convinced of ultimate victory and so devoted to Hitler that to other Germans their mental attitude almost defied comprehension. Their fanaticism was so strong that it sometimes seemed to have penetrated the subconscious. Dr. Ferdinand Sauerbruch, in Charité Hospital, working on the anesthetized form of a seriously wounded SS man just in from the Oder front, was suddenly, momentarily frozen. In the stillness of the operating theater, from the depths of his anesthesia, the SS man began to speak. Quietly and distinctly he repeated over and over, "Heil Hitler! . . . Heil Hitler! . . . Heil Hitler!"

Although these were the real extremists, there were hundreds of thousands of civilians almost as bad. Some were walking caricatures of what the free world thought the fanatical Nazi to be. One of them was 47-year-old Gotthard Carl. Although Gotthard was only a minor civil servant, an accountant on temporary service to the Luftwaffe, he wore the dashing blue air force uniform with all the pride and arrogance of an ace fighter pilot. As he entered his apartment in the late afternoon, he clicked his heels sharply together, shot his right arm out and shouted, "Heil Hitler." This performance had been going on for years.

His wife, Gerda, was thoroughly bored with her husband's fanaticism, but she was worried, and anxious to discuss with him some sort of plan for their survival. The Russians, she pointed out, were getting very close to Berlin. Gotthard cut her off. "Rumors!" he fumed, "rumors! Deliberately put out by the enemy." In Gotthard's disoriented Nazi world everything was going along as planned. Hitler's victory was certain. The Russians were *not* at the gates of Berlin.

Then there were the enthusiastic and impressionable—those who had never considered defeat possible—like Erna Schultze. The 41-year-old secretary in the headquarters of the Oberkommando der Kriegsmarine (Navy High Command) had just realized her life's ambition: she had been made an admiral's secretary and this was her first day on the job.

53

Shell House, where the headquarters was located, had been badly bombed in the previous forty-eight hours. Still, the dust and wreckage did not bother Erna—neither was she perturbed by the order that had just reached her desk. It stated that all *Geheime Kommandosache* (Top Secret) files were to be burned. But Erna was saddened on this first day of her new job to be told at closing time that she and the other employees were to take "indefinite leave" and that their pay checks would be forwarded.

Still Erna remained unshaken. Her faith was so strong that she even refused to believe the official communiqués when defeats were reported. Morale was good throughout Berlin, she believed, and it was only a question of time before the Reich triumphed. Even now, as she left the building, Erna was quite certain that within a few days the Navy would call her back.

There were others so trusting and so involved with the upper clique of the Nazi hierarchy that they thought little of the war or its consequences. Caught up in the heady atmosphere and glamor of their privileged positions, they felt not only secure, but in their blind devotion to Hitler, totally protected. Such a person was attractive, blue-eyed Käthe Reiss Heusermann.

At 213 Kurfürstendamm the blond and vivacious 35-year-old Käthe was immersed in her work as assistant to Professor Hugo J. Blaschke, the Nazi leaders' top dentist. Blaschke, because he had served Hitler and his court since 1934, had been honored with the military rank of SS *Brigadeführer* (Brigadier General) and placed in charge of the dental staff of the Berlin SS Medical Center. An ardent Nazi, Blaschke had parlayed his association with Hitler into the largest and most lucrative private practice in Berlin. Now he was preparing to parlay it a step farther. Unlike Käthe, he could clearly see the writing on the wall—and he planned to leave Berlin at the earliest opportunity. If he remained, his SS rank and position might prove embarrassing: under the Russians, today's prominence might well become tomorrow's liability.

Käthe was almost completely oblivious of the situation. She was much too busy. From early morning until late at night she was on the move, assisting Blaschke at various clinics and headquarters or at his private surgery on the Kurfürstendamm. Competent and well liked, Käthe was so completely trusted by the Nazi elite that she had attended nearly all of Hitler's entourage—and once, the Führer himself.

That occasion had been the highlight of her career. In November, 1944, she and Blaschke had been urgently summoned to the Führer's headquarters in Rastenburg, East Prussia. There they had found Hitler in acute pain. "His face, particularly the right cheek was terribly swollen," she later recalled. "His teeth were extremely bad. In all he had three bridges. He had only eight upper teeth of his own and even these were backed by gold fillings. A bridge completed his upper dental work and it was held securely in place by the existing teeth. One of them, the wisdom tooth on the right side, was badly infected."

Blaschke took one look at the tooth and told Hitler that it had to come out, there was no way he could save it. Blaschke explained that he would need to remove two teeth—a false tooth at the rear of the bridge as well as the infected one next to it. That meant cutting through the porcelain and gold bridge at a point in front of the false tooth, a procedure that called for a considerable amount of drilling and sawing. Then, after making the final extraction, at some later date he would either make an entirely new bridge or re-anchor the old one.

Blaschke was nervous about the operation: it was intricate and there was no telling how Hitler would behave. Complicating matters even further was the Führer's dislike of anesthetics. He told Blaschke, Käthe remembered, that he would accept "only the bare minimum." Both Blaschke and Käthe knew he would suffer excruciating pain; furthermore the operation might last as long as thirty to forty-five minutes. But there was nothing they could do about it.

Blaschke gave Hitler an injection in the upper jaw and the operation began. Käthe stood by the Führer's side with one hand pulling back his cheek, the other holding a mirror. Swiftly Blaschke's rasping drill bored into the bridge. Then he changed the bit and began sawing. Hitler sat motionless—"as though frozen," she recalled. Finally Blaschke cleared the tooth and quickly made the extraction. "Throughout," Käthe said later, "Hitler neither moved nor uttered a single word. It was an extraordinary performance. We wondered how he stood the pain."

That had been five months ago; as yet nothing had been done about the Führer's dangling bridge. Outside of Hitler's immediate circle, few knew the details of the operation. One of the cardinal rules for those who worked for the Führer was that everything about him, especially his illnesses, remain top secret.

Käthe was good at keeping secrets. For example, she knew that a special denture was being constructed for the Reich's acknowledged, but unwed first lady. Blaschke intended to fit the gold bridge next time she was in Berlin. Hitler's mistress, Eva Braun, certainly needed it.

Finally, Käthe knew one of the most closely guarded secrets of all. It was her responsibility to send a complete set of dental tools and supplies everywhere the Führer went. Moreover, she was preparing a new bridge with gold crowns for one of Hitler's four secretaries: short, stout, 45-year-old Johanna Wolf. Soon Käthe would fit "Wolfie's" new bridge, over in the surgical room of the Reichskanzlei. She had been traveling back and forth between Blaschke's surgery and the Reichskanzlei almost daily for the last nine weeks. Adolf Hitler had been there since January 16.

THE CIVILIANS

Milkman Richard Poganowska, photographed in 1945. To the left, the wagon with the two horses, Lisa and Hans. "Each day now Poganowska watched for certain signs that helped keep him from losing heart."

Unless otherwise credited, all photographs are from the author's private collection.

Robert and Ingeborg
Kolb in 1945.

The Kolbs' house in Spandau. "The war will pass us by," Robert told Ingeborg. The first sign that it would not was when an army field kitchen pulled up in front of their door.

Left, Dr. Arthur Leckscheidt, Evangelical pastor of the gutted Melanchthon Church. " . . . eyes filled with tears, he played his farewell. As bombs burst all over Kreuzberg people sheltering in adjacent shelters heard the organ pealing out the ancient hymn, 'From Deepest Need I Cry to Thee.' " *Right,* Carl Johann Wiberg. " . . . this Swede who was more German than the Germans was also an Allied spy."

Mother Superior Cunegundes, head of the Haus Dahlem, the orphanage and maternity home run by the Mission Sisters of the Sacred Heart. "How do you tell sixty nuns and lay sisters that they are in danger of being raped?"

Erna Saenger (center) with her daughters-in-law and grandchildren, in 1945. "To believe faithfully means to be stupid and blind . . . we'll stay in Berlin. If everyone left like the neighbors the enemy would have what he wants."

Left, Juliane Bochnik in 1945. "The first pair of Russian boots I see, I'm going to commit suicide," a friend confided to her. *Right,* Pia van Hoeven, who waited for the end in "a resplendent shelter, complete with Oriental rugs. . . ."

Hildegard Radusch, *left,* and her friend Else Kloptsch. Hildegard, a Communist, was on the Nazi "Wanted" list, and eagerly awaited the arrival of the Red Army.

Bruno Zarzycki (second from left), with the Russians who entered his village. "He suffered so badly from ulcers he could hardly eat, but the day the Red Army arrived his ulcers would disappear; he knew it."

THE PRISONERS

Herbert Kosney.

Kurt Kosney.

Captain Helmuth Cords, who, like Herbert Kosney, awaited execution for his complicity in the July 20th plot against Hitler. *At right,* Cords with his fiancée, Jutta Sorge, also imprisoned. Cords was released in the last days of the war, and married Jutta.

Lehrterstrasse Prison.

THE ZOO-KEEPERS

Dr. Lutz Heck, the zoo director, and a good friend of Hermann Goering, shown in 1945.

Walter Wendt (shown here with Dr. Heinroth), who was in charge of the cattle and survived the fighting in and around the zoo.

Gustav Riedel, the lion-keeper who was forced to kill his animals, but found some of them "good eating."

Dr. Katherina Heinroth, who was later to become director of the zoo, with her pet monkey.

63

HITLER'S DENTISTS

Käthe Heusermann today.
Below, Käthe and Professor Hugo
Blaschke operate on Propaganda
Minister Dr. Joseph Goebbels.
" . . . she knew one of the most
closely guarded secrets of all—the
whereabouts of Adolf Hitler."

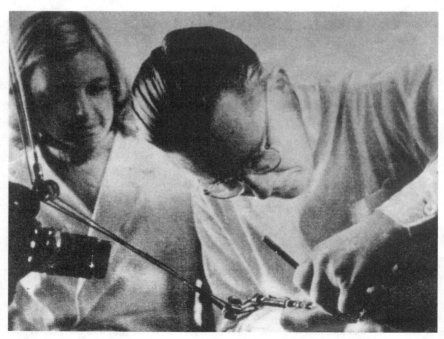

As the spring night closed in, the city took on a deserted look. The ruined colossus of Berlin, ghostly and vulnerable, stretched out in the pale moonlight, offering a clear target for the nighttime enemy. Below ground, Berliners waited for the bombers and wondered who among them would be alive by morning.

At 9 P.M. the R.A.F. came back. The sirens wailed for the fourth time in twenty-four hours, and the 317th attack on the city began. At his military headquarters on the Hohenzollerndamm, Major General Hellmuth Reymann, working steadily at his desk, paid scant attention to the hammering of anti-aircraft fire and the explosion of bombs. He was desperately fighting for time—and there was little of it left.

Only sixteen days before, the telephone had rung in Reymann's Dresden home. General Wilhelm Burgdorf, Hitler's adjutant, was on the line. "The Führer," said Burgdorf, "has appointed you military commander of Dresden." At first Reymann could not even reply. The 16th-century Saxony capital with its fairy-tale spires, castles and cobbled streets, had been almost totally destroyed in three massive air attacks. Reymann, heartbroken by the destruction of the lovely old city, lost his temper. "Tell him there's nothing here to defend except rubble," he shouted, and hung up. His angry words were a rash indulgence. An hour later Burgdorf called again and said, "The Führer has named you commander of Berlin instead."

On March 6 Reymann assumed command. Within a few hours he made an appalling discovery. Although Hitler had declared Berlin a *Festung*, the fortifications existed only in the Führer's imagination. Nothing had been done to prepare the city against attack. There was no plan, there were no defenses and there were virtually no troops. Worse, no provision had been made for the civilian population; an evacuation plan for the women, children and old people simply did not exist.

Now, Reymann was working around the clock trying feverishly to untangle the situation. His problems were staggering: where was he to get the troops, guns, ammunition and equipment to hold the city? Or the engineers, machinery and materials to build defenses? Would he be allowed to evacuate the women, children and aged? If not, how would he feed and protect them when the siege began? And again and again his mind returned to the big question: time—how much time was left?

Even securing senior command officers was difficult. Only now, at this late date, had Reymann been assigned a chief of staff, Colonel Hans Refior. The able Refior had arrived several hours earlier, and he was more startled than Reymann by the confusion in Berlin. A few days before in the illustrated magazine *Das Reich*, Refior had seen an article which claimed that Berlin was virtually impregnable. He recalled particularly one line: "Hedgehog-position Berlin simply bristles with defenses." If so, they must be carefully hidden. Refior had not been able to spot more than a few.

In all his years as a professional soldier, the gray-haired, 53-year-old Reymann had never imagined being faced with such a task. Yet he had to find answers for each problem—and quickly. Was it possible to save Berlin? Reymann was determined to do all he could. There were numerous examples in military history where defeat had seemed inevitable and yet a victory was achieved. He thought of Vienna which had been successfully defended against the Turks in 1683, and of General Graf von Gneisenau, Blücher's Chief of Staff, who defended Kolberg in 1806. True, these were pale comparisons, but perhaps they offered some hope. Yet, Reymann knew that everything would depend on the German armies holding the Oder front, and on the general commanding them.

The great ones were gone—Rommel, Von Rundstedt, Von Kluge, Von Manstein—the victorious leaders whose names were once household words. They had all disappeared, were all dead, discredited or forced into retirement. Now, more than ever, the nation and the armies needed a master soldier—another dashing Rommel, another meticulous Von Rundstedt. Berlin's safety and perhaps even the survival of Germany as a nation would depend on this. But where was that man?

Part Two

THE GENERAL

❖ 1 ❖

MARCH 22 dawned misty and cold. South of the city, Reichs-strasse 96 stretched away through the dripping pine forests, patches of frost gleaming dimly on the broad asphalt. Early on this chill second day of spring the road was crowded with traffic —traffic that even for wartime Germany had an unreal quality.

Some of the heavy lorries that came down the road carried bulky filing cabinets, document cases, office equipment and cartons. Others were piled high with works of art—fine furniture, crated pictures, brasses, ceramics and statuary. Atop one open truck a sightless bust of Julius Caesar rocked gently back and forth.

Scattered among the trucks were heavy passenger cars of every kind—Horchs, Wanderers, Mercedes limousines. All bore the silvered swastika medallion that marked them as official vehicles of the Nazi Party. And all were traveling along Reichsstrasse 96 in one direction: south. In the cars were the party bureaucrats of the Third Reich—the "Golden Pheasants," those privileged to wear the gilded swastika of the Nazi elite. Together with their wives, children and belongings, the Golden Pheasants were emigrating. Hardfaced and somber in their brown uniforms, the men gazed fixedly ahead, as though haunted by the possibility that they might be halted and sent back to the one place where they did not want to be: Berlin.

Speeding northward on the opposite side of the road came a Wehrmacht staff car, a big Mercedes with the checkerboard black, red and white metal flag of a *Heeresgruppe* commander on its left mudguard. Hunched in an ancient sheepskin coat, a muffler at his throat, Colonel General Gotthard Heinrici sat beside his driver, and looked out bleakly at the road. He knew this highway, as did all of the Reich's general officers. Heinrici's cousin, Field Marshal Gerd von Rundstedt, had once caustically called it *"der Weg zur Ewigkeit"*—the road to eternity. It had carried many a senior officer to military oblivion, for Reichsstrasse 96 was the direct route to the German General Staff headquarters eighteen miles from Berlin. Outside high-ranking military circles, few Germans knew the location of this headquarters. Not even local inhabitants were aware that, heavily camouflaged and hidden deep in the woods, the military nerve center of Hitler's Germany lay just outside their 15th-century town of Zossen. Zossen was Heinrici's destination.

If the oncoming traffic, with its disquieting evidence of government departments on the move, made any impression on the General, he did not communicate it to his 36-year-old aide, Captain Heinrich von Bila, sitting in back with Heinrici's batman, Balzen. There had been little conversation during the long hours of their 500-mile journey. They had left before dawn from northern Hungary, where Heinrici had commanded the First Panzer and Hungarian First armies. They had flown to Bautzen, near the Czecho-German border, and from there had continued by car. And now each hour that passed was bringing the 58-year-old Heinrici, one of the Wehrmacht's masters of defense, closer to the greatest test of his forty-year military career.

Heinrici would learn the full details of his new post at Zossen— but he knew already that his concern would not be with the Western Allies, but with his old enemies, the Russians. It was a bitter and, for Heinrici, a classic assignment: he was to take command of Army Group Vistula with orders to hold the Russians on the Oder and save Berlin.

Suddenly an air raid siren blared. Heinrici, startled, swung around to look back at the cluster of half-timbered houses they had just passed. There was no sign of bombing or Allied planes. The wailing continued, the warbling sound fading now in the distance. It was not the sound that had startled him. He was no stranger to bombing attacks. What had surprised him was the realization that this deep inside Germany, even little villages were having air raid alerts. Slowly Heinrici turned back. Although he had commanded units from the very beginning of the war in 1939, first on the western front, then after 1941 in Russia, he had not been in Germany for more than two years and he had little idea of the impact of total war on the home front. He realized that he was a stranger in his own country. He was depressed; he had not expected anything like this.

Yet few German generals had experienced more of the war—and, conversely, few of such high rank had achieved less prominence. He was no dashing Rommel, lionized by the Germans for his successes and then honored by a propaganda-wise Hitler with a field marshal's baton. Outside of battle orders, Heinrici's name had scarcely appeared in print. The fame and glory that every soldier seeks had eluded him, for in his long years as a combat commander on the eastern front, he had fought the Russians in a role that by its very nature relegated him to obscurity. His operations had dealt not with the glories of blitzkrieg advance, but with the desperation of grinding retreat. His specialty was defense, and at that he had few peers. A thoughtful, precise strategist, a deceptively mild-mannered commander, Heinrici was nevertheless a tough general of the old aristocratic school who had long ago learned to hold the line with the minimum of men and at the lowest possible cost. "Heinrici," one of his staff officers once remarked, "retreats only when the air is turned to lead—and then only after considerable deliberation."

In a war that for him had been a slow and painful withdrawal all the way from the Moscow suburbs to the Carpathian Mountains, Heinrici had held out again and again in near-hopeless positions.

Stubborn, defiant and demanding, he had grabbed every chance —even when it was just a matter of holding one more mile for one more hour. He fought with such ferocity that his officers and men proudly nicknamed him *"Unser Giftzwerg"*—our tough little bastard.* Those meeting him for the first time were often nonplussed by the description "tough." Short, slightly built, with quiet blue eyes, fair hair and a neat moustache, Heinrici seemed at first glance more schoolmaster than general—and a shabby schoolmaster at that.

It was a matter of great concern to his aide, Von Bila, that Heinrici cared little about looking the part of a colonel general. Von Bila constantly fretted about Heinrici's appearance—particularly his boots and overcoat. Heinrici hated the highly polished, knee-high jackboot so popular with German officers. He preferred ordinary low-cut boots, worn with old-fashioned, World War I leather leggings that buckled at the side. As for his overcoats, he had several, but he liked his somewhat ratty sheepskin coat, and despite all of Von Bila's efforts he refused to part with it. Similarly, Heinrici wore his uniforms until they were threadbare. And, as he believed in traveling light, Heinrici rarely had more than one uniform with him—the one on his back.

It was Von Bila who had to take the initiative when Heinrici needed new clothes—and Von Bila dreaded these encounters, for he usually came out the loser. When Von Bila last ventured to bring up the subject he adopted a cautious approach. Tentatively, he inquired of Heinrici, "Herr Generaloberst, shouldn't we perhaps try to find a moment to be measured for a new uniform?" Heinrici had looked at Von Bila over the top of his reading glasses and had asked mildly, "Do you really think so, Bila?" For just a moment Von Bila thought he had succeeded. Then the *Giftzwerg* asked icily, "What for?" Von Bila had not raised the question since.

But if Heinrici did not look the part of a general, he acted like

---

* *Unser Giftzwerg* literally means "our poison dwarf"—and the term was often applied to Heinrici in this sense by those who disliked him.

one. He was every inch the soldier, and to the troops he commanded, particularly after his stand at Moscow, he was a legendary one.

In December, 1941, Hitler's massive blitzkrieg offensive into Russia had finally ground to a frozen halt before the very approaches to Moscow. All along the German front more than 1,250,-000 lightly clad troops had been trapped by an early and bitter winter. As the Germans floundered through ice and snow, the Russian armies that Hitler and his experts had virtually written off appeared as if from nowhere. In an all-out attack, the Soviets threw one hundred divisions of winter-hardened soldiers against the invaders. The German armies were thrown back with staggering losses, and for a time it seemed as if the terrible retreat of Napoleon's armies in 1812 would be repeated—on an even greater and bloodier scale.

The line had to be stabilized. It was Heinrici who was given the toughest sector to hold. On January 26, 1942, he was placed in command of the remnants of the Fourth Army, which, holding the ground directly facing Moscow, was the kingpin of the German line. Any major withdrawal on its part would jeopardize the armies on either flank and might trigger a rout.

Heinrici took over on a bitterly cold day; the temperature stood at minus 42 degrees Fahrenheit. Water froze inside the boilers of locomotives; machine guns would not fire; trenches and foxholes could not be dug because the ground was like iron. Heinrici's ill-equipped soldiers were fighting in waist-deep snow, with icicles hanging from their nostrils and eyelashes. "I was told to hold out until the big attack that this time would surely take Moscow," he later recalled. "Yet all around me my men were dying—and not only from Russian bullets. Many of them froze to death."

They held out for almost ten weeks. Heinrici used every method available to him, orthodox and unorthodox. He exhorted his men, goaded them, promoted, dismissed—and again and again defied Hitler's long-standing and inflexible order, "*Starre Verteidigung*" —stand fast. That spring it was estimated by the staff of the

Fourth Army that during the long winter the *Giftzwerg* had at times been outnumbered by at least twelve to one.

Outside Moscow Heinrici had developed a technique for which he became famous. When he knew a Russian attack was imminent in a particular sector, he would order his troops to retreat the night before to new positions one or two miles back. The Russian artillery barrages would land on a deserted front line. As Heinrici put it: "It was like hitting an empty bag. The Russian attack would lose its speed because my men, unharmed, would be ready. Then my troops on sectors that had not been attacked would close in and reoccupy the original front lines." The trick was to know when the Russians were preparing for an attack. From intelligence reports, patrols and the interrogation of prisoners, plus an extraordinary sixth sense, Heinrici was able to pinpoint the time and place with almost mathematical precision.

It was not always possible to employ these methods, and when he did, Heinrici had to use great caution—Hitler had imprisoned and even shot generals for defying his no-withdrawal order. "While we could hardly move a sentry from the window to the door without his permission," Heinrici was later to record, "some of us, where we could, found ways to evade his more suicidal orders."

For obvious reasons Heinrici had never been a favorite of Hitler or his court. His aristocratic and conservative military background demanded that he faithfully observe his oath of allegiance to Hitler, but the call of a higher dictatorship had always come first. Early in the war Heinrici had fallen afoul of the Führer because of his religious views.

The son of a Protestant minister, Heinrici read a Bible tract daily, attended services on Sundays and insisted on church parades for his troops. These practices did not sit well with Hitler. Several broad hints were dropped to Heinrici that Hitler thought it unwise for a general to be seen publicly going to church. On his last trip to Germany, while on leave in the town of Münster, Westphalia, Heinrici was visited by a high-ranking Nazi

Party official sent from Berlin specifically to talk with him. Heinrici, who had never been a member of the Nazi Party, was informed that "the Führer considers your religious activities incompatible with the aims of National Socialism." Stonily Heinrici listened to the warning. The following Sunday he, his wife, son and daughter attended church as usual.

Thereafter, he was promoted slowly and reluctantly. Promotion might have been denied him entirely except for his undeniably brilliant leadership, and the fact that the various commanders under whom he served—particularly Field Marshal Günther von Kluge—kept insisting on his promotion.

Late in 1943, Heinrici incurred the enmity of Reichsmarschall Hermann Goering, once again on religious grounds. Goering vehemently complained to Hitler that during the retreat of the Fourth Army in Russia Heinrici had failed to carry out the Führer's scorched-earth policy. Specifically he charged that the General had deliberately defied the orders "to burn and lay waste every habitable building" in Smolensk; among other buildings left standing had been the town's great cathedral. Heinrici explained solemnly that "had Smolensk been fired I could not have withdrawn my forces through it." The answer failed to satisfy either Hitler or Goering, but there was just sufficient military logic in it to prevent a court-martial.

Hitler, however, did not forget. Heinrici, a victim of poison gas in World War I, had suffered ever since from various stomach disorders. Some months after the incident with Goering, Hitler, citing these ailments, placed Heinrici on the non-active list because of "ill health." He was retired to a convalescent home in Karlsbad, Czechoslovakia, and there, in Heinrici's words, "they simply let me sit." A few weeks after his dismissal, the Russians for the first time broke through his old command, the Fourth Army.

During the opening months of 1944, Heinrici remained in Karlsbad, a remote spectator to the apocalyptic events that were slowly bringing Hitler's empire down in ruins: the invasion of Normandy by the Western Allies in June; the Anglo-American advance up the

75

boot of Italy and the capture of Rome; the abortive plot to assassinate Hitler on the twentieth of July; the overwhelming offensives of the Russians as they drove across eastern Europe. As the situation grew increasingly critical, Heinrici found his inaction unbearably frustrating. He might have had a command by entreating the Führer, but that he refused to do.

At last, in the late summer of '44, after eight months of enforced retirement, Heinrici was ordered back to duty—this time to Hungary and command of the hard-pressed First Panzer and Hungarian First armies.

In Hungary Heinrici resumed his old ways. At the height of the battle there, Colonel General Ferdinand Schörner, Hitler's protégé, and Heinrici's superior in Hungary, issued a directive that any soldier found behind the front without orders was to be "executed immediately and his body exhibited as a warning." Heinrici, disgusted by the command, angrily retorted: "Such methods have never been used under my command, and never shall be."

Although he was forced to retreat from northern Hungary into Czechoslovakia, he contested the ground so tenaciously that on March 3, 1945, he was informed that he had been decorated with the Swords to the Oak Leaves of his Knight's Cross—a remarkable accomplishment for a man who was disliked so intensely by Hitler. And now, just two weeks later, he was rushing to Zossen, with orders in his pocket to take over the command of Army Group Vistula.

As he watched Reichsstrasse 96 rushing away beneath the wheels of his speeding Mercedes, Heinrici wondered where it would ultimately lead him. He remembered the reaction of his staff in Hungary when his appointment became known and he was ordered to report to General Heinz Guderian, Chief of the General Staff of OKH (Oberkommando des Heeres)—the Army High Command. They were shocked. "Do you really want the job?" asked his chief of staff.

To his worried subordinates, the outspoken Heinrici seemed headed for certain trouble. As the commander of the Oder front, the last major line of defense between the Russians and Berlin, he would be constantly under the supervision of Hitler and the "court jesters," as one of Heinrici's officers called them. Heinrici had never been a sycophant, had never learned to varnish the facts; how could he avoid clashing with the men around the Führer? And everyone knew what happened to those who disagreed with Hitler.

As delicately as they could, officers close to Heinrici had suggested that he find some excuse to turn the command down—perhaps for "health reasons." Surprised, Heinrici replied simply that he would follow his orders—"just like Private Schultz or Schmidt."

Now as he approached the outskirts of Zossen, Heinrici could not help remembering that at his departure his staff had looked at him "as though I was a lamb being led to the slaughter."

✢ 2 ✢

AT THE MAIN GATES of the base, Heinrici's car was quickly cleared. The inner red-and-black guardrail swung up, and in a flurry of salutes the car passed into the Zossen headquarters. It was almost as though they had driven into another world. In a way it was just that—a hidden, camouflaged, orderly, military world, known only to a few and identified by the code words "Maybach I" and "Maybach II."

The complex through which they drove was Maybach I—the headquarters of OKH, the Army High Command, headed by General Guderian. From here he directed the armies on the eastern front. A mile farther in was another completely separate encampment: Maybach II, the headquarters of OKW, Armed Forces High Command. Despite its secondary designation Maybach II was the higher authority—the headquarters of the Supreme Commander, Hitler.

Unlike General Guderian, who operated directly from his OKH headquarters, the top echelon of OKW—its Chief of Staff, Field Marshal Wilhelm Keitel, and Chief of Operations, Colonel General Alfred Jodl—stayed close to Hitler wherever he chose to be. Only the operational machinery of OKW remained at Zossen. Through it Keitel and Jodl commanded the armies on the western front, besides using it as a clearinghouse for all of Hitler's directives to the entire German armed forces.

Thus Maybach II was the holy of holies, so cut off from Guderian's headquarters that few of his officers had even been permitted inside it. The sealing was so complete that the two headquarters were physically separated by high barbed-wire fences constantly patrolled by sentries. No one, Hitler had declared in 1941, was to know more than was necessary for the carrying out of his duties. In Guderian's headquarters it was said that "if the enemy ever captures OKW we'll go right on working as usual: we won't know anything about it."

Beneath the protective canopy of the forest, Heinrici's car followed one of the many narrow dirt roads that crisscrossed the complex. Spotted among the trees in irregular rows were low concrete buildings. They were so spaced that they got maximum protection from the trees, but just to be sure, they had been painted in drab camouflage colors of green, brown and black. Vehicles were off the roads—parked by the sides of the barracks-like buildings beneath camouflaged netting. Sentries stood everywhere, and at strategic points around the camp the low humps of manned bunkers rose above the ground.

These were part of a warren of underground installations extending beneath the entire encampment, for there was more of Maybach I and Maybach II below ground than above. Each building had three floors underground and was connected to the next by passageways. The largest of these subterranean installations was "Exchange 500"—the biggest telephone, teletype and military radio communications exchange in Germany. It was completely self-contained, with its own air conditioning (including a special filtration system against enemy gas attacks), water supply, kitchens and living quarters. It was almost seventy feet beneath the surface—the equivalent of a seven-story building below ground.

Exchange 500 was the only facility shared by OKH and OKW. Besides connecting all the distant senior military, naval and Luftwaffe commands with the two headquarters and Berlin, it was the main exchange for the Reich government and its various administrative bodies. It had been completed in 1939, designed to serve a far-flung empire. In the main trunk or long-lines room, scores of operators sat before boards with blinking lights; above each was a small card bearing the name of a city—Berlin, Prague, Vienna, Copenhagen, Oslo and so on. But the lights had gone out on some consoles—boards that still carried labels such as Athens, Warsaw, Budapest, Rome and Paris.

Despite all the camouflaging precautions, the Zossen complex had been bombed—Heinrici could see the evidence plainly as his car rolled to a stop outside Guderian's command building. The area was pitted with craters, trees had been uprooted, and some buildings were badly damaged. But the effect of the bombing had been minimized by the heavy construction of the buildings—some of which had walls up to three feet thick.*

* Zossen was, in fact, heavily bombed by the Americans just seven days before, on March 15, at the request of the Russians. The message from Marshal Sergei V. Khudyakov of the Red Army staff, to General John R. Deane, chief of the U.S. Military Mission in Moscow, now on file in Washington and Moscow, and appearing here for the first time, is an astonishing document for the insight it offers into the extent of Russian intelligence in Germany: "Dear General Deane: According to information we have, the General Staff of the German Army is situated 38 kms. south of Berlin, in a specially fortified underground shelter called by the Germans 'The Citadel.' It is located . . . 5½ to 6 kms. south-southeast of Zossen and from 1 to 1½ kms. east of a wide highway . . . [Reichsstrasse 96] which runs parallel to the railroad from Berlin to Dresden. The area occupied by the underground fortifications . . . covers about 5 to 6 square kilometers. The whole territory is surrounded by wired entanglements several rows in depth, and is very strongly guarded by an SS regiment. According to the same source the construction of

There was more evidence of the attack inside the main building. The first person Heinrici and Von Bila saw was Lieutenant General Hans Krebs, Guderian's Chief of Staff, who had been injured in the raid. Monocle rammed in his right eye, he sat behind a desk in an office close to Guderian's, his head wrapped in a large white turban of bandages. Heinrici did not care much for Krebs. Though the Chief of Staff was extremely intelligent, Heinrici saw him as "a man who refused to believe the truth, who could change black to white so as to minimize the true situation for Hitler."

Heinrici looked at him. Foregoing the niceties, he asked abruptly, "What happened to you?"

Krebs shrugged. "Oh, it was nothing," he replied. "Nothing." Krebs had always been unperturbable. Before the war he had been military attaché at the German Embassy in Moscow, and he spoke near-perfect Russian. After the signing of the Russo-Japanese Neutrality Pact in 1941, Stalin had embraced Krebs, saying, "We shall always be friends." Now, chatting casually with Heinrici, Krebs mentioned that he was still learning Russian. "Every morning," he said, "I place a dictionary on a shelf beneath the mirror and while shaving, learn a few more words." Heinrici nodded. Krebs might find his Russian useful soon.

Major Freytag von Loringhoven, Guderian's aide, joined them at that moment. With him was Captain Gerhard Boldt, another member of Guderian's personal staff. They formally greeted Heinrici and Von Bila, then escorted them to the General's offices. To Von Bila, everyone seemed immaculately dressed in shining, high boots, well-cut, well-pressed field-gray uniforms with the red tabs of staff rank at the collar. Heinrici, walking ahead with Von Lor-

---

the underground fortification was started in 1936. In 1938 and 1939 the strength of the fortifications was tested by the Germans against bombing from the air and against artillery fire. I ask you, dear General, not to refuse the kindness as soon as possible to give directions to the Allies' air forces to bomb 'The Citadel' with heavy bombs. I am sure that as a result . . . the German General Staff, if still located there, will receive damage and losses which will stop its normal work . . . and [may] have to be moved elsewhere. Thus the Germans will lose a well-organized communications center and headquarters. Enclosed is a map with the exact location of the German General Staff [headquarters]."

inghoven, seemed, as usual, sartorially out of place—especially from behind. The fur-collared sheepskin coat made Von Bila wince.

Von Loringhoven disappeared into Guderian's office, returned a few moments later and held the door open for Heinrici. "Herr Generaloberst Heinrici," he announced as Heinrici passed through. Von Loringhoven closed the door and then joined Boldt and Von Bila in the anteroom.

Guderian was sitting behind a large, paper-strewn desk. As Heinrici entered, he rose, warmly greeted the visitor, offered him a chair and for a few moments talked about Heinrici's trip. Heinrici saw that Guderian was tense and edgy. Broad-shouldered, of medium height, with thinning gray hair and a straggling moustache, Guderian seemed much older than his fifty-six years. Although it was not generally known, he was a sick man, suffering from high blood pressure and a weak heart—a condition that was not alleviated by his constant frustrations. These days the creator of Hitler's massive panzer forces—the General whose armored techniques had brought about the capture of France in 1940 in just twenty-seven days and who had nearly succeeded in accomplishing as much in Russia—found himself almost completely powerless. Even as Chief of the General Staff he had virtually no influence with Hitler. A hot-tempered officer at the best of times, Guderian was now so thwarted, Heinrici had heard, that he was subject to violent rages.

As they talked Heinrici looked about him. The office was spartan: a large map table, several straight-backed chairs, two phones, a green-shaded lamp on the desk, and nothing on the yellow-beige walls except the usual framed picture of Hitler, which hung over the map table. The Chief of the General Staff did not even have an easy chair.

Though Guderian and Heinrici were not intimate friends, they had known each other for years, respected each other's professional competence and were close enough to converse freely and informally. As soon as they got down to business, Heinrici spoke

81

frankly. "General," he said, "I've been in the wilds of Hungary. I know almost nothing about Army Group Vistula, what it's composed of or what the situation is on the Oder."

Guderian was equally blunt. Briskly he replied, "I should tell you, Heinrici, that Hitler didn't want to give you this command. He had somebody else in mind."

Heinrici remained silent.

Guderian continued: "I was responsible. I told Hitler that you were the one man needed. At first he wouldn't consider you at all. Finally, I got him to agree."

Guderian spoke in a businesslike, matter-of-fact fashion, but as he warmed to his subject the tone of his voice changed. Even twenty years later Heinrici would remember in detail the tirade that followed.

"Himmler," Guderian snapped. "That was the biggest problem. Getting rid of the man you're to replace—Himmler!"

Abruptly he got up from his chair, walked around the desk and began pacing the room. Heinrici had only recently learned that Reichsführer Heinrich Himmler was commander of the Army Group Vistula. The news had so astonished him that at first he did not believe it. He knew of Himmler as a member of Hitler's inner cabinet—probably the most powerful man in Germany next to the Führer. He did not know that Himmler had any experience commanding troops in the field—let alone directing the activities of a group of armies.

Bitterly Guderian recounted how in January, as the Polish front began to collapse before the tidal wave of the Red Army, he had desperately urged the formation of Army Group Vistula. At that time it was envisioned as a northern complex of armies holding a major defense line between the Oder and the Vistula, roughly from East Prussia to a point farther south where it would link with another army group. If the line held it would prevent the Russian avalanche from driving directly into the very heart of Germany, through lower Pomerania and Upper Silesia, then into Brandenburg and finally—Berlin.

To command the group Guderian had suggested Field Marshal Freiherr von Weichs. "At the time he was just the man for this situation," Guderian said. "What happened? Hitler said Von Weichs was too old. Jodl was present at the conference and I expected him to support me. But he made some remark about Von Weichs's religious feelings. That ended the matter.

"Then," thundered Guderian, "whom did we get? Hitler appointed Himmler! Of all people—Himmler!"

Guderian had, in his own words, "argued and pleaded against the appalling and preposterous appointment" of this man who had no military knowledge. But Hitler remained adamant. Under Himmler the front had all but collapsed. The Red Army had moved exactly as Guderian had predicted. Once the Russians were across the Vistula, part of their forces swung north and reached the Baltic at Danzig, cutting off and encircling some twenty to twenty-five divisions in East Prussia alone. The remaining Soviet armies sliced through Pomerania and upper Silesia, and reached the Oder and Neisse rivers. Everywhere along the eastern front the German line was overwhelmed. But no sector had collapsed so fast as Himmler's. His failure had opened the gates to the main drive across Germany and the link-up with the Western Allies. Above all, it had placed Berlin in jeopardy.

Guderian told Heinrici that, just forty-eight hours before, he had driven to the Army Group Vistula headquarters at Birkenhain, roughly fifty miles north of Berlin, to try to persuade Himmler to give up the command. There, he was informed that Himmler was ill. He had finally located the SS commander twenty miles away, near the town of Lychen, "cowering in a sanatorium with nothing more than a head cold."

Guderian quickly saw that Himmler's "illness" could be used to advantage. He expressed sympathy with the Reichsführer, and suggested that perhaps he had been overworking, that the number of posts he held would "tax the strength of any man." Besides being the commander of Army Group Vistula, the ambitious Himmler was also Minister of the Interior; Chief of the Gestapo, the

German police forces and security services; head of the SS, and Commander of the Training Army. Why not relinquish one of these posts, Guderian suggested—say, the Army Group Vistula?

Himmler grasped at the proposal. It was all too true, he told Guderian; his many jobs did, indeed, call for enormous endurance. "But," Himmler asked, "how can *I* possibly suggest to the Führer that I give up Vistula?" Guderian quickly told Himmler that, given the authorization, *he* would suggest it. Himmler quickly agreed. That night, added Guderian, "Hitler relieved the overworked, overburdened Reichsführer, but only after a lot of grumbling and with obvious reluctance."

Guderian paused, but only for a moment. His acrimonious recital of disaster had been punctuated by bursts of anger. Now he flared again. His voice choking with rage, he said: "The mess we're in is fantastic. The way the war is being run is unbelievable. Unbelievable!"

Through the previous months, Guderian recalled, he had tried to get Hitler to understand that "the real danger lay on the eastern front," and that "drastic measures were necessary." He urged a series of strategic withdrawals from the Baltic States—particularly from Courland in Latvia—and from the Balkans, and even suggested abandoning Norway and Italy. Everywhere lines needed shortening; each division relieved could be sped to the Russian front. According to intelligence, the Russians had twice as many divisions as the Western Allies—yet there were fewer German divisions fighting in the east than the west. Furthermore, the best German divisions were facing Eisenhower. But Hitler refused to go on the defensive; he would not believe the facts and figures that were placed before him.

Then, Guderian declared, "Hitler made possibly his greatest error." In December, 1944, he unleashed his massive, last-throw-of-the-dice offensive against the Western Allies through the rolling forests of the Ardennes in Belgium and northern Luxembourg. The attack, Hitler boasted, would split the Allies and change the whole course of the war. Against the center of the Allied line he hurled three fully equipped armies—a total of twenty divisions of which twelve were armored. Their objective: to break through, reach the Meuse, and then swing north to capture the vital supply port of Antwerp. Caught off balance, the Allies reeled under the blow and fell back with heavy losses. But the offensive soon petered out. Swiftly recovering, Allied troops drove Hitler's shattered armies back behind Germany's borders in just five weeks.

"When it became obvious that the offensive had failed," Guderian said, "I begged Hitler to get our troops out of the Ardennes and put them on the eastern front, where we expected the Russian offensive at any moment. It was no use—he refused to believe our estimates of their strength."

On January 9 Guderian told Hitler that the Russians could be expected to launch their attack from the Baltic to the Balkans with a massive force totaling some 225 divisions and 22 armored corps. The situation estimate had been prepared by General Reinhard Gehlen, Guderian's Chief of Intelligence. It indicated that the Russians would outnumber the Germans in infantry by eleven to one, in armor by seven to one, in both artillery and aircraft by at least twenty to one. Hitler pounded the table and in a frenzy denounced the author of the report. "Who prepared this rubbish?" he roared. "Whoever he is, he should be committed to a lunatic asylum!" Three days later the Russians attacked, and Gehlen was proved right.

"The front virtually collapsed," Guderian told Heinrici, "simply because most of our panzer forces were tied down in the west. Finally Hitler agreed to shift some of the armor, but he would not let me use the tanks to attack the Russian spearheads east of Berlin. Where did he send them? To Hungary, where they were thrown into a perfectly useless attack to recapture the oilfields.

"Why, even now," he fumed, "there are eighteen divisions sitting in Courland—tied down, doing nothing. They are needed here—not in the Baltic States! If we're going to survive, everything has got to be on the Oder front."

Guderian paused and, with an effort, calmed himself. Then he said: "The Russians are looking down our throats. They've halted their offensive to reorganize and regroup. We estimate that you'll have three to four weeks—until the floods go down—to prepare. In that time the Russians will try to establish new bridgeheads on the western bank and broaden those they already have. These have to be thrown back. No matter what happens elsewhere, the Russians must be stopped on the Oder. It's our only hope."

✛ 3 ✛

Now Guderian called for maps. In the anteroom outside, one of the aides peeled several from the top of the prepared pile, brought them into the office and spread them on the map table before the two Generals.

This was Heinrici's first look at the overall situation. More than one third of Germany was gone—swallowed by the advancing Allies from the west and east. All that remained lay between two great water barriers: on the west, the Rhine; on the east, the Oder and its linking river, the Neisse. And Heinrici knew the great industrial areas of the Reich that had not yet been captured were being bombed night and day.

In the west, Eisenhower's armies, as Heinrici had heard, were indeed on the Rhine, Germany's great natural defense line. The Anglo-American forces stretched for nearly five hundred miles along the western bank—roughly from the North Sea to the Swiss border. At one point the Rhine had even been breached. On March 7, the Americans had seized a bridge at Remagen, south of Bonn, before it could be completely destroyed. Now a bridgehead twenty miles wide and five miles deep sprawled along the eastern bank. Other crossings were expected momentarily.

In the east the Soviets had swarmed across eastern Europe and held a front of more than eight hundred miles—from the Baltic to the Adriatic. In Germany itself they stood along the Oder-Neisse river lines all the way to the Czechoslovakian border. Now, Guderian told Heinrici, they were feverishly preparing to resume their offensive. Reconnaissance planes had spotted reinforcements pouring toward the front. Every railhead was disgorging guns and equipment. Every road was clogged with tanks, motor- and horse-drawn convoys, and marching troops. What the Red Army's strength might be at the time of attack nobody could even estimate, but three army groups had been identified in Germany—concentrated for the most part directly opposite Army Group Vistula's positions.

Looking at the front he had inherited, Heinrici saw for the first time what he would later describe as "the whole shocking truth."

On the map the thin wavering red line marking the Vistula's positions ran for 175 miles—from the Baltic coast to the juncture of the Oder and Neisse in Silesia, where it linked with the forces of Colonel General Schörner. Most of the front lay on the western bank of the Oder, but there were three major bridgeheads still on the eastern bank: in the north, Stettin, the 13th-century capital of Pomerania; in the south, the town of Küstrin and the old university city of Frankfurt-on-Oder—both in the vital sector directly opposite Berlin.

To prevent the Russians from capturing the capital and driving into the very heart of Germany, he had only two armies, Heinrici discovered. Holding the front's northern wing was the Third Panzer Army under the command of the diminutive General Hasso von Manteuffel—after Guderian and Rommel probably the greatest panzer tactician in the Wehrmacht. He held positions extending about 95 miles—from north of Stettin to the juncture of the Hohenzollern Canal and the Oder, roughly 28 miles northeast of Berlin. Below that, to the confluence of the Neisse 80 miles away, the defense was in the hands of the bespectacled 47-year-old General Theodor Busse and his Ninth Army.

Depressed as he was by the overall picture, Heinrici was not unduly surprised by the huge forces arrayed against him. On the eastern front it was customary to fight without air cover, with a minimum of tanks, and while outnumbered by at least nine or ten to one. But everything, Heinrici knew, depended on the caliber of the troops. What alarmed him now was the makeup of these two armies.

To the experienced Heinrici the name of a division and its commander usually served as an indication of its history and fighting abilities. Now, examining the map, he found that there were few regular divisions in the east that he even recognized. Instead of the usual identifying numbers, most of them had odd names such as "Gruppe Kassen," "Döberitz," "Nederland," "Kurmark," "Berlin" and "Müncheberg." Heinrici wondered about the composition of these units. Were they splinter troops—the remnants of divisions simply thrown together? Guderian's map did not give him a very clear picture. He would have to see for himself, but he had a dawning suspicion that these were divisions in name only. Heinrici did not comment on his suspicions, for Guderian had other, more immediate problems to discuss—in particular, Küstrin.

Heinrici's biggest army was Busse's Ninth, the defense shield directly before Berlin. From the rash of red marks on the map it was clear that Busse faced pressing problems. The Russians, Guderian said, were concentrating opposite the Ninth Army. They were making a mighty effort to wipe out the two German-held bridgeheads on the eastern banks at Küstrin and in the area of Frankfurt. The situation at Küstrin was the more dangerous.

In that sector during the preceding weeks, the Red Army had succeeded in crossing the Oder several times and gaining footholds on the western bank. Most of these attempts had been thrown back, but despite every defense effort the Russians still held on around Küstrin. They had secured sizable bridgeheads on either side of the town. Between these pincer-like lodgments,

88

a single corridor remained, linking the defenders of Küstrin with the Ninth Army. Once these pincers snapped shut, Küstrin would fall and the linking of the two bridgeheads would provide the Russians with a major springboard on the western bank for their drive on Berlin.

And now Guderian tossed Heinrici another bombshell. "Hitler," he said, "has decided to launch an attack to wipe out the bridge-head south of Küstrin, and General Busse has been preparing. I believe it's to take place within forty-eight hours."

The plan, as Guderian outlined it, called for the attack to be launched from Frankfurt, thirteen miles below Küstrin. Five Panzer Grenadier divisions were to cross the river into the German bridgehead and from there attack along the eastern bank and hit the Russian bridgehead south of Küstrin from the rear.

Heinrici studied the map. Frankfurt-on-Oder straddles the river, with its greatest bulk on the western bank. A single bridge connects the two sections of the city. To the new commander of the Army Group Vistula two facts were starkly clear: the hilly terrain on the eastern bank offered ideal conditions for Russian artillery—from the heights they could stop the Germans dead in their tracks. But worse, the bridgehead across the river was too small for the assembly of five motorized divisions.

For a long moment Heinrici pored over the map. There was no doubt in his mind that the assembling German divisions would be instantly detected, and first pulverized by artillery, then hit by planes. Looking at Guderian, he said simply, "It's quite impossible."

Guderian agreed. Angrily he told Heinrici that the only way the divisions could assemble was "to roll over the bridge, one after the other—making a column of men and tanks about fifteen miles long." But Hitler had insisted on the attack. "It will succeed," he had told Guderian, "because the Russians won't expect such a daring and unorthodox operation."

Heinrici, still examining the map, saw that the sector between Küstrin and Frankfurt was jammed with Russian troops. Even if the attack could be launched from the bridgehead, the Russians were so strong that the German divisions would never reach Küstrin. Solemnly Heinrici warned: "Our troops will be pinned with their backs to the Oder. It will be a disaster."

Guderian made no comment—there was nothing to say. Suddenly he glanced at his watch, and said irritably, "Oh, God, I've got to get back to Berlin for the Führer's conference at three." The mere thought of it set off another furious outburst. "It's impossible to work," Guderian spluttered. "Twice a day I stand for hours listening to that group around Hitler talking nonsense—discussing nothing! I can't get anything done! I spend all of my time either on the road or in Berlin listening to drivel!"

Guderian's rage was so violent that it alarmed Heinrici. The Chief of Staff's face had turned beet red, and for a moment Heinrici feared Guderian would drop dead on the spot from a heart attack. There was an anxious silence as Guderian fought for control. Then he said: "Hitler is going to discuss the Küstrin attack. Perhaps you'd better come with me."

Heinrici declined. "If I'm supposed to launch this insane attack the day after tomorrow," he said, "I'd better get to my headquarters as soon as possible." Then stubbornly he added: "Hitler can wait a few days to see me."

In the anteroom, Heinrich von Bila was timing the meeting by the diminishing pile of maps and charts as they were taken into Guderian's office. There were only one or two left, so the briefing, he thought, must be almost over. He wandered over to the table and looked idly at the top map. It showed the whole of Germany but the lines on it seemed somehow different. Von Bila was about to turn away when something caught his eye. He looked closer. The map *was* different from all the others. It was the lettering that now caught his attention—it was in English. He bent down and began to study it carefully.

✢4✢

IT WAS ALMOST SIX when the weary Heinrici reached his headquarters at Birkenhain, near Prenzlau. During the two-and-a-half-
hour drive from Zossen, he had remained silent. At one point Von
Bila tried to open a conversation by asking the General if he had
seen the map. Von Bila assumed that Guderian had shown a separate copy to Heinrici and explained its contents. Heinrici, in fact,
knew nothing about it, and Von Bila got no answer. The General
simply sat tight-lipped and worried. Von Bila had never seen him
so dejected.

Heinrici's first glimpse of his new headquarters depressed him
even more. The Army Group Vistula command post consisted of a
large, imposing mansion flanked on either side by wooden barracks. The main building was an architectural monstrosity—a
massive, ornate affair with a row of oversized columns along its
front. Years before, Himmler had built the place as his own personal refuge. On a nearby siding stood his luxuriously appointed
private train, the "Steiermark."

Like Zossen, this headquarters was hidden in the woods, but
there the comparison ended. There was none of the military
bustle Heinrici had come to expect of an active army group headquarters. Except for an SS corporal in the foyer of the main building, the place seemed deserted. The corporal asked their names,
ushered them to a hard bench and disappeared.

Some minutes passed, then a tall, immaculately dressed SS
lieutenant general appeared. He introduced himself as Himm-

ler's Chief of Staff, Heinz Lammerding, and smoothly explained that the Reichsführer was "engaged in a most important discussion" and "could not be disturbed right now." Polite but cool, Lammerding did not invite Heinrici to wait in his office, nor did he make any of the usual gestures of hospitality. Turning on his heel, he left Heinrici and Von Bila to wait in the foyer. In all his years as a senior officer Heinrici had never been treated in such a cavalier fashion.

He waited patiently for fifteen minutes, then spoke quietly to Von Bila. "Go tell that Lammerding," he said, "that I have no intention of sitting out here one minute longer. I demand to see Himmler immediately." Seconds later Heinrici was escorted down a corridor and into Himmler's office.

Himmler was standing by the side of his desk. He was of medium build, his torso longer than his legs—which one of Heinrici's staff remembers as being like "the hind legs of a bull." He had a narrow face, a receding chin, squinting eyes behind plain wire spectacles, a small moustache and a thin mouth. His hands were small, soft and effeminate, the fingers long. Heinrici noted the texture of his skin, which was "pale, sagging and somewhat spongy."

Himmler came forward, exchanged greetings, and immediately launched into a long explanation. "You must understand," he said, taking Heinrici's arm, "that it is a most difficult decision for me to leave the Army Group Vistula." Still talking, he showed Heinrici to a chair. "But as you must know, I have so many posts, so much work to do—and also, I'm not in very good health."

Seating himself behind the desk, Himmler leaned back and said: "Now, I'm going to tell you all that has happened. I've asked for all the maps, all the reports." Two SS men came into the room; one was a stenographer, the other carried a large stack of maps. Behind them came two staff officers. Heinrici was happy to see that the officers wore Wehrmacht, not SS, uniforms. One of them was Lieutenant General Eberhard Kinzel, the Deputy Chief of Staff; the other, Colonel Hans Georg Eismann, the Chief of Operations. Heinrici was particularly glad to see Eismann, whom he knew as an exceptionally efficient staff officer. Lammerding was not present.

Himmler waited until all had taken seats. Then he launched into a dramatic speech of personal justification. It seemed afterward to Heinrici that "he began with Adam and Eve," and then went into such laborious explanatory details that "nothing he said made sense."

Both Kinzel and Eismann knew that Himmler could talk like this for hours. Kinzel after a few minutes took his leave because of "pressing business." Eismann sat watching Himmler and Heinrici, mentally comparing them. He saw Heinrici, a "persevering, graying old soldier—a serious, silent, taut little man for whom courtesy was a thing taken for granted," being subjected to the flamboyant ranting of an unsoldierly upstart "who could not read the scale on a map." Looking at the wildly gesturing Himmler "repeating over and over the most unimportant facts in a theatrical tirade," he knew that Heinrici must be both shocked and disgusted.

Eismann waited as long as he could, then he, too, asked to be excused because "there was much to do." A few minutes later, Heinrici noticed that the stenographer, unable to keep abreast of Himmler's verbal torrent, had put down his pencil. Heinrici, bored beyond belief, sat silently, letting the words flow over him.

Suddenly the phone on Himmler's desk rang. Himmler picked it up and listened for a moment. He looked startled. He handed the phone to Heinrici. "You're the new commander," he said. "You'd better take this call."

Heinrici picked up the phone. He said: "Heinrici here, who is this?"

It was General Busse, commander of the Ninth Army. Heinrici froze as he listened. Disaster had already befallen his new command. The Russians had spotted Busse's preparations for the Küstrin attack. The 25th Panzer Division, one of Busse's best, which for months had held the corridor open between the Russian bridgeheads on either side of Küstrin, had been quietly pulling out of its positions in preparation for the offensive. Another division, the 20th Panzer, had been moving into the 25th's positions. The Russians had seen the exchange and attacked from the north and south. The pincers had snapped shut, just as Guderian had feared. The 20th Panzer Division was cut off, Küstrin was isolated —and the Russians now had a major bridgehead for the assault on Berlin.

Heinrici cupped the phone and grimly told Himmler the news. The Reichsführer looked nervous and shrugged his shoulders. "Well," he said, "you are commander of Army Group Vistula."

Heinrici stared. "Now look here," he said sharply. "I don't know a damn thing about the army group. I don't even know what soldiers I have, or who's supposed to be where."

Himmler looked blankly at Heinrici and Heinrici saw that he could expect no help. He turned back to the phone and immediately authorized Busse to counterattack, at the same time promising the Ninth Army commander that he would get to the front as soon as possible. As he replaced the receiver, Himmler began his rambling discourse again as though nothing had happened.

But Heinrici was now thoroughly exasperated. Bluntly he interrupted. It was necessary, he told Himmler, that he get the Reichsführer's considered opinion of the overall situation as far as Germany and her future were concerned. The question, he later remembered, "was visibly disagreeable" to Himmler. The Reichsführer rose from his chair, came around the desk and, taking Heinrici's arm, ushered him across to a sofa on the far side of the room, out of earshot of the stenographer. Then in a quiet voice Himmler dropped a bombshell. "Through a neutral country," he confided, "I have taken the necessary steps to start negotiations with the West." He paused, and added: "I'm telling you this in absolute confidence, you understand."

There was a long silence. Himmler looked at Heinrici expectantly—presumably awaiting some comment. Heinrici was stunned. This was treason—betrayal of Germany, its armies and its leaders. He struggled to control his thoughts. Was Himmler telling the truth? Or was it a ruse to trick him into an indiscretion? The ambitious Himmler, Heinrici believed, was capable of anything— even of treason in order to grab power for himself. The experienced front-line General sat speechless, revolted by Himmler's very presence.

Suddenly the door opened and an SS officer appeared. Himmler seemed relieved at the interruption. "Herr Reichsführer," the officer announced, "the staff has assembled to say good-bye." Himmler rose and, without uttering another word, left the room.

By 8 P.M. Himmler, his SS officers and bodyguard were gone. They took everything with them, including, as Balzen, Heinrici's batman, soon discovered, the mansion's flatware, plates, even cups and saucers. Their departure was so complete that it was almost as though Himmler had never set foot inside the headquarters. Aboard his luxurious private train, Himmler headed swiftly into the night away from the Oder front, toward the west.

Behind him he left a furious Heinrici. The new commander's anger and disgust mounted as he looked about his headquarters; one of his officers remembers that "Heinrici's temper rose several degrees" as he examined the effeminate decor of Himmler's mansion. The enormous office and everything in it was white. The bedroom was decorated in soft green—drapes, carpeting, upholstery, even the quilts and coverlets. Heinrici acidly remarked that the place was more "appropriate for an elegant woman than a soldier trying to direct an army."

Later that night Heinrici telephoned his former Chief of Staff in Silesia, as he had promised, and told him what had occurred. He had regained control of his emotions, and could think of the encounter more coolly. Himmler's disclosures, he had decided, were too fantastic to believe. Heinrici decided to forget about it. On the phone to his old colleague in Silesia, Heinrici said, "Himmler was only too happy to leave. He couldn't get out of here fast enough. He didn't want to be in charge when the collapse comes. No. He wanted just a simple general for that—and I'm the goat."

In the room assigned him, Heinrici's aide, Captain Heinrich von Bila, paced restlessly up and down. He was unable to get his mind off the map he had seen at Guderian's headquarters at Zossen. It was odd, he thought, that no one had objected when he studied it—yet the map was obviously a confidential command document. Guderian must have shown it to him, but Heinrici had made no comment. Was it possible therefore that the map was less important than he believed? Maybe it had even been prepared at Guderian's headquarters—as a German estimate of Allied intentions. Still, Von Bila found that hard to accept—why print it in English, not German? There was only one other explanation: that it *was* an Allied map, captured somehow by German Intelligence. Where else could it have come from? If this was true—and Von Bila could think of no other answer—then somehow he had to warn his wife and three children. According to that map, if Germany was defeated, his home in Bernberg would lie in the zone controlled by the Russians. For unless Von Bila was imagining things, he had actually seen a top-secret plan showing how the Allies proposed to occupy and partition Germany.

✢ 5 ✢

FIFTY MILES AWAY, the original of the map and its supporting papers lay in a safe at Auf dem Grat 1, Dahlem, Berlin—the emergency headquarters of Colonel General Alfred Jodl, Chief of Operations of OKW (Armed Forces High Command). And of all the fantastic secrets that had come into the hands of German Intelligence during the war, this red-covered dossier was the most brutally revealing document Jodl had ever read.

The file contained a letter and a seventy-page background memorandum; stitched into the back cover were two pull-out maps, each approximately twenty by eighteen inches and drawn to a scale of one inch to twenty-nine miles. Jodl wondered if the Allies had yet discovered that a copy of the preamble to one of their top-secret war directives was missing. It had been captured from the British in late January, in the closing days of the Ardennes offensive.

The Allied plan was considered so explosive by Hitler that only a few at OKW headquarters were permitted to see it. In the first week of February, the Führer, after spending one entire evening studying the dossier, classified the papers as "State Top Secret." His military advisers and their staffs could study the plan, but no one else. Not even the members of his own cabinet were informed. But, despite these restrictions, one civilian saw the documents and maps: Frau Luise Jodl, the General's bride of only a few weeks.

One evening, just before their marriage, General Jodl decided to show the papers to his fiancée. She was, after all, the recipient of many military secrets: she had been a confidential secretary to the German High Command. Placing the entire file in his briefcase, General Jodl took it to her apartment, a block away from his headquarters. Almost as soon as the front door was safely closed behind him, he produced the papers and said to his fiancée: "That's what the Allies intend to do with Germany."

Luise took the red-covered file over to a table and began looking through the pages. She had long ago learned to read military documents and maps, but in this instance that ability was hardly necessary—the papers were crystal clear. Her heart sank. What she held in her hands was the Allied blueprint for the occupation of the Fatherland after Germany's defeat. Someone at Eisenhower's headquarters, she thought, had a vindictive bent in choosing code words. Across the cover of the file was the chilling title, "Operation Eclipse."

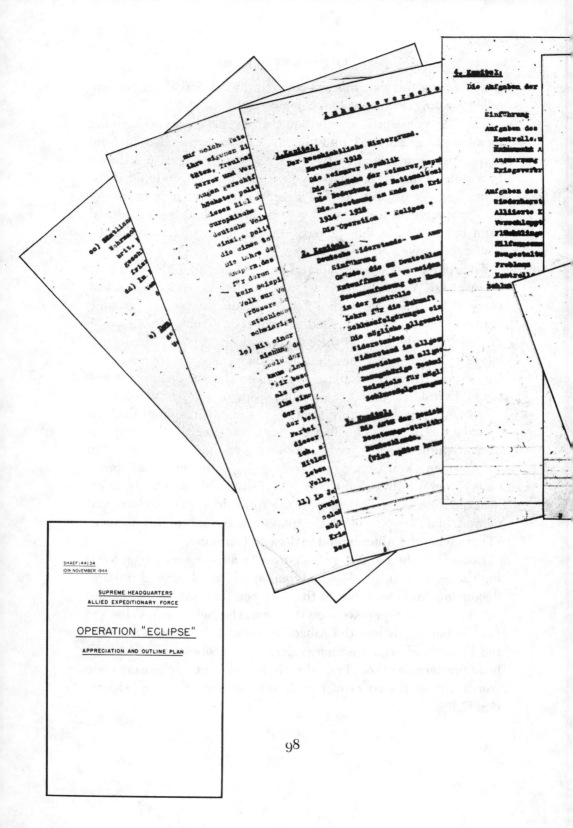

SHAEF (44) 34
IOth NOVEMBER 1944

SUPREME HEADQUARTERS
ALLIED EXPEDITIONARY FORCE

OPERATION "ECLIPSE"

APPRECIATION AND OUTLINE PLAN

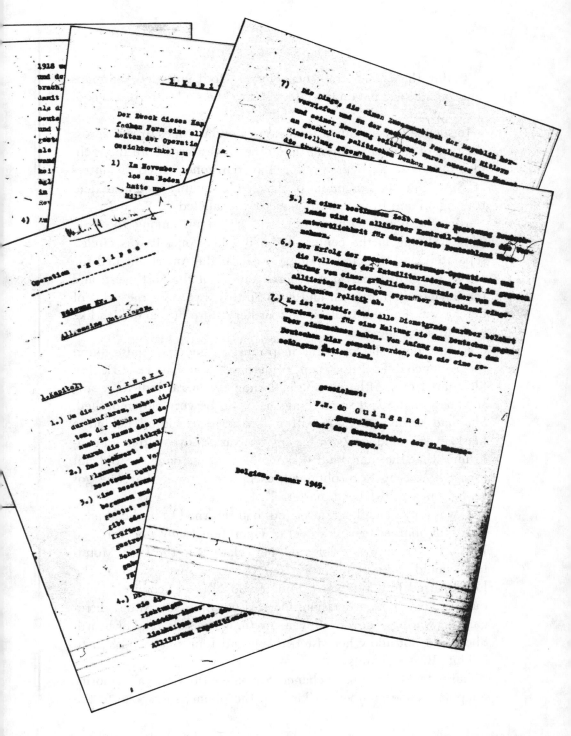

Jodl's actual headquarters translation of the original British copy of Operation Eclipse. This picture shows the covering letter, signed by Montgomery's Chief of Staff, Sir Francis de Guingand. It was on Jodl's desk less than three months after it had been circulated to only the highest officers of the Allied Armies, and one month before it was even ratified at Yalta, in February, 1945. At left is the cover of one of SHAEF's copies of Eclipse. Note the date.

Taking the dossier from her, General Jodl unfolded the maps and spread them flat on the table. "Look," he said bitterly, "look at the frontiers."

In silence Luise studied the heavy boundary lines drawn across the face of the map. The north and northwest area bore the inch-high initials "U.K." The southern, Bavarian zone carried the letters "U.S.A.," and the remainder of the Reich, roughly the entire central region and from there due east, was labeled "U.S.S.R." Even Berlin, she noted with dismay, was sliced up among the "Big Three." Lying in the center of the Russian zone, it was circled separately and trisected among the Allies: the Americans had the south; the British part of the north and all of the northwest; and the Soviets the northeast and east. So this was to be the price of defeat, she thought. Luise looked at her future husband. "It's like a nightmare," she said.

Even though she knew the map must be genuine, Luise found the evidence difficult to accept. Where, she asked, had the Eclipse file come from? Although she had known General Jodl for years, she knew that about some things he could be very closemouthed. She had always thought Alfred "withdrawn, hiding behind a mask, even from me." Now his answer was evasive. Although confirming that the maps and documents were genuine, he did not reveal how they were obtained, except to remark that "we got them from a British headquarters."

It was only much later, after Jodl had returned to his headquarters, that another fearful aspect of Operation Eclipse occurred to Luise. If Germany was defeated, her relatives in the Harz Mountains would be living in the Russian-occupied zone. Although she loved Alfred Jodl and was completely loyal to her country, Luise made a very human decision. On this occasion she would disregard his warnings never to reveal anything she saw, read or heard. She could not allow her sister-in-law and four small children to fall into Russian hands.

Luise decided to take a chance. She knew the General's priority telephone code number. Picking up the phone, she spoke to the operator and called her relatives. Within minutes she got through. After a brief and innocuous conversation with her surprised sister-in-law, Luise casually remarked in closing, "You know the east wind is very strong these days. I really think you and the children should move west beyond the river."

Slowly she put down the receiver—hoping that her clumsily coded message had been understood. At the other end of the line, her sister-in-law heard the click as the receiver was replaced. She wondered why Luise had called so late at night. It was good to hear from her, but she had no idea what Luise was talking about. She thought no more about it.

The General and Luise were married on March 6. Since then Frau Jodl had worried that somehow her husband might find out about the call. She need not have been concerned. The overburdened General had more pressing problems.

By now Jodl and his staff officers had studied and analyzed Operation Eclipse so thoroughly that they knew every paragraph almost by heart. Although it was not a strategic document—that is, it did not warn of imminent enemy moves that called for corresponding German countermoves—the Eclipse plan was almost as important. For one thing, it helped answer a series of questions that had bedeviled Jodl and the OKW for years: How strong, they had wondered, was the alliance between the Western Powers and the Soviet Union? Would it fall asunder when they sat down to divide the spoils? Now that Russian forces held most of Central Europe, did the "unconditional surrender" declaration made by Churchill and Roosevelt after the 1943 Casablanca Conference still stand? And did the Allies seriously intend to impose such terms on a defeated Germany? As Jodl and the German High Command studied the Eclipse file, all such questions about Allied intentions disappeared. The Allied document spelled out the answers in unmistakable terms.

Not until the second week in February, however, did Jodl realize the full importance of the file—in particular, of its maps. On February 9 and for the next three days, Roosevelt, Churchill and

Stalin met in secret conclave at Yalta. In spite of intelligence efforts to find out exactly what had transpired at the meeting, about all Jodl learned was contained in the official communiqué issued to the world's press on February 12—but that was enough. Vague and guarded as the announcement was, it left no doubt that the Eclipse papers and maps were the key to the announced Allied intentions.

One paragraph in the official communiqué stated: "We have agreed on common policies and plans for enforcing the unconditional surrender terms which we shall impose together . . . These terms will not be made known until the final defeat of Germany. . . . Under the agreed plan, the forces of the Three Powers will each occupy a separate zone of Germany. . . ." It was not necessary for the Allies to state the "terms"—Jodl had already read them in the Eclipse file. And though the Yalta communiqué did not reveal the proposed zones of occupation, Jodl knew them, too. The position and precise boundaries of each zone were shown on the Eclipse maps.

There were many other conclusions that could be deduced, but one was particularly bitter for Jodl. It was clear that whatever else had occurred at Yalta, the Allied plans for Germany had been merely ratified at the meeting of the Big Three. While the Yalta communiqué gave the impression that the partitioning and occupation blueprint had originated at the meeting, the dates on the Eclipse documents and maps proved beyond doubt that the basic decisions had been reached months before. The covering letter attached to the Eclipse background memorandum was signed in January. The maps had been prepared before that: they had been printed in late '44 and carried a November date. Plainly, Operation Eclipse, which was defined as "planning and operations for the occupation of Germany," could never have been produced at all unless there was complete unity among the Allies—a sobering fact that withered one of Germany's last hopes.

From the moment the Red Army crossed the Reich's eastern frontiers, Hitler and his military advisers had waited for the first cracks of disunity to appear among the Allies. It would surely happen, they believed, because the West would never allow Soviet Russia to dominate Central Europe. Jodl shared these views. He was banking especially on the British, for he felt that they would never tolerate such a situation.* But that was before he set eyes on Operation Eclipse. Eclipse indicated clearly that the alliance was still intact and Yalta had confirmed it.

Beyond that, the very first paragraph of the covering letter—a foreword to the entire file—showed the complete agreement among the Allies. It read: "In order to carry out the surrender terms imposed on Germany, the governments of the United States, the Soviet Union and the United Kingdom (the latter also in the name of the Dominions) have agreed that Germany is to be occupied by the Armed Forces of the three powers." † And there was no disputing the authority of the letter. It had been signed in January, 1945, at the British Twenty-first Army Group Headquarters, then in Belgium, by no less a personage than Major General Sir Francis de Guingand, Field Marshal Montgomery's Chief of Staff.

The most crushing blow of all for Jodl was the repeated emphasis on unconditional surrender; it was mentioned again and again. From the beginning the Germans had felt sure the unconditional surrender declaration had been intended much as morale-building propaganda for the Allied home fronts. Now they knew better:

* At his conference on January 27, 1945, Hitler asked Goering and Jodl: "Do you think that deep down inside, the English are enthusiastic over all the Russian developments?" Jodl answered without hesitation. "Certainly not," he replied. "Their plans were quite different . . . later . . . the full realization will come." Goering was also confident. "They certainly didn't plan that we hold them off while the Russians conquer all of Germany," he said. "They had not counted on us . . . holding them off in the West like madmen, while the Russians drive deeper and deeper into Germany." Jodl fully agreed, pointing out that the British "have always regarded the Russians with suspicion." Goering was so certain that the British would attempt some sort of compromise with the Reich, rather than see the heart of Europe fall into the Communist orbit, that he said: "If this goes on we will get a telegram [from the British] in a few days."

† There may be some slight variations between this translation and the original document. When Eclipse was captured, it was translated into German and then photographed. The version given above is a translation of the captured document back into English.

the Allies had obviously meant every word of it. "The only possible answer to the trumpets of total war," Eclipse said, "is total defeat and total occupation. . . . It must be made clear that the Germans will not be able to negotiate in our sense of that word."

The Allied intent promised no hope, no future for Germany. It was clear that even if the Reich wished to capitulate, there was no way she could do so short of unconditional surrender. To Jodl, this meant that there was nothing left for Germany but to fight to the bitter end.*

It was during the last week of March—the exact day no one could later remember—that General Reinhard Gehlen, Guderian's Chief of Intelligence, drove to Prenzlau for a meeting with the new commander of Army Group Vistula. In his briefcase was a copy of Operation Eclipse. Gehlen outlined for Heinrici the latest known dispositions of the Russian troops on the Oder, then he produced the Eclipse file and explained what it was. Heinrici slowly looked through the pages. Then he pored over the maps. For a long time he studied them. Finally, Heinrici looked at Gehlen and in one line summarized what everyone in the High Command really knew the document to mean. *"Das ist ein Todesurteil"*—This is a death sentence—he said.

---

* At Jodl's trial in Nuremberg in 1946, he was asked why he had not advised Hitler to capitulate early in 1945. Jodl said: "The reasons against it were primarily . . . unconditional surrender . . . and even if we had any doubt as to what faced us, it was completely removed by the fact that we captured the English Eclipse." At this point in his testimony, Jodl looked at the British officers present and said with a half-smile, "The gentlemen of the British delegation will know what that is." The fact is that the remark was lost on the Britishers at the trial: Eclipse had been kept so secret that they knew nothing about it. It was this mysterious reference, plus several interviews with Frau Jodl, that led the author to Operation Eclipse and its contents, revealed here for the first time.

THE DEFENDERS

THE GENERAL

Colonel General Gotthard Heinrici, commander of Army Group Vistula. *Below, right,* Heinrici in his sheepskin coat; *below, left,* Heinrici today, with the author.

Heinrici's Chief of Staff, Major General von Trotha.

General Max Pemsel, the fortifications expert who found Berlin's defenses "utterly futile."

Major General Hellmuth Reymann, Military Commander of Berlin, examining an Italian rifle.

Colonel Hans Refior (right), Reymann's Chief of Staff.

Top, Frau Jodl, in 1945; *below,* as she is today. *Right,* Colonel General Alfred Jodl and his wife on their wedding day, March 7, 1945.

Colonel General Heinz Guderian, Chief of the General Staff in 1945. "The mess we're in is fantastic." This photograph was taken in May, 1940, when Guderian commanded the spearhead of the German panzer thrust to the Channel.

Major General Reinhard Gehlen, Guderian's Chief of Intelligence; now head of the West Germany Intelligence Service. This is the only picture known to exist of him.

General Walther Wenck, in whose hurriedly organized Twelfth Army Hitler placed his last hopes. *At left*, he is shown in 1945, *above*, today.

SS General Felix Steiner, commander of "Group Steiner" (photographed today), whose orders were to save Berlin and free the Führer.

Colonel Theodor von Dufving, *above,* in 1945 and today. Von Dufving was Chief of Staff to General Karl Weidling, commander of the 56th Panzer Corps, whom Hitler first ordered shot, then appointed Commandant of Berlin. Weidling and Von Dufving surrendered the city to Chuikov on May 2, 1945. The Russian photograph below purports to show Weidling after the capitulation, but it is probably a posed shot, since the actual surrender took place in a house in Tempelhof, rather than in a bunker.

THE COMMANDERS

General Theodor Busse, commander of the Ninth Army, *at left,* in 1945; *at right,* today.

General Hasso von Manteuffel, commander of the Third Panzer Army.
"We have an army of ghosts."

Colonel Hans Oscar Wöhlermann, artillery commander, 56th Panzer Corps. "Everywhere," he said, were soldiers, "running away like madmen."

PHOTO BY THE AUTHOR

Colonel Günther Reichhelm, Twelfth Army Chief of Staff, in 1945 and today.

Lieutenant General Wolf Hagermann, Ninth Army.

Captain Hellmuth Lang (shown standing behind Rommel, 1944) joined Heinrici in the closing hours of the war with a message of warning.

THE HITLER YOUTH

"The dream was gone. . . ."

Willy Feldheim, who fought as a Hitler Youth in Berlin. The top photograph shows him at the age of 15, in 1945. The middle photograph shows him after his release by the Russians from two years in a POW camp; the bottom photograph shows him today.

PHOTO BY THE AUTHOR

The "soldiers" of the Berlin defense, aged between 12 and 15, photographed after capture. This picture was released to the author by the Russians. *Below,* the Volkssturm Home Guard, some in their seventies.

A rare view toward the Brandenburg Gate, showing one of the enormous camouflage canopies that were hung umbrella-like over various parts of the city as protection against air-raid reconnaissance aircraft.

THE CITY BEFORE THE ATTACK

The Tiergarten, littered with wreckage; in the background, the Reichstag.

A few days later—on Palm Sunday, March 25—Colonel General Jodl examined the Eclipse maps again. He had good reason to do so. Units of General George S. Patton's U.S. Third Army had crossed the Rhine on Thursday night at the farming village of Oppenheim, near Mainz, and were now heading for Frankfurt. The following day, in the north, Field Marshal Montgomery's forces swept across the river in a massive assault on a 25-mile front. Despite everything, the Rhine line was crumbling—and the Western Allies were driving fast. Now Jodl, anxiously re-examining the Eclipse maps, wondered how deeply the Allies intended to drive into Germany. That was one question the Eclipse background memorandum did not answer. Jodl wished he had the other sections of the plan—particularly the part covering military operations.

Still, the maps provided a clue. He had even mentioned the matter to his wife. It was only a hunch, but Jodl thought he was right. The maps showed that the line of demarcation between the Anglo-Americans and the Russians ran roughly along the river Elbe from Lübeck to Wittenberge, and from there coiled south to the vicinity of Eisenach, then swung due east to the Czech border. Was that line, besides being a zonal boundary, also the terminating point of the Anglo-American advance? Jodl was nearly certain that it was. He told his wife he did not think the Americans and British were driving for Berlin; he believed they had decided to leave the capture of the capital to the Red Army. Unless the Eclipse maps had been changed, it looked to Jodl as though Eisenhower's forces would grind to a halt on the Eclipse boundary line.

Part Three

THE OBJECTIVE

✤ 1 ✤

A LITTLE BEFORE MIDNIGHT on Palm Sunday, an American staff car pulled up outside the gray stone headquarters of the 82nd Airborne Division in Sissonne, northern France. Two officers got out. One was in American uniform, the other was dressed in British battle dress without insignia. The second man, tall and lanky, wore a neat green beret and, in vivid contrast to his blond hair, sported a large, fierce-looking red moustache. To the British and Americans his name was almost unpronounceable: Arie D. Bestebreurtje. He was widely known among them as "Arie," or "Captain Harry." Even those names changed from mission to mission, for he spent most of his time behind German lines. Arie was a Special Forces Agent and a member of the Dutch Intelligence Service.

A few days before, Arie had been called to Brussels by his superiors and told that he was being assigned to the 82nd Division for a special operation. He was to report to the youthful 38-year-old Major General James M. Gavin, 82nd Division commander, to take part in a top-secret briefing. Now, Arie and his escorting officer entered the headquarters, hurried up a flight of stairs to the second floor and down a corridor to a well-guarded map room. Here, their credentials were checked by a military policeman who then saluted and opened the door.

Inside, Arie was warmly greeted by General Gavin and his Chief of Staff, Colonel Robert Wienecke. Most of the men in the room,

Arie saw, were old friends: he had jumped and fought with them during the 82nd's assault on Nijmegen, Holland. His superiors in Brussels had not exaggerated the security measures he could expect. There were only fifteen officers present—regimental commanders and certain members of their staffs, all clearly hand-picked. The room itself was quite plain. There were a few benches and tables, some charts on the walls. At one end of the room a curtain covered a large, wall-sized map.

Each man's name was now called out by a security officer who checked it off against a roster; then General Gavin quickly opened the proceedings. Standing by the curtained map, he motioned everyone to gather around. "Only those of you with an absolute reason to know have been asked to this briefing," he began, "and I must emphasize that, until further orders, nothing you hear to-night is to go beyond this room. In a way, you will be training your men in the dark, for you will not be able to reveal to them the objective. Actually, you've already been giving them part of their training, although most of you were completely unaware of it. Over the last few weeks you and your men have been jumping or flying onto a specific training area deliberately marked and laid out to simulate the actual dimensions of our next assault target.

"Gentlemen, we're going in for the kill. This is the Sunday punch." He yanked the cords at the side of the map. The curtains slid back, revealing the target: Berlin.

Arie looked closely at the faces of the officers as they stared at the map. He thought he saw eagerness and anticipation. It did not surprise him. These commanders had been frustrated for months. Most of them had jumped with their units into Sicily, Italy, Normandy and Holland, but lately the division had been relegated to ground actions, mainly in the Ardennes during the Battle of the Bulge. Arie knew that as crack airborne troops they felt they had been denied their true role: assaulting objectives in front of the advancing armies and then holding on until relieved. The truth was that the Allied advance had been so fast that planned parachute drops had been canceled again and again.

The assault on Berlin, Gavin explained, would be part of a First Allied Airborne Army operation calling for units from three divisions. The 82nd, designated "Task Force A," was to have the major role. Unrolling a transparent overlay from the top of the map, Gavin pointed to a series of squares and ovals marked in black grease pencil that outlined the various objectives and drop zones. "As plans now stand," he said, "the 101st Airborne Division will grab Gatow Airfield, west of the city. A brigade from the British 1st Airborne Corps is to seize Oranienburg Airfield to the northwest." He paused and then continued. "Our piece of real estate is right in Berlin itself—Tempelhof Airport."

The 82nd's target seemed incredibly small. In the sprawling 321 square miles of the city and its environs, the airport looked like a postage stamp—a smudge of green barely one and a half miles square, lying in a heavily built-up area. On its north, east and southern fringes there were, rather ominously, no less than nine cemeteries. "Two regiments will hold the perimeters," Gavin said, "and the third will move into the buildings north of the field, toward the center of Berlin. We'll hang on to this airhead until the ground forces get to us. That should not be long—not more than a few days at the most."

"Blind" training of the paratroopers, Gavin said, was to be intensified. Terrain models of Tempelhof and the surrounding areas would be set up in a "secure" room of the headquarters; photographic coverage of the drop zone, intelligence appreciations and other materials would be made available to the regimental commanders and their staffs for specific planning. "We are also lucky," said Gavin, "to have the services of Captain Harry. He is an expert on Berlin—particularly on Tempelhof and the surrounding region. He will be jumping with us and from now on will be available for briefings and to answer all your questions."

Gavin paused again and looked at his officers. "I'm sure all of you want to know the answer to the big question: how soon? That's up to the Germans. The airborne plan has been in the works since last November. There have been constant changes and we must expect many more before we get a target date. 'A-Day,' as that day has been designated, will depend on the speed of the Allied advance toward Berlin. Certainly the drop won't be scheduled until the ground forces are within a reasonable distance of the city. But A-Day may only be a matter of two or three weeks away. So we don't have much time. That's all I can tell you now."

Gavin stepped back and turned the meeting over to his staff officers. One after the other they went into each phase of the operation, and as they talked Gavin sat half listening. As he later recalled, he regretted the fact that security had prevented him from revealing the details fully. He had been less than candid, for he had told his men only one part of the First Allied Airborne operation—the operational section calling for the assault in conjunction with the Allied drive to capture Berlin. What he had not mentioned was that the same airborne drop might be ordered under a different military condition: the sudden collapse or surrender of Germany and her armed forces. But that part of the plan was still top secret. It was the logical extension to Operation Overlord— the invasion of Europe—and for a time had been known as Operation Rankin, Case C, and later as Operation Talisman. That last title had been changed in November, 1944, for security reasons. Now it bore the code name Operation Eclipse.

Eclipse was so secret that, apart from high-ranking staff officers at Supreme Headquarters, only a score of generals had been permitted to study it. They were army or corps commanders or those in the other services with equivalent responsibilities. Few division commanders knew anything about Eclipse. Gavin had learned only some of the plan's objectives and those parts of it that specifically concerned him and his division.

During the previous months, at numerous conferences attended by General Lewis H. Brereton, Commander of the First Allied Airborne Army, and Gavin's immediate superior, Major General Matthew B. Ridgway, Commander of the 18th Corps, Eclipse had been referred to as the occupation plan for Germany. It detailed the operational moves which would immediately take place in the event of a German surrender or collapse. Its main objectives were the enforcement of unconditional surrender and the disarmament and control of all German forces.

Under Eclipse conditions the airborne assault plan on Berlin called for the paratroopers to move swiftly to "gain control over the enemy's capital and foremost administrative and transportation center . . . and display our armed strength." They were to subdue any remaining pockets of fanatics who might continue to resist; rescue and care for prisoners of war; seize top-secret documents, files and films before they could be destroyed; control information centers such as postal and telecommunications offices, radio stations, newspaper and printing plants; capture war criminals and surviving principals of the government, and establish law and order. The airborne troops were to initiate all these moves pending the arrival of land forces and military government teams.

That was as much as Gavin had been told about Operation Eclipse. As to what the plan contained regarding the manner in which Germany or Berlin was to be occupied or zoned after the defeat, he had no knowledge. Right now Gavin's only concern was to prepare the 82nd. But as a result of all the requirements, this meant the preparation of two distinct plans. The first was the operational assault to capture the city. The second, as conceived under Eclipse conditions, called for airborne units to drop on Berlin as an advance guard, but charged with a police action only. Gavin had told his commanders all he dared—even though he knew that if the war were to end suddenly the entire airborne mission would change dramatically. As things stood his orders were explicit. He was to follow the operational plan and get the 82nd ready for an airborne assault to capture Berlin.

Gavin was suddenly aware that the Dutch intelligence officer was concluding his part of the briefing. "I must repeat that if you are expecting help from anyone in Berlin, forget it," Captain Harry was saying. "Will you find guides willing to help? Answer: No. Is there an underground such as we had in France and Holland? Answer: No. Even if some Berliners are privately sympathetic, they will be too frightened to show it. We can discuss all these matters in greater detail later, but right now let me assure you of this: do not have any illusions that you will be greeted as liberators with champagne and roses. The army, the SS and the police will fight until the last bullet, and then they will come out with their hands in the air, tell you that the whole thing was really a dreadful mistake, that it was all Hitler's fault and thank you for getting to the city before the Russians."

The big Dutchman tugged at his moustache. "But they are going to fight like blazes," he said, "and it may be a bit sticky for a time. It will be worth it and I'm proud to be going with you. My friends, when we take Berlin, the war is over."

Taking Berlin would not be easy, Gavin knew, but he thought that the psychological shock of the assault might in itself overwhelm the German defenders. It would be one of the war's biggest airborne attacks. In the initial planning, the operation called for 3,000 protective fighters, 1,500 transport planes, probably more than 1,000 gliders and some 20,000 paratroopers—more than had been dropped in Normandy on D-Day. "All we need now," Gavin told his officers as the meeting broke up, "is a decision and the word 'Go.'"

Thirty miles away, at Mourmelon-le-Grand, the tough 101st Airborne Division was also in training and stood ready for any operation, but nobody in the 101st knew which one would be ordered. So many paratroop assault plans had "come down the pipe" from higher headquarters that the commander, Major General Maxwell D. Taylor, his assistant, Brigadier General Gerald J. Higgins, and the staff found themselves in a quandary. They had to prepare for all of them, but they seriously wondered if any of the projected drops would ever take place.

Besides the Berlin project there were plans for an airborne attack on the German naval base at Kiel (Operation Eruption); for a series of drops on prisoner-of-war camps (Operation Jubilant); and for an assault to seize objectives ahead of the U. S. Seventh Army as it drove toward the Black Forest (Operation Effective). Many others were under study—and some were quite fantastic. The 101st headquarters had learned that the staff of the First Allied Airborne Army was even considering a jump on the mountains around Berchtesgaden, in Bavaria, to seize the Eagle's Nest on the Obersalzberg and perhaps its owner, Adolf Hitler.

Obviously not all the drops could be scheduled. As General Higgins told the staff: "There just aren't that many transport planes to accommodate the airborne demands if all these operations are ordered. Anyway, we're not greedy—all we want is one!" But which operation would the airborne army get—and, in particular, what would be the role of the 101st? The Berlin drop seemed the most likely—even though the operations chief, Colonel Harry Kinnard, thought it would be "quite a hairy bit of business." Everyone was bitter that in the event of a Berlin drop the men of the 101st had drawn Gatow Airfield, while their arch rivals, the 82nd, had been given the primary objective, Tempelhof. Still, Berlin was the biggest target of the war; there was enough for everyone.

To Colonel Kinnard an airborne drop seemed the perfect way to end the war in Europe. On the war room map he had even drawn a red line from the staging areas in France to the 101st's drop zones in Berlin: the German capital was only 475 air miles away. If they got the green light he thought the first Americans could be in Berlin in just about five hours.

General Taylor, the 101st's Commander, and his assistant, General Higgins, while eager for the attack, wondered if the airborne would even get the chance. Higgins morosely studied the map. "The way the ground forces are moving," he said, "they're going to put us out of business."

On this same day, Sunday, March 25, the military leaders of the Western Allies received gratifying news from Supreme Headquarters of the Allied Expeditionary Force (SHAEF). In Washington and London, General George C. Marshall, U.S. Chief of Staff, and Field Marshal Sir Alan Brooke, Chief of the Imperial General Staff, studied a cable from General Dwight D. Eisenhower that had arrived the night before. "The recent series of victories west of the Rhine has resulted as planned in the destruction of a large proportion of available enemy forces on the Western Front. While not desiring to appear over-optimistic it is my conviction that the situation today presents opportunities for which we have struggled and which must be seized boldly. . . . It is my personal belief that the enemy strength . . . is becoming so stretched that penetrations and advances will soon be limited only by our maintenance. . . . I am directing the most vigorous actions on all fronts . . . I intend to reinforce every success with utmost speed."

✛ 2 ✛

FROM 800 FEET UP, the lines of men and vehicles seemed endless. Peering out of his unarmed Piper Cub, the scouting plane *Miss Me*, Lieutenant Duane Francies gazed down fascinated at the spectacle below. The landscape swarmed with troops, tanks and vehicles. Ever since late March, when the last of the armies crossed the Rhine, Francies had watched the breakout develop. Now the great river was far behind, and off to the right and left and stretching ahead as far as Francies could see was a vast khaki panorama.

Francies pushed the stick forward and *Miss Me* swooped down along the boundary of the British Second and U. S. Ninth armies.

He waggled the wings, saw the answering waves of the troops, and headed due east to take up his task as the "eyes" of the leading tank columns of the 5th Armored Division. Victory was near, of that he was sure. Nothing could stop this advance. It seemed to the 24-year-old pilot, he later recalled, that "the very crust of the earth itself had shaken loose and was rushing like hell for the Elbe," the last major water barrier before Berlin.

What Francies saw was only a minuscule part of the great Allied assault. For days now, in biting cold, in driving rain and through mud, in sleet and over ice, all along the Western Front from Holland almost to the Swiss border, a 350-mile-wide torrent of men, supplies and machines had been flooding into the German plains. The last great offensive was on. To destroy the German military might, seven powerful armies—eighty-five huge divisions, five of them airborne and twenty-three armored, the bulk of the immense Western Allied force of 4,600,000 men—were swarming into the Reich for the kill.

Makeshift flags of surrender—white sheets, towels, scraps of cloth—hung everywhere. In the towns and villages frightened Germans, still dazed by the battles that had washed over them, stared in amazement from doorways and shattered windows at the vast strength of the Allies that flowed all about them. The operation was gigantic, its speed breathtaking.

Hammering down every road were convoys of tanks, self-propelled guns, heavy artillery, armored cars, Bren gun carriers, ammunition conveyors, ambulances, gasoline trucks and huge Diesel transporters towing block-long trailers loaded with equipment—bridging sections, pontoons, armored bulldozers and even landing craft. Division headquarters were on the move, with their jeeps, staff cars, command caravans and massive radio trucks sprouting forests of trembling antennae. And in wave after wave, choking every road, were the troops—in trucks and on the backs of armored vehicles, marching by the sides of the motorized columns or slogging through the adjoining fields.

They formed a violent, gaudy parade, and in their midst were

127

battle flags, regimental badges and insignia that had made history in World War II. In the divisions, brigades and regiments were Guardsmen who had fought the rearguard action during the evacuation of Dunkirk, bearded Commandos in faded green berets, veterans of Lord Lovat's brigade who had raided the coasts of occupied Europe in the darkest years of the war, tough Canadians of the famous 2nd Division who had landed at Dieppe in the bloody rehearsal for the Normandy invasion. In the armored columns, pennants fluttering, were a few of the original "Desert Rats" of the 7th Armored Division who had helped run Field Marshal Erwin Rommel to ground in the Libyan sands. And riding high above the tremendous din of men and arms was the skirling music of the "Devils in Skirts," the 51st Highland Division, their pipes sounding the prelude to battle as they had always done.

In the phalanxes of Americans were divisions with impudent names and colorful legends—the "Fighting 69th," the 5th Armored "Victory Division," "The Railsplitters" of the 84th Infantry, the 4th Infantry "Ivy Division." There was the 2nd Armored, "Hell on Wheels," whose unconventional tank tactics had caused havoc for the Germans all the way from the wadis of North Africa to the banks of the Rhine. There was the 1st Division, "The Big Red One," with a record of more assault landings than any other American unit: the 1st, together with one of the oldest U.S. forces, the tough, tradition-steeped 29th "Blue and Gray" Division, had hung on when all seemed lost to a narrow strip of Normandy beach called "Omaha."

One unit, the illustrious 83rd Infantry Division, which was moving as fast as an armored task force, had recently been nicknamed "The Rag-Tag Circus" by the correspondents. Its resourceful commander, Major General Robert C. Macon, had given orders to supplement the division's transport with anything that moved; "no questions asked." Now the Rag-Tag Circus was going flat out in a weird assortment of hurriedly repainted captured German vehicles: Wehrmacht jeeps, staff cars, ammunition trucks, Mark V and Tiger panzers, motor bikes, buses and two cherished fire engines. Out in front, with infantrymen hanging all over it, was one of the fire trucks. On its rear bumper was a large, flapping banner. It read, NEXT STOP: BERLIN.

There were three great army groups. Between Nijmegen in Holland and Düsseldorf on the Rhine, Field Marshal Sir Bernard Law Montgomery's Twenty-first Army Group had erupted across the Rhine on March 23 and was now racing across the Westphalian plains, north of the great Ruhr Valley, Germany's industrial mainspring. Under Montgomery's command and holding his northern flank was the Canadian First Army under Lieutenant General Henry D. Crerar. In the center was Lieutenant General Sir Miles Dempsey's British Second Army (the most "allied" of all the Allied armies, the Second had, besides British, Scottish and Irish units, contingents of Poles, Dutch, Belgians, Czechs—and even a U.S. division, the 17th Airborne). Driving along the Army Group's southern flank was Montgomery's third force: Lieutenant General William H. Simpson's powerful U. S. Ninth Army. Already Montgomery's forces had left the Rhine almost fifty miles behind.

Next in the Allied line, holding a front of about 125 miles along the Rhine from Düsseldorf to the Mainz area, was the Twelfth Army Group under the quiet, unassuming General Omar N. Bradley. Like Montgomery, Bradley had three armies. However, one of them, the U. S. Fifteenth under Lieutenant General Leonard Gerow, was a "ghost" army; it was being prepared for occupation duties and for the moment was playing a relatively non-active role, holding the western bank of the Rhine, directly in front of the Ruhr, from the Düsseldorf area to Bonn. Bradley's strength lay with the powerful U. S. First and Third armies, a force totaling close to 500,000 men. General Courtney Hodges' U. S. First Army —the "workhorse" of the European theater and the army that had led the Normandy invasion—was surging south of the Ruhr, charging east at a breakneck pace. Ever since the capture of the Remagen bridge on March 7, Hodges had steadily enlarged the bridgehead on the Rhine's eastern bank. Division after division packed into it. Then on March 25 the men of the First had burst out of the lodgement with incredible force. Now, three days later, they were more than forty miles from their jump-off point. Storming across central Germany next to the First Army was General George S. Patton's famous U. S. Third Army. The controversial and explosive Patton—whose boast was that his Third Army had traveled farther and faster, liberated more square miles of the continent and killed and captured more Germans than any other—racked up another first. He had stolen Montgomery's thunder by secretly crossing the Rhine on the run more than twenty-four hours before the Twenty-first Army Group's much-publicized assault on March 23. Now Patton's tank columns were advancing eastward at the rate of thirty miles a day.

Next to Patton and on the right flank of General Bradley's command was the third great Allied ground force, General Jacob Devers' Sixth Army Group. Devers' two armies—Lieutenant General Alexander Patch's U. S. Seventh and General Jean de Lattre de Tassigny's French First—held the front's southern wing for roughly 150 miles. The armies of Patch and Patton were driving almost abreast of each other. De Tassigny's army was fighting over some of the most rugged terrain on the entire front, through the mountainous Vosges and Black Forest. His force, the first post-liberation French army, had not existed six months before. Now its 100,000 soldiers hoped there was still time before the war ended to settle accounts with *les boches*.

Everyone had a score to settle. But along the Western Front the German Army scarcely existed any longer as a cohesive, organized force. Decimated during the Ardennes offensive, the Reich's once-powerful armies had been finally smashed in the month-long campaign between the Moselle and the Rhine. Hitler's decision to fight west of the Rhine rather than withdraw his battered forces to prepared positions on the eastern banks had proved disastrous;

it would be recorded as one of the greatest military blunders of the war. Nearly 300,000 men had been taken prisoner and 60,000 were killed or wounded. In all, the Germans lost the equivalent of more than twenty full divisions.

Now it was estimated that although more than sixty German divisions remained, they were merely paper divisions, with only 5,000 men apiece instead of the full-strength complement of 9- to 12,000 each. In fact, it was believed that there were barely twenty-six complete divisions left in the West, and even these were ill-equipped, lacking ammunition, drastically short of fuel and transport, artillery and tanks. In addition, there were the shattered remnants of divisions, splintered SS groups, anti-aircraft gun troops, thousands of Luftwaffe men (the German air force had almost disappeared), quasi-military organizations, Home Guard Volkssturm units composed of untrained old men and boys, and even cadres of teen-age officer cadets. Disorganized, lacking communications and often without competent leaders, the German Army was unable to stop or even slow up the systematic onslaught of Eisenhower's armies.

With the offensive from the Rhine barely a week old, the racing armies from Montgomery's and Bradley's groups were already closing in on the last German stronghold: the heavily defended Ruhr. Simultaneous with the developing drive eastward, three U.S. armies had suddenly and abruptly wheeled to take on the envelopment of the Ruhr from north and south. On the north, Simpson's Ninth Army changed direction from due east and was beginning to march southeast. To the south, Hodges' First and Patton's Third armies, moving parallel, with Patton on the outside, were also turning and heading northeast for a link-up with Simpson. The trap had been sprung so quickly that the Germans—principally Field Marshal Walter Model's Army Group B, a force of no less than twenty-one divisions—seemed almost unaware of the pincers closing around them. Now they were threatened with encirclement, caught up in a pocket some 70 miles long and 55 miles wide—a pocket that Allied Intelligence said contained more men and equipment than the Russians had captured at Stalingrad.

In the overall plan to defeat Germany, the crossing of the Rhine and the capture of the Ruhr had always been considered essential —and formidable—objectives. The sprawling industrial Ruhr basin, with its coal mines, oil refineries, steel mills and armament factories covered almost 4,000 square miles. It had been thought that its capture might take months—but that was before the German debacle on the Rhine. Now the pincer maneuver—the stratagem of the quiet Missourian, Omar Bradley—was being executed at breathtaking pace. The Americans were moving so fast that division commanders now talked of completing the encirclement in a matter of days. Once the Ruhr was sealed, Germany would have little strength left to impede the progress of the great Allied offensive. Even now the enemy was so disrupted that there was no continuous defense line.

So disorganized were the German forces, in fact, that Major General Isaac D. White, commanding the U. S. 2nd Armored Division, ordered his men to bypass any major resistance and keep on going. The 2nd, spearheading the Ninth Army's pincer movement along the northern rim of the Ruhr, had thereupon dashed more than fifty miles in just under three days. The Germans fought hard in isolated pockets but the 2nd encountered more trouble from blown bridges, hurriedly erected roadblocks, minefields and bad terrain than from enemy action. It was the same nearly everywhere.

Lieutenant Colonel Wheeler G. Merriam, leading the 2nd's dash with his 82nd Reconnaissance Battalion, was encountering a great deal of confusion and very little fighting. On March 28, with his tanks spread out on either side of a main railway line running east and west, Merriam called a halt to report his new position. As his radio man tried to raise headquarters, Merriam thought he heard a steam whistle. Suddenly a German train, filled with troops and hauling flat cars loaded with armored vehicles and guns, puffed along the line, passing right through his units. Germans and Americans gazed at each other in amazement. Merriam, looking up at the Wehrmacht soldiers leaning out of the train windows, was so close that he distinctly noted "the individual hairs on men's faces where they hadn't shaved." His men, flabbergasted, gazed after the train as it headed west. Not a single shot was fired by either side.

At last, galvanized into action, Merriam grabbed the radio telephone. Some miles to the west, the Division Commander, Major General White, saw the train come into sight at almost the same time that he heard Merriam's excited warning on his jeep radio. White saw an MP, directing the 2nd's columns, suddenly halt the traffic that was moving across the tracks—and then White, like Merriam, stood mesmerized as the train rolled by. Seconds later, field telephone in hand, White was calling for artillery fire. Within minutes, the 92nd Field Artillery, set up farther west, let loose a salvo that cut the train cleanly in two. Later it was discovered that the flat cars carried numerous anti-tank guns, field pieces and a 16-inch railway gun. Captured soldiers who had been on the train said that they had been completely ignorant of the Allied advance. They had thought the Americans and British were still west of the Rhine.

Confusion was both an ally and a foe. Lieutenant Colonel Ellis W. Williamson of the 30th Infantry Division was moving so fast that he was even fired on by the artillerymen of another Allied division. They thought Williamson's men were Germans retreating to the east. Lieutenant Clarence Nelson of the 5th Armored had an equally bizarre experience. His jeep was shot out from under him and Nelson jumped into a half-track which came under heavy fire. He ordered a tank to wipe out the enemy strongpoint. It moved out, breasted a hill, and fired two rounds—into a British armored car. The occupants were irate but unhurt. They had been lying in wait hoping to find a target of their own. And Chaplain Ben L. Rose of the 113th Mechanized Cavalry remembers a tank commander reporting solemnly to the group leader: "We advanced the last hundred yards, sir—under grass. Resistance is heavy—both enemy and friendly."

So rapid were the maneuvers and so fast were the German de-

133

fenses crumbling that many commanders worried more about fatalities from road accidents than from enemy fire. Captain Charles King of the famed British 7th Armored Division begged his men to "be careful driving on these roads. It would be a pity," he warned, "to die in an accident just now." A few hours later King, one of the original Desert Rats, was dead; his jeep had hit a German landmine.

Most men had no idea where they were or who was on their flanks. Forward units, in many instances, were already running off their maps. The resourceful scouts of the 82nd Reconnaissance Battalion were not in the least concerned. They were using emergency charts: silken handkerchief-size U. S. Air Force escape maps supplied to all combat fliers earlier in the war to help them slip out of enemy territory if they were shot down. The 82nd scouts confirmed their positions simply by checking with German signposts. In the 84th Division sector, Lieutenant Colonel Norman D. Carnes discovered that in his whole battalion there were only two maps left showing proposed advances. He was not worried either—not so long as his radios worked and he could keep in touch with headquarters. Lieutenant Arthur T. Hadley, a psychological warfare expert attached to the 2nd Armored Division, who used a loudspeaker on his tank instead of a gun to demand the surrender of German towns, was now using the maps in an ancient Baedeker guide intended for tourists. And Captain Francis Schommer of the 83rd Division always knew where he had led his battalion. He just grabbed the first German he saw, stuck a gun in his ribs, and in fluent German demanded to know where he was. He hadn't had a wrong answer yet.

To the men of the armored divisions, the advance from the Rhine was their kind of warfare. The snaking lines of armor that now thrust, bypassed, encircled and carved through the German towns and armies were offering a classic example of armored tactics at their best. Some men tried to describe in letters the great armored race to the east. Lieutenant Colonel Clifton Batchelder, commander of the 1st Battalion, 67th Armored Regiment, thought that the drive had "all the dash and daring of the great cavalry operations of the Civil War." Lieutenant Gerald P. Leibman, noting that as the 5th Armored Division cut through the enemy, thousands of Germans were left behind fighting in isolated pockets, wrote tongue-in-cheek that "We are exploiting the enemy's rear areas *after* breaching his frontal positions." To Leibman the attack was reminiscent of General Patton's armored dash out of the Normandy hedgerows, in which he had also participated. "No one eats or sleeps," he noted. "All we do is attack and push on, attack and push on. It is France all over again—except this time the flags flying from the houses are not French Tricolors, but flags of surrender." In the Devonshire Regiment racing along with the British 7th Armored Division, Lieutenant Frank Barnes told his friend Lieutenant Robert Davey that "it is wonderful to be going forward all the time." Both men were elated, for at the briefing before the attack, they had been told that this was the last great push and that the ultimate objective was Berlin.

Field Marshal Montgomery had always known that Berlin was the ultimate objective. Quick to anger, impatient of delays, temperamental and often tactless, but always both realistic and courageous, Montgomery had fixed his sights on Berlin as far back as his great victory in the desert at El Alamein. The one man who had unreservedly said "Go" when weather might have delayed the invasion of Normandy, he now demanded the green light again. In the absence of any clear-cut decision from the Supreme Commander, Montgomery had announced his own. At 6:10 P.M. on Tuesday, March 27, in a coded message to Supreme Headquarters, he informed General Eisenhower: "Today I issued orders to Army Commanders for the operations eastwards which are now about to begin. . . . My intention is to drive hard for the line of the Elbe using the Ninth and Second Armies. The right of the Ninth Army will be directed on Magdeburg and the left of the Second Army on Hamburg. . . .

"Canadian Army will operate . . . to clear Northeast Holland and West Holland and the coastal area to the north of the left boundary of the Second Army. . . .

"I have ordered Ninth and Second Armies to move their armored and mobile forces forward at once to get through to the Elbe with utmost speed and drive. The situation looks good and events should begin to move rapidly in a few days.

"My tactical headquarters move to northwest of Bonninghardt on Thursday, March 29. Thereafter . . . my headquarters will move to Wesel-Münster-Wiedenbrück-Herford-Hanover—thence by autobahn to Berlin, I hope."

*　　*　　*

Turning slowly in midair on the end of their ropes, Aunt Effie and Uncle Otto gazed mournfully down on the rubble-filled Berlin courtyard. From the back balcony of his second-story Wilmersdorf flat, Carl Wiberg spoke softly and encouragingly to the dachshunds as he pulled them up to safety. He was putting them through the air raid escape procedure he had devised, and the dogs, after weeks of training, were now well conditioned. So were Wiberg's neighbors, although they thought that the Swede's concern for his pets was excessive. Everyone had grown accustomed to the sight of Aunt Effie and Uncle Otto, coats brushed and gleaming, going up and down past the windows. No one paid much attention to the dangling ropes, either, which was exactly the way Wiberg wanted it. One day, if the Gestapo ever closed in, he might have to go over the back balcony and make his getaway down the same ropes.

He had thought out everything very carefully. A single slip could mean his exposure as an Allied spy, and now, with Berliners growing daily more suspicious and anxious, Wiberg was taking no chances. He had still not discovered Hitler's whereabouts. His casual and innocent-seeming questions apparently evoked no suspicion, but they turned up no information, either. Even his high-ranking friends in the Wehrmacht and Luftwaffe knew nothing. Wiberg was beginning to believe that the Führer and his court were not in Berlin.

Suddenly, as he lifted the dogs onto the balcony, the doorbell rang. Wiberg tensed; he was not expecting visitors, and he lived with a gnawing fear that one time he would go to the door and find the police. He carefully freed the dogs and then went to the door. Outside stood a stranger. He was tall and husky, dressed in working clothes and a leather jacket. Balanced on his right shoulder was a large carton.

"Carl Wiberg?" he asked.

Wiberg nodded.

The stranger dumped the carton inside the door. "A little present from your friends in Sweden," he said with a smile.

"My friends in Sweden?" said Wiberg warily.

"Oh, you know damned well what it is," said the stranger. He turned and went quickly down the stairs.

Wiberg softly closed the door. He stood frozen, looking down at the carton. The only "presents" he got from Sweden were supplies for the Berlin espionage operation. Was this a trap? Would the police come bursting into the apartment the moment he opened the box? Quickly he crossed the living room and looked cautiously down into the street. It was empty. There was no sign of his visitor. Wiberg returned to the door and stood for some time listening. He heard nothing out of the ordinary. At last he lugged the carton onto the living-room sofa and opened it. The box which had been so casually delivered contained a large radio transmitter. Wiberg suddenly discovered he was sweating.

Some weeks before, Wiberg had been notified by his superior, a Dane named Hennings Jessen-Schmidt, that henceforth he was to be "storekeeper" for the spy network in Berlin. Ever since, he had been receiving a variety of supplies through couriers. But up to now he had always been warned beforehand, and the actual deliveries had always been handled with extreme caution. His phone would ring twice, then stop; that was the signal that a delivery was to be made. The supplies arrived only during the hours of darkness, and generally during an air raid. Never before had Wiberg been approached in broad daylight. He was furious. "Somebody," he was later to put it, "had acted in a very naïve and amateurish way and seemed bent on wrecking the entire operation."

Wiberg's position had become increasingly dangerous; he could not afford a visit from the police. For his apartment was now a virtual warehouse of espionage equipment. Cached in his rooms were a large quantity of currency, some code tables and a variety of drugs and poisons—from quick-acting "knockout" pellets, capable of producing unconsciousness for varying durations of time, to deadly cyanide compounds. In his coal cellar and in a rented garage nearby was a small arsenal of rifles, revolvers and ammunition. Wiberg even had a suitcase of highly volatile explosives. Because of air raids, this consignment had worried him considerably. But he and Jessen-Schmidt had found the perfect hiding place. The explosives were now in a large safety deposit box in the vault of the Deutsche Union Bank.

Wiberg's apartment had miraculously survived the air raids up to now, but he dreaded to think of the consequences if it were hit. He would be immediately exposed. Jessen-Schmidt had told Wiberg that at the right time the supplies would be issued to various groups of operatives and saboteurs who would shortly arrive in Berlin. The operations of these selected agents were to begin on the receipt of a signal sent either by radio or through the courier network from London. Wiberg expected the distribution to be made soon. Jessen-Schmidt had been warned to stand by for the message sometime during the next few weeks, for the work of the teams would coincide with the capture of the city. According to the information Jessen-Schmidt and Wiberg had received, the British and Americans would reach Berlin around the middle of April.

✛ 3 ✛

IN THE QUIET of his study at No. 10 Downing Street, Winston Churchill sat hunched in his favorite leather chair, telephone cupped to his ear. The Prime Minister was listening to his Chief of Staff, General Sir Hastings Ismay, read a copy of Montgomery's message to the Supreme Commander. The Field Marshal's promise of "utmost speed and drive" was good news indeed; even better was his declared intention of heading for Berlin. "Montgomery," the Prime Minister told Ismay, "is making remarkable progress."

After months of stormy discussion between British and U.S. military leaders, Allied strategy seemed to have smoothed out. General Eisenhower's plans, outlined in the fall of 1944 and approved by the Combined Chiefs of Staff at Malta in January, 1945, called for Montgomery's Twenty-first Army Group to make the main drive over the Lower Rhine and north of the Ruhr; this was the route that Churchill, in a letter to Roosevelt, had called "the shortest road to Berlin." In the south, American forces were to cross the river and head into the Frankfurt area, drawing off the enemy from Montgomery. This supplementary advance could become the main line of attack if Montgomery's offensive faltered. But as far as Churchill was concerned, the matter was settled. The "Great Crusade" was nearing its end, and for Churchill it was immensely satisfying that of all the Allied commanders it was the hero of El Alamein who seemed destined to capture the enemy capital. The Twenty-first Army Group had been specially reinforced for the offensive, with top priority in troops, air support, supplies and equipment. In all, Montgomery had under his command almost one million men in some thirty-five divisions and attached units, including the U. S. Ninth Army.

Four days before, Churchill had traveled with General Eisenhower to Germany to witness the opening phase of the river assault. As he stood on the banks of the Rhine watching the monumental offensive unfold, Churchill said to Eisenhower, "My dear General, the German is whipped. We've got him. He's all through."

And indeed, enemy resistance proved surprisingly light in most areas. In the U. S. Ninth Army sector, where two divisions—about 34,000 men—crossed shoulder to shoulder with the British, there were only thirty-one casualties. Now, Montgomery had more than twenty divisions and fifteen hundred tanks across the river and was driving for the Elbe. The road to Berlin—which Churchill had called "the prime and true objective of the Anglo-American armies"—seemed wide open.

It was open politically, too. There had never been any Big Three discussions about which army would take the city. Berlin was an open target, waiting to be captured by the Allied army that reached it first.

However, there *had* been discussions, plenty of them, regarding the occupation of the rest of the enemy nation—as the sectors laid out in the Operation Eclipse maps indicated. And the decisions regarding the occupation of Germany were to have a crucial effect on the capture and political future of Berlin. At least one of the Allied leaders had realized this from the start. "There will definitely be a race for Berlin," he had said. That man was Franklin Delano Roosevelt.

It had been seventeen months earlier, on November 19, 1943, that the matter was brought before Roosevelt. On that occasion the President had sat at the head of the table in a conference room of Admiral Ernest J. King's suite aboard the battleship, U.S.S. *Iowa*. Flanking him were assistants and advisors, among them the U. S. Joint Chiefs of Staff. Roosevelt was en route to the

Middle East for the Cairo and Teheran conferences—the fifth and sixth of the Allied leaders' wartime meetings.

These were momentous days in the global struggle with the Axis powers. On the Russian front the Germans had suffered their biggest and bloodiest defeat: Stalingrad, encircled and cut off for twenty-three days, had fallen, and more than 300,000 Germans had been killed, wounded or taken prisoner. In the Pacific, where more than one million Americans were fighting, the Japanese were being forced back on every front. In the West, Rommel had been routed from North Africa. Italy, invaded from Africa via Sicily, had surrendered; the Germans were hanging on grimly to the northern part of the country. And now the Anglo-Americans were preparing plans for the *coup de grâce*—Operation Overlord, the all-out invasion of Europe.

Aboard the *Iowa*, Roosevelt was showing sharp annoyance. The documents and maps before him were the essentials of a plan called Operation Rankin, Case C, one of many studies developed in connection with the forthcoming invasion. Rankin C considered the steps that should be taken if there was a sudden collapse or capitulation of the enemy. In that event the plan suggested that the Reich and Berlin should be divided into sectors, with each of the Big Three occupying a zone. What troubled the President was the area that had been chosen for his country by the British planners.

Rankin C had been created under peculiar and frustrating circumstances. The one man most directly affected by its provisions would be the Allied Supreme Commander in Europe. But this officer was still to be appointed. The difficult task of trying to plan ahead for the Supreme Commander—that is, to prepare both the cross-channel offensive, Operation Overlord, and a plan in the event Germany crumbled, Operation Rankin—had been given to Britain's Lieutenant General Frederick E. Morgan,* known by the

---

* As originally conceived in 1943 there were actually three parts to Operation Rankin: Case A dealt with a situation in which the Germans might become so weak that only a "miniature Overlord" invasion might be necessary; Case B con-

code name "COSSAC" (Chief of Staff to the Supreme Allied Commander, designate). It was a staggering and thankless job. When he was named to the post, Morgan was told by Sir Alan Brooke, Chief of the Imperial General Staff: "Well there it is; it won't work, of course, but you must bloody well make it!"

In preparing Rankin C Morgan had to consider all sorts of imponderables. What would happen if the enemy capitulated so abruptly that the Allies were caught off balance, as they were in World War I by the unforeseen German surrender of November, 1918? Whose troops would go where? What parts of Germany would be occupied by American, British and Russian forces? Who would take Berlin? These were the basic questions, and they had to be solved in clear and decisive ways if the Allies were not to be surprised by a sudden collapse.

Up to that time no specific plan for the war's end had ever been set down. Although in the United States and Britain various governmental bodies discussed the problems that would arise on the cessation of hostilities, little headway was made in the formulation of an overall policy. There was agreement on only one point: that the enemy country would be occupied.

The Russians, by contrast, had no difficulty arriving at a policy. Occupation had always been taken for granted by Josef Stalin and he had always known exactly how he would go about it. As far back as December, 1941, he bluntly informed Britain's Foreign Secretary, Anthony Eden, of his post-war demands, naming the territories he intended to occupy and annex. It was an impressive list: included in his victory booty Stalin wanted recognition of his claims to Latvia, Lithuania and Estonia; that part of Finland which he had taken when he attacked the Finns in 1939; the province of Bessarabia in Rumania; that part of eastern Poland which the Soviets had overrun in 1939 by agreement with

---

ceived a strategic German withdrawal from some parts of the occupied countries while still leaving the bulk of their forces along the European coastline to repel an invasion; and Case C dealt with a sudden German collapse either before, during or after the actual invasion itself. Cases A and B were early abandoned and received, as Morgan recalls, only the briefest consideration.

the Nazis; and most of East Prussia. As he calmly laid down his terms guns were firing only fifteen miles from the Kremlin, in the Moscow suburbs, where German forces were still fighting desperately.

Although the British considered Stalin's 1941 demands premature to say the least,* by 1943 they were preparing plans of their own. The British Foreign Secretary, Anthony Eden, had recommended that Germany be totally occupied and divided among the Allies into three zones. A cabinet body called the Armistice and Post-war Committee was thereupon set up under Deputy Prime Minister Clement Attlee, head of the Labour Party. The Attlee group issued a broad recommendation which also advocated a tripartite division, with Britain occupying the industry- and commerce-rich northwestern areas. Berlin, it was suggested, should be jointly occupied by the three powers. The only Ally with virtually no plans for a defeated Germany was the United States. The official U.S. view was that post-war settlements should await a time nearer the final victory. Occupation policy, it was felt, was primarily a military concern.

But now, with the collective strength of the Allies beginning to be felt on every front and with the tempo of their offensives mounting, the need for coordinating political planning had become acute. In October, 1943, at the Foreign Ministers Conference in Moscow, the first tentative step was taken to define a common Allied post-war policy. The Allies accepted the idea of joint

---

* Stalin's proposals reached Churchill while he was crossing the Atlantic aboard the battleship H.M.S. *Duke of York* en route to meet with Roosevelt. The U.S. had just entered the war and Churchill had qualms about raising the matter with his powerful new ally at this time. He wired Eden: "Naturally you will not be rough with Stalin. We are bound to U.S. not to enter into secret and special pacts. To approach President Roosevelt with these proposals would be to court a blank refusal and might cause lasting trouble. . . . Even to raise them informally . . . would in my opinion be inexpedient." The State Department was informed of Eden's conversation with Stalin, but there is no evidence that anyone ever bothered to tell the President of the United States at the time. But by March of 1943 Roosevelt was fully apprised and according to Eden, who discussed the matter with him, the President foresaw no great difficulties with the Soviet Union. "The big question which rightly dominated Roosevelt's mind," said Eden, "was whether it was possible to work with Russia now and after the war."

responsibility in the control and occupation of Germany, and set up a tripartite body, the European Advisory Commission (EAC), to "study and make recommendations to the three governments upon European questions connected with the termination of hostilities."

But in the meantime Morgan had produced *his* plan—a rough blueprint for the occupation of Germany—"prepared," he later explained, "only after a powerful amount of crystal-ball gazing." Initially, without political guidance, Morgan had produced a plan calling for a limited occupation. But his final Rankin C proposals reflected the Attlee committee's more elaborate scheme. Morgan had sat down with a map and divided Germany into mathematical thirds, "faintly sketching in blue pencil along the existing provincial boundaries." It was obvious that the Russians, driving from the east, must occupy an eastern sector. The division between the Anglo-Americans and the Russians in the revised Rankin C plan was a suggested line running from Lübeck on the Baltic to Eisenach in central Germany and from there to the Czech border. What the extent of the Soviet zone would be was of no concern to Morgan. He had not been asked to consider that since it "would naturally be the affair of the Russians who were not included in our COSSAC party." But Berlin did bother him, for it would lie within the Russian sector. "Were we to continue to regard the place as a capital or was there to be a capital at all?" he wondered. "The internationality of the operation suggested that occupation of Berlin or any other capital, were there to be one, should be in equal tripartite force, by a division each of United States, British and Russian troops."

As for the British and American zones, their north-south relationship seemed to Morgan to have been predetermined by one seemingly ridiculous but relevant fact: the location of the British and American bases and depots back in England. From the time the first American troops arrived in the United Kingdom they had been quartered first in Northern Ireland and later in the south and southwest of England. British forces were situated in the north and southeast. Thus the concentration of troops, their supplies and communications were separate—the Americans always on the right, the British on the left facing the continent of Europe. As Morgan foresaw Overlord, this design was to continue across the Channel to the invasion beaches of Normandy—and, presumably, through Europe to the heart of Germany itself. The British were to enter northern Germany and liberate Holland, Denmark and Norway. On the right, the Americans, following their line of advance through France, Belgium and Luxembourg, would end up in the southern German provinces.

"I do not believe," Morgan said later, "that anyone at the time could have realized the full and ultimate implications of the quartering decision—which in all probability was made by some minor official in the War Office. But from it flowed all the rest."

Aboard the *Iowa*, the President of the United States realized the full and ultimate implications perfectly well. Those implications were precisely what he did not like about the Rankin C plan. Immediately the afternoon session began at 3 P.M., Roosevelt launched into the subject, and he was plainly irritated. Commenting on the accompanying memorandum, in which the Chiefs of Staff asked for guidance on Morgan's revised plan, Roosevelt rebuked his military advisors for "making certain suppositions"—in particular, that the U.S. should accept the British proposal to occupy southern Germany. "I do not like that arrangement," declared the President. He wanted northwest Germany. He wanted access to the ports of Bremen and Hamburg, and also those of Norway and Denmark. And Roosevelt was firm on something else: the extent of the U.S. zone. "We should go as far as Berlin," he said. "The U.S. should have Berlin." Then he added: "The Soviets can take the territory to the east."

Roosevelt was also displeased by another aspect of Rankin C. The U.S., in the south, would have a sphere of responsibility that included France, Belgium and Luxembourg. He was worried about France, and especially about the leader of the Free French Forces, General Charles de Gaulle, whom he saw as a "political headache." As forces advanced into that country, the President told his advisors, De Gaulle would be "one mile behind the troops," ready to take over the government. Above all, Roosevelt feared that civil war might break out in France when the war ended. He did not want to be involved, he said, "in reconstituting France. France," declared the President, "is a British baby."

And not only France. He felt that Britain should have the responsibility for Luxembourg and Belgium as well—and for the southern zone of Germany. As for the American zone—as the President visualized it, it would sweep across northern Germany (including Berlin) all the way to Stettin on the Oder. Then once again, measuring his words, he emphasized his displeasure over proposed zonal arrangements. "The British plan for the U.S. to have the southern zone," Roosevelt said, "and I do not like it."

The President's suggestions startled his military advisors. Three months before, at the Quebec Conference, the Joint Chiefs had approved the plan in principle. So had the Combined American and British Chiefs of Staff. At that time, President Roosevelt expressed great interest in the division of Germany and added his weight to the urgency of the planning by expressing the desire that troops should "be ready to get to Berlin as soon as the Russians."

The Joint Chiefs had believed the issues involved in Rankin C were all settled. They had brought up the plan on the *Iowa* only because political and economic matters, as well as military policy, were involved. Now the President was challenging not only the occupation plan but the very basis of Operation Overlord itself. If the projected zones of occupation were switched to accommodate the President's wishes, a troop changeover would have to be made in England *before* the invasion. This would delay—and might thus jeopardize—the cross-Channel offensive, one of the most complicated operations ever undertaken in any war. It seemed clear to his military advisors that President Roosevelt either did not understand the immense logistical movements involved—or understood them perfectly well and was simply prepared to pay a phenomenal cost in order to get the northwest zone and Berlin for the United States. In their view, the cost was prohibitive.

General Marshall began diplomatically to elaborate on the situation. He agreed "that the matter should be gone into." But, he said, the Rankin C proposals stemmed from prime military considerations. From a logistical standpoint, he reasoned, "We must have U.S. forces on the right . . . the whole matter goes back to the question of the ports of England."

Admiral Ernest King, U.S. Chief of Naval Operations, backed Marshall; the invasion plans were so far developed, he said, that it would be impractical to accept any change in the deployment of troops.

The immensity of the problem was such that Marshall believed an entire new scheme would be needed just for the switching of troops—one flexible enough to be applied "at any stage of development" in order to get the President what he wanted in Germany.

Roosevelt didn't think so. He felt that if there was a total collapse of Hitler's Reich the U.S. would have to get as many men as possible into Germany, and he suggested that some of them could be sent "around Scotland"—thereby entering Germany on the north. It was at this point that he expressed certainty that the Allies would race for Berlin; in that case, U.S. divisions would have to get there "as soon as possible." Harry Hopkins, Roosevelt's confidant and advisor, who was present on the *Iowa*, had the same sense of urgency: he thought that the U.S. would have to be "ready to put an airborne division into Berlin within two hours of the collapse."

Again and again the President's military advisors tried to impress on him the seriousness of the problems that a change in Rankin C would entail. Roosevelt remained adamant. Finally he pulled toward him a *National Geographic* map of Germany that lay on the table and began drawing. First he drew a line across Germany's western frontier to Düsseldorf and south along the Rhine to Mainz. From there, with a broad stroke, he cut Germany in half along the 50th parallel roughly between Mainz on the west and Asch on the Czech border to the east. Then his pencil moved northeast to Stettin on the Oder. The Americans would have the area above the line, the British the sector below it. But as Roosevelt outlined it, the eastern boundary of the U.S. and British zones would form a rough wedge. Its apex was at Leipzig; from there it ran northeast to Stettin and southeast to Asch. The President did not say so, but this shallow triangle was obviously to be the Soviet zone. It contained less than half of the area allotted to Russia in the Rankin C proposal. Nor was Berlin located within the territory he left to Russia. It lay on the boundary line between the Soviet and U.S. zones. It was Marshall's understanding that the President intended Berlin to be jointly occupied by U.S., British and Soviet troops.

The map showed unmistakably what the President had in mind. If the U.S. took the southern zone proposed by COSSAC in the Rankin paper, the President told his military chiefs, the "British will undercut us in every move we make." It was quite evident, Roosevelt said, that "British political considerations are in back of the proposals."

The discussion ended without any clear-cut decision, but Roosevelt had left no doubt in the minds of his military chiefs as to what he expected. United States occupation as envisaged by Roosevelt meant the quartering of one million troops in Europe "for at least one year, or maybe two." His post-war plan was similar to the American approach to the war itself—an all-out effort, but with a minimum of time and involvement in European affairs. He foresaw a swift and successful thrust into the enemy's heartland—"a railroad invasion of Germany with little or no fighting"—that would carry U.S. troops into the northwest zone and from there, into Berlin. Above all, the President of the United States was determined to have Berlin.*

---

* The account of the events aboard the *Iowa* comes from handwritten minutes which were made by General George C. Marshall. The actual memorandum contains no direct quotes, only notes made as points of reference. I have directly quoted the President and others where it was clearly indicated that a sentence was being attributed to them.

❁   ❁   ❁

Thus was offered the first concrete U.S. plan for Germany. There was just one trouble. Roosevelt, often criticized for acting as his own Secretary of State, had told no one his views except his military chiefs. They were to sit on the plan for almost four months.

After the *Iowa* conference, General Marshall gave the Roosevelt map—the one tangible evidence of administration thinking about the occupation of Germany—to Major General Thomas T. Handy, Chief of the War Department's Operations Division. When General Handy returned to Washington the map was filed away in the archives of the top secret Operations Division. "To the best of my knowledge," he was later to recall, "we never received instructions to send it to anyone at the Department of State."

The shelving of the Roosevelt plan by his own military advisors was just one of a series of strange and costly blunders and errors of judgment that occurred among American officials in the days following the *Iowa* meeting. They were to have a profound influence on the future of Germany and Berlin.

On November 29, Roosevelt, Churchill and Stalin met for the first time at the Teheran Conference. At this meeting the Big Three named the representatives who would sit in London on the all-important European Advisory Commission—the body charged with drafting surrender terms for Germany, defining the zones of occupation, and formulating plans for Allied administration of the country. To the EAC the British named a close friend of Anthony Eden, Under Secretary for Foreign Affairs Sir William Strang. The Russians chose a hard-headed bargainer, already known for his obstinacy—Fedor T. Gusev, Soviet Ambassador to the United Kingdom. Roosevelt appointed his envoy to the Court of St. James's, the dedicated but shy and often inarticulate John G. Winant. Winant was never briefed on his new job, nor was he told of the President's objectives in Germany.

However, an opportunity soon arose for the Ambassador to learn the nature of the policy he was supposed to espouse on the EAC—

but the opportunity was lost. The Cairo Conference (Roosevelt, Churchill, Chiang Kai-shek) ran from November 22 to 26; the Teheran meeting (Roosevelt, Churchill, Stalin) began on November 28 and continued until December 1; after Teheran, Roosevelt and Churchill met again at Cairo on December 4. That night, at a long dinner meeting with Churchill, Eden and the President's Chief of Staff, Fleet Admiral William D. Leahy, Roosevelt once again voiced objections to the Rankin C proposals. He told the British—apparently without divulging the contents of his map or the extent of his revisions—that he felt the U.S. should have the northwest zone of Germany. Churchill and Eden strongly opposed the suggestion, but the matter was passed on to the Combined Chiefs of Staff for study. They, in turn, recommended that COSSAC, General Morgan, should consider the possibility of revising the Rankin C plan.

Winant, although part of the delegation in Cairo, was not invited to the dinner meeting and apparently was never informed about the matters discussed there. As Roosevelt set out for home, Winant flew back to London for the first meeting of the EAC, only vaguely aware of what the President and the administration really wanted.

Ironically, only a few miles away from the U. S. Embassy in London, at Norfolk House in St. James's Square, was a man who knew only too well what President Roosevelt wanted. Lieutenant General Sir Frederick Morgan, flabbergasted by his new orders to re-examine his Rankin C plan with a view to switching the British and U.S. zones, put his hard-pressed staff to work immediately. He very quickly reached the conclusion that it was impossible—at least until after Germany was defeated. He so reported to his superiors—and "that," he later recorded, "ended the affair" so far as he was concerned.

*　　*　　*

Meanwhile, the U.S. military chiefs, despite their protestations that they did not want to be involved in politics, were, in fact, left to decide U.S. policy in post-war Europe. To them, the zoning and occupation of Germany were strictly military matters, to be handled by the Civil Affairs Division of the War Department. As an inevitable result, the War Department found itself at odds with the State Department over Germany. The consequence was a tug of war, in the course of which any hope of achieving a coherent, unified U.S. policy on the subject was irretrievably lost.

First, it was clear to all that something had to be done to direct Ambassador Winant in his negotiations with the EAC in London. To coordinate the conflicting U.S. views, a special group called the Working Security Committee was established in Washington early in December, 1943, with representatives from the State, War and Navy departments. The War Department representatives, officers from the Civil Affairs Division, actually refused at first to sit on the committee—or for that matter, to recognize the need for a European Advisory Commission at all. The entire problem of the surrender and occupation of Germany, the Army officers maintained, was purely a military matter that would be decided at the right time, and "at a military level," by the Combined Chiefs of Staff. Because of this farcical situation, the proceedings were held up for two weeks. Meanwhile, Winant sat in London without instructions.

At last, the military men agreed to the meetings and the committee settled down to work—but little was accomplished. Each group on the committee had to clear recommendations with its departmental superiors before anything could be cabled to Winant in London. Worse, each of the department heads could veto a suggested directive—a prerogative the War Department exercised repeatedly. The Acting Chairman of the Committee, Professor Philip E. Mosely of the State Department, who was to become Political Advisor to Ambassador Winant, commented later that the Civil Affairs officers "had been given strict instructions to agree to nothing, or almost nothing, and could only report the discussions back to their superiors. The system of negotiating at arm's length, under rigid instructions and with the exercise of the veto, resembled the procedures of Soviet negotiators in their more intransigent moods."

All through December, 1943, the haggling went on. In the Army's opinion the zones of occupation probably would be determined more or less by the final position of troops when the surrender was signed. Under the circumstances, the Army representatives saw no sense in permitting Winant to negotiate *any* agreement about zones in the EAC.

So adamant were the military men that they even turned down a State Department plan which, though similar to the British scheme—it, too, divided Germany into three equal parts—had one vital additional element: a corridor linking Berlin, deep inside the Soviet area, with the Western zones. The author of the corridor was Professor Mosely. He fully expected the Soviets to object but he pressed for its inclusion for, as he was later to explain, "I believed, if the plan was presented first with impressive firmness, it might be taken into account when the Soviets began framing their own proposals." Provision had to be made, he contended, "for free and direct territorial access to Berlin from the west."

The State Department's plan was submitted to the War Department's Civil Affairs Division for study prior to a meeting of the full committee. For some time it was held up. Finally Mosely visited the offices of the Civil Affairs Division and sought out the colonel who was handling the matter. He asked the officer if he had received the plan. The colonel opened a bottom drawer of his desk and said, "It's right there." Then he leaned back in his chair, put both feet in the drawer and said, "It's damn well going to stay there, too." The plan was never transmitted to Winant.

In London the EAC met informally for the first time on December 15, 1943, and for Ambassador Winant it was perhaps just as well that the meeting dealt only with rules of procedure. He was still without official instructions. He had learned unofficially from British sources about the plan which had so upset Roosevelt but he did not know it as Morgan's Rankin C: it was described to him as the Attlee Plan. He had also been informed, again unofficially (by U. S. Assistant Secretary of War John J. McCloy), that the President wanted the northwest zone. Winant did not expect the British to switch.* Winant's estimate was absolutely right.

On January 14, 1944, General Dwight D. Eisenhower, the newly appointed Supreme Commander, arrived in London to take over his post, and all the machinery of military planning, heretofore in the hands of General Morgan, was officially transferred to his authority. But there was one plan that even he could hardly influence at this late date. The day following Eisenhower's arrival, at the first formal meeting of the EAC, Morgan's Rankin C plan was presented by Sir William Strang to Ambassador Winant and the Russian envoy, Fedor Gusev. The U.S., because of the deadlock in Washington, had lost the initiative. It would never regain it. Strang was later to write that he had an advantage over his colleagues, "in that, whereas they had to telegraph for instructions to a remote and sometimes unsympathetic and uncomprehending government, I was at the center of things, usually able at short notice to have my line of action defined for me. I had a further advantage in that the Government had begun post-war planning in good time and in an orderly way."

On February 18, at the EAC's second formal meeting, in what was surely a record for a Soviet diplomatic decision, the inscru-

* "The British have had a long economic affiliation with the northern zone," McCloy wrote General Marshall on December 12, "and Winant tells me that the plan was brought out after consultation with their political and economic people. I do not know to what extent the President wishes to adhere to the occupation of these areas in the face of heavy English opposition. . . . On the whole I would favor the northern area, but I do not think it is worth the big fight." The State Department apparently did not care one way or the other. In his own handwriting, McCloy added that Cordell Hull had called and said "he had no preference as between the northern and southern areas."

table Gusev, without argument of any kind, solemnly accepted the British zonal proposals.

The British proposal gave the Soviets almost 40 per cent of Germany's area, 36 per cent of its population and 33 per cent of its productive resources. Berlin, though divided between the Allies, lay deep inside the proposed Soviet zone, 110 miles from the western Anglo-American demarcation line. "The division proposed seemed fair as any," Strang later recalled, "and if it perhaps erred somewhat in generosity to the Soviets, this was in line with the desire of our military authorities who had preoccupations about post-war shortages of manpower, not to take on a larger area of occupation than need be." There were many other reasons. One of them was the fear of both British and American leaders that Russia might make a separate peace with Germany. Another, which particularly concerned the U.S. military, was the fear that Russia would not join the war against Japan. And finally, the British believed that Russia, if not forestalled, might actually demand up to 50 per cent of Germany because of her wartime sufferings.

As far as the U.S. was concerned, the die now seemed cast. Although the Big Three still had to approve the British plan, the hard fact for the U.S. was that Britain and Russia were in agreement.* In a way it was a *fait accompli* and there was little that Winant could do except inform his government.

The Soviets' quick acceptance of the British plan caught Washington and the President off balance. Roosevelt hurriedly dashed off a note to the State Department. "What are the zones in the British and Russian drafts and what is the zone we are propos-

---

* One of the great myths that has developed since the end of World War II is that Roosevelt was responsible for the zones of occupation. The fact is that the plan was British throughout. It was conceived by Anthony Eden, developed by the Attlee Committee (which used Morgan's strictly military concept as the vehicle), approved by Churchill and his cabinet, and presented by Strang at the EAC. Many U.S. and British accounts refer to the zonal division as a Russian plan. This erroneous conclusion derives from the fact that when Gusev, at the second meeting of the EAC, accepted the British proposal, he also submitted a Soviet draft covering surrender terms for Germany. One section dealt with the zones: it was the British plan *in toto*.

ing?" he asked. "I must know this in order that it conform with what I decided on months ago." State Department officials were baffled and for a very good reason: they did not know what decisions Roosevelt had made at Teheran and Cairo regarding the zones.

There was a flurry of calls between the Joint Chiefs of Staff and the State Department before the President got his information. Then, on February 21, having seen the Anglo-Russian plan, Roosevelt reacted. "I disagree with the British proposal of the demarcation of boundaries," he bluntly stated in a formal memorandum to the State Department. He made no mention of the Soviet zone, but instead took sharp exception once again to the sector proposed for the U.S., repeating even more forcefully what he had told his military advisors on the *Iowa*. The President's memo was a revelation to the State Department.

"Our principal object," he wrote, "is not to take part in the internal problems in southern Europe but is rather to take part in eliminating Germany as a possible and probable cause of a third World War. Various points have been raised about the difficulties of transferring our troops . . . from a French front to a northern German front—what is called a 'leap-frog.' These objections are specious because no matter where British and American troops are on the day of Germany's surrender it is physically easy for them to go anywhere—north, east or south. . . . All things considered, and remembering that supplies come 3,500 miles or more by sea, the United States should use the ports of Northern Germany—Hamburg and Bremen—and . . . the Netherlands. . . . Therefore, I think American policy should be to occupy northwestern Germany. . . .

"If anything further is needed to justify this disagreement with the British . . . I can only add that political considerations in the United States make *my decision conclusive*." Then, to make absolutely sure that his Secretary of State really understood what he wanted, Roosevelt added, underlining the words: *"You might speak to me about this if the above is not wholly clear."*

155

In a more jocular vein, he explained his position to Churchill. "Do please don't ask me to keep any American forces in France," he wrote the Prime Minister. "I just cannot do it! As I suggested before, I denounce in protest the paternity of Belgium, France and Italy. You really ought to bring up and discipline your own children. In view of the fact that they may be your bulwark in future days, you should at least pay for the schooling now!"

The U.S. Chiefs of Staff apparently heard from the President, too. Almost immediately the Army officers from the Civil Affairs Division reversed their position in the Working Security Committee. A few days after the London EAC meeting, a colonel strode into Professor Mosely's office in the State Department and spread a map before him. "That's what the President really wants," he said. Mosely looked at the map. He had no idea when or under what circumstances it had been prepared. He had never seen it before—nor had anyone else in the State Department. The map was the one President Roosevelt had marked aboard the *Iowa*.

As mysteriously as it had emerged, the Roosevelt map thereupon again dropped out of sight. Mosely expected it to be brought up at the next meeting of the Washington committee. It never was. "What happened to it, I do not know," Mosely said years later. "The next time we met, the Civil Affairs officers produced a brand-new map, a variation which they explained was based on the President's instructions. Who received these instructions I was never able to discover."

The new concept was somewhat similar to the President's *Iowa* map, but not quite. The U.S. zone still lay in the northwest, the British in the south, but the dividing line between them running along the 50th parallel now stopped short of the Czech border. Furthermore, the eastern boundary of the U.S. zone swung sharply due east above Leipzig to encompass even more territory. There was one other change, more important than all the others: the U.S. zone no longer included Berlin. In Roosevelt's original version, the eastern boundary of the U.S. zone had passed through the capital; now that line swung west in a wavering semi-circle around the city. Had Roosevelt—after insisting to his military chiefs that "We should go as far as Berlin" and that "the U.S. should have Berlin"—now changed his mind? The Civil Affairs officers did not say. But they demanded that the new proposal be immediately transmitted to London, where Winant was to demand its acceptance by EAC!

It was a preposterous proposal anyway, and the State Department knew it. Under the new plan both Britain and Russia would get smaller occupation areas; it seemed hardly likely that they would accept such an arrangement after both had approved an earlier, more favorable division of territory. The Civil Affairs officers had produced the proposal without any accompanying memoranda to assist Winant in rationalizing it before the EAC; when asked to prepare such background papers they refused and said that was the State Department's job. The proposal was finally submitted to Winant without papers of any sort. The Ambassador frantically cabled for more detailed instructions. When they were not forthcoming, he shelved the plan; it was never submitted.

That was the last effort made to introduce a U.S. plan. Roosevelt continued to hold out against accepting the British scheme until late March, 1944. At that time, George F. Kennan, Ambassador Winant's political advisor, flew to Washington to explain to the President the problems that had arisen in the EAC because of the deadlock. Roosevelt reviewed the situation and after examining the British proposal once again, told Kennan that "considering everything, it is probably a fair decision." He then approved the Soviet zone and the overall plan, but with one proviso: the U.S., he insisted, must have the northwestern sector. According to the account that Kennan later gave Mosely, as the meeting broke up Kennan asked the President what had happened to his own plan. Roosevelt laughed. "Oh," he said, "that was just an idea."

All through the momentous months of 1944, as Anglo-American troops invaded the continent, routed the Germans out of France and began driving for the Reich, the behind-the-scenes political battles went on. Roosevelt clung firmly to his demands for the northwest zone of Germany. Churchill just as tenaciously refused to budge from his position.

In April Winant verbally informed the EAC of his government's position, but he did not immediately put the President's desires before the delegates in writing. The Ambassador was not prepared to do so until he received instructions on one matter that he thought was crucial. In the British plan there was still no provision for Western access to Berlin.

The British foresaw no problem about access. They assumed that when hostilities ended some form of German authority would sign the surrender and administer the country under the control of the Supreme Commander. No zone would be sealed off from any other and, as Strang saw it, there would be "some free movement of Germans from zone to zone and from western zones to the capital . . . also freedom of movement for all proper purposes for Allied military and civilian staffs in Germany." Furthermore, whenever the subject had been mentioned in the EAC, Russia's Gusev had smoothly assured Strang and Winant that he foresaw no difficulties. After all, as Gusev repeatedly put it, the mere presence of U.S. and British forces in Berlin automatically carried with it rights of access. It was a matter that was taken for granted, a kind of gentlemen's agreement.

Nevertheless, Winant thought the provision should be nailed down. He believed that "corridors" such as those originally suggested by Mosely had to be included before the Big Three formally accepted the British scheme. He intended to present such a proposal at the same time he formally placed the President's views on the zones before EAC. He wanted guarantees of specific rail, highway, and air routes through the Soviet zone to Berlin.

In May the Ambassador flew to Washington, saw the President, and then outlined his corridor provisions to the War Department. The Civil Affairs Division flatly turned down Winant's plan.* Its

---

* What transpired between Roosevelt and Winant at their meeting, or what the President's position was on the Berlin transit question is not known. There is further confusion as to whether the War Department did or did not oppose Winant's

officers assured him that the question of access to Berlin was "strictly a military matter anyway" and would be handled by local commanding officers through military channels when Germany was occupied. Winant, defeated, returned to London. On June 1 he formally agreed to the British plan and the proposed Soviet sector, with the one exception that the U.S. should have the northwestern zone. The document contained no clause providing for access to Berlin.* In tentative form, at least, the Allies had decided the future of the city: when the war ended it would be a jointly occupied island almost in the center of the Soviet zone.

The power struggle now moved swiftly to its conclusion. In late July, 1944, Gusev, eager to formalize Soviet gains in the EAC, deliberately brought matters to a head. Unless the Anglo-American dispute was settled so that the Big Three could sign the agreement, he said blandly, the U.S.S.R. could see little reason for further EAC discussions. The implied threat to pull out of the Advisory Commission, thus nullifying the work of months, had the desired effect.

On both sides of the Atlantic, anxious diplomats and military advisors urged their leaders to give in. Both Churchill and Roosevelt remained adamant. Roosevelt seemed to be the least flustered by the Soviet threat. Winant was told that since the U.S. had al-

---

"corridor" plan. Major General John H. Hildring, Chief of the Civil Affairs Division, is reported to have told Winant that "access to Berlin should be provided for." The version here reflects the views of the three principal U.S. historians on this period: Professor Philip Mosely (*The Kremlin and World Politics*); Herbert Feis (*Churchill Roosevelt Stalin*); and William M. Franklin, Director of the State Department's Historical Office (*Zonal Boundaries and Access to Berlin—World Politics*, October 1963). "Winant," Franklin writes, "apparently made no memoranda of these conversations. . . . This much, however, is clear: Winant received neither instructions nor encouragement from anyone in Washington to take the matter up with the Russians."

* For reasons which would always remain obscure, Winant's position on access to Berlin had changed after his return from Washington. Veteran diplomat Robert Murphy recalls that soon after joining Supreme Headquarters in September, 1944, he lunched with Winant in London and discussed the Berlin transit question. Murphy urged Winant to reopen the matter. In his memoirs, *Diplomat Among Warriors*, he writes: "Winant argued that our right of free access to Berlin was implicit in our right to be there. The Russians . . . were inclined to suspect our motives anyway and if we insisted on this technicality we would intensify their distrust." According to Murphy, Winant was not willing to force the issue in the EAC.

ready agreed on the Soviet zone, the President could not understand why "any further discussion with the Soviets is necessary at
this time."

But Roosevelt was now being pressed from all sides. While the
political squabbles went on, the great Anglo-American armies
were swarming toward Germany. In the middle of August, General Eisenhower cabled the Combined Chiefs of Staff, warning
that they might be "faced with the occupation of Germany sooner
than had been expected." Once again the disposition of troops as
originally foreseen by Morgan in his Rankin C plan had returned
to plague the planners: British troops on the left were heading for
northern Germany, Americans on the right were advancing toward the south. Eisenhower now sought political guidance on the
occupation zones—the first U.S. military man to do so. "All we can
do," he said, "is approach the problem on a purely military basis"
and that would mean keeping the "present deployment of our
armies. . . ." Eisenhower added: "Unless we receive instructions
to the contrary, we must assume this solution is acceptable . . .
considering the situation which may confront us and the absence
of basic decisions as to the zones of occupation."

The crisis, long inevitable, had now been reached. The U.S.
War and State departments, for once in complete agreement,
were faced with a dilemma: no one was prepared to reopen the
issue with the President again. In any case, the matter was due to
be discussed at a new Roosevelt-Churchill meeting scheduled for
the fall; any final decision would have to be put off till then. In the
meantime, Eisenhower's planning could not be delayed. Since the
U.S. Chiefs had plans already prepared for a U.S. occupation of
either the northwest or southern zones, on August 18 they advised
Eisenhower that they were "in complete agreement" with his solution. Thus, although Roosevelt had not yet announced his decision, the assumption that the U.S. would occupy the southern
zone was allowed to stand.

Roosevelt and Churchill met once again in Quebec in September, 1944. Roosevelt had changed visibly. The usually vital Presi-

dent looked frail and wan. The crippling polio which his renowned charm and witty informality cloaked was now evident in the painful hesitancy of his every move. But there was more than that. He had been in office since 1933—longer than any other U. S. President—and even now was seeking a fourth term. The campaigning, the diplomacy at home and abroad, the strain of the heavy burdens of the war years, were fast taking their toll. It was easy to see why his doctors, family and friends were begging him not to run again.To the British delegation at Quebec, Roosevelt appeared to be failing rapidly. Churchill's Chief of Staff, General Sir Hastings Ismay, was shocked by his appearance. "Two years before," he said, "the President had been the picture of health and vitality, but now he had lost so much weight that he seemed to have shrunk: his coat sagged over his broad shoulders and his collar looked several sizes too big. We knew the shadows were closing in."

Tired, frustrated, trapped by circumstances and under pressure from his advisors and Churchill, the President finally gave in and accepted the southern zone. The British met him halfway. Among other concessions, they agreed to give the U.S. control of the great harbors and staging areas of Bremen and Bremerhaven.*

The final wartime meeting of the Big Three occurred at Yalta, in February, 1945. It was a crucial conference. Victory lay ahead, but it was clear that the bonds binding the Allied leaders were weakening as political considerations replaced military realities. The Russians were becoming more demanding and arrogant with every mile they advanced into central Europe. Churchill, long a foe of Communism, was particularly concerned about the future of countries like Poland, which the Red Army had liberated and now controlled.

---

* At the Conference, another controversial issue boiled up when the President and the U. S. Secretary of the Treasury, Henry Morgenthau, introduced a severe and far-reaching economic plan calling for Germany to be turned into an agricultural nation, without industry. At first Churchill subscribed to this scheme, but under pressure from his advisors later retreated from his original position. Months later Roosevelt abandoned the controversial Morgenthau plan.

Roosevelt, gaunt and much weaker than he had been at Quebec, still saw himself in the role of the Great Arbiter. In his view a peaceful post-war world could be achieved only with the cooperation of Stalin. He had once expressed his policy toward the Red leader in these terms: "I think that if I give him everything I can and ask for nothing in return, *noblesse oblige*, he won't try to annex anything and will work with me for a world of democracy and peace." The President believed that the U.S. could "get along with Russia" and that he could "manage Stalin" for, as he had once explained, "on a man-to-man basis . . . Uncle Joe . . . is get-at-able." Although the President was growing increasingly concerned about Soviet post-war intentions, he still seemed almost determinedly optimistic.

At Yalta the last great wartime decisions were made. Among them was one giving France full partnership in the occupation of Germany. The French zone of Germany and the French sector of Berlin were carved out of the British and U.S. areas; Stalin, who was opposed to French participation, refused to contribute any part of the Russian zone. On February 11, 1945, the Big Three formally accepted their respective zones.

Thus, after sixteen months of confusion and squabbling, the U.S. and Britain at last were in accord. The occupation plan, based on a scheme originally called Rankin C but now known to the military as Operation Eclipse, contained one staggering omission: there was no provision whatever for Anglo-American access to Berlin.

It took just six weeks for Stalin to violate the Yalta agreement. Within three weeks of the conference, Russia had ousted the government of Soviet-occupied Rumania. In an ultimatum to King Michael, the Reds bluntly ordered the appointment of Petru Groza, the Rumanian Communist chief, as Prime Minister. Poland was lost, too: the promised free elections had not taken place.

Roosevelt's desire to have Berlin for the United States was clearly evident from the lines he drew on the National Geographic map while en route to Teheran for the first Big Three Conference. Military minds prevailed and one of the plans that was substituted for F. D. R.'s was the one below—notice that Berlin is no longer included in the projected American zone. In the end, after almost two years of discussions, the final occupation zones were chosen as shown on the back endpaper map. The typed inset is a note by Major General Handy.

AMERICAN

PROPOSAL

FOR ZONES

OCCUPATION

SECRET
DO NOT REMOVE
FROM DEPARTMENT

Contemptuously, Stalin seemed to have turned his back on the very heart of the Yalta pact, which stated that the Allied powers would assist "peoples liberated from the dominion of Nazi Germany and . . . former Axis satellite states . . . to create democratic institutions of their own choice." But Stalin saw to it that any Yalta provisions that favored him—such as the division of Germany and Berlin—were carried out scrupulously.

Roosevelt had been warned often of Stalin's ruthless territorial ambitions by his Ambassador to Moscow, W. Averell Harriman, but now the Soviet leader's flagrant breach of faith came to him as a staggering shock. On the afternoon of Saturday, March 24, in a small room on the top floor of the White House, Roosevelt had just finished lunch with Mrs. Anna Rosenberg, his personal representative charged with studying the problems of returning veterans, when a cable arrived from Harriman on the Polish situation. The President read the message and erupted in a violent display of anger, repeatedly pounding the arms of his wheelchair. "As he banged the chair," Mrs. Rosenberg later recalled, "he kept repeating: 'Averell is right! We can't do business with Stalin! He has broken every one of the promises he made at Yalta!' " *

In London, Churchill was so disturbed by Stalin's departure from the spirit of Yalta that he told his secretary he feared the world might consider that "Mr. Roosevelt and I have underwritten a fraudulent prospectus." On his return from Yalta he had told the British people that "Stalin and the Soviet leaders wish to live in honorable friendship and equality with the western democracies. I feel . . . their word is their bond." But on this same Saturday, March 24, the worried Prime Minister remarked to his aide: "I hardly like dismembering Germany until my doubts about Russia's intentions have been cleared away."

With Soviet moves becoming "as plain as a pikestaff," Churchill felt that the Western Allies' most potent bargaining force would

---

* This incident comes from a private conversation with Mrs. Rosenberg (now Mrs. Paul Hoffman). Mrs. Roosevelt was also present; the two women later compared notes and agreed on the President's exact words.

be the presence of Anglo-American troops deep inside Germany, so they could meet with the Russians "as far to the east as possible." Thus, Field Marshal Montgomery's message announcing his intention of dashing for the Elbe and Berlin was heartening news indeed: to Churchill, the quick capture of Berlin now seemed vital. But, despite the Montgomery message, no commander along the western front had as yet been ordered to take the city. That order could come from only one man: the Supreme Commander, General Eisenhower.

✤ 4 ✤

THE RAID took Berlin's defenders completely by surprise. Shortly before 11 A.M. on Wednesday, March 28, the first planes appeared. Immediately, batteries all over the city crashed into action, belching shells into the sky. The racket of the guns, coupled with the belated wailing of air raid sirens, was earsplitting. These planes were not American. U.S. raids were almost predictable: they usually occurred at 9 A.M. and then again at midday. This attack was different. It came from the east, and both the timing and tactics were new. Screaming in at rooftop level, scores of Russian fighters emptied their guns into the streets.

In Potsdamer Platz, people ran in all directions. Along the Kurfürstendamm, shoppers dived for doorways, ran for subway entrances, or headed for the protective ruins of the Kaiser-Wilhelm Memorial Church. But some Berliners, who had been standing for hours in long queues waiting to buy their weekly rations, refused to budge. In Wilmersdorf, 36-year-old Nurse Charlotte Winckler was determined to get food for her two children, Ekkehart, six, and Barbara, nine months old. In Adolf-Hitler-Platz, Gertrud Ketz-ler and Inge Rühling, long-time friends, waited calmly with others before a grocery store. Some time ago both had decided to commit suicide if the Russians ever reached Berlin, but they weren't think-ing about that now. They intended to bake an Easter cake, and for days had been shopping and storing the items they would require. Over in Köpenick, plump 40-year-old Hanna Schultze was hoping to get some extra flour for a holiday marble cake. During the day's shopping, Hanna also hoped to find something else: a pair of suspenders for her husband, Robert. His last remaining pair was almost beyond saving.

During air raids Erna Saenger always worried about "Papa," as she called her husband Konrad. He obstinately refused to go into a Zehlendorf shelter and, as usual, he was out. Konrad was trudging toward his favorite restaurant, the Alte Krug, on Königin-Luise Strasse. No air raid yet had ever stopped the 78-year-old veteran from meeting with his World War I comrades every Wednesday. He wouldn't be stopped today, either.

One Berliner was actually enjoying every minute of the attack. Wearing an old army helmet, young Rudolf Reschke ran back and forth between the door of his Dahlem home and the center of the street, deliberately taunting the low-flying planes. Each time Ru-dolf waved to the pilots. One of them, apparently seeing his an-tics, dived right for him. As Rudolf ran, a burst of fire ripped across the sidewalk behind him. It was just part of the game for Rudolf. As far as he was concerned, the war was the greatest thing that had ever happened in his fourteen years of life.

Wave after wave of planes hit the city. As fast as squadrons exhausted their ammunition, they peeled off to the east, to be re-placed by others swarming in to the attack. The surprise Russian raid added a new dimension of terror to life in Berlin. Casualties were heavy. Many civilians were hit not by enemy bullets, but by the returning fire from the city's defenders. To get the low-flying planes in their sights, anti-aircraft crews had to depress their gun barrels almost to tree-top level. As a result, the city was sprayed with red-hot shrapnel. The shell fragments came mainly from the six great flak towers that rose above the city at Humboldthain, Friedrichshain, and from the grounds of the Berlin Zoo. These massive bombproof forts had been built in 1941-42 after the first Allied attacks on the city. Each was huge, but the largest was the anti-aircraft complex built, incongruously, near the bird sanctuary in the zoo. It had twin towers. The smaller, called L Tower, was a communications control center, bristling with radar antennae. Next to it, guns now erupting with flame, stood G Tower.

G Tower was immense. It covered almost the area of a city block and stood 132 feet high—equivalent to a 13-story building. The reinforced concrete walls were more than 8 feet thick, and deep-cut apertures, shuttered by 3- to 4-inch steel plates, lined its sides. On the roof a battery of eight 5-inch guns was firing continuously, and in each of the four turreted corners multiple-barreled, quick-firing "pom pom" cannons pumped shells into the sky.

Inside the fort the noise was almost intolerable. Added to the firing of the batteries was the constant rattling of automatic shell elevators, which carried ammunition in an endless stream from a ground floor arsenal to each gun. G Tower was designed not only as a gun platform but as a huge five-story warehouse, hospital and air raid shelter. The top floor, directly underneath the batteries, housed the 100-man military garrison. Beneath that was a 95-bed Luftwaffe hospital, complete with X-ray rooms and two fully equipped operating theaters. It was staffed by six doctors, twenty nurses and some thirty orderlies. The next floor down, the third, was a treasure trove. Its storerooms contained the prize exhibits of Berlin's top museums. Housed here were the famous Pergamon sculptures, parts of the huge sacrificial altar built by King Eumenes II of the Hellenes around 180 B.C.; various other Egyptian, Greek and Roman antiquities, including statues, reliefs, vessels and vases; "The Gold Treasure of Priam," a huge collection of gold and silver bracelets, necklaces, earrings, amulets, ornaments and jewels, excavated by the German archaeologist Heinrich Schliemann in 1872 on the site of the ancient city of Troy. There were priceless Gobelin tapestries, a vast quantity of paintings—among them the fine portraits of the 19th-century German artist Wilhelm Leibl—and the enormous Kaiser Wilhelm coin collection. The two lower floors of the tower were mammoth air raid shelters, with large kitchens, food storerooms and emergency quarters for the German broadcasting station, Deutschlandsender.

Entirely self-contained, G Tower had its own water and power, and easily accommodated fifteen thousand people during air raids. The complex was so well stocked with supplies and ammunition that the military garrison believed that, no matter what happened to the rest of Berlin, the zoo tower could hold out for a year if need be.

As suddenly as it had begun, the raid was over. The guns atop G Tower stuttered to a stop. Here and there over Berlin black smoke curled up from fires started by incendiary bullets. The raid had lasted slightly longer than twenty minutes. As quickly as they had emptied, the Berlin streets filled again. Outside the markets and shops, those who had left the queues now angrily tried to regain their former places from others who just as stubbornly refused to give them up.

In the zoo itself, one man hurried outside as soon as the guns of G Tower stopped firing. Anxious as always after a raid, 63-year-old Heinrich Schwarz headed for the bird sanctuary, carrying with him a small pail of horse meat. "Abu, Abu," he called. A strange clapping sound came from the edge of a pond. Then the weird-looking bird from the Nile, with the blue-gray plumage and the huge beak resembling an up-ended Dutch clog, stepped daintily out of the water on thin stilt-like legs and came toward the man. Schwarz felt an immense relief. The rare Abu Markub stork was still safe.

Even without the raids, the daily encounter with the bird was becoming more and more of an ordeal for Schwarz. He held out the horse meat. "I have to give you this," he said. "What can I do? I have no fish. Do you want it or not?" The bird closed its eyes. Schwarz sadly shook his head. The Abu Markub made the same refusal every day. If its stubbornness persisted, the stork would surely die. Yet there was nothing Schwarz could do. The last of the tinned tuna was gone and fresh fish was nowhere to be found in Berlin—at least not for the Berlin Zoo.

Of the birds still remaining, the Abu Markub was the real pet of head bird-keeper Schwarz. His other favorites had long since gone—"Arra," the 75-year-old parrot which Schwarz had taught to say "Papa," had been shipped to the Saar for safety two years ago. All the German "Trappen" ostriches had died from concussion or shock during the air raids. Only Abu was left—and he was slowly dying of starvation. Schwarz was desperate with worry. "He is getting thinner and thinner," he told his wife Anna. "His joints are beginning to swell. Yet each time I try to feed him, he looks at me as though to say, 'Surely you have made a mistake. This is not for me.'"

Of the fourteen thousand animals, birds, reptiles and fish which had populated the zoo in 1939, there were now only sixteen hundred of all species left. In the six years of the war, the sprawling zoological gardens—which included an aquarium, insectarium, elephant and reptile houses, restaurants, movie theaters, ballrooms and administration buildings—had been hit by more than a hundred high-explosive bombs. The worst raid had been in November, 1943, when scores of animals had been killed. Soon after, many of those remaining had been evacuated to other zoos in Germany. Finding supplies for the remaining sixteen hundred animals and birds was becoming daily more difficult in food-rationed Berlin. The zoo's requirements, even for its reduced menagerie, were staggering: not only large quantities of horse meat and fish, but thirty-six different kinds of other food, ranging from noodles, rice and cracked wheat to canned fruit, marmalade and ant larvae. There was plenty of hay, straw, clover and raw vegetables, but nearly everything else had become almost unobtainable. Although ersatz food was being used, every bird or animal was on less than half-rations—and looked it.

Of the zoo's nine elephants, only one now remained. Siam, his skin hanging in great gray folds, had become so bad-tempered that keepers were afraid to enter his cage. Rosa, the big hippo, was miserable, her skin dry and crusted, but her 2-year-old baby, Knautschke, everybody's favorite, still maintained his youthful jauntiness. Pongo, the usually good-natured 530-pound gorilla, had lost more than 50 pounds and sat in his cage, sometimes motionless for hours, glowering morosely at everyone. The five lions (two of them cubs), the bears, zebras, hartebeests, monkeys and the rare wild horses, all were showing effects of diet deficiencies.

There was a third threat to the existence of the zoo creatures. Every now and then, Keeper Walter Wendt reported the disappearance of some of his rare cattle. There was only one possible conclusion: some Berliners were stealing and slaughtering the animals to supplement their own meager rations.

Zoo Director Lutz Heck was faced with a dilemma—a dilemma that not even the friendship of his hunting companion, Reichsmarschall Hermann Goering, or anyone else for that matter, could alleviate. In the event of a prolonged siege, the birds and animals would surely die from starvation. Worse, the dangerous animals— the lions, bears, foxes, hyenas, Tibetan cats and the zoo's prize baboon, one of a rare species which Heck had personally brought back from the Cameroons—might escape during the battle. How soon, wondered Heck, should he destroy the baboon and the five lions he loved so much?

Gustav Riedel, the lion-keeper, who had bottle-fed the 9-month-old lion cubs, Sultan and Bussy, had made up his mind about one thing: despite any orders, he intended to save the little lions. Riedel was not alone in his feeling. Almost every keeper had plans for the survival of his favorite. Dr. Katherina Heinroth, wife of the 74-year-old director of the bombed-out aquarium, was already caring for a small monkey, Pia, in her apartment. Keeper Robert Eberhard was obsessed with protecting the rare horses and the zebras entrusted to his care. Walter Wendt's greatest concern were the ten wisent—near cousins of the American bison. They were his pride and joy. He had spent the best part of thirty years in scientific breeding to produce them. They were unique and worth well over one million marks—roughly a quarter of a million dollars.

As for Heinrich Schwarz, the bird-keeper, he could no longer stand the suffering of the Abu Markub. He stood by the pond and called the great bird once more. When it came, Schwarz bent over and tenderly lifted it into his arms. From now on the bird would live—or die—in the Schwarz family bathroom.

In the baroque red and gold Beethoven Hall, the sharp rapping of the baton brought a sudden hush. Conductor Robert Heger raised his right arm and stood poised. Outside, somewhere in the devastated city, the sound of a fire engine's wailing siren faded slowly away. For a moment longer Heger held the pose. Then his baton dropped and, heralded by four muffled drumbeats, Beethoven's *Violin Concerto* welled softly out from the huge Berlin Philharmonic Orchestra.

As the woodwinds began their quiet dialogue with the drums, soloist Gerhard Taschner waited, his eyes on the conductor. Most of the audience that crowded the undamaged concert hall on Köthenerstrasse had come to hear the brilliant 23-year-old violinist, and as the bell-clear notes of his violin suddenly soared, faded away and soared again, they listened, rapt. Witnesses present at this afternoon concert in the last week of March recall that some Berliners were so overcome by Taschner's playing that they quietly wept.

All during the war the 105-man Philharmonic had offered Berliners a rare and welcome release from fear and despair. The orchestra came under Joseph Goebbels' Propaganda Ministry, and its members had been exempted from military service, since the Nazis considered the Philharmonic good for morale. With this, Berliners completely agreed. For music lovers the orchestra was like a tranquilizer transporting them away from the war and its terrors for a little while.

One man who was always deeply moved by the orchestra was Reichsminister Albert Speer, Hitler's Armament and War Production chief, now sitting in his usual seat in the middle of the orchestra section. Speer, the most cultured member of the Nazi hierarchy, rarely missed a performance. Music, more than anything else, helped him shed his anxieties—and he had never needed its help more than he did now.

Reichsminister Speer was facing the greatest problem of his career. All through the war, despite every conceivable kind of setback, he had kept the Reich's industrial might producing. But long ago his statistics and projections had spelled out the inevitable: the Third Reich's days were numbered. As the Allies penetrated ever deeper into Germany the realistic Speer was the only cabinet minister who dared tell Hitler the truth. "The war is lost," he wrote the Führer on March 15, 1945. "If the war is lost," Hitler snapped back, "then the nation will also perish." On March 19, Hitler issued a monstrous directive: Germany was to be totally destroyed. Everything was to be blown up or burned—power plants, water and gas works, dams and locks, ports and waterways, industrial complexes and electrical networks, all shipping and bridges, all railroad rolling stock and communications installations, all vehicles and stores of whatever kind, even the country's highways.

The incredulous Speer appealed to Hitler. He had a special, personal stake in getting this policy reversed. If Hitler succeeded in eliminating German industry, commerce and architecture, he would be destroying many of Speer's own creations—his bridges, his broad highways, his buildings. The man who, more than anyone else, was responsible for forging the terrible tools of Hitler's total war could not face their total destruction. But there was another, more important consideration as well. No matter what happens to the regime, Speer told Hitler, "we must do everything to maintain, even if only in a primitive manner, a basis for the existence of the nation. . . . We have no right to carry out demolitions which might affect the life of the people. . . ."

Hitler was unmoved. "There is no need to consider the basis of even a most primitive existence any longer," he replied. "On the contrary, it is better to destroy even that, and to destroy it ourselves. The nation has proved itself weak. . . ." With these words Hitler wrote off the German people. As he explained to Speer, "those who remain after the battle are of little value, for the good have fallen."

Speer was horrified. The people who had fought so hard for their leader apparently now meant less than nothing to the Führer. For years Speer had closed his eyes to the more brutal side of the Nazis' operations, believing himself to be intellectually above it all. Now, belatedly, he came to a realization which he had refused to face for months. As he put it to General Alfred Jodl, "Hitler is totally mad . . . he must be stopped."

Between March 19 and 23 a stream of "scorched earth" orders flashed out from Hitler's headquarters to gauleiters and military commanders all over Germany. Those who were slow to comply were threatened with execution. Speer immediately went into action. Fully aware that he was placing his own life in jeopardy, he set out to stop Hitler's plan, aided by a small coterie of high-ranking military friends. Speer telephoned industrialists, flew to military garrisons, visited provincial officials, everywhere insisting, even to the most die-hard Nazis, that Hitler's plan spelled the end of Germany forever.

Considering the serious purpose of the Reichsminister's campaign, his presence at the Philharmonic concert might have seemed frivolous—were it not for one fact: high on the list of German resources Speer was fighting to preserve was the Philharmonic itself. A few weeks earlier, Dr. Gerhart von Westermann, the orchestra manager, had asked violinist Taschner, a favorite of Speer's, to seek the Reichsminister's help in keeping the Philharmonic intact. Technically, the musicians were exempt from military service. But with the battle for Berlin approaching, Von Westermann feared that any day now the entire orchestra might be ordered into the Volkssturm, the Home Guard. Although the orchestra's affairs were supposed to be administered by Joseph Goebbels' Propaganda Ministry, Von Westermann knew there was no hope of assistance from that quarter. He told the violinist, "You've got to help us. Goebbels has forgotten us . . . go to Speer and ask him for help . . . we'll all be on our knees to you."

Taschner was extremely reluctant: any talk of shirking or flight was considered treasonable and could lead to disgrace or imprisonment. But at last he agreed.

At his meeting with Speer, Taschner began hesitantly. "Mr. Minister," he said, "I would like to speak with you about a rather delicate matter. I hope you will not misunderstand . . . but nowadays some things are difficult to talk about. . . ." Looking at him sharply, Speer quickly put him at his ease and, encouraged, Taschner poured out the story of the orchestra's plight. The Reichsminister listened intently. Then Speer told Taschner that Von Westermann was not to worry. He had thought of a plan to do much more than keep the musicians out of the Volkssturm. At the very last moment he intended secretly to evacuate the entire 105-man orchestra.

Speer had now carried out the first part of the plan. The 105 men seated on the stage of Beethoven Hall were wearing dark business suits instead of the usual tuxedos, but of all the audience, only Speer knew the reason. The tuxedos—along with the orchestra's fine pianos, harps, famous Wagner tubas and musical scores —had been removed quietly from the city by truck convoy three weeks before. The bulk of the precious cargo was cached at Plassenburg near Kulmbach, 240 miles southwest of Berlin—conveniently in the path of the advancing Americans.

The second part of Speer's plan—saving the men—was more complicated. Despite the intensity of the air raids, and the proximity of the invading armies, the Propaganda Ministry had never suggested cutting short the Philharmonic's schedule. Concerts were scheduled at the rate of three or four a week, in between air raids, right through to the end of April, when the season would officially end. Any evacuation of the musicians before that time was out of the question: Goebbels undoubtedly would charge the musicians with desertion. Speer was determined to evacuate the orchestra to the west; he had absolutely no intention of allowing the men to fall into Russian hands. But his scheme was entirely dependent on the speed of the Western Allies' advance: he was counting on the Anglo-Americans to beat the Russians to Berlin.

Speer did not intend to wait until the Western Allies entered the city. As soon as they were close enough to be reached by an overnight bus trip, he would give the order to evacuate. The crux of the plan lay in the signal to leave. The musicians would all have to leave at once, and after dark. That meant the flight must start right after the concert. To avoid a breach of security, word of the move would have to be withheld as long as possible. Speer had come up with an ingenious method of alerting the musicians: at the very last minute the orchestra conductor would announce a change in the program and the Philharmonic would then play a specific selection which Speer had chosen. That would be the musicians' cue; immediately after the performance they would board a convoy of buses waiting in the darkness outside Beethoven Hall.

In Von Westermann's possession was the music Speer had requested as the signal. When it was delivered by Speer's cultural affairs specialist, Von Westermann had been unable to hide his surprise. He queried Speer's assistant. "Of course you are familiar with the music of the last scenes," he said. "You know they picture the death of the gods, the destruction of Valhalla and the end of the world. Are you sure this is what the Minister ordered?" There was no mistake. For the Berlin Philharmonic's last concert, Speer had requested music from Wagner's *Die Götterdämmerung*—The Twilight of the Gods.

In this choice, if Von Westermann had known it, lay a clue to

Speer's final and most ambitious project. The Reichsminister, determined to save as much of Germany as he could, had decided that there was just one way to do it. For weeks now, perfectionist Albert Speer had been trying to find just the right way to murder Adolf Hitler.

*   *   *

THE ATTACKERS

The Allied high commanders meet. *Left to right,* Marshal Sokolovskii, Robert Murphy, Field Marshal Montgomery, Marshal Zhukov, General Eisenhower, General Koenig of France.

Lieutenant General William Simpson, commander U.S. Ninth Army, talks with Field Marshal Montgomery. To the left of Montgomery, in background, is General Omar Bradley, commander of the U.S. 12th Army Group; behind Montgomery is Field Marshal Sir Alan Brooke, Chief of the Imperial Green Staff.

General George S. Patton, commander of the U.S. Third Army.

General Courtney Hodges, commander of the U.S. First Army.

Lieutenant General Henry D. Crerar, commander of the Canadian First Army, with Montgomery.

IMPERIAL WAR MUSEUM

Major General James M. Gavin (right), the 38-year-old commander of the U.S. 82nd Airborne Division, ordered to drop on Berlin, discusses his plans with Lieutenant General Sir Miles Dempsey of the British Second Army.

General Jacob Devers, commander of the 6th Army Group.

Major General Raymond S. McLain, 19th Corps commander, who expected to reach Berlin "six days after crossing the Elbe."

Major General Isaac D. White, 2nd Armored Division. "No damned infantry division is going to beat my outfit to the Elbe."

Major General Robert C. Macon, commander 83rd Infantry Division, "The Rag-Tag Circus."

Colonel Paul A. Disney, commander 67th Armored Regiment. "What's the objective?" "Berlin!"

Major General Alexander R. Bolling, commander 84th Infantry Division. "Alex, keep going . . . and don't let anybody stop you."

Except where noted, all photographs on this page are courtesy of the U.S. Army.

Brigadier General Sidney R. Hinds, commander of the 2nd's Combat Command B, receives the French Légion d'Honneur in March of 1945. "We're on the Elbe."

Major James Hollingsworth, 67th Armored Regiment, receives the Silver Star from General Isaac White. "He lined up 34 tanks and gave a command rarely heard in modern warfare: 'Charge!' "

THE PLANNERS

The Big Three at Teheran.

Above, Lieutenant General Frederick E. Morgan, planner of Rankin C—". . . it won't work, of course, but you must bloody well make it!"

Left, U.S. Ambassador John G. Winant, with Winston Churchill.

Above, Ambassador to the U.S.S.R. W. Averell Harriman, who often warned the President of Stalin's ruthless territorial ambitions.

Right, Fedor T. Gusev, Soviet Ambassador to the United Kingdom. "A hard bargainer, already known for his obstinacy."

Left, George F. Kennan, Ambassador Winant's political advisor. Like Harriman he warned again and again of his distrust of Soviet intentions. *Right,* Professor Philip E. Mosley, Acting Chairman of the Working Security Committee, charged with working out American policy in postwar Europe in December, 1943. He contended that provision had to be made "for free and direct territorial access to Berlin from the west."

THE RUSSIANS

Marshal Ivan S. Koniev, commander of the 1st Ukranian Front (at left), in 1945.

Koniev with the author, during a four-hour discussion of his part in the capture of Berlin. This is one of the rare occasions on which he has permitted himself to be photographed.

BRITISH ARMY PHOTO

Marshal Konstantin K. Rokossovskii, commander of the 2nd Belorussian Front (at right), in 1945, with Montgomery.

IMPERIAL WAR MUSEUM

PHOTO BY THE AUTHOR

Marshal Georgi Zhukov, commander of the 1st Belorussian Front, Koniev's rival, photographed in 1945.

Marshal Vasili I. Chuikov today. In 1945, he was a Colonel General commanding the 8th Guards Army in the attack on Berlin.

Marshall Vasili Sokolovskii with the author. In 1945 he was appointed Deputy Commander to Zhukov the day before the attack on Berlin.

Lieutenant (now Colonel) Konstantin Y. Samsonov. In 1945 he was battalion commander of the 171st Rifle Division, which captured the Reichstag.

Major General (now General) Ivan I. Yushchuk, commander of the 11th Tank Corps.

The Americans and the Russians meet, April, 1945.

An American MP and a Russian military policewoman guard a bridge on the Elbe.

American soldiers hold a makeshift flag made from a bedsheet painted with watercolors with which they identified themselves to the Russians. Second from the right is Pfc. Paul Staub.

American troops cross the Elbe to meet the Russians (waving, at right) in a captured racing eight!

Lieutenant Duane Francies (right), pilot of the unarmed Piper Cub scout plane *Miss Me*, stands beside his kill.

R.A.F. Warrant Officer James "Dixie" Deans (fifth from left, with left hand showing at waist and R.A.F. pilot's wings) with German officers of Stalag 357.

BELSEN

Brigadier Hugh Glyn Hughes, Senior Medical Officer, British Second Army. "No description could bring home the horrors I saw."

Berlin, April, 1945.

All along the eastern front the great Russian armies were massing, but they were still far from ready to open the Berlin offensive. The Soviet commanders chafed at the delay. The Oder was a formidable barrier and the spring thaw late: the river was still partly covered with ice. Beyond it lay the German defenses—the bunkers, minefields, anti-tank ditches and dug-in artillery positions. Each day now the Germans grew stronger, and this fact worried the Red Army generals.

No one was more anxious to get started than the 45-year-old Colonel General Vasili Ivanovich Chuikov, commander of the crack Eighth Guards Army, who had earned great renown in the Soviet Union as the defender of Stalingrad. Chuikov blamed the holdup on the Western Allies. After the surprise German attack in the Ardennes in December, the British and Americans had asked Stalin to ease the pressure by speeding up the Red Army's drive from the east. Stalin had agreed and had launched the Russian offensive in Poland sooner than planned. Chuikov believed, as he was later to say, that "if our lines of communications had not been so spread out and strained in the rear, we could have struck out for Berlin itself in February." But so fast was the Soviet advance out of Poland that when the armies reached the Oder they found that they had outrun their supplies and communications. The offensive came to a halt, as Chuikov put it, because "we needed ammunition, fuel and pontoons for forcing the Oder, the riverways and canals that lay in front of Berlin." The need to regroup and prepare had already given the Germans nearly two months in which to organize their defenses. Chuikov was bitter. Each day's wait meant more casualties for his Guardsmen when the attack began.

Colonel General Mikhail Yefimovich Katukov, Commander of the First Guards Tank Army, was equally eager for the offensive to begin, yet he was grateful for the delay. His men needed the rest, and his maintenance crews needed a chance to repair the armored vehicles. "The tanks have traveled, in a straight line, perhaps 570 kilometers," he had told one of his corps commanders,

General Getman, after they reached the Oder. "But, Andreya Levrentevich," he continued, "their speedometers show more than 2,000. A man has no speedometer and nobody knows what wear and tear has taken place there."

Getman agreed. He had no doubt that the Germans would be crushed and Berlin captured, but he, too, was glad of the opportunity to reorganize. "The alphabet of war, Comrade General," he told Katukov, "says that victory is achieved not by taking towns but by destroying the enemy. In 1812, Napoleon forgot that. He lost Moscow—and Napoleon was no mean leader of men."

The attitude was much the same at other army headquarters all along the front. Everyone, though impatient of delay, was tirelessly taking advantage of the respite, for there were no illusions about the desperate battle that lay ahead. Marshals Zhukov, Rokossovskii and Koniev had received chilling reports of what they might encounter. Their intelligence estimates indicated that more than a million Germans manned the defenses and that up to three million civilians might help fight for Berlin. If the reports were true, the Red Army might be outnumbered more than three to one.

When would the attack take place? As yet, the marshals did not know. Zhukov's huge army group was scheduled to take the city—but that, too, could be changed. Just as Anglo-American armies on the western front waited for the word "Go" from Eisenhower, the Red Army commanders waited on their Supreme Commander. What worried the marshals more than anything else was the speed of the Anglo-American drive from the Rhine. Each day now they were drawing closer to the Elbe—and Berlin. If Moscow failed to order the offensive soon, the British and Americans might beat the Red Army into the city. So far the word "Go" had not come down from Josef Stalin. He almost seemed to be waiting himself.

Part Four

THE DECISION

✢1✢

A GREAT PROCESSION of Army supply trucks rolled along the narrow, dusty main street of the French city. In endless lines the convoys roared through, heading northeast on the long haul to the Rhine and the Western Front. No one was permitted to stop; MP's stood everywhere to keep the traffic flowing. To the drivers, there was no reason to stop anyway. This was just another sleepy French city with the usual cathedral, just another checkpoint on the high-speed "Red Ball Highway." They did not know that at this moment in the war Reims was perhaps the most important city in Europe.

For centuries battles had raged about this strategic crossroad in northeast France. The Gothic cathedral rising majestically from the city's center had endured countless bombardments, and again and again its fabric had been restored. On its site or within its sanctuary every French monarch, from Clovis I in 496 to Louis XVI in 1774, had been crowned. In this war, mercifully the city and its monument had been spared. Now, in the shadow of the great twin-spired cathedral stood the headquarters of another great leader. His name was Dwight D. Eisenhower.

Supreme Headquarters of the Allied Expeditionary Forces was tucked away on a back street close to the railway station in a plain, modern three-story building. The building was the Collège Moderne et Technique, a former technical school for boys. Box-

197

like, its four sides surrounding an inner courtyard, the red brick school was originally designed to hold more than 1,500 students. Staff members called it the "little red school house." Perhaps because of SHAEF's requirements, it seemed small: the headquarters had almost doubled its strength since 1944 and now had nearly 1,200 officers and some 4,000 enlisted men. As a result, the college could accommodate only the Supreme Commander, his immediate general staff officers and their departments. The remainder worked in other buildings throughout Reims.

In the second-floor classroom that he used for an office, the General had worked almost without pause all day. The room was small and spartan. Blackout curtains hung by the two windows overlooking the street. There were a few easy chairs on the highly polished oak floor, but that was all. Eisenhower's desk, set in an alcove at one end of the room, was on a slightly raised platform— once used by the teacher. On the desk were a blue leather desk set, an intercom, leather-framed photos of his wife and son, and two black phones—one for regular use, the other a special instrument for "scrambled" calls to Washington and London. There were also several ashtrays, for the Supreme Commander was a chain-smoker who consumed more than sixty cigarettes a day.* Behind the desk stood the General's personal flag and, in the opposite corner, Old Glory.

The previous afternoon Eisenhower had made a quick flight to Paris for a press conference. The big news was the victory on the Rhine. The Supreme Commander announced that the enemy's main defense in the west had been shattered. Although Eisenhower told reporters he did not want to "write off the war for the Germans are going to stand and fight where they can," in his opinion the German was "a whipped enemy." Buried in the conference was a reference to Berlin. Someone asked who would get to the capital first, "the Russians or us?" Eisenhower answered that he thought "mileage alone ought to make them do it," but he quickly

---

* In 1948, following a sudden rise in pulse rate, his doctors told him to give up tobacco. Eisenhower never smoked again.

added that he did not "want to make any predictions"; although the Russians had a "shorter race to run" they were faced with "the bulk of the German forces."

Eisenhower spent the night at the Hotel Raphael; then, leaving Paris shortly after dawn, he flew back to Reims. At 7:45 A.M. he was in his office and conferring with his Chief of Staff, Lieutenant General Walter Bedell Smith. Waiting for Eisenhower, in General Smith's blue leather snap-top folder, were a score of overnight cables that only the Supreme Commander could answer. They were labeled with the highest security tag: "For Eisenhower's Eyes Only." Among them was Montgomery's message, seeking approval for his dash to the Elbe and Berlin. But the most important cable was from Eisenhower's superior, the U.S. Army Chief of Staff, General George C. Marshall. By coincidence Marshall's and Montgomery's messages had arrived at SHAEF within two hours of each other the previous evening—and both were to have a major influence on Eisenhower. On this Wednesday, March 28, they would act as catalysts in finally crystallizing for the Supreme Commander the strategy he would follow to the war's end.

Months before, Eisenhower's mission as Supreme Commander had been spelled out by the Combined Chiefs of Staff in one sentence: "You will enter the continent of Europe and, in conjunction with the other United Nations, undertake operations aimed at the heart of Germany and the destruction of her armed forces." He had carried out this directive brilliantly. By dint of personality, administrative ability and tact, he had welded the soldiery of more than a dozen nations into the most awesome force in history. Few men could have achieved this while keeping animosities to such a minimum. Yet the 55-year-old Eisenhower did not conform to the traditional European concept of the military leader. Unlike British generals, he was not trained to consider political objectives as part of military strategy. Eisenhower, though a master diplomat in the politics of compromise and placation, was in international terms politically unaware—and proud of it. In the American military tradition he had been schooled never to usurp civilian supremacy. In short, he was content to fight and win; politics he left to the statesmen.

Even now, at this crucial turning point of the war, Eisenhower's objectives remained, as always, purely military. He had never been given a political directive regarding post-war Germany, nor did he regard that problem as his responsibility. "My job," he later said, "was to get the war over quickly . . . to destroy the German Army as fast as we could."

Eisenhower had every reason to be elated with the way the job was going: in twenty-one days his armies had catapulted across the Rhine and burst into the German heartlands far ahead of schedule. Yet their headline-making advances, so eagerly followed by the free world, were now presenting the Supreme Commander with a series of complex command decisions. The unanticipated speed of the Anglo-American offensive had made obsolete some strategic moves planned months before. Eisenhower had to tailor his plans to meet the new situation. This meant changing and redefining the roles of some armies and their commanders—in particular, Field Marshal Montgomery and his powerful Twenty-first Army Group.

Montgomery's latest message was a clarion call for action. The 58-year-old Field Marshal was not asking how the battle would be fought; he was demanding the right to lead the charge. Quicker than most commanders to realize the political implications of a military situation, Montgomery felt that the Allied capture of Berlin was vital—and he was convinced that it should be undertaken by the Twenty-first Army Group. His cable, indicative as it was of Montgomery's intractability, made clear there were still vital differences of opinion between him and the Supreme Commander. Eisenhower's reaction to the Field Marshal's cable, as General Smith and others at SHAEF were to recall, was "like that of a horse with a burr under his saddle."

The crucial difference between the military philosophies of Montgomery and Eisenhower concerned the single thrust versus the broad-front strategy. For months Montgomery and his supe-

rior, Chief of the Imperial General Staff Field Marshal Sir Alan
Brooke, had agitated for a lightning-like single thrust into the
heart of Germany. Almost immediately after the fall of Paris,
while the Germans were still disorganized and fleeing France,
Montgomery had first put his plan up to Eisenhower. "We have
now reached a stage," he wrote, "where one really powerful and
full-blooded thrust toward Berlin is likely to get there and thus
end the German war."

Montgomery spelled out his scheme in nine terse paragraphs.
He reasoned that the Anglo-American forces lacked the supply
and maintenance capabilities for two side-by-side drives into Germany. In his view there could be only one—his own—and it
would need "all the maintenance resources . . . without qualifi-
cation." Other operations would have to get along with whatever
logistical support remained. "If," warned Montgomery, "we attempt a compromise solution and split our maintenance resources
so that neither thrust is full-blooded, we will prolong the war."
Time was "of such vital importance . . . that a decision is required at once."

The plan was boldly imaginative and, from Montgomery's
viewpoint, accurately timed. It also marked a strange reversal in
the Field Marshal's usual approach to battle. As Lieutenant General Sir Frederick Morgan, now Eisenhower's Assistant Chief of
Staff, later described the situation: "Put succinctly, Montgomery,
principally celebrated hitherto for cautious deliberation, had conceived the notion that were he to be accorded every priority to the
detriment of the American Army Groups, he could, in the shortest
order, overwhelm the enemy, drive to Berlin and bring the war to
a speedy end."

Obviously the plan involved a gigantic gamble. To hurl two
great army groups of more than forty divisions northeast into Germany in a single massive thrust might invite speedy and decisive
victory—but it might also result in total and perhaps irreversible
disaster. To the Supreme Commander, the risks far outweighed
any chance of success, and he had said as much in a tactful

message to Montgomery. "While agreeing with your conception of a powerful thrust towards Berlin," Eisenhower said, "I do not agree that it should be initiated at this moment." He felt that it was essential first to open the ports of Le Havre and Antwerp "to sustain a powerful thrust deep into Germany." Further, Eisenhower said, "no reallocation of our present resources would be adequate to sustain a thrust to Berlin." The Supreme Commander's strategy was to advance into Germany on a broad front, cross the Rhine and capture the great industrial valley of the Ruhr before driving for the capital.

That exchange had taken place in the first week of September, 1944. A week later in a message to his three army group commanders, Montgomery, Bradley and Devers, Eisenhower further elaborated on his plan: "Clearly Berlin is the main prize and the prize in defense of which the enemy is likely to concentrate the bulk of his forces. There is no doubt whatsoever in my mind that we should concentrate all our energies and resources on a rapid thrust to Berlin. Our strategy, however, will have to be coordinated with that of the Russians, so we must also consider alternative objectives."

The possible objectives as Eisenhower saw them, varied widely: the northern German ports ("they might have to be occupied as a flank protection to our thrust on Berlin"); the important industrial and communication centers of Hanover, Brunswick, Leipzig and Dresden ("the Germans will probably hold them as intermediate positions covering Berlin"); and finally, in southern Germany, the Nuremberg-Munich areas, which would have to be taken ("to cut off enemy forces withdrawing from Italy and the Balkans"). Thus, warned the Supreme Commander, "We must be prepared for one or more of the following:

"A. To direct forces of both north and central army groups on Berlin astride the axes Ruhr-Hanover-Berlin *or* Frankfurt-Leipzig-Berlin *or* both.

"B. Should the Russians beat us to Berlin, the northern group of armies would seize the Hanover area and the Hamburg group of ports. The central group . . . would seize part, or the whole of the area Leipzig-Dresden depending on the progress of the Russian advance.

"C. In any event the southern group of armies would seize Augsburg-Munich. The area Nuremberg-Regensburg would be seized by the central or southern groups . . . depending on the situation at the time."

Eisenhower summarized his strategy in these words: "Simply stated, it is my desire to move on Berlin by the most direct and expeditious route, with combined U. S.-British forces supported by other available forces moving through key centers and occupying areas on the flanks, all in one coordinated, concerted operation." But, he added, all this would have to wait, for it was "not possible at this stage to indicate the timing of these thrusts or their strengths."

Whether the broad-front strategy was right or wrong, Eisenhower was the Supreme Commander and Montgomery had to take his orders. But he was bitterly disappointed. To the British people he was the most popular soldier since Wellington; and to his troops Monty was a legend in his own time. Many Britons considered him the most experienced field commander in the European theater (as he was well aware), and the denial of his plan, which he believed could have ended the war within three months, left Montgomery deeply aggrieved.* This strategic dispute in the autumn of 1944 had opened up a split between the two commanders that had never completely healed.

In the seven months since then, Eisenhower had not deviated from his concept of a broad coordinated pattern of attack. Nor had Montgomery ceased to express his opinions on how, where, and by whom the war should be won. His own Chief of Staff, Major General Sir Francis de Guingand, later wrote, "Montgomery . . . feels justified in bringing all influences to bear in order

---

* His pride was somewhat restored when, shortly after this incident, the British showed their confidence in Montgomery and his policies by naming him a Field Marshal. For the man who had turned the tide of British defeat in the desert and chased Rommel out of North Africa, it was an honor long overdue.

to win his point: in fact the end justifies almost any means." One of the influences he brought to bear was powerful indeed: the Chief of the Imperial General Staff, Field Marshal Brooke, saw Eisenhower as vague and indecisive. He once summarized the Supreme Commander as a man with "a most attractive personality and, at the same time, a very, very limited brain from a strategic point of view."

Eisenhower was perfectly well aware of the biting comments that emanated out of the War Office and Montgomery's headquarters. But if this whispering campaign over his strategic policies hurt, Eisenhower did not reveal it. And he never hit back. Even when Brooke and Montgomery advocated the appointment of a "Land Forces Commander"—a sort of field marshal sandwiched in between Eisenhower and his army groups—the Supreme Commander displayed no anger. Finally, after months of "sitting with clenched teeth"—to use General Omar Bradley's expression—Eisenhower lost his temper. The issue came to an explosive boil after the German attack through the Ardennes.

Because the enemy drive split the Anglo-American front, Eisenhower was forced to place all troops on the northern salient under Montgomery's command. These forces included two thirds of General Bradley's Twelfth Army Group—that is, the First and Ninth U.S. armies.

After the Germans had been thrown back, Montgomery gave an extraordinary press conference in which he implied that he had almost singlehandedly rescued the Americans from disaster. He had neatly tidied up the front, the Field Marshal declared, and "headed off . . . seen off . . . and . . . written off" the enemy. "The battle has been most interesting. I think possibly one of the most tricky . . . I have ever handled." He had, Montgomery said, "employed the whole available power of the British group of armies . . . you thus have the picture of British troops fighting on both sides of the Americans who have suffered a hard blow."

Montgomery had indeed mounted the main counteroffensive from the north and east and had directed it superbly. But, at the

Field Marshal's press conference, to use Eisenhower's words, "he unfortunately created the impression that he had moved in as the savior of the Americans." Montgomery failed to mention the part played by Bradley, Patton and the other American commanders, or that for every British soldier there were thirty to forty Americans engaged in the fighting. Most important, he neglected to point out that for every British casualty forty to sixty Americans had fallen. [*] [†]

German propagandists were quick to make matters worse. Enemy radio transmitters put out an exaggerated, distorted version of the conference and beamed the broadcasts directly toward the American lines; it was this version that gave many Americans their first news of the incident.

On the heels of the press conference and the uproar it caused, the old controversy about a land forces commander flared again, this time supported by an active campaign in the British press. Bradley blew up. If the Field Marshal were appointed ground forces commander, he declared, he would resign his command. "After what has happened," he told Eisenhower, "if Montgomery is to be put in charge . . . you must send me home . . . this is one thing I cannot take." Patton told Bradley: "I'll be quitting with you."

Never had there been such a rift in the Anglo-American camp. As the "promote-Montgomery" campaign intensified—a campaign which seemed to some Americans to originate directly from Montgomery's headquarters—the Supreme Commander finally found the situation intolerable. He decided to end the bickering once

[*] These figures were given by Winston Churchill on Jaunary 18, 1945, in a speech before the House of Commons. Appalled by the breakdown in amity, he announced that "U.S. troops have done almost all the fighting" in the Ardennes, suffering losses "equal to those of both sides at the Battle of Gettysburg." Then, in what could only be interpreted as a direct slap at Montgomery and his supporters, he warned the British not to "lend themselves to the shouting of mischief makers."

[†] "I should never have held the press conference at all," Montgomery told the author in 1963. "The Americans seemed over-sensitive at the time and many of their generals disliked me so much that no matter what I said, it would have been wrong."

and for all: he would fire Montgomery by making an issue of the whole matter before the Combined Chiefs of Staff.

At that point Montgomery's Chief of Staff, General de Guingand, learned of the impending blow-up and hastened to the rescue of Anglo-American unity. He flew to SHAEF and met with the Supreme Commander. "He showed me a signal that he was about to send to Washington," De Guingand later recounted. "I was stunned when I read it." With the aid of General Bedell Smith he prevailed on Eisenhower to delay the message twenty-four hours. Eisenhower agreed with great reluctance.

Returning to Montgomery's headquarters, De Guingand bluntly laid the facts before the Field Marshal. "I told Monty that I had seen Ike's message," De Guingand said, "and that, in effect, it said 'It is either me or Monty.' " Montgomery was shocked. De Guingand had never seen him "so lonely and deflated." He looked up at his Chief of Staff and said quietly, "Freddie, what do you think I should do?" De Guingand had already drafted a message. Using this as a basis, Montgomery sent Eisenhower a thoroughly soldierly dispatch in which he made clear that he had no desire to be insubordinate. "Whatever your decision may be," he said, "you can rely on me one hundred per cent." The message was signed "Your very devoted subordinate, Monty." *

There the matter had ended—for the moment anyhow. But now, at his headquarters in Reims, on this day of decision, March 28, 1945, Eisenhower was hearing again the distinct echo of an old refrain: not the agitation for a land forces commander once more, but the older, more basic issue—single thrust versus broad front. Without conferring with Eisenhower, Montgomery had, in his own words, "issued orders to Field Commanders for the operations eastwards" and now hoped to make a single great push toward the Elbe and Berlin, obviously intending to enter the capital in a blaze of glory.

The fact was that in making the main thrust north of the Ruhr,

---

* "Montgomery," Eisenhower later stated, "believed in the appointment of a field commander as a matter of principle. He even offered to serve under Bradley if I would approve."

Montgomery was actually following agreed strategy—the Eisenhower plan approved by the Combined Chiefs of Staff at Malta in January. What Montgomery now proposed was simply a logical extension of that drive—a move that would carry him to Berlin. If he was acting in haste, his eagerness was understandable. Like Winston Churchill and Field Marshal Brooke, Montgomery believed that time was running out, that the war might be lost politically unless Anglo-American forces reached Berlin before the Russians.

The Supreme Commander, on the other hand, had received no policy directive from his superiors in Washington reflecting this British sense of urgency. And although he was Commander of the Allied Forces, Eisenhower still took his orders from the U.S. War Department. In the absence of any redefinition of policy from Washington, his objective remained the same: the defeat of Germany and the destruction of her armed forces. And, as he now saw it, the method by which he could most quickly achieve that military objective had changed radically since the presentation of his plans to the Combined Chiefs of Staff in January.

Originally, under Eisenhower's plan, General Bradley's Twelfth Army Group in the center was to have a limited role, supplementing Montgomery's main effort in the north. But who could have foreseen the spectacular successes achieved by Bradley's armies since the beginning of March? Good fortune and brilliant leadership had produced dazzling results. Even before Montgomery's massive Rhine assault, the U.S. First Army had captured the Remagen bridge and had quickly crossed the river. Farther south, Patton's Third Army had slipped across the Rhine almost unimpeded. Since then, Bradley's forces had been on a rampage, going from victory to victory. Their achievements had fired the imagination of the U.S. public, and Bradley was now seeking a larger role in the final campaign. In this respect Bradley and his generals were no different from Montgomery: they, too, wanted the prestige and glory of ending the war—and, if they got the chance, of capturing Berlin.

At the right moment, Eisenhower had promised, he would

launch one massive drive to the east, but he had not specified what group—or groups—would make the final thrust. Now, before making a decision, Eisenhower had to consider a variety of factors, all of which affected the design of his final campaign.

The first of these was the unexpected speed of the Russian advance to the Oder. At the time the Supreme Commander formulated his plans for the Rhine assault and Montgomery's offensive north of the Ruhr, it looked as if months might pass before the Russians got to within striking distance of Berlin. But now the Red Army was barely 38 miles from the city—while British and American forces were still more than 200 miles away. How soon would the Russians launch their offensive? Where and how did they intend to mount the attack—with Zhukov's army group in the center opposite Berlin, or with all three groups simultaneously? What was their estimate of the German strength opposing them and how long would it take the Red Army to break through those defenses? And, after they crossed the Oder, how long would it take the Soviets to reach and capture Berlin? The Supreme Commander could not answer these questions, all of them vitally important in his planning.

The simple truth was that Eisenhower knew almost nothing of the Red Army's intentions. There was no day-to-day military coordination between Anglo-American and Soviet commanders in the field. There was not even a direct radio link between SHAEF and the Anglo-American military liaison mission in Moscow. All messages between the two fronts were funneled through normal diplomatic channels—a method totally inadequate now because of the speed of events. Although Eisenhower knew the Russians' approximate strength, he had no idea of their battle order. Apart from occasional data collected from various intelligence sources—most of it of doubtful accuracy*—SHAEF's chief source of information

* On March 11, for example, SHAEF intelligence reported that Zhukov's "spearheads" had reached Seelow, west of the Oder and just twenty-eight miles from Berlin. When the author interviewed Soviet defense officials in Moscow in 1963, he learned that Zhukov did not actually reach Seelow, in the center of the German Oder defense system, until April 17.

on Russian moves was the Soviet communiqué broadcast each evening by the BBC.

One fact, however, was clear: the Red Army had almost reached Berlin. With the Russians so close should the Supreme Commander try for the city at all?

The problem had many dimensions. The Russians had been on the Oder for more than two months, and with the exception of some local advances and patrol activity they appeared to have come to a full stop. Their lines of supply and communications must be stretched to the utmost, and it hardly seemed likely that they could attack until after the spring thaw. Meanwhile the western armies, moving at astonishing speeds, were driving deeper and deeper into Germany. At places they were averaging better than thirty-five miles per day. The Supreme Commander had no intention of letting up, no matter what Russian plans were. But he was reluctant to enter into a contest with the Russians for Berlin. That might prove not only embarrassing for the loser but —in the event of an unexpected meeting between the onrushing armies—catastrophic for both forces.

A headlong collision involving the Russians had occurred once before, when they were allied by treaty with the Germans. In 1939, after Hitler's undeclared blitzkrieg into Poland and the subsequent division of that country between Germany and Russia, Wehrmacht troops advancing east had smashed head on into Red Army forces racing west: no prearranged line of demarcation had been established. The result was a minor battle, with fairly heavy casualties on both sides. A similar clash could occur now, but between the Anglo-Americans and the Russians—and on a much larger scale. It was a nightmarish thought. Wars had been set off by less. Obviously coordination of movement had to be effected with the Russians, and quickly.

Furthermore, there was one tactical problem that hung over Eisenhower like a thunderhead. In the great map room near his office there was a carefully drawn intelligence chart bearing the legend "Reported National Redoubt." It showed an area of mountainous territory lying south of Munich and straddling the alpine regions of Bavaria, western Austria and northern Italy. In all, it covered almost twenty thousand square miles. Its heart was Berchtesgaden. On the nearby Obersalzberg—surrounded by peaks seven to nine thousand feet high, each studded with concealed anti-aircraft guns—was Hitler's mountaintop hideaway, the "Eagle's Nest."

Covering the map's face was a rash of red marks, each one a military symbol denoting some kind of defense installation. There were food, ammunition, gasoline and chemical warfare dumps; radio and power stations; troop concentration points, barracks and headquarters; zigzagging lines of fortified positions, ranging from pillboxes to massive concrete bunkers; even bombproof underground factories. Each day now, more and more symbols were added to the chart, and though all of them were labeled "unconfirmed," to SHAEF this formidable mountain defense system was the greatest threat remaining in the European war. The area was sometimes referred to as the *Alpenfestung*, Alpine Fortress, or the "National Redoubt." In this craggy citadel, according to intelligence, the Nazis, with Hitler at their head, intended to make a last-ditch, Wagnerian stand. The rugged stronghold was considered almost impregnable and its fanatical defenders might hold out for as long as two years. There was another, even more chilling aspect; specially trained commando-type forces—Goebbels called them "Werewolves"—were expected to sally out from the alpine bastion and create havoc among the occupation armies.

Did the *Alpenfestung* really exist? In Washington the military seemed to think so. Information had been accumulating ever since September, 1944, when the Office of Strategic Services (OSS), in a general study of southern Germany, predicted that as the war neared its end the Nazis would probably evacuate certain government departments to Bavaria. Since then, intelligence reports and appreciations had poured in, from the field, from neutral countries, even from sources inside Germany. Most of these evaluations were guarded, but some bordered on the fantastic.

The Southern Redoubt. This map was drawn up at Supreme Headquarters to show the so-called defenses, which existed only in the minds of Allied intelligence officers. The details of nonexistent ammunition dumps and defense lines were so believable that the map played a large part in the decision not to advance to Berlin.

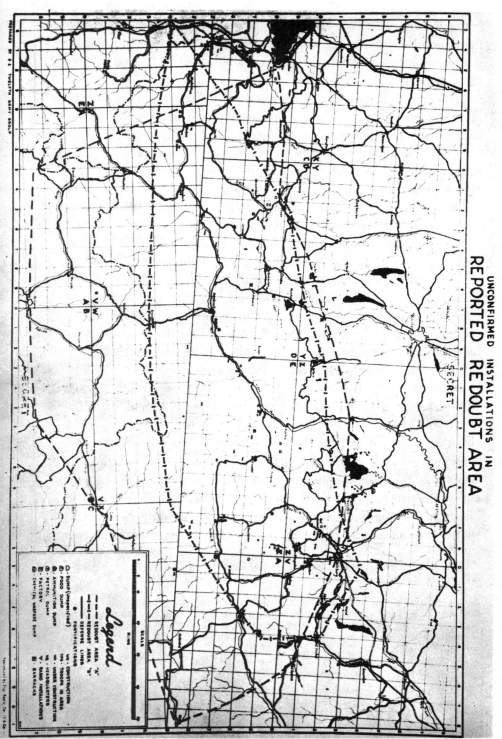

UNCONFIRMED INSTALLATIONS IN
REPORTED REDOUBT AREA

On February 12, 1945, the War Department issued a straight-faced counterintelligence paper which said: "Not enough weight is given the many reports of the probable Nazi last stand in the Bavarian Alps. . . . The Nazi myth which is important when you are dealing with men like Hitler requires a *Götterdämmerung*. It may be significant that Berchtesgaden itself, which would be the headquarters, is on the site of the tomb of Barbarossa who, in German mythology, is supposed to return from the dead." * The memo urged that field commanders "down to corps level" be alerted to the danger.

On February 16, Allied agents in Switzerland sent Washington a bizarre report obtained from neutral military attachés in Berlin: "The Nazis are undoubtedly preparing for a bitter fight from the mountain redoubt. . . . Strongpoints are connected by underground railroads . . . several months' output of the best munitions have been reserved and almost all of Germany's poison gas supplies. Everybody who participated in the construction of the secret installations will be killed off—including the civilians who happen to remain behind . . . when the real fighting starts."

Although British intelligence agencies and the OSS both issued cautious statements intended to dampen the scare reports, over the next twenty-seven days the specter of the National Redoubt grew. By March 21, the threat had begun to influence tactical thinking. Headquarters of Bradley's Twelfth Army Group put out a memorandum entitled "Re-Orientation of Strategy" in which it was stated that Allied objectives had changed, rendering "obsolete the plans we brought with us over the beaches." One of the changes: the significance of Berlin was much diminished. "The metropolitan area can no longer occupy a position of importance,"

---

* Whoever prepared the counterintelligence paper was in error about Barbarossa's last resting place. Barbarossa (Red Beard)—the surname of Frederick I (1121-1190)—is not buried in Berchtesgaden. As the myth goes, "he never died, but merely sleeps" in the hills of Thuringia. He sits at a "stone table with his six knights waiting for the fullness of time when he will rescue Germany from bondage and give her the foremost place in the world . . . his beard has already grown through the stone slab, but must wind itself thrice around the table before his second advent."

the report read. ". . . all indications suggest that the enemy's political and military directorate is already in the process of displacing to the 'Redoubt' in lower Bavaria."

To meet the threat, instead of making a thrust in the north, Bradley suggested that his army group split Germany in two by driving through the center. This would "prevent German forces from withdrawing" toward the south and "into the Redoubt." In addition it would drive the enemy "northwards where they can be rounded up against the shores of the Baltic and North Seas." Later, suggested the memorandum, Twelfth Army Group forces would pivot south to reduce any remaining resistance in the *Alpenfestung*.

The most alarming analysis came on March 25 from the Intelligence Chief of Lieutenant General Patch's Seventh Army, which was fighting along the southern wing of the front. It foresaw the possible creation in the redoubt of "an elite force, predominantly SS and mountain troops, of between 200,000 and 300,000 men." Already, the report said, supplies were arriving in the redoubt area at the rate of "three to five very long trains . . . each week (since 1 Feb. 1945). . . . A new type of gun has been reported observed on many of these trains. . . ." There was even mention of an underground aircraft factory "capable of producing . . . Messerschmitts."

Day after day the reports had flooded into SHAEF. No matter how the evidence was analyzed and re-analyzed, the picture remained the same: though the *Alpenfestung* might be a hoax, the possibility of its existence could not be ignored. SHAEF's own concern was clearly indicated in a March 11 intelligence evaluation on the redoubt: "Theoretically . . . within this fortress . . . defended both by nature and the most efficient secret weapons yet invented, the powers that have hitherto guided Germany will survive to organize her resurrection. . . . The main trend of German defense policy does seem directed primarily to the safeguarding of the Alpine zone. . . . The evidence indicates that considerable numbers of SS and specially chosen units are being systematically withdrawn to Austria. . . . It seems reasonably certain that some of the most important ministries and personalities of the Nazi regime are already established in the redoubt area. . . . Goering, Himmler, Hitler . . . are said to be in the process of withdrawing to their respective personal mountain strongholds. . . ."

SHAEF's Intelligence Chief, British Major General Kenneth W. D. Strong, commented to the Chief of Staff: "The redoubt may not be there, but we have to take steps to prevent it being there." Bedell Smith agreed. There was, in his opinion, "every reason to believe that the Nazis intend to make their last stand among the crags."

As the considered views of the SHAEF staff and U.S. field commanders piled up in Eisenhower's office, there arrived the most significant message of all. It came from the Supreme Commander's superior, General Marshall, a man Eisenhower venerated almost above all others. *

"From the current operations report," Marshall's cable read, "it looks like the German defense system in the west may break up. This would permit you to move a considerable number of divisions rapidly eastwards on a broad front. What are your views on . . . pushing U.S. forces rapidly forward on, say, the Nuremberg-Linz or Karlsruhe-Munich axes? The idea behind this is that . . . rapid action might prevent the formation of any organized resistance areas. The mountainous country in the south is considered a possibility for one of these.

"One of the problems which arises with disintegrating German resistance is that of meeting the Russians. What are your ideas on control and coordination to prevent unfortunate instances. . . ? One possibility is an agreed line of demarcation. The arrangements we now have . . . appear inadequate . . . steps should be initiated without delay to provide for communication and liaison . . ."

* One of Marshall's senior staff officers, General John Hull, who in 1945 was the U.S. Army's Acting Chief of Staff for Operations, says that "Ike was Marshall's protégé and, though Ike might resent me saying this, there was between the two men a sort of father-son relationship."

Marshall's carefully worded message finally jelled the Supreme Commander's plans. Having weighed all the problems, having consulted with his staff, having discussed the situation over the weeks with his old friend and West Point classmate, General Bradley, and, most important, having been acquainted with the views of his superior, Eisenhower now molded his strategy and made his decisions.

On this chill March afternoon he drafted three cables. The first was historic and unprecedented: it was sent to Moscow with a covering message to the Allied Military Mission. SHAEF's operations, Eisenhower wired, had now reached a stage "where it is essential I should know the Russians' plans in order to achieve the most rapid success." Therefore, he wanted the Mission to "transmit a personal message from me to Marshal Stalin" and do everything possible "to assist in getting a full reply."

Never before had the Supreme Commander communicated directly with the Soviet leader, but now the matter was urgent. He had been authorized to deal with the Russians directly on military matters pertaining to coordination, so Eisenhower saw no particular reason to consult beforehand with the Combined Chiefs of Staff nor with the U.S. or British governments. Indeed, not even the Deputy Supreme Commander, Air Chief Marshal Sir Arthur Tedder, knew about it. Copies were prepared for them, however.

The Supreme Commander approved the draft of the Stalin cable shortly after three. At 4 P.M., after it had been encoded, Eisenhower's "Personal Message to Marshal Stalin" was dispatched. In it the General asked the Generalissimo for his plans, and at the same time revealed his own. "My immediate operations," he said, "are designed to encircle and destroy the enemy defending the Ruhr. . . . I estimate that this phase . . . will end late in April or even earlier, and my next task will be to divide the remaining enemy forces by joining hands with your forces. . . . The best axis on which to effect this junction would be Erfurt-Leipzig-Dresden. I believe . . . this is the area to which main German Government Departments are being moved. It is along this axis that I propose to make my main effort. In addition, as soon as possible, a secondary advance will be made to effect junction with your forces in the area Regensburg-Linz, thereby preventing the consolidation of German resistance in the Redoubt in southern Germany.

"Before deciding firmly on my plans, it is most important that they should be coordinated . . . with yours both as to direction and timing. Could you . . . tell me your intentions and . . . how far the proposals outlined . . . conform to your probable action. If we are to complete the destruction of German armies without delay, I regard it as essential that we coordinate our action and . . . perfect the liaison between our advancing forces . . ."

Next he prepared cables for Marshall and Montgomery. These were dispatched at 7 P.M. and within five minutes of each other. Eisenhower told the U.S. Chief of Staff that he had communicated with Stalin "on the question of where we should aim to link up . . ." He then pointed out that "my views agree closely with your own, although I think that the Leipzig-Dresden area is of primary importance . . ." because it offered the "shortest route to present Russian positions" and also would "overrun the one remaining industrial area in Germany to which . . . the High Command Headquarters and Ministries are reported moving."

Regarding Marshall's fears of a "National Redoubt," Eisenhower reported that he too was aware of the "importance of forestalling the possibilities of the enemy forming organized resistance areas" and would make "a drive towards Linz and Munich as soon as circumstances allowed." Eisenhower added that as regards coordination with the Russians he did not think that "we can tie ourselves down to a demarcation line" but would approach them with the suggestion that "when our forces meet, either side will withdraw to its own occupational zone at the request of the opposite side."

The third Eisenhower cable of the day, to Montgomery, contained disappointing news. "As soon as you have joined hands with Bradley . . . [east of the Ruhr] . . . the Ninth U.S. Army will revert to Bradley's command," the Supreme Commander said; "Bradley will be responsible for mopping up . . . the Ruhr and with the minimum delay will deliver his main thrust on the axis Erfurt-Leipzig-Dresden to join hands with the Russians. . . ." Montgomery was to head for the Elbe; at that point it might be "desirable for the Ninth Army to revert to your operational control again to facilitate the crossing of that obstacle." Eisenhower, after reading the draft, added one last line in pencil, "As you say, the situation looks good."

The Supreme Commander had refined his plans to this extent: instead of making the major drive across northern Germany as originally considered, he had decided to strike directly across the center of the country. The U.S. Ninth Army had been returned to Bradley, who would now have the major role. He would launch the last offensive, aiming to put his forces in the Dresden area, about one hundred miles south of Berlin.

Although Eisenhower had accepted part of Marshall's recommendations, his moves were similar to those suggested by General Bradley's Twelfth Army Group in its "Re-Orientation of Strategy" memorandum. But, in all three of Eisenhower's cables on his campaign plans, there was one significant omission: the objective which the Supreme Commander had once referrred to as "clearly the main prize." There was no mention of Berlin.

✿   ✿   ✿

The battered Brandenburg Gate loomed large in the dusk. From his villa nearby, Dr. Joseph Goebbels stared out at the monument through the partly boarded-up windows of his study. Almost contemptuously, Hitler's gnomelike propaganda chief had turned his back on his visitors—at least so it appeared to the man who was speaking, the Berlin Commandant, Major General Hellmuth Reymann. The General was trying to get a decision on the one matter that he considered of the utmost urgency: the fate of the city's population on this eve of battle.

It was the fourth time within a month that Reymann and his Chief of Staff, Colonel Hans Refior, had met with Goebbels. Next to Hitler, the 47-year-old Goebbels was now the most important man in Berlin. He was not only Reichsminister for Public Enlightenment and Propaganda; he was also Gauleiter of Berlin. As such he was a Reich Defense Commissioner, responsible for all measures regarding the city's civilian population, the organization and training of Home Guard units and the construction of fortifications. At a time when the absence of any clearly defined division of authority between the military and civilian agencies was creating trouble for soldiers and civil leaders alike, Goebbels had added to the confusion. Though he was totally ignorant of military or municipal matters, he had made it quite clear that he alone was assuming responsibility for defending Berlin. As a result, Reymann found himself in an impossible position. From whom was he to take his orders—from Hitler's military headquarters or from Goebbels? He was not sure, and no one seemed eager to clarify the command position. Reymann was desperate.

At each of the previous meetings Reymann had raised the issue of evacuation. At first Goebbels said that it "was out of the question." Then he informed the General that a scheme did exist, prepared by "higher SS authorities and the police." Reymann's Chief of Staff had promptly investigated. Refior had indeed found a plan. "It consists," he told Reymann, "of a map, scale 1 to 300,000, on which the responsible official, a police captain, has neatly marked evacuation routes running out of Berlin to the west and south with red ink." There were, he reported, "no sanitation stations, no food points, no transportation for the sick or weak." He added that, "as far as I can see, the plan calls for evacuees to set out along these roads with only hand luggage, march 20 to 30 kilometers to entraining stations where they will be transported to Thüringen, Sachsen-Anhalt and Mecklenburg. All this is supposed to take place when Goebbels presses a button. But exactly where the rail transport is to come from has not been made clear."

Reymann tried to discuss the matter with Hitler. He had seen him only twice: on assuming command and a few days later when he was invited to attend one of the Führer's nightly conferences. At that meeting the discussion was mostly about the Oder front and Reymann did not get an opportunity of explaining the situation in Berlin. But at one point during a lull in the proceedings, he spoke to Hitler and urged that he immediately order the evacuation of all children under ten from the capital. In the sudden silence that followed Reymann's suggestion, Hitler turned toward him and asked icily, "What do you mean? What exactly do you mean?" Then, slowly, emphasizing each word, he said, "There are no children in that age group left in Berlin!" No one had dared contradict him. Hitler quickly passed on to other matters.

The rebuff did not deter the Berlin Commandant. Reymann now pressed Goebbels on the same subject. "Herr Reichsminister," he said, "how will we support the population in the event of a siege? How will we feed them? Where is the food to come from? According to the mayor's statistics there are 110,000 children under ten with their mothers in the city right now. How are we to provide babies with milk?"

Reymann paused, waiting for an answer. Goebbels continued to stare out the window. Then, without turning, he snapped: "How will we feed them? We'll bring livestock in from the surrounding countryside—that's how we'll feed them! As for the children, we have a three months' supply of canned milk." The canned milk was news to Reymann and Refior. The livestock proposal seemed madness. In a battle cows would prove more vulnerable than human beings, who could at least take shelter. Where did Goebbels plan to herd the animals? And what would they feed on? Reymann spoke up earnestly: "Surely we must consider an immediate evacuation plan. We cannot wait any longer. Each day that passes will multiply the difficulties later on. We must at least move out the women and children now—before it's too late."

Goebbels did not answer. There was a long silence. Outside it was growing dark. Suddenly he reached up, grabbed a cord by the window, and yanked it. The blackout curtains closed with a rattle. Goebbels turned. Club-footed from birth, he limped across to his desk, snapped on the light, looked at the watch lying on the blotting pad and then at Reymann. "My dear General," he said mildly, "when and if an evacuation becomes necessary *I* will be the one to make the decision." Then he snarled: "But I don't intend to throw Berlin into panic by ordering it now! There's plenty of time! Plenty of time!" He dismissed them. "Good evening, gentlemen."

As Reymann and Refior left the building, they paused for a moment on the steps. General Reymann gazed out over the city. Although the sirens had not sounded, in the far distance searchlights had begun fingering the night sky. As Reymann slowly pulled on his gloves he said to Refior: "We are faced with a task that we cannot solve; that has no chance of success. I can only hope that some miracle happens to change our fortunes, or that the war ends before Berlin comes under siege." He looked at his Chief of Staff. "Otherwise," he added, "God help the Berliners."

A short while later, at his command post on the Hohenzollerndamm, Reymann received a call from the OKH (Army High Command). Besides the Supreme Commander, Hitler and the Berlin Gauleiter, Goebbels, Reymann now learned that he was subordinated to yet another authority. Arrangements were being made, he was told, for the Berlin Defense Area to come eventually under the direction of the Army Group Vistula and its commander, Colonel General Gotthard Heinrici. Reymann felt the first stirrings of hope at reading Heinrici's name. He directed Refior to brief the Army Group Vistula staff at the earliest opportunity. There was only one thing that worried him. He wondered how Heinrici would feel about taking Berlin under his wing while at the same time preparing to hold the Russians on the Oder. Reymann knew Heinrici well. He could imagine the *Giftzwerg's* reaction when he heard the news.

"It's absurd!" growled Heinrici. "Absurd!"

Army Group Vistula's new Chief of Staff, Lieutenant General Eberhard Kinzel, and its Operations Chief, Colonel Hans Eismann, looked at each other and remained silent. There was nothing to say. "Absurd" seemed an understatement. The proposal to attach the Berlin Defense Area to Heinrici's hard-pressed command at this particular moment seemed impossible to both officers. Neither could see how Heinrici was supposed to direct or even oversee Reymann's defense operations. Distance alone made the plan impractical; Vistula's headquarters was more than fifty miles from Berlin. And it was clear that whoever had suggested the idea appeared to know very little about the staggering problems facing Heinrici.

Earlier in the evening, operations department officers of OKH (Army High Command) had carefully presented the Berlin defense proposal to Kinzel. The idea was put forth tentatively—almost as a suggestion. Now, as Heinrici paced his office, the mud of the front still on his old-fashioned leggings, he made it plain to his subordinates that so far as he was concerned the plan would remain just that—a suggestion. Army Group Vistula had one task: to stop the Russians on the Oder. "Unless I'm forced," said Heinrici, "I do not intend to accept responsibility for Berlin."

That did not mean he was unaware of the plight of the city's people. Indeed, the fate of Berlin's population of almost three million was often in Heinrici's thoughts. He was haunted by the possibility of Berlin's becoming a battlefield; he knew better than most what happened to civilians caught in the fury of artillery fire and street fighting. He believed that the Russians were merciless, and in the heat of battle he did not expect them to discriminate between soldiers and civilians. Nevertheless, at this moment it was unthinkable that he should be expected to take on the problem of Berlin and its civilian population. The Army Group Vistula was the sole barrier between Berlin and the Russians, and as always Heinrici's main concern was with his soldiers. The crusty, belligerent *Giftzwerg* was furious at Hitler and the Chief of OKH,

Guderian, for what seemed to him the deliberate sacrifice of his soldiers' lives.

Turning to Kinzel, he said: "Get me Guderian."

Since assuming command a week before, Heinrici had been constantly at the front. Tirelessly he had traveled from headquarters to headquarters, mapping out strategy with division commanders, visiting front-line troops in their dugouts and bunkers. He had quickly discovered that his suspicions were well founded: his forces were armies in name only. He was appalled to find that most units had been fattened with splinter troops and the remnants of once-proud divisions long since destroyed. Among his forces Heinrici even found non-German units. There were the "Nordland" and "Nederland" divisions composed of pro-Nazi Norwegian and Dutch volunteers, and a formation of former Russian prisoners of war under the leadership of the erstwhile defender of Kiev, a distinguished soldier named Lieutenant General Andrei A. Vlasov. After his surrender in 1942 he had been persuaded to organize a pro-German anti-Stalinist Russian army. Vlasov's troops worried Heinrici: it seemed to him that they were likely to desert at the slightest opportunity. Some of Heinrici's panzer forces were in good shape, and he was depending greatly on them. But the overall picture was bleak. Intelligence reports indicated that the Russians might have as many as three million men. Between Von Manteuffel's Third Panzer Army in the north and Busse's Ninth Army in the southern sector, Heinrici had a total of about four hundred eighty-two thousand, and there were almost no reserves.

Besides being desperately short of combat-tested troops, Heinrici was handicapped by acute shortages of equipment and supplies. He needed tanks, motorized guns, communications equipment, artillery, gasoline, ammunition, even rifles. So short were supplies that Colonel Eismann, the Operations officer, discovered that some replacements had arrived at the front with bazooka-like anti-tank weapons instead of rifles—and only one rocket-projectile apiece for the weapons.

"It's madness!" Eismann told Heinrici. "How are these men supposed to fight after they fire their one round? What does OKH expect them to do—use their empty weapons like billy clubs? It's mass murder." Heinrici agreed. "OKH expects the men to wait for what fate may bring them. I do not." By every means in his power Heinrici was trying to rectify his equipment and supply situation, even though some commodities had all but disappeared.

His greatest lack was artillery. The Russians were beginning to construct bridges across the Oder and its marshy approaches. In some places the flood-swollen river was more than two miles wide. Special naval forces attached to Heinrici's command had floated mines down the river to destroy the pontoons, but the Russians had promptly countered by erecting protective nets. Bombing the bridge construction from the air was out of the question. Luftwaffe officials had informed Heinrici that they had neither the aircraft nor the gasoline for the job. The most they could provide was single planes for reconnaissance missions. There was only one way left to stop the Russians' feverish bridge building: artillery. And Heinrici had precious little of that.

To make up for this crippling shortage he had ordered anti-aircraft guns to be used as field pieces. Although it meant less protection from Russian air attacks, Heinrici reasoned that the guns would be used to better advantage in the field. And, indeed, the move had alleviated the situation. From the Stettin area alone, Von Manteuffel's Third Panzer Army acquired 600 flak guns. Each had to be set in concrete; for they were too large and unwieldy to be mounted on vehicles, but they were helping to fill out the gaps. Yet, though they stood menacingly in place, they fired only when absolutely necessary. The lack of ammunition was so severe that Heinrici was determined to husband what little he had for the opening of the Red Army's onslaught. Still, as he told his staff, "While we do not have enough guns or ammunition to stop the Russians' building, at least we're slowing them up." Colonel Eismann viewed the situation more pessimistically. "The Army Group could be compared to a rabbit," he later recalled, "watching spellbound a snake which wants to devour him. He can't move a muscle, but waits for the moment when the snake will strike in a lightning-fast manner. . . . General Heinrici did not want to admit the fact that the Army Group could not take any more meaningful measures on the basis of its own strength."

Yet in just one week of command, Heinrici had bulldozed his way through scores of seemingly insurmountable difficulties. Like the Heinrici of Moscow he had cajoled and goaded his troops, growled at and praised them in an effort to give them a fighting morale that would gain him time and help save their lives. Whatever his private feelings, to his officers and men he was the unintimidated, unbreakable Heinrici of legend. And true to character he was still fighting the "madness and bad judgment" of the higher command.

Right now his fiery temper was directed at Hitler and the Chief of OKH, Guderian. On March 23 General Busse's Ninth Army had attacked twice in a desperate effort to break through to the isolated defenders of Küstrin, the city the Russians had encircled the day Heinrici had assumed command from Himmler. Heinrici had agreed to Busse's tactics. He felt they offered the only chance to free the city before the Russians consolidated their positions. But the Russians were much too strong; both attacks proved disastrous.

Heinrici, reporting the outcome to Guderian, was told bluntly: "There must be another attack." Hitler wanted it; so did Guderian. "It's crazy," Heinrici replied stiffly. "I would suggest that the panzer units in Küstrin receive orders to break out. It's the only sensible thing left to do." Guderian flared at the proposal. "The attack must be mounted," he had shouted. On March 27 Busse had once again thrown his troops at Küstrin. So ferocious was the attack that some of his panzer forces actually did break through to the city. But then the Russians smashed the German drive with artillery fire. At staff headquarters, Heinrici minced no words. "The attack," he said, "is a massacre. The Ninth Army has suffered incredible losses for absolutely nothing."

Even now, the day after, his anger had not abated. As he waited for his call to Guderian, he paced his office muttering over and over the one word, "Fiasco!" Regardless of what might happen to him personally, when Guderian came on the phone Heinrici intended to charge his superior with the bloody massacre of eight thousand men—nearly a division had been lost in the Küstrin attack.

The phone rang and Kinzel answered. "It's Zossen," he told Heinrici.

The smooth voice of Lieutenant General Hans Krebs, OKH Chief of Staff, was not what Heinrici expected. "I meant to talk to Guderian," he said. Krebs began speaking again. Heinrici's face hardened as he listened. The staff officers watching him wondered what was happening. "When?" asked Heinrici. He listened again, then abruptly said, "Thank you," and put down the phone. Turning to Kinzel and Eismann, Heinrici said quietly, "Guderian is no longer Chief of OKH. Hitler relieved him of command this afternoon." To his astonished staff Heinrici added, "Krebs says that Guderian is sick, but that he doesn't really know what happened." Heinrici's rage had completely evaporated. He made only one further observation. "It's not like Guderian," he said thoughtfully. "He didn't even say good-bye."

It was late that night before Heinrici's staff was able to piece the story together. Guderian's dismissal had followed one of the wildest scenes ever witnessed in the Reichskanzlei. Hitler's midday conference had begun quietly enough but there were undertones of barely repressed hostility. Guderian had written the Führer a memorandum explaining why the Küstrin attack had failed. Hitler disliked not only the tone Guderian adopted but also Guderian's defense of the Ninth Army and of General Busse in particular. The Führer had settled on Busse as the scapegoat and had ordered him to attend the meeting and make a full report.

As usual Hitler's top military advisors were in attendance. In addition to Guderian and Busse there were Hitler's Chief of Staff, Keitel; his Operations Chief, Jodl; the Führer's adjutant, Burgdorf; several other senior officers and various aides. For several minutes Hitler listened to a general briefing on the current situation, then Busse was invited to give his report. He began by briefly outlining how the attack was launched and the forces that were employed. Hitler began to show annoyance. Suddenly he interrupted. "Why did the attack fail?" he yelled. Without pausing, he answered his own question. "Because of incompetence! Because of negligence!" He heaped abuse on Busse, Guderian and the entire High Command. They were all "incompetent." The Küstrin attack was launched, he ranted, "without sufficient artillery preparation!" Then he turned on Guderian: "If Busse didn't have enough ammunition as you claim—why didn't you get him more?"

There was a moment of silence. Then Guderian began to speak quietly. "I have already explained to you . . ." Hitler, waving his arm, cut him off. "Explanations! Excuses! That's all *you* give me!" he shouted. "Well! Then *you* tell me who let us down at Küstrin— the troops or Busse?" Guderian suddenly boiled. "Nonsense!" he spluttered. "This is nonsense!" He almost spat the words out. Furious, his face reddening, he launched into a tirade. "Busse is not to blame!" he bellowed. "I've told you that! He followed orders! Busse used all the ammunition that was available to him! All that he had!" Guderian's anger was monumental. He struggled for words. "To say that the troops are to blame—look at the casualties!" he raged. "Look at the losses! The troops did their duty! Their self-sacrifice proves it!"

Hitler yelled back. "They failed!" he raged. "They failed."

Guderian, his face purpling, roared at the top of his voice: "I must ask you . . . I must ask you *not* to level any further accusations at Busse or his troops!"

Both men were beyond reasonable discussion, but they did not stop. Facing each other, Guderian and Hitler engaged in such a furious and terrifying exchange that officers and aides stood frozen in shock. Hitler, lashing out at the General Staff, called them all "spineless," "fools" and "fatheads." He ranted that they had constantly "misled," "misinformed" and "tricked" him. Guderian challenged the Führer on his use of the words "misinformed" and "misled." Had General Gehlen in his intelligence estimate "misinformed" about the strength of the Russians? "No!" roared Guderian. "Gehlen is a fool!" Hitler retorted. What of the surrounded eighteen divisions still in the Baltic States, in Courland? "Who," barked Guderian, "has misled you about them? Exactly when," he demanded of the Führer, "do you intend to evacuate the Courland army?"

So loud and violent was the encounter that afterward no one could remember exactly the sequence of the quarrel.* Even Busse, the innocent perpetrator of the argument, was unable to tell Heinrici later what had transpired in any detail. "We were almost paralyzed," he said. "We couldn't believe what was happening."

Jodl was the first to snap into action. He grabbed the yelling Guderian by the arm. "Please! Please," he implored, "calm down." He pulled Guderian to one side. Keitel and Burgdorf began ministering to Hitler who had slumped, exhausted, into a chair. Guderian's horrified aide, Major Freytag von Loringhoven, certain that his chief would be arrested if he did not get him immediately out of the room, ran outside and called Krebs, the Chief of Staff, at Zossen and told him what was happening. Von Loringhoven implored Krebs to speak to Guderian on the phone, on the pretense that there was urgent news from the front and to hold him in conversation until the General calmed down. With diffi-

* There are many versions of the row, ranging from a detailed report in Juergen Thorwald's *Flight in the Winter* to a two-line account in *Die Leitzen Tage der Reichskanzlei* by Gerhard Boldt, one of Guderian's aides. Passing lightly over the matter, Boldt writes that Hitler advised the OKH Chief "to go to a spa for treatment" and Guderian "took the hint." He gives the conference date as March 20, seven days *before* the fateful Küstrin attack. Guderian, in his memoirs *Panzer Leader*, gives the time and date as precisely 14.00 hours on March 28. For the most part, my reconstruction is based on Guderian's memoirs, supplemented by interviews with Heinrici, Busse and their respective staffs.

culty, Guderian was persuaded to leave the room. Krebs, a past master at the art of manipulating information to suit the occasion, had no trouble in claiming Guderian's undivided attention for more than fifteen minutes—and by that time the Chief of the Army High Command was in control of his emotions again.

During the interval the Führer had calmed down, too. When Guderian returned, Hitler was conducting the conference as though nothing had happened. Seeing him enter, the Führer ordered everyone out of the room except Keitel and Guderian. Then he said, coldly, "Colonel General Guderian, your physical health requires that you immediately take six weeks' convalescent leave." His voice betraying no emotion, Guderian said, "I'll go." But Hitler was not quite finished. "Please wait until the conference is over," he ordered. It was several hours before the meeting broke up. By that time, Hitler was almost solicitous. "Please do your best to get your health back," he said. "In six weeks the situation will be very critical. Then I shall need you urgently. Where do you think you will go?" Keitel wanted to know, too. Suspicious at their sudden concern, Guderian prudently decided not to tell them his plans. Excusing himself, he left the Reichskanzlei. Guderian was out. The innovator of the panzer techniques, the last of Hitler's big-name generals was gone; with him went the last vestiges of sound judgment in the German High Command.

By 6 A.M. the following morning, Thursday, March 29, Heinrici had good reason to feel Guderian's loss. He had just been handed a teletyped message informing him that Hitler had appointed Krebs as Chief of the OKH. Krebs was a smooth-talking man who was a fanatical supporter of Hitler; he was widely and cordially disliked. Among the Vistula staff, the news of his appointment, following so closely that of Guderian's departure, produced an atmosphere of gloom. The Operations Chief, Colonel Eismann, summed up the prevailing attitude. As he was later to record: "This man, with his eternally friendly smile, reminded me somehow of a fawn . . . it was clear what we could expect. Krebs had only to spout out a few confident phrases—and the situation was rosy again. Hitler would get much better support from him than from Guderian."

Heinrici made no comment on the appointment. Guderian's spirited defense of Busse had saved that commander and there would be no more suicidal attacks against Küstrin. For that Heinrici was grateful to a man with whom he had often disagreed. He would miss Guderian, for he knew Krebs of old and expected little support from him. There would be no outspoken Guderian to back up Heinrici when he saw Hitler to discuss the problems of the Oder front. He was to see the Führer for a full-dress conference on Friday, April 6.

The car pulled up outside Vistula's main headquarters building a little after 9 A.M., on March 29, and the broad-shouldered, six-foot Berlin Chief of Staff bounded out. The energetic Colonel Hans "Teddy" Refior was looking forward enthusiastically to his meeting with Heinrici's Chief of Staff, General Kinzel. He had high hopes that the conference would go well; coming under Heinrici's command would be the best thing that could happen to the Berlin Defense Area. Lugging maps and charts for his presentation, the husky 39-year-old Refior entered the building. Small though the Berlin garrison was, Refior believed, as he later wrote in his diary, that Heinrici "would be delighted at this increase in his forces."

He had his first moments of doubt on meeting the Chief of Staff. Kinzel's greeting was restrained, though not unfriendly. Refior had hoped that his old classmate Colonel Eismann would be present—they had gone over the Berlin situation together a few weeks before—but Kinzel received him alone. The Vistula Chief of Staff seemed harassed, his manner bordering on impatience. Taking his cue from Kinzel, Refior opened his maps and charts and quickly began the briefing. The lack of a major authority to direct Reymann had produced an almost impossible situation for the Berlin command, he explained. "When we asked the OKH if we came under them," he elaborated, "we were told 'the OKH is responsible only for the eastern front. You people come under the OKW [Armed Forces High Command].' So we went to OKW. They said, 'Why come to us? Berlin's front faces east—you are the responsibility of OKH.'" As Refior talked, Kinzel examined the maps and disposition of the Berlin forces. Suddenly Kinzel looked up at Refior and quietly told him of Heinrici's decision of the night before not to accept responsibility for the city's defense. Then, as Refior later recorded, Kinzel spoke briefly of Hitler, Goebbels and the other bureaucrats. "As far as I am personally concerned," he said, "those madmen in Berlin can fry in their own juice."

On the drive back to Berlin, Refior, his buoyant enthusiasm shattered, realized for the first time what it meant to be "a rejected orphan." He loved Berlin. He had attended the War Academy, married and raised his two children—a boy and girl—in the capital. Now, it seemed to him that he was working in ever-increasing loneliness to defend the city in which he had spent the happiest years of his life. No one in the chain of command was prepared to make what Refior saw as the gravest of all decisions: the responsibility for the defense and preservation of Berlin.

All that was left to do was to put the few possessions on his desk into a small case. He had said good-bye to his staff, briefed his successor, Krebs, and now Colonel General Heinz Guderian was ready to leave his Zossen headquarters, his eventual destination a well-guarded secret. First, however, he intended to go with his wife to a sanatorium near Munich where Guderian could get treatment for his ailing heart. Afterward he planned to head for the only peaceful place left in Germany: Southern Bavaria. The only activities in that region centered around army hospitals and convalescent homes, retired or dismissed generals and evacuated government officials and their departments. The General had chosen carefully. He would sit out the war in the unwarlike climate of the Bavarian Alps. As former Chief of the OKH, Guderian knew that absolutely nothing was happening down there.

✢2✢

It was Good Friday, March 30, the beginning of the Easter weekend. In Warm Springs, Georgia, President Roosevelt had arrived for a stay at the Little White House; near the railroad station crowds stood in the hot sun waiting, as always, to greet him. At the first appearance of the President a murmur of surprise swept the onlookers. He was being carried from the train in the arms of a Secret Service man, almost inert, his body sagging. There was no jaunty wave, no good-humored joke shared with the crowd. To many, Roosevelt seemed almost comatose, only vaguely aware of what was happening. Shocked and apprehensive, the people watched in silence as the Presidential limousine moved slowly away.

In Moscow the weather was unseasonably mild. From his second-floor apartment in the embassy building on Mokhavaya Street, Major General John R. Deane gazed out across the square at the green Byzantine domes and minarets of the Kremlin. Deane, the Chief of the U.S. Military Mission, and his British counterpart, Admiral Ernest R. Archer, were awaiting confirmation from their respective ambassadors, W. Averell Harriman and Sir Archibald Clark-Kerr, that a meeting with Stalin had been arranged. At that conference they would deliver to Stalin "SCAF 252," the cable which had arrived from General Eisenhower the day before (and which the ailing U.S. President had not seen).

In London Winston Churchill, cigar jutting from his mouth, waved to onlookers outside No. 10 Downing Street. He was preparing to leave by car for Chequers, the 700-acre official residence of British Prime Ministers in Buckinghamshire. Despite his cheerful appearance, Churchill was both worried and angry. Among his papers was a copy of the Supreme Commander's cable to Stalin. For the first time in almost three years of close cooperation, the Prime Minister was furious with Eisenhower.

British reaction to Eisenhower's cable had been mounting for more than twenty-four hours. The British had been bewildered at first, then shocked, and finally angered. Like the Combined Chiefs of Staff in Washington, London had learned of the message at second hand—through copies passed along "for information." Not even the British Deputy Supreme Commander, Air Chief Marshal Sir Arthur Tedder, had known of the cable beforehand; London had heard nothing from him. Churchill himself was caught completely off balance. Remembering Montgomery's signal of March 27 announcing his drive to the Elbe and "thence by autobahn to Berlin, I hope," the Prime Minister whipped off an anxious note to his Chief of Staff, General Sir Hastings Ismay. Eisenhower's message to Stalin, he wrote, "seems to differ from Montgomery who spoke of Elbe. Please explain." For the moment Ismay could not.

At that point Montgomery gave his superiors another surprise. The powerful U.S. Ninth Army, he reported to Field Marshal Brooke, was to be switched back from his command to General Bradley's Twelfth Army Group, which would then make the central thrust to Leipzig and Dresden. "I consider we are about to make a terrible mistake," Montgomery said.

Once again the British were incensed. In the first place, such information should have come from Eisenhower, not Montgomery. But worse, the Supreme Commander seemed to London to be taking too much into his own hands. In the British view he had not only stepped far beyond his authority by dealing directly with Stalin, but he had also changed longstanding plans without warning. Instead of attacking across Germany's northern plains with Montgomery's Twenty-first Army Group, which had been specially built up for the offensive, Eisenhower had suddenly tapped Bradley to make the last drive of the war through the heart of the Reich. Brooke bitterly summed up the British attitude: "To start with, Eisenhower has no business to address Stalin direct, his communications should be through the Combined Chiefs of Staff; secondly, he produced a telegram which was unintelligible; and finally, what was implied in it appeared to be adrift and a change from all that had been agreed on." On the afternoon of March 29, an irate Brooke, without consulting Churchill, fired off a sharp protest to Washington. A bitter and vitriolic debate was slowly building up about SCAF 252.

At about the same time, General Deane in Moscow, having taken the first steps to arrange a meeting with Stalin, sent an urgent cable to Eisenhower. Deane wanted "some additional background information in case [Stalin] wishes to discuss your plans in more detail." After months of frustrating dealings with the Russians, Deane knew full well what the Generalissimo would ask for, and he spelled it all out for Eisenhower: "1) The present composition of Armies; 2) A little more detail on the scheme of maneuver; 3) Which Army or Armies you envisage making the main and secondary advances . . . ; 4) Brief current estimate of enemy dispositions and intentions." SHAEF quickly complied. At eight-fifteen that night the intelligence was on its way to Moscow. Deane got the composition of the Anglo-American armies and their order of battle from north to south. So detailed was the information that it even included the fact that the U.S. Ninth Army was to revert back from Montgomery to Bradley.

Fifty-one minutes later SHAEF heard from Montgomery. He was understandably distressed. With the loss of Simpson's Army the strength of his drive was sapped and his chance of triumphantly capturing Berlin seemed gone. But he still hoped to persuade Eisenhower to delay the transfer. He sent an unusually tactful message. "I note," he said, "that you intend to change the command set up. If you feel this is necessary I pray you not to do so until we reach the Elbe as such action would not help the great movement which is now beginning to develop."

Montgomery's British superiors were in no mood to be tactful, as Washington officials quickly discovered. At the Pentagon Brooke's protest was formally delivered to General Marshall by the British representative to the Combined Chiefs of Staff, Field Marshal Sir Henry Maitland Wilson. The British note condemned the procedure Eisenhower had adopted in communicating with Stalin and charged that the Supreme Commander had changed plans. Marshall, both surprised and concerned, promptly radioed Eisenhower. His message was mainly a straightforward report on the British protest. It argued, he said, that existing strategy should be followed—that Montgomery's northern drive would secure the German ports and thereby "to a great extent annul the U-boat war," and that it would also free Holland, Denmark and open up communications with Sweden again, making available "nearly two million tons of Swedish and Norwegian shipping now lying idle in Swedish ports." The British Chiefs, Marshall quoted, "feel strongly that the main thrust . . . across the open plains of N.W. Germany with the object of capturing Berlin should be adhered to . . ."

To fend off Eisenhower's British critics and to patch up Anglo-American unity as quickly as possible, Marshall was prepared to give latitude and understanding to both sides. Yet his own puzzlement and annoyance with the Supreme Commander's actions showed through the last paragraph of his message: "Prior to your dispatch of SCAF 252 had the naval aspects of the British been considered?" He ended with: "Your comments are requested as a matter of urgency."

One man above all others felt urgency—and, indeed, impending chaos—in the situation. Winston Churchill's anxiety had been mounting almost hourly. The Eisenhower incident had arisen at a moment when relations among the three allies were not going well. It was a critical period, and Churchill felt very much alone.

He did not know how ill Roosevelt was, but for some time previous he had been puzzled and uneasy about his correspondence with the President. As he was later to put it: "In my long telegrams I thought I was talking to my trusted friend and colleague . . . [but] I was no longer being fully heard by him . . . various hands drafted in combination the answers which were sent in his name . . . Roosevelt could only give general guidance and approval . . . these were costly weeks for all."

Even more worrisome was the rapid political deterioration that was evident between the West and Russia. Churchill's suspicions about Stalin's post-war aims had grown steadily since Yalta. The Soviet Premier had contemptuously disregarded the promises made there; nearly every day now, new and ominous trends appeared. Eastern Europe was slowly being swallowed up by the U.S.S.R.; Anglo-American bombers, downed behind Red Army lines because of fuel or mechanical problems, were being interned along with their crews; air bases and facilities promised by Stalin for the use of American bombers had been suddenly denied; the Russians, granted free access to liberated prisoner-of-war camps in western Germany for the repatriation of their troops, refused similar permission to Western representatives to enter, evacuate or in any way aid Anglo-American soldiers in eastern European camps. Worse, Stalin had charged that "Soviet ex-prisoners of war in U.S. camps . . . were subjected to unfair treatment and unlawful persecution, including beating." When the Germans in Italy tried to negotiate secretly the surrender of their forces, Russian reaction was to fire off an insulting note accusing the Allies of treacherously dealing with the enemy "behind the back of the Soviet Union, which is bearing the brunt of the war . . ." *

And now had come the Eisenhower message to Stalin. At a time when the choice of military objectives might well determine the future of post-war Europe, Churchill considered that Eisen-

* Churchill had shown this Russian note to Eisenhower on March 24 and the Supreme Commander, he later wrote, "seemed deeply stirred with anger at what he considered most unjust and unfounded charges about our good faith."

hower's communication with the Soviet dictator constituted a dangerous intervention into global and political strategy—realms that were strictly the concern of Roosevelt and the Prime Minister. To Churchill, Berlin was of crucial political importance and it now looked as though Eisenhower did not intend to make an all-out effort to capture the city.

Before midnight on March 29 Churchill had called Eisenhower on the scrambler telephone and asked for a clarification of the Supreme Commander's plans. The Prime Minister carefully avoided mentioning the Stalin cable. Instead he stressed the political significance of Berlin and argued that Montgomery should be allowed to continue the northern offensive. It was of paramount importance, Churchill felt, that the Allies capture the capital before the Russians. Now, on this March 30, as he began the 60-odd-mile drive to Chequers, he pondered Eisenhower's answer with profound concern. "Berlin," the Supreme Commander had said, "is no longer a major military objective."

In Reims, Dwight Eisenhower's temper was mounting in pace with the British protests. The London reaction to the curbing of Montgomery's northern drive had surprised him by its vehemence, but more astonishing to Eisenhower was the storm raging over his cable to Stalin. He could see no reason for any controversy. He believed his action was both correct and militarily essential, and he was incensed to find his decision challenged. Short-tempered at best, Eisenhower was now the angriest Allied leader of all.

On the morning of March 30 he began to respond to the messages from Washington and London. His first move was to send a brief acknowledgment of Marshall's overnight cable. He promised a more detailed answer within a few hours, but for the moment simply stated that he had not changed plans, and that the British charge "has no possible basis in fact. . . . My plan will get the ports and all the other things on the north coast more speedily and decisively than will the dispersion now urged upon me by Wilson's message to you."

Next, in reply to the Prime Minister's nighttime telephone request, he sent Churchill additional details clarifying the orders which had been issued Montgomery. "Subject to Russian intentions" a central drive to Leipzig and Dresden under Bradley's command seemed called for because it would cut the German armies "approximately in half . . . and destroy the major part of the remaining enemy forces in the West." Once its success was assured, Eisenhower intended "to take action to clear the northern ports." Montgomery, said the Supreme Commander, would be "responsible for these tasks, and I propose to increase his forces if that should seem necessary." Once "the above requirements have been met," Eisenhower planned to send General Devers and his Sixth Army Group southeast toward the Redoubt area "to prevent any possible German consolidation in the south, and to join hands with the Russians in the Danube valley." The Supreme Commander closed by remarking that his present plans were "flexible and subject to changes to meet unexpected situations." Berlin was not mentioned.

Eisenhower's message to the Prime Minister was restrained and correct; it did not reflect his anger. But his fury was clearly evident in the detailed cable he sent, as promised earlier, to Marshall. Eisenhower told the U.S. Chief of Staff that he was "completely in the dark as to what the protest concerning 'procedure' involved. I have been instructed to deal directly with the Russians concerning military coordination." As for his strategy, Eisenhower insisted again that there was no change. "The British Chiefs of Staff last summer," he said, "always protested against my determination to open up the [central] . . . route because they said it would be futile and . . . draw strength away from a northern attack. I have always insisted that the northern attack would be the principal effort in . . . the isolation of the Ruhr, but from the very beginning, extending back before D-Day, my plan . . . has been to link up . . . primary and secondary efforts . . . and then make

one great thrust to the eastward. Even cursory examination . . .
shows that the principal effort should . . . be toward the Leipzig
region, in which area is concentrated the greater part of the remaining German industrial capacity and to which area German
ministries are believed to be moving."

Harking back to the old Montgomery–Brooke agitation for a
single-thrust strategy, Eisenhower said: "Merely following the
principle that Field Marshal Brooke has always shouted to me, I
am determined to concentrate on one major thrust and all that my
plan does is to place the Ninth U.S. Army back under Bradley for
that phase of operations involving the advance of the center . . .
the plan clearly shows that Ninth Army may again have to move
up to assist the British and Canadian armies in clearing the whole
coastline to the westward of Lübeck." Afterward, "we can launch
a movement to the southeastward to prevent Nazi occupation of
the mountain citadel."

The National Redoubt, which Eisenhower called "the mountain citadel," was now clearly a major military goal—of more
concern, in fact, than Berlin. "May I point out," the Supreme Commander said, "that Berlin itself is no longer a particularly important objective. Its usefulness to the German has been largely destroyed and even his government is preparing to move to another
area. What is now important is to gather up our forces for a single
drive, and this will more quickly bring about the fall of Berlin,
the relief of Norway and the acquisition of the shipping and the
Swedish ports than will the scattering around of our effort."

By the time Eisenhower reached the final paragraph of his message his anger at the British was barely contained. "The Prime
Minister and his Chiefs of Staff," he declared, "opposed 'Anvil'
[the invasion of Southern France]; they opposed my idea that the
German should be destroyed west of the Rhine before we made
our great effort across the river; and they insisted that the route
leading northeastward from Frankfurt would involve us merely in
slow, rough-country fighting. Now they apparently want me to
turn aside on operations in which would be involved many thou-

sands of troops before the German forces are fully defeated. I submit that these things are studied daily and hourly by me and my advisors and that we are animated by one single thought which is the early winning of this war." *

In Washington, later that day, General Marshall and the Combined Chiefs of Staff received an amplification of the British Chiefs of Staff protest of the day before. For the most part the second telegram was a lengthy reiteration of the first, but there were two important additions. In the interim the British had learned from Admiral Archer in Moscow of the supplementary intelligence forwarded from SHAEF to Deane. The British strongly urged that this information be withheld from the Russians. In the event that discussions had already begun, London wanted the talks suspended until the Combined Chiefs of Staff had reviewed the situation.

But by now the British were beginning to disagree among themselves—not just over the propriety of the Eisenhower message, but over which parts of it should be attacked. The British Chiefs of Staff had neglected to show Churchill their protests before sending them off to Washington. And Churchill's objections differed from those of his military advisors. To him, the "main criticism of the new Eisenhower plan is that it shifts the axis of the main advance upon Berlin to the direction through Leipzig and Dresden." As the Prime Minister saw it, under this plan British forces "might be condemned to an almost static role in the North." Worse, "all prospect also of the British entering Berlin with the Americans is ruled out."

Berlin, as always now, was uppermost in the Prime Minister's thoughts. It seemed to him that Eisenhower "may be wrong in supposing Berlin to be largely devoid of military or political importance." Although government departments had "to a great ex-

* Eisenhower's 1,000-word cable does not appear in the official histories, and the version in his own *Crusade in Europe* has been cut and edited. For example, the phrase "always shouted to me" has been changed to "always emphasized," while the angry last paragraph cited above has been dropped altogether. Ironically, the cable was originally drafted by a Britisher, SHAEF's Deputy Operations Chief, Major General John Whiteley, but by the time it left headquarters it bore Eisenhower's clear imprint.

tent moved to the south, the dominating fact on German minds of the fall of Berlin should not be overlooked." He was haunted by the danger involved in "neglecting Berlin and leaving it to the Russians." He declared: "As long as Berlin holds out and withstands a siege in the ruins as it may easily do, German resistance will be stimulated. The fall of Berlin might cause nearly all Germans to despair."

While agreeing in principle with the arguments of his Chiefs of Staff, Churchill felt they had brought into their objections "many minor extraneous matters." He pointed out that "Eisenhower's credit with the U.S. Chiefs of Staff stands very high . . . the Americans will feel that, as the victorious Supreme Commander, he had a right, and indeed a vital need, to try to elicit from the Russians . . . the best point for making contact by the armies of the West and of the East." The British protest, Churchill feared, would only provide "argumentative possibilities . . . to the U.S. Chiefs of Staff." He expected them to "riposte heavily." And they did.

On Saturday, March 31, the American military chiefs gave Eisenhower their unqualified support. They agreed with the British on only two points: that Eisenhower should amplify his plans for the Combined Chiefs of Staff and that additional details to Deane should be held up. In the view of the U.S. Chiefs, "the battle of Germany is now at the point where the Commander in the Field is the best judge of the measures which offer the earliest prospect of destroying the German armies or their power to resist. . . . General Eisenhower should continue to be free to communicate with the Commander-in-Chief of the Soviet Army." To the American military leaders there was only one aim, and it did not include political considerations. "The single objective," they said, "should be quick and complete victory."

Still, the controversy was far from over. In Reims, a harassed Eisenhower was still explaining and re-explaining his position. During the day, following Marshall's instructions, Eisenhower sent the Combined Chiefs of Staff a long and detailed exposition of his plans. Next, he cabled Moscow and ordered Deane to withhold from Stalin the additional information sent from SHAEF. After that he assured Marshall in still another message, "You may be •sure that, in future, policy cables passing between myself and the military mission in Moscow will be repeated to the Combined Chiefs of Staff and the British." And finally, he came to Montgomery's still-unanswered plea, which had arrived nearly forty-eight hours before.

It was more than the urgency of his previous cables that caused Eisenhower to answer Montgomery last. Relations between the two men had become so strained that Eisenhower was now communicating with the Field Marshal only when absolutely necessary. As the Supreme Commander explained years later:* "Montgomery had become so personal in his efforts to make sure that the Americans—and me, in particular—got no credit, that, in fact, we hardly had anything to do with the war, that I finally stopped talking to him." The Supreme Commander and his staff—including, interestingly, the senior British generals at SHAEF—saw Montgomery as an egocentric troublemaker who in the field was overcautious and slow. "Monty wanted to ride into Berlin on a white charger wearing two hats," recalled British Major General John Whiteley, SHAEF's Deputy Operations Chief, "but the feeling was that if anything was to be done quickly, don't give it to Monty." Lieutenant General Sir Frederick Morgan, SHAEF's Deputy Chief of Staff, put it another way: "At that moment Monty was the last person Ike would have chosen for a drive on Berlin—Monty would have needed at least six months to prepare." Bradley was a different sort. "Bradley," Eisenhower told his aide, "has never held up, never paused to regroup, when he saw an opportunity to advance."

Now, Eisenhower's anger over the criticism of his cable to Stalin, coupled with his longstanding antagonism toward Montgomery, was clearly reflected in his reply to the Field Marshal. It exuded annoyance. "I must adhere," it said, "to my decision about Ninth Army passing to Bradley's command. . . . As I have already told

* In a long and detailed taped interview with the author.

you, it appears from this distance that an American formation will again pass to you at a later stage for operations beyond the Elbe. You will note that in none of this do I mention Berlin. That place has become, as far as I am concerned, nothing but a geographical location, and I have never been interested in these. My purpose is to destroy the enemy's forces . . ."

Even as Eisenhower was making his position evident to Montgomery, Churchill at Chequers was writing the Supreme Commander a historic plea. It was in nearly every respect the antithesis of Eisenhower's words to Montgomery. A little before 7 P.M. the Prime Minister wired the Supreme Commander: "If the enemy's position should weaken, as you evidently expect . . . why should we not cross the Elbe and advance as far eastward as possible? This has an important political bearing, as the Russian army . . . seems certain to enter Vienna and overrun Austria. If we deliberately leave Berlin to them, even if it should be in our grasp, the double event may strengthen their conviction, already apparent, that they have done everything.

"Further, I do not consider myself that Berlin has lost its military and certainly not its political significance. The fall of Berlin would have a profound psychological effect on German resistance in every part of the Reich. While Berlin holds out, great masses of Germans will feel it their duty to go down fighting. The idea that the capture of Dresden and the juncture with the Russians there would be a superior gain does not commend itself to me. . . . Whilst Berlin remains under the German flag, it cannot in my opinion fail to be the most decisive point in Germany.

"Therefore I should greatly prefer persistence in the plan on which we crossed the Rhine, namely that the Ninth U.S. Army should march with the 21st Army Group to the Elbe and beyond to Berlin . . ."

In Moscow, as darkness fell, the American and British Ambassadors, together with Deane and Archer, met with the Soviet Premier and delivered Eisenhower's message. The conference was brief. Stalin, as Deane later reported to the Supreme Commander, "was impressed with the direction of the attack in central Germany" and he thought "Eisenhower's main effort was a good one in that it accomplished the most important objective of dividing Germany in half." He felt too that the Germans' "last stand would probably be in western Czechoslovakia and Bavaria." While approving of Anglo-American strategy, Stalin was noncommittal about his own. The final coordination of Soviet plans, the Premier said, would have to wait until he had a chance to consult with his staff. At the conclusion of the meeting he promised to reply to Eisenhower's message within twenty-four hours.

Moments after his visitors left, Stalin picked up the phone and called Marshals Zhukov and Koniev. He spoke tersely but his orders were clear: the two commanders were to fly to Moscow immediately for an urgent conference the following day, Easter Sunday. Although he did not explain the reason for his orders, Stalin had decided that the Western Allies were lying; he was quite sure Eisenhower planned to race the Red Army for Berlin.

THE THOUSAND-MILE FLIGHT to Moscow from the eastern front had been long and tiring. Marshal Georgi Zhukov sat wearily back in his field-gray staff car as it joggled up the cobblestone hill and into the vastness of Red Square. The car sped past the Cathedral of St. Basil the Blessed with its multihued, candy-striped cupolas, swung left and entered the Kremlin's fortress walls through the western gate. Immediately behind Zhukov, in another army sedan, was Marshal Ivan Koniev. On the clockface of the great Savior's Tower guarding the entrance, the gilt hands showed almost 5 P.M.

Crossing the windswept interior courtyards, the two staff cars advanced into the architectural thicket of frescoed palaces, golden-domed cathedrals and massive yellow-fronted government build-ings, once the domain of Russian czars and princes, and headed for the center of the Kremlin compound. Near the monumental 17th-century white brick bell tower of Ivan the Great, the cars slowed, rolled past a line of ancient cannon and came to a stop outside a long, three-story, sand-colored building. Moments later the two men, in well-cut dun-colored uniforms with heavy gold epaulettes bearing the one-inch-wide single star of a Soviet field marshal, were in the elevator headed for Stalin's second-floor of-fices. In those brief moments, surrounded by aides and escorting officers, the two men chatted affably together. A casual observer might have thought them close friends. In truth, they were bitter rivals.

Both Zhukov and Koniev had reached the peak of their profes-sion. Each was a tough, pragmatic perfectionist, and throughout the officer corps it was considered both an honor and an awesome responsibility to serve under them. The short, stocky, mild-looking Zhukov was the better known, idolized by the public and Russian enlisted men as the Soviet Union's greatest soldier. Yet there were those among the commissioned ranks who saw him as a monster.

Zhukov was a professional who had begun his career as a private in the Czar's Imperial Dragoons. When the Russian Revolution be-gan in 1917 he had joined the revolutionaries; as a Soviet cavalry-man, he had fought the anti-Bolsheviks with such courage and fe-rocity that in the post–civil war Red Army he was rewarded with a commission. Although he was gifted with a brilliant imagination and a natural flair for command, he might have remained a rela-tively unknown officer but for Stalin's brutal purging of the Red Army's generals in the thirties. Most of those purged were veterans of the Revolution, but Zhukov, possibly because he was more "Army" than "Party," escaped. The ruthless removal of the old guard speeded up his promotion. By 1941 he had risen to the highest military job in the U.S.S.R.: Chief of the Soviet General Staff.

Zhukov was known as "the soldier's soldier." Perhaps because he had once been a private himself, he had a reputation for leniency with enlisted men. So long as his troops fought well, he considered the spoils of war no more than their just deserts. But with his officers he was a harsh disciplinarian. Senior commanders who failed to measure up were often fired on the spot and then punished for failing. The punishment usually took one of two forms: the officer either was sent to join a penal battalion or was ordered to serve on the most exposed part of the front line—as a private. Sometimes he was given a choice.

Once during the Polish campaign of 1944 Zhukov had stood with Marshal Konstantin Rokossovskii and General Pavel Batov, Commander of the Sixty-fifth Army, watching the troops advance. Suddenly Zhukov, viewing the scene through binoculars, yelled at Batov: "The corps commander and the commander of the 44th Rifle Division—penal battalion!" Both Rokossovskii and Batov began to plead for the two generals. Rokossovskii was able to save the corps commander. But Zhukov remained firm regarding the second officer. The general was immediately reduced in rank, sent to the front lines, and ordered to lead a suicidal attack. He was killed almost instantly. Zhukov thereupon recommended Russia's highest military award, Hero of the Soviet Union, for the fallen officer.

Zhukov himself was a Hero of the Soviet Union thrice over—as was his arch competitor, Koniev. Honors had been heaped on both marshals, but while Zhukov's fame had spread throughout the U.S.S.R., Koniev remained virtually unknown—and the anonymity rankled.

Koniev was a tall, gruff, vigorous man with a shrewd twinkle in his blue eyes. He was 48 years old, a year younger than Zhukov, and in some respects his career had paralleled the other man's. He, too, had fought for the Czar, crossed over to the revolutionaries and continued to serve with the Soviet forces. But there was one difference, and to men like Zhukov it was a big one. Koniev had come into the Red Army as a political commissar and, although he switched to the command side in 1926 and became a regular officer, to other soldiers his background was forever tainted. Political officers had always been heartily disliked by the regular military. So powerful were they that a commander could not issue an order unless it was countersigned by the ranking commissar. Zhukov, though a loyal Party man, had never regarded former commissars as true army professionals. It had been a constant irritant to him that in the pre-war years he and Koniev had commanded in the same theaters and had been promoted at about the same pace. Stalin, who had handpicked them both for his cadre of young generals in the thirties, was cannily aware of the intense rivalry between the men: he had made it a point to play one off against the other.

Koniev, despite his rough, outspoken manner, was generally regarded by the military as the more thoughtful and better educated of the two. A voracious reader, he kept a small library at his headquarters and occasionally surprised his staff by quoting passages from Turgenev and Pushkin. The rank and file of his armies knew him as a stern disciplinarian. But unlike Zhukov, he was considerate of his officers, reserving his wrath for the enemy. On the battlefield he could be barbarous. During one phase of the Dnieper campaign, after his troops had surrounded several German divisions, Koniev demanded their immediate surrender. When the Germans refused he ordered his saber-wielding Cossacks to attack. "We let the Cossacks cut for as long as they wished," he told Milovan Djilas, head of the Yugoslav Military Mission to Moscow, in 1944. "They even hacked off the hands of those who raised them to surrender." In this respect at least, Zhukov and Koniev saw eye to eye: they could not forgive Nazi atrocities. For Germans, they had neither mercy nor remorse.

Now, as the two marshals walked along the second-floor corridor toward Stalin's suite of offices, both were reasonably certain that the matter to be discussed was Berlin. Tentative plans called for Zhukov's First Belorussian group of armies, in the center, to take the city. Marshal Rokossovskii's Second Belorussian forces to the north and Koniev's First Ukrainian Army Group on the south could be called in to help. But Zhukov was determined to take Berlin by himself. He had no intention of asking for assistance—especially not from Koniev. Koniev, however, had been giving Berlin a lot of thought himself. Zhukov's forces could be held up by terrain—especially in the heavily defended Seelow Heights region lying just beyond the western banks of the Oder. If that happened, Koniev thought he saw a chance to steal Zhukov's thunder. He even had a rough scheme of action in mind. Of course, everything would depend on Stalin but this time Koniev fervently hoped to beat out Zhukov and reap a long-awaited glory. If the opportunity presented itself, Koniev thought that he just might race his rival for Berlin.

Midway along the red-carpeted corridor, the escorting officers ushered Zhukov and Koniev into a conference room. It was high-ceilinged, narrow and almost filled by a long, massive, highly polished mahogany table surrounded by chairs. Two heavy chandeliers with clear, unfrosted bulbs blazed over the table. At an angle in one corner was a small desk and leather chair and on the wall nearby hung a large picture of Lenin. The windows were draped and there were no flags or insignia in the room. There were, however, chrome-lithographs, in identical dark frames, of two of Russia's most famous military technicians: Catherine II's brilliant Field Marshal Aleksandr Suvorov, and General Mikhail Kutuzov, who had destroyed Napoleon's armies in 1812. At one end of the room double doors led to Stalin's private office.

The marshals were not unfamiliar with the surroundings. Zhukov had worked down the hall when he was Chief of Staff in 1941; and both men had met here with Stalin many times before. But this conference was not to be a small private session. Within minutes after the two marshals entered the room, they were followed by the seven most important men, after Stalin, in the wartime U.S.S.R.—the members of the State Defense Committee, the all-powerful decision-making body of the Soviet war machine.

Without formality or deference to rank, the Soviet leaders filed into the room: Foreign Minister Vyacheslav M. Molotov, the committee's Deputy Chairman; Lavrenti P. Beria, the thickset, myopic Chief of the Secret Police and one of the most feared men in Russia; Georgi M. Malenkov, the rotund Secretary of the Central Committee of the Communist Party and Military Procurement Administrator; Anastas I. Mikoyan, thin-faced and hawk-nosed, the Production Coordinator; Marshal Nikolai A. Bulganin, the distinguished-looking, goateed Supreme Headquarters Representative to the Soviet fronts; stolid, mustachioed Lazar M. Kaganovich, Transportation Specialist and the lone Jew on the committee; and Nikolai A. Voznesenskii, the Economic Planner and Administrator. Representing the operational side of the military were the Chief of the General Staff, General A. A. Antonov and the Operations Chief, General S. M. Shtemenko. As the top Soviet leaders took chairs, the doors to the Premier's office opened and the short, stocky figure of Stalin appeared.

He was simply dressed in a mustard-colored uniform, without epaulettes or rank insignia; his trousers, each seamed with a thin red stripe, were tucked into soft black, knee-length boots. On the left side of his tunic, he wore a single decoration: the red-ribboned gold star of a Hero of the Soviet Union. Clamped in his teeth was one of his favorite pipes: a British Dunhill. He wasted little time in formalities. As Koniev was later to recall, "We barely managed to greet each other before Stalin began to talk." *

Stalin asked Zhukov and Koniev a few questions about conditions

---

* Russian quotes not otherwise attributed, like other Soviet material used throughout the book, were obtained during a research trip to Moscow, in April, 1963. The Soviet Government allowed the author, assisted by Professor John Erickson of the University of Manchester, to interview participants—from marshals to privates—in the battle for Berlin (for a full list of names, see the appendix). The only Soviet marshal the author was prohibited from interviewing was Zhukov. The others—Koniev, Sokolovskii, Rokossovskii and Chuikov—each contributed an average of three hours of private conversations. In addition, the author was given access to military archives and allowed to copy and take out of Russia voluminous documentation, including battle maps, after-action reports, monographs, photographs and military histories hitherto circulated only within Soviet government circles.

on the front. Then abruptly he got to the point. In his low voice, characterized by the peculiar singsong accent of Georgia, he said quietly and with great effect: "The little allies (*soyuznichki*) intend to get to Berlin ahead of the Red Army."

He waited a moment before continuing. He had received information about Anglo-American plans, Stalin said, and it was clear that "their intentions are less than 'allied.' " He did not mention Eisenhower's message of the night before, nor did he give any other source for his information. Turning to General Shtemenko he said: "Read the report."

Shtemenko stood up. Eisenhower's forces planned to surround and destroy the Ruhr concentrations of the enemy, he announced, then advance to Leipzig and Dresden. But just "on the way" they intended to take Berlin. All of this, said the General, "will look like helping the Red Army." But it was known that taking Berlin before the arrival of Soviet troops was "Eisenhower's main aim." Furthermore, he intoned, it had been learned by the *Stavka* (Stalin's Supreme Headquarters) that "two Allied airborne divisions are being rapidly readied for a drop on Berlin." *

Koniev, in his version of the meeting, was later to remember that the Allied plan, as described by Shtemenko, also included a drive by Montgomery north of the Ruhr "along the shortest route separating Berlin from the basic groupings of the British forces." Shtemenko finished, Koniev recalled, "by saying that 'according to all the data and information, this plan—to take Berlin earlier than the Soviet Army—is looked upon at the Anglo-American headquarters as fully realistic and that preparation for its fullfillment is in full swing.' " †

* As, of course, they were.
† Stalin's crucial conference with his marshals is well known to the upper echelon of the Soviet military, although it has never before been published in the West. A number of versions have appeared in Russian military histories and journals. One such is Zhukov's account of the meeting to his staff officers, as recorded by the Russian historian, Lieutenant General N. N. Popiel. Marshal Koniev explained the background of the conference to the author and supplied details hitherto unknown. He also recounts part of the details in the first part of his memoirs, published in Moscow in 1965. There are some differences between his version and Zhukov's.

As Shtemenko ended the military evaluation, Stalin turned to his two marshals. "So," he said softly. "Who will take Berlin? We or the Allies?"

Koniev later remembered proudly that he was the first to answer. "We will," he said, "and before the Anglo-Americans."

Stalin looked at him, a slight smile flickering over his face. "So," he said again softly. With ponderous humor, he added, "Is that the sort of fellow you are?" Then, in an instant, as Koniev remembers, Stalin was once more cold and businesslike, stabbing out questions. Exactly how was Koniev, on the south, prepared to capture Berlin in time? "Wouldn't a great regrouping of your forces be necessary?" he asked. Too late Koniev saw the trap. Stalin was up to his old tricks again, pitting one man against the other, but by the time he realized this Koniev had already begun to answer. "Comrade Stalin," he said, "all the measures needed will be carried out. We shall regroup in time to take Berlin."

It was the moment Zhukov had waited for. "May I speak?" he asked quietly, almost condescendingly. He did not wait for an answer. "With due consideration," he said, nodding to Koniev, "the men of the First Belorussian Front need no regrouping. They are ready now. We are aimed directly at Berlin. We are the shortest distance from Berlin. We will take Berlin."

Stalin looked at the two men in silence. Once again a smile showed briefly. "Very well," he said mildly. "You will both stay in Moscow and, with the General Staff, prepare your plans. I expect them ready within forty-eight hours. Then you can return to the front with everything approved."

Both men were shocked by the brief time period allotted for the preparation of their plans. Up to now they had understood that the target date for attacking Berlin was early May. Now Stalin obviously expected them to attack weeks earlier. To Koniev, in partic-

---

For example, Zhukov did not mention Montgomery's drive on Berlin; Koniev makes no reference to a proposed Anglo-American airborne drop on the city.

The source material for the report read by General Shtemenko has never been revealed. In the author's judgment it was a grossly exaggerated military evaluation of Eisenhower's message of the night before—an evaluation based partly on suspicion of Eisenhower's motives, partly as a concoction intended to furnish a rationale for Stalin's own aims.

ular, this was a sobering thought. Although he had a tentative plan which he believed would get him into Berlin before Zhukov, he had nothing on paper. The meeting now made him desperately aware of immense logistical problems that he must solve quickly. All kinds of equipment and supplies would now have to be rushed to the front. Worse, Koniev was short of troops. After the fighting in Upper Silesia, a considerable part of his forces was still spread out to the south. Some were miles from Berlin. These would have to be transferred immediately, posing a major transportation problem.

Zhukov, listening to Stalin speak, was equally worried. Although his staff officers had been preparing for the attack, he was far from ready. His armies were in position but he, too, was still bringing up supplies and rushing replacements to the front to fill out his badly depleted forces. Some of his divisions, usually 9,000 to 12,-000 men strong, were down to 3,500. Zhukov believed the Berlin operations would be enormously difficult and he wanted to be ready for every eventuality. His intelligence had reported that "the city itself and its environs have been carefully prepared for stubborn defense. Each street, square, crossroad, house, canal and bridge is a component part of the overall defense. . . ." Now, everything would have to be speeded up if he was to beat the Western forces to Berlin. How soon could he attack? That was the question Stalin wanted answered—and quickly.

As the meeting broke up Stalin spoke once again. There was no warmth in his voice. To the two marshals he said, with great emphasis: "I must tell you that the dates of the beginning of your operations will attract our special attention."

The rivalry between the two commanders, never far beneath the surface, was being exploited once again. With a brief nod to the men around him, Stalin turned and left the room.

Now, having set his plans in motion, the Soviet Premier still faced one important task: the careful detailing of an answer to Eisenhower's cable. Stalin began work on the prepared draft. By 8 P.M. his reply was finished and dispatched. "I have received your telegram of March 28," Stalin wired Eisenhower. "Your plan

251

to cut the German forces by joining . . . [with] Soviet Forces entirely coincides with the plan of the Soviet High Command." Stalin fully agreed that the link-up should be in the Leipzig-Dresden area, for the "main blow of the Soviet Forces" would be made "in that direction." The date of the Red Army's attack? Stalin gave that particular notice. It would be "approximately the second half of May."

The most important part of his message came in the third paragraph. There he implanted the impression that he had no interest in Germany's capital. "Berlin," he stated, "has lost its former strategic importance." In fact, Stalin said, it had become so unimportant that "the Soviet High Command therefore plans to allot secondary forces in the direction of Berlin."

*   *   *

Winston Churchill had conferred with the British Chiefs of Staff nearly all afternoon. He was feeling embarrassed and upset. His embarrassment stemmed from an Eisenhower message that had been garbled in transmission. One sentence in the cable Churchill received had read: "Montgomery will be responsible on patrol tasks. . . ." Sharply, Churchill had replied that he thought His Majesty's forces were being "relegated . . . to an unexpected restricted sphere." The bewildered Eisenhower had wired back: "I am disturbed, if not hurt . . . Nothing is further from my mind and I think my record . . . should eliminate any such idea." It turned out that Eisenhower had never used the words "on patrol tasks." He had said, "on these tasks," and somehow the expression had been transmitted wrong. Churchill was chagrined by the incident which, trivial though it was, had compounded the mounting confusion.

Far from trivial, in the Prime Minister's eyes, was the continuing American apathy toward Berlin. With the tenacity that had characterized him all his life he now took on both problems— Allied relations and Berlin—at once. In a long telegram to the

252

ailing Roosevelt—his first to FDR since the beginning of the SCAF 252 controversy—the Prime Minister first recorded at length his complete confidence in Eisenhower. Then, "having disposed of these misunderstandings between the truest friends and allies that have ever fought side by side," Churchill hammered away at the urgency of taking the German capital. "Nothing will exert a psychological effect of despair upon German forces . . . equal to that of the fall of Berlin," he argued. "It will be the supreme signal of defeat . . . If the [Russians] take Berlin, will not their impression that they have been the overwhelming contributor to the common victory be unduly imprinted in their minds, and may this not lead them into a mood which will raise grave and formidable difficulties in the future? I therefore consider that from a political standpoint . . . should Berlin be in our grasp we should certainly take it . . . "

The following day Churchill's concern deepened still more when he received a copy of Stalin's message to Eisenhower. Its contents, the Prime Minister believed, were highly suspicious. At ten forty-five that night he cabled Eisenhower, "I am all the more impressed with the importance of entering Berlin which may well be open to us by the reply from Moscow to you which in paragraph three says 'Berlin has lost its former strategic importance.' This should be read in the light of what I mentioned of the political aspects." Churchill added fervently that he now deemed it "highly important that we should shake hands with the Russians as far to the east as possible . . ."

Despite everything, Churchill's determination to win Berlin had not flagged. He was still optimistic. He ended his message to Eisenhower: "Much may happen in the West, before the date of Stalin's main offensive." His great hope now was that the momentum and enthusiasm of the Allied drive would carry the troops forward into Berlin well ahead of Stalin's target date.

❂   ❂   ❂

At Stalin's headquarters, Marshals Zhukov and Koniev had worked around the clock. By Tuesday, April 3, within the 48-hour deadline, their plans were ready. Once again they saw Stalin.

Zhukov gave his presentation first. He had been considering the attack for months and the projected moves of his massive First Belorussian group of armies were at his fingertips. His main attack would take place in the pre-dawn, he said, from the 44-kilometer-long bridgehead over the Oder west of Küstrin—directly opposite Berlin. Additional attacks on the north and south would support this stroke.

The logistics of the Zhukov plan were staggering. No less than four field and two tank armies would be thrown into his main thrust and two armies each would be employed for the supporting assaults. Including secondary forces coming up behind, he would have 768,100 men. Leaving nothing to chance, Zhukov hoped to secure for the Küstrin bridgehead a minimum of 250 artillery pieces *for each kilometer*—approximately one cannon for every thirteen feet of front! He planned to open his assault with a stupefying barrage from some 11,000 guns, not counting smaller caliber mortars.

Now he came to his favorite part of the plan. Zhukov had devised an unorthodox and bizarre stratagem to befuddle the enemy. He would launch his offensive in the hours of darkness. At the very instant of attack he intended to blind and demoralize the Germans by turning upon them the fierce glare of 140 high-powered anti-aircraft searchlights beamed directly at their positions. He fully expected his plan to result in massacre.

Koniev's plan was equally monumental and, fed by his burning ambition, more complex and difficult. As he was later to say: "Berlin for us was the object of such ardent desire that everyone, from soldier to general, wanted to see Berlin with their own eyes, to capture it by force of arms. This too was my ardent desire . . . I was overflowing with it."

But the fact was that at their closest point Koniev's forces were more than seventy-five miles from the city. Koniev was counting on speed to see him through. Craftily he had massed his tank armies on the right so that when a breakthrough was achieved he could wheel northwest and strike out for Berlin, perhaps slipping into the city ahead of Zhukov. This was the idea he had been nurturing for weeks. Now, in light of Zhukov's presentation, he hesitated to tip his hand. Instead, for the moment he stuck to operational details. His plans called for a dawn attack across the Neisse, under the protection of a heavy smoke screen laid down by low-flying squadrons of fighter planes. Into the assault he planned to hurl five field and two tank armies—511,700 men. Remarkably, he was requesting the same almost incredible artillery density as Zhukov—250 guns per kilometer of front—and he meant to get even greater use from them. "Unlike my neighbor," Koniev recalled, "I planned to saturate the enemy positions with artillery fire for two hours and thirty-five minutes."

But Koniev badly needed reinforcements. Whereas Zhukov had eight armies along the Oder, Koniev, on the Neisse, had a total of only five. To put his plan into effect he needed two more. After some discussion Stalin agreed to give him the Twenty-eighth and Thirty-first armies, because "the fronts have been reduced in the Baltic and East Prussia." But much time might elapse before these armies would reach the First Ukrainian Front, Stalin pointed out. Transport was at a premium. Koniev decided to gamble. He could begin the attack while the reinforcements were still en route, he told Stalin, then commit them the moment they arrived.

Having listened to the two propositions, Stalin now approved them both. But to Zhukov went the responsibility of capturing Berlin. Afterward, he was to head for the line of the Elbe. Koniev was to attack on the same day as Zhukov, destroy the enemy along the southern fringes of Berlin and then let his armies flood west for a meeting with the Americans. The third Soviet army group, Marshal Rokossovskii's Second Belorussians, massing along the lower Oder and all the way to the coast north of Zhukov, would not be involved in the Berlin assault. Rokossovskii, with 314,000 men, would attack later, driving across northern Germany for a link-up with the British. Together, the three Russian army groups would have a total of 1,593,800 men.

It appeared that Koniev had been relegated to a supporting role in the Berlin attack. But then, leaning over the map on the table, Stalin drew a dividing line between Zhukov's and Koniev's army groups. It was a curious boundary. It began east of the Russian front, crossed the river and ran straight to the 16th-century town of Lübben on the Spree, approximately sixty-five miles southeast of Berlin. There, Stalin suddenly stopped drawing. Had he continued the line right across Germany, thereby marking a boundary that Koniev was not to cross, the First Ukrainian armies would clearly have been denied any participation in the Berlin attack. Now Koniev was elated. Although "Stalin did not say anything . . ." he recalled later, "the possibility of a show of initiative on the part of the command of the front was tacitly assumed." Without a word being spoken the green light to Berlin had been given Koniev's forces—if he could make it. To Koniev, it was as though Stalin had read his mind. With what he was to term this "secret call to competition . . . on the part of Stalin," the meeting ended.

Immediately the marshals' plans were incorporated into formal directives. The next morning the rival commanders, orders in hand, drove out in a swirling fog to Moscow airport, each eager to reach his headquarters. Their orders called for them to mount the offensive a full month earlier than the date Stalin had given Eisenhower. For security reasons, the written directives were undated, but Zhukov and Koniev had been given the word by Stalin himself. The attack on Berlin would begin on Monday, April 16.

❋   ❋   ❋

Even as Zhukov and Koniev began feverishly preparing to hurl thirteen armies with more than a million men at Berlin, Adolf Hitler had another of his famous intuitive flashes. The massing of the Russian armies at Küstrin, directly opposite the capital, was nothing more than a mighty feint, he concluded. The main Soviet offensive would be aimed at Prague in the south—not at Berlin. Only one of Hitler's generals was gifted with the same insight. Colonel General Ferdinand Schörner, now commander of Army Group Center on Heinrici's southern flank, had also seen through the Russian hoax. "My Führer," warned Schörner, "it is written in history. Remember Bismarck's words, 'Whoever holds Prague holds Europe.' " Hitler agreed. The brutal Schörner, a Führer favorite and among the least talented of the German generals, was promptly promoted to Field Marshal. At the same time, Hitler issued a fateful directive. On the night of April 5 he ordered the transfer south of four of Heinrici's veteran panzer units—the very force Heinrici had been depending on to blunt the Russian drive.

✤4✤

COLONEL GENERAL HEINRICI'S car moved slowly through the rubble of Berlin, making for the Reichskanzlei and the full-dress meeting ordered by Hitler nine days earlier. Sitting in back alongside his Operations Chief, Colonel Eismann, Heinrici stared silently out at the burned and blackened streets. In two years he had made only one other trip to the city. Now, the evidence of his own eyes overwhelmed him. He would never have recognized the place as Berlin.

In normal times the trip from his headquarters to the Reichskanzlei would have taken about ninety minutes, but they had been en route nearly twice that long. Again and again clogged streets forced them to make complicated detours. Even main thoroughfares were often impassable. Elsewhere, crazily canted buildings threatened to collapse at any moment, making every street a danger. Water gushed and gurgled from immense bomb holes; escaping gas flared from ruptured mains; and all over the city, areas were cordoned off and marked with signs that warned, *"Achtung! Minen!"* signifying the location of still-unexploded aerial mines. Heinrici, his voice bitter, said to Eismann. "So this is what we've finally come to—a sea of rubble."

Although buildings on both sides of the Wilhelmstrasse were in ruins, apart from some splinter damage nothing about the Reichskanzlei appeared to have changed. Even the faultlessly dressed SS sentries just outside the entrance seemed the same. They snapped smartly to attention as Heinrici, Eismann behind him, entered the building. Despite the delays, the General was on time. The conference with Hitler was scheduled for 3 P.M., and Heinrici had given it much thought over the past few days. As bluntly and precisely as possible, he intended to tell Hitler and those around him the true facts of the situation confronting the Army Group Vistula. Heinrici knew perfectly well the danger of speaking out, but the possible consequences did not seem to bother him. Eismann, on the other hand, was greatly disturbed. "It looked to me," he later said, "as if Heinrici was planning an all-out attack against Hitler and his advisors, and there were very few men who could do that and survive."

In the main hall an SS officer, immaculate in a white tunic, black breeches and highly polished cavalry boots, greeted Heinrici and informed him that the meeting would take place in the Führerbunker. Heinrici had heard that a vast labyrinth of underground installations existed beneath the Chancellery, the adjoining buildings and the enclosed gardens at back, but he had never before been in any of them. Following a guide, he and Eismann walked down to the basement and out into the gardens. Though the façade of the Reichskanzlei was intact, the rear of the building showed severe damage. Once, magnificent gardens with a complex of fountains had been here. They were gone now, along with Hitler's tea pavilion and the botanical greenhouses that had stood to one side of it.

To Heinrici the area resembled a battlefield, with "huge craters, lumps of concrete, smashed statuary and uprooted trees." In the soot-stained walls of the Chancellery were "great black holes where windows used to be." Eismann, looking at the desolation, was reminded of a line from "The Singer's Curse," by the 19th-century German balladier, Uhland. It went, "Only one high column tells of the vanished glory; this one can fall overnight." Heinrici was more literal-minded. "Just think," he murmured to Eismann. "Three years ago Hitler had Europe under his command, from the Volga to the Atlantic. Now he's sitting in a hole under the earth."

They crossed the garden to an oblong blockhouse guarded by two sentries. Their credentials were examined and then the guards opened a heavy steel door, allowing the officers to pass through. As the door clanged shut behind them, Heinrici was always to remember, "We stepped into an unbelievable underworld." At the bottom of a winding concrete staircase two young SS officers received them in a brilliantly lighted foyer. Courteously their coats were taken and then, with equal courtesy, Heinrici and Eismann were searched. Eismann's briefcase, in particular, received attention: it had been a briefcase containing explosives that had nearly ended Hitler's life in July, 1944. Since then, the Führer's elite guards had allowed no one near him without first subjecting them to a search. Heinrici, despite the apologies of the SS men, seethed at the indignity. Eismann felt "ashamed that a German general should be treated in this manner." The search over, they were shown into a long narrow corridor, partitioned into two sections, the first of which had been converted into a comfortable lounge. Domed lights protruded from the ceiling, giving the light beige stucco walls a yellowish cast. An Oriental carpet on the floor had apparently been brought down from a larger Chancellery room, for its edges were folded under at each side. Although the room was comfortable, the furniture—like the carpet—seemed out of keeping. There were various chairs, some plain, some covered in rich upholstery. A narrow oak table was set against one wall and several large oil paintings, landscapes by the German architect and painter Schinkel, were hung about the room. To the right of the entrance an open door gave onto a small conference room set up for the meeting. Heinrici could only make a guess as to the size and depth of the Führerbunker. From what he could see, it appeared relatively spacious, with doors leading to rooms on either side of the corridor lounge and beyond. Because of its low ceiling, narrow metal doors and the absence of windows, this might have been the passageway in a small liner—except that, by Heinrici's estimate, they were at least forty feet below ground.

Almost immediately a tall, elegantly dressed SS officer appeared. He was Hitler's personal aide and bodyguard, Colonel Otto Günsche. Pleasantly he inquired about their trip and offered them refreshments; Heinrici accepted a cup of coffee. Soon, other conference members began to arrive. Hitler's adjutant, General Wilhelm Burgdorf, came next. He greeted them, as Eismann remembers, "with some noises about success." Then Field Marshal Wilhelm Keitel, the OKW Chief of Staff, arrived, followed by Himmler, Admiral Karl Doenitz and the man reputed to be Hitler's closest confidant, Martin Bormann. In Eismann's words, "All greeted us loudly. Seeing them, I was really proud of my commander. With his familiar stiff posture, serious and measured, he was a soldier from head to toe among court asses."

Eismann saw Heinrici tense as Himmler started across the room toward him. In an undertone the General growled, "That man is never going to set foot in my headquarters. If he ever announces a visit, tell me quickly so I can leave. He makes me vomit." And, indeed, Eismann thought Heinrici looked pale as Himmler dragged him into conversation.

At that moment General Hans Krebs, Guderian's successor, came into the room and, seeing Heinrici, came across to him immediately. Earlier in the day Heinrici had learned from Krebs of the transfer of his vital armored units to Schörner's army group. Though he blamed Krebs for not vigorously protesting the decision, Heinrici now seemed almost cordial to the new Chief of the

OKH. At least he did not have to continue talking with Himmler.

Krebs, as usual, was diplomatic and solicitous. He had no doubt that everything would work out all right at the conference, he assured Heinrici. Doenitz, Keitel and Bormann now joined them and listened as Heinrici mentioned some of his problems. All three promised their support when Heinrici made his presentation to Hitler. Turning to Eismann, Bormann asked, "What's your opinion about the Army Group situation—since all this has a direct bearing on Berlin and Germany in general?" Eismann was dumbfounded. With the Russians only thirty-eight miles from the capital and the Allies racing across Germany from the west, the question seemed to border on madness. Bluntly he replied, "The situation is serious. That's why we're here." Bormann patted him soothingly on the shoulder. "You shouldn't worry so much," he told Eismann. "The Führer is sure to grant you help. You'll get all the forces you need." Eismann stared. Where did Bormann think the forces were to come from? For a moment he had the uncomfortable feeling that he and Heinrici were the only sane people in the room.

More and more officers and staff were filing into the already crowded corridor. Hitler's Operations Chief, General Alfred Jodl, aloof and composed, arrived with his deputy; the Luftwaffe's Chief of Staff, General Karl Koller, and OKW's Staff Chief in charge of supplies and reinforcements, Major General Walter Buhle, came in together. Nearly every man seemed to be followed by an aide, an orderly or a deputy. The resulting noise and confusion reminded Eismann of a swarm of bees.

In the packed corridor Heinrici now stood silent, listening impassively to the din of conversation. For the most part, it consisted of small talk, trivial and irrelevant. The bunker and its atmosphere were stifling and unreal. Heinrici had the disquieting feeling that the men around Hitler had retreated into a dream world in which they had convinced themselves that by some miracle catastrophe could be averted. Now, as they waited for the man who, they believed, would produce this miracle, there was a sudden movement in the corridor. General Burgdorf, hands high above his head, waved the group into silence. "Gentlemen, gentlemen," he said, "the Führer is coming."

"Gustav! Gustav!" Radios sputtered out the warning code for Tempelhof as the planes approached the district. In stationmasters' offices along the route of the U-Bahn, loudspeakers blared out, "Danger 15!" Another city-wide saturation raid had begun.

Earth erupted. Glass ripped through the air. Chunks of concrete smashed down into the streets, and tornadoes of dust whirled up from a hundred places, covering the city in a dark gray, choking cloud. Men and women raced one another, stumbling and clawing their way into shelters. Ruth Diekermann, just before she reached safety, looked up and saw the bombers coming over in waves, "like an assembly line." In the Krupp und Druckenmüller plant, French forced laborer Jacques Delaunay dropped the ghastly remnant of a human arm he had just recovered from the battle-scarred tank he was overhauling, and ran for shelter. In the Sieges Allee the marble statues of Brandenburg-Prussian rulers rocked and groaned on their pedestals; and the crucifix held aloft by the 12th-century leader, Margrave Albert the Bear, shattered against the bust of his eminent contemporary, Bishop Otho of Bamberg. Nearby in Skagerrak Square, police ran for cover, leaving the swaying body of a suicide still hanging from a tree.

A shower of incendiaries smashed through the roof of Wing B of the Lehrterstrasse Prison and set off a dozen flaring magnesium fires on the second floor. Frantic prisoners, turned loose to fight the flames, stumbled through the acrid smoke with buckets of sand. Two men suddenly stopped working. The prisoner from Cell 244 stared at the man from Cell 247. Then they embraced. The brothers Herbert and Kurt Kosney discovered they had been on the same floor for days.

In Pankow, in the Möhrings' ground-floor two-room apartment where the Weltlinglers hid, Siegmund hugged his sobbing wife

Margarete as they stood together in the kitchen. "If this keeps up," he shouted over the din of anti-aircraft fire, "even Jews can go openly to the shelters. They're all too scared of the bombs to turn us in now."

Fourteen-year-old Rudolf Reschke had only time enough to see that the planes glinted like silver in the sky—too high for the dangerous game of tag he liked to play with strafing fighters. Then his mother, yelling and nearly hysterical, dragged him down into the cellar where his 9-year-old sister, Christa, sat shivering and crying. The whole shelter seemed to be shaking. Plaster fell from the ceiling and the walls; then the lights flickered and went out. Frau Reschke and Christa began to pray aloud, and after a minute Rudolf joined them in the "Our Father." The noise of the bombing was getting worse and the shelter now seemed to be shuddering all the time. The Reschkes had been through many raids, but nothing like this. Frau Reschke, her arms about both children, began to sob. Rudolf had seldom heard his mother cry before, even though he knew that she was often worried, especially with his father at the front. Suddenly he was angry at the planes for making his mother frightened—and for the first time Rudolf felt frightened himself. With some embarrassment he discovered that he was crying, too.

Before his mother could detain him, Rudolf rushed out of the shelter. He ran up the stairs to the family's ground-floor apartment; there he headed straight for his room and his collection of toy soldiers. He chose the most imposing figure among them, with distinct features painted on its china face. He went to the kitchen and took down his mother's heavy meat cleaver. Oblivious now of the air raid, Rudolf went out into the apartment house courtyard, laid the doll on the ground, and with one stroke chopped off its head. "There!" he said, standing back. Tears still staining his face, he looked down without remorse upon the severed head of Adolf Hitler.

٭   ٭   ٭

He came shuffling into the bunker corridor—half bent, dragging his left foot, the left arm shaking uncontrollably. Although he was 5 feet 8½ inches tall, now, with his head and body twisted to the left, he looked much smaller. The eyes that admirers had called "magnetic" were feverish and red, as if he had not slept for days. His face was puffy, and its color was a blotchy, faded gray. A pair of pale green spectacles dangled from his right hand; bright light bothered him now. For a moment he gazed expressionlessly at his generals as their hands shot up and out to a chorus of "Heil Hitler." *

The corridor was so crowded that Hitler had some difficulty getting past everyone to reach the small conference room. Eismann noticed that the others began talking again as soon as the Führer passed; there was not the respectful silence he had expected. As for Heinrici, he was shocked by the Führer's appearance. Hitler, he thought, "looked like a man who had not more than twenty-four hours to live. He was a walking corpse."

Slowly, as though in pain, Hitler scuffled to his place at the head of the table. To Eismann's surprise, he seemed to crumple "like a sack into the armchair, not uttering a word, and held that prostrate condition, his arms propped up on the sides of the chair." Krebs and Bormann moved in behind the Führer to sit on a bench against the wall. From there, Krebs informally presented Heinrici and

---

* Contrary to generally accepted belief, the deterioration of Hitler's health was not the result of injuries sustained during the attempted bomb plot on his life in 1944, though it seems to have marked the beginning of a rapid debilitation. After the war, U.S. counterintelligence teams interrogated nearly every doctor who had attended Hitler. The author has read all their reports and, while none of them give a specific cause for Hitler's palsied condition, the general opinion is that, in origin, it was partly psychogenic, and partly caused by the manner in which he lived. Hitler hardly ever slept; night and day had little distinction for him. In addition, there is abundant evidence that he was slowly being poisoned by the indiscriminate use of drugs administered to him in massive injections by his favorite physician, Professor Theodor Morell. These ranged from prescriptions containing morphia, arsenic and strychnine to various artificial stimulants and mysterious "miracle drugs" which the doctor himself compounded.

Eismann. Hitler feebly shook hands with them both. Heinrici noted that he "could hardly feel the Führer's hand, for there was no returning pressure."

Because of the smallness of the room, not everyone could sit, and Heinrici stood on the Führer's left, Eismann on his right. Keitel, Himmler and Doenitz took chairs on the opposite side of the table. The remainder of the group stayed outside in the corridor; to Heinrici's amazement, they continued to talk, although their voices were now subdued. Krebs began the conference. "In order that the commander"—he looked at Heinrici—"can get back to his army group as soon as possible," he said, "I propose that he give his report immediately." Hitler nodded, put on his green glasses, and gestured to Heinrici to begin.

In his measured and precise manner, the General got straight to the point. Looking directly at each man around the table, then at Hitler, he said, "My Führer, I must tell you that the enemy is preparing an attack of unusual strength and unusual force. At this moment they are preparing in these areas—from south of Schwedt to south of Frankfurt." On Hitler's own map lying on the table, Heinrici slowly ran his finger down along the threatened section of the Oder front, a line roughly seventy-five miles long, touching briefly on the cities where he expected the heaviest blows—at Schwedt, in the Wriezen area, around the Küstrin bridgehead, and south of Frankfurt. He entertained no doubts, he said, that "the main attack will hit Busse's Ninth Army" holding this central area; also, "it will strike the southern flank of Von Manteuffel's Third Panzer Army around Schwedt."

Carefully Heinrici described how he had juggled his forces to build up Busse's Ninth Army against the expected Russian onslaught. But because of this need to strengthen Busse, Von Manteuffel had suffered. Part of the Third Panzer Army front was now being held by inferior troops: aged Home Guardsmen, a few Hungarian units and some divisions of Russian defectors—whose dependability was questionable—under General Andrei Vlasov. Then, said Heinrici flatly: "While the Ninth Army is now in better shape than it was, the Third Panzer Army is in no state to fight at all. The potential of Von Manteuffel's troops, at least in the middle and northern sectors of his front, is low. They have no artillery whatsoever. Anti-aircraft guns cannot replace artillery and, in any case, there is insufficient ammunition even for these."

Krebs hastily interrupted. "The Third Panzer Army," he said emphatically, "will receive artillery shortly."

Heinrici inclined his head but made no comment—he would believe Krebs when he actually saw the guns. Continuing as though there had been no interruption, he explained to Hitler that the Third Panzer owed its present safe situation to one thing only— the flooded Oder. "I must warn you," he said, "that we can accept the Third Panzer's weak condition only as long as the Oder remains flooded." Once the waters drop, Heinrici added, "the Russians will not fail to attack there, too."

The men in the room listened attentively, if a little uneasily, to Heinrici's presentation. Such directness at a Hitler conference was unusual; most officers presented the gains and skipped the drawbacks. Not since Guderian's departure had anyone spoken so frankly—and it was clear that Heinrici was only beginning. Now he turned to the matter of the garrison holding out at Frankfurt-on-Oder. Hitler had declared the city a fortress, like the ill-fated Küstrin. Heinrici wanted Frankfurt abandoned. He felt the troops there were being sacrificed on the altar of Hitler's "fortress" mania. They could be saved and used to advantage elsewhere. Guderian, who had shared the same opinion regarding Küstrin, had been broken for his views about that city. Heinrici might meet the same fate for his opposition now. But the Vistula commander saw the men of Frankfurt as his responsibility; whatever the consequences, he was not to be intimidated. He raised the issue.

"In the Ninth Army's sector," he began, "one of the weakest parts of the front is around Frankfurt. The garrison strength is very low, as is their ammunition. I believe we should abandon the defense of Frankfurt and bring the troops out."

Suddenly Hitler looked up and uttered his first words since the meeting began. He said harshly, "I refuse to accept this."

Up to this point Hitler had sat not only silent but unmoving, as though completely disinterested. Eismann had had the impression that he wasn't even listening. Now, the Führer suddenly "came awake and began to take an intense interest." He began asking about the garrison's strength, supplies and ammunition, and even, for some incomprehensible reason, about the deployment of Frankfurt's artillery. Heinrici had the answers. Step by step he built his case, taking reports and statistics from Eismann and placing them on the table before the Führer. Hitler looked at the papers as each was handed over and seemed impressed. Sensing his opportunity, Heinrici said quietly but emphatically, "My Führer, I honestly feel that giving up the defense of Frankfurt would be a wise and sound move."

To the astonishment of most of those in the room, Hitler, turning to the Chief of OKH, said, "Krebs, I believe the General's opinion on Frankfurt is sound. Make out the necessary orders for the Army Group and give them to me today."

In the stunned silence that followed, the babble of voices in the corridor outside seemed unduly loud. Eismann sensed a sudden and new respect for Heinrici. "Heinrici himself seemed completely unmoved," he remembered, "but he gave me a look which I interpreted as 'Well, we've won.'" The victory, however, was short-lived.

At that moment there was a loud commotion in the corridor and the vast bulk of Reichsmarschall Hermann Goering filled the doorway of the little conference room. Pushing his way in, Goering heartily greeted those present, pumped Hitler's hand vigorously and excused himself for being late. He squeezed in next to Doenitz, and there was an uncomfortable delay while Krebs brought him quickly up to date on Heinrici's briefing. When Krebs had finished, Goering got up and, placing both hands on the map table, leaned toward Hitler as though to make some comment on the proceedings. Instead, smiling widely and with obvious good humor, he said, "I must tell you a story about one of my visits to the 9th Parachute Division . . ."

He got no further. Hitler sat suddenly bolt upright in his chair and then jerked himself to his feet. Words poured from his mouth in such a torrent that those present could scarcely understand him. "Before our eyes," recalled Eismann, "he went into a volcanic rage."

His fury had nothing to do with Goering. It was a diatribe against his advisors and generals for deliberately refusing to understand him on the tactical use of forts. "Again and again," he yelled, "forts have fulfilled their purpose throughout the war. This was proven at Posen, Breslau and Schneidemühl. How many Russians were pinned down by them? And how difficult they were to capture! Every one of those forts was held to the very last man! History has proved me right and my order to defend a fort to the last man is right!" Then, looking squarely at Heinrici, he screamed, "That's why Frankfurt is to retain its status as a fort!"

As suddenly as it had begun, the tirade ended. But Hitler, though slack with exhaustion, could no longer sit still. He seemed to Eismann to have lost all control of himself. "His entire body trembled," he recalled. "His hands, in which he was holding some pencils, flew wildly up and down, the pencils beating on the arms of the chair in the process. He gave the impression of being mentally deranged. It was all so unreal—especially the thought that the fate of an entire people lay in the hands of this human ruin."

Despite Hitler's choleric outburst, and despite his mercurial change of mind about Frankfurt, Heinrici doggedly refused to give up. Quietly, patiently—almost as though the outburst had not occurred—he went over all the arguments again, underlining every conceivable reason for abandoning Frankfurt. Doenitz, Himmler and Goering supported him. But it was token support at best. The three most powerful generals in the room remained silent. Keitel and Jodl said nothing—and just as Heinrici had expected, Krebs offered no opinion one way or the other. Hitler, apparently spent, only made tired gestures with his hands as he dismissed each argument. Then, with renewed vitality he demanded to know the credentials of the commander of the Frankfurt garrison, Colonel Bieler. "He is a very reliable and experienced officer," replied Heinrici, "who has proven himself time and again in battle."

"Is he a Gneisenau?" snapped Hitler, referring to General Graf von Gneisenau, who had successfully defended the fortress of Kolberg against Napoleon in 1806.

Heinrici kept his composure. Evenly, he replied that "the battle for Frankfurt will prove whether he is a Gneisenau or not." Hitler snapped back, "All right, send Bieler to see me tomorrow so that I can judge him. Then I shall decide what's to be done about Frankfurt." Heinrici had lost the first battle for Frankfurt and, he believed, the second, too, in all probability. Bieler was an unprepossessing man who wore thick-lensed glasses. He was not likely to make much of an impression on Hitler.

There now approached what Heinrici regarded as the crisis of the meeting. As he began to speak again, he regretted that he had no skill in diplomatic niceties. He knew only one way to express himself; now, as always, he spoke the unvarnished truth. "My Führer," he said, "I do not believe that the forces on the Oder front will be able to resist the extremely heavy Russian attacks which will be made upon them."

Hitler, still trembling, was silent. Heinrici described the lack of combat fitness among the hodgepodge of troops—the very scrapings of Germany's manpower—that made up his forces. Most units in the line were untrained, inexperienced or so watered down by green reinforcements as to be unreliable. The same was true of many of the commanders. "For example," explained Heinrici, "the 9th Parachute Division worries me. Its commanders and noncommissioned officers are nearly all former administration officers, both untrained and unaccustomed to lead fighting units."

Goering suddenly bristled. "My paratroopers!" he said in a loud voice. "You are talking about my paratroopers! They are the best in existence! I won't listen to such degrading remarks! I personally guarantee their fighting capabilities!"

"Your view, Herr Reichsmarschall," remarked Heinrici icily, "is somewhat biased. I'm not saying anything against your troops, but experience has taught me that untrained units—especially those led by green officers—are often so terribly shocked by their first exposure to artillery bombardment that they are not much good for anything thereafter."

Hitler spoke again, his voice now calm and rational. "Everything must be done to train these formations," he declared. "There is certainly time to do this before the battle."

Heinrici assured him that every effort would be made in the time still remaining, but he added, "Training will not give them combat experience, and that is what's lacking." Hitler dismissed this theory. "The right commanders will provide the experience, and anyway the Russians are fighting with substandard troops, too." Stalin, claimed Hitler, is "nearing the end of his strength and about all he has left are slave soldiers whose capabilities are extremely limited." Heinrici found Hitler's misinformation incredible. Emphatically he disagreed. "My Führer," he said, "the Russian forces are both capable and enormous."

The time to hammer home the truths of the desperate situation had, to Heinrici's mind, arrived. "I must tell you," he said bluntly, "that since the transfer of the armored units to Schörner, all my troops—good and bad—must be used as front-line troops. There are no reserves. None. Will they resist the heavy shelling preceding the attack? Will they withstand the initial impact? For a time, perhaps, yes. But, against the kind of attack we expect, every one of our divisions will lose a battalion a day. This means that all along the battle front we will lose divisions themselves at the rate of one per week. We cannot sustain such losses. We have nothing to replace them with." He paused, aware that all eyes were upon him. Then Heinrici plunged ahead. "My Führer, the fact is that, at best, we can hold out for just a few days." He looked around the room. "Then," he said, "it must all come to an end."

There was dead silence. Heinrici knew that his figures were indisputable. The men gathered there were as familiar with casualty statistics as he. The difference was that they would not have spoken of them.

Goering was the first to break the paralyzing silence. "My

Führer," he announced, "I will place immediately at your disposal 100,000 Luftwaffe men. They will report to the Oder front in a few days."

Himmler glanced owlishly up at Goering, his arch rival, then at Hitler, as if sampling the Führer's reaction. Then he, too, made an announcement. "My Führer," he said, in his high-pitched voice, "the SS has the honor to furnish 25,000 fighters for the Oder front."

Doenitz was not to be outdone. He had already sent a division of marines to Heinrici; now he declared that he, too, would subscribe further forces. "My Führer," he announced, "12,000 sailors will be released immediately from their ships and rushed to the Oder."

Heinrici stared at them. They were volunteering untrained, unequipped, unqualified forces from their own private empires, spending lives instead of money in a sort of ghastly auction. They were bidding against one another, not to save Germany, but to impress Hitler. And suddenly the auction fever became contagious. A chorus of voices sounded as each man tried to suggest other forces that might be available. Someone asked for the reserve army figures and Hitler called out, "Buhle! Buhle!"

Outside in the corridor, where the crowd of waiting generals and orderlies had turned from coffee to brandy, the cry was taken up. "Buhle! Buhle! Where is Buhle?" There was a further commotion as Major General Walter Buhle, Staff Chief in charge of supplies and reinforcements, pushed through the crowd and entered the conference room. Heinrici looked at him, and then away in disgust. Buhle had been drinking and he smelled of it.* Nobody else seemed to notice or care—including Hitler. The Führer put a number of questions to Buhle—about reserves, supplies of rifles, small arms and ammunition. Buhle answered thickly and, Heinrici thought, stupidly, but the answers seemed to satisfy Hitler. According to what he made of Buhle's replies, another 13,000 troops could be scraped up from the so-called reserve army.

Dismissing Buhle, Hitler turned to Heinrici. "There," he said.

---

* As Heinrici put it in an interview with the author, "Buhle was waving a large brandy flag in front of him."

"You have 150,000 men—about twelve divisions. There are your reserves." The auction was over. Hitler apparently considered the Army Group's problems settled. Yet all he had done was to buy, at most, twelve more days for the Third Reich—and probably at a tremendous cost in human lives.

Heinrici struggled to preserve his control. "These men," he stated flatly, "are not combat-trained. They have been in rear areas and in offices or on ships, in maintenance work at Luftwaffe bases. . . . They have never fought at the front. They have never seen a Russian." Goering cut in. "The forces I have presented are, for the most part, combat fliers. They are the best of the best. And also there are the troops who were at Monte Cassino—troops whose fame outshone all others." Flushed and voluble, he hotly informed Heinrici, "These men have the will, the courage, and certainly the experience."

Doenitz, too, was angry. "I tell you," he snapped at Heinrici, "the crews of warships are every bit as good as your Wehrmacht troops." For just a moment Heinrici himself flared. "Don't you think there's a big difference between fighting at sea and fighting on land?" he asked scathingly. "I tell *you*, all these men will be slaughtered at the front! Slaughtered!"

If Heinrici's sudden outburst shocked Hitler, he did not show it. As the others fumed, Hitler seemed to have grown icily calm. "All right," he said. "We will place these reserve troops in the second line about eight kilometers behind the first. The front line will absorb the shock of the Russian preparatory artillery fire. Meanwhile, the reserves will grow accustomed to battle and if the Russians break through, they will then fight. To throw back the Russians if they break through, you will have to use the panzer divisions." And he gazed at Heinrici as though awaiting agreement on what was really a very simple matter.

Heinrici did not find it so. "You have taken away my most experienced and combat-ready armored units," he said. "The Army Group has made a request for their return." Enunciating each word clearly, Heinrici said: "I must have them back."

There was a startled movement behind him and Hitler's adjutant, Burgdorf, whispered angrily in Heinrici's ear. "Finish!" he ordered Heinrici. "You must finish." Heinrici stood his ground. "My Führer," he repeated, ignoring Burgdorf, "I must have those armored units back."

Hitler waved his hand almost apologetically. "I am very sorry," he replied, "but I had to take them from you. Your panzers are needed much more by your southern neighbor. The main attack of the Russians is clearly not aimed at Berlin. There is a stronger concentration of enemy forces to the south of your front in Saxony." Hitler waved his hand over the Russian positions on the Oder. "All of this," he announced in an exhausted, bored voice, "is merely a support attack in order to confuse. The main thrust of the enemy will not be directed at Berlin—but there." Dramatically, he placed a finger on Prague. "Consequently," the Führer continued, "the Army Group Vistula should be well able to withstand the secondary attacks."

Heinrici stared unbelievingly at Hitler.* Then he looked at Krebs; certainly all this must seem equally irrational to the Chief of OKH. Krebs spoke up. "Based on the information we have," he explained, "there is nothing to indicate that the Führer's assessment of the situation is wrong."

Heinrici had done all he could. "My Führer," he concluded, "I have completed everything possible to prepare for the attack. I cannot consider these 150,000 men as reserves. I also cannot do anything about the terrible losses we must surely sustain. It is my duty to make that absolutely clear. It is also my duty to tell you that I cannot guarantee that the attack can be repelled."

Hitler came suddenly to life. Struggling to his feet, he pounded on the table. "Faith!" he yelled. "Faith and strong belief in success will make up for all these insufficiencies! Every commander must

---

* Heinrici was later to say: "Hitler's statement killed me completely. I could hardly argue against it, for I did not know what the situation opposite Schörner's group was. I did know that Hitler was completely wrong. All I could think of was, 'How can anyone delude themselves to this extent?' I realized that they were all living in a cloud-cuckoo-land (*Wolkenkuckucksheim*)."

be filled with confidence! You!" he pointed a finger at Heinrici. "*You* must radiate this faith! *You* must instill this belief in your troops!"

Heinrici stared unflinchingly at Hitler. "My Führer," he said, "I must repeat—it is my duty to repeat—that hope and faith alone will not win this battle."

Behind him a voice whispered, "Finish! Finish!"

But Hitler was not even listening to Heinrici. "I tell you, Colonel General," he yelled, "if you are conscious of the fact that this battle should be won, it will be won! If your troops are given the same belief—then you will achieve victory, and the greatest success of the war!"

In the tense silence which followed, Heinrici, white-faced, gathered his papers and handed them to Eismann. The two officers took their leave of the still-silent room. Outside, in the corridor lounge, they were told that an air raid was in progress. Numbly, both men stood waiting, each in a kind of stupor, almost unaware of the continuing chatter around them.

After a few minutes they were permitted to leave the bunker. They climbed the stairs and went out into the garden. There, for the first time since he left the conference room, Heinrici spoke. "It's all of no use," he said, wearily. "You might just as well try to bring the moon down to earth." He looked up at the heavy smoke palls over the city and repeated softly to himself, "It's all for nothing. All for nothing." °

The blue waters of the Chiem See, like a series of moving mirrors, reflected the great stands of pine that blanketed the foothills all the way up to the snow line. Leaning heavily on his stick, Walther

° The research for Hitler's conference comes principally from Heinrici's diaries, supplemented by a long (186-page) memoir from Colonel Eismann. Heinrici kept meticulous notes of everything that happened, including the exact words Hitler used. There are some differences between Heinrici's account and that of Eismann's but these variations were resolved by a long series of interviews with Heinrici over a three-month period in 1963.

Wenck gazed across the lake and beyond to the vast panoramic tumble of mountains around Berchtesgaden a few miles away. It was a scene of extraordinary beauty and peace.

Everywhere the early flowers were out; the snow caps had begun to disappear from the high ranges and, although it was only April 6, even the air was redolent of spring. The peacefulness of his surroundings had done much to speed the convalesence of Guderian's former Chief of Staff, at 45, the Wehrmacht's youngest general.

Here, in the heart of the Bavarian Alps, the war seemed a thousand miles away. Except for men recuperating from war wounds or, as in Wenck's case, accidents, there was hardly a soldier to be seen in the entire area.

Although still weak, Wenck was on the mend. Considering the seriousness of the accident, he was lucky to be alive. He had sustained head wounds and multiple fractures in a car wreck on February 13, and had been hospitalized for nearly six weeks. So many ribs had been smashed that he was still encased in a surgical corset from chest to thighs. The war seemed over for him, and in any case its outcome was sadly clear. He did not believe the Third Reich could survive more than a few weeks longer.

Although Germany's future seemed bleak, Wenck had much to be thankful for: his wife, Irmgard, and their 15-year-old twins, son Helmuth and daughter Sigried were safe, and staying with him in Bavaria. With painful slowness Wenck walked back to the picturesque little inn where they were living. As he entered the foyer, Irmgard met him with a message. Wenck was to ring Berlin immediately.

Hitler's adjutant, General Burgdorf, came on the line. Wenck, Burgdorf said, was to report to Hitler in Berlin the following day. "The Führer," said Burgdorf, "has named you commander of the Twelfth Army." Wenck was both surprised and puzzled. "The Twelfth Army?" he asked. "Which one is that?"

"You'll learn all about that when you get here," Burgdorf replied.

Wenck was still not satisfied. "I've never heard of a Twelfth

Army," he pressed. "The Twelfth Army," Burgdorf said irritably, as though explaining everything, "is being organized now." Then he hung up.

Hours later, in uniform once more, Wenck said good-bye to his distressed wife. "Whatever you do," he warned her, "stay in Bavaria. It's the safest place." Then, totally ignorant of his assignment, he set out for Berlin. Within the next twenty-one days the name of this virtually unknown general would become synonymous with hope in the mind of almost every Berliner.

The staff was accustomed to seeing an occasional outburst of temper, but nobody had ever seen Heinrici quite like this before. The commander of the Army Group Vistula was in a towering rage. He had just received a report from Bieler, the officer in charge of the "fortress" at Frankfurt, on the young colonel's visit to Hitler. As Heinrici had feared, the bespectacled, thin-faced officer had not measured up to Hitler's idea of a Nordic hero. After a few inconsequential remarks, during which Frankfurt was not even mentioned, Hitler shook hands and dismissed the young officer. As soon as Bieler had left the bunker, Hitler ordered a change in the Frankfurt command. "Get someone else," the Führer told Krebs, "Bieler is certainly no Gneisenau!"

General Busse, whose Ninth Army included the Frankfurt garrison, had heard from Krebs of the impending change and had promptly informed Heinrici. Now, as Bieler stood beside Heinrici's desk, the blazing *Giftzwerg* put in a call to Krebs. His staff watched silently. They had learned to tell the measure of Heinrici's temper by the way he drummed on the table top with his fingers. Now his right hand was beating out a violent tattoo. Krebs came on the phone. "Krebs," barked Heinrici, "Colonel Bieler is here in my office. I want you to listen carefully. Bieler is to be reinstated as commander of the Frankfurt garrison. I have told this to Burgdorf and now I'm telling you. I refuse to accept any other officer.

Do you understand that?" He did not wait for an answer. "Something else. Where is Bieler's Iron Cross? He has been waiting for that decoration for months. Now he is to get it. Do you understand that?" Still Heinrici did not pause. "And now listen to me, Krebs," he said. "If Bieler does not get his Iron Cross, if Bieler is not reinstated as commander of Frankfurt, I shall lay down *my* command! Do you understand *that?*" Heinrici, still drumming furiously, pressed on. "I expect your confirmation on this matter today! Is that clear?" And he slammed down the phone. Krebs had not uttered a word.

On the afternoon of April 7, Colonel Eismann later recalled, "the Army Group received two teletype messages from the Führer's headquarters. In the first, Bieler was confirmed as commander of Frankfurt; in the second the Iron Cross was bestowed upon him."

General Alfred Jodl, Hitler's Chief of Operations, sat in his Dahlem office awaiting the arrival of General Wenck. The new Twelfth Army commander had just left Hitler and now it was Jodl's job to brief Wenck on the situation on the western front. On Jodl's desk was a sheaf of reports from Field Marshal Albert Kesselring, Commander-in-Chief, West. They painted a picture that was growing darker almost hourly. Everywhere the Anglo-Americans were breaking through.

In theory, the Twelfth Army was to be the western shield before Berlin, holding about 125 miles of the lower Elbe and Mulde rivers to prevent an Anglo-American drive on the city. Wenck, Hitler had decided, would command an army of ten divisions, composed of panzer training corps officers, Home Guardsmen, cadet forces, various splinter groups, and the remnants of the shattered Eleventh Army in the Harz Mountains. Even if such a force could be organized in time, Jodl was skeptical that it could have much, if any, effect. And on the Elbe it might never get into action at all—although he had no intention of telling Wenck this. In his office safe, Jodl still held the captured Eclipse plan—the document detailing the moves the Anglo-Americans would make in the event of a German surrender or collapse—and the attached maps showing the agreed zones each Ally would occupy at war's end. Jodl remained convinced that the Americans and British would halt on the Elbe—roughly the dividing line between the Anglo-American and Russian post-hostility zones of occupation. It seemed perfectly clear to him that Eisenhower was going to leave Berlin to the Russians.

* * *

"Naturally," ran the last paragraph of General Eisenhower's latest cable to Churchill, "if at any moment 'Eclipse' conditions [a German collapse or surrender] should come about anywhere along the front we would rush forward . . . and Berlin would be included in our important targets." It was as much of a commitment as the Supreme Commander was willing to make. It did not satisfy the British, and their Chiefs of Staff continued to press for a clear-cut decision. They messaged Washington urging a meeting to discuss Eisenhower's strategy. Stalin's cable had roused their suspicions. While the Generalissimo had stated that he planned to begin his offensive in the middle of May, said the British Chiefs, he had not indicated when he intended to launch his "secondary forces" in the direction of Berlin. Thus it still seemed to them that Berlin should be captured as soon as possible. Further, they believed it would be "appropriate for the Combined Chiefs of Staff to give Eisenhower guidance on the matter."

The reply from General Marshall firmly and decisively ended the discussion. "Such psychological and political advantages as would result from the possible capture of Berlin ahead of the Russians," he said, "should not override the imperative military consideration, which in our opinion is the destruction and dismembering of the German armed forces."

Marshall did not entirely close the door on the possibility of taking Berlin for, "as a matter of fact, it is within the center of the impact of the main thrust." But there was no time for the Combined Chiefs of Staff to give the problem any lengthy consideration. The speed of the Allied advance into Germany was now so fast, he said, that it outstripped the possibility of "review of operational matters by this or any other form of committee action." And Marshall ended with an unequivocal endorsement of the Supreme Commander: "Only Eisenhower is in a position to know how to fight his battle and to exploit to the full the changing situation."

The harassed Eisenhower, for his part, had declared himself willing to change his plans but only if ordered to do so. On April 7 he wired Marshall, "At any time that we can seize Berlin at little cost we should, of course, do so." But because the Russians were so close to the capital, he regarded it "as militarily unsound at this stage of the proceedings to make Berlin a major objective." He was the first, said Eisenhower, "to admit that war is waged in pursuance of political aims, and if the Combined Chiefs of Staff should decide that the Allied effort to take Berlin outweighs purely military considerations in this theater, I would cheerfully re-adjust my plans and thinking so as to carry out such an operation." He stressed his belief, however, that "the capture of Berlin should be left as something that we should do if feasible and practicable as we proceed on the general plan of (A) dividing the German forces . . . (B) anchoring our left firmly in the Lübeck area, and (C) attempting to disrupt any German effort to establish a fortress in the southern mountains."

He gave almost the same answer to Montgomery the following day. Monty had picked up the cudgels where Churchill and the British Chiefs left off. He asked Eisenhower for ten extra divisions to attack toward Lübeck and Berlin. Eisenhower turned him down. "As regards Berlin," declared the Supreme Commander, "I am quite ready to admit that it has political and psychological significance, but of far greater importance will be the location of the remaining German forces in relation to Berlin. It is on them that I am going to concentrate my attention. Naturally if I can get a chance to take Berlin cheaply, I shall do so."

At this point Churchill decided to end the controversy before there was further deterioration of the Allied relationship. He informed President Roosevelt that he considered the affair closed. "To prove my sincerity," he cabled the President, "I will use one of my very few Latin quotations: *Amantium irae amoris integratio est.*" Translated, it meant, Lovers' quarrels are a renewal of love.

But while the controversy over SCAF 252 and the Anglo-American objectives had been taking place behind the scenes, the men of the Anglo-American forces had been driving deeper by the hour into Germany. Nobody had told them that Berlin was no longer a major military objective.

✤ 5 ✤

T HE RACE WAS ON. Never in the history of warfare had so many men moved so fast. The speed of the Anglo-American offensive was contagious, and all along the front the drive was taking on the proportions of a giant contest. As the armies concentrated on gaining the banks of the Elbe, to secure the bridgeheads for the last victorious dash that would end the war, every division along the north and center of the western front was determined to reach the river first. Beyond, Berlin, as always, was the final goal.

In the British zone, the 7th Armored Division—the famed Desert Rats—had hardly paused since leaving the Rhine. Once across, Major General Louis Lyne, the 7th's commander, had emphasized that "for all ranks, your eyes should now be firmly fixed on the river Elbe. Once we get started I do not propose to stop by day or by night till we get there . . . Good hunting on the next lap." Now, even against heavy opposition, the Desert Rats were averaging upward of twenty miles a day.

Squadron Sergeant Major Charles Hennell thought it "right and proper for the 7th to take the capital as a reward for our long and arduous efforts in the war from the Western Desert onwards." Hennell had been with the Desert Rats since El Alamein. Sergeant Major Eric Cole had an even more compelling reason to reach Berlin. A veteran of Dunkirk, he had been driven into the sea by the Germans in 1940. Now Cole was grimly preparing to even the score. He constantly badgered the armored crews to get their mechanized equipment in tiptop running condition. Cole planned to drive the Germans in front of the 7th Armored tanks all the way back to Berlin.

The men of the British 6th Airborne Division had led their countrymen into Normandy on D-Day; they were determined to lead them on to the end. Sergeant Hugh McWhinnie had heard from German prisoners that the moment the British crossed the Elbe, the enemy would "open the door and let them through to Berlin." He doubted it. The 6th was used to fighting for every mile. Captain Wilfred Davison of the 13th Parachute Battalion was certain that there would be a race for the city but, like most of the division, he had no doubt that "the 6th was in the running to lead the way." But at division headquarters, Captain John L. Shearer was becoming a little anxious. He had heard a rumor that "Berlin was being left to the Americans."

U.S. Airborne divisions had heard the same rumor. The trouble was that it made no mention of paratroopers. At General James Gavin's 82nd Airborne staging area, where chutists had been training for days, it was now all too clear that a fighting drop on Berlin was out. Apparently an airborne operation would result only if a sudden enemy collapse put the Eclipse plan into action, making it necessary for the troopers to go to Berlin on a policing mission. But this seemed remote. SHAEF had already instructed

General Lewis Brereton's First Airborne Army that it would soon be making relief drops on Allied POW camps, under the code name "Operation Jubilant." Much as they wanted POWs freed, the prospect of a rescue operation instead of a fighting assignment filled the men of the airborne army with something less than jubilance.

Similar frustration characterized other airborne groups. General Maxwell Taylor's "Screaming Eagles" of the 101st Airborne Division were once more fighting as foot soldiers, this time in the Ruhr. One regiment of Gavin's 82nd had been ordered there, too. The 82nd had also been alerted to help Montgomery's Twenty-first Army Group in a later operation across the Elbe.

It was Private Arthur "Dutch" Schultz of the 505th Parachute Regiment who perhaps best summed up the feelings of the men of the airborne divisions. Climbing aboard a truck headed for the Ruhr, he cynically told his pal, Private Joe Tallett, "So. I lead 'em into Normandy, yes? Into Holland, yes? Look at me, kid. I'm a blue-blooded American and the country's got only one of me. They want to get their money's worth. They ain't gonna waste *me* on Berlin. Hell, no! They're saving me up! They're gonna drop me on Tokyo!"

But if the airborne divisions were dispirited, the land armies were brimming over with anticipation.

In the center, U.S. forces were going all out and their strength was enormous. With the return of Simpson's massive Ninth Army from Montgomery's Twenty-first Army Group, Bradley had become the first general in American history to command four field armies. Besides the Ninth, his forces included the First, Third and Fifteenth—close to a million men.

On April 2, just nine days after crossing the Rhine, his troops had finished springing the trap encircling the Ruhr. Caught in the 4,000-square-mile pocket was Field Marshal Walter Model's Army Group B, numbering no fewer than 325,000 men. With Model contained, the western front was wide open and Bradley swept boldly on, leaving part of the Ninth and First armies to mop up the pocket. Now his forces were in full cry. With the British in the north and General Devers' U.S. Sixth Army Group in the south holding the flanks, Bradley was driving furiously through Germany's center, toward Leipzig and Dresden. In the north-to-south line-up of U.S. armies the Ninth was the shortest distance from the Elbe, and it looked to commanders as if Bradley had given Simpson the go-ahead for the dash that, by its very momentum, should take U.S. forces to Berlin.

The day the encirclement of the Ruhr was completed, Eisenhower issued orders to his forces. Bradley's group was to "mop up the . . . Ruhr . . . launch a thrust with its main axis: Kassel-Leipzig . . . seize any opportunity to capture a bridgehead over the River Elbe and be prepared to conduct operations beyond the Elbe." On April 4, the day the Ninth was returned to him, Bradley himself gave new commands to his armies. In the Twelfth Army Group's "Letter of Instructions, No. 20," the Ninth was directed, first, to drive for a line roughly south of Hanover with the army center in the approximate area of the town of Hildesheim—about seventy miles from the Elbe. Then, "on order," the second phase would begin. It was this vital paragraph that spelled out the role of the Ninth Army and, to its commander, left no doubt as to the destination of his forces. It read: "Phase 2. Advance on order to the east . . . exploit any opportunity for seizing a bridgehead over the Elbe and be prepared to continue the advance on BERLIN or to the northeast." Phase 1—the drive toward Hildesheim—seemed to be simply a directional order. No one expected to be held there. But Phase 2 was the starting flag that every division in the Ninth Army had been awaiting, none more eagerly than the commander, Lieutenant General William "Big Simp" Simpson.*

"My people were keyed up," General Simpson was to recall later. "We'd been the first to the Rhine and now we were going

---

* Simpson had every reason to believe he had been given the go-ahead. In the same Twelfth Army Group order, the U.S. First and Third armies were instructed in the second phase to seize bridgeheads on the Elbe and be prepared to drive east—in the case of Patton's Third, the expression used was "east or southeast." But only in Ninth Army's order were the words "on Berlin" included.

to be the first to Berlin. All along we thought of just one thing—capturing Berlin, going through and meeting the Russians on the other side." From the time the Letter of Instructions came down from the Army Group, Simpson had not wasted a minute. He expected to reach the Hildesheim phase line in a matter of days. After that, Simpson told his staff officers, he planned "to get an armored and an infantry division set up on the autobahn running just above Magdeburg on the Elbe to Potsdam, where we'll be ready to close in on Berlin." Then Simpson intended to commit the rest of the Ninth "as fast as we can . . . if we get the bridgehead and they turn us loose." Jubilantly he told his staff, "Damn, I want to get to Berlin and all you people, right down to the last private, I think, want it, too."

Major General Isaac D. White, the determined, wiry commander of the 2nd Armored "Hell on Wheels" Division, was a good step ahead of Simpson: his plan to take Berlin had been ready even before his men crossed the Rhine. White's Operations Chief, Colonel Briard P. Johnson, had plotted the drive on the capital weeks before. So thorough was his plan that detailed orders and map overlays were ready by March 25.

The 2nd's assault plan was somewhat similar to Simpson's own concept. It, too, followed the autobahn from Magdeburg on the Elbe. Proposed day-by-day advances were drawn on the map overlays and each stage was given a code name. The last dash of about sixty miles from Magdeburg carried phase lines with the names: "Silver," "Silk," "Satin," "Daisy," "Pansy," "Jug," and finally, imposed on a huge blue swastika covering Berlin, the code word "Goal." At the rate the 2nd was moving, against only spotty opposition, often achieving upward of thirty-five miles a day, White was confident of grabbing the capital. If his men could secure a bridgehead at Magdeburg, now only eighty miles away, White expected to dash into Berlin within forty-eight hours.

Now, along the Ninth Army's fifty-odd miles of front, White's 2nd Armored was spearheading the drive. The division was one of the largest formations on the western front. With its tanks, self-propelled guns, armored cars, bulldozers, trucks, jeeps and artillery, it formed a stream more than seventy-two miles long. To create maximum fighting effectiveness, the force had been broken into three armored units—Combat Commands A, B and R, the latter held in reserve. Even so, the division, moving in tandem and averaging about two miles an hour, took nearly twelve hours to pass a given point. This ponderous armored force was running ahead of every other unit of the Ninth Army—with one notable exception.

On its right flank, tenaciously pacing the 2nd mile for mile and fighting all the way, was a wildly assorted collection of vehicles crammed with troops. From the air it bore no resemblance to either an armored or an infantry division. In fact, but for a number of U.S. Army trucks interspersed among its columns, it might easily have been mistaken for a German convoy. Major General Robert C. Macon's highly individualistic 83rd Infantry Division, the "Rag-Tag Circus," was going hell-for-leather toward the Elbe in its captured booty. Every enemy unit or town that surrendered or was captured subscribed its quota of rolling stock for the division, usually at gunpoint. Every newly acquired vehicle got a quick coat of olive-green paint and a U.S. star slapped on its side; then it joined the 83rd. The men of the Rag-Tag Circus had even managed to liberate a German airplane and, harder, had found someone to fly it, and it was spreading consternation all over the front. First Sergeant William G. Presnell of the 30th Infantry Division, who had fought all the way from Omaha Beach, knew the silhouette of every Luftwaffe fighter. So when he saw what was obviously a German plane heading in his direction, he yelled "ME-109!" and dived for cover. Puzzled when there was no burst of machine gun fire, he raised his head and stared as the fighter sped away. The plane was painted a blotchy olive-green. On the undersides of the wings were the words "83rd Inf. Div."

If their compatriots were confused by the 83rd's vehicles, the Germans were even more so. As the division rushed pell mell toward the Elbe, Major Haley Kohler heard the insistent blowing of

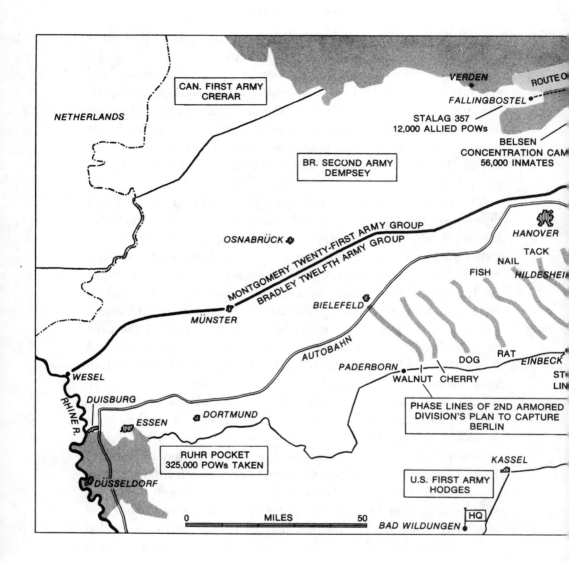

CAN. FIRST ARMY
CRERAR

NETHERLANDS

VERDEN

ROUTE O

FALLINGBOSTEL

STALAG 357
12,000 ALLIED POWs

BELSEN
CONCENTRATION CAM
56,000 INMATES

BR. SECOND ARMY
DEMPSEY

MONTGOMERY TWENTY-FIRST ARMY GROUP

BRADLEY TWELFTH ARMY GROUP

OSNABRÜCK

HANOVER

TACK

NAIL

FISH

HILDESHEI

MÜNSTER

BIELEFELD

AUTOBAHN

DOG

RAT

EINBECK

PADERBORN

ST

LIN

WALNUT   CHERRY

WESEL

DUISBURG

RHINE R.

ESSEN

DORTMUND

PHASE LINES OF 2ND ARMORED
DIVISION'S PLAN TO CAPTURE
BERLIN

RUHR POCKET
325,000 POWs TAKEN

KASSEL

DÜSSELDORF

U.S. FIRST ARMY
HODGES

0   MILES   50

HQ

BAD WILDUNGEN

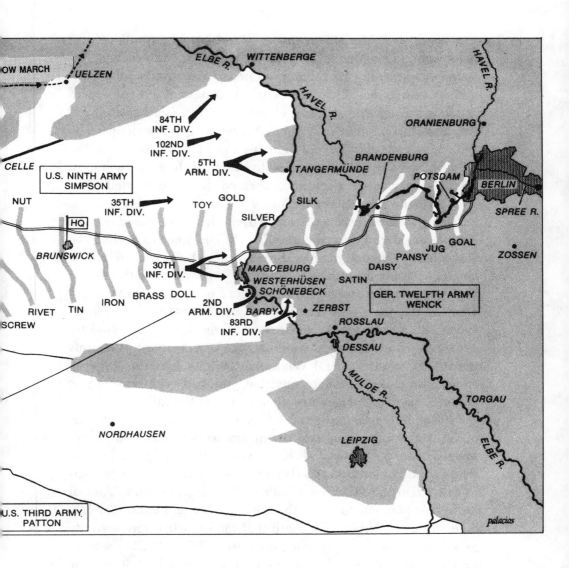

This map shows the U.S. Ninth Army's plan for the advance to Berlin.

287

a car horn. "This Mercedes came up behind us," he recalled, "and then began passing everything on the road." Captain John J. Devenney saw it, too. "The car weaved in and out of our column, going in our direction," he remembered. As it passed, Devenney was astounded to see that it was a chauffeur-driven German staff car with a full load of officers. A burst of machine gun fire stopped the vehicle, and the bewildered Germans were taken prisoner in the middle of what they had supposed to be one of their own columns. The Mercedes, in top condition, received the usual hurried paint job and was immediately put to use.

General Macon was determined that the 83rd would be the first infantry division to cross the Elbe and advance to Berlin. The rivalry between the 83rd and the 2nd Armored was now so intense that when leading units of the two divisions reached the Weser River at the same time on April 5 "there was considerable argument," as Macon put it, "as to who was to cross the river first." Eventually a compromise was reached: the divisions crossed together, by sandwiching their units. Back at 83rd headquarters rumor had it that General White was furious with the Rag-Tag Circus. "No damned infantry division," the 2nd's commander was quoted as saying, "is going to beat *my* outfit to the Elbe."

The 2nd was running into other competition, too. The 5th Armored "Victory Division" was rolling almost as fast as White's columns, and its men had plans of their own for taking the capital. "The only big question at the time was who was going to get Berlin first," remembers Colonel Gilbert Farrand, the 5th's Chief of Staff. "We planned to cross the Elbe at Tangermünde, Sandau, Arneburg and Werben. We heard that the Russians were ready to go, so we made every possible preparation." The division was on the move so continuously that, as Farrand remembers it, no one slept more than four or five hours a night—and often no one slept at all. Because of the steadiness of the advance, Farrand's own half-track was now the division's headquarters. The 5th's progress was greatly helped by the spottiness of the opposition. "The advance was really nothing more," Farrand recalls, "than cracking rear guard actions." But these could be deadly, as Farrand discovered when a shell plowed through his half-track.

Among the infantry divisions, the 84th, 30th and 102nd had their eyes on Berlin, too. Everywhere in the Ninth, tired and dirty men, eating on the move, were hoping to be in on the kill. The very momentum of the drive was exhilarating. Still, despite the absence of a general pattern of German defense, there was fighting—and at times it was heavy.

In some areas diehards put up fierce resistance before surrendering. Lieutenant Colonel Roland Kolb of the 84th "Railsplitters" Division noticed that the worst fighting came from scattered SS units that hid in the woods and harassed the advancing troops. The armored columns usually bypassed these fanatic remnants and left them to the infantry to mop up. Desperate encounters often took place in small towns. At one point in the advance, Kolb was shocked to find children of twelve and under manning artillery pieces. "Rather than surrender," he remembers, "the boys fought until killed."

Other men also experienced moments of horror. Near the wooded ridges of the Teutoburger Wald, Major James F. Hollingsworth, leading the 2nd Armored's advance guard, found himself suddenly surrounded by German tanks. His column had run directly into a panzer training ground. Luckily for Hollingsworth, the tanks were relics from which the engines had been long since removed. But their guns were in place for use in training recruits, and the Germans quickly opened fire. Staff Sergeant Clyde W. Cooley, a veteran of North Africa and the gunner on Hollingsworth's tank, swung into action. Revolving his turret, he knocked out a German tank at 1,500 yards. Turning again, he blasted another 75 yards away. "All hell broke loose as everyone opened up," recalls Hollingsworth. Then just as the fight ended, a German truck filled with soldiers came barreling down the road toward the 2nd Armored's column. Hollingsworth hastily ordered his men to wait until the truck was in range. At 75 yards, he gave the order to open fire. The truck, riddled by .50 caliber machine gun bullets, blazed, turned over and threw its uniformed occupants out onto the road. Most were dead by the time they hit the ground, but a few were still alive and screaming horribly. It was only when he came up to inspect the torn and riddled bodies that Hollingsworth discovered the soldiers were uniformed German women—the equivalent of U.S. WACs.

The opposition was completely unpredictable. Many areas capitulated without firing a shot. In some towns and cities burgomasters surrendered while the withdrawing German troops were still moving through the populated areas, often no more than a block away from American tanks and infantry. At Detmold, where one of Germany's largest armament works was located, a civilian met the lead tank of Lieutenant Colonel Wheeler G. Merriam's 82nd Reconnaissance Battalion, scouting ahead of the 2nd Armored. The German representative announced that the superintendent of the factory wished to surrender. "Shells were falling all about us as we drove in," Merriam recalls. "Lined up outside the factory were the superintendent, the factory manager and the workers. The superintendent made a little speech of surrender and then presented me with a beautifully chromed Mauser pistol." A few blocks farther on, Merriam took the surrender of an entire German paymaster company—complete with vast quantities of bank notes. But a few hours later, U.S. infantry coming up behind Merriam fought a bitter and prolonged battle to clean out the same town. Detmold, as it turned out, was in the center of an SS training area.

Similar incidents occurred everywhere. In some small cities the silence of surrender in one area would be suddenly shattered by the din of fierce fighting a few blocks away. On the main street of one such city, General Macon, the 83rd's commander, remembers "walking quite safely through the front entrance of my headquarters, but when I tried to leave by the back door, I almost had to fight my way out." On the outskirts of one town, troops of the 30th Infantry were met by German soldiers with white handkerchiefs tied to their rifles. As the Germans tried to surrender to the Americans, they were machine gunned in the back by SS stragglers who still fought on.

Some men developed new techniques for securing surrenders. Captain Francis Schommer of the 83rd Division, who spoke fluent German, several times conducted capitulations by telephone—bolstered by a Colt .45. Schommer, his pistol pointed at a newly captured burgomaster, would inform the mayor that "it might be wise for you to telephone the burgomaster of the next town and inform him that, if he wants the place to remain standing, he better surrender it right now. Tell him to get the people to hang sheets from their windows—or else." The frightened burgomaster "would usually pour it on, telling his neighbor that the Americans in his town had hundreds of tanks and artillery pieces, and thousands upon thousands of troops. The ruse worked again and again."

As the great drive gathered momentum, the roads became jammed with motorized troops and armored columns pushing east past thousands of German prisoners going west. There was not even time to take charge of the prisoners. Exhausted and unshaven, Wehrmacht officers and privates trudged back toward the Rhine unaccompanied. Some of them still carried weapons. Chaplain Ben L. Rose of the 113th Mechanized Cavalry Group recalls the hopeless look of two officers who, in full dress uniform, walked alongside his column "trying to get someone to notice them long enough to surrender their side arms." But the troopers, intent on piling up mileage, simply thumbed them west.

Cities and towns fell to the onrushing forces one after another. Few men had heard their names before and, in any case, no one stayed long enough to remember them. Places like Minden, Bückeburg, Tündern and Stadthagen were merely checkpoints on the way to the Elbe. But the troops of the 30th Division encountered a familiar name—so familiar that most men remember being surprised that it actually existed. The town was Hamelin, of Pied Piper fame. Suicidal opposition from a few SS strongpoints bypassed earlier by the 2nd Armored, and heavy retaliatory shelling by the 30th, reduced the storybook city of gingerbread houses and cobblestoned streets to a burned and blasted rubble by April 5. "This time," said Colonel Walter M. Johnson of the 117th Regiment, "we got the rats out with a slightly different kind of flute."

By April 8, the 84th Division had reached the outskirts of 15th-century Hanover. On the long drive from the Rhine, Hanover, with a population of 400,000, was the largest city to fall to any division of the Ninth Army. Major General Alexander R. Bolling, commander of the 84th, had expected to bypass the city, but instructions came down to capture it instead. Bolling was less than happy. To commit his troops at Hanover would lose him precious time in his race against other infantry divisions for the Elbe. The battle was fierce; yet within forty-eight hours resistance had been reduced to small isolated actions. Bolling, proud of the 84th's prowess, yet chafing to get on with the advance, was both surprised and pleased to be visited in Hanover by the Supreme Commander, his Chief of Staff, General Smith, and the Ninth Army's General Simpson. At the end of their formal meeting, Bolling remembered, "Ike said to me, 'Alex, where are you going next?' I replied, 'General, we're going to push on ahead, we have a clear go to Berlin and nothing can stop us.'"

Eisenhower, according to Bolling, "put his hand on my arm and said, 'Alex, keep going. I wish you all the luck in the world and don't let anybody stop you.'" When Eisenhower left Hanover, Bolling believed that he had a "clear verbal acknowledgement from the Supreme Commander that the 84th was going to Berlin."

On that same Sunday, April 8, the 2nd Armored Division, slightly ahead of the 83rd for the moment, pulled up at the first phase line, Hildesheim. Now the 2nd must await orders for the opening of the second stage of the attack. General White was glad of the pause. With the division traveling at such speed, maintenance had become a problem and White needed at least forty-eight hours for repairs. The temporary halt, he understood, would also enable other units to come abreast. But the majority of soldiers, after the frenzied speed of the last few days, wondered why they were being held. Men chafed at the delay; in the past, such stand-downs had given the enemy a chance to reorganize and consolidate. With the end so close no one wanted to push his luck. First Sergeant George Petcoff, a Normandy veteran, was worried about "the fight for Berlin, because I was beginning to think my number was up." Chaplain Rose remembers that one tanker was so superstitious about the future that he climbed out of his tank, looked at the words "Fearless Joe" painted on the front and painstakingly proceeded to scratch out the word "Fearless." "From now on," he announced, "it's just plain Joe!"

If the men were anxious and fearful of delay, their commanders —including General White's immediate superiors at 19th Corps headquarters—were even more concerned. Major General Raymond S. McLain, the Corps Commander, hoped nothing would upset his plans. Despite the speed, he was not worried about supplies. The strength of his corps, totaling well over 120,000 men, was now greater than the Union Army's at Gettysburg, and he had 1,000 armored vehicles. With all this power, McLain, as he later expressed it, had "absolutely no doubt that six days after crossing the Elbe" the entire 19th Corps would be in Berlin.

McLain had heard from Simpson's headquarters that the pause was only temporary—and that the reason for the delay was both tactical and political. As it turned out, his information was right on both counts. Ahead lay the future frontier of the Soviet zone of occupation, and the halt gave SHAEF time to consider the situation. No geographic "stop line" had yet been decided upon for either the Anglo-American or the Russian forces. Thus, the danger of head-on collision still existed. In the absence of any concentrated German opposition, higher headquarters had no intention of stopping the attack, yet one serious consideration had to be taken into account: once the Soviet occupation line was crossed, every mile captured would, sooner or later, have to be handed back to the Russians.

At the closest point of advance, Berlin was now only 125 miles away, and all along the Ninth Army front, men waited to go, oblivious of the delicate problem that faced the High Command.

They had all sorts of reasons for being eager. P.F.C. Carroll Stewart was looking forward to his first glimpse of the German capital because he had heard that, of all the cities in Europe, Berlin could not be matched for its scenic views.

*   *   *

RAF Warrant Officer James "Dixie" Deans stamped to attention before the desk and smartly saluted the German colonel. Hermann Ostmann, commandant of Stalag 357, the Allied prisoner-of-war camp near Fallingbostel, north of Hanover, returned the salute with equal briskness. It was just one of a series of military formalities that Prisoner-of-War Deans and Captor Ostmann played out whenever they met. Each, as always, was a model of correctness.

Between the two men there existed a grudging and wary respect. Deans regarded the commandant—a middle-aged World War I officer whose palsied arm disqualified him from more active service—as a fair-minded warden, doing a job he disliked. For his part, Ostmann knew that the 29-year-old Deans, elected by the prisoners as their spokesman, was an obstinate, determined bargainer who could, and often did, make Ostmann's life miserable. The Colonel was always aware that the real control of Stalag 357 lay in the slender Deans's firm handling of the prisoners, and in their unswerving loyalty to him.

Deans was a legend. A navigator who had been shot down over Berlin in 1940, he had been in POW camps ever since. In each, he had learned something more about how to obtain maximum privileges for himself and his fellow inmates. He had also learned much about dealing with prison commandants. According to Deans, the procedure was basic: "You simply give the blighters hell all the time."

Now, Deans stared down at the aging colonel, waiting to learn the reason for his latest summons to the commandant's office.

"I have here some orders," said Ostmann, holding up some forms.

"And I am afraid that we must move you and your men."

Deans was immediately on guard. "Where to, Colonel?" he asked.

"Northeast of here," said Ostmann. "Exactly where I do not know, but I'll get instructions along the way." Then he added, "Of course you understand we are doing this for your own protection." He paused and smiled weakly. "Your armies are getting a little close."

Deans had been aware of that for days. "Recreational" activities in the camp had resulted in the production of two highly functional and secret radios. One lay hidden in an old-fashioned, constantly used gramophone. The other, a tiny battery-operated receiver, made the rounds of Stalag 357 broadcasting the latest news from its owner's mess kit. From these precious sources, Deans knew that Eisenhower's armies were over the Rhine and fighting in the Ruhr. The extent of the Anglo-American advance was still unknown to the prisoners—but the troops must be near if the Germans were moving the camp.

"How will the transfer be made, Colonel?" Deans asked, knowing full well that the Germans almost always moved POWs one way only—on foot.

"They'll march in columns," said Ostmann. Then, with one of his courteous gestures, he offered Deans a special privilege. "You can drive with me if you like." With equal courtesy, Deans declined.

"How about the sick?" he asked. "There are many men here who can hardly walk."

"They'll be left behind with whatever help we can give them. And some of your men can stay with them, too."

Now Deans wanted to know how soon the prisoners were leaving. There were times when Ostmann suspected that Deans knew almost as much of the war situation as the commandant himself— but there was one thing he was certain Deans could not have heard. According to headquarters information, the British were advancing in the general direction of Fallingbostel and were now only about fifty to sixty miles away, while the Americans, by all reports, were already in Hanover fifty miles to the south.

"You go immediately," he informed Deans. "Those are my orders."

As he left the commandant's office, Deans knew there was little he could do to prepare the men for the march. Food was short and almost all the prisoners were weak and emaciated from malnutrition. A prolonged, arduous journey was almost certain to finish off many of them. But as he returned to barracks to pass the word of the march around camp, he made himself a solemn vow: using every ruse he could think of, from slow-ups to sit-downs to minor mutinies, Dixie Deans somehow intended to reach the Allied lines with all twelve thousand men of Stalag 357.

The whereabouts of the headquarters of the newly organized Twelfth Army had so far eluded the commanding officer, General Walther Wenck. The command post was supposed to be in the area north of the Harz Mountains, about seventy to eighty miles from Berlin, but Wenck had been driving about for hours. The roads were black with refugees and vehicles heading in both directions. Some refugees were milling east, away from the advancing Americans; others, fearful of the Russians, were hurrying to the west. Convoys carrying soldiers seemed equally aimless. Dorn, Wenck's driver, pressed down the horn again and again as he edged the car along. As they drove deeper, heading south by west, conditions bordered on the chaotic. Wenck was becoming ever more uneasy and restless. What, he wondered, would he find when headquarters was finally reached?

Wenck was taking a roundabout way to reach his command post. He had decided to make a wide swing which would take him first to the city of Weimar, lying southwest of Leipzig, before he headed up to headquarters somewhere near Bad Blankenburg. Though the diversion was adding almost a hundred miles to his journey, Wenck had a reason for the detour. In a Weimar bank were his life savings, some ten thousand marks, and he intended to withdraw the entire sum. But as his car approached the city, the roads became strangely empty and the crack of gunfire sounded in the distance. A few kilometers further, the car was halted and Wehrmacht military police informed the General that tanks of Patton's U.S. Third Army were already on the outskirts. Wenck felt both shocked and deceived. The situation was much worse than he had been told at Hitler's headquarters. He could not believe that the Allies had advanced so fast—or that so much of Germany was already overrun. It was also hard to concede that, in all probability, his ten thousand marks were gone, too.*

From local headquarters Wehrmacht officers told Wenck that the entire Harz region was endangered, troops were retreating and areas were being outflanked. Obviously, his headquarters had already pulled out of the area. Wenck headed back toward Dessau, where some of his army was supposedly gathering. Near Rosslau, about eight miles north of Dessau, he discovered his headquarters in a former Wehrmacht engineering school. There, too, Wenck discovered the truth about the Twelfth Army.

Its front ran along the Elbe and its tributary, the Mulde, for a distance of about 125 miles—roughly from Wittenberge on the Elbe to the north, then south to a point just below and east of Leipzig on the Mulde. On the northern flank, facing the British, were the forces of Field Marshal Ernst Busch, Commander-in-Chief, North West. On the south were the badly mauled units of Field Marshal Albert Kesselring, Commander-in-Chief, West. Wenck had little information about the strength of these forces. In his section, between the two, the Twelfth Army existed mainly on paper. Other than troops holding scattered positions along the

* The persistent Wenck tried to lay claim to his money after the war but by then Weimar was in the Soviet zone and under the administration of Ulbricht's East German Government. Curiously, the bank continued to send Wenck monthly statements up to July 4, 1947. He acknowledged the statements repeatedly, asking that the money be transferred to his own bank in West Germany. No action was taken until October 23, 1954, when the Weimar bank informed Wenck that he must take up the matter with the Ministry of Internal Affairs, District of Weimar. "We have annulled your very old account," the bank's letter said, "along with the interest accrued. . . ."

Elbe he had little but the scant remains of ghost divisions. Other groups, he found, were not yet operational, and there were even shadow units still to be formed. The bulk of his artillery was immobile, set in fixed positions around such towns as Magdeburg, Wittenberge, and near bridge or crossing sites along the Elbe. There were some self-propelled guns, a group of armored cars, and some forty small jeeplike Volkswagen troop carriers. But Wenck's Twelfth Army at this moment had at best only about a dozen tanks.

Although presumably the scattered and splinter troops would eventually bring his forces up to about 100,000 men, right now he had nowhere near the ten divisions he had been promised. Amid the remnants of units with impressive names—"Clausewitz," "Potsdam," "Scharnhorst," "Ulrich von Hutten," "Friedrich Ludwig Jahn," "Theodor Körner"—there remained at most five and a half divisions, about 55,000 men.

Apart from forces already committed to set positions or in actual combat, the bulk of the new Twelfth Army was made up of eager cadets and training officers. Neither Wenck nor his Chief of Staff, Colonel Günther Reichhelm, had any doubt about the eventual outcome of the battles ahead. But Wenck refused to give in to disillusionment. Young and eager himself, he saw what many an older general might have missed: what the Twelfth lacked in strength it might well make up by the fierceness and dedication of young officers and cadets.

Wenck thought he saw a way to use his green but enthusiastic forces as mobile shock troops, rushing them from area to area as needed—at least until his other forces were regrouped and in position. Wenck believed in this fashion his energetic youngsters might buy Germany precious time. Almost his first move as commander was to order his strongest and best-equipped formations into central positions for use on either the Elbe or Mulde rivers. Looking at his map, Wenck circled the areas of probable action—Bitterfeld, Dessau, Belzig, Wittenberge. There was one other site, he thought, where the Americans would surely try to cross the Elbe. Lying within three arms of the river, devastated during the Thirty Years' War and almost wholly destroyed, the town of Magdeburg had risen again. Now, the great fortress with its island citadel and 11th-century cathedral stood like a beacon in the path of the American armies. Around this area—particularly south of Magdeburg—Wenck assigned the best-equipped of his "Scharnhorst," "Potsdam" and "Von Hutten" units to stand off the U.S. assault as well as they could.

His defenses were planned down to the last detail, his tactics committed to memory by his officers. Now, at Army Group Vistula headquarters, approximately 120 miles northeast of Wenck, Gotthard Heinrici was ready for the battle.

Behind his first *Hauptkampflinie*—the main line of resistance—Heinrici had developed a second line. Just before the expected Russian artillery barrage, Heinrici had told his commanders, he would order the evacuation of the front line. Immediately all troops would retreat to the second *Hauptkampflinie*. It was Heinrici's old Moscow trick of letting the Russians "hit an empty bag." As quickly as the Russian bombardment lifted, the troops were to move forward and take up their front-line positions again. The ruse had worked in the past and Heinrici was counting on its success again. The trick, as always, was to determine the exact moment of attack.

There had been several feints already. In Von Manteuffel's Third Panzer Army sector north of Berlin, General Martin Gareis, commanding the weak 46th Panzer Corps, was convinced that the attack would take place on April 8. The heavy forward movement of vehicles and the deepening concentration of artillery directly in front of Gareis' area seemed to indicate an imminent assault—and captured Russian soldiers had even boasted of the date. Heinrici did not believe the reports. His own intelligence, plus his old habit of trusting his instinct, told him the date was too early. As it turned out, he was right. All along the Oder front, April 8 was quiet and uneventful.

Yet Heinrici's vigilance was now unceasing. Each day he flew over the Russian lines in a small reconnaissance plane, observing troop and artillery dispositions. Each night he painstakingly studied late intelligence reports and prisoner interrogations, searching always for the clue that might pinpoint the time of attack.

It was during this tense and critical period that Reichsmarschall Hermann Goering summoned Heinrici to his castle for lunch. Though Heinrici was desperately weary and loath to be gone from his headquarters even for a few hours, he could not refuse. Karinhall, the Reichsmarschall's huge estate, lay only a few miles from the Vistula headquarters at Birkenhain. The grounds were so vast that Goering even had his own private zoo. As they approached, Heinrici and his aide, Captain von Bila, were amazed by the magnificence of Goering's parklike holdings, with the vistas of lakes, gardens, landscaped terraces and tree-lined drives. Lining the road from the main gates to the castle itself were units of sprucely uniformed Luftwaffe paratroopers—Goering's personal defense force.

The castle, like Goering himself, was both massive and opulent. The reception hall reminded Heinrici of "a church so large, so huge, that one's eye automatically traveled up to the roof beams." Goering, resplendent in a white hunting jacket, greeted Heinrici coolly. His attitude was a portent of what was to come, for the luncheon was a disaster.

The Reichsmarschall and the General disliked each other intensely. Heinrici had always blamed Goering for the loss of Stalingrad where, despite all his promises, the Luftwaffe had been unable to supply the cut-off troops of Von Paulus' Sixth Army. But Heinrici would have disliked the Reichsmarschall in any case for his arrogance and pomposity. For his part, Goering found Heinrici dangerously insubordinate. He had never forgiven the General for leaving Smolensk unscorched, and in the past few days, his distaste for Heinrici had greatly increased. Heinrici's remarks about the 9th Paratroopers at the Führer's conference had rankled deeply.

The day following that meeting, Goering had telephoned Vistula headquarters and had spoken to Colonel Eismann. "It is inconceivable to me," said the Reichsmarschall angrily, "that Heinrici would talk about my paratroopers the way he did. It was a personal insult! I still have the 2nd Parachute Division and you can tell your commander from me that he's not getting them. No! I'm giving them to Schörner. There's a real soldier! A true soldier!"

Now, at the luncheon, Goering turned his attack directly on Heinrici. He began by sharply criticizing the troops he had seen during recent trips along the Vistula front. Sitting back in a huge thronelike chair and waving a large silver beaker of beer, Goering accused Heinrici of poor discipline throughout his command. "I've driven all over your armies," he said, "and in one sector after another I found men doing nothing! I saw some in foxholes playing cards! I found men from the labor organization who didn't even have spades to do their jobs. In some places, I found men without field kitchens! In other sections almost nothing has been done to build defenses. Everywhere I found your people loafing, doing nothing." Taking a great swallow of beer, Goering said menacingly, "I intend to bring all this to the attention of the Führer."

Heinrici saw no point in arguing. All he wanted to do was get away. Keeping his temper in check, Heinrici somehow got through the meal. But, as Goering saw his two visitors to the door, Heinrici paused, looking slowly around the magnificent grounds and the impressive castle with its turrets and wings. "I can only hope," he said, "that my loafers can save this beautiful place of yours from the battles that lie ahead." Goering stared icily for a moment, then turned on his heel and walked back inside.

Goering would not have Karinhall much longer, Heinrici thought as he drove away. He was beginning to reach a conclusion about the timing of the Russian attack, based on intelligence reports, aerial observations, the steadily dropping flood waters of the Oder and that intuition which had never yet betrayed him. Heinrici believed the attack would begin within the week—somewhere around the fifteenth or sixteenth of April.

* * *

Pulling back the covering sheet on the table, Marshal Georgi Zhukov exposed the huge relief map of Berlin. It was more a model than a map, with miniature government buildings, bridges and railroad stations showing in exact replica against the principal streets, canals and airfields. Expected defensive positions, flak towers and bunkers were all neatly marked, and small green tags, each with a number, flagged principal objectives. The Reichstag was labeled 105, the Reichskanzlei 106; 107-8 were the offices of the Ministries of Internal and Foreign Affairs.

The Marshal turned to his officers. "Look at Objective 105," he said. "Who is going to be the first to reach the Reichstag? Chuikov and his 8th Guards? Katukov and his tanks? Berzarin and his Fifth Shock Army? Or maybe Bogdanov with his 2nd Guards? Who will it be?"

Zhukov was deliberately baiting his officers. Each was in a frenzy to reach the city first and, in particular, to capture the Reichstag. As General Nikolai Popiel later remembered the scene, Katukov, presumably already there in his mind's eye, said suddenly, "Just think. If I reach 107 and 108, I might grab Himmler and Ribbentrop together!"

All day the briefings had been in progress; along the front preparations for the attacks were nearly complete. Guns and ammunition were positioned in the forests; tanks were moving up so their guns could supplement the artillery when the bombardment began. A vast store of supplies, bridging materials, rubber boats and rafts was ready in the attack areas, and convoy after convoy jammed the roads bringing divisions up to the assembly areas. So frantic were demands for troops that the Russians for the first time were airlifting men from rear areas. It was obvious to Russian soldiers everywhere that the attack would come soon, yet no one below headquarters level had been given the date.

Captain Sergei Ivanovich Golbov, the Red Army correspondent, drove along Zhukov's front watching the massive preparations. Golbov had tapped all his sources in an effort to find out the date of the attack, but without success. Never before had he witnessed activity such as this prior to an attack and he was convinced that the Germans must be watching every move. But, he commented long afterward, "No one seemed to give a damn what the Germans saw."

One aspect of the preparations puzzled Golbov. For days now, anti-aircraft searchlights of all sizes and shapes had been arriving at the front. The crews were women. Moreover, these units were being held well back from the front and carefully hidden beneath camouflage netting. Golbov had never seen so many searchlights before. He wondered what they could possibly have to do with the attack.

* * *

At the Berlin *Reichspostzentralamt*, the Postal Services Administration building in Tempelhof, Reich Postal Minister Wilhelm Ohnesorge leaned over the brilliantly colored sheets of stamps on his desk. They were the first run, and Ohnesorge was inordinately pleased by them. The artist had done a fine job and the Führer was certain to be gratified by the results. With delight he examined two of the stamps more closely. One showed an SS soldier with a Schmeisser machine pistol at his shoulder; the other depicted a uniformed Nazi Party leader, a torch upraised in his right hand. Ohnesorge thought the special commemorative issues did justice to the occasion. They would be on sale on Hitler's birthday, April 20.

STAMPS—COURTESY OF COLONEL HANS REFIOR

A special date was also uppermost in Erich Bayer's mind. The Wilmersdorf accountant had been worrying for weeks about what he would do on Tuesday, April 10—tomorrow. The payment had to be made by then; otherwise all sorts of trouble and red tape could result. Bayer had the money; that was not his problem. But did it matter now? Would the army that captured Berlin—American or Russian—insist on payment? And what if neither got the city? Bayer considered the matter from all sides. Then he went to his bank and withdrew fourteen hundred marks. Entering the office nearby, he made the required down payment on his income tax for 1945.

*　*　*

It happened so fast that everyone was taken by surprise. On the western front, at his Ninth Army headquarters, General Simpson immediately passed the word down to his two corps commanders, Major General Raymond S. McLain of the 19th and the 13th's Major General Alvan Gillem. Official orders would follow, Simpson said, but the word was "Go." Phase 2 was on. It was official. The divisions were to jump off for the Elbe—and beyond. At the 2nd Armored Division headquarters, General White got the news and promptly sent for Colonel Paul A. Disney, commanding the 67th Armored Regiment, the 2nd's lead unit. Upon arrival, Disney remembered, "I barely had time to say 'hello' when White said, 'Take off for the east.' " For just a moment Disney was taken aback. The stand-down had lasted a bare twenty-four hours. Still confused, he asked, "What's the objective?" White answered with just one word: "Berlin!"

✠6✠

I<small>N FIVE GREAT</small> columns, the men of the 2nd Armored Division
sped toward the Elbe and Berlin. They passed lighted German
headquarters without slowing their pace. They swept through
towns where aged Home Guardsmen, guns in their hands, stood
helpless in the streets, too shocked to take action. They raced past
German motorized columns moving out in the same direction.
Guns blazed but nobody stopped on either side. GIs riding on
tanks took potshots at Germans on motorcycles. Where enemy
troops tried to make a stand from dug-in positions, some U.S. commanders used their armor-like cavalry. Major James F. Hollingsworth, coming upon one such situation, lined up thirty-four tanks
and gave a command rarely heard in modern warfare: "Charge!"
Guns roaring, Hollingsworth's tanks raced down toward the enemy positions, and the Germans broke and ran. Everywhere tanks
chewed through enemy positions and across enemy terrain. By
Wednesday evening, April 11, in an unparalleled armored dash,
the Shermans had covered fifty-seven miles—seventy-three road
miles—in just under twenty-four hours. Shortly after 8 P.M., Colonel Paul Disney flashed headquarters a laconic message: "We're
on the Elbe."

One small group of armored vehicles had reached the outskirts
of Magdeburg even earlier. In the afternoon Lieutenant Colonel
Wheeler Merriam's reconnaissance scout cars, traveling at speeds
up to fifty-five miles per hour, had dashed into a suburban area
on the western bank of the Elbe. There the cars were stopped,

not by German defenses, but by civilian traffic and shoppers. The platoon let loose a high burst of machine gun fire in order to clear the streets. The result was chaos. Women fainted. Shoppers huddled in fearful groups or threw themselves flat on the ground. German soldiers ran helter-skelter, firing wildly. Merriam's group lacked the strength to hold the area, but scout cars did manage to disentangle themselves from the mess and get to the airport which had been their objective. As they drove along the edge of the field, planes were landing and taking off. American guns began spraying everything in sight, including a squadron of fighters ready to take to the air. Then the defenses rallied and the platoon of scout cars was pinned down under heavy fire. The vehicles got out with the loss of only one armored car, but their appearance had alerted Magdeburg's defenders. Now, as one American unit after another reached the Elbe on either side of the city, they began to encounter increasingly stiffening resistance. Merriam's scouts, as they pulled back, had reported one vital piece of information: the *Autobahn* bridge to the north of the city was still standing. This immediately became the division's prime objective, for it could carry the 2nd to Berlin. But from the gunfire that met the Americans it was clear that the bridge could not be taken on the run. Magdeburg's defenders were determined to fight. Meanwhile there were other bridges to the north and south. If any one of these could be grabbed before the enemy destroyed it, the 2nd would be on its way.

Seven miles to the south, at Schönebeck, another bridge crossed the Elbe. It was the objective of Major Hollingsworth of the 67th Armored Regiment. All through Wednesday afternoon, Hollingsworth's tanks raced unimpeded through town after town until they reached a place called Osterwieck. There, a regiment of Home Guard units forced a halt in the advance. Hollingsworth was puzzled. Many of the elderly Germans seemed ready to surrender—some had even tied handkerchiefs to their rifles and had raised them above their foxholes—yet there was no letup in the fighting. A prisoner, taken within the first few minutes, explained:

eleven SS soldiers in the town were forcing the Home Guardsmen to fight. Angrily, Hollingsworth swung into action.

Calling for his jeep, and taking along an extra sergeant and a radio operator as well as the driver, the major circled the area and entered the town along a cow path. He cut a strange figure. Twin Colt automatics were strapped low on his hips, Western style; for added measure, he carried a tommy gun. Hollingsworth was a deadly shot who had personally killed over 150 Germans. Grabbing a passing civilian, he demanded to know where the SS troops were quartered. The terrified man immediately pointed to a large house and barn nearby, surrounded by a high fence. Noting a doorway in the fence, Hollingsworth and his men leaped from the car and, from a running start, smashed the door with their shoulders, ripping it off its hinges. As they crashed into the yard, an SS man rushed toward them, machine pistol raised; Hollingsworth riddled the man with his tommy gun. The other three Americans began throwing grenades into the windows. Looking quickly about, the major spotted another SS man in the open hayloft doors of the barn and beat him to the draw with his .45. Inside the buildings they found the bodies of six grenade victims; the three other SS men surrendered. Hollingsworth rushed back to his column. He had been held up for forty-five precious minutes.

Three hours later, Hollingsworth's tanks breasted the high ground overlooking the towns of Schönebeck and Bad Salzelmen. Beyond, glittering in the early evening light, lay the Elbe, at this point almost five hundred feet wide. As he surveyed the area through binoculars, Hollingsworth saw that the highway bridge was still standing—and with good reason. German armored vehicles were using it to flee east across the river. How, Hollingsworth wondered, with enemy armor all around could he grab the bridge before it was blown?

As he watched, a plan began to form. Calling two of his company commanders, Captain James W. Starr and Captain Jack A. Knight, Hollingsworth outlined his idea. "They are moving along this north-to-south road running into Bad Salzelmen," he said. "Then they swing east at the road junction, head into Schönebeck and cross the bridge. Our only hope is to charge into Bad Salzelmen and grab the junction. Now, here's what we'll do. When we get to the junction, your company, Starr, will peel off and block the road, holding the Germans coming up from the south. I'll join onto the rear of the German column that has already swung east into Schönebeck and follow it across the bridge. Knight, you come up behind. We've got to get that bridge and, by God, we're going to do it."

Hollingsworth knew that the plan would work only if they could move fast enough. The light was fading; with luck, the German tanks would never know they had company behind them as they crossed the bridge.

Within moments, Hollingsworth's tanks were on their way. Hatches buttoned up, they charged into Bad Salzelmen; before the Germans were aware of what was happening, Starr's vehicles had blocked the road from the south and were engaging the line of panzers. The German tanks leading the column had already made the turn, heading for the bridge. Apparently hearing the sound of firing behind, they began to speed up. At that moment Hollingsworth's tanks filled the gap in their column and followed along at the same speed.

But then they were spotted. Artillery mounted on flat cars in the nearby railway yard opened fire on the rear of the U.S. column. As Hollingsworth's Shermans turned into Schönebeck, a German Mark V tank, its turret revolving, drew a bead on the lead American. Staff Sergeant Cooley, Hollingsworth's gunner, opened fire and blew up the Mark V. Slewing sideways, the panzer smashed into a wall and began burning furiously. There was barely room for Hollingsworth's tank to get by, but weaving ponderously it edged through, followed by the rest of the column. Firing at the rear of each enemy vehicle and squeezing by the burning panzers, the American tanks charged through the town. By the time they reached its center, as Hollingsworth remembered, "everyone was firing at everyone else. It was the damnedest mess. Germans were hanging out of windows, either shooting at us with their *Panzerfäuste* or just dangling in death."

Hollingsworth's tank had not been hit and he was now only three or four blocks from the bridge. But the last stretch was the worst. As the remaining tanks pressed on, enemy fire seemed to come from everywhere. Buildings were blazing and, although by now it was 11 P.M., the scene was so brightly lit that it might still have been day.

Ahead lay the approach to the bridge. The tanks rushed forward. The entrance, blocked from Hollingsworth's earlier view from the heights, was a maze of stone walls jutting out at irregular intervals from either side of the road; the vehicles had to slow and make sharp left and right maneuvers before reaching the center span. Jumping from his tank, Hollingsworth reconnoitered to see if he could both lead the way and direct his gunner's fire via the telephone hooked to the back of the tank. At that instant an anti-tank shell exploded fifteen yards ahead of Hollingsworth. Cobblestone fragments flew through the air and suddenly the major found his face was a mass of blood.

A .45 in one hand and the tank telephone in the other, he doggedly moved toward the bridge. His tank collided with a jeep and Hollingsworth called for infantrymen. Leading them onto the approach, he began working his way through the roadblocks, exchanging steady fire with the Germans who were fiercely defending the way. A bullet struck him in the left knee but he kept the lead, urging the infantry on. At last, staggering and half-blinded by his own blood, Hollingsworth was stopped. A rain of fire was coming from the German positions and Hollingsworth was forced to order a withdrawal. He had come to within forty feet of the bridge. When Colonel Disney, his commanding officer, arrived on the scene he found the major "unable to walk and bleeding all over the place. I ordered him back to the rear." Hollingsworth had missed taking the bridge by minutes. Had he succeeded, he believed he could have reached Berlin within eleven hours.

At dawn on April 12, as infantry and engineers tried once again to seize the Schönebeck bridge, the Germans blew it up in their faces.

High above the Ninth Army front Lieutenant Duane Francies put the unarmed spotting plane, the Piper Cub *Miss Me,* into a wide turn. Riding behind Francies was his artillery observer, Lieutenant William S. Martin. The two men had scouted for the 5th Armored all the way from the Rhine, locating strongpoints and radioing the positions to the oncoming tanks. It was not all routine work; more than once Francies and Martin had buzzed enemy troops, taking potshots at columns with their Colt .45's.

Off to the east the clouds had opened and the fliers could see chimney stacks faint in the distance. "Berlin!" Francies shouted, pointing ahead. "The factories at Spandau." Each day now, as the 5th advanced steadily, Francies searched for different city landmarks from his lofty vantage point. When the *Miss Me* led the tanks into Berlin, the young pilot wanted to be able to recognize instantly the main roads and buildings so as to inform the tankers about them. He intended to give "the boys" the full tour treatment as they approached Berlin.

Francies was almost ready to head back to a pasture near the lead columns when he suddenly pushed the stick forward. He had spotted a motorcyclist with a sidecar speeding out of a road close by some of the 5th's tanks. As he began a dive to check out the vehicle, he glanced to his right and stiffened in amazement. Flying only a few hundred feet above the trees and almost indistinguishable was a Fieseler Storch, a German artillery-spotting plane. As the *Miss Me* drew closer, the white crosses on fuselage and wings showed prominently against the Storch's gray-black body. Like the Cub, this was a fabric-covered, high-wing monoplane, but it was larger than *Miss Me* and, as Francies knew, at least a good thirty miles an hour faster. The American, however, had the advantage of altitude. Even as Francies yelled, "Let's get him!" he heard Martin urging the same thing.

By radio Martin reported that they had spotted a German plane and announced calmly "we are about to give combat." On the ground, astounded 5th Armored tankers, hearing Martin's call, craned their necks skyward searching out the impending dogfight.

Martin got the side doors open as Francies dived. Swinging the Cub into a tight circle over the German plane, both men blasted away with their .45's. Francies hoped the fire would force the German over the waiting tanks where machine gunners could easily bring it down. But the pilot of the enemy plane, though obviously confused by the unexpected attack, was not that obliging. Violently sideslipping, the Storch began circling wildly. Above it, Francies and Martin, like frontier stagecoach guards, were leaning out of their own plane emptying their automatics as fast as they could pull the triggers. To Francies' amazement, there was no answering fire from the German. Even as the Americans reloaded, the Storch pilot, instead of putting distance between them, kept on circling. Later, Francies could only surmise that the pilot was still trying to figure out what was happening to him.

Now, dropping to within twenty feet of the enemy plane, the two Americans put bullet after bullet into the German's windshield. They were so close that Francies saw the pilot "staring at us, his eyeballs as big as eggs." Then suddenly the German maneuvered wildly and spun in. Martin, who had been giving a rapid running account of the fight on the radio, yelled, "We got him! We got him!" His voice was so blurred with excitement that Lieutenant Colonel Israel Washburn, sitting in his half-track, thought Martin said "We got hit!"

The Storch spiraled down, its right wing hit the ground, snapped off, and the plane cartwheeled and came to rest in the middle of a pasture. Francies set the *Miss Me* down in the next field and ran across to the downed plane. The German pilot and his observer were already out, but the observer had been hit in the foot and fell to the ground. The pilot dived behind a huge pile of sugar beets until a warning shot from Martin brought him out, hands in the air. As Martin covered the pilot with his gun, Francies examined the wounded observer. When he removed the German's boot, a .45 slug fell out. As he bandaged the superficial wound, the German kept repeating, *"Danke. Danke. Danke."*

Later that day, Francies and Martin posed happily beside their captured prize. They had fought what was probably the last World War II dogfight in the European theater and they were undoubtedly the only airmen in this war to bring down a German plane with a pistol. For Francies "it was a day of pure joy." The only thing that could top this experience would be guiding the 5th Armored into Berlin. Francies believed he would have only a day or two to wait before the order came.*

As the platoon of tanks led by Lieutenant Robert E. Nicodemus approached Tangermünde at noon, they were met by an ominous silence. The objective of this unit of the 5th Armored Division was the bridge in the picturesque little city, which was some forty miles northeast of Magdeburg. Now that the bridge at Schönebeck was gone, the Tangermünde bridge was the most important one in the war, to the Ninth Army at least.

Nicodemus' tank rolled down the main street of Tangermünde and into the square. The streets here, as elsewhere in the city, were deserted. Then, as the tanks pulled up in the square, air raid sirens began to wail and, Nicodemus said later, "everything happened at once. All hell broke loose."

From windows, doorways and rooftops that had seemed empty moments earlier, Germans opened fire with bazooka-like anti-tank guns. The Americans answered back. At one moment Sergeant

---

* Francies' extraordinary feat, unequaled in World War II, has never been acknowledged by the U. S. Defense Department. He was recommended for a Distinguished Flying Cross, but never received it. Curiously Martin, though not a flyer, was awarded the Air Medal for his part in the action.

Charles Householder stood in the turret of his tank, blasting away with his tommy gun fire until the tank was hit and he had to jump out. Sergeant Leonard Haymaker's tank, just behind Householder's, was also hit; it burst into flames. Haymaker leaped to safety, but his crewmen were pinned inside by enemy fire. Crouching low and revolving in a slow circle, Haymaker fired short bursts from his tommy gun, covering his men as they escaped.

At the height of the battle, an American soldier jumped on the back of Nicodemus' tank and, shouting above the din, identified himself as an escaped prisoner of war. About five hundred prisoners were being held in the town, he said, in two separate compounds. Nicodemus found himself in a dilemma. He had been about to call for artillery support, but he could hardly shell a town full of American prisoners. He decided to try breaking into the nearest compound to get the prisoners out of the line of fire.

Led by the POW, Nicodemus made his way through buildings and backyards and over fences to an enclosure down by the river. The instant the American prisoners in the compound saw the approaching officer they jumped their guards. The skirmish was brief. As soon as the guards had been disarmed, Nicodemus led the prisoners out. As the group approached the last enemy-held street and saw American tanks beyond, one GI turned to Nicodemus and exulted: "I'm a free man now. They can't kill me." He walked into the middle of the street and a German sniper shot him through the head.

While Nicodemus had been freeing the prisoners, desperate house-to-house fighting had been taking place throughout the city. At last, when the bridge was almost in sight, representatives of the German garrison met the U.S. advance guard and announced their wish to surrender. As the negotiations got under way, there was a tremendous explosion. A huge cloud of dust billowed up and rubble stormed down on the city. German engineers had blown the bridge. The Victory Division, closest American unit to the capital, had been stopped a tantalizing fifty-three miles from Berlin.

Anxiety began to spread through the Ninth Army Command. Up to mid-afternoon of April 12 there had been every reason for confidence. The 5th Armored had traveled a phenomenal 200 miles in just thirteen days; the 2nd had advanced the same distance in just one day more. Altogether, Simpson's army had raced nearly 226 miles since leaving the Rhine. Ninth Army divisions were charging up to the Elbe all along the front.

But no bridges had yet been seized, no bridgeheads established on the river's eastern bank. Many men had hoped for a repetition of the famous capture of the Rhine bridge at Remagen, which in early March had changed Anglo-American strategy overnight. But there had been no such luck. Now, at 2nd Armored headquarters a decision was reached: the river must be forced. Troops would make an amphibious assault on the Elbe's eastern bank to secure a bridgehead. Then a pontoon bridge would be built across the river.

At his headquarters, Brigadier General Sidney R. Hinds, commander of the 2nd's Combat Command B, laid his plans. The operation would take place south of Magdeburg, at a small town called Westerhüsen. At best, the plan was a gamble. Enemy artillery fire might destroy the bridge before its completion or, worse, prevent bridging operations altogether. But the longer Hinds waited, the more concentrated the enemy's defenses might become. And with each hour of delay, the chance of beating the Russians into Berlin grew slimmer.

At 8 P.M. on April 12, two battalions of armored infantry were quietly ferried across to the eastern bank in the amphibious vehicles known as DUKWs. The crossing was unopposed. By midnight the two battalions were over and by first light a third had joined them. On the eastern bank, troops quickly deployed, digging defensive positions in a tight semicircle about the selected pontoon site. Jubilantly, General White put in a telephone call to the Ninth Army commander, General Simpson: "We're across!"

* * *

The Germans learned of the crossing almost as soon as Simpson. At Magdeburg, the combat commander, a veteran of Normandy, immediately got word to General Wenck at Twelfth Army headquarters.

The Magdeburg officer, an expert artilleryman, had long ago learned not to underestimate the enemy. Early on the morning of June 6, 1944, he had looked out from his forward artillery post and had seen the Allied invasion fleet. Then, as now, he had promptly informed his superiors of the situation. "It's the invasion," he had said. "There must be ten thousand ships out there." His incredible message was not believed. "What way are these ships headed?" he was asked. His reply was stark and simple: "Right for me."

Now Major Werner Pluskat, the man who had directed the German fire from the center of Omaha Beach, prepared to make a stand on the Elbe. His gunners along the river, north and south of Magdeburg, would hold back the Americans as long as they could. But Pluskat had been around too long to have any doubts about the outcome.

However, the young cadets on whom General Wenck was depending had no pessimistic thoughts. Eager and fresh, they were looking forward to the battles ahead. Now mobile combat units of the Potsdam, Scharnhorst and Von Hutten divisions were rushing into position, preparing to erase the American bridgehead on the eastern bank of the Elbe.

* * *

On the west bank of the Elbe, engineers worked frantically. Searchlights, hurriedly positioned, were pointed straight up to reflect off the clouds, and in this artificial moonlight the first pontoons were secured and pushed into the river. One after another, the floating units were locked in place.

Standing close by, Colonel Paul A. Disney, the 67th Armored Regiment commander, watched the bridging operation with growing impatience. Suddenly shells screamed in. As they exploded about the first few pontoons, fountains of water shot up in the air. The fire pattern was unusual: the shells did not land in salvos; they came in singly, apparently from several widely positioned guns. Disney, certain that the fire was being directed by an artillery observer hidden nearby, ordered an immediate search of the rundown four-story apartment houses overlooking the river. The search yielded nothing; the fire continued, accurate and deadly.

Ripped pontoons sank, and the shrapnel lashing the water repeatedly forced the bridge-builders to take cover. Wounded men were dragged to the safety of the river bank; others took their places. All through the night the firing went on, nullifying the grim persistence of the American engineers. The one thing Hinds had feared most had happened. Grimly he ordered an infantry unit on a forced march south. Its instructions: find another site.

The following morning the rest of the bridge was destroyed by German gunfire. When the last shells screamed in and demolished the twisted and battered span, the bridge was only seventy-five yards from the eastern shore. Hinds, set-faced and weary, ordered the site abandoned. As the men assembled with their wounded, a message arrived: infantry on the eastern bank had found a suitable bridging area farther down the river.

By the afternoon of Friday the thirteenth, DUKWs were towing a heavy cable across the river to the newest bridgehead. The cable was intended as a stopgap. Once in place it would haul a string of pontoons back and forth across the river, bearing vehicles, tanks and guns. Although this system was desperately slow it would have to serve until bridging materials could be brought up.

The matter of greatest concern to Hinds now was the fate of the three battalions on the east bank of the river. With their backs to the Elbe, the troops were manning a rough semicircle in the area of the twin villages of Elbenau and Grünewalde. It was a small beachhead, and they had no armor support or artillery except for the batteries on the western banks. If the three battalions were hit by any attack in strength, the situation could become perilous. Hinds now ordered Colonel Disney across the Elbe in a DUKW to take command of the infantry.

Disney found the first of the three battalion command posts, headed by Captain John Finnell, in a patch of woods. Finnell was worried. German pressure was building up. "If we don't get tanks over here real quick," he said, "there's going to be bad trouble."

After briefing Hinds on the situation by radio, Disney set out to find the second battalion. As he moved down near the river, shells began to land all around him. Disney dived into a ditch, but the shells came closer, so he climbed out and started for another one. This time luck was against him. He felt a rain of shrapnel, then another. A third burst knocked him down. Disney lay there, barely conscious and severely wounded. His left upper arm was gouged and riddled and a large piece of shrapnel had torn away the upper part of his right thigh.

Within thirty-six hours, Hollingsworth and Disney, two of the men most fiercely dedicated to leading American forces to Berlin, had been put out of action.

At 1:15 P.M. on April 12, at about the time lead tanks of the 5th Armored Division were rolling into Tangermünde, President Franklin D. Roosevelt died at his desk in Warm Springs.

An artist was working on a portrait of him when suddenly the President put a hand to his head and complained of a headache. A short while later he was dead. On his desk lay a copy of the Atlanta *Constitution*. The headline read: 9TH—57 MILES FROM BERLIN.

It was nearly twenty-four hours later before news of the President's death began filtering down to the front-line troops. Major Alcee Peters of the 84th Division heard the news from a German.

At a railroad crossing near Wahrenholz an aging flagman came up to offer him sympathy because "the news is so terrible." Peters felt shock and disbelief but before he fully absorbed what he had heard, his column moved out again, heading for the Elbe, and he had other matters to think about. Lieutenant Colonel Norman Carnes, commanding a battalion of the 333rd Infantry Regiment, was traveling through a bombed-out oil field north of Brunswick when he learned of FDR's death. He felt regret, but his mind, too, was on his work. "It was just another crisis," he later said. "My next objective was Wittingen and I was busy thinking about that. Roosevelt, dead or alive, couldn't help me now." Chaplain Ben Rose wrote to his wife Anne: "All of us were sorry . . . but we've seen so many men die that most of us know that even Roosevelt is not indispensable. . . . I was surprised how calmly we heard the news and talked about it."

✵   ✵   ✵

Joseph Goebbels could scarcely contain himself. The moment he heard the news he telephoned Hitler in the Führerbunker. "My Führer, I congratulate you! Roosevelt is dead!" he exulted. "It is written in the stars. The last half of April will be the turning point for us. This is Friday, April 13. It *is* the turning point!"

Sometime earlier Goebbels had passed along two astrological predictions to Count Schwerin von Krosigk, Reichsminister of Finance. One had been prepared for Hitler the day he took power, January 30, 1933. The other, dated November 9, 1918, had dealt with the future of the Weimar Republic. Krosigk noted in his diary: "An amazing fact had become evident. Both horoscopes predicted the outbreak of war in 1939, the victories until 1941, and the subsequent series of reversals—with the hardest blows during the first months of 1945, especially in the first half of April. Then, there was to be an overwhelming victory in the second half of April, stagnation until August, and peace the same month. For the following three years Germany would have a difficult time, but starting in 1948 she would rise again."

Goebbels also had been reading Thomas Carlyle's *History of Friedrich II of Prussia,* and it had given him further cause for delight. One chapter told of the Seven Years' War (1756-1763) when Prussia had stood alone against a coalition of forces that included France, Austria and Russia. In the sixth year of this struggle, Frederick had told his advisors that if by February 15 there was no change in his fortunes, he would commit suicide. Then on January 5, 1762, Czarina Elizabeth died and Russia withdrew from the conflict. "The miracle of the House of Brandenburg," wrote Carlyle, "had come to pass." The whole character of the war had changed for the better. Now, in the sixth year of World War II, Roosevelt was dead. The parallel was inescapable.

The Propaganda Minister was in ecstasy. At the Ministry of Propaganda he ordered champagne for everyone.

* * *

"Get across! Get across! And keep moving!" Colonel Edwin "Buckshot" Crabill of the 83rd Division stalked up and down the river bank, pushing men into assault boats and, here and there, helping slow starters with the toe of his boot.

"Don't waste this opportunity," he yelled at another boatload. "You're on your way to Berlin!" As other men began to move across in DUKWs, the short, peppery Crabill admonished them, "Don't wait to organize! Don't wait for someone to tell you what to do! Get over there in any shape you can! If you move *now,* you can make it without a shot being fired!"

Crabill was right. At the town of Barby, fifteen miles southeast of Magdeburg and just below the spot where their arch rivals, the 2nd Armored, were desperately trying to make use of their cable ferry, the men of the 83rd were crossing the river in droves, unopposed. They had entered the town to find that the bridge had been blown but, without waiting for orders from the 83rd's commanding officer, Crabill had ordered an immediate crossing. Assault boats had been rushed up and in a matter of hours a full battalion had been put across. Now another was en route. Simultaneously, artillery was being floated over on pontoons and engineers were building a treadway bridge that should be finished by nightfall. Even Crabill was impressed by the frenetic activity his orders had set off. As he dashed from group to group urging more speed, he kept repeating triumphantly to the other officers, "They'll never believe this back at Fort Benning!"

Watching the feverish scene in silence was an audience of Germans, standing on a balcony below the clock tower of the town hall. For hours, as Lieutenant Colonel Granville Sharpe, commanding an infantry battalion, cleaned up what little resistance there was in the town, he had been aware of the audience, and he had grown increasingly annoyed. "My men were being shot at, but there stood the Germans watching the fighting and the river assault with intense interest," he recalled. Now Sharpe had had enough. Going up to a tank, he told the gunner. "Put one round through the clock face at, say, about five o'clock." The tanker obliged, scoring a clean bull's-eye on the number five. The gallery suddenly dispersed.

In any case, the show was over. The 83rd was across. The first solid bridgehead had been established on the east bank of the Elbe.

By the evening of the thirteenth, engineers had finished their task and, thorough to the end, had put up a sign on the approach to the bridge. In honor of the new President and, with the division's customary high morale and keen appreciation for the value of advertising, it read: TRUMAN BRIDGE. GATEWAY TO BERLIN. COURTESY OF THE 83RD INFANTRY DIVISION.

The news was flashed back to General Simpson and from there to General Bradley. He immediately telephoned Eisenhower. Suddenly the 83rd's bridgehead was uppermost in everybody's thoughts. The Supreme Commander listened carefully to the news. Then, at the end of the report, he put a question to Bradley. As Bradley later reconstructed the conversation, Eisenhower asked: "Brad, what do you think it might cost us to break through from the Elbe and take Berlin?"

Bradley had been considering that same question for days. Like Eisenhower, he did not now see Berlin as a military objective, but if it could be taken easily he was for its capture. Still, Bradley, like his chief, was concerned about too deep a penetration into the future Soviet zone and about the casualties that would occur as U.S. troops moved forward into areas from which, eventually, they would have to withdraw. He did not believe losses on the way to Berlin would be too high, but it might be a different story in the city itself. Taking Berlin might be costly.

Now he answered the Supreme Commander, "I estimate that it might cost us 100,000 men."

There was a pause. Then Bradley added, "It would be a pretty stiff price to pay for a prestige objective, especially when we know that we've got to pull back and let the other fellow take over." *

There the conversation ended. The Supreme Commander did not reveal his intentions. But Bradley had made his own opinion unmistakably clear: U.S. lives were more important than mere prestige or the temporary occupation of meaningless real estate.

---

* Bradley's estimate has given rise to much confusion, both as to when he gave it to Eisenhower and as to how he arrived at the figure. The incident was first revealed by Bradley himself in his memoir, A Soldier's Story. No date was given. Thus, as Bradley has told the author, he is partly responsible for the uncertainty that resulted. One version that has seen print depicts Bradley as telling Eisenhower at SHAEF as early as January, 1945, that the Berlin casualty figure would reach 100,000. Bradley himself says: "I gave the estimate to Ike on the phone immediately after we got the Elbe bridgehead. Certainly I did not expect to suffer 100,000 casualties driving from there to Berlin. But I was convinced that the Germans would fight hard for their capital. It was in Berlin, as I saw it, that we would have suffered the greatest losses."

At headquarters of the 19th Corps, General McLain stood before his map studying the situation. In his opinion the enemy line on the eastern bank of the Elbe was a hard crust, nothing more. Once his divisions got across and broke through it, nothing would stop them from rolling into Berlin. Colonel George B. Sloan, McLain's Operations Officer, believed the Americans would hit the same sort of opposition they had encountered en route from the Rhine—pockets of last-ditch resistance that could be bypassed by fast-moving forces. He had every confidence that within forty-eight hours of resuming the attack, leading elements of U. S. armored units would enter Berlin.

McLain made a few quick decisions. The surprising accomplishment of the Rag-Tag Circus in grabbing a bridgehead, rushing troops across and then straddling the Elbe with a bridge, all within a few hours, had changed the whole river picture. The men of the 83rd were not merely expanding the beachhead on the eastern bank; they were advancing out of it. McLain was sure that the 83rd's bridgehead was permanent. He was not so sure that the 2nd Armored's puny cable ferry operation would survive the shelling. Still, the 2nd had three battalions across and they were holding. Arrangements had been made for part of the 2nd Armored to begin crossing the 83rd's "Truman Bridge." McLain, therefore, saw no reason for the 30th Division, now moving into position, to attack Magdeburg and go for the *Autobahn* bridge. At the rate the troops were moving now, the 83rd's bridgehead could be quickly expanded to link with the cut-off battalions opposite the 2nd's cable ferry site. From this vastly enlarged bridgehead, the drive could continue. McLain decided to bypass Magdeburg entirely. The Truman Bridge, as the 83rd had anticipated, would be the gateway to Berlin.

At dawn, Saturday, April 14, at the 2nd Armored's cable ferry, General Hinds waited for the three pontoons to be strapped together. They would form the ferry platform which the cable would pull back and forth pending construction of a bridge. Shells were still falling about both banks of the bridgehead and troops on the eastern side were involved in heavy fighting. They could hold out for some time against opposing infantry, but Hinds's great fear was of a panzer attack. The Americans on the east bank were still without supporting artillery or armor.

The first vehicle to roll onto the pontoon ferry was a bulldozer; the eastern bank of the river had to be scraped and graded before tanks and heavy weapons could climb it. A DUKW would tow the platform, speeding the ferry by helping the cable move faster. Hinds watched anxiously. Two cables had been damaged and washed downstream. He had only one left; and his last outsized pontoons had gone to make the ferry.

The cumbersome operation began. As men watched, the ferry moved slowly out into the middle of the Elbe. Then, as it neared the eastern shore, the unbelievable happened. A single shell screamed in and, in a million-to-one shot, severed the cable. Hinds stood frozen in shock as cable, ferry and bulldozer disappeared down the river. Bitterly he said, "There it goes to hell!"

As though the incredible bull's-eye had been a signal for total disaster, word now came that the troops on the eastern bank were being attacked by armored vehicles.

On the eastern side of the Elbe, through the wisps of morning haze and the smoke from artillery fire, Lieutenant Colonel Arthur Anderson watched the German armor smashing through his infantry defense lines. There were seven or eight armored vehicles, among them a couple of tanks. Through his glasses Anderson saw the group, well out of range of his own anti-tank bazookas, firing methodically into the American foxholes. Even as he watched, one of his companies holding positions on the far right of his command post was overrun. Troops dashed from their foxholes, making for the safety of the woods. Now the Germans were working over the positions of Anderson's other two companies, blasting the foxholes one by one. Frantically Anderson radioed the batteries on the Elbe's western bank for help. But the attack had taken place so fast that even as the 2nd Armored's shells came screaming in, Anderson knew they were too late.

Farther along the bridgehead, Lieutenant Bill Parkins, commanding I Company, suddenly heard his machine guns open up and then the answering fire of German burp guns. A platoon runner dashed up. Three German vehicles with infantry, he reported, were coming down along the line, "cleaning out everything as they go." Parkins sent back word to the troops to remain in position and to keep firing. Then he dashed out of his command post to find out for himself what was happening. "I saw three Mark V tanks about a hundred yards away, approaching from the east," he later reported, "and each one appeared to have a platoon of infantry with it. They had American prisoners marching in front. Their guns were firing right through them." Some of Parkins' men returned the fire with their bazookas, but the range was too great; those projectiles that hit merely ricocheted off the tanks. His men were being chewed up. Parkins ordered them to pull back, before they were all captured or killed.

From north, east and south of the bridgehead German vehicles came in fast. Staff Sergeant Wilfred Kramer, in charge of an infantry platoon, saw a German tank about 220 yards away. Infantry was fanned out about it and coming up behind. Kramer ordered his men to wait. Then, when the Germans were about forty yards away, he yelled to open fire. "We were doing all right and holding our own," he later explained. "But then the tank opened up. The first round landed about ten yards from our machine gun. Then Jerry went right down the line. He could see where every one of our holes was. It was point-blank fire." Kramer held out for as long as he dared; then he, too, ordered his men back.

The fighting was so fierce around Grünewalde that Lieutenant Colonel Carlton E. Stewart, commanding a battalion, got a call for artillery from one of his companies and was told to "throw it right on our positions as our men are in the cellars of the houses." Everyone was asking for air strikes to knock out the tanks, but only a few planes showed up during the entire dawn-to-noon battle. In the dash to the Elbe, fighter strips had been left so far behind that the planes had to carry extra gasoline wing tanks to keep up with the ground advance and that meant they couldn't carry bombs.

By noon General Hinds had ordered all infantry on the east bank to withdraw back across the Elbe. Although casualties were at first thought to be high, men kept trickling in for days. Total east bank casualties were ultimately set at 304; one battalion lost 7 officers and 146 enlisted men killed, wounded or missing. The fight ended the last hope of getting a 2nd Armored bridge or bridgehead across the Elbe. Now General White, the 2nd's commander, had no choice but to use the 83rd's bridge at Barby. The Germans had halted successfully, and with lightning speed, the great momentum that the 2nd Armored had built up.

The erasing of the bridgehead had been so sudden and the fighting so fierce that American commanders did not even know what units had attacked them. In fact, they were scarcely units at all. As General Wenck had foreseen, his fledgling cadets and training officers had served him well. Ambitious and eager for glory, they had pushed themselves and their meager equipment to the limit, buying the time Wenck needed. In throwing back the 2nd Armored Division these mobile shock troops had accomplished something no other German unit had managed in thirty months of combat. Had the division been able to secure either a bridge or a bridgehead across the Elbe, the 2nd might have roared right on to Berlin without ever waiting for orders.

The Supreme Commander's plan of attack on Germany had unfolded brilliantly; indeed, the speed of the great Anglo-American advance had clearly surprised even him. In the north Montgomery's Twenty-first Army Group was moving steadily. The Canadians, closing on Arnhem, were ready to begin clearing out the big enemy pocket that remained in northeast Holland. The British Second Army had crossed the river Leine, captured the town of Celle and were on the outskirts of Bremen. In the center of the Reich the surrounded Ruhr was almost reduced and, most important, Simpson's Ninth Army, along with the U.S. First and Third armies, had almost cut Germany in two. The First was advancing on Leipzig. Patton's Third was nearing the Czech border.

But these whirlwind gains had taken a toll: they had stretched Eisenhower's supply lines almost to the limit. Apart from truck convoys, there was virtually no land transport available to Bradley's forces; only one railroad bridge was still in operation over the Rhine. The fighting forces remained well supplied, but SHAEF staff officers were disturbed by the total picture. To serve the farflung armies, hundreds of Troop Carrier Command planes had been ordered to fly around the clock, bringing up supplies. On April 5 alone, a flying train of C-47s had carried more than 3,500 tons of ammunition and supplies and almost 750,000 gallons of gasoline to the front.

In addition, as the Allies pushed deeper and deeper into Germany, they had to supply increasing thousands of noncombatants. Hundreds of thousands of German prisoners of war had to be fed. Forced laborers from a score of countries and liberated British and American POWs had to be given shelter, food and medical services. Hospitals, ambulance convoys and medical supplies were only now moving up. And although these medical facilities were vast, an unforeseen demand was suddenly thrust upon them.

In recent days, what would prove to be the greatest hidden horror of the Third Reich had begun to be uncovered. All along the front in this tremendous week of advance, men had recoiled in shock and revulsion as they encountered Hitler's concentration camps, their hundreds of thousands of inmates, and the evidence of their millions of dead.

Battle-hardened soldiers could scarcely believe what they were seeing as scores of camps and prisons fell into their hands. Twenty years later men would remember those scenes with grim anger: the emaciated walking skeletons who tottered toward them, their will to survive the only possession they had saved from the Nazi regime; the mass graves, pits and trenches; the lines of crematoriums filled with charred bones, mute and awful testimony to the systematic mass extermination of "political prisoners"—who had been put to death, as one Buchenwald guard explained, because "they were only Jews."

Troops found gas chambers, set up like shower rooms except that cyanide gas instead of water sprayed from the nozzles. In the Buchenwald commandant's home there were lampshades made from human skin. The commandant's wife, Ilse Koch, had book covers and gloves made from the flesh of inmates; two human heads, shrunken and stuffed, were displayed on small wooden stands. There were warehouses full of shoes, clothing, artificial limbs, dentures and eyeglasses—sorted and numbered with detached and methodical efficiency. Gold had been removed from the dentures and forwarded to the Reich finance ministry.

How many had been exterminated? In the first shock of discovery no one could even estimate. But it was clear as reports came in from all along the front that the total would be astronomical. As to who the victims were, that was only too obvious. They were, by the Third Reich's definition, the "non-Aryans," the "culture-tainting inferiors," peoples of a dozen nations and of a dozen faiths, but predominantly Jews. Among them were Poles, Frenchmen, Czechs, Dutchmen, Norwegians, Russians, Germans. In history's most diabolical mass murder, they had been slain in a variety of unnatural ways. Some were used as guinea pigs in laboratory experiments. Thousands were shot, poisoned, hanged or gassed; others were simply allowed to starve to death.

In the camp at Ohrdruf, overrun by the U.S. Third Army on April 12, General George S. Patton, one of the U.S. Army's most hard-bitten officers, walked through the death houses, then turned away, his face wet with tears, and was uncontrollably ill. The next day Patton ordered the population of a nearby village, whose inhabitants claimed ignorance of the situation within the camp, to view it for themselves; those who hung back were escorted at rifle point. The following morning the mayor of the village and his wife hanged themselves.

Along the British route of advance, the discoveries were equally terrible. Brigadier Hugh Glyn Hughes, the British Second Army's Senior Medical Officer, had been worrying for days about the possibility of infectious diseases in a camp he had been warned about at a place called Belsen. Upon arrival there, Hughes discovered that typhus and typhoid were the least of his worries. "No photograph, no description could bring home the horrors I saw," he said, years later. "There were 56,000 people still alive in the camp. They were living in 45 huts. There were anywhere from 600 to 1,000 people living in accommodations which could take barely 100. The huts overflowed with inmates in every state of emaciation and disease. They were suffering from starvation, gastroenteritis, typhus, typhoid, tuberculosis. There were dead everywhere, some in the same bunks as the living. Lying in the compounds, in uncovered mass graves, in trenches, in the gutters, by the side of the barbed wire surrounding the camp and by the huts, were some 10,000 more. In my thirty years as a doctor, I had never seen anything like it."

To save those still living, armies all along the front had to get immediate medical help. In some instances military needs had to take second place. "I do not believe," Hughes later said, "that anyone realized what we were going to be faced with or the demands that would be made on the medical services." Doctors, nurses, hospital beds and thousands of tons of medical stores and equipment were urgently needed. Brigadier Hughes alone required a 14,000-bed hospital—even though he knew that, no matter what steps were taken, at least 500 inmates would die each day until the situation could be brought under control.

General Eisenhower made a personal tour of a camp near Gotha. Ashen-faced, his teeth clenched, he walked through every part of the camp. "Up to that moment," he later recalled, "I had known about it only generally or through secondary sources. . . . I have never at any other time experienced an equal sense of shock."

The psychological effect of the camps on officers and men was beyond assessment. On the Ninth Army front in a village near Magdeburg, Major Julius Rock, a medical officer with the 30th Infantry, came up to inspect a freight train which the 30th had stopped. It was loaded with concentration camp inmates. Rock, horrified, immediately unloaded the train. Over the local burgomaster's vehement protests, Rock billeted the inmates in German homes—but not until his battalion commander had given a crisp command to the complaining burgomaster. "If you refuse," he said simply, "I'll take hostages and shoot them."

A cold determination to win and win quickly was replacing every other emotion in the men who had seen concentration camps. The Supreme Commander felt much the same way. On his return to SHAEF from Gotha he wired Washington and London urging that editors and legislators be sent immediately to Germany to see the horror camps at first hand so that the evidence could be "placed before the American and British publics in a fashion that would leave no room for cynical doubt."

But before Eisenhower could press on to end the war, he had to consolidate his farflung forces. On the night of the fourteenth, from his office in Reims, Eisenhower cabled Washington of his future plans.

Having successfully completed his thrust in the center, Eisenhower said, he was confronted by two main tasks: "the further sub-division of the enemy's remaining forces; and the capture of those areas where he might form a last stand effectively." Those latter places, Eisenhower thought, would be Norway and the National Redoubt of Bavaria. In the north, he planned to throw Montgomery's forces forward across the Elbe, to secure Hamburg and drive for Lübeck and Kiel. In the south, he planned to send General Devers' Sixth Army Group toward the Salzburg area.

"Operations in the winter," Eisenhower stated, "would be extremely difficult in the National Redoubt. . . . The National Redoubt could remain in being even after we join the Russians . . . so we must move rapidly before the Germans have the opportunity to thoroughly prepare its defenses with men and material."

As for the German capital, Eisenhower thought it would also be "most desirable to make a thrust to Berlin as the enemy may group forces around his capital and, in any event, its fall would greatly affect the morale of the enemy and that of our own peoples." But, said the Supreme Commander, that operation "must take a low priority in point of time unless operations to clear our flanks proceed with unexpected rapidity."

In brief, then, his plan was: (1) "to hold a firm front in the central area on the Elbe"; (2) to begin operations toward Lübeck and Denmark; and (3) to initiate a powerful thrust" to meet Soviet troops in the Danube valley and break up the National Redoubt. "Since the thrust on Berlin must await the outcome of the first three above," Eisenhower said, "I do not include it as a part of my plan."

On the Elbe, all through the night of the fourteenth, men of the Rag-Tag Circus and the 2nd Armored moved across the 83rd's bridges at Barby. Although a second bridge had been built near the first, the movement across remained slow. General White's armored column, however, planned to begin the Berlin drive again the moment it reassembled on the western bank. Among the troops of the 83rd the story was going the rounds that Colonel Crabill had offered to lend the 2nd Armored a large, newly confiscated red bus, capable of holding fifty soldiers, which he had liberated in Barby. The 83rd had every reason to feel triumphant. Already its patrols were north of the town of Zerbst, less than forty-eight miles from Berlin.

Early Sunday morning, April 15, the Ninth Army commander, General Simpson, got a call from General Bradley. Simpson was to fly immediately to the Twelfth Army Group headquarters at Wiesbaden. "I've something very important to tell you," Bradley said, "and I don't want to say it on the phone."

Bradley was waiting for his commander at the airfield. "We shook hands," Simpson recalled, "and there and then he told me the news. Brad said, 'You must stop on the Elbe. You are not to advance any farther in the direction of Berlin. I'm sorry, Simp, but there it is.'"

"Where in the hell did you get this?" Simpson demanded.

"From Ike," Bradley said.

Simpson was so stunned he could not "even remember half of the things Brad said from then on. All I remember is that I was heartbroken and I got back on the plane in a kind of a daze. All I could think of was, How am I going to tell my staff, my corps commanders and my troops? Above all, how am I going to tell my troops?"

From his headquarters Simpson passed the word along to his corps commanders; then he left immediately for the Elbe. General Hinds encountered Simpson at the 2nd's headquarters and seeing him became worried. "I thought," Hinds recalled, "that maybe the old man didn't like the way we were crossing the river. He asked how I was getting along." Hinds answered, "I guess we're all right now, General. We had two good withdrawals. There was no excitement and no panic and our Barby crossings are going good."

"Fine," said Simpson. "Keep some of your men on the east bank if you want to. But they're not to go any farther." He looked at Hinds. "Sid," he said, "this is as far as we're going." Hinds was shocked into insubordination. "No, sir," he said promptly. "That's not right. We're going to Berlin." Simpson seemed to struggle to control his emotions. There was a moment of uneasy silence. Then

Simpson said in a flat, dead voice, "We're not going to Berlin, Sid. This is the end of the war for us."

Between Barleben and Magdeburg where elements of the 30th Division troops were still advancing toward the river, the news spread quickly. Men gathered in groups, gesturing and talking both angrily and excitedly. P.F.C. Alexander Korolevich of the 120th Regiment, Company D, took no part in the conversation. He wasn't sure if he was sad or happy, but he simply sat down and cried.

*　*　*

Heinrici recognized all the signs. At one part of the front the Russians had laid down a short artillery barrage; in another section they had launched a small attack. These were feints and Heinrici knew it. He had learned all the Russian ruses years before. These small actions were the prelude to the main attack. Now, his main concern was how soon he should order his men back to the second line of defense.

While he was pondering the question, Reichsminister Albert Speer, the Armament and Production Chief, arrived. This was one day Heinrici did not want visitors—especially someone as nervous and obviously harassed as Speer. In the confines of Heinrici's office, Speer explained the nature of his visit. He wanted the General's support. Heinrici must not follow Hitler's "scorched-earth" orders to destroy German industry, power plants, bridges and the like. "Why," Speer asked, "should everything be destroyed with Germany even now defeated? The German people must survive."

Heinrici heard him out. He agreed that the Hitler order was "vicious," he told Speer, and he would do everything in his power to help. "But," cautioned Heinrici, "all I can do right now is to try and fight *this* battle as well as I can."

332

Suddenly Speer pulled a pistol out of his pocket. "The only way to stop Hitler," he said suddenly, "is with something like this."

Heinrici looked at the gun, his eyebrows raised.

"Well," he said coldly, "I must tell you that I was not born to murder."

Speer paced the office. He seemed not even to have heard Heinrici. "It is absolutely impossible to make it clear to Hitler that he should give up," he said. "I have tried three times, in October, 1944, in January and in March of this year. Hitler's reply to me on the last occasion was this: 'If a soldier had talked to me this way I would consider he had lost his nerve and I would order him shot.' Then he said, 'In this serious crisis leaders must not lose their nerves. If they do they should be done away with.' It is impossible to persuade him that everything is lost. Impossible."

Speer put the pistol back in his pocket. "It would be impossible to kill him anyway," he said in a calmer voice. He did not tell Heinrici that for months he had been thinking of assassinating Hitler and his entire court. He had even thought up a scheme to introduce gas into the ventilating system of the Führerbunker, but it had proved impossible: a twelve-foot-high chimney had been built around the air intake pipe. Now Speer said: "I could kill him if I thought I could help the German people, but I can't." He looked at Heinrici. "Hitler has always believed in me," he said. Then he added, "Anyway it would somehow be indecent."

Heinrici did not like the tone of the conversation. He was also worried about Speer's manner and inconsistencies. If it ever became known that Speer had talked to him this way, everyone at his headquarters would probably be shot. Heinrici deftly brought the conversation back to the original subject, the protection of Germany from the scorched-earth policy. "All I can do," the Vistula commander reiterated, "is to perform my duty as a soldier as well as I can. The rest lies in the hands of God. I will assure you of this. Berlin will not become a Stalingrad. I will not let that happen."

The fighting in Stalingrad had been street by street, block by block. Heinrici had no intention of letting his troops fall back to

Berlin under Russian pressure and there fight a similar kind of battle. As for Hitler's instructions to destroy vital installations, throughout his army group area Heinrici had already privately countermanded that order. He told Speer that he expected the Berlin Commandant, General Reymann, momentarily. He had invited Reymann, Heinrici said, to discuss these very matters and to explain personally why it was impossible to take the Berlin garrison under the Vistula command. A few moments later Reymann arrived. With him was Heinrici's Chief of Operations, Colonel Eismann. Speer remained throughout the military conference.

Heinrici told Reymann, as Eismann was later to note, "not to depend on the Vistula Army Group for support." Reymann looked as though his last hope was gone. "I do not know, then," he said, "how I can defend Berlin." Heinrici expressed the hope that his forces could bypass Berlin. "Of course," he added, "I may be *ordered* to send units into Berlin, but you should not depend on it."

Reymann told Heinrici that he had received orders from Hitler to destroy bridges and certain buildings in the city. Heinrici replied angrily, "Any demolition of bridges or anything else in Berlin will merely paralyze the city. If by any chance I am ordered to include Berlin in my command I will forbid such demolitions."

Speer added his weight to the discussion, begging Reymann not to carry out the orders. In such a case, he said, most of the city would be cut off from water and electric supplies. As Eismann recalled Speer's words, he said, "If you destroy these supply lines, the city will be paralyzed for at least a year. It will lead to epidemic and hunger for millions. It's your duty to prevent this catastrophe! It's your responsibility not to carry out these orders!"

The atmosphere, as Eismann remembered, was charged with tension. "A hard struggle was going on within Reymann," he said. "Finally he answered in a hoarse voice that he had done his duty as an officer in an honorable manner; his son had fallen at the front; his home and possessions were gone; all he had left was his honor. He reminded us of what had happened to the officer who failed to blow up the Remagen bridge: he had been executed like a common criminal. The same, Reymann thought, would happen to him if he did not carry out his orders."

Both Heinrici and Speer tried to dissuade him, but they could not change his mind. At last Reymann took his leave. Shortly thereafter Speer drove away, too. Finally Heinrici was alone—to concentrate on the one thing uppermost in his mind: the timing of the Russian attack.

The latest batch of intelligence reports had arrived at the headquarters and they seemed to point to an immediate assault. General Reinhard Gehlen, OKH Chief of Intelligence, had even included the most recent prisoner interrogations. One report told of a Red Army soldier from the 49th Rifle Division who "stated that the major offensive operation will begin in about five to ten days." There was talk, the prisoner had said, "among Soviet soldiers that Russia will not allow the U.S. and England to claim the conquest of Berlin." A second report was similar and contained even more speculation. A prisoner of the 79th Corps taken earlier in the day near Küstrin said that when the attack began, its main purpose would be "to get to Berlin ahead of the Americans." According to the soldier, "brushes were expected with the Americans" who would be "covered 'by mistake' with artillery fire so that they will feel the force of Russian artillery."

*   *   *

In Moscow on this same day, Sunday, April 15, Ambassador Averell Harriman met with Stalin to discuss the war in the Far East. Prior to the meeting, General Deane of the U. S. Military Mission had drawn Harriman's attention to German radio reports which stated that the Russians were expected to attack Berlin at any moment. Harriman, as the conference with Stalin ended, casually brought up the matter. Was it true, he asked, that the Red Army was about to renew its offensive on Berlin? The Marshal's answer, as General Deane was to cable Washington that evening, was: "Stalin said there was indeed going to be an offensive and that he did not know if it would be successful. However the main blow of this attack would be aimed toward Dresden, not Berlin, as he had already told Eisenhower."

✴   ✴   ✴

THE FUHRER'S COURT

Hitler with his personal pilot, Baur. Between them is the famous portrait of Frederick the Great, which hung in the Führerbunker and which Hitler gave to Baur as a parting gift.

Hitler with Erich Kempka, his chauffeur.

Hitler and Eva Braun, in happier days.

WIDE WORLD PHOTO

Reichsmarschall Hermann Goering.

Reichsführer Heinrich Himmler.

Martin Bormann.

Minister of Propaganda Joseph Goebbels.

Frau Goebbels and five of her six children by Goebbels. The older boy, a child by her previous marriage, survived the war.

From left to right:
Albert Speer, Admiral Doenitz, Colonel General Jodl, seen here after their capture.

The dining hall in Hitler's Reichskanzlei, with the shattered
chandeliers hanging to the floor.

The Reichskanzlei in ruins.

Below, the entrance to Hitler's bunker. On
the left is the area in which the bodies of
Hitler and Eva Braun were drenched in
gasoline and set alight.

All through the remainder of the afternoon, Heinrici went over intelligence reports and talked with his staff and army officers on the telephone. Then, a little after 8 P.M., he made a decision. He had analyzed all the reports from the field; he had assessed and evaluated every nuance of his old enemy's moves. Now, as he walked the length of his office, hands clasped behind his back, his head bowed in concentration, he paused; to an intently watching aide "it was as though he had suddenly sniffed the very air." He turned to his staff. "I believe," he said quietly, "the attack will take place in the early hours, tomorrow." Beckoning to his Chief of Staff, he issued a one-line order to General Busse, commanding the German Ninth Army. It read: "Move back and take up positions on the second line of defense." The time was now 8:45 P.M. In exactly seven hours and fifteen minutes, on Monday, April 16, the *Giftzwerg* would begin to fight Germany's last battle.

Part Five

THE BATTLE

✤ 1 ✤

ALONG THE FIRST Belorussian Front, in the deep darkness of the forests, there was complete silence. Beneath the pines and camouflage netting the guns were lined up for mile after mile and stepped back caliber by caliber. The mortars were in front. Behind them were tanks, their long rifles elevated. Next came self-propelled guns and, following these, batteries of light and heavy artillery. Along the rear were four hundered *Katushkas*—multibarreled rocket launchers capable of firing sixteen projectiles simultaneously. And massed in the Küstrin bridgehead on the Oder's western bank were the searchlights. Everywhere now in these last few minutes before the attack the men of Marshal Georgi Zhukov's armies waited for zero hour—4 A.M.

Captain Sergei Golbov's mouth was dry. With each passing moment it seemed to him that the stillness was becoming more intense. He was with troops north of Küstrin on the eastern bank of the Oder, at a point where the flooded river was almost five hundred yards wide. Around him, he would later relate, were "swarms of assault troops, lines of tanks, platoons of engineers with sections of pontoon bridges and rubber boats. Everywhere the bank of the river was jammed with men and equipment and yet there was complete silence." Golbov could sense "the soldiers almost trembling with excitement—like horses trembling before the hunt." He kept telling himself that "somehow I had to survive this day, for

345

there was so much I had to write." Over and over he kept repeating, "This is no time to die."

In the center, troops were jammed into the bridgehead on the river's western bank. This key lodgment—it was now thirty miles long and ten miles deep—which the Russians had wrested from General Busse in late March, was to be the springboard for Zhukov's drive on Berlin. From here the men of the crack Eighth Guards Army would launch the assault. Once they seized the critical Seelow Heights directly ahead and slightly to the west, the armor would follow. Guards Lieutenant Vladimir Rozanov, 21-year-old leader of an artillery reconnaissance section, stood on the west bank near the Red Army girls who would operate the searchlights. Rozanov was sure that the lights would drive the Germans mad; he could hardly wait for the girls to switch them on.

In one respect, however, Rozanov was unusually concerned about the forthcoming attack. His father was with Marshal Koniev's forces to the south. The young officer was angry with his father; the older man had not written the family in two years. Nevertheless, he had high hopes that they might meet in Berlin—and perhaps go home together after the battle. Although he was fed up with the war, Rozanov was glad to be on hand for the last great assault. But the waiting was almost unbearable.

Farther along the bridgehead, Gun Crew Chief Sergeant Nikolai Svishchev stood by his battery. A veteran of many artillery barrages, he knew what to expect. At the moment the firing began, he had warned his crew, "roar at the top of your voices to equalize the pressure, for the noise will be terrific." Now, gun lanyard in hand, Svishchev awaited the signal to open fire.

South of Küstrin, in the bridgehead around Frankfurt, Sergeant Nikolai Novikov of a rifle regiment was reading the slogans scrawled on the sides of nearby tanks. "Moscow to Berlin," read one. Another said: "50 kilometers to the lair of the Fascist Beast." Novikov was in a frenzy of excitement. His enthusiasm had been whetted by a morale-building speech given by one of the regiment's political officers. The impassioned and optimistic pep talk had so stirred Novikov that he had promptly signed an application to join the Communist Party.*

In a bunker built into a hill overlooking the Küstrin bridgehead, Marshal Zhukov stood gazing impassively into the darkness. With him was Colonel General Chuikov, the defender of Stalingrad and commander of the spearhead Eighth Guards Army. Ever since Stalingrad, Chuikov had suffered from eczema. The rash had particularly affected his hands; to protect them, he wore black gloves. Now, as he waited impatiently for the offensive to begin, he nervously rubbed one gloved hand against the other. "Vasili Ivanovich," Zhukov suddenly asked, "are all your battalions in position?" Chuikov's answer was quick and assured. "For the last forty-eight hours, Comrade Marshal," he said. "Everything you have ordered, I have done."

Zhukov looked at his watch. Settling himself at the bunker's aperture, he tilted back his cap, rested both elbows on the concrete ledge and carefully adjusted his field glasses. Chuikov turned up the collar of his greatcoat and, pulling the flaps of his fur cap over his ears to muffle the sound of the bombardment, took up a position beside Zhukov and sighted his own binoculars. Staff officers clustered behind them or left the bunker to watch from the hill outside. Now everyone gazed silently into the darkness. Zhukov glanced once more at his watch and again looked through the glasses. The seconds ticked away. Then Zhukov said quietly, "Now, Comrades. Now." It was 4 A.M.

Three red flares soared up suddenly into the night sky. For one interminable moment the lights hung in midair, bathing the Oder in a garish crimson. Then, in the Küstrin bridgehead Zhukov's phalanx of searchlights flashed on. With blinding intensity the 140 huge anti-aircraft lights, supplemented by the lights of tanks, trucks and other vehicles, focused directly ahead on the German

---

* Many soldiers joined the Party on the Oder, for reasons which were not always political. Unlike American or British forces, the Red Army had no system of registration of identification discs or "dog tags"; families of Red Army men killed or wounded in action were rarely officially informed. But if a Communist soldier became a casualty, the Party notified his family or next of kin.

positions. The dazzling glare reminded war correspondent Lieutenant Colonel Pavel Troyanoskii of "a thousand suns joined together." Colonel General Mikhail Katukov, Commander of the First Guards Tank Army, was taken completely by surprise. "Where the hell did we get all the searchlights?" he asked Lieutenant General N. N. Popiel of Zhukov's staff. "The devil only knows," Popiel replied, "but I think they stripped the entire Moscow anti-aircraft defense zone." For just a moment there was silence as the searchlights illuminated the area ahead of Küstrin. Then three green flares soared into the heavens and Zhukov's guns spoke.

With an earsplitting, earthshaking roar the front erupted in flame. In a bombardment that had never been equaled on the eastern front, more than twenty thousand guns of all calibers poured a storm of fire onto the German positions. Pinned in the merciless glare of the searchlights, the German countryside beyond the western Küstrin bridgehead seemed to disappear before a rolling wall of bursting shells. Whole villages disintegrated. Earth, concrete, steel, parts of trees spewed into the air and in the distance forests began to blaze. To the north and south of Küstrin thousands of gun flashes stabbed the darkness. Pinpoints of light, like deadly firecrackers, winked in rapid succession as tons of shells slammed into targets. The hurricane of explosives was so intense that an atmospheric disturbance was created. Years later German survivors would vividly recall the strange hot wind that suddenly sprang up and howled through the forests, bending saplings and whipping dust and debris into the air. And men on both sides of the line would never forget the violent thunder of the guns. They created a concussion so tremendous that troops and equipment alike shook uncontrollably from the shock.

The storm of sound was stupefying. At Sergeant Svishchev's battery the gunners yelled at the tops of their voices but the concussion of their guns was so great that blood ran from their ears. The most fearsome sound of all came from the *Katushkas* or "Stalin Organs," as the troops called them. The rocket projectiles whooshed off the launchers in fiery batches and screeched through the night, leaving long white trails behind them. The terrifying noise they made reminded Captain Golbov of huge blocks of steel grinding together. Despite the terrible racket, Golbov found the bombardment exhilarating. All around him he saw "troops cheering as though they were fighting the Germans hand-to-hand and everywhere men were firing whatever weapon they had even though they could see no target." As he watched the guns belching flames, he remembered some words his grandmother had once uttered about the end of the world, "when the earth would burn and the bad ones would be devoured by fire."

Amid the tumult of the bombardment Zhukov's troops began to move out. Chuikov's well-disciplined Eighth Guards led the way from the Küstrin bridgehead on the Oder's western banks. As they surged forward, the artillery barrage remained always in front of them, carpeting the area ahead. North and south of Küstrin, where assault crossings had to be made across the flooded river, engineers were in the water laying pontoons and fitting together prefabricated sections of wooden bridges. All around them waves of shock troops were crossing the Oder without waiting for the bridges, tossing and bobbing in a variety of assault boats.

In the ranks were troops who had stood at Leningrad, Smolensk, Stalingrad and before Moscow, men who had fought their way across half a continent to reach the Oder. There were soldiers who had seen their villages and towns obliterated by German guns, their crops burned, their families slain by German soldiers. For all these the assault had special meaning. They had lived for this moment of revenge. The Germans had left them nothing at home to return to; they had nowhere to go but forward. Now they attacked savagely. Equally avid were the thousands of recently released prisoners of war: reinforcements had been so urgently needed by the Red Army that the newly freed prisoners—tattered, emaciated, many still showing the effects of brutal treatment—had been given arms. Now they, too, rushed forward, seeking a terrible vengeance.

Cheering and yelling like wild tribesmen, the Russian troops advanced on the Oder's eastern banks. Caught up in a kind of frenzy, they found it impossible to wait for boats or bridges. Golbov watched in amazement as soldiers dived in, fully equipped, and began swimming the river. Others floated across clutching empty gasoline cans, planks, blocks of wood, tree trunks—anything that would float. It was a fantastic spectacle. It reminded Golbov of "a huge army of ants, floating across the water on leaves and twigs. The Oder was swarming with boatloads of men, rafts full of supplies, log floats supporting guns. Everywhere were the bobbing heads of men as they floated or swam across." At one point Golbov saw his friend, the regimental doctor, "a huge man named Nicolaieff, running down the river bank dragging behind him a ridiculously small boat." Golbov knew that Nicolaieff was "supposed to stay behind the lines at the field hospital, but there he was in this tiny boat, rowing like hell." It seemed to Golbov that no power on earth could stop this onslaught.

Abruptly the bombardment ended, leaving a stunning silence. The cannonade had lasted a full thirty-five minutes. In Zhukov's command bunker, staff officers suddenly became aware that the phones were ringing. How long the sound had been going on, no one could say; all were suffering from some degree of deafness. Officers began taking the calls. Chuikov's commanders were making their first reports. "So far everything is going as planned," Chuikov told Zhukov. A few moments later he had even better news. "The first objectives have been taken," he announced proudly. Zhukov, a tense figure since the opening of the attack, became suddenly expansive. As General Popiel recalled, Zhukov "seized Chuikov by the hand and said, 'Excellent! Excellent! Very good indeed!' " But pleased as he was, Zhukov had too much experience to underestimate his enemy. The stocky Marshal would feel better when the vital Seelow Heights near Küstrin was seized. Then, he felt, success would be assured. Still, that should not take long. Apart from everything else, Russian bombers were now airborne and beginning to pound the areas ahead. More than 6,500 planes were scheduled to support his and Koniev's attacks. But Zhukov believed that the artillery bombardment alone must certainly have demoralized the enemy.

* * *

In the operations room of his advance command post in the Schönewalde forest north of Berlin, Colonel General Gotthard Heinrici paced the floor, hands behind his back. Around him telephones shrilled and staff officers took reports, carefully transcribing the information onto the war map lying on a table in the center of the room. Every now and then Heinrici paused in his pacing to glance at the map or to read a message handed him by Colonel Eismann. He was not surprised by the way the Russian offensive was being carried out, although most of his officers were awestruck by the massiveness of the bombardment. General Busse of the Ninth Army described it as "the worst ever," and Colonel Eismann, basing his opinion on early reports, believed the "annihilating fire had practically destroyed our front-line fortifications."

Under darkness on the night of the fifteenth, the majority of the Vistula troops had swung back to the second line of positions as Heinrici had ordered. But there had been difficulties. Some officers had bitterly resented giving up their front-line positions. It looked to them as though they were retreating. Several commanders had complained to Heinrici. "Has it ever occurred to you," he inquired icily of one protesting general, "that nothing will be left of your nice front-line fortifications or of your men after the Russians open fire? If you're in a steel mill you don't put your head under a trip hammer, do you? You pull it back in time. That is precisely what we're doing."

The difficult stratagem had taken most of the night. From all reports, in the areas where troops had been withdrawn the maneuver had proved successful. Now in the second line the men waited for the advancing Russians. On one part of the front Heinrici had the advantage: west of Küstrin was the sandy, horseshoe-shaped plateau of the Seelow Heights. It ranged in height from one hundred to two hundred feet and it overlooked a spongy valley known, for the streams veining through it, as the Oder Bruch. The Russians would have to cross this valley in their advance from the Oder, and all along the crescent-shaped plateau Heinrici's guns were trained on the lines of approach.

Here, on these critical heights, lay Heinrici's only chance to blunt Zhukov's attack, and Heinrici knew Zhukov would undoubtedly have given this fact great consideration in his planning. The Russian would need to seize the plateau quickly, before Heinrici's guns could shell the Red Army's Oder bridges and create havoc among the troops advancing across the low-lying, marshy terrain. Obviously Zhukov had hoped to knock out almost all resistance with his massive bombardment, making the capture of the Heights that much easier. But because of the German withdrawal from the front lines, the majority of Heinrici's army and artillery were intact and in position. The defensive plan had gone well. There was only one thing wrong: Heinrici did not have enough of either men or guns. Without Luftwaffe help in the air and without reserves in men, guns, panzers, ammunition or fuel, Heinrici could only delay Zhukov's offensive. Eventually his enemy must break through.

Along the entire front Heinrici's two armies had fewer than 700 operable tanks and self-propelled guns. These had been dispersed among the various units of the Ninth and Third armies. The heaviest division, the 25th Panzer, had seventy-nine such vehicles; the smallest unit had two. In contrast to Zhukov's artillery strength— 20,000 guns of all calibers*—Heinrici had 744 guns, plus 600 anti-aircraft guns being used as artillery. Ammunition and fuel supplies

---

* Zhukov told General Eisenhower and the press in June, 1945, that he opened the attack with 22,000 guns of all calibers. His original plan called for 11,000 cannon, but whether he had acquired that many by the time of the attack is not known. While Russian accounts give a variety of figures, ranging from twenty to forty thousand guns, most military experts believe that Zhukov had at least seven to eight thousand field pieces and probably the same again in guns of lesser caliber.

were equally critical. Apart from shells stored at battery sites, the Ninth Army had reserves sufficient for only two and a half days.

Heinrici could not hold the Russians for any appreciable length of time—nor could he counterattack, because he had dispersed what little armor and artillery there was to give each unit a fighting chance. He could do only what he had known was possible all along: he could buy a little time. As Heinrici looked at the map and the thick red arrows marking the Russian advances, he thought bitterly of the panzers that had been transferred to Field Marshal Schörner's southern army group to stem the Russian attack which Hitler and Schörner had insisted was heading for Prague. Those armored units would have given Heinrici seven panzer divisions in all. "If I had *them*," he told Eismann sourly, "the Russians wouldn't be having much fun now."

Bad as matters were, the crisis still lay ahead. Zhukov's attack was only the beginning. There were Rokossovskii's forces in the north to reckon with. How soon would they attack Von Manteuffel's Third Army? And when would Koniev launch his offensive in the south?

Heinrici did not have to wait long to learn of Koniev's intentions. The Russians' second blow came along the extreme southern edge of the line held by Busse's army, and into Field Marshal Ferdinand Schörner's sector. At exactly 6 A.M. the troops of Koniev's First Ukrainian Front attacked across the river Neisse.

❂   ❂   ❂

In tight V-formations, the Red fighter planes banked and headed for the river through bursts of bright pink flak and streams of red, yellow and white tracer bullets. Then with dense clouds of white smoke pouring out behind them they screamed up the valley, less than fifty feet above the metallic-gray river Neisse. Again and again the fighters bored through the anti-aircraft barrage, laying a thick, fluffy blanket of smoke that obscured not only the river but the eastern and western banks as well. Marshal Ivan

Koniev, watching from an observation post on a high point directly above the river, was well pleased. Turning to General N. P. Pukhov, whose Thirteenth Army would soon join in the assault, Koniev said, "Our neighbors use searchlights, for they want more light. I tell you, Nikolai Pavlovich, we need more darkness."

Although Koniev was attacking on a front of about fifty miles, he had ordered the smoke screen laid over a distance almost four times as long to confuse the Germans. Now watching through artillery glasses mounted on a tripod, Koniev noted that the smoke was holding. The wind velocity had been figured at only half a meter a second—no more than a mile an hour. With satisfaction he announced that the screen was "the right thickness and density, and exactly the correct height." Then, as the planes continued to lay smoke, Koniev's massed artillery opened up with a tremendous roar.

His bombardment was as merciless as Zhukov's had been, but Koniev was using his artillery strength more selectively. Prior to the attack Koniev's artillery commanders, knowing their observers would be blinded by the smoke screen, had pinpointed every known defense line and enemy strongpoint on topographical maps and had then zeroed in their guns. Besides hitting these pre-selected targets, the First Ukrainian guns were deliberately blasting out avenues running west from the Neisse for the assault troops and tanks that would follow. Rolling barrages, like fiery scythes, methodically chopped paths several hundred yards wide through the German positions. As they did, forests began blazing as they had in Zhukov's area, and seas of flame stretched away from the river for miles ahead.

Koniev was leaving nothing to chance. He was driven not only by his ambition to reach Berlin before Zhukov but by another even more important reason: the unexpected speed of the Western Allies, who were now only forty miles from the city. Koniev thought one or both of two things might happen: Eisenhower's forces might try to reach the capital before the Red Army—and the Germans probably would attempt to make a separate peace with the Western Allies. As Koniev was later to put it: "We did not want to believe that our Allies would enter into any sort of separate agreement with the Germans. However in the atmosphere . . . which abounded in both fact and rumor, we as military men had no right to exclude the possibility. . . . This gave the Berlin operation special urgency. We had to consider the possibility that . . . the Fascist leaders would prefer to surrender Berlin to the Americans and British rather than to us. The Germans would open the way for them, but with us they would fight fiercely and to the last soldier." * In his planning Koniev had "soberly considered the prospect." In order to beat either Marshal Zhukov or the Western Allies to Berlin, Koniev knew that he had to overwhelm the enemy within the first few hours of his attack. Unlike Zhukov, Koniev had no infantry-filled bridgehead on the Neisse's western bank. He had to hurdle the river in force, and it was a formidable obstacle.

The Neisse was an icy, swift-flowing river. In places it was 150 yards wide, and although the eastern banks were relatively flat, the western shore sloped up steeply. The Germans had taken full advantage of these natural defenses; they were now entrenched in a number of heavily fortified concrete bunkers overlooking the river and its eastern approaches. Koniev had to overwhelm the enemy quickly if he was to avoid being pinned down by fire from these bunkers. His plan called for armored divisions to be thrown into the attack the moment footholds were secured on the western banks. But that meant building bridges across the river even be-

---

* Koniev was echoing Stalin's own suspicions. In early April Stalin had cabled Roosevelt that an agreement had been reached at Berne with the Germans whereby they would "open the front to the Anglo-American troops and let them move east, while the British and Americans have promised, in exchange, to ease the armistice terms for the Germans. . . . The Germans on the Western Front have in fact ceased the war . . . [while] . . . they continue the war against Russia, the Ally of Britain and the U.S.A. . . ." Roosevelt answered that he was astonished at the allegation "that I have entered into an agreement with the enemy without first obtaining your full agreement. . . . Frankly I cannot avoid a feeling of bitter resentment toward your informers, whoever they are, for such vile misrepresentations of my actions or those of my trusted subordinates." Stalin and his marshals remained unconvinced. Even today, the latest U.S.S.R. Ministry of Defense history, *The Great Fatherland War of the Soviet Union 1941-45*, says that "to avoid permitting the Red Army from seizing Berlin . . . the Hitlerites . . . were prepared to surrender the capital to the Americans or to the English. Our Allies also counted on seizing . . . [it] . . . in spite of existing agreements . . . consigning Berlin to the operational zone of the Soviet Army. . . ." The fact is, of course, that no such agreement ever existed.

fore the protective smoke screen dissipated and, if the bombardment had not knocked out the enemy, it might have to be done under heavy fire. He intended to make his main crossing in the area of Buchholz and Triebel. But there would also be others. Koniev, convinced that he must achieve the complete and rapid smothering of the enemy, had ordered an enormous river assault, with crossings at more than 150 places. At each site, his engineers had vowed to have bridges or ferries available in one to three hours.

At 6:55 A.M. the second stage of Koniev's plan unfolded. All along the eastern bank first-wave troops emerged from the forests under cover of the continuing artillery fire and, in a miscellaneous collection of boats, headed across the Neisse. Immediately behind them came a second wave of men and behind them a third. In the Buchholz-Triebel area, shock troops of Pukhov's Thirteenth Army swarmed across the choppy waters, dragging sections of pontoon bridges. Leading the way was the 6th Guards Rifle Division, commanded by Major General Georgi Ivanov, a tough 44-year-old Cossack. Ivanov had put everything that would float into the water. Besides pontoons, he used empty aviation fuel tanks and large German fertilizer bins which he had ordered welded to make them airtight; these were manhandled into position as bridging supports. In the water were hundreds of engineers; as fast as prefabricated wooden bridge sections were pushed off the eastern bank the engineers bolted them together. Scores of men stood neck-deep in the icy Neisse holding heavy bridging beams above their heads, while others drove wooden supports into the river bed. Special teams of engineers hauled cables across the Neisse in boats equipped with hand-operated winches. On the western bank they set up ferry heads and then manually wound in the cables, pulling floats with guns and tanks across the river. At some places engineers got guns across without the ferry-floats: they simply dragged them along the river bed on the end of the cables. The operations were moving steadily forward despite enemy fire nearly everywhere along the line. To protect the crossings Ivanov used shore batteries which fired directly above the heads of his troops and into the German defenses on the western bank. He supported these batteries with a hail of fire from no less than two hundred machine guns, "just to keep their heads down."

At 7:15 A.M. Koniev got good news: the first bridgehead had been seized on the western bank. One hour later he learned that tanks and self-propelled guns had been ferried across and were already engaging the enemy. By 8:35, A.M., at the end of a two hour and thirty-five minute bombardment, Koniev knew with absolute certainty that his troops were well established west of the Neisse. They had so far secured 133 of the 150 crossings. Units of Pukhov's Thirteenth Army, together with forces of the Third Guards Tank Army, had already punched through the center in the assault area at Triebel, and by all accounts the enemy in front of them seemed to have cracked. The armor of the Fourth Guards Tank Army was now moving across in the same sector, and to the south men of the Fifth Guards Army were over the river. It looked to Koniev as if his tanks might achieve a breakthrough at any moment.

Once that was accomplished, Koniev planned to dash for the cities of Spremberg and Cottbus. Past Cottbus he would head out on the roadnet for Lübben. That area held special interest for Koniev. It was the terminal point of the boundary line laid down by Stalin, separating Zhukov's First Belorussian Front and his own First Ukrainian Front. If Koniev got there fast enough, he planned to ask Stalin immediately for permission to swing north and head for Berlin. Confident of the go-ahead, Koniev had already sent written orders to Colonel General Pavel Semenovich Rybalko of the Third Guards Tank Army "to be prepared to break into Berlin from the south with a tank corps reinforced with a rifle division from the Third Guards Army." It looked to Koniev as though he might just beat Zhukov to the city. He was so engrossed in the progress of his attack that he did not realize how lucky he was to be alive. In the first moments of the assault a sniper's bullet had drilled a neat hole through the tripod of his artillery glasses, inches away from Koniev's head.*

---

* Koniev did not learn about the incident until twenty years later when he read of it in General Pukhov's memoirs.

* * *

On the eastern fringes of Berlin the hammering of the guns, less than thirty-five miles away, was like the sullen thunder of a far-off storm. In small villages and towns nearer the Oder there were some strange concussion effects. In the police station at Mahlsdorf books fell off their shelves and telephones rang for no reason. Lights dimmed and flickered in many areas. In Dahlwitz-Hoppegarten an air raid siren suddenly went berserk and no one could switch it off. Pictures fell from walls, windows and mirrors shattered. A cross hurtled down from the steeple of a church in Müncheberg, and everywhere dogs began to howl.

In the eastern districts of Berlin the muffled sound echoed and re-echoed in the skeletal, fire-blackened ruins. The fragrant smell of burning pines wafted across the fringes of Köpenick. Along the edges of Weissensee and Lichtenberg a sudden wind caused curtains to whip and flap with ghostly abandon, and in Erkner some inhabitants of air raid shelters were jolted out of sleep, not by noise but by a sickening vibration of the earth.

Many Berliners knew the sound for what it was. In the Möhrings' Pankow apartment where the Weltlingers were hiding, Siegmund, who had been a World War I artilleryman, instantly recognized the far-off sound as that of a massive artillery bombardment; he woke his wife Margarete to tell her about it. At least one Berliner claimed to have actually seen Zhukov's rolling barrage. Shortly after 4 A.M. 16-year-old Horst Römling climbed a seven-story tower on the western edge of Weissensee and stared eastward through field glasses. Horst quickly informed the neighbors he had seen the "flash and glare of Russian guns," but few believed him—he was considered a wild, fanciful boy at best.

The sound did not penetrate the central districts, although here and there some Berliners claimed they heard something unusual. Most thought it was probably anti-aircraft fire, or the detonation of unexploded bombs dropped during the night's two hour and twenty-five minute air raid, or perhaps the sudden collapse of a bomb-blasted building.

One small group of civilians learned almost immediately that the Russian offensive had started. They were the operators in the main post office telephone building on Winterfeldtstrasse in Schöneberg. Within minutes of the opening barrage, long-distance and trunk-line sections of the exchange were jammed with calls. Nervous Nazi Party officials in areas near the Oder and Neisse called administrative heads in Berlin. Fire brigade chiefs asked whether they should try to put out the forest fires or move their equipment out of the areas. Police chiefs phoned their superiors and everybody tried to get through to relatives. As operators were to recall years later, nearly all those completing calls began their conversations with two words: "It's begun!" Switchboard supervisor Elisabeth Milbrand, a devout Catholic, took out her beads and silently said the Rosary.

By 8 A.M. on April 16, most of Berlin had heard on the radio that "heavy Russian attacks continue on the Oder front." The news announcements were guarded, but the average Berliner needed no elaboration. By word of mouth or from relatives outside the city, people learned that the moment they had dreaded had finally arrived. Curiously, at this time the man in the street knew more than Hitler. In the Führerbunker the leader was still sleeping. He had retired a little before 3 A.M. and General Burgdorf, his adjutant, had given strict instructions that the Führer was not to be awakened.

The strange subterranean world of the bunker had an almost cheerful look this morning: there were vases of bright tulips in the little anteroom, the corridor lounge and the small conference room. Earlier one of the Reichskanzlei gardeners had cut them from the few flowerbeds that still remained in the bomb-pitted gardens. It had seemed a good idea to Burgdorf because Eva Braun loved tulips. The Reich's unwed first lady had arrived the night before. With her she had brought some presents for the Führer from old friends in Munich. One was a book sent by Baroness Baldur von

Schirach, wife of the former Reich Youth Leader. The novel's hero bore every misfortune without losing hope. "Optimism," he was made to say "is a mania for maintaining that all is well when things are going badly." The Baroness had thought the book a most appropriate choice. It was Voltaire's *Candide*.

❋   ❋   ❋

At first Zhukov did not believe the news. Standing in the Küstrin command post surrounded by his staff, he stared incredulously at Chuikov and then spluttered in rage. "What the hell do you mean—your troops are pinned down?" he yelled at the Eighth Guards Army commander, and this time there was no friendly use of the General's given names. Chuikov had seen Zhukov angry before and he remained perfectly calm. "Comrade Marshal," he said, "whether we are pinned down temporarily or not, the offensive will most certainly succeed. But resistance has stiffened for the moment and is holding us up."

Heavy artillery fire from the Seelow Heights had hit the troops and supporting tank units as they advanced, Chuikov explained. Also the terrain through which they were moving was proving extremely difficult for armor. In the marshes and irrigation canals of the Oder Bruch self-propelled guns and tanks were thrashing and churning helplessly. A number of mired tanks had been hit, one after another, and had gone up in flames. Up to now, said Chuikov, his Eighth Guards had advanced only fifteen hundred yards. Zhukov, according to General Popiel, gave vent to his fury with "a stream of extremely forceful expressions."

What had happened to the supposedly irresistible offensive? There were a variety of opinions, as General Popiel quickly discovered when he checked Zhukov's senior officers. General Mikhail Shalin, a corps commander of the First Guards Army, told Popiel he was certain "the Germans had been pulled out of the front lines before the attack and placed in a second defensive line along the Seelow Heights. Therefore," said Shalin, "the majority of our shells fell in open country." General Vasili Kuznetsov, commander of the Third Shock Army, was bitterly critical of the First Belorussian plan. "As usual," he told Popiel, "we stuck to the book and by now the Germans know our methods. They pulled back their troops a good eight kilometers. Our artillery fire hit everything but the enemy." General Andreya Getman, a ranking tank expert and corps commander in Katukov's First Guards Tank Army was both critical and angry, particularly about the searchlights. "They didn't blind the main forces of the enemy," he said. "But I'll tell you what they did do—they absolutely spotlighted our tanks and infantry for the German gunners."

Zhukov had never expected the attack to be easy, but although he had anticipated heavy casualties he had deemed it virtually impossible for the Germans to halt his advance. As he later put it, he had counted on "a rapid reduction of the enemy's defenses"; instead, he added in a massive understatement, "the blow by the front's first echelon had proved to be inadequate." He had no doubt that by sheer weight of armies alone he could overwhelm the enemy, but he was bothered by "the danger which now arose that the offensive might be slowed." Zhukov decided to change his tactics. Quickly he rapped out a series of orders. His bomber fleets were to concentrate on the enemy gun positions; at the same time, artillery was to begin pounding the Heights. Then Zhukov took one more step. Although originally his tank armies were not to be committed until after the Seelow Heights had been seized, Zhukov now decided to throw them in immediately. General Katukov, Commander of the First Guards Tank Army, who happened to be in the bunker, got his orders direct. Zhukov left no doubt as to what he wanted: the Heights was to be captured, whatever the cost. Zhukov was going to bludgeon the enemy into submission and, if necessary, bulldoze his way to Berlin. Then, followed by his staff, the stocky Marshal left the command post, his anger over the delay still evident. Zhukov had no intention of being slowed up by a few well-placed enemy guns—nor did he intend to be beaten into Berlin by Koniev. On his way out of the bunker, as offi-

cers stood aside respectfully to let him pass, he suddenly turned
to Katukov and snapped, "Well! Get moving!"

* * *

The Führer's Order of the Day reached General Theodor Busse's
Ninth Army headquarters a little after midday. It was dated April
15 but apparently had been held until Hitler's staff was certain
that the main Russian offensive had begun. Commanders were ordered to disseminate the paper at once, down to company level,
but on no account was it to be published in the public newspapers.

"Soldiers of the German Eastern Front," it read. "For the last
time the deadly Jewish Bolshevist enemy is going over to the attack with his hordes. He is trying to smash Germany and extermi-
nate our people. You soldiers in the East already know the fate
which threatens . . . German women, girls and children. The old
men and children will be murdered; women and girls will be reduced to army camp whores. The remainder will go to Siberia.

"We have expected this attack, and since January everything
has been done to build up a strong front. The enemy is confronted
by a tremendous amount of artillery. Losses in our infantry have
been filled in with countless new units. Alarm units, newly organized units and the Volkssturm are reinforcing our front. This time
the Bolshevist will experience the old fate of Asia: he must and
shall fall before the capital city of the German Reich.

"Whoever does not do his duty at this moment is a traitor to our
people. Any regiment or division which leaves its position acts so
disgracefully that it must be ashamed before the women and children who are withstanding the bomb terror in our cities. Take
heed especially of the few traitorous officers and soldiers who,
in order to save their miserable lives, will fight against us for Russian pay, perhaps even wearing German uniforms. Anyone ordering you to retreat, unless you know him well, is to be taken prisoner at once and if necessary killed on the spot, no matter what
his rank may be. If every soldier at the Eastern Front does his duty

in the coming days and weeks, the last onrush of Asia will be broken, exactly as in the end the penetration of our enemy in the West will fail in spite of everything.

"Berlin will remain German, Vienna* will be German once more and Europe will never be Russian.

"Swear a solemn oath to defend, not the empty concept of a Fatherland but your homes, your wives, your children and thus, our future.

"In these hours the whole German people look to you, my warriors in the East, and only hope that thanks to your constancy, your fanaticism, your weapons, and your leadership the Bolshevist onrush will be smothered in its own blood. At the moment when fate has removed the greatest war criminal † of all time from the earth, the turning point of this war will be decided."

Busse did not need an Order of the Day to tell him that the Russians had to be stopped. Months ago he had told Hitler that if the Russians broke through the Oder line Berlin and the remainder of Germany would fall. But he was angry to read the talk of a strong front; of an enemy confronted by "a tremendous amount of artillery" and "countless new units." Bold words would not stop the Russians. Hitler's Order of the Day was, for the most part, fiction. On one point, however, it was crystal clear: Hitler intended German soldiers to fight to the death—against both West and East.

Busse had harbored a secret hope, so guarded that he had never voiced it aloud to anyone except Heinrici and certain of his closest commanders. He had wanted to stand fast on the Oder long enough for the Americans to arrive. As he put it to Heinrici, "If we can hold until the Americans get here we will have fulfilled our mission before our people, our country and history." Heinrici had responded tartly. "Don't you know about Eclipse?" he asked. Busse had never heard of it. Heinrici told him of the captured plan showing the Allied lines of demarcation and projected zones of occupa-

* Vienna was captured by the Red Army on April 13.
† Hitler was obviously referring to President Roosevelt.

tion. "I doubt," said Heinrici, "that the Americans will even cross the Elbe." Despite all, Busse had continued for a time to cling to the idea. Now he finally abandoned it. Even if Eisenhower's forces were to cross the Elbe and drive for Berlin, it was probably too late. Among other things, Hitler was obviously prepared to contest bitterly every mile of an American advance; he was making no distinction between the democracies and the Communists. Germany's position was hopeless; so, Busse believed, was the Ninth Army's, but as long as Hitler continued the war and refused to capitulate Busse could only try to hold the Russians, as he was doing, up to the very last moment.

The Ninth had taken the full brunt of the Russian attacks; it could not take much more. Yet Busse's forces were still holding nearly everywhere. At Frankfurt, they had actually thrown the Russians back. The guns and troops on the Seelow Heights, though mercilessly bombed and shelled, had doggedly persisted, and had pinned the enemy down. But although Busse's men were stopping the Russians nearly everywhere, it was at terrible cost. In some areas officers reported that they were outnumbered at least ten to one. "They come at us in hordes, in wave after wave, without regard to loss of life," one division commander had telephoned. "We fire our machine guns, often at point-blank range, until they turn red hot. My men are fighting until they run out of ammunition. Then they are simply wiped out or completely overrun. How long this can continue I don't know." Nearly every message was alike. There were frantic calls for reinforcements: guns, tanks and, above all, ammunition and gasoline were needed. One item was irreplaceable: troops. Busse's few reserves were either already committed or were moving up. Most of them were being hurriedly thrown into battle in the crucial Seelow region.

Holding this central area of the Ninth Army was the 56th Panzer Corps. It bore a famous name, but that was about all. The 56th had been shattered and reconstituted many times. Now, once more, it was undergoing a rebuilding process. About all that remained of the original corps was a group of key staff members.

But despite all, the corps had one definite asset—a highly experienced, much decorated commander, Lieutenant General Karl Weidling, a rough-spoken officer known to his friends as "Smasher Karl."

Busse had placed the miscellaneous units in the vital Seelow region under Weidling's command. At the moment Weidling had three divisions: Goering's skittish and unreliable 9th Parachute, the badly mauled 20th Panzer Grenadiers and the understrength Müncheberg Division. Supported by a corps on either side—the 101st on the left, the 11th SS on the right—Weidling's 56th Corps was opposing the Russians' main thrust on Berlin. Although Weidling had arrived only a few days before and was fighting in unfamiliar terrain with weak and often inexperienced forces, the 60-year-old veteran had so far repulsed all attacks.

But he badly needed the remainder of his units and as yet, on this April 16 morning, they had not arrived. Weidling's problems were only beginning. Before the week was out he would be facing crises far greater than any he had ever encountered on a battlefield. Smasher Karl was shortly destined to be condemned to death both by Busse and Hitler—and then, in a strange quirk of fate, in Germany's last hours he would become the defender of Berlin.

On the western front General Walther Wenck, commander of the Twelfth Army, was both pleased and puzzled. The success of his young and inexperienced units in throwing back the enemy and wiping out their bridgehead south of Magdeburg was a greater achievement than Wenck had dared hope for. The bridgehead at Barby, however, was a different story. Wenck's men had tried everything they could think of to destroy the Barby bridges, from floating mines down the river to using frogmen. Some of the last remaining Luftwaffe planes in the area had also made a bombing attack; that, too, had failed. The bridgehead was well established by now and American troops and armor had been pouring across the river for more than forty-eight hours. What puzzled Wenck was that, although the Americans were strengthening and consolidating their hold on the Elbe's eastern bank, they were making no effort whatever to drive toward Berlin. Wenck could not understand it.

The furious assault by the Americans between April 12 and 15 had given Wenck every reason to believe he would be forced to fight a bloody defensive battle in the west. Yet now the Americans gave every appearance of having come to a halt. "Frankly, I'm astonished," Wenck told Colonel Reichhelm, his Chief of Staff. "Maybe they've outrun their supplies and need to reorganize." Whatever the reason, Wenck was glad of the respite. His forces were widely scattered and in many places were still being organized. He needed all the time he could get to whip his army into shape and to reinforce his troops with whatever armor he could lay his hands on. Some tanks and self-propelled guns had arrived, but Wenck had little hope of getting more. Nor did he have any illusions that he would receive the full complement of divisions he had been promised. Wenck suspected that there was simply nothing left to send him. One thing was certain: the Twelfth Army, spread thinly along the Elbe before Berlin, could not hold any sort of onslaught for long. "If the Americans launch a major attack they'll crack our positions with ease," he told Reichhelm. "After that, what's to stop them? There's nothing between here and Berlin."

*　*　*

The news was like a blow to Carl Wiberg. He stared incredulously at his boss, Hennings Jessen-Schmidt, the head of the OSS Berlin unit. "Are you sure?" Wiberg asked. "Are you quite sure?"

Jessen-Schmidt nodded. "That's the information I've received," he said, "and I've no reason to doubt it." The two men looked at each other in silence. For months they had been sustained by the conviction that Eisenhower's forces would capture Berlin. But the news that had brought Jessen-Schmidt across town to Wiberg's apartment had dashed all their hopes. A network courier had just arrived from Sweden with a message of prime importance from London. It warned them not to expect the Anglo-Americans.

In all the long months that he had led his double life in Berlin, Wiberg had considered almost every possibility but this. Even now he could not quite believe it. The change in plan would not affect their jobs, at least for the time being: they were to continue sending out information, and Wiberg, in his role as "storekeeper," would still distribute supplies to operatives when and if the order came. But as far as Wiberg knew, few, if any, of the trained specialists and saboteurs who were supposed to use the equipment had arrived in the city. Jessen-Schmidt had been waiting for weeks for just one man—a radio technician who was to assemble the transmitter and receiver that still lay hidden beneath a pile of coal in Wiberg's cellar. With sinking heart Wiberg wondered if anybody would come now or if the equipment could ever be put to use. That cache of supplies was dangerous. The Germans might yet find it. Worse, the Russians might. Wiberg hoped London had told the Eastern allies about the little group of spies in Berlin. If not, the large store of military material was going to be difficult to explain.

Wiberg also had a personal reason to be anxious. After his long years as a widower he had recently met a young woman named Inge Müller. They planned to marry when the war ended. Now Wiberg wondered how safe Inge would be if the Russians arrived. It seemed to him that the little group of conspirators was doomed in the fiery cauldron that Berlin would soon become. He tried to put aside his fears but he had never felt such dejection. They had been abandoned.

* * *

The commander of the First Guards Tank Army, Colonel General Mikhail Katukov, slammed down the field phone and, whirling around, violently kicked the door of his headquarters. He had just received a report from the officer leading the 65th Guards Tank Brigade on the Seelow Heights front. The Russians were getting nowhere. "We are standing on the heels of the infantry," General Ivan Yushchuk had told Katukov. "We are stuck on our noses!"

His anger somewhat appeased, Katukov turned from the door to face his staff. Hands on his hips, he shook his head in disbelief. "Those Hitlerite devils!" he said. "I have never seen such resistance in the whole course of the war." Then Katukov announced that he was going to find out for himself "what the hell is holding things up." No matter what, he must take the Heights by morning, so Zhukov's breakout could begin.

To the south, Marshal Koniev's forces had smashed through the German defenses on an eighteen-mile front west of the Neisse. His troops were pouring across the river. They now had in operation twenty tank-carrying bridges (some capable of supporting sixty tons), twenty-one ferry and troop-crossing sites and seventeen light assault bridges. With "Stormovik" dive bombers blasting a path, Koniev's tankers had driven more than ten miles through the enemy defenses in less than eight hours of battle. Now Koniev was just twenty-one miles from Lübben, the point at which Stalin had terminated the boundary between his forces and Zhukov's. There, Koniev's tankers would veer northwest and head for the main road leading through Zossen and into Berlin. On the maps this route was labeled Reichsstrasse 96—the highway that Field Marshal Gerd von Rundstedt had called *"Der Weg zur Ewigkeit"*—the road to eternity.

* * *

It almost seemed as if the authorities were not prepared to face the fact that Berlin was endangered. Although the Red Army was now barely thirty-two miles away, no alarm had been given and no official announcement had been made. Berliners knew very well that the Russians had attacked. The muffled thunder of artillery had been the first clue; now from refugees, by telephone, by word of mouth, the news had spread. But it was still fragmentary and contradictory, and in the absence of any real information there was wild speculation and rumor. Some people said the Russians were fewer than ten miles away, others heard that they were already in the eastern suburbs. No one knew precisely what the situation was, but most Berliners now believed that the city's days were numbered, that its death throes had begun.

And yet, astonishingly, people still went about their business. They were nervous, and it was increasingly difficult to preserve the outward appearance of normality, but everyone tried.

At every stop, milkman Richard Poganowska was besieged with questions. His customers seemed to expect him to know more than anyone else. The usually cheerful Poganowska could not provide any answers. He was as fearful as those he served. On the Kreuznacherstrasse the portrait of Adolf Hitler still hung in the living room of the Nazi postal official, but even that no longer seemed reassuring to Poganowska.

He was happy to see his young friend, 13-year-old Dodo Marquardt, waiting patiently for him on a corner in Friedenau. She often rode with him for a block or two, and she helped immeasurably to keep up his morale. Now, sitting next to his dog Poldi, Dodo chattered happily. But Poganowska found it difficult to listen to her this morning. Some newly painted slogans had appeared on the half-demolished walls in the area, and he eyed them without enthusiasm. "Berlin will remain German," one announced. Others read: "Victory or Slavery," "Vienna Will Be German Again," and "Who Believes in Hitler Believes in Victory." At Dodo's usual stop, Poganowska lifted her down from the wagon. With a little smile she said, "Until tomorrow, Mr. Milkman." Poganowska replied, "Until tomorrow, Dodo." As he climbed back on the wagon Richard Poganowska wondered just how many tomorrows there were left.

Pastor Arthur Leckscheidt, presiding over a burial service in the cemetery near his wrecked church, did not think the suffering that lay ahead could be any worse than it was right now. It seemed an eternity since his beautiful Melanchthon Church had been destroyed. During the past few weeks so many had been killed in the raids that his parish clerk no longer registered the deaths. Leckscheidt stood at the edge of a mass grave in which lay the bodies of forty victims killed during the night's air raids. Only a few persons were present as he said the funeral service. As he finished, most of them moved away but one young girl remained behind. She told Leckscheidt that her brother was one of the dead. Then tearfully she said: "He belonged to the SS. He was not a member of the church." She hesitated. "Will you pray for him?" she asked. Leckscheidt nodded. Much as he disagreed with the Nazis and the SS, in death, he told her, he "could deny no man the words of God." Bowing his head he said, "Lord, do not hide your face from me . . . my days have gone like a shadow . . . my life is like nothing before you . . . my time lies in your hands. . . ." On a wall nearby, during the night somebody had scrawled the words "Germany is Victorious."

Mother Superior Cunegundes longed for the end of it all. Even though Haus Dahlem, the convent and maternity home run by the Mission Sisters of the Sacred Heart in Wilmersdorf, was almost a little island in its religious seclusion, the short, round, energetic Mother Superior was not without outside sources of information. The Dahlem Press Club, in the villa of Foreign Minister Joachim von Ribbentrop directly across from the convent, had closed down the night before. From newspaper friends who had come to say good-bye she had heard that the end was near and that the battle for the city would take place within a few days. The resolute Mother Superior hoped the fighting would not be prolonged. What with an allied plane crashing in her orchard and the roof of her convent being blown off a few days before, the danger was coming much too close. It was long past time for this foolish and terrible war to end. In the meantime, she had more than two hundred people to care for: 107 newborn babies (of whom 91 were illegitimate), 32 mothers, and 60 nuns and lay sisters.

As though the Sisters did not have enough to do, Mother Superior had piled even more work upon them. With the janitor's help, some of the nuns had painted huge white circles surmounted by bright red crosses on the sides of the building and on the new tar paper roof which covered the entire second floor (the third floor had disappeared with the roof). Realist that she was, Mother Superior had set her student nurses to converting the dining hall and recreation rooms into first-aid stations. The nurses' dining hall had become the chapel, illuminated by candles night and day; the basement was now partitioned into nurseries and a series of smaller rooms for confinement cases. Mother Superior had even seen to it that all windows in this area were cemented, bricked up and sandbagged from the outside. She was as ready for what might come as she would ever be. But there was one thing she simply did not know how to prepare for: she shared the anxiety of their confessor and mentor, Father Bernhard Happich, that the women might be molested by the occupying forces. Father Happich had arranged to speak to the Sisters about this matter on April 23. Now, in the light of the news her journalist friends had brought, Mother Superior Cunegundes hoped they hadn't waited too long. It looked to her as if the Russians might arrive at any time.

As people waited for news, they hid their anxiety in grim humor. A new greeting swept the city. Total strangers shook hands and urged each other *"Bleib übrig"*—Survive. Many Berliners were burlesquing Goebbels' broadcast of ten days before. Insisting that Germany's fortune would undergo a sudden change, he had said: "The Führer knows the exact hour of its arrival. Destiny has sent us this man so that we, in this time of great external and internal stress, shall testify to the miracle." Now those words were being repeated everywhere, usually in a derisive imitation of the Propaganda Minister's spellbinding style. One other saying was going the rounds. "We've got nothing at all to worry about," people solemnly assured one another. "Gröfaz will save us." Gröfaz had long been the Berliner's nickname for Hitler. It was the abbreviation of *"Grösster Feldherr aller Zeiten"*—the greatest general of all time.

Even with the city almost under the Russian guns, the vast majority of Berlin's industrial concerns were still producing. Shells and ammunition were being rushed to the front as fast as factories in Spandau could make them. Electrical equipment was being turned out at the Siemens plant in Siemensstadt; vast quantities of ballbearings and machine tools were being made in factories at Marienfelde, Weissensee and Erkner; gun barrels and mounts rolled out of the Rheinmetall-Borsig factory at Tegel; tanks, lorries and self-propelled guns rumbled off the assembly lines at Alkett in Ruhleben; and as fast as tanks were repaired at the Krupp und Druckenmüller plant in Tempelhof, workers delivered them directly to the armies. So great was the urgency that the management had even asked foreign workers to volunteer as emergency drivers. French forced laborer Jacques Delaunay was one who flatly refused. "You were very wise," a tank driver who returned to the plant that afternoon told Delaunay. "Do you know where we took those tanks? Right up to the front lines."

Not only industrial plants but services and utilities continued to function. At the main meteorological station in Potsdam, weathermen noted routinely that the noontime temperature was 65 degrees with an expected drop to about 40 by nightfall. The sky was clear with occasional scattered clouds and there was a mild southwest wind which would swing southeast by evening. A change was predicted for the seventeenth—overcast skies with the possibility of thundershowers.

Partly because of the fine weather, streets were crowded. Housewives, not knowing what the future might hold, shopped for unrationed commodities wherever they could. Every shop seemed to have its own long queue. In Köpenick, Robert and Hanna Schultze spent three hours in a line for bread. Who knew when they would be able to buy more? Like thousands of other

Berliners, the Schultzes had tried to find some way to forget their worries. On this day, braving the now capricious transportation system, they changed buses and trams six times to get to their Charlottenburg destination—a movie theater. It was their third such venture in a week. In various districts they had seen pictures called *Ein Mann wie Maximilian* (A Man Like Maximilian); *Engel mit dem Saitenspiel* (Angel with a Lyre) and *Die Grosse Nummer* (The Big Number). *Die Grosse Nummer* was a circus picture, and Robert thought it the best of the week's film fare by far.

French POW Raymond Legathière saw that there was so much confusion at the military headquarters on Bendlerstrasse that his presence would not be missed and he calmly took the afternoon off. These days, the guards did not seem to care anyway. Legathière had managed to wrangle a ticket for a movie theater near the Potsdamer Platz that was reserved for German soldiers. Now he relaxed in the darkness as the picture, specially reissued by Goebbels' Propaganda Ministry, came on. It was a historical full-color epic called *Kolberg*, and it dealt with Graf von Gneisenau's heroic defense of the Pomeranian city during the Napoleonic Wars. During the movie Legathière was as fascinated by the behavior of the soldiers around him as he was by the picture. They were enthralled. Cheering, clapping, exclaiming to one another, they were almost transported by this saga of one of Germany's legendary military figures. It occured to Legathière that before too long some of these soldiers might get a chance to become heroes themselves.

The signal came without warning. In his office in the Philharmonie, the complex of buildings that housed the concert halls and practice studios of the Berlin Philharmonic, Dr. Gerhart von Westermann, the orchestra's manager, received a message from

Reichsminister Albert Speer: the Philharmonic would play its last concert that evening.

Von Westermann had always known that the news would come like this—suddenly and within just a few hours of a concert. Speer's instructions were that all the musicians who would leave were to do so immediately after the performance. They were to end their journey in the Kulmbach-Bayreuth region, about 240 miles southwest of Berlin—the same area to which Speer had earlier sent most of the Philharmonic's prized instruments. According to the Reichsminister, the Americans would overrun the Bayreuth area in a matter of hours.

There was just one trouble. Speer's original design had been to spirit away the entire Philharmonic; this plan had collapsed. To begin with, fearing that the plan might reach Goebbels' ear, Von Westermann had sounded out only certain trusted members of the orchestra. To his amazement the great majority, because of family, sentimental or other ties with the city, were reluctant to leave. When the plan was put to a vote it was turned down. Gerhard Taschner, the young violin virtuoso and concertmaster, was asked to inform Speer. The Reichsminister had taken the news philosophically, but the offer was left open: Speer's own car and driver would be waiting on the final night to take those who wanted to go. Taschner, his wife and two children, along with the daughter of fellow musician Georg Diburtz, were definitely leaving. But they were the only ones. Even Von Westermann, in view of the vote, felt that he must stay.

But if there were any wavering Philharmonic members, they would have to be told that this was their last chance. There was still a possibility that those who were in on the secret might change their minds and decide to leave. So, with the evening's performance barely three hours away, Von Westermann revised the program. It was too late even to schedule a rehearsal, and the musicians who knew nothing of the evacuation plan would be startled by the change. But for the knowing and unknowing alike, the music Speer had picked as the signal marking the last concert would have a dark and moving significance. The scores that Von Westermann now ordered placed on the musicians' stands bore the label, *Die Götterdämmerung*—Wagner's climactic and tragic music of the death of the gods.

By now it was fast becoming clear to all Berliners that "Fortress Berlin" was a myth; even the least knowledgeable could see how ill-prepared the city was to withstand an attack. The main roads and highways were still open. There were few guns or armored vehicles in evidence, and apart from aged Home Guardsmen, some in uniform, others with only armbands sewn on the sleeves of their jackets, there were virtually no troops to be seen.

To be sure, there were roadblocks and crude defense barriers everywhere. In side streets, courtyards, around government buildings and in parks, large stockpiles of fortification materials had been collected. There were occasional rolls of barbed wire, masses of steel anti-tank obstacles and old trucks and disused tram cars filled with stones. These were to be used to block main thoroughfares when the city came under attack. But would barricades such as these stop the Russians? "It will take the Reds at least two hours and fifteen minutes to break through," a current joke went: "Two hours laughing their heads off and fifteen minutes smashing the barricades." Defense lines—trenches, anti-tank ditches, barricades and gun positions—were apparent only on the outskirts, and even these, as Berliners could plainly see, were far from completion.

One man, driving out of the city this day, found the defense preparations "utterly futile, ridiculous!" He was an expert on fortifications. General Max Pemsel had been the Chief of Staff of the Seventh Army defending Normandy on D-Day. Because his forces had failed to stop the invasion, Pemsel, along with others, had been in disgrace with Hitler ever since. He had been put in command of an obscure division fighting in the north and had re-signed himself to this "dead command."

Then on April 2 a surprised Pemsel had received instructions from General Jodl to fly to Berlin. Bad weather had delayed his planes everywhere and he had not reached the capital until April 12. Jodl had admonished him for his tardiness. "You know, Pem-sel," he said, "you were supposed to be appointed commander of Berlin, but you've arrived too late." As he heard these words, Pemsel said later, "a large stone fell off my heart."

Now, instead of taking over the Berlin command, Pemsel was en route to the Italian front: Jodl had appointed him Chief of Staff to Marshal Rodolfo Graziani's Italian Army. Pemsel found the situation almost dreamlike. He considered it doubtful that Graziani's force still existed; nevertheless, Jodl had briefed him on his duties as thoroughly as though the war were proving a bril-liant success and were destined to go on for years. "Your job," he cautioned Pemsel, "will be very difficult because it demands not only great military knowledge but diplomatic skills." Unrealistic as Jodl's outlook was, Pemsel was pleased to be going to Italy. On the way he would pass through Bavaria, and for the first time in two years he would see his wife and family. By the time he reached Italy, perhaps the war would be over.

As Pemsel left Berlin, he felt that fate and the weather had been exceptionally kind to him. It was clear that the city could not be defended. Passing a hodgepodge of tree trunks, steel spikes and cone-shaped concrete blocks that would be used as anti-tank obstacles, he shook his head in disbelief. Still farther along, the car sped by elderly Home Guardsmen slowly digging trenches. As he left the city behind, Pemsel later recounted, "I thanked God for allowing this bitter chalice to pass from me."

At his headquarters on the Hohenzollerndamm, the city's Com-mandant, General Reymann, stood before a huge wall map of Berlin looking at the defense lines marked on it and wondering, as he afterward put it, "what in God's name I was supposed to do." Reymann had hardly slept for the past three days and he was bone-weary. Since morning he had taken countless telephone calls, attended several meetings, visited sections of the perimeter defense lines and issued a batch of orders—most of which, he privately believed, stood little chance of being completed before the Russians reached the city.

Earlier in the day, Goebbels, Berlin's Gauleiter and self-appointed defender, had held his usual weekly "war council." To Reymann, these meetings seemed almost farcical now. In the afternoon he described this latest one to his Chief of Staff, Colonel Refior. "He told me the same old thing. He said, 'If the battle for Berlin was on right now you would have at your disposal all sorts of tanks and field pieces of different calibers, several thousand light and heavy machine guns, and several hundred mortars, in addition to large quantities of corresponding ammunition.'" Reymann paused. "According to Goebbels," he told Refior, "we'll get everything we want—*if* Berlin is encircled."

Then Goebbels had suddenly switched the conversation. "Once the battle for Berlin begins, where do you intend to set up your headquarters?" he had asked. Goebbels himself planned to go to the Zoo Bunker. He suggested that Reymann operate from there also. Reymann thought he saw immediately what the Gauleiter had in mind; Goebbels intended to keep Reymann and the defense of Berlin completely under his own thumb. As tactfully as he could, Reymann had sidestepped the offer. "I would like to refrain from that," he said, "since both the military and political could be eliminated at the same time by a freakish hit." Goebbels had dropped the subject but Reymann noticed an immediate coolness in the Gauleiter's manner. Goebbels was well aware that it would be almost impossible for the massive Zoo Bunker to be destroyed by even a score of large bombs.

Reymann knew the Reichsminister would not forget that his invitation had been turned down. But at the moment, while he was faced with the almost hopeless task of trying to prepare a defense for the city, the last person Reymann wanted in close proximity was Goebbels. He placed no stock in either the Gauleiter's pronouncements or in his promises. Only a few days earlier, again discussing supplies, Goebbels had said that the Berlin defense would be bolstered with "at least one hundred tanks." Reymann had asked for a written list of the promised supplies. When he finally got the information, the hundred tanks turned out to be "twenty-five tanks completed, seventy-five now being built." No matter how many there were, Reymann knew he would see no part of any of them. The Oder front would have priority on all such vital weapons.

In Reymann's view, only one Cabinet member really understood what lay ahead for Berlin. That was Reichsminister Albert Speer, and even he had his blind spot. Immediately after the Gauleiter's war council, Reymann had been ordered to present himself before Speer. At the former French Embassy on the Pariser Platz where Hitler's wartime production chief now had his offices, the usually urbane Speer was furious. Pointing to the great highway running across a map of the city, Speer demanded to know what Reymann "was up to on the East-West Axis." Reymann looked at him in amazement. "I'm building a landing strip between the Brandenburg Gate and the Victory Column," he answered. "Why?"

"Why?" exploded Speer. "Why? You are chopping down my lamp posts—that's why! And you cannot do it!"

Reymann had thought Speer knew all about the plan. In the battles for Breslau and Königsberg, the Russians had grabbed the airports on the outskirts of both cities almost immediately. To circumvent a similar situation in Berlin should one occur, it had been decided to build a landing strip almost in the very center of the government district, along the East-West Axis where it passed through the Tiergarten. "For this reason," Reymann said later, "in agreement with the Luftwaffe, the strip between the Brandenburg Gate and the Victory Column was chosen. It meant that the ornamental bronze lamp posts would have to be removed, and the trees, for a depth of 30 meters [about 100 feet] on either side, would have to come down. When I mentioned this plan to

Hitler, he said that the lamp posts could go but the trees had to remain. I did my utmost to persuade him to change his mind, but Hitler would not hear of the trees being cut. Even though I explained that if the trees were not taken out only small planes would be able to take off and land, he still would not change his mind. What his reasons were I do not know, but the removal of a few trees would hardly have ruined the city's beauty at this late date." And now Speer was objecting to the removal of the lamp posts.

Reymann explained the situation to Speer, pointing out in conclusion that he had the Führer's permission to remove the posts. But that made no impression on the Reichsminister. "You cannot take down those lamp posts," he insisted. "I object to that." Then Speer added, "You do not seem to realize that I am responsible for the reconstruction of Berlin."

In vain Reymann tried to persuade Speer to change his mind. "It is vital that we keep an airstrip open, especially in this location," he argued. The Reichsminister would hear no more. As Reymann remembered it, "the conversation ended with Speer expressing his intention of taking up the whole matter with the Führer. Meanwhile his lamp posts remained, and the work on the strip was to stop—even though the Russians were advancing steadily toward us."

Just before the meeting ended, Speer brought up the matter of Berlin's bridges. Again he argued with Reymann, as he had at Heinrici's headquarters the day before, that to destroy the bridges was futile, that water, power and gas mains were carried over many of them and that the "severing of these lifelines would paralyze large parts of the city and make my task of reconstruction that much more difficult." Reymann knew that Speer's influence with Hitler was great: he had already received a direct order from the Reichskanzlei to strike off his list several of those bridges slated for destruction. Now, Speer was insisting that they all be saved. Reymann turned as stubborn as Speer. Unless counter orders were received from Hitler, Reymann intended to carry out his instructions and blow up the remaining bridges. He did not like the idea any more than Speer, but he had no intention of risking his own life and career to save them.

From Speer's office Reymann made a quick visit to one of the defense sectors on Berlin's outskirts. Each of these inspections only served to deepen Reymann's conviction that Berlin's defenses were an illusion. In the strutting, triumphant years, the Nazis had never considered the possibility that one day a last stand would be made in the capital. They had built fortifications everywhere else—the Gustav Line in Italy, the Atlantic Wall along the European coast, the Siegfried Line at Germany's western borders—but not even a trench had been built around Berlin. Not even when the Russians drove with titanic force across eastern Europe and invaded the Fatherland did Hitler and his military advisors act to fortify the city.

It was only when the Red Army reached the Oder early in 1945 that the Germans began to strengthen Berlin's defenses. Slowly a few trenches and anti-tank obstacles appeared on the eastern outskirts of the city. Then, incredibly, when the Red Army pulled up before the frozen river to wait for the spring thaws, the preparations for the capital's protection stopped, too. Not until March was the defense of Berlin given any serious consideration—and by then it was too late. There were no longer the forces, the supplies, or the equipment to set up the necessary fortifications.

In two grueling months of frenetic activity, a makeshift series of defense lines had been thrown together. Sometime in late February, an "obstacle belt" had been hurriedly established in a broken ring twenty to thirty miles outside the capital. This line ran through wooded areas and marshes and along lakes, rivers and canals, mostly north, south and east of the city. Before Reymann took command, orders had been issued declaring the obstacle areas "fortified places." In keeping with Hitler's fortress mania, local Home Guard contingents were told that they would be expected to stand fast at these locations and fight to the last man. To turn such localities into a solid zone of resistance, staggering quantities of men, guns and materials would have been needed, for the obstacle belt girdled nearly 150 miles of territory around Greater Berlin.

As Reymann soon discovered, except where the obstacle zone came under direct army supervision, the so-called fortified places were often nothing more than a few trenches covering main roads, some scattered gun positions, or a few concrete-reinforced structures hurriedly converted into blockhouses with bricked-up windows and slits for machine guns. These feeble positions, most of them not even manned, were marked on Reichskanzlei defense maps as major strongpoints.

The main line of resistance lay in the city itself. Three concentric rings made up the inner defense pattern. The first, sixty miles in circumference, ran around the outskirts. In the absence of proper fortifications, everything and anything had been used to create barriers: ancient railroad cars and wagons, ruined buildings, massive concrete-block walls, converted air raid bunkers and, nature's contribution, Berlin's lakes and rivers. Now, gangs of men were working night and day to tie these natural and man-made devices into a continuous defense line and anti-tank barrier. The work was being done by hand. There was no power equipment. Most heavy earth-moving machines had long since been sent east to work on the Oder front fortifications. The use of the few remaining machines was restricted because of the shortage of fuel—every available gallon had gone to the panzer divisions.

There were supposed to be 100,000 laborers working on the fortification rings. In fact there were never more than 30,000. There was even a shortage of hand tools; appeals through the newspapers for picks and shovels had brought little results. As Colonel Refior put it, "Berlin gardeners apparently consider the digging of their potato plots more important than the digging of tank traps." To Reymann, it was all futile anyhow. The perimeter ring would never be finished in time. It was a hopeless job, hopelessly far from completion.

The second or middle ring could be a formidable obstacle, if manned by veteran troops amply supplied with weapons. It had a circumference of about twenty-five miles and its barriers had long been in place. The Berlin railway system had been converted into a deadly trap. In some places there were deep track cuttings and sidings, some of them one hundred to two hundred yards wide, which made perfect anti-tank ditches. From fortified houses overlooking the tracks, gunners could pick off tanks caught in the gullies. Along other stretches the line followed the elevated railway (*S-Bahn*), giving defenders the advantage of high rampart-like embankments.

If even these defenses gave way, there still remained the third or inner ring, in the city's center. Called the Citadel, this last-ditch area lay within the arms of the Landwehr Canal and the Spree River, in the Mitte district. Nearly all the major buildings of the government crowded this last island of defense. In great structures linked together by barricades and concrete block walls, the last defenders would hold out—in Goering's immense Air Ministry (Reichsluftfahrtministerium), in the huge Bendler Block military headquarters, and in the empty, echoing hulks of the Reichskanzlei and the Reichstag.

Radiating out from the Citadel through all three of the defense rings were eight pie-shaped sectors, each with its own commander. Beginning with the Weissensee district on the east, the sectors were labeled clockwise from A through H. The inner ring itself was Z. Supporting the rings, six formidable bombproof flak towers were spotted about the city—at Humboldthain, Friedrichshain, and in the grounds of the Berlin Zoo.

But many vital links were missing in *Festung* Berlin. The most crucial one was manpower. Even under ideal conditions, Reymann believed, 200,000 fully trained and combat-seasoned soldiers would have been needed to defend the city. Instead, what he had to hold Berlin's 321 square miles, an area almost equal to that of New York City, was a miscellaneous collection of troops ranging from 15-year-old Hitler Youths to men in their seventies. He had policemen, engineering units and flak battery crews, but his only infantry consisted of 60,000 untrained Home Guardsmen.

These tired old men of the Volkssturm now digging trenches or moving slowly into positions along the approaches to Berlin, would have to assume the largest burden of the city's defense. The Volkssturm occupied a kind of nether world among the military. Although they were expected to fight alongside the Wehrmacht in times of emergency, they were not considered part of the army. They, like the Hitler Youth, were the responsibility of the local party officials; Reymann would not even assume command of their forces until after the battle began. Even the Volkssturm equipment was the responsibility of the party. The Home Guardsmen had no vehicles, field kitchens or communications of their own.

In all, one third of Reymann's men were unarmed. The remainder might as well have been. "Their weapons," he was to relate, "came from every country that Germany had fought with or against. Besides our own issues, there were Italian, Russian, French, Czechoslovakian, Belgian, Dutch, Norwegian and English guns." There were no less than fifteen different types of rifles and ten kinds of machine guns. Finding ammunition for this hodgepodge of arms was almost hopeless. Battalions equipped with Italian rifles were luckier than most: there was a maximum of twenty bullets apiece for them. Belgian guns, it was discovered, would accept a certain type of Czech bullet, but Belgian ammunition was useless in Czech rifles. There were few Greek arms, but for some reason there were vast quantities of Greek munitions. So desperate was the shortage that a way was found to re-machine Greek bullets so that they could be fired in Italian rifles. But such frantic improvisations hardly alleviated the overall problem. On this opening day of the Russian attack, the average ammunition supply of each Home Guardsman was about five rounds per rifle.

Now, as Reymann toured positions along the eastern outskirts, he felt certain that the Russians would simply roll over the German positions. Too many defense necessities were missing. There were almost no mines available, so the belts of minefields that were essential to a defensive position hardly existed. One of the most ancient and effective of all defense items, barbed wire, had become almost impossible to obtain. Reymann's artillery consisted of some mobile flak guns, a few tanks dug in up to the turrets so that their guns covered avenues of an approach, and the massive flak tower guns. Powerful as they were, these high-angled batteries had limited usefulness. Because of their fixed positions they could not be deflected toward the ground to stave off close-range infantry and tank attacks.

Reymann knew his own situation was hopeless. He was almost equally pessimistic about the outlook elsewhere. He did not believe that the Oder front would hold, nor did he expect help from troops falling back on the city. Colonel Refior had discussed the possibility of obtaining aid with officers at General Busse's headquarters. He got a blunt answer: "Don't expect us," said Busse's Chief of Staff, Colonel Artur Hölz. "The Ninth Army stays and will stay on the Oder. If necessary we will fall there, but we will not retreat."

Reymann kept thinking of an exchange he'd had with a Volkssturm official in one sector. "What would you do right now," Reymann had asked, "if you suddenly saw Russian tanks in the far distance? How do you let us know? Let's assume that tanks are heading this way. Show me what you would do."

To his amazement the man turned abruptly and ran back to the village just behind the positions. A few minutes later he returned, breathless and dejected. "I couldn't get to the telephone," he explained sheepishly. "I forgot. The post office is closed between one and two."

As he headed back into the city, Reymann stared unseeing out the car window. He felt that an awful doom was gathering and that in its blackness Berlin might disappear forever.

The line was cracking slowly but surely under the massive enemy pressure. Heinrici had been at the front all day, going from headquarters to headquarters, visiting field positions, talking to commanders. He marveled that Busse's soldiers had done so well against such terrible odds. First the Ninth Army had stood off three days of heavy preliminary attacks; now, for more than twenty-four hours, they had been taking the full force of the main Russian offensive. Busse's troops had fought back ferociously. In the Seelow area alone, they had knocked out more than 150 tanks and had shot down 132 planes. But they were weakening.

As he drove in darkness back to his headquarters, Heinrici found himself slowed by crowds of refugees. He had seen them everywhere this day—some carrying bundles, some pulling hand carts filled with their last possessions, some in farm wagons drawn by horses or oxen. In many places their numbers were posing almost as great a problem to Heinrici's troops as the Russians.

At his command post, anxious staff officers gathered to hear the General's firsthand impression of the situation. Gravely Heinrici summed up what he had seen. "They cannot last much longer," he said. "The men are so exhausted that their tongues are hanging out. Still," he continued, "we are holding. It is something Schörner couldn't do. That great soldier has not been able to hold Koniev even for one day."

A short time later, the OKH Chief, General Hans Krebs, rang up. "Well, we all have good reason to feel satisfied," he told Heinrici smoothly. Heinrici conceded the point. "Considering the size of the attack we have not lost much ground," he said. Krebs would have preferred a more optimistic response, and he said as much, but Heinrici did not make it. "I have learned," he told Krebs dryly, "never to praise the day until the twilight comes."

In the darkness, Private Willy Feldheim grasped his bulky *Panzerfaust* more firmly. He did not know for certain where he was, but he had heard that this line of foxholes covering the three roads in the Klosterdorf area was about eighteen miles from the front.

A little while ago, waiting for the Russian tanks to come up the road, Willy had felt a sense of great adventure. He had thought about what it would be like when he saw the first tank and could finally fire the anti-tank gun for the first time. The three companies holding the crossroads had been told to let the tanks get as close as possible before firing. Willy's instructor had said that a sixty-yard range was about right. He wondered how soon they would come.

Crouched in the damp foxhole, Willy thought about the days when he was a bugler. He remembered in particular one brilliant, sunshiny day in 1943 when Hitler spoke in Olympic Stadium and Willy had been among the massed buglers who had sounded the fanfare at the Führer's entrance. He would never forget the leader's words to the assembled Hitler Youth: "You are the guarantee of the future. . . ." And the crowds had yelled *"Führer Befiehl! Führer Befiehl!"* It had been the most memorable day of Willy's life. On that afternoon he had known beyond doubt that the Reich had the best army, the best weapons, the best generals and, above all, the greatest leader in the world.

The dream was gone in the sudden flash that illuminated the night sky. Willy peered out toward the front and now he heard again the low rumbling of the guns he had momentarily forgotten, and he felt the cold. His stomach began to ache and he wanted to cry. Fifteen-year-old Willy Feldheim was badly scared, and all the noble aims and the stirring words could not help him now.

The drum beat was almost imperceptible. Softly the tubas answered. The muffled drum roll came again. Low and ominously the tubas replied. Then the massed basses came alive and the awesome grandeur of *Die Götterdämmerung* rolled out from the Berlin Philharmonic. The mood in the darkness of Beethoven Hall seemed as tragic as the music. The only illumination came from the lights on the orchestra's music stands. It was cold in the hall and people were wearing overcoats. Dr. Von Westermann sat in a box with his wife and brother. Nearby was the sister of the conductor Robert Heger, with three friends. And in his usual seat in the orchestra section was Reichsminister Albert Speer.

Immediately after playing the Beethoven Violin Concerto, Taschner, his family and the daughter of Georg Diburtz had left the hall. They were now on their way to safety—but they were the only ones. Speer had kept his promise. His car was waiting. He had even sent his adjutant to escort the little group safely to their destination. Now the architect of Hitler's monstrous war-making industrial machine listened to the tempest of music as it told of the evildoing of the gods, of Siegfried on his funeral bed of fire, of Brünnhilde on horseback ascending the pyre to join him in death. Then, with cymbals crashing and drums rolling, the orchestra thundered to its climax: the terrible holocaust that destroyed Valhalla. And as the mournful majestic music filled the auditorium, those who listened felt a sorrow too deep for tears.*

⚜ 2 ⚜

ALMOST NOTHING of the once mighty Third Reich remained. Crushed from both sides, on the map it resembled an hourglass: the North Sea and the Baltic formed the top, and Bavaria, parts of Czechoslovakia, Austria and northern Italy—which Germany now

---

* There are probably as many accounts of the last concert as there are survivors of the orchestra. Some tell one story, others another. There are differences of opinion about the date, the program and even the performers. Those who knew nothing of Speer's plan refuse to believe that any such scheme existed. The version which appears here is based on Dr. Von Westermann's account and records, with subsidiary information from Gerhard Taschner.

occupied—made up the lower half. Across the narrow neck between these areas, only about ninety miles separated the Americans and the Russians. Fighting was still heavy in the north and, to a lesser degree, in the south. In the center General William Simpson's U. S. Ninth Army was simply holding its positions along the Elbe, mopping up pockets of resistance bypassed during the dash for the river and repulsing occasional sharp counterattacks against its bridgeheads. There was one sore spot for the Ninth: Magdeburg. Again and again its commander had refused to surrender. Now Simpson had had enough: he called in bombers and leveled more than one third of the city. Then he sent in his troops.

On the afternoon of the seventeenth, as units of the 30th Infantry and 2nd Armored divisions began the attack, General Bradley joined Simpson at his headquarters. The phone rang. Simpson picked it up, listened for a moment and then, putting his hand over the receiver, said to Bradley, "It looks as if we may get the bridge in Magdeburg after all. What'll we do then, Brad?"

Bradley knew only too well what Simpson wanted him to say: that the *Autobahn* bridge was the most direct and fastest route to Berlin. But he shook his head. "Hell's bells," he replied. "We don't want any more bridgeheads on the Elbe. If you get it you'll have to throw a battalion across it, I guess. But let's hope the other fellows blow it up before you're stuck with it."

Bradley's instructions from SHAEF were clear; he could offer Simpson no hope of moving forward. The orders read: "Take the necessary action to avoid offensive action in force, including the formation of new bridgeheads east of the Elbe-Mulde line. . . ." Simpson's forces were to remain as a threat to Berlin, but that was all.

Minutes later a second call settled the issue. As he put down the phone, Simpson told Bradley: "No need to worry any longer. The Krauts just blew it up."

The blowing of the bridge brought to an end the dream of "Big Simp" Simpson, who had wanted to take his mighty Ninth Army into Berlin, the city which the Supreme Commander had once described as "clearly the main prize."

* * *

In the hamlets north of Boizenburg on the Elbe, the household-
ers were startled by a distant wailing. The strange sound grew
louder, and soon an astonishing apparition came in sight. Down
the road tramped two Scottish bagpipers, their pipes skirling. Behind them came Warrant Officer "Dixie" Deans's POWs, twelve
thousand strong, marching in columns under a light German
guard. The prisoners' uniforms were in tatters. Their few belongings were bundled and slung on their backs. They were emaciated, cold and hungry, but their heads were high. The determined
Deans had seen to that. "When you pass through the villages," he
told the men, "spruce up even if it hurts, and show these bloody
supermen exactly who won this war."

Dixie's own transport was an ancient bicycle that threatened to
fall apart at any moment. A patch covered a large swelling on the
front tire. But, bumpy as the ride was, Dixie was thankful for the
mobility. He rode continuously from column to column, watching
over his men and observing the German guards that marched on
either side of each column. Every road was filled with POWs.
There were nearly two thousand to a column, and although
Deans tried resolutely to cover the entire area, it was an ex-
hausting job. After almost ten days of seemingly aimless marching, Deans's men were in bad shape. There were a few German
supply trucks in the procession, but for the most part the men were
living off the countryside. The German Commandant, Colonel
Ostmann, appeared almost embarrassed by the meandering march
and the shortage of food, but he told Deans, "There is just nothing
I can do." Dixie believed him. "I don't think he has a clue from
one day to the next where the devil we're going," Deans told fellow R.A.F. Warrant Officer Ronald Mogg.

The POWs had wandered like nomads since leaving Fallingbostel. Now they were heading for the town of Gresse, where trucks
with Red Cross food parcels were said to await them. Deans
hoped that they would halt there and go no farther. He told

Ostmann that the march was useless, for the British would soon overrun them. Deans hoped he was right. From what the men were able to pick up on the precious secret radios they had carried out of the camp, the Allied news was good. Mogg, a shorthand expert, took down the BBC news twice a day. Whenever they could plug into an outlet, the radio in the gramophone was used; during the march they relied on the battery-operated receiver. One of the German guards, Ostmann's interpreter, Corporal "Charlie" Gumbach, thought Sergeant John Bristow was foolish to carry the heavy, old-fashioned gramophone on his back. "Why don't you drop it somewhere?" the German suggested. "I've grown attached to it, Charlie," said Bristow seriously. "And anyway, the chaps would never forgive me if we didn't have music in the evenings." Bristow looked at the German suspiciously. "Don't you like to dance, Charlie?" he asked. Gumbach shrugged helplessly; all these British were madmen.

As Deans's column swung down the road toward a new village the pipers hoisted their instruments into position, and the tired men in the ranks squared their shoulders and got into step. "At least," said Ron Mogg, stepping out smartly alongside Deans on the bicycle, "we're impressing the natives no end."

*   *   *

On the eastern front, Chuikov's Guards and Katukov's tankers had finally gained a foothold on the Seelow Heights by sheer weight of numbers. A little before midnight on the sixteenth, General Popiel afterward remembered, "the first three houses in the northern suburbs of the town of Seelow had been captured. . . . It was a bitter operation." All through the night of the sixteenth, Red Army attacks were smashed again and again by point-blank fire from anti-aircraft guns. "The Germans didn't even have to aim," Popiel said. "They just fired over open sights." Chuikov himself reached Seelow about noon on the seventeenth. He found the resistance so fierce that he pessimistically estimated it would take "one day to pierce each line of resistance between the Oder and Berlin." Not until the night of the seventeenth were the Heights taken. It had indeed taken more than forty-eight hours to break through the first two lines. The Russians believed that there were at least three more such lines lying before Berlin.

Popiel, trying to make his way to Katukov's headquarters some distance from Seelow, saw that the fight had caused great confusion. Troops and tanks were everywhere, crammed into every corner, alley, street and garden. German artillery was still firing. In their effort to take the Heights, Zhukov's troops had become disorganized; now they had to be reassembled before moving again. Zhukov, furious, and well aware of the pace Koniev was setting, demanded an all-out effort.

During the fighting, Soviet tankers had come up with an ingenious solution to the bulky anti-tank rockets fired from *Panzerfäuste*. To his amazement, General Yushchuk saw that his tankers had taken every bedspring they could find from German homes. These coiled-wire contraptions were now hitched to the front of tanks to break the impact of the blunt-nosed rockets. Preceded by bedsprings, the Soviet cannon now prepared to lead the assault on the city.

Near Cottbus, in a medieval castle overlooking the Spree, Marshal Koniev waited for his call to go through to Moscow. Somewhere a lone enemy battery was still firing. It was typical German artillery fire, Koniev thought as he listened to the carefully timed, methodical bursting of the shells. He wondered what they were firing at—perhaps the castle or the antenna of his headquarters radio station. Whatever the target, the fire was not hindering his tanks, which had been crossing the Spree since noon. By now they were miles away, smashing through a disintegrating enemy and rumbling toward Lübben, near the point where the boundary between his army and Zhukov's ended. For Koniev, the time had come to call Stalin and ask permission to swing his tanks north toward Berlin.

Koniev had every reason to be in high spirits. His tankers had moved with unforeseen speed, although the fighting had been brutally hard in some areas and casualties had been heavy. Earlier on this morning of the seventeenth, driving toward the front to watch the crossing of the Spree, Koniev had realized for the first time just how terrible the battle had been. His car had passed through smoldering forests and along fields cratered by artillery fire. There were, he recalled, "huge quantities of decommissioned and burned-out tanks, equipment mired in streams and swamps, heaps of twisted metal, and there were dead everywhere—all that remained of the forces that had met and battled and passed through this land."

Koniev had expected great difficulty crossing the Spree, which was 180 feet wide in places. By the time he reached the headquarters of General Rybalko's Third Guards Tank Army, a few tanks had actually been ferried across, but ferrying was much too slow. The Spree line had to be forced fast. Koniev and Rybalko hurried to an area where reconnaissance patrols had reported evidence that some sort of ford existed. Although the river at this site was close to 150 feet wide, Koniev, after inspecting the terrain, decided to risk sending a tank on a trial crossing. Rybalko selected the best tank crew in his lead detachment and explained what they were to attempt. The tank plunged in. Under fire from the west bank, it began slowly to move across. The water rose up over its treads—but it got no deeper. At this one point, the river was only three and a half feet deep. One behind another, Rybalko's tanks lumbered through the water. The German line on the Spree was cracked. Koniev's forces moved across the river in strength and charged ahead at full speed.

Now, in the Cottbus castle, the Marshal's call to Moscow came through. An aide handed Koniev the radio-telephone. As he spoke he reverted to the military formality that Stalin always demanded. "This is the Commander of the First Ukrainian Front," he said. Stalin replied, "Comrade Stalin. Go ahead."

"This is my tactical situation," Koniev reported. "My armored forces are now twenty-three kilometers [about fourteen miles] northwest of Finsterwalde, and my infantry are on the banks of the Spree." He paused. "I suggest that my armored formations move immediately in a northerly direction." He carefully avoided mentioning Berlin.

"Zhukov," Stalin said, "is having a difficult time. He is still breaking through the defenses on the Seelow Heights. Enemy resistance there appears stiff and unyielding." There was a brief pause. Then Stalin said, "Why not pass Zhukov's armor through the gap created on your front and let him go for Berlin from there? Is that possible?"

"Comrade Stalin," Koniev said quickly, "it would take much time and cause great confusion. There is no necessity for transferring armor from the First Belorussian Front. Operations in my section are going favorably." He took the plunge. "I have adequate forces and we are in a perfect position to turn our tank armies toward Berlin."

Koniev explained that he could send his forces toward the city by way of Zossen, twenty-five miles south of Berlin. "What scale map are you using?" Stalin asked suddenly. "One to two hundred thousands," Koniev answered. There was a pause while Stalin referred to his own map. Then he said, "Are you aware that Zossen is the headquarters of the German General Staff?" Koniev said he was. There was another pause. Finally Stalin said, "Very well. I agree. Turn your tank armies toward Berlin." The Generalissimo added that he would issue new army boundary lines, and then, abruptly, he hung up. Koniev put down his own phone, immensely satisfied.

Zhukov learned of Koniev's drive on Berlin from Stalin himself —and for the General it apparently was not a pleasant conversation. What was said no one knew, but the headquarters staff could see its effect on the commander. As Lieutenant Colonel Pavel

Troyanoskii, senior correspondent for the military paper *Red Star,* was later to recall the incident: "The attack had stalled and Stalin reprimanded Zhukov. It was a serious situation and a reprimand from Stalin was often couched in not very mild language." Troyanoskii could plainly see that "Zhukov, a man with all the marks of an iron will about his face and a man who did not like to share his glory with anyone, was extremely worked up." General Popiel described Zhukov's state of mind more succinctly. "We have a lion on our hands," he told his fellow staff members. The lion was not long in showing his claws. That evening the word went out from a grim Zhukov to the entire First Belorussian army group: "Now take Berlin!"

* * *

By now confusion was beginning to sweep the German lines. Shortages were apparent everywhere and in everything. A critical lack of transport, an almost total absence of fuel, and roads thronged with refugees made large-scale troop movements almost impossible. This immobility was producing dire consequences: as units shifted position, their equipment, including precious artillery, had to be abandoned. Communication networks, too, were faltering and in some places no longer existed. As a result, orders were often obsolete when they reached their destinations—or even when they were issued. The chaos was compounded as officers arriving at the front to take over units discovered nothing to take over, because their commands had already been captured or annihilated. In some areas, inexperienced men, left leaderless, did not know exactly where they were or who was fighting on their flanks. Even in veteran outfits, headquarters were forced to move with such frequency that often the troops did not know where their command post was or how to contact it.

Units were trapped and captured or simply overrun and slaughtered. Others, demoralized, broke and ran. In only two places did the Vistula front remain intact. The northern area held by General

Hasso von Manteuffel's Third Panzer Army had not been hit by Zhukov's massive assault—but Von Manteuffel was expecting an attack at any moment by Marshal Konstantin Rokossovskii's Second Belorussians. Farther south, part of Busse's Ninth Army was still holding. But it was beginning to be affected by the general disintegration: its left flank had already started to crumble before Zhukov's avalanche of tanks; the right was halfway encircled by Koniev's sledgehammer drive south of Berlin. In truth, the Army Group Vistula was breaking up piece by piece, in chaos, confusion and death—exactly as Heinrici had known it would.

Von Manteuffel, like Heinrici, had never underestimated the Russians; he, too, had fought them many times before. Now, in his Storch reconnaissance plane over the Oder, he studied the enemy. Rokossovskii's men were making no effort to hide their assault preparations. Artillery and infantry units were being openly moved up into position. Von Manteuffel marveled at the Russians' cockiness. For days now, as he flew back and forth over their lines, they had not even bothered to look up.

Von Manteuffel knew that when the drive came he would not be able to hold for very long. He was a panzer general without panzers. To halt Zhukov's drive in the Ninth Army sector, Heinrici had denuded Von Manteuffel's army of the few panzer divisions it had left. They had come from the 3rd SS Corps, holding the southern edge of his sector in the forests of Eberswalde. SS General Felix Steiner, who was regarded by Wehrmacht officers as one of the best of the SS generals, reported that though he had lost the tanks he had been given other reinforcements. Solemnly he reported to Von Manteuffel: "I have just received five thousand Luftwaffe pilots, each with his little Iron Cross hanging around his neck. Tell me, what do I do with them?"

"I have no doubt," Von Manteuffel told his staff, "that on Hitler's maps there is a little flag saying 7TH PANZER DIV., even though it got here without a single tank, truck, piece of artillery or even a machine gun. We have an army of ghosts."

Now, looking down on the Russians' preparations from his

plane, Von Manteuffel figured that he could expect their main assault sometime around the twentieth. He knew exactly what he was going to do then. He would hold as long as possible and then he intended to retreat "step by step, with my soldiers arm to arm, shoulder to shoulder, all the way to the west." Von Manteuffel had no intention of allowing even one of them to fall into Russian hands.

The situation of the Ninth Army was now bordering on the catastrophic, yet its commander was not considering pulling back. To General Theodor Busse, retreat, except under orders, was comparable to treason—and Hitler's orders were to stand fast. Zhukov's tanks, storming on after their breakthrough on Seelow Heights, had ripped a gash in the army's northern flank, and now the First Belorussians were charging at breakneck speed toward Berlin. The near-absence of communications made it impossible for Busse to assess the extent of the breakthrough. He did not even know if counterattacks could close the tear in his lines. His best information was that Zhukov's tanks were already within twenty-five miles of Berlin's outskirts. Even more alarming was Koniev's blistering drive along the Ninth's southern flank. The First Ukrainians, now beyond Lübben, were arching back behind the Ninth and racing northward for the city. Would the Ninth be cut off, Busse wondered, just as Model's army group had been in the Ruhr? Model had been lucky in one respect: he had been encircled by the Americans.*

The situation was particularly galling for General Karl Weidling, whose 56th Panzer Corps had absorbed the full brunt of Zhukov's breakthrough on the Seelow Heights. His corps had held off Zhukov for forty-eight hours, inflicting staggering casualties. But the promised reserve divisions that Weidling so anxiously awaited—the SS Nordland Division and the powerful, fully operational 18th Panzer Grenadier Division—had not arrived in time for the counterattacks that might have stopped Zhukov's tanks.

* The Ruhr pocket was completely erased by April 18. Three days later Model committed suicide.

One man from the Nordland Division did show up—the commander, SS Major General Jürgen Ziegler. Arriving by car at Weidling's headquarters north of Müncheberg, Ziegler announced calmly that his division was miles away; it had run out of fuel. Weidling was livid. Every panzer division carried reserves for just such emergencies. But Ziegler, who disliked fighting under Wehrmacht officers, apparently did not consider his division's arrival urgent. Now, twenty precious hours had been lost in refueling and Ziegler was still not in position. The 18th Panzer Grenadier Division, which should have reached Weidling the day before, on the seventeenth, had just arrived. The counterattacks that had been planned for this force would not take place: the division had arrived just in time to retreat.

Weidling seemed dogged by bad luck. When Zhukov's massive columns of tanks surged out from the plateau, among the German units hit hardest had been the one force that Heinrici had worried about most: Goering's 9th Parachute Division. Already demoralized by their initial exposure to the battle on the Heights, Goering's paratroopers panicked and broke as the Russian tanks, guns blazing, smashed into their lines. Colonel Hans Oscar Wöhlermann, Weidling's new artillery commander, who had arrived on the opening day of the Russian offensive across the Oder, witnessed the rout that followed. Everywhere, he said, were soldiers "running away like madmen." Even when he drew his pistol, the frantic paratroopers did not halt. Wöhlermann found the division's commander "utterly alone and completely disheartened by the flight of his men, trying to hold back whatever there was left to hold back." Eventually the headlong flight was stopped, but Goering's much-vaunted paratroopers "remained"—in Wöhlermann's words—"a threat to the course of the whole battle." As for Heinrici, when he heard the news he rang Goering at Karinhall. "I have something to tell you," he said acidly. "Those Cassino troops of yours, those famous paratroopers—well, they have run away."

Although Weidling tried desperately to stem the Russian armored assaults, the 56th Corps front could not hold. Weidling's

Chief of Staff Lieutenant Colonel Theodor von Dufving, saw that the Russians were "beginning to force us back by applying terrific pressure in a kind of horseshoe-like maneuver—hitting us from both sides and encircling us again and again." The Corps was also subjected to merciless air attack: Von Dufving had to take cover thirty times within four hours. The Soviet pincer tactics had forced Weidling to evacuate two headquarters since noon. As a result, he had lost communications with Busse's headquarters.

At nightfall Weidling found himself in a candlelit cellar at Waldsieversdorf, northwest of Müncheberg. There he received a visitor: Foreign Minister Joachim von Ribbentrop, looking shaky and apprehensive. "He kept looking at us expectantly," Wöhlermann was to remember, "with anxious, sad eyes." When he heard the truth about the 56th Corps situation, "it seemed to have a crushing effect upon him." Hesitantly, the Foreign Minister asked a few questions in a hoarse, quiet voice, and shortly thereafter he took his leave. Wöhlermann and other members of the headquarters staff had half expected Von Ribbentrop "to tell us that negotiations had begun from our side with the English and the Americans. It would have given us hope at this last hour." He left no such word.

On the heels of the Foreign Minister arrived the one-armed 32-year-old leader of the Hitler Youth, Artur Axmann. He brought news he was sure would please Weidling. The youngsters of the Hitler Youth, Axmann announced, were ready to fight and were even now manning the roads in the 56th Corps rear. Weidling's reaction to the news was not what Axmann had expected. As Wöhlermann remembers, Weidling was so enraged that for a moment he was almost inarticulate. Then, "using extremely coarse language," he denounced Axmann's plan. "You cannot sacrifice these children for a cause that is already lost," he angrily told the Youth Leader. "I will not use them and I demand that the order sending these children into battle be rescinded." The pudgy Axmann hurriedly gave Weidling his word that the order would be countermanded.

If such a directive was issued, it never reached hundreds of Hitler Youth boys lying under arms on the approaches to the city. They remained in position. In the next forty-eight hours they were steamrollered by Russian attacks. Willy Feldheim and the 130 boys in his company were swamped; they fell back helter-skelter and finally stopped and tried to hold a line in the protection of some ditches and a bunker. At last Willy, exhausted by fear, stretched out on a bench during a lull in the fighting and fell asleep.

Hours later he woke up with a strange sense that something was wrong. A voice said, "I wonder what's up? It's so silent."

The boys rushed out of the bunker—and were confronted by a "fantastic, incredible scene, like an old painting of the Napoleonic Wars." The sun was shining and there were bodies everywhere. Nothing was standing. Houses were in ruins. There were cars wrecked and abandoned, some of them still burning. The worst shock was the dead. They were heaped in piles, in "a weird tableau, with their rifles and *Panzerfäuste* lying beside them. It was lunatic. And then we realized that we were all alone."

They had slept through the entire attack.

In Berlin the tension was building hour by hour. General Reymann's scanty forces, manning the outer perimeter rings, had been warned that the signal "Clausewitz," code name for the attack on the city, might come at any time. Various emergency measures had gone into effect, making clear to all Berliners that the moment of truth was at hand. Among other things, along the main roads and thoroughfares the closing of the barricades had begun.

Not even Goebbels could ignore the threat any longer. A torrent of hysterical news and slogans poured out of the Propaganda Ministry. The official Nazi Party newspaper, *Völkischer Beobachter,* announced the Soviet drive across the Oder, and said: "A new and heavy trial, perhaps the heaviest of all, is before us." The newspaper continued, "Each square meter of territory which the enemy has to battle for, each Soviet tank which a Grenadier, a Volkssturm man, or a Hitler lad destroys bears more weight today than at any other time in this war. The word for the day is: *Clench your teeth! Fight like the devil! Don't give up one foot of soil easily! The hour of decision demands the last, the greatest, effort!"* Berliners were warned that the Russians had already decided the fate of the city's inhabitants. Those who were not killed at the barricades, Goebbels warned, would be liquidated "by deportation as slave labor."

On the afternoon of the eighteenth, General Reymann received an order from the Reichskanzlei, later confirmed by a personal call from Goebbels, that "all forces available, including Volkssturm, have been requested by the Ninth Army to hold second-line positions." In other words, the city was to be stripped to man the outer defenses. Reymann was astounded. Hurriedly ten Volkssturm battalions were rounded up, along with a regiment of anti-aircraft defense units of the "Great Germany" Guard regiment. After hours of search and requisition, a miscellaneous collection of vehicles was assembled and the force headed east. As he watched them go, Reymann turned to Goebbels' deputy. "Tell Goebbels," he said angrily, "that it is no longer possible to defend the Reich capital. The inhabitants are defenseless."

* * *

Carl Wiberg's face betrayed no emotion but he noticed that his hands were trembling. After the long months of his quest, he could hardly believe his ears. Standing among other customers near the main counter of the black market food store, he leaned down and patted his little dachshunds; the action also enabled him to hear a little better, although the two well-dressed women standing next to him had made no attempt at secrecy.

Most Berliners knew nothing about this well-stocked shop. It sold only to selected customers, including those well up in Nazi echelons. Wiberg had been patronizing the place for a long time, and he had picked up many choice and accurate items of information just by listening to such customers as these two well-fed ladies. Their information ought to be accurate, he thought; their husbands were both important Nazis.

Wiberg decided he had heard enough. He collected his purchases, doffed his Homburg to the proprietor and strolled out of the store. In the street his pace quickened as he hurried to find Jessen-Schmidt.

Several hours later, after a lengthy discussion, both men agreed that Wiberg's news had to be true. By the afternoon of Wednesday, April 18, a message was en route to London. Though all their other hopes had been dashed, Wiberg fervently hoped the Allies would act on this report. According to what he had overheard in the food shop, Hitler was definitely in the Berlin area—at a headquarters in Bernau, only about fourteen miles northeast of the city. What better present could they give him for his fifty-sixth birthday, April 20, than a massive air raid?

❀   ❀   ❀

General Alfred Jodl, Hitler's Chief of Operations, returned home at 3 A.M. on April 20. His face was lined with worry and exhaustion. The crisis had been reached, he told his wife Luise. "You'd better start packing and get ready to leave," he said. Luise argued; she wanted to continue with her Red Cross work. But Jodl was insistent. "With your name, the Russians would not wait a single day before shipping you off to Lubianka," he said. Where were they going? she asked. Jodl shrugged. "To the north or south—nobody knows," he said. "But I hope we can face the end together." They talked most of the night. A little before 10 A.M. the sirens sounded. "I'll bet Berlin gets an extra ration of bombs today," Jodl said. "It always happens on Hitler's birthday."

Jodl hurried upstairs to shave before going back to the Führer-bunker. This birthday was to be no different from the Führer's others: there would be the usual parade of government officials and Cabinet members arriving to congratulate Hitler, and Jodl was expected to be present. As he came down the stairs, Luise handed him his cap and belt. He picked up his map case and kissed her good-bye. "I must hurry for the congratulations," he said. Luise wondered, as she did every day now, whether they would ever see each other again. "Bless you," she called after her husband as he got into his car.

Another of Hitler's court was also ready to leave for the ceremonies. Reichsmarschall Hermann Goering intended to show up just to prove he was still loyal, but from there he was heading south. Goering had decided that the moment had come for him to bid farewell to his huge castle and estate at Karinhall, about fifty miles northwest of Berlin. He had reached the decision shortly after the Soviet bombardment began at 5:30 A.M. Goering had promptly called Heinrici's headquarters in nearby Prenzlau. The attack in the north had begun, he was told: Rokossovskii's Second Belorussians had finally launched their offensive against Von Manteuffel's Third Panzer Army. Goering was well aware that Von Manteuffel's strength was inadequate. The Reichsmarschall had toured that front several times in the previous weeks, loudly telling one general after another that because of "all the loafing around nothing is prepared. The Russians will just laugh their way through your lines."

Goering himself had prepared well for this moment. Lined up on the main road outside the gates of his estate were twenty-four Luftwaffe trucks loaded with the contents of Karinhall—his antiques, paintings, silver and furniture. This convoy was to head south immediately. Most of the Luftwaffe headquarters people in Berlin, along with their equipment, were to leave in other convoys later in the day.*

---

* Goering may have had even more than twenty-four trucks. Heinrici believes he had "four columns." This, however, may have included the additional Luftwaffe convoys that left Berlin later in the day. The fantastic fact is that at this moment

Now, standing by the main gates, Goering spoke a few final words to the commander of the truck column. Surrounded by motorcylists, it moved off. Goering stood looking at the huge castle with its magnificent wings and buttresses. A Luftwaffe engineering officer came up; everything, he said, was ready. As a few of his men and some of the local villagers watched, Goering walked across the road, bent over a detonator and pushed down the plunger. With a tremendous roar Karinhall blew up.

Without waiting for the dust to settle, Goering walked back to his car. Turning to one of his engineering officers he said calmly, "Well, that's what you have to do sometimes when you're a crown prince." Slamming the car door he set out for Berlin and the Führer's birthday celebration.

Hitler rose at 11 A.M. and from noon on he received the tributes of his inner clique—among them Joseph Goebbels, Martin Bormann, Joachim von Ribbentrop, Albert Speer, and his military leaders Karl Doenitz, Wilhelm Keitel, Alfred Jodl, Hans Krebs and Heinrich Himmler. After them came Berlin area Gauleiters, staff members and secretaries. Then, as the guns rumbled in the distance, Hitler, followed by his entourage, emerged from the bunker. There in the bombed wilderness of the Reichskanzlei gardens he inspected men from two units—the SS "Frundsberg" Division, a recently arrived unit from the Courland Army,* and a proud little group from Axmann's Hitler Youth. "Everyone," Axmann said long afterward, "was shocked at the Führer's appearance. He walked with a stoop. His hands trembled. But it was surprising how much will power and determination still radiated from this man." Hitler shook hands with the boys and decorated

---

with planes grounded and vehicles unable to move because of fuel, Goering had at his disposal not only trucks but ample supplies of gasoline.

* Completely surrounded in the Baltic States, the remnants of the Courland Army were finally evacuated by boat and arrived at Swinemünde at the beginning of April. Of the eighteen divisions only a few boatloads of men, minus equipment, reached Germany.

some whom Axmann introduced as having "recently distinguished themselves at the front."

Then Hitler walked down the line of SS men. He shook hands with each one, and confidently predicted that the enemy would be defeated before the approaches to Berlin. Looking on was Heinrich Himmler, the head of the SS. Since April 6 he had been meeting secretly from time to time with Count Folke Bernadotte, head of the Swedish Red Cross. In a vague way, Himmler had sounded out Bernadotte about the possibility of negotiating peace terms with the Allies, but now he stepped forward and reaffirmed his loyalty and that of the SS to Hitler. In a few hours he was scheduled to meet once more with Bernadotte.

Immediately after the inspection ceremonies, Hitler's military conference began. By this time Goering had arrived. General Krebs conducted the briefing, although everyone was familiar with the situation. Berlin would be encircled within a matter of days, if not hours. Even before that happened, Busse's Ninth Army would be surrounded and trapped, unless orders for its withdrawal were given. To Hitler's military advisors one point was clear: the Führer and vital government ministries and departments still in Berlin must leave the capital for the south. Keitel and Jodl particularly urged the move, but Hitler refused to acknowledge that things were that serious. According to Colonel Nicolaus von Below, the Führer's Luftwaffe adjutant, "Hitler stated that the battle for Berlin presented the only chance to prevent total defeat." He did make one concession: in the event that the Americans and Russians linked up on the Elbe, the Reich would be commanded in the north by Admiral Doenitz and in the south possibly by Field Marshal Albert Kesselring. Meanwhile, various government agencies were given authorization to leave immediately.

Hitler did not reveal his own plans. But at least three people in the bunker were convinced he would never leave Berlin. Fräulein Johanna Wolf, one of Hitler's secretaries, had heard him remark only a few days earlier that "he would take his own life, if he felt the situation was beyond saving." Von Below, too, believed that "Hitler had made up his mind to stay in Berlin and die there." Jodl, when he returned home, told his wife that Hitler, in a private talk, had said, "Jodl, I shall fight as long as the faithful fight next to me and then I shall shoot myself." *

Most of the government had already left Berlin, but the remaining Reich administrative agencies almost seemed to have been preparing for this moment for days, like runners awaiting a starter's pistol. The real exodus now began; it was to continue until the city was finally surrounded. The Luftwaffe's Chief of Staff, General Karl Koller, noted in his diary that Goering had departed. "Naturally," Koller wrote, "he leaves me here to let all Hitler's anger pass over me." Bureaucrats big and small made their getaway. Philippe Hambert, a young French forced laborer who worked as a draftsman in the offices of Dr. Karl Dustmann, one of the Todt Labor Organization architects, was dumbfounded when his boss suddenly gave him a present of a thousand marks (about $250) and then left town. Margarete Schwarz, in the garden of her apartment house in Charlottenburg, glanced down the street and saw a large chauffeur-driven blue car pull up outside a nearby house. Her neighbor, Otto Solimann, joined her, and together they watched as "an orderly in a neat white jacket along with a naval officer with lots of gold on his uniform" left the house. Quickly the car was packed with baggage. Then the men jumped in "and drove off at top speed." Solimann said to Margarete: "The rats are leaving the sinking ship. That was Admiral Raeder."

In all, the Berlin Commandant's office issued over two thousand permits to leave the capital. "There was something almost comic about the reasons with which state and party functionaries backed up their requests to leave the city," the Chief of Staff, Colonel Hans Refior, later recalled. "Even though Goebbels had or-

---

* Hitler's remark to Jodl was written down by Luise Jodl in her detailed diary. The entry is followed by this note: "My husband remarked that 'save for one other occasion, after the death of my first wife, this is the only personal remark Hitler has ever made to me.'"

dered that 'No man capable of carrying arms is to leave Berlin,' we put no difficulties in the way of these 'home fighters' who wanted passes. Why should we hold up these contemptible characters? They all believed that flight would save their precious lives. The majority of the population remained behind. Flight for them was beyond their means anyway because of the transport shortage."

In the dental offices at 213 Kurfürstendamm, blond Käthe Heusermann got a phone call from her employer. The Nazis' top dentist, Professor Hugo J. Blaschke, was leaving immediately. A few days earlier, Blaschke had instructed Käthe to pack all dental records, X-rays, molds and other equipment in boxes so they could be collected and sent south. Blaschke said that he expected "the Chancellery group to leave any day and we are going with them." Käthe had told him she was staying in Berlin. Blaschke was furious. "Do you realize what it's going to be like when the Russians get here?" he asked. "First you'll be raped. Then you'll be strung up. Have you any idea what the Russians are like?" But Käthe just "could not believe it was going to be that bad." Later she was to recall, "I didn't understand the seriousness of the situation. Maybe it was foolishness, but I was so busy that I didn't realize how desperate everything had become." Now Blaschke was insistent. "Pack up and get out," he urged. "The Chancellery group and their families are leaving." But Käthe was adamant. She intended to stay in the city. "Well," Blaschke said, "remember what I told you." Then he hung up.

Suddenly Käthe remembered something Blaschke had asked her to do some days before. If he left the city and she remained, she was to warn a certain friend of his—using a code sentence because, said Blaschke, "the phones might be tapped"—that the top Nazis were fleeing. If the entire entourage had gone she was to say, "The bridge was removed last night." If only some had departed the sentence was to be, "Only a tooth was extracted last night." She had no idea who Blaschke's friend was except that "his name was Professor Gallwitz or Grawitz and I think he mentioned that he was a senior dentist for the SS." Blaschke had given her only a telephone number. Now, under the impression that the entire "Chancellery group" had left, she called the number. When a man spoke, Käthe said, "The bridge was removed last night."

A few hours later that evening, Professor Ernst Grawitz, head of the German Red Cross and friend of Heinrich Himmler, sat down to dinner with his family. When everyone was seated Grawitz reached down, pulled the pins on two hand grenades, and blew himself and his family to oblivion.*

The great exodus would always be remembered by the Berliners as "the flight of the Golden Pheasants." But most people that day were more aware of advancing Russians than of fleeing Nazis. Helena Boese, wife of film director Karl Boese, recalled that the only concern now "was to somehow stay alive." Soviet troops were already at Müncheberg and Strausberg, about fifteen miles to the east; and now the news was filtering through the city that another Russian drive was heading toward the capital from the south, toward Zossen. Georg Schröter, a screenwriter living in Tempelhof, learned of this Russian advance firsthand. Worried about a girl friend of his, a cabaret artist named Trude Berliner who lived in one of the outlying districts south of Berlin, Schröter phoned her home. She answered and then said, "Wait a minute." There was a pause. "I have someone here who would like to speak to you," she said. Schröter found himself conversing with a Soviet colonel who spoke perfect German. "You can count on us," he told the astonished Schröter, "to be there in two or three days."

Everywhere—north, south and east—the fronts were shrinking. And now almost all the machinery of the shattered, ruined metropolis was either slowing down or coming to a halt. Factories were

* Testimony at the Nuremberg trials disclosed that Grawitz in his additional capacity as Himmler's Chief Surgeon had authorized medical experiments on concentration camp inmates.

closing; streetcars had ceased to run; the subway had stopped except for the transport of essential workers. Ilse König, a laboratory technician in the city health department, remembers the *Roter Ausweis* (red pass) she received in order to continue riding to her job. Garbage was no longer being collected; mail could not be delivered. Gertrud Evers, working in the main post office on Oranienburgerstrasse, remembered the "terrific stench of spoiled, undelivered food packages that hung over the building." Because most of the police were now either in fighting units or the Volkssturm, the streets were no longer patrolled.

For many people on this twentieth of April the seriousness of the situation was really brought home by a single occurrence: the zoo closed its gates. Electricity there stopped at exactly 10:50 A.M., making it impossible to pump in water. The current would come on again four days later, but for only nineteen minutes. Thereafter it would remain off until the battle was over. But from this day onward the keepers knew that many of the animals must surely die—particularly the hippos in the pools and the inhabitants of the aquarium that had been saved earlier. Heinrich Schwarz, the bird keeper, already worried about the condition of the rare Abu Markub stork, which was slowly but surely starving to death in the Schwarz bedroom, now wondered how the bird could possibly survive without water. He would carry pails of water until he collapsed, the 63-year-old Schwarz decided—and not only for Abu, but for Rosa, the big hippo, and her two-year-old baby, Knautschke.

Zoo director Lutz Heck was in a quandary. He knew that eventually the dangerous animals must be destroyed, in particular the zoo's prize baboon, but he kept putting off the moment. Distraught and in need of a moment's peace, Heck did something he had never before done in his life: he went fishing in the Landwehr Canal along with one of the keepers. There, while "thinking things out," the men caught two pike.

That day Fritz Kraft, the municipal subway director, met with Berlin's Mayor, Julius Lippert. The Mayor gave Kraft and the assembled subway managers some realistic instructions. "If the Western Allies get here first," Lippert told the group, "hand over the subway installations intact. If the Russians get here before them . . ." He paused, shrugged, and said, "Destroy as much as possible." Small automatic telephone exchanges got similar instructions. Mechanics at the Buckow exchange were told to destroy the installations rather than let the Russians capture them. But maintenance man Herbert Magder suddenly realized that nobody had been given any instructions about how to do it. To the best of Magder's knowledge not a single exchange was destroyed. Nearly all of them continued to work throughout the battle.

Factories also were ordered leveled, in keeping with Hitler's scorched-earth policy. Professor Georg Henneberg, head of the Schering chemical department in Charlottenburg, remembers the plant director calling in all the chemists and reading an order he had just received. As the enemy got closer, the edict said, water, gas, electrical and boiler installations were to be destroyed. Henneberg's boss finished reading the order, paused a moment, then said, "Now, gentlemen, you know what you are *not* supposed to do." He bid them all good-bye and closed down the plant, intact. As Henneberg remembers, "We all bid farewell to one another until life after death."

For years, Berliners would remember that April 20 for still another reason. Whether in celebration of the Führer's birthday or in anticipation of the climax to come no one knew, but that day the government gave the hungry populace extra allocations of food called "crisis rations." As Jurgen-Erich Klotz, a 25-year-old one-armed veteran, remembered the extra food allocation, it consisted of one pound of bacon or sausage, one half pound of rice or oatmeal, 250 dried lentils, peas or beans, one can of vegetables, two pounds of sugar, about one ounce of coffee, a small package of a coffee substitute and some fats. Although there were almost five hours of air raids on Berlin this day, housewives braved the bombs to pick up the extra rations. They were to last eight days, and, as Anne-Lise Bayer said to her husband, "With these rations we shall now ascend into heaven." The same thought apparently occurred to Berliners everywhere; the extra food came to be known as *Himmelfahrtsrationen*—Ascension Day rations.

* * *

At Gresse, north of the Elbe, the Red Cross packages had arrived for Warrant Officer Dixie Deans's twelve thousand POWs. Deans had made all the arrangements. He had even persuaded the Commandant, Colonel Ostmann, to let R.A.F. men go to the International Red Cross center in Lübeck and drive trucks back, to get delivery faster. Now, columns of men covered the roads all around the town where the distribution of parcels was taking place. "Two parcels to a man," Deans had announced. "The effect on the morale of the men," Flight Sergeant Calton Younger remembered, "was electric. The arrival of the parcels was a plain miracle and we promptly invested Deans with the qualities of a saint."

Deans cycled from column to column on his frail bicycle with the distorted tire, seeing that every man got his quota, and warning the half-starved POWs, who had been subsisting for the most part on raw vegetables, not to eat too much but to "save as much as you can because we don't know what Jerry still has up his sleeve for us." Nevertheless, most men, Deans saw, "were eating as though it was their last meal." Flight Sergeant Geoffrey Wilson wolfed his way through the parcel: corned beef, biscuits, chocolate—and, above all, 120 cigarettes. He was "eating like mad, and smoking like mad because I intended to die full and not hungry."

The British planes found them as they sat there eating: nine R.A.F Typhoon fighters. They circled overhead, and then, in what Wilson was to remember as a "kind of a dreamlike, fascinating way," they peeled off and dived. Someone said, "My God! They're coming for us!" Men scattered wildly in all directions. Some tried to put out colored identifying cloth strips which they were carrying for just such an emergency. Others threw themselves into ditches, lay behind walls, ran for cover in barns or took shelter in the town itself. But many were too late. One after another, the Typhoons swooped in, firing rockets and dropping anti-personnel bombs among the columns. Men yelled: "We're your mates! We're your mates!" Eight planes made individual attacks; the ninth, perhaps realizing the mistake, pulled up. It was all over in minutes. Sixty POWs were dead. A score of others were injured, and some would die of their wounds in German hospitals.

Deans was sick with despair as he walked along the roads and saw the carnage. He immediately ordered identification of the dead. Some bodies were riddled almost beyond recognition—"just bits and pieces that had to be shoveled into the graves," Deans was later to recall.

After the dead had been buried and the wounded moved into German hospitals, a cold and determined Deans cycled over to Colonel Ostmann at his temporary headquarters. There was no military courtesy this time from Deans. "Ostmann," he said, "I want you to write me out a pass that will carry me through to the British lines. This sort of thing must never happen again."

Ostmann looked at Deans in amazement. "Mr. Deans," he said, "I couldn't do that."

Deans stared back at him. "We don't know who is going to overrun our group," he warned. "It could be the British—or it could be the Russians. We don't give a damn who liberates us. But which do you want to surrender to?" Deans looked squarely at the German. "Somehow I don't think you'll have much of a future with the Russians." He paused to let his last statement sink in. Then he said quietly, "Colonel, write out the pass."

Ostmann sat down at a table and on Wehrmacht paper wrote out a note which would carry Deans through enemy territory. "I don't know how you'll get through the front lines," he told Deans, "but at least this will get you up to them." Deans said: "I would like to take the guard Charlie Gumbach with me." Ostmann thought about that for a moment and said, "Agreed." He wrote out a pass for Gumbach. "And I could do with a bicycle that isn't falling apart," said Dixie. Ostmann looked at him and then, shrugging, said that he would arrange that, too. As he left the office, Deans had one final remark. "I will be back with Charlie to bring my men out, I promise you that." Then with a crisp salute, Deans said, "Thank you, Colonel." The Colonel saluted too. "Thank you, Mr. Deans," he said.

That night, accompanied by German Corporal Charlie Gumbach, the indomitable Dixie Deans set out for the long ride to the British lines.

❀   ❀   ❀

By nightfall Koniev, watching the map anxiously as Zhukov's tanks streaked toward Berlin, was urging his men on to even greater speed. "Don't worry about your flanks, Pavel Semenovich," he told General Rybalko, Commander of the Third Guards Tank Army. "Don't worry about being detached from the infantry. Keep going." Years afterward, Koniev remarked, "At that moment I knew what my tank commanders must be thinking: 'Here you are throwing us into this manhole, forcing us to move without strength on our flanks—won't the Germans cut our communications, hit us from the rear?'" The tall Koniev, clapping his Marshal's epaulettes with his hands, told the tank commanders, "I will be present. You need not worry. My observation post will be traveling with you in the very middle of the drive." Rybalko and General D. D. Lelyushenko, Commander of the Fourth Guards Tank Army, responded brilliantly. In a dash resembling that of the U.S. 2nd and 5th Armored divisions to the Elbe, the Soviet tankers sliced through the enemy—even though, as Rybalko noted, "German divisions that had not been wiped out still remained behind us." In twenty-four hours, fighting all the way, Rybalko made a blazing run of thirty-eight miles. Lelyushenko's tanks drove twenty-eight miles. Now Rybalko exultantly phoned Koniev. "Comrade Marshal," he said, "we are fighting on the outskirts of Zossen." Elements of the First Ukrainians were now only twenty-five miles from Berlin.

＊　　＊　　＊

At Zossen the alarm had been sounded. It now seemed likely that the Soviets would reach the High Command headquarters within twenty-four hours, and the order had been given to move. Key officers had left already for a new command post near Potsdam. The remainder of the headquarters personnel, along with the office typewriters, decoding machines, safes and crates of documents, were loaded into buses and trucks. As the packing and loading went on, people walked about anxiously, eager to get going. At that moment, said General Erich Dethleffsen, who had taken over Krebs's old job as Assistant Chief of Staff, "we offered the enemy air force a rewarding target." Shortly before dark the convoys moved out, heading for Bavaria. Dethleffsen, driving toward Berlin to attend the Führer's night conference, was happy to see a flight of Luftwaffe planes heading over him going south. Later at the briefing he heard a Luftwaffe officer tell Hitler about a "successful attack upon Soviet tanks pushing toward Zossen, to defend the area from attack." The bombers of the Luftwaffe had been more than successful: the "Soviet tanks" had been the buses and trucks of the OKH command column heading south. The Germans had shot up their own convoy.

At midnight on April 20 Heinrici grimly surveyed his maps and tried to analyze the situation. A few hours earlier, one of his fears had been realized: he now commanded not only the Army Group Vistula but Berlin as well. Almost immediately upon receiving the order he had called Reymann and told him that no bridges were to be destroyed in the city. Reymann had complained that the city was defenseless anyway, now that the best part of his Volkssturm had been pulled out to man defense lines. Heinrici knew all about it; in fact, he now told Reymann to send along the remainder of the Home Guard. "Reymann," said Heinrici wear-

413

ily, "don't you understand what I'm trying to do? I'm trying to make sure that fighting takes place *outside* the city, and not in it."

Under the present circumstances, Heinrici knew, Berlin could not be defended. He had no intention of allowing his armies to fall back into the city. Tanks would not be able to maneuver there. Because of the buildings, artillery could not be used: they would have no field of fire. Furthermore, if any attempt was made to fight in the city there would be an enormous loss of civilian life. At all costs Heinrici hoped to avoid the horror of block-to-block, street-to-street fighting.

His main concern at the moment was Busse's army; he was sure that if it was not pulled back quickly it would be encircled. Before leaving for the front early in the morning, he had given a message to his Chief of Staff for Krebs: "I cannot accept responsibility or direct this situation if Busse's army is not withdrawn immediately—and have him tell that to the Führer."

Then he had driven all over the front. Signs of disintegration were everywhere. He saw "roads covered with the vehicles of refugees, often with military transport among them." For the first time, he ran into troops who were obviously retreating. On the way to Eberswalde, he noted, "I didn't find one soldier who didn't claim to have orders to get munitions, fuel or something else from the rear." He was appalled, and swung into action. North of Eberswalde he "found men marching toward the northwest, saying that their division was to be reformed near Joachimsthal"; he stopped them and reorganized them near Eberswalde. At canal crossing-points in the same area he found "parts of the 4th SS Police Division being unloaded. They were young, newly organized, but only partially armed. They had been told they would get weapons in Eberswalde." South of there he found the road jammed with a mass of civilians and soldiers. Heinrici got out of his car and ordered the noncommissioned officers to turn their men around. "Go back to the front," he said.

In the town of Schönholz he saw "younger officers inactive and just looking around. They had to be energetically ordered to build

414

a line to catch scattered troops." The forests between there and Trampe were "filled with groups of soldiers either resting or retreating. No one claimed to have any orders or assignments." In another area he discovered "a tank reconnaissance section resting next to its parked vehicles." He ordered the unit to "move on Biesenthal at once and recapture this very important crossroads." There was so much confusion around Eberswalde, Heinrici later recalled, that "no one could tell me if a front existed at all." But by midnight he had restored order in the region and had issued fresh commands.

It was clear that his forces were undermanned, underarmed and often without competent leadership, and Heinrici knew that the front could not hold for long. Von Manteuffel's Third Panzer Army in the north had achieved some defensive success against Rokossovskii, but it was only a question of time before Von Manteuffel would be forced to retreat also.

At 12:30 A.M. he called Krebs. He told him that the situation was becoming almost impossible to control. In particular he talked about the 56th Panzer Corps which, "in spite of all counterattacks against the Soviets, is being pushed farther and farther back." The situation there, he said, was "tense to the point of bursting." Twice during the day he had talked personally to Krebs about the Ninth Army's rapidly worsening situation; each time Krebs had again given him the Führer's decision: "Busse is to hold on the Oder." Now Heinrici fought for Busse again.

"Consistently," Heinrici told Krebs now, "I have been denied freedom of movement for the Ninth Army. Now I demand it—before it's too late. I must point out that I am not resisting the Führer's orders because of stubbornness or unjustified pessimism. From my record in Russia you know that I do not give up easily. But it is essential to act now in order to save the Ninth from destruction.

"I have received the order," he said, "that the Army Group must hold the front line in its present positions and that all available forces must be pulled out to close the gap between the Ninth and Schörner on the southern flank. I regret what I'm going to say with all my heart, but the order cannot be carried out. The move simply has no chance of success. I demand the approval of my request to withdraw the Ninth Army. It is in the interest of the Führer himself that I make this request.

"Actually," said Heinrici, "what I should do is go to the Führer and say, 'My Führer, since this order endangers your well-being, has no chance of success and cannot be carried out, I request you to relieve me of command and give it to somebody else. Then I could do my duty as a Volkssturm man and fight the enemy.'" Heinrici was putting his cards squarely on the table: he was stating to his superior officer that he would rather fight in the lowest ranks than carry out an order that could result only in the useless sacrifice of lives.

"Do you really want me to pass this on to the Führer?" asked Krebs. Heinrici's answer was short. "I demand it," he said. "My Chief of Staff and my operations officers are my witnesses."

A short while later Krebs rang back. The Ninth was to hold its position. At the same time, all forces that could be made available were to try to close the gap with Schörner on the southern flank, "so as to set up a continuous front once more." Heinrici knew then that the Ninth was as good as lost.

In the Führerbunker Hitler's nightly military conference broke up at 3 A.M. During the meeting Hitler had blamed the Fourth Army—the army that had been crushed by Koniev's attack in the opening day of his offensive—for all the problems that had since arisen. He accused the army of treason. "My Führer," asked General Dethleffsen, shocked, "do you really believe that the command committed treason?" Hitler looked at Dethleffsen "with pitying eyes, as if only a fool could ask such a stupid question." Then he said: "All our failures in the east can be traced to treachery—nothing else but treachery."

As Dethleffsen was about to leave the room, Ambassador Walter Hewel, Von Ribbentrop's representative from the Foreign Ministry, entered, his expression deeply concerned. "My Führer," he said, "do you have any orders for me?" There was a pause, and then Hewel said: "If we still want to achieve anything on a diplomatic level, now is the time." According to Dethleffsen, Hitler, "in a voice soft and completely changed," said: "Politics. I have nothing to do with politics any more. That just disgusts me." He walked toward the door—"slowly," recalls Dethleffsen, "tired and with flagging gait." Then he turned and said to Hewel, "When I am dead you will have to busy yourself plenty with politics." Hewel pressed. "I think we should do something now," he said. As Hitler got to the door Hewel added most earnestly: "*My Führer, it is five seconds before twelve.*" Hitler seemed not to hear.

✤ 3 ✤

THE SOUND WAS unlike anything Berliners had heard before, unlike the whistle of falling bombs, or the crack and thud of anti-aircraft fire. Puzzled, the shoppers who were queued up outside Karstadt's department store on Hermannplatz listened: it was a low keening coming from somewhere off in the distance, but now it rose rapidly to a terrible piercing scream. For an instant the shoppers seemed mesmerized. Then suddenly the lines of people broke and scattered. But it was too late. Artillery shells, the first to reach the city, burst all over the square. Bits of bodies splashed against the boarded-up store front. Men and women lay in the street screaming and writhing in agony. It was exactly 11:30 A.M., Saturday, April 21. Berlin had become the front line.

Shells now began to strike everywhere. Tongues of flame leaped from rooftops all over the center of the city. Bomb-weakened buildings collapsed. Automobiles were up-ended and set afire. The Brandenburg Gate was hit and one cornice crashed down into the street. Shells plowed the Unter den Linden from one end to the other; the Royal Palace, already wrecked, burst into flames again. So did the Reichstag; the girders that had once supported the building's cupola collapsed and hunks of metal showered down. People ran wildly along the Kurfürstendamn, dropping briefcases and packages, bobbing frantically from doorway to doorway. At the Tiergarten end of the street, a stable of riding horses received a direct hit. The screams of the animals mingled with the cries and shouts of men and women; an instant later the horses stampeded out of the inferno and dashed down the Kurfürstendamm, their manes and tails blazing.

Barrage after barrage pounded the city, systematically and methodically. Correspondent Max Schnetzer of the Swiss paper *Der Bund,* standing by the Brandenburg Gate, noted that in the center of the government section of the Wilhelmstrasse at least one shell was landing every five seconds. Then there would be a pause of half a minute or a minute and once again the shells would start to fall. From where he stood the newspaperman could see fires shooting up toward the skies from the direction of the Friedrichstrasse Station. "Because the smoke and haze diffuses the light," he later wrote, "it looks as if the very clouds are on fire."

The shelling was just as intense in other parts of the city. In Wilmersdorf, Ilse Antz, her mother and sister felt their building shudder. The two girls threw themselves to the floor. Their mother clung to the doorpost, screaming, "My God! My God! My God!" In Neukölln, Dora Janssen watched her husband, a Wehrmacht major, walk down the driveway to his limousine. The major's batman opened the car door and suddenly was "torn completely to pieces" by a shell. When the dust cleared she saw her husband still standing by the car, his head high but his face distorted with pain. As Frau Janssen ran toward the major, she saw that "one leg

418

of his trousers was soaked in blood which was running over his boot and onto the sidewalk." Later, as she watched him being carried away on a stretcher, she found a curious emotion competing with her concern for her husband's safety. She could not help thinking, "How upright he stood in spite of his injury. A real officer!"

Not far away was another officer who had never believed that the Russians could come this close. The fanatical Luftwaffe accountant, Captain Gotthard Carl, who still greeted his family with the Hitler salute, was growing desperate. As the Russians had come closer, Carl's sartorial splendor had gleamed undiminished; indeed, it had become even more evident. Though she would never dare tell him so, his wife Gerda thought Carl looked ridiculous in his gala dress uniform, complete with gold cufflinks and those rows of meaningless ribbons. These days, too, he was never without his signet ring, on which a swastika was outlined in diamonds.

But Gotthard Carl was fully aware of the turn events were taking. Returning home at noon from his Tempelhof office, he threw up his hand in his usual "Heil Hitler" greeting and then gave his wife some instructions. "Now that the bombardment has begun," he told her, "you are to go to the cellar and remain there permanently. I want you to sit right opposite the cellar entrance." Gerda looked at him in amazement; it seemed the least safe place to be. But Gotthard was insistent. "I have heard that in other cities the Russians enter the cellars with flame throwers and most people are burned alive. I want you to sit directly before the cellar door so that you will be killed first. You won't have to sit and wait your turn." Then, without another word he clasped his wife's hands, gave the Nazi salute and walked out of the apartment.

Numbly, Gerda did as she was told. Sitting well ahead of the other occupants and just inside the entrance to the shelter, she prayed steadily as the bombardment raged overhead. For the first time since their marriage she did not include Gotthard in her prayers. In the afternoon, at the time her husband usually arrived home, Gerda, defying his orders, ventured upstairs. Trembling and frightened, she waited awhile, but Gotthard did not return. She never saw him again.

The artillery shelling had begun just as the aerial bombing ended. The last Western air raid on Berlin, the 363rd of the war, was delivered at 9:25 A.M. by elements of the U. S. Eighth Air Force. For forty-four months the Americans and British had pounded "Big B," as the U.S. fliers called it. Berliners had shaken their fists at the bombers, and they had mourned the deaths of friends and relatives and the destruction of their homes. Yet their anger, like the bombs themselves, had been impersonal, directed at men they would never see. The shelling was different. It came from an enemy who stood outside their doors, who would soon be facing them.

There was another difference, too. Berliners had learned to live with the bombing and to anticipate the almost clocklike regularity of the raids. Most people could tell by the very whistle of a falling bomb approximately where it would land; many had grown so accustomed to the raids that often they did not even bother to seek shelter. Artillery fire was somehow more dangerous. Shells landed suddenly and unexpectedly. The razor-sharp, scythelike shrapnel ripped and cut in every direction, often striking yards away from the initial explosion.

Journalist Hans Wulle-Wahlberg, making his way across Potsdamer Platz as it was raked by shell bursts, saw dead and dying everywhere. It seemed to him that some people had been killed by the blast of air pressure "which had torn out their lungs." As he dodged the bursts the thought struck him that Berliners, formerly bound together against their common enemy, the bombers, "now had no time to bother about the dead and the wounded. Everyone was too busy trying to save his own skin."

The merciless shelling had no pattern. It was aimless and incessant. Each day it seemed to increase in intensity. Mortars and the grinding howl of rocket-firing *Katushkas* soon added to the din. Most people now spent much of their time in cellars, air raid shelters, flak tower bunkers and subway stations. They lost all sense of time. The days blurred amid the fear, confusion and death that was all about them. Berliners who had kept meticulous diaries up to April 21 suddenly got their dates mixed. Many wrote that the Russians were in the center of the city on April 21 or 22, when the Red Army was still fighting in the suburbs. Their terror of the Russians was often intensified by a certain guilty knowledge. Some Germans, at least, knew all about the way German troops had behaved on Soviet soil, and about the terrible and secret atrocities committed by the Third Reich in concentration camps. Over Berlin, as the Russians drew closer, hung a nightmarish fear unlike that experienced by any city since the razing of Carthage.

Elfriede Wassermann and her husband Erich had taken shelter in the huge bunker next to the Anhalter railway station. Erich had lost his left leg on the Russian front in 1943, and could walk only with the aid of crutches. He had quickly recognized the sound of the artillery fire for what it was, and had rushed his wife off to the bunker. Elfriede had packed their belongings in two suitcases and two other large bags. Over her own clothes she put on a pair of Erich's old military pants and, on top of everything, both her woolen and fur coats. Since her husband needed both hands for his crutches, she had strapped one bag on his back, the other across his chest. One of the parcels contained food: some hard-crusted bread, and a few tins of meat and vegetables. In one of her suitcases Elfriede had a large pot of butter.

By the time they reached the Anhalter Station, its bunker was already jammed. Elfriede finally found them a place on one of the stairway landings. A single weak light hung above their heads. In its glow, people could be seen crowding every foot of floor space and every stairway of the building. Conditions in the bunker were unbelievable. The floor above was reserved for wounded, and their screams could be heard night and day. Toilets could not be used because there was no water; excrement was everywhere. The stench was nauseating at first, but after a time Elfriede and

Erich no longer noticed it. They passed the hours in a state of complete apathy, hardly talking, unaware of what was happening outside.

Only one thing intruded on their private thoughts: the continuous screaming of children. Many parents had run out of supplies of food and milk. Elfriede saw "three small babies being carried down from the floor above, all of them dead from lack of food." Next to Elfriede sat a young woman with a 3-month-old infant. At some point during their stay in the bunker, Elfriede noticed that the baby was no longer in the mother's arms. It was lying on the concrete floor next to Elfriede, dead. The mother seemed dazed. So was Elfriede; she remembers "that I simply saw that the child was dead without being upset in any way."

On Potsdamerstrasse, the House of Tourist Affairs was being shelled. In the 44-room underground shelter there were more than two thousand people, and Margarete Promeist, who was in charge of the shelter, had her hands full. Besides civilians, two battalions of Volkssturm had recently been moved in because, Margarete was told, "the Russians are getting closer." Harried and near exhaustion, Margarete had been more than grateful for the telephone call she had received a short time before. A close friend had volunteered to bring her some food. Now, as she moved about the shelter, forty-four wounded civilians were brought down from the street. Margarete hurried over to assist with the casualties. One of them was beyond help—and as she sat quietly beside the dead body of the woman who had come to bring her food, Margarete "envied her quiet and peaceful smile. She, at least, has been spared our *via dolorosa*."

While most people were going underground for the duration of the battle, druggist Hans Miede patrolled his beat as air raid warden for the public shelter at Bismarckstrasse 61 in Charlottenburg. As shells exploded all about him, he looked balefully at a poster on the wall of the building opposite the shelter. The text, printed in gigantic letters, read, THE HOUR BEFORE SUNRISE IS THE DARKEST.

For Dr. Rudolf Hückel the sunrise was far away. For weeks now the eminent pathologist had been a source of deep worry to his wife Annemaria. She believed he was headed for a nervous breakdown. Some time earlier he had shown her a cyanide capsule whose deadly potency he had improved upon by the addition of acetic acid. He had told her then that if Berlin's situation worsened, they would commit suicide. Since then Frau Hückel had seen how "the intensity of the war, its senselessness, and my husband's rage against Hitler had all gotten the best of him." Now the limit of Dr. Hückel's endurance had been reached. After hours of listening to the screaming of shells, the doctor suddenly got up, ran to the open window and yelled out at the top of his voice, *"Der Kerl muss umgebracht werden!"*—That fellow [Hitler] must be bumped off!

Hitler's finger stabbed the map. "Steiner! Steiner! Steiner!" he shouted. The Führer had found the answer. SS General Felix Steiner and his troops, he cried, were to attack immediately from their positions in the Eberswalde on the flank of Von Manteuffel's Third Panzer Army; then they were to head south, cutting off the Russians' drive on Berlin. Steiner's attack would close the gap that had opened when the northern flank of Busse's Ninth Army crumpled. On Hitler's map it appeared a brilliant move. Zhukov's drive now looked like an arrowhead, its base on the Oder, its tip pointing directly at Berlin. Along Zhukov's northern flank was the little flag that said, "Group Steiner." Hitler was confident once more. Steiner's attack would re-establish contact between the Third and Ninth armies.

There was only one thing wrong with the Führer's scheme. Steiner had virtually no men. Earlier, Heinrici had decided to place under Steiner the Ninth Army troops that had been shoved to the north by the Russian drive. Unfortunately, the widespread confusion at the front and the lack of time had made it impossible

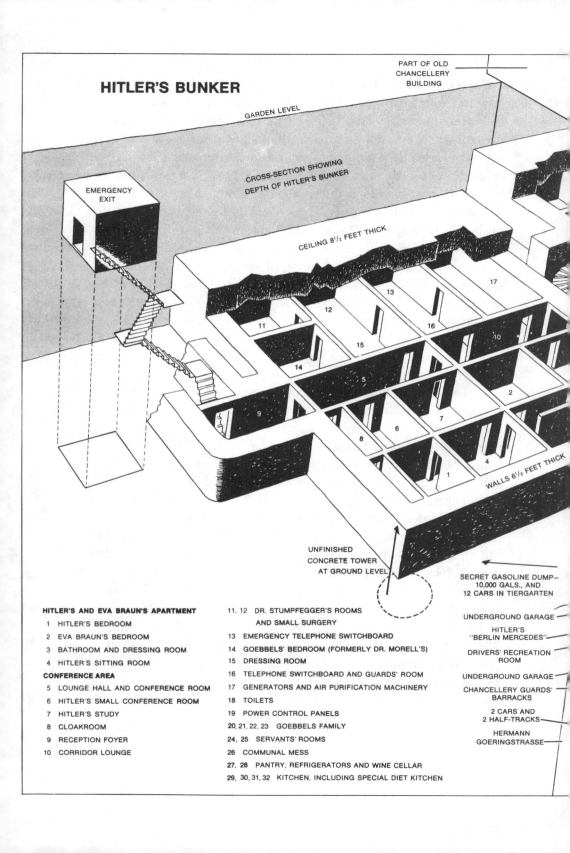

HITLER'S BUNKER

PART OF OLD CHANCELLERY BUILDING

GARDEN LEVEL

CROSS-SECTION SHOWING DEPTH OF HITLER'S BUNKER

EMERGENCY EXIT

CEILING 8½ FEET THICK

WALLS 6½ FEET THICK

UNFINISHED CONCRETE TOWER AT GROUND LEVEL

SECRET GASOLINE DUMP— 10,000 GALS., AND 12 CARS IN TIERGARTEN

UNDERGROUND GARAGE

HITLER'S "BERLIN MERCEDES"

DRIVERS' RECREATION ROOM

UNDERGROUND GARAGE

CHANCELLERY GUARDS' BARRACKS

2 CARS AND 2 HALF-TRACKS

HERMANN GOERINGSTRASSE

HITLER'S AND EVA BRAUN'S APARTMENT

1 HITLER'S BEDROOM
2 EVA BRAUN'S BEDROOM
3 BATHROOM AND DRESSING ROOM
4 HITLER'S SITTING ROOM

CONFERENCE AREA

5 LOUNGE HALL AND CONFERENCE ROOM
6 HITLER'S SMALL CONFERENCE ROOM
7 HITLER'S STUDY
8 CLOAKROOM
9 RECEPTION FOYER
10 CORRIDOR LOUNGE

11, 12 DR. STUMPFEGGER'S ROOMS AND SMALL SURGERY
13 EMERGENCY TELEPHONE SWITCHBOARD
14 GOEBBELS' BEDROOM (FORMERLY DR. MORELL'S)
15 DRESSING ROOM
16 TELEPHONE SWITCHBOARD AND GUARDS' ROOM
17 GENERATORS AND AIR PURIFICATION MACHINERY
18 TOILETS
19 POWER CONTROL PANELS
20, 21, 22, 23 GOEBBELS FAMILY
24, 25 SERVANTS' ROOMS
26 COMMUNAL MESS
27, 28 PANTRY, REFRIGERATORS AND WINE CELLAR
29, 30, 31, 32 KITCHEN, INCLUDING SPECIAL DIET KITCHEN

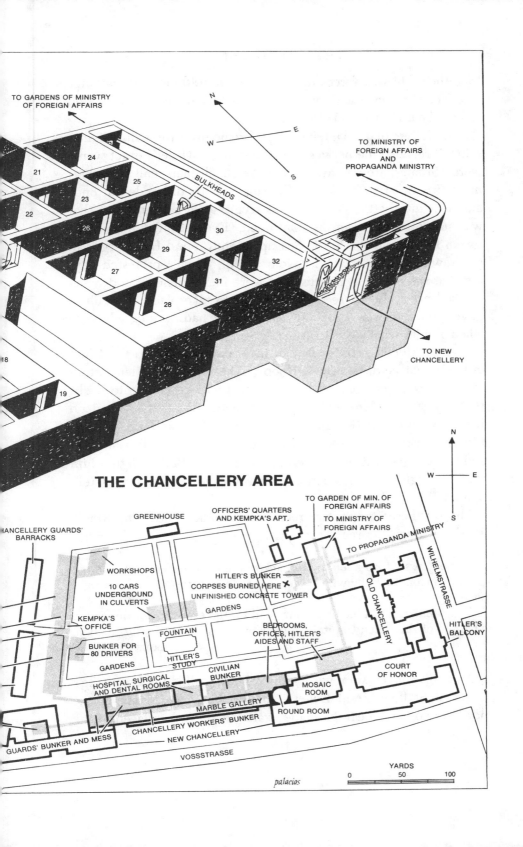

TO GARDENS OF MINISTRY
OF FOREIGN AFFAIRS

N

W — E

S

24

21

25

23

22

26.

BULKHEADS

TO MINISTRY OF
FOREIGN AFFAIRS
AND
PROPAGANDA MINISTRY

30

29

32

27

31

28

18

19

TO NEW
CHANCELLERY

N

W — E

S

THE CHANCELLERY AREA

GREENHOUSE

OFFICERS' QUARTERS
AND KEMPKA'S APT.

TO GARDEN OF MIN. OF
FOREIGN AFFAIRS

TO MINISTRY OF
FOREIGN AFFAIRS

TO PROPAGANDA MINISTRY

CHANCELLERY GUARDS'
BARRACKS

WILHELMSTRASSE

OLD CHANCELLERY

WORKSHOPS

HITLER'S BUNKER
CORPSES BURNED HERE ✗
UNFINISHED CONCRETE TOWER

10 CARS
UNDERGROUND
IN CULVERTS

GARDENS

KEMPKA'S
OFFICE

HITLER'S
BALCONY

BUNKER FOR
80 DRIVERS

FOUNTAIN

BEDROOMS,
OFFICES, HITLER'S
AIDES AND STAFF

GARDENS

HITLER'S
STUDY

CIVILIAN
BUNKER

COURT
OF HONOR

HOSPITAL, SURGICAL
AND DENTAL ROOMS

MOSAIC
ROOM

MARBLE GALLERY

ROUND ROOM

CHANCELLERY WORKERS' BUNKER

GUARDS' BUNKER AND MESS

NEW CHANCELLERY

VOSSSTRASSE

palacios

YARDS

0   50   100

to gather sufficient forces to make the Group Steiner operational. In effect, there *was* no Group Steiner. But the name had stuck, and so had the little flag on Hitler's map.

Now Hitler phoned Steiner. "As I remember the call," Steiner said, "it reached me between 8:30 and 9 P.M. Hitler's exact words were: 'Steiner, are you aware that the Reichsmarschall [Goering] has a private army at Karinhall? This is to be disbanded at once and sent into battle.' While I was trying to figure out what that was supposed to mean, he continued, 'Every available man between Berlin and the Baltic Sea up to Stettin and Hamburg is to be drawn into this attack I have ordered.' When I protested, saying that the troops at my disposal were inexperienced, and when I asked precisely where the attack was to take place, the Führer gave me no answer. He simply hung up. I had no idea where or when or with what I was to attack."

Steiner called Krebs, explained his situation and told the Chief of OKH that he did not have troops. "Then I recall Hitler cutting in on the conversation. At that moment I was explaining to Krebs that my troops were totally inexperienced and that we had no heavy weapons. Hitler gave me a long lecture and closed with these words, 'You will see, Steiner. You will see. The Russians will suffer their greatest defeat before the gates of Berlin.' I told him that I thought the Berlin situation was hopeless. I was completely ignored."

Shortly thereafter Steiner received the official order to attack. The last paragraphs read:

It is expressly forbidden to fall back to the west. Officers who do not comply unconditionally with this order are to be arrested and shot right away.

You, Steiner, are liable with your head for the execution of this order. The fate of the Reich Capital depends on the success of your mission.

ADOLF HITLER.

After his conversation with Steiner, Hitler called the Luftwaffe's Chief of Staff, General Koller. "All Air Force personnel in the northern zone who can be made available are to be placed at the

426

disposal of Steiner and brought to him," Hitler said, his voice rising. "Any commanding officer who keeps back personnel will forfeit his life within five hours. They must be told of this." Then he screamed: "You, yourself, will guarantee with your own head that absolutely every man is employed."

Koller was dumbfounded. It was the first he had heard of Group Steiner. He called General Dethleffsen at OKH and asked, "Where is Steiner? Where should our troops be sent?" Dethleffsen did not know, but promised to find out as quickly as possible.

Throughout this frantic period, one man, Heinrici, knew nothing at all about the scheme. When he finally heard, he called Krebs. "Steiner does not have the strength to make such an attack," Heinrici said angrily. "I reject the order. I insist on the withdrawal of the Ninth Army. Otherwise, Krebs, the only troop units still in position to defend Hitler and Berlin will be lost. Now, I tell you if this final request is not approved, then I must demand to be released from my post." Could he, Heinrici suggested, have an appointment with Hitler to discuss the situation? Krebs flatly vetoed the idea. "It's just not possible," he said. "The Führer is overworked."

For the record, Heinrici noted the outcome of the conversation in his personal war diary: "My appeal to the highest officials to bear in mind the responsibilities they bore to the troops was rejected with the words, 'That responsibility is borne by the Führer.'"

The life of Army Group Vistula was drawing to a close. Heinrici knew that it could last only a few days longer. His career, too, seemed to be running out. The General was well aware that his unbending obstinacy over how to fight his losing battle was considered the worst kind of defeatism by Krebs. Now, without warning, during the night of April 21, Heinrici received word that General Eberhard Kinzel, Vistula's Chief of Staff, was to be replaced. The man who was to take over his job was Major General

Thilo von Trotha, one of Hitler's most ardent disciples. Heinrici believed that Krebs had deliberately put Von Trotha in the post to try to influence his decisions. If so, it was a senseless move. "I know this Von Trotha," Heinrici told Colonel Eismann. "Maybe he's intelligent, but he embellishes the facts; he has a kind of flashy optimism. His feet," the General observed tartly, "are in the air." When Von Trotha arrived, Heinrici decided, he would isolate him completely and deal only with Eismann. It was a dangerous procedure to adopt with a Hitler favorite, but Heinrici could not concern himself with that now.

Before dawn of the twenty-second, a second announcement reached Heinrici. The Berlin Commandant, General Reymann, telephoned. "I am being replaced," he told Heinrici. The events that followed Reymann's removal had some of the qualities of slapstick. His successor was another high-ranking Nazi Party official, a certain Colonel Kaether, a man so obscure that his first name is lost to history. Kaether was immediately promoted to major general, jumping the interim rank of brigadier general. He spent the rest of that day delightedly phoning his friends the news. By nightfall Kaether was a colonel again, having been removed from the post: Hitler himself had decided to take command temporarily.

Meanwhile, the man whose future was to be most closely bound to the city's last days was getting himself into serious trouble. General Karl Weidling was completely out of communication with any headquarters, including that of his immediate superior, General Busse. Weidling's 56th Panzer Corps had been so battered and so often encircled by General Katukov's First Guards Tank Army that he had lost all contact with his colleagues. Rumors were flying that Weidling had deliberately retreated, and Weidling was not on hand to refute them. Hitler had heard these stories. So had Busse. After waiting almost twenty-four hours for news, both men issued orders for Weidling's immediate arrest and execution.

✿   ✿   ✿

When the smoke cleared on the outskirts of Bernau, Captain Sergei Golbov saw the first prisoners coming out of their defenses. The fighting here had been murderous. It had taken Chuikov's troops almost half a day to advance five miles in this sector, fourteen miles northeast of Berlin. Now parts of the town were in flames, but tanks were pushing through, heading southwest for the Berlin districts of Pankow and Weissensee. Golbov sat on his newly confiscated motorcycle watching the prisoners. They were a sorry-looking lot, he thought—"gray-faced, dusty, bodies sagging with fatigue." Golbov looked about him and was struck by the disparity between the works of man and those of nature. Fruit trees were beginning to bloom. "The blossoms looked like white snowballs, and in the suburbs every little garden had flowers, but then the huge black war machines, the tanks, crawling through the gardens—what a contrast!"

Golbov took out of his tunic pocket a folded copy of the newspaper *Red Star*, carefully tore off a small strip of the paper, shook some tobacco onto it and rolled a cigarette. Everyone used *Red Star* paper; it was thinner and seemed to burn better than *Pravda* or *Izvestia*. It was as he lit the cigarette that he saw the German major staggering up the road toward him.

"Leave my wife alone!" the man was shouting in Polish. "Leave my wife alone!" Golbov watched, puzzled, as the wild-eyed officer staggered toward him. When the German got closer, Golbov got off his cycle and went toward him. Blood was pouring down the major's hands.

The German lifted his blood-streaked arms and Golbov saw that he had slashed his wrists. "I'm dying," the man gasped. "I've committed suicide. Look!" He thrust his bleeding hands toward Golbov. "Now! Will you leave my wife alone?"

Golbov stared at him. "You stupid fool," he said. "I've got other things to do than bother your wife." He called out for the medics, then held the man's wrists to stanch the flow of blood until the first-aid men arrived. It was probably too late anyway, Golbov thought, as the medics led the major away. "Leave my wife alone! Leave her alone!" the German kept yelling. Golbov leaned back against the motorcycle and relit his cigarette. Goebbels has done his work well, he thought; what do they think we are, monsters?

* * *

Bruno Zarzycki, tears staining his face, stood in the street as the liberators he had waited so long to see passed by. The Communist leader in the Neuenhagen-Hoppegarten area, twelve miles east of Berlin, was delighted because now everyone could see what he had known all along: that Goebbels' propaganda about the Soviets was fabricated of the most vicious lies. Red Army troops, trim and efficient, had entered Neuenhagen and had quickly passed through, heading west for the Berlin districts of Weissensee and Lichtenberg. There had been practically no fighting in the town. Most of the local Nazis had left on April 15. At that time Bruno had told Mayor Otto Schneider, "When I see the first Russians I'm going out to meet them with a white flag. Fighting would be useless." The Mayor agreed. Only one man had put up a fight: the fanatical Hermann Schuster, head of the party's social welfare unit. He had barricaded his house and opened fire on the first reconnaissance units. It was a one-sided battle. The Russians had efficiently wiped out Schuster and his house with hand grenades. Bruno and the other members of his Communist cell burned their Volkssturm arm bands and met the Russian troops with a white flag. Bruno was happier than he ever remembered being. He shared all his information with the Soviet troopers and told them that he and his friends were "anti-fascists and always had been." For Bruno the arrival of Zhukov's soldiers brought on the miracle cure he had anticipated weeks before: his ulcers disappeared. For the first time, he could eat without nausea or pain.

The cure was to be short-lived. Bruno's detailed plan for the future socialistic administration of the town, which he confidently offered to the conquerors a few weeks later, was turned down. A Russian official heard him out and then had responded with one word: *"Nyet."* On that day—three months after Bruno Zarzycki had watched with pride and wonder the arrival of his idols—the ulcers which he had always called "fascist-inspired" returned, worse than ever.

In the Lehrterstrasse Prison, condemned Corporal Herbert Kosney did not know how much longer his luck would hold. The confirmation of the death sentence pronounced on him by civil authorities was still pending action by a military court. Herbert was living on borrowed time. On the twentieth he had been informed that the military tribunal would hear his case the following day. He knew what its verdict would be, and that he probably would be executed immediately. But the next morning, when he arrived under guard at the courthouse at Plötzensee, the building was empty: everybody had fled to the shelters.

Although the surprise Russian bombardment had saved him, the reprieve was only temporary. Kosney had now been told that his trial would take place Monday, the twenty-third. The Russians were Herbert's last hope. If they did not reach the prison before that date, he would surely die.

Because of the shelling, the prisoners had been moved down into the cellars. Herbert noticed that the guards had suddenly become friendly. There were rumors that some prisoners had already been released and that others might be allowed to leave within the next few hours. Herbert was certain he would be held, but he hoped that his brother Kurt might get out.

Kurt, too, was aware of the rumors, but he knew what Herbert did not—that they were at least partly true. The names of some Jehovah's Witnesses—convicted conscientious objectors who performed various menial chores in the prison—had been called out, and the men had been given release slips which would permit them to leave the prison. One Witness did not seem to be in much of a hurry to depart, Kurt noticed. The man was sitting at a table in the cellar, carefully cleaning the last morsel of food from his tin plate. "Why aren't you leaving with the others?" Kurt asked. The man's explanation was simple. "My home is in the Rhineland, behind the Western Allies' lines," he said. "There's no possibility of getting there. I'm just going to sit tight and stay here until the whole thing is over."

Kurt looked at the man's release slip. If the Witness was not going to use it, he knew someone who could. As the prisoner continued eating, Kurt kept him in conversation, moving closer to the yellow paper that signified freedom. After a few more moments of amiable chatting, Kurt managed to slip the paper into his pocket; undetected, he walked off.

Quickly he found Herbert and offered him the precious release order. To his astonishment, Herbert refused it. Because he was condemned to death, the Gestapo would capture him no matter what, Herbert said. Kurt had been imprisoned only as a suspected Communist; he had not been charged with anything. "You'll have a better chance," Herbert told his brother. "You go." Then he added with false enthusiasm, "We'll all probably get out today, in any case. So you might as well go first."

A short time later, his bedroll over his shoulder, Kurt Kosney walked into the guard room on the main floor and joined a line of Jehovah's Witnesses being processed out. One of the guards, an SS sergeant named Bathe who knew Kurt, looked right at him. For one awful moment Kurt expected to be grabbed and hauled back to the cellar. But Bathe turned away. The man behind the desk said, "Next." Kurt presented his slip. Five minutes later, his official stamped release in hand, Kurt Kosney stood in the street outside the prison. He was a free man. The street was being swept with gunfire and "the air was thick with shrapnel," but Kurt Kosney hardly noticed. He felt "deliriously happy—as though I had drunk about twenty brandies."

*　　*　　*

The Russians were in Zossen. General Rybalko's Third Guards tankers had captured the High Command headquarters intact, along with a handful of engineers, soldiers and technicians. Everyone else had gone.

432

Rybalko's tired, begrimed tankers blinked in amazement at the brilliant lighting in the vast underground rooms. As they wandered through galleries, living quarters and offices, evidences of a speedy exodus were apparent everywhere. Major Boris Polevoi, a political commissar attached to Koniev's headquarters, saw that the floors were littered with maps and papers. In one room a dressing gown lay on a desk; nearby was a leather case filled with family photographs.

Exchange 500, the huge telephone complex, had been seized undamaged. Men stood on the threshold and gaped at the flickering lights on the consoles, all now unmanned. Large signs, attached to the telephone boards, warned in schoolbook Russian: "Soldiers! Do not damage this apparatus. It will be valuable to the Red Army." Polevoi and the other officers speculated that fleeing German workers "had put up the signs in order to save their own necks."

Among the men captured in the command center had been Hans Beltow, the chief engineer of the complex electrical systems, and now he showed the Russians around Exchange 500. One operator, Beltow explained through Russian women interpreters, had stayed until just before the headquarters was overrun. As wire recorders played out his last conversations, the Russians stood listening in the great immaculate room. During Zossen's final minutes in German hands, calls had continued to come in from all over the swiftly contracting Reich, and they were all there on the recorders.

"I have an urgent message for Oslo," a voice said in German.

"Sorry," said the Zossen operator, "but we're not transmitting. I'm the last man here."

"My God, what's happening . . . ?"

Another voice: "Attention, attention. I have an urgent message . . ."

"We aren't accepting any messages."

"Is there any contact with Prague? How are they feeling in Berlin?"

"Ivan is almost at the door. I'm closing down now."

Zossen had fallen. Except for this brief inspection, Koniev's armies had hardly paused there. One tentacle of tanks was heading for Potsdam; another had already crossed the Nuthe Canal and reached Lichtenrade, south of the Berlin district of Tempelhof. Other tankers pushed on to Teltow and were now crashing through the defenses south of the Teltow Canal. Beyond lay the districts of Zehlendorf and Steglitz.

By nightfall of April 22, Koniev's armies had cracked Berlin's southern defenses and had beaten Zhukov into Berlin by more than a full day.

* * *

In the Führerbunker the customary military conference began at 3 P.M. In the twelve-year history of the Third Reich, there had never been a day like this. The usual outpourings of optimism were missing. The Oder front had all but crumpled. The Ninth Army was virtually encircled. Its strongest unit, the 56th Panzer Corps, was lost for the moment and could not be found.* Steiner had been unable to attack. Berlin was almost encircled. Commanders were being replaced almost hourly. The Reich was in its death agonies, and the man who had brought it all about now gave up.

Hitler's announcement climaxed a wild, uncontrolled torrent of abuse in which he denounced his generals, his advisors, his armies and the people of Germany whom he had led to disaster. The end had come, Hitler sputtered; everything was falling apart; he was no longer able to continue; he had decided to remain in Berlin; he intended to take over the defense of the city personally—and at the last moment he meant to shoot himself. General Krebs and the Luftwaffe representative, General Eckhardt Christian, were horror-stricken. To both, Hitler seemed to have suffered a complete

---

* In Heinrici's war diary, in which all telephone conversations were taken down verbatim in shorthand, an astonishing entry appears: "12:30 April 21: Busse to Heinrici: 'Just got word that 56th Corps last night moved into Olympic Village from Hoppegarten without specific orders. Request arrest . . .' " No one knows where Busse got his information, but it was wrong: the Olympic Village was at Döberitz on the western side of Berlin. Weidling was fighting on the eastern outskirts of the city.

breakdown. Jodl alone remained calm, for Hitler had told the Operations chief all of this forty-eight hours before.

Everyone present tried to persuade the almost deranged Führer that all was not lost. He must remain in charge of the Reich, they said, and he must leave Berlin, for it was impossible to control matters from the capital any longer. The man who had held their world together now brutally rejected them. He was remaining in Berlin, Hitler said. The others could go where they pleased. Everyone was thunderstruck. To emphasize that he meant what he said, Hitler stated that he intended to make a public announcement of his presence in Berlin. There and then he dictated a statement to be broadcast immediately. The others managed to persuade him not to release it right away. The announcement would not be made until the next day. Meanwhile, the officers and aides in the bunker called on their colleagues outside the city to bring additional pressure on the Führer. Himmler, Doenitz and even Goering telephoned, pleading, like their comrades, for a change of mind. Hitler would not be dissuaded.

Jodl was called away to the phone. While he was gone Keitel, trying to reason with Hitler, asked to speak to him privately. The conference room was cleared. According to Keitel's account, he told Hitler that he saw two courses of action still open: to "make an offer of capitulation before Berlin became a battlefield," or to arrange "for Hitler to fly to Berchtesgaden and from there instantly begin negotiations." Hitler, according to Keitel, "did not let me get beyond these words. He interrupted and said, 'I have made this decision already. I shall not leave Berlin. I shall defend the city to the end. Either I win this battle for the Reich's capital or I shall fall as a symbol of the Reich.'"

Keitel thought this decision was madness. "I must insist," he told Hitler, "that you leave for Berchtesgaden this very night." Hitler refused to hear any more. He called back Jodl and, in a private conference with the two officers, "gave us his order that we were to fly to Berchtesgaden and from there take over the reins together with Goering, who was Hitler's deputy."

"In seven years," Keitel protested, "I have never refused to carry out an order from you, but this one I shall not carry out. You can't leave the Wehrmacht in the lurch." Hitler replied, "I am staying here. That is certain." Then Jodl suggested that Wenck's army could drive toward Berlin from its positions on the Elbe.* Keitel declared that he would immediately travel to the western front, see General Wenck, "relieve him of all previous commands and order him to march toward Berlin and link up with the Ninth Army."

At last Hitler had heard a suggestion he could approve. It seemed to Keitel that the proposal brought a "certain relief to Hitler in this absolutely dreadful situation." Soon after, Keitel left for Wenck's headquarters.

Some officers who were not at the conference, such as the Luftwaffe's Chief of Staff, General Karl Koller, were so astonished by the news of the Führer's collapse that they refused to believe the reports of their own representatives on the scene. Koller rushed to Jodl's latest headquarters at Krampnitz, five miles northeast of Potsdam, and got a verbatim report. "What you've heard is correct," Jodl told Koller. He also told the Luftwaffe Chief of Staff that Hitler had given up and intended to commit suicide at the last minute. "Hitler said that he could not take part in the fighting for physical reasons and that he would not do so because of the danger of falling into the enemy's hands, perhaps when he was only wounded. We all tried to dissuade him. Hitler," Jodl went on, "said he was no longer able to continue and that now it was up to the Reichsmarschall. In answer to a remark that troops would not fight for Goering, the Führer said: 'What do you mean, fight? There's not much fighting to be done and when it comes to negotiating, the Reichsmarschall can do that better than I.'" Jodl added that "Hitler said the troops are no longer fighting, the tank barricades in Berlin are open and are no longer being defended."

---

* The Eclipse documents he had studied so thoroughly had convinced Jodl that Wenck's drive east would not be hindered by the Americans who, he was sure, were permanently halted on the Elbe.

In the Führerbunker it was clear by now that Hitler had meant every word he had said. He spent hours selecting documents and papers which were then taken out into the courtyard and burned. Then he sent for Goebbels, Frau Goebbels and their children. They were to stay with him in the bunker until the end. Dr. Werner Naumann, Goebbels' assistant, had known for some time that "Goebbels felt that the only decent course of conduct in the event of collapse was to fall in battle or commit suicide." Magda Goebbels, the Reichsminister's wife, felt the same way. When he heard of the Goebbels' impending move to the Chancellery, Naumann knew that "they would all die there together."

Goebbels' contempt for the "traitorous and unworthy" was almost equal to Hitler's. The day before the Führer's outburst, he called his propaganda staff together and said, "The German people have failed. In the east they are running away, in the west they are receiving the enemy with white flags. The German people themselves chose their destiny. I forced no one to be my co-worker. Why did you work with me? Now your little throats are going to be cut! But believe me, when we take our leave, earth will tremble."

By Hitler's standards it almost seemed that the only loyal Germans were those who now planned suicide and buried themselves in their own tombs. On this very evening, gangs of SS men were searching houses looking for deserters. Punishment was swift. On nearby Alexanderplatz, 16-year-old Eva Knoblauch, a refugee recently arrived in Berlin, saw the body of a young Wehrmacht private hanging from a lamp post. There was a large white card tied to the dead man's legs. It read: "Traitor. I deserted my people."

All through this decisive day Heinrici had waited for the news that he felt must come, that Hitler had given permission for the

Ninth Army to withdraw. Busse's force, almost encircled, cut off from the armies on its flanks, was close to annihilation. Yet Krebs had continued to insist that it hold its positions. He had gone even further: he had suggested that some of the Ninth's forces attempt to fight their way south and link up with Field Marshal Schörner. Busse himself was complicating matters. Heinrici had tried to get him to pull back without orders; Busse refused even to consider withdrawal unless a specific command arrived from the Führer.

At 11 A.M. on April 22, Heinrici warned Krebs that the Ninth would be split into several parts by nightfall. Krebs confidently predicted that Field Marshal Schörner would right the situation by driving north to link up with Busse. Heinrici knew better. "It will take Schörner several days to mount an attack," he told Krebs. "By then the Ninth will no longer exist."

Hour by hour the situation grew more desperate, and Heinrici repeatedly urged Krebs to do something. "You nail my forces down," he stormed, "while you tell me that I must do all I can to avoid the shame of the Führer being encircled in Berlin. Against my will, in spite of my request to be relieved of my duties, I am being prevented from pulling out the only forces that can be used for the protection of the Führer and Berlin." The Führer's headquarters was not only making difficulties over Busse; now it was demanding that Von Manteuffel's Third Army throw Rokossovskii's forces back across the Oder—an order so impossible to carry out that Heinrici could only gasp when he received it.

At 12:10 P.M. Heinrici warned Krebs: "It is my conviction that this is the last moment to withdraw the Ninth Army." Two hours later he called again but Krebs had already left for the Führer's conference. To General Dethleffsen, Heinrici said, "We *must* have a decision." At 2:50 Krebs called Heinrici. The Führer had agreed that some of the Ninth Army's forces could be moved back along the outer northern wing, giving up Frankfurt. Heinrici snorted. It was a half-measure that would do little to improve the situation. He did not point out to Krebs that the city had been held steadily by Colonel Bieler, the man Hitler had decided was "no Gneisenau." Now Bieler would find it difficult to disengage. In any event, the approval had come too late. The Ninth was encircled.

Nearly two hours later, Krebs again came on the phone. This time he informed Heinrici that at the Führer's conference it had been decided to turn General Wenck's Twelfth Army away from its positions on the western front. Wenck would launch an attack toward the east and Berlin, relieving the pressure. It was a surprising announcement; Heinrici commented dryly: "They will be most welcome." But still no order of complete withdrawal had come for the Ninth. Although they were encircled, Heinrici believed Busse's troops were still strong enough to begin moving toward the west. Now Krebs's news of Wenck—whom Heinrici had never even heard of before this moment—offered a new possibility. "The news gave rise to the hope," Heinrici said later, "that the Ninth could still be rescued from its precarious situation after all." Heinrici called Busse. "Krebs just told me that the Army Wenck is to turn about and march in your direction," he said. He instructed Busse to pull out his strongest division, break through the Russians, and head west to meet Wenck. Busse protested that this would lose him the bulk of his strength. Heinrici had had enough. "This is the order for the Ninth Army," he interrupted in a steely voice. "Pull out one division and get it under way to join with Wenck." He was finished arguing.

All around the rim of the city a red glow tinged the night sky. Fires pockmarked nearly every district, and the shelling was ceaseless. But in the cellar of the Lehrterstrasse Prison a feeling of jubilance and excitement had been mounting steadily. During the afternoon twenty-one men had been freed. Later, some of the remaining prisoners' valuables had been returned. According to the guards, the action had been authorized to speed up the processing of releases. At any moment now the prisoners expected to be freed. Some thought they might be home before morning. Even Herbert Kosney now felt that he had beaten the executioner.

A guard came into the cellar. From a list in his hand, he quickly began to read off names. The men listened tensely as each name was called. There was a Communist, a Russian POW and several men whom Kosney recognized as suspects in the Hitler plot of 1944. The guard reeled off the names: ". . . Haushofer . . . Schleicher . . . Munzinger . . . Sosinow . . . Kosney . . . Moll. . . ." Suddenly Herbert realized with a surge of hope that his name had been called

Altogether some sixteen prisoners had been singled out. When they had been counted, the guard led them to the security office. There they waited outside the door as, one after another, each man was called in. When Kosney's turn came, he saw that there were six SS men in the room, all quite drunk. One of them looked up his name and gave him the personal belongings taken from him at the time of his arrest. They were pitifully few: his army paybook, a pencil and a cigarette lighter. Herbert signed a receipt for his effects and then a form stating that he had been released. One of the SS men told him, "Well, you'll see your wife pretty soon."

Back in the cellar the men were told to pack their belongings. Kosney could hardly believe his luck. He packed quickly, carefully folding the good suit his wife had given him on their fourth wedding anniversary. When he had finished, he began to help his fellow prisoner, Haushofer. Among Haushofer's belongings was some food, including a bottle of wine and a loaf of pumpernickel. Haushofer could not get the bread into his rucksack, so he gave it to Kosney. There was a long wait. Then, after almost an hour and a half, the sixteen men were lined up in a double row and led up the cellar steps, through a door and into a dark hall. Suddenly a door slammed shut behind them and they were left standing in total darkness. Almost immediately a flashlight was switched on. As Herbert's eyes grew accustomed to the dimness, he saw that the light was hanging from an SS officer's belt. The man, a lieutenant colonel, was wearing a helmet and he carried a gun. "You are being transferred," he told the men. "If there are any attempts at escape you will be shot down. Load your things onto the truck outside. We'll march to the Potsdam railroad station."

Kosney's hopes were dashed. For a moment he thought of darting into one of the nearby cells. He was now certain that the Russians would be in the area within a few hours. But even as he considered hiding, he realized that other SS men, carrying machine pistols, were standing all about the room.

The prisoners were herded out into the Lehrterstrasse and marched off in the direction of Invalidenstrasse. It was raining; Herbert turned up his jacket collar and tied a towel he was using as a scarf tighter around his throat. Halfway down the street the men were stopped and searched, and their personal effects, which had been returned to them only a short while earlier, were taken again. The column set off once more, each prisoner flanked by an SS man with a machine pistol on his back and a gun in his hand. As they reached Invalidenstrasse an SS sergeant suggested taking a shortcut through the bombed-out Ulap exhibition hall. They marched through the rubble and entered the ruins of the massive building with its skeletal concrete pillars. Suddenly each prisoner was grabbed by the collar by his SS guard. One group of prisoners went to the left, the other to the right. They were marched right up to the wall of the building and positioned about six to seven feet apart. And then they all knew what was going to happen.

Some prisoners began to plead for their lives. The man next to Kosney began to scream, "Let me live! I haven't done anything." At that moment Herbert felt the cold barrel of a pistol touching the back of his neck. Just as the sergeant shouted "Fire," Herbert turned his head. There was a ragged volley as each SS man fired. Kosney felt a sudden sharp blow. Then he was on the ground. He lay motionless.

Now the lieutenant colonel walked along the line of fallen men, firing an additional shot into the head of each prisoner. When he got to Herbert, he said: "This pig has had enough."

Then he said: "Come on, men. We must hurry. We have more work to do tonight."

Kosney never knew how long he lay there. After a time, very cautiously, he put his hand up to his neck and cheek. He was bleeding profusely. But his life had been saved in that split second when he turned his head. He found that he could not use his right arm or leg. Crawling, he slowly made his way through the ruins until he reached Invalidenstrasse. Then he got up, found he could walk, tied the towel even more tightly about his wounded throat and slowly, painfully started in the direction of the Charité Hospital. He collapsed several times. Once he was stopped by a group of Hitler Youths; they first demanded his identity papers, but then, seeing that he was badly hurt, they allowed him to pass.

At some point in his journey he took his shoes off because "they felt too heavy." At another time he encountered heavy artillery fire. How long the walk took he could never remember—he was never more than half conscious—but finally he reached his home off Franseckystrasse. Then, with his last ounce of strength, Herbert Kosney, the only living witness to the Lehrterstrasse Prison massacre, banged again and again on the door. His wife Hedwig opened the door. The man who stood there was unrecognizable. His face was a mass of blood, as was the front of his coat. Horrified, she said, "Who are you?" Just before he collapsed, Kosney managed to say, "I'm Herbert." *

At 1 A.M. on April 23, the phone rang in the Wiesenburg forest headquarters of General Walther Wenck, commander of the Twelfth Army. The Wehrmacht's youngest general was still in

---

* The other fifteen bodies were found three weeks later. Still clutched in the hand of Albrecht Haushofer were some of the sonnets he had written in jail. One line read: "There are times which are guided by madness; And then they are the best heads that one hangs."

uniform, dozing in an armchair. His command post, *Alte Hölle* —Old Hell—about thirty-five miles east of Magdeburg was the former home of a gamekeeper.

Wenck picked up the phone himself. One of his commanders reported that Field Marshal Wilhelm Keitel had just passed through the lines, en route to the headquarters. Wenck called his Chief of Staff, Colonel Günther Reichhelm. "We have a visitor coming," he said. "Keitel." Wenck had always heartily disliked Hitler's Chief of Staff. Keitel was the last man in the world he wanted to talk to now.

In the last few weeks Wenck had seen more sorrow, hardship and suffering than he had ever witnessed in battle. As Germany's boundaries shrank, his area had become a vast refugee encampment. Homeless Germans were everywhere—along the roads, in the fields, villages and forests, sleeping in wagons, tents, broken-down trucks, railway carriages, and in the open. Wenck had turned every habitable building in the area—homes, churches, even village dance halls—into shelters for the refugees. "I felt," he said later, "like a visiting priest. Every day I went around trying to do what I could for the refugees, in particular the children and the sick. And all the time we wondered how soon the Americans would attack from their bridgeheads across the Elbe."

His army was now feeding more than half a million people a day. Trains from all over the Reich had reached this narrow area between the Elbe and Berlin and had been unable to proceed farther. The freight they carried was both a boon and a burden to the Twelfth Army. Every conceivable kind of cargo, from aircraft parts to carloads of butter, had been found on the trains. A few miles away, on the eastern front, Von Manteuffel's panzers were halted for lack of fuel; Wenck, on the other hand, was almost awash in gasoline. He had reported these surpluses to Berlin, but as yet no arrangements had been made to collect them. Nobody had even acknowledged his reports.

Now as he waited for Keitel, Wenck reflected with some concern that if the OKW Chief of Staff learned of his social work among the refugees he would hardly approve. Under Keitel's code of soldierly ethics, such actions were simply inconceivable. Wenck heard a car drive up and one of his staff said, "Now watch Keitel play the hero."

In the full trappings of a field marshal, even to baton, Keitel entered the little house followed by his adjutant and aide. "The arrogance and pomp of Keitel and his group, strutting as though they had just taken Paris," seemed disgraceful to Wenck, "when every road told its tale of misery and Germany lay defeated."

Formally Keitel saluted, touching his cap with his field marshal's baton. Wenck saw immediately that for all his punctilious behavior his visitor was anxious and excited. Keitel's adjutant produced maps and spread them out; without preamble, Keitel leaned over, tapped Berlin, and said: "We must save the Führer."

Then, as though he felt he had been too abrupt, Keitel dropped that subject and asked for a briefing on the Twelfth Army's situation. Wenck did not mention the refugees or the army's part in caring for them. Instead, he spoke in general terms of the Elbe area. Even when coffee and sandwiches were served, Keitel did not relax. Wenck did little to put his visitor at ease. "The truth was," he later explained, "that we felt terribly superior. What could Keitel tell us that we did not already know? That the end had come?"

Keitel suddenly stood up and began pacing the room. "Hitler," he said gravely, "has broken down completely. Worse, he has given up. Because of this situation, you must turn your troops around and drive toward Berlin, together with the Ninth Army of Busse." Wenck listened quietly as Keitel described the situation. "The battle for Berlin has begun," he said. "No less than the fate of Germany and Hitler are at stake." He looked solemnly at Wenck. "It is your duty to attack and save the Führer." Irrelevantly, Wenck suddenly thought that this was probably the closest Keitel had ever been to the front lines in his life.

Long ago in his dealings with Keitel, Wenck had learned that "if you gave an argument, one of two things happened: you got two hours of blistering talk or you lost your command." Now he replied automatically, "Of course, Field Marshal, we will do what you order."

Keitel nodded. "You will attack Berlin from the sector Belzig-Treuenbrietzen," he said, pointing to two small towns about twelve miles northeast of the Twelfth's front lines. Wenck knew that this was impossible. Keitel was talking about a plan which was based on forces—men, tanks and divisions—that had long since been destroyed, or had simply never existed. With virtually no tanks or self-propelled guns and with few men, Wenck could not simultaneously hold the line against the Americans at the Elbe and attack toward Berlin to save the Führer. In any case, it would be immensely difficult to attack northeast into Berlin. There were too many lakes and rivers in his path. With the limited forces at his disposal, he could only get into Berlin from the north. He suggested to Keitel that the Twelfth drive on Berlin "north of the lakes, via Nauen and Spandau. I think," Wenck added, "that I can mount the attack in about two days." Keitel stood for a moment in silence. Then he told Wenck stonily, "We can't wait two days."

Again, Wenck did not argue. He could not waste the time. Quickly he agreed to Keitel's plan. As the Field Marshal left the headquarters, he turned to Wenck and said, "I wish you complete success."

When Keitel's car had driven away, Wenck called together his staff. "Now," he said, "here's how we will actually do it. We will drive as close to Berlin as we can, but we will not give up our positions on the Elbe. With our flanks on the river we keep open a channel of escape to the west. It would be nonsense to drive toward Berlin only to be encircled by the Russians. We will try for a link-up with the Ninth Army, and then let's get out every soldier and civilian who can make it to the west."

As for Hitler, Wenck said only that "the fate of one person does not matter any more." While he was giving orders for the attack, it occurred to Wenck that in all the long night's discussion Keitel had never once mentioned the people of Berlin.

*   *   *

As dawn came up at Magdeburg, three Germans slipped across the Elbe and surrendered to the U. S. 30th Infantry Division. One of them was 57-year-old Lieutenant General Kurt Dittmar, a Wehrmacht officer who had daily broadcast the latest communiqués from the front, and who was known throughout the Reich as the "voice of the German High Command." With him were his 16-year-old son Eberhard and Major Werner Pluskat, the D-Day veteran whose Magdeburg guns had played an important part in preventing General Simpson's U. S. Ninth Army from crossing the Elbe.

Dittmar, who was considered the most accurate of all German military broadcasters, had a large following, not only in Germany but among the Allied monitoring staffs. He was immediately taken to the 30th's headquarters for questioning. He surprised intelligence officers with one piece of information: Hitler, he said, firmly, was in Berlin. It was enlightening news to the Allied officers. Up to now no one had been certain of the Führer's whereabouts.* Most rumors had placed him in the National Redoubt. But Dittmar could not be shaken from his story. The Führer was not only in Berlin, he told his interrogators, but he believed that "Hitler will either be killed there or commit suicide."

"Tell us about the National Redoubt," somebody urged. Dittmar looked puzzled. The only thing he knew about a national redoubt, he said, was something he had read in a Swiss newspaper the previous January. He agreed that there were pockets of resistance in the north, "including Norway and Denmark, and one in the south in the Italian Alps. But," he added, "that is less by intention than by force of circumstance." As his interrogators pressed him about the redoubt, Dittmar shook his head. "The National Redoubt? It's a romantic dream. It's a myth."

And that is all it was—a chimera. As General Omar Bradley,

---

* Apparently there had not been time to circulate Wiberg's report after its receipt in London.

the Twelfth Army Group commander, was later to write, "the Redoubt existed largely in the imagination of a few fanatical Nazis. It grew into so exaggerated a scheme that I am astonished we could have believed it as innocently as we did. But while it persisted, this legend . . . shaped our tactical thinking."

❋   ❋   ❋

Amid clouds of dust, columns of German tanks hammered through the cobbled streets of Karlshorst, on the outskirts of Berlin's eastern district of Lichtenberg. Eleanore Krüger, whose Jewish fiancé Joachim Lipschitz was hiding in the cellar of her home, watched in amazement. Where had the tanks come from? Where were they going? Instead of heading into the city, they were dashing south toward Schöneweide, as though fleeing Berlin. Were the Russians right behind? If they were, it would mean freedom at last for Joachim. But why were German troops leaving the city? Were they abandoning it? Retreating?

Eleanore did not know it, but she was watching the lost and battered remnant of General Weidling's 56th Panzer Corps in the process of restoring contact with the main force. After being pushed back to the very outskirts of the city, Weidling's men had re-established communications with Busse's now-encircled Ninth Army in a most roundabout way: the moment they hit the edge of the city they had used the public telephone to call High Command headquarters in Berlin, and they had thereupon been connected by radio with the Ninth. The 56th had immediately received orders to head south of the capital, cut their way through the surrounding ring of Russians, and link up with the Ninth again about fifteen miles from the city in the area of Königswusterhausen and Klein Kienitz. From there they would join the effort to cut off Koniev's forces.

But first Weidling had some unfinished business to attend to. He had now heard that officers from both Busse's and Hitler's headquarters had been sent to bring him in on charges that he had deliberately fled the battlefield, leaving his corps leaderless.

Angrily, he ordered his men to push on without him while he headed into the city to confront Krebs.

Some hours later Weidling, having crossed Berlin to the Reichskanzlei, made his way through the basement to the so-called aide-de-camp bunker where Krebs and Burgdorf had their office. They greeted him coolly. "What's going on?" demanded Weidling. "Tell me why I'm supposed to be shot." His headquarters, said Weidling sharply, had been located almost on the front line from the moment the battle began: how could anyone say he had fled? Someone mentioned the Olympic Village at Döberitz. The 56th had been nowhere near Döberitz, growled Weidling; to have gone there "would have been the greatest stupidity." Slowly Krebs and Burgdorf thawed; soon they were promising to clear up matters with the Führer "without delay."

Weidling then gave the two men a briefing on his situation. He told them that his corps was about to attack south of Berlin— and then, "in passing, I casually added that before leaving I had received a report that Russian tank spearheads had been seen near Rudow." Rudow lay just beyond the edge of the southeastern district of Neukölln. Krebs immediately saw danger. In that case, he said, the Ninth's order for the 56th Corps had to be changed: Weidling's corps would have to stay in Berlin. Then both Krebs and Burgdorf hurried off to see Hitler.

Shortly thereafter Weidling was told that Hitler wanted to see him. The walk to the Führerbunker was a long one, through what Weidling later called an "underground city." From Krebs's office he proceeded first along a subterranean tunnel, then through a kitchen and dining room, and finally down a staircase and into the Führer's personal quarters.

Krebs and Burgdorf introduced him. "Behind a table loaded with maps," Weidling wrote, "sat the Führer of the Reich. When I entered, he turned his head. I saw a puffy face with feverish eyes. When he tried to stand up, I noticed to my horror that his hands and legs were constantly trembling. He succeeded with great effort in getting up. With a distorted smile he shook hands with me and asked in a hardly audible voice whether we hadn't met before." Once before, said Weidling; the Führer had given him a decoration a year earlier. Hitler said: "I do remember the name, but cannot remember the face." When Hitler sat down, Weidling noticed that even in a sitting position "his left leg kept moving, the knee swinging like a pendulum, only faster."

Weidling told Hitler what the 56th's situation was. Then Hitler confirmed Krebs's instructions that the Corps was to stay in Berlin. The Führer thereupon launched into his plan for the defense of Berlin. He proposed to pull in the armies of Wenck from the west, Busse from the southeast and Group Steiner from the north, and thus, somehow, cut off the Russians. "It was," wrote Weidling, "with ever-growing astonishment that I listened to the big talk of the Führer." Only one thing was clear to Weidling: "Short of a miracle, the days until final defeat were numbered."

That evening the 56th Corps, suffering heavy losses, managed to disengage from the Russians in the south, then pivot and enter Berlin. Twenty-four hours later, to Weidling's horror, he was named Commandant of the city.

❖　❖　❖

The order from Stalin was numbered 11074. It was addressed to both Zhukov and Koniev; and it divided up the city between them. As of this day, April 23, the order said, the boundary line between the First Belorussian Front and First Ukrainian Front would be "Lübben, thence to Teupitz, Mittenwalde, Mariendorf, Anhalter Station of Berlin."

Although he could not complain publicly, Koniev was crushed. Zhukov had been given the prize. The boundary line, which ran straight through Berlin, placed Koniev's forces roughly 150 yards *west* of the Reichstag—which the Russians had always considered the city's prize plum, the place where the Soviet flag was to be planted.

❖　❖　❖

Now the city began to die. In most places, water and gas services had stopped. Newspapers began to close down; the last was the Nazis' own *Völkischer Beobachter*, which shut up on the twenty-sixth (it was replaced by a Goebbels-inspired four-page paper called *Der Panzerbar* [The Armored Bear], described as the "Combat Paper for the Defenders of Greater Berlin," which lasted six days). All transportation within the city was grinding to a halt as streets became impassable, gasoline scarce, and vehicles crippled. Distribution services broke down; there were almost no deliveries of any kind. Refrigeration plants no longer functioned. On April 22, the city's 100-year-old telegraph office closed down for the first time in its history. The last message it received was from Tokyo; it read: "GOOD LUCK TO YOU ALL." On the same day, the last plane left Tempelhof Airport, bound for Stockholm with nine passengers aboard, and Berlin's 1,400 fire companies were ordered to the west.*

And now, with all the police serving in either the army or the Home Guard, the city slowly started to go out of control. People began to plunder. Freight trains stalled in the marshaling yards were broken into in broad daylight. Margarete Promeist, who made an extremely dangerous journey to the rail yards under heavy shelling, came away with a single piece of bacon; "looking back on it," she said afterward, "I thought this was sheer madness." Elena Majewski and Vera Ungnad rushed all the way to the railway freight yards in Moabit. They saw people grabbing cases of canned apricots, plums and peaches. There were also sacks of a strange kind of beans, but the girls passed these by. They did not recognize green coffee beans. They got a case of canned goods labeled "Apricots" and when they got home discovered it was applesauce. Both girls had always hated it. Robert Schultze fared even worse: he spent five hours as part of a mob trying to get at some potatoes in a large food store—but by the time his turn came they were all gone.

* Two operations continued without a break: the meteorological records, kept at the station in Potsdam, did not miss a day throughout 1945, and eleven of the city's seventeen breweries--engaged, by government decree, in "essential" production—continued making beer.

Storekeepers who would not give supplies away were often forced to do so. Hitler Youth Klaus Küster walked into a store with his aunt and asked for some supplies. When the owner insisted that he had only some cereals left, Küster pulled a gun and demanded food. The shopowner quickly produced an assortment of foodstuffs, literally from under the counter. Küster gathered up as much as he could carry, and he and his scandalized aunt left the store. "You are a godless youth," his aunt cried when they were outside, "using American gangster methods!" Klaus replied: "Aw, shut up! It's now a matter of life and death."

Elfriede Maigatter heard a rumor that the giant Karstadt department store on the Hermannplatz was being looted. She hurried to the store and found it jammed with people. "Everyone was pushing and kicking to get through the doors," she later reported. "There were no queues any more. There was no sales staff, and nobody seemed to be in charge." People were just grabbing everything in sight. If it turned out to be something useless they simply dropped it on the floor. In the food department there was a carpet of several inches of sticky mud on the floor, made up of condensed milk, marmalade, noodles, flour, honey—anything that had been overturned or dropped by the mob."

A few supervisors seemed to be left, for now and then a man would shout, "Get out! Get out! The store is going to be blown up!" Nobody paid any attention to him; it was too obvious a trick. Women were grabbing coats, dresses and shoes in the clothing department. Bedding, linens and blankets were being dragged from shelves by others. In the candy section Elfriede saw a man grab a box of chocolates from a little boy. The child began to cry. Then he yelled, "I'm going to get another one." And he did.

But at the exit door came the denouement: two supervisors were stopping everyone as they tried to get out with their booty. They were letting people take food, but nothing else. Soon a great pile of merchandise began to grow near the door. People plowed through it, pushing and shoving, trying to force their way past the supervisors. When Elfriede tried to get through with the coat she had taken, one of the store officials grabbed it away from her. "Please let me have it," she begged. "I'm cold." He shrugged, took it back off the pile and gave it to her. "Beat it," he said. And all the time, as the mob pushed and shoved and grabbed everything in sight, someone kept yelling: "Get out! Get out! The store is going to be blown up!"

One witness to the looting at Karstadt's was Pastor Leckscheidt. His presence on the scene had come about in a surprising way. One of his parishioners had given birth to a stillborn baby and the infant had been cremated. The mother, deeply distressed, wanted the urn containing the ashes properly buried and Leckscheidt had agreed to be present—even though it meant walking several miles, under constant shelling, to the cemetery in Neukölln where the woman wanted her child buried. As they tramped along, the woman carrying the little urn in her shopping bag, they passed by Karstadt's and saw the mobs looting. His parishioner stared. Suddenly she said, "Wait!" Leckscheidt stood in amazement as "she left my side and disappeared into the store, urn, market bag and all." Moments later she returned, triumphantly swinging a pair of sturdy boots. Turning to Leckscheidt, she said: "Shall we go?"

On the way back, Leckscheidt was careful to keep her away from Karstadt's. It was just as well. That afternoon the huge store rocked as explosives tore it apart. The SS, which reportedly had stored 29 million marks' worth of supplies in the basement, had blown up the emporium to deny the Russians the treasure. A number of women and children were killed in the blast.

In the face of the plunderers many store owners simply gave up. Rather than let their shops get smashed by unruly mobs, they emptied their shelves and gave supplies away without accepting either ration stamps or money. There was another reason: shopkeepers had heard that if the Russians found hoarded food, they burned the shop down. In Neukölln a week before, film projectionist Günther Rosetz, had tried to buy some marmalade at Tengelmann's grocery store and had been refused. Now Rosetz saw that Tengelmann's was selling tubs of marmalade, oats, sugar and flour—all at ten marks a pound. In panic the store was giving goods away just to move everything out of the shop. In the Caspary wine shop on the corner of Hindenburgstrasse, Alexander Kelm could hardly believe his eyes: bottles of wine were given away to all comers. The Hitler Youth, Klaus Küster, making another foray through his neighborhood, got two hundred free cigarettes at one place, two bottles of brandy at another. The owner of the liquor shop in his area said: "Here, you might as well drink it up. Hard times are coming."

Even for looters there was virtually no meat to be had. At first a few butchers had supplies which they doled out to special customers, but soon that, too, was gone. Now, all over Berlin, people started carving up horses, which lay dead in the streets from the shelling. Charlotte Richter and her sister saw people armed with knives cutting up a gray-white horse that had been killed on Breitenbachplatz. "The horse," Charlotte saw, "had not fallen over on its side, but sort of sat on its haunches, its head still high, eyes wide open. And there were women with carving knives cleaving at its shanks."

Ruby Borgmann found that she enjoyed brushing her teeth with champagne; it made the toothpaste very foamy. In the luxurious cellar beneath Heinrich Schelle's fashionable Gruban-Souchay restaurant, Ruby and her husband Eberhard were living an almost exotic existence. Schelle had kept his promise; when the shelling began, he invited the Borgmanns to join him in his resplendent underground quarters. The restaurant's reserves of silver, crystal and fine china were stored there and Schelle had provided creature comforts as well. The floor was carpeted with Oriental rugs. On either side of the entrance, sleeping accommodations were screened by heavy gray-green draperies. Luxurious overstuffed chairs, a sofa and small tables—each covered with beige and rust-colored linen cloths from the restaurant—were placed about the room. There had been no water for days but there was champagne aplenty. "We drank champagne morning, noon and night," Ruby remembered. "It flowed like water—the water we didn't have."

Food was the real problem. The Borgmanns' good friend, Pia van Hoeven, who sometimes shared the cellar's comforts with them, was occasionally able to produce some bread and even a little meat on her visits. Mostly, however, the occupants lived on tuna fish and potatoes. Ruby wondered just how many ways there were to fix these staples. The restaurant's temperamental French chef, Mopti, had yet to repeat himself, but he could not go on forever. Still, now that there seemed no hope that the Americans would come, the little group had decided to live it up. At any hour they might be dead.

"Papa" Saenger was gone.

Through four years of bombing and through the shelling of the last few days, the 78-year-old World War I veteran had refused to be intimidated. In fact, it had taken all of Erna Saenger's powers of persuasion to prevent her husband Konrad from going out for his customary meeting with his World War I comrades-in-arms. She had put Papa to work digging a shallow hole in the garden to hide her preserves. Konrad also thought it might be a good idea to hide his old army sword along with the jams and jellies, so the Russians would find no weapons in the house.

But once the work was done, Papa had gone out into the streets despite the pleadings of the entire family. They had found his shrapnel-riddled body in the bushes outside the burning wreckage of Pastor Martin Niemöller's house, only a short way from home. While shells blanketed the district, the family brought Papa home in a wheelbarrow. As she walked alongside the cart, Erna remembered that during their last conversation she had a slight difference of opinion with Konrad as to which Biblical quotation was more appropriate for the times. Papa maintained that "one can only live by the 90th Psalm, especially the fourth verse: 'For a thousand years in thy sight are but as yesterday when it is past, and as a watch in the night.' " Erna had disagreed. "Personally," she told him, "I think that psalm is much too pessimistic. I prefer the 46th: 'God is our refuge and strength, a very present help in trouble.' "

There was not a coffin to be found, and a trip to the cemetery was too dangerous to attempt in any case. Still, they could not keep the body in the warm house. They left it on the porch. Erna found two small pieces of wood and nailed them together for a cross. Gently, she placed the crucifix between her husband's hands. As she looked down at Papa, she wished she could tell him that he had been right, for the 90th Psalm continued: "We are consumed by thine anger, and by thy wrath are we troubled."

Father Bernhard Happich looked down at the notes for his sermon. The chapel of Haus Dahlem was softly lit by candles, but outside the sky to the east of Wilmersdorf was almost blood red, and the shelling which had awakened the Sisters at three that morning was still going on nearly twelve hours later. Somewhere nearby, glass shattered and a tremendous concussion shook the building. Father Happich heard loud shouts from the street and then the heavy thudding sound of the Czech anti-aircraft gun just across the road from the maternity home and orphanage.

The nuns sitting before him did not stir. As he gazed out at them, he saw that, in keeping with an order from Mother Superior Cunegundes, the women had removed the heavy silver crosses they normally wore. Instead, small, inconspicuous metal crucifixes—so-called Death Crosses—were attached to their habits. The silver ones had been hidden, along with all rings and watches.

Father Happich had made some preparations of his own. In the Dahlem villa where the priest lived, a large box had been packed. In it Father Happich had placed some medical instru-

455

ments, the contents of the medicine chests, plus drugs, bandages and white sheets contributed by neighbors. Before becoming a priest Father Happich had received a medical degree, and now he was working again at both vocations; each day now he cared for casualties of the shellings, attended to accident victims and treated hysteria and shock. His white medical coat was beginning to see as much wear as his clerical robes.

He looked once more at his little flock of nuns, nurses and lay sisters, said a silent prayer that God would give him the right words, and began.

"Within the near future we expect Soviet occupation," he said. "Very bad rumors have been spread about the Russians. In part they have proven to be true. But one should not generalize.

"If one of you present here should experience something bad, remember the story of little St. Agnes. She was twelve when she was ordered to worship false gods. She raised her hands to Christ and made the Sign of the Cross and for this her clothes were ripped off and she was tortured before a pagan crowd. Yet this did not daunt her, though the heathens were moved to tears. Her public exposure brought flattery from some and even offers of marriage. But she answered, 'Christ is my Spouse.' So the sentence of death was passed. For a moment she stood in prayer and then she was beheaded and the angels bore her swiftly to Paradise."

Father Happich paused. "You must remember," he said. "Like St. Agnes, if your body is touched and you do not want it, then your eternal reward in Heaven will be doubled, for you will have worn the crown of the martyr. Therefore, do not feel guilty." He stopped and then said emphatically: *"You are not guilty."*

As he walked back down the aisle, the voices of his congregation sang a recessional. "I need Thy presence every passing hour . . . what but Thy grace can foil the tempter's power?" They were the words of the ancient hymn, "Abide with Me."

At the main switchboard in the long-distance exchange on Winterfeldtstrasse in Schöneberg, the lights were going out one by one as outlying communities were cut off by the Russian attack. Yet, in the exchange itself people were as busy as ever. Rather than go down to the basement shelter, supervisor Elisabeth Milbrand and operator Charlotte Burmester had brought steamer chairs with mattresses and pillows into their office; the two women intended to stick it out on the fifth floor, where the main exchange was located, as long as they could.

Suddenly the loudspeakers in the building blared. In the shelter hospital, Operator Helena Schroeder was overjoyed by what she heard. On the fifth floor, operators Milbrand and Burmester were taking down the news so they could phone it to all areas still connected to the exchange. "Attention! Attention!" said the announcer. "Don't get restless. General Wenck's army has joined with the Americans. They are attacking toward Berlin. Hold up your courage! Berlin is not lost!"

*　　*　　*

They cracked the outer ring of the city's defenses and gouged their way into the second ring. They crouched behind the T-34 tanks and self-propelled guns and fought up the streets, the roads, the avenues and through the parklands. Leading the way were the battle-toughened assault troops of Koniev's and Zhukov's Guards, and with them the leather-capped soldiers of four great tank armies. Behind came line upon line of infantry.

They were a strange soldiery. They came from every republic of the Soviet Union and, apart from the crisp Guards regiments, they varied as much in physical appearance as in battle dress. There were so many different languages and dialects among them that officers often could not communicate with elements of their own troops.* In the ranks were Russians and Belorussians, Ukrain-

* In Normandy, in 1944, the author remembers being present when two captured soldiers in German uniform posed a strange problem to intelligence interrogaters of the U. S. First Army: nobody could understand their language. Both men were sent to England where it was discovered they were Tibetan shepherds, press-ganged

457

ians and Karelians, Georgians and Kazakhs, Armenians and Azer-
baijanis, Bashkirs, Mordvinians, Tartars, Irkutsks, Uzbeks, Mongols and Cossacks. Some men wore dark brown uniforms, some
wore khaki or gray-green. Others were dressed in dark pants with
high-necked blouses; the blouses ranged in color from black to
beige. Their headwear was equally varied—leather hoods with
bobbing earflaps, fur hats, battered, sweat-stained khaki caps. All
of them seemed to carry automatic weapons. They came on horseback, on foot, on motorcycles, in horse-drawn carts and captured
vehicles of every sort, and they threw themselves on Berlin.

* * *

In the Schöneberg telephone exchange, the voice coming over
the loudspeaker commanded: "Everyone pay attention. Discard
your party badges, your party books and please take off your uniforms. Throw the stuff into the big sandpile in the yard or go to
the engine room where it will be burned."

Milkman Richard Poganowska stopped his milk cart and gaped
as five Russian tanks, surrounded by infantry, rumbled up the
street. Poganowska turned his wagon around and drove back to
the Domäne Dahlem dairy. There he joined his family in the
cellar.

For a time they waited. Suddenly the shelter door was kicked
open and Red Army soldiers entered. They looked around silently.
Then they left. A short while later some soldiers returned, and
Poganowska and the other employees of the dairy were ordered
to the administration building. As he waited, he noticed that all
the horses were gone but the cows were still there. A Soviet officer,
speaking perfect German, ordered the men back to work. They
were to care for the animals and milk the cows, he said. Poganow-

---

into the Red Army, captured on the eastern front and press-ganged once again into
the German Army.

ska could hardly believe it. He had expected a great deal worse.

It was the same in all the outer districts where people were seeing their first Russian troops. The forward elements of the Soviet Army, hard-bitten but scrupulously correct in behavior, were not at all what the terrified citizens had expected.

At 7 P.M. Pia van Hoeven was sitting in the cellarway of her apartment house in Schöneberg, peeling a few potatoes. Nearby, several other women from the house chatted together, their backs to the open shelter door. Suddenly Pia looked up and stared openmouthed into the muzzles of submachine guns held by two Russian soldiers. "Quietly I raised my arms, knife in one hand, potato in the other," she remembers. The other women looked at her, turned, and put their hands up, too. To Pia's surprise, one of the soldiers asked in German, "Soldiers here? Volkssturm? Any guns?" The women shook their heads. "Good Germans," said the soldier approvingly. They walked in and took the women's watches, and then they disappeared.

As the night wore on, Pia saw more and more Russians. "They were fighting troops and many spoke German," she remembered. "But they seemed to be interested only in moving up and getting on with the battle." Pia and the women in her apartment house decided that all Goebbels' talk about the rapacious Red Army was just another pack of lies. "If all the Russians behave like this," Pia told her friends, "then we have nothing to worry about."

Marianne Bombach felt the same way. She came out of her Wilmersdorf cellar one morning and saw a Russian field kitchen set up just outside her back door. The soldiers, fighting units bivouacked in Schwarze Grund Park, were sharing food and candy with the neighborhood children. Their manners particularly impressed Marianne. They had upended some square garbage cans and were using them as tables. Each was covered with a doily, apparently taken from villas nearby. There they sat in the middle of the field on somebody's straight-backed chairs eating off the garbage cans. Except for their fraternization with the children, the Russians seemed to be ignoring the civilians. They remained for just a few hours and then moved on.

Dora Janssen and the widow of her husband's batman were shocked and frightened. After the fatal shelling of the aide and the wounding of Major Janssen, Dora had invited the widow to stay with her. The two defenseless women, their nerves raw from grief and fear, were in the cellar of the Janssens' building when Dora saw "a huge shadow appear on the wall." In the shadow's hands was a gun. To Dora the apparition "appeared like a cannon being held in the paws of a gorilla and the soldier's head seemed huge and deformed." She was unable to breathe. The Russian came into view, followed by another, and ordered them out of the cellar. "Now," Dora thought, "it is going to take place." The two women were led outdoors, where the Russians handed them brooms and pointed to the debris and broken glass that littered the walk. The women were dumbfounded. Their surprise and relief was so obvious that the Russians broke into laughter.

Other people had more harrowing encounters with the newly arrived front-line troops. Elisabeth Eberhard was almost shot. A social worker employed by Catholic Bishop Konrad von Preysing, Elisabeth had been hiding Jews for years. She was visiting a friend when she met her first two Russians—a young blond officer accompanied by a woman interpreter. Both entered the house heavily armed; the woman carried a submachine gun. The phone rang just as the Russians came in. As Elisabeth's friend picked it up, the elegant officer grabbed it from her. "You are both traitors," the interpreter told them, "you have contact with the enemy." The women were rushed out of the house and into the garden and were backed against the wall. The officer announced that he intended to shoot them. Elisabeth, knees shaking, shouted at him, "We have been waiting for you! We have always been against Hitler! My husband has been in prison as a political offender for twelve years!"

The Red Army woman interpreted. Slowly the officer lowered his gun. He seemed greatly embarrassed. Then he came toward Elisabeth, took her right hand and kissed it. Elisabeth was equal to the Russian's poise. In as casual a voice as she could muster, she politely inquired, "Will you both join us in a glass of wine?"

The discipline and orderliness of the first troops amazed almost everyone. Druggist Hans Miede noticed that Soviet soldiers "seemed to avoid firing into houses unless they were sure German defenders were hiding there." Helena Boese, who had lived in dread of the Russians' arrival, came face to face with a Red Army trooper on her cellar steps. He was "young, handsome and wearing an immaculately clean uniform." He just looked at her when she came out of the cellar and then, gesturing to indicate good will, gave her a stick with a white handkerchief tied to it as a sign of capitulation. In the same Wilmersdorf area, Ilse Antz, who had always believed that the Berliners were going to be "thrown like fodder to the Russians," was asleep in the basement of her apartment house when the first Russian entered. She awakened and stared at him in terror, but the young, dark-haired trooper just smiled at her and said in broken German: "Why afraid? Everything all right now. Go to sleep."

For one group of Berliners the arrival of the Soviet troops produced no terror at all. The Jews had long ago come to terms with fear. Leo Sternfeld, the former Tempelhof businessman forced to work as a garbage collector for the Gestapo, had sweated out every mile of the Russian advance. A half-Jew, he had lived all through the war in anguished suspense, never knowing when he and his family would be sent to a concentration camp. For most of the war, his name had made Sternfeld and his family unwelcome in air raid shelters. But when the shelling began, Leo noticed a remarkable change in his neighbors. "The residents of the house," he recalled, "almost dragged us into the shelter."

Sternfeld was overjoyed when he saw the first troops in the Tempelhof district. They were orderly and peaceful, and to Leo they were liberators. The Russian battalion commander asked if they might have a room in Leo's house to hold a celebration. "You can have anything I've got," Leo told him. He had already lost half his house when the nearby post office had blown up some days before, but there were three rooms left. "You can have the one with the ceiling," Leo assured the Russian. In return, he, his family and some friends were invited to the party. The Russians arrived, bringing baskets of food and drink. "It seemed to me at one time," Leo said, "as if the entire Russian Army joined the party." The Russians drank enormous quantities of vodka. Then, to the accompaniment of an accordion, the battalion commander, an opera star in private life, began to sing. Leo sat enthralled. For the first time in years, he felt free.

Joachim Lipschitz came out of hiding in the Krügers' cellar in Karlshorst to meet the Red Army troopers. Speaking in the slow, halting Russian he had taught himself in his months underground, he tried to explain who he was and to express his gratitude for liberation. To his amazement the Russians howled with laughter. Slapping him boisterously on the back, they said that they, too, were happy, but they added, choking again with laughter, that he spoke terrible Russian. Joachim didn't mind. For him and for Eleanore Krüger the long wait was over. They would be the first couple married when the battle ended. As soon as they received their marriage certificate, it would represent, as Eleanore was to put it, "our own personal victory over the Nazis. We had won and nothing could hurt us any more." *

Everywhere, as areas were overrun, the Jews came out of hiding. Some, however, were still so fearful that they remained in their secret places long after the danger from the Nazis was past. Twenty-year-old Hans Rosenthal was to stay in his six- by five-foot cubicle in Lichtenberg until May—a total of twenty-eight months in hiding. In some areas, Jews were freed and then faced with the prospect of having to go underground again when the Russians were thrown back in temporary but violent and widely scattered counterattacks.

The Weltlingers in Pankow had one of the strangest experiences of all. They were liberated early. The Russian officer who entered their hiding place in the Möhrings' apartment would always be remembered by Siegmund as "the personification of Michael the archangel." When he saw them, the officer called out in poor Ger-

* Joachim Lipschitz was eventually to become one of West Berlin's most famous officials. As Senator of Internal Affairs in 1955, he was in charge of the city's police force. He remained an unrelenting foe of the East German Communist regime until his death in 1961.

man, "Russki no barbarian. We good to you." At one time he had been a student in Berlin.

Then suddenly there was a tense moment. The officer and his men searched the entire apartment house—and found six revolvers. To the assembled occupants, the Russian announced that he had found them hidden with discarded uniforms. Everyone was ordered out of the house and lined up against a wall. Siegmund stepped forward and said, "I'm a Jew." The young officer smiled, shook his head, made a motion as though cutting his throat and said, "No more Jews alive." Over and over Siegmund repeated that he was a Jew. He looked at the others lined up against the wall. A few weeks earlier, many of these people would have turned him in had they known his whereabouts. Yet Siegmund now said in a clear, loud voice: "These are good people. All of them have sheltered us in this house. I ask you not to harm them. These weapons were thrown away by the Volkssturm."

His statement saved the lives of all the tenants. Germans and Russians began hugging each other. "We were drunk," Siegmund said, "with happiness and joy." The Soviet officer immediately brought food and drink for the Weltlingers and stood anxiously watching them, and urging them to eat. Both Weltlingers nearly became ill from the food because they were not used to anything so rich. "Immediately," Siegmund said, "people became very kind to us. We were given an empty flat, food and clothing, and for the first time we were able to stand in the fresh air and walk a street."

But then the Russians were thrown out of the area by an SS attack—and the same residents Weltlinger had saved the day before suddenly became hostile again. "It was," said Weltlinger, "unbelievable." The next day the Russians retook the area and once more they were liberated, but by a different Soviet unit—and this time the Russians would not believe that Weltlinger was a Jew. All the men in his building were loaded onto a truck and driven away for questioning. As Siegmund said good-bye to his wife he wondered if all this deprivation, all this hiding was now going to have a senseless end. They were taken to the northeastern suburbs and one by one were questioned in a cellar. Weltlinger was brought into the room and placed beneath a bright light. Sitting in the darkness were some officers at a long table. Once again Weltlinger insisted that he was a Jew who had been in hiding for more than two years. Then a woman's voice came out of the darkness: "Prove to me you are a Jew." "How?" She asked him to recite the Hebrew profession of faith.

In the silence of the room Siegmund looked at the shadowy faces sitting in the darkness before him. Then, covering his head with his right hand, his voice filled with emotion, he said one of the most ancient of all prayers, the *Sh'mah Yisroël*. In Hebrew he slowly intoned:

> *Hear, O Israel!*
> *The Lord our God,*
> *The Lord is One.*

Then the woman spoke again. "Go," she said. "You are a Jew and a good man." She, too, was Jewish, she said. The next day Siegmund was reunited with his wife. "No words," he said, "can describe how we felt when we met again." Hand in hand, they walked in the sunshine, "free and as happy as children."

If Mother Superior Cunegundes felt any fear it did not show on her round, peaceful face. The battle was raging all about Haus Dahlem. The building shook every time the tanks fired, and even in the sandbagged cellar the concussion could be felt. But Mother Superior Cunegundes no longer paid any attention to the rattle of the machine guns and the scream of the shells. She was praying in the little dining room now turned into a chapel when the firing lifted; for a moment the noise of battle seemed to fade. Still Mother Superior Cunegundes remained on her knees. One of the Sisters came into the chapel and whispered to the Mother Superior: "The Russians. They are here."

Mother Superior Cunegundes calmly blessed herself, genuflected, and quickly followed the Sister out of the chapel. The Soviet troops had first approached the home from the rear, through the gardens. They had appeared at the kitchen windows, grinning and pointing their guns at the nuns and lay sisters. Now, ten troopers led by a young lieutenant waited on the Mother Superior. Lena, the cook, a Ukrainian, was hurriedly sent for to act as interpreter. The officer, noted the Mother Superior, "looked very smart, and his behavior was excellent."

He asked about Haus Dahlem. Mother Superior Cunegundes explained that it was a maternity home, hospital and orphanage. Lena added that there were only "nuns and babies" there. The lieutenant seemed to understand. "Are there any soldiers or weapons here?" he asked. Mother Superior Cunegundes said: "No. Of course not. There is nothing like that in this building." Some of the soldiers now began to demand watches and jewelry. The lieutenant spoke sharply, and the men pulled back, abashed.

The Mother Superior then told the young officer that Haus Dahlem needed some guarantee of protection because of the children, the expectant mothers and the Sisters. The lieutenant shrugged: he was a fighting man, and all he was interested in was clearing out the enemy and moving up.

As the Russians left the building, some of the soldiers stopped to look at the great statue of St. Michael, "God's fighting knight against all evil." They walked around the statue, touching the sculptured folds of the gown and looking up into the face. The lieutenant said good-bye to the Mother Superior. Something seemed to be troubling him. For just a moment he gazed at his men looking at the statue. Then he said to Mother Superior Cunegundes:

"These are good, disciplined and decent soldiers. But I must tell you. The men who are following us, the ones coming up behind, are pigs."

There was no stopping the tide of the Russian advance. Desperate orders flashed out from the deranged man in the Führerbunker as the remains of both the Reich and its capital were dissected by the invaders. Commands were superseded by counter-commands. Then counter-commands were canceled and new orders issued. Weidling's Chief of Staff, Lieutenant Colonel von Dufving, summed it up: "Confusion led to chaos; order led to counterorder; and finally everything led to disorder."

The German command system had all but collapsed. As the Western Allies and the Russians drew closer together, the OKW, charged with handling the western front, became hopelessly entangled with the OKH, which controlled the eastern front. General Erich Dethleffsen, OKH Assistant Chief of Staff, got a desperate call from the commander of Dresden as Koniev's tanks, heading west to link up with the Americans, approached the city. He was told to put everything he had on the *east* bank of the Elbe, which runs through the city. Ten minutes later the OKW ordered the Dresden commander to put his forces on the *west* bank.

It was the same all over. Communications hardly existed any more. The OKW headquarters, now established in Rheinsberg, about fifty miles northeast of Berlin, was dependent for its communications on a single transmitting antenna attached to a barrage balloon. In Berlin, those of Hitler's orders that could not be telephoned were radioed via the communications complex in the smaller of the two Zoo flak towers. Luftwaffe Lieutenant Gerda Niedieck, sitting at her teleprinter and deciphering machines in the vast telecommunications room in L Tower, noted that most of Hitler's messages at this time had one theme: frantic queries for information—usually about armies that no longer existed. Over and over, the radio teletype machines clacked out his messages. *"What is Wenck's position?"* *"Where is Steiner?"* *"Where is Wenck?"* Sometimes it was just too much for 24-year-old Gerda. Sometimes she just wept silently at her teleprinter as she sent out Hitler's messages and his threats, and his orders that the dying nation was to fight to the last German.

At last, after six years of war, the headquarters of the OKH and the OKW—whose armies had once been separated by three thousand miles—were pulled together in a unified command. The officials of the combined OKH-OKW were promptly addressed by Field Marshal Wilhelm Keitel. "Our troops," he said with great assurance, "are not only willing to fight, they are completely able to fight." He paced the floor of the new headquarters, under the watchful eyes of General Alfred Jodl, OKW Operations Chief, and General Erich Dethleffsen, OKH Assistant Chief of Staff. Keitel had painted the same bright picture for Hitler on the twenty-fourth, just before the Führer had ordered his top officers to leave the capital so they could conduct operations for the relief of Berlin from outside the city. That had been Dethleffsen's last visit to the underground world of the Führerbunker. When he arrived he had found utter confusion. There was no guard at the entrance. To his amazement he had found some twenty workers sheltering behind the bunker door: they had been ordered, because of the artillery fire, to "dig a trench from the parking area to the entrance," but they could not work because of the shelling. As he went down the stairs he found that there were no guards in the anteroom either. No one searched his briefcase or "checked to see if he was carrying weapons." His impression was one of "complete disintegration."

In the little hall outside Hitler's small briefing room "stood empty glasses and half-full bottles." It seemed to him that "the soldierly principle of remaining calm, and thus preventing a panic situation from developing, had been completely disregarded." Everyone was nervous and irritable—except the women. "The secretaries, the female personnel . . . Eva Braun and Frau Goebbels and her children . . . were amiable and friendly and shamed many of the men by their example."

Keitel's report to Hitler had been short. "In rosy words," Dethleffsen remembered, "he reported on the mood of Wenck's Twelfth Army and the prospects for the relief of Berlin." Dethleffsen had found it hard to judge "how much Keitel believed his own words:

perhaps his optimism was grounded only in the wish not to burden the Führer."

But now, before the OKH-OKW leaders, away from Hitler, Keitel was talking in the same vein. As he paced the floor he said: "Our defeats are really due to a lack of courage, a lack of will in the upper and intermediate commands." It could have been Hitler speaking. Dethleffsen thought that Keitel was a "true student of his master." And from his glowing report of how Berlin would be relieved, it was "clear that he had not the slightest understanding of the plight of the troops." Keitel kept talking: everything would be all right; the rapidly closing Russian ring about Berlin would be cracked; the Führer would be saved. . . .

In Bavaria, Reichsmarschall Hermann Goering found himself in a preposterous situation: he was under house arrest by SS guards.

His Chief of Staff, General Koller, had flown to Bavaria to see Goering after Hitler's fateful conference of April 22. On receiving Koller's report that "Hitler has broken down" and that the Führer had said, "When it comes to negotiating the Reichmarschall can do better than I," Goering had acted. He had sent the Führer a very carefully worded message. *"My Führer,"* he wired, *"in view of your decision to remain in the fortress of Berlin do you agree that I take over at once the total leadership of the Reich with full freedom of action at home and abroad as your deputy, in accordance with your decree of June 29, 1941? If no reply is received by ten o'clock tonight I shall take it for granted that you have lost your freedom of action, and shall act for the best interests of our country and people. . . ."*

Goering received a fast reply—one undoubtedly inspired by his arch rival, the ambitious Martin Bormann. Hitler fired off a message accusing Goering of treason and announced that he would be executed unless he immediately resigned. On the evening of April

25, Berlin radio solemnly reported that "Reichsmarschall Goering's heart condition has now reached an acute state. Therefore he has requested that he be released from command of the Air Force and all the duties connected with it. . . . The Führer has granted this request. . . ." Goering told his wife, Emmy, that he thought the whole business was ridiculous; that in the end he would have to do the negotiating anyway. She later told Baroness von Schirach that Goering was wondering "what uniform he should wear when he first met Eisenhower."

❋   ❋   ❋

While Berlin burned and the Reich died, the one man Hitler never suspected of treachery had already surpassed Goering's grab for power.

In Washington on the afternoon of April 25, General John Edwin Hull, the U. S. Army's Acting Chief of Staff for Operations, was called into the Pentagon office of General George C. Marshall, the Chief of Staff. Marshall told him that President Truman was en route from the White House to the Pentagon to talk with Winston Churchill on the scrambler telephone. A German offer to negotiate had been received via Count Folke Bernadotte, head of the Swedish Red Cross. The peace feeler came from no less a person than the man Hitler called *Der treue Heinrich*—Heinrich Himmler.

Himmler's secret proposals were supposed to be en route in a coded message from the American Ambassador in Sweden. Marshall told Hull to get the phone room set up and to find out right away from the State Department if the text of the message had arrived. "I phoned Dean Acheson at State," Hull said, "who told me that he knew nothing about any cable containing Himmler's proposals. Actually, the message was then coming in to the State Department, but nobody had yet seen it."

Then President Truman arrived, and at 3:10 P.M. American time he spoke to the Prime Minister from the Pentagon phone room.

"When he got on the phone," recalls Hull, "the President did not even know what the German proposal was." Churchill, according to Hull, "started off by saying, 'What do you think of the message?' The President replied, 'It is just coming in now.'"

Churchill then read the version which he had received from the British Ambassador to Sweden, Sir Victor Mallet. Himmler, he told Truman, wished to meet with General Eisenhower and capitulate. The SS chief reported that Hitler was desperately ill, that he might even be dead already, and in any case would be within a few days. It was clear that Himmler wished to capitulate—but only to the Western Allies, not to the Russians. "What happens," Bernadotte had asked Himmler, "if the Western Allies refuse your offer?" Himmler replied: "Then I shall take command on the eastern front and die in battle." Hull, listening on another phone, then heard Churchill say, "Well, what do you think?"

The new American President, only thirteen days in office, answered without hesitation. "We cannot accept it," he said. "It would be dishonorable, because we have an agreement with the Russians not to accept a separate peace."

Churchill promptly agreed. As he was later to put it, "I told him [Truman] that we were convinced the surrender should be unconditional and simultaneous to the three major powers." When both Churchill and Truman informed Stalin of the Himmler proposal and their response to it, the Generalissimo thanked them both, and in similar replies promised that the Red Army would "maintain its pressure on Berlin in the interests of our common cause."

Lieutenant Albert Kotzebue of the U. S. 69th Division, sitting in his jeep, saw the farm from far away and he thought it was much too quiet. He got out and moved up ahead of his 26-man patrol so he could approach the house alone.

This whole countryside near the Elbe had been strangely silent. Villages had white flags of surrender flying, but there was no movement; the villagers were staying behind doors. Kotzebue had talked to several burgomasters and it was always the same story: the Russians were coming, and they were sure to be killed and their women raped.

Warily Kotzebue went to the front of the house. The door was half open. He stood to one side and pushed it wide with his rifle. It swung back with a creaking noise, and Kotzebue stared. Sitting around the dining table were the farmer, his wife and their three children. It was a peaceful, homelike scene—except that they were all dead. They must have been terribly afraid, for they had all taken poison.

The rest of the patrol came up, and the Lieutenant jumped back into his jeep. They sped on toward the Elbe, and then, just before they reached the river, Albert Kotzebue made history. In the village of Leckwitz he saw a strange-looking man in an unusual uniform astride a pony. The man swung around in the saddle and looked at Kotzebue. The Lieutenant looked back. Kotzebue and the man on the horse had fought across half a world for this moment. It seemed to Kotzebue that he had met the first Russian.

Someone who spoke Russian questioned the horseman. Yes, he was a Russian, he said. "Where's his unit?" asked Kotzebue. The man answered curtly, "On the Elbe." The patrol set out again for the river. The man watched them go. At the river Kotzebue and a few others found a rowboat and crossed to the other bank, using their rifles as oars. As they stepped out of the boat, Kotzebue saw that the shore for hundreds of yards was covered with dead civilians—men, women and children. There were overturned wagons and carts; baggage and clothing were strewn everywhere. There was nothing to indicate how or why the slaughter had occurred. A few moments later the Americans met the first group of Russians. Kotzebue saluted. So did the Soviet soldiers. There was no joyful meeting, no back-slapping or hugging. They just stood there looking at each other. The time was 1:30 P.M. on April 25. The Western and Eastern allies had joined at the little town of Strehla.

At 4:40 P.M. at Torgau on the Elbe, about twenty miles to the north, Lieutenant William D. Robinson, also of the 69th Division, encountered some other Russians. He brought four Soviet soldiers back with him to his headquarters. His meeting would go into history books as the official link-up. In any case, whether at 1:30 or 4:40, Hitler's Reich had been cut in half by the men of General Hodges' U. S. First Army and Marshal Koniev's First Ukrainians. And on this same day—no one seems sure of the exact time— Berlin was encircled.

* * *

The entire northern flank of the Ninth Army had collapsed. Totally encircled, the Ninth was being hammered night and day by Russian bombers. The supply situation was critical. The Luftwaffe tried an air drop, but everything went wrong. There were not enough planes for the job and not enough gasoline for the planes —and such drops as were made landed in the wrong places. Yet, despite everything, the Ninth was doggedly battling toward Wenck's Twelfth Army.

But now Heinrici knew the truth about Wenck: contrary to what Krebs had said, the Twelfth Army had almost no strength. Bitterly he had phoned Krebs and accused him of deliberately giving false information. "It's a phantom army," Heinrici raged. "It simply does not have the strength to drive toward the Ninth, join with it and head north to relieve Berlin. There'll be little left of either army by the time they meet—and you know it!"

Von Manteuffel's Third Panzer Army was, in effect, all that was left of the Army Group Vistula. Von Manteuffel was holding tenaciously, but the center of his line bulged in ominously. Worse, Zhukov's tanks, driving along the southern flank, were now in position to swing north and encircle Von Manteuffel. The only force that stood in their way was the rag-tag group of SS General Felix Steiner.

Hitler's plan for the relief of Berlin called for Steiner to attack southward across the path of the Russians from one side of the city, while the Ninth and Twelfth together drove northward from the other side. Theoretically it was a workable plan. Actually it stood no chance of success. Steiner was one of the drawbacks. "He kept finding all sorts of excuses not to attack," Heinrici said. "Gradually I got the impression that something was wrong."

The Vistula commander knew that Steiner did not have sufficient forces to reach Spandau, as Hitler was demanding, but Heinrici wanted the attack to take place just the same. Steiner was at least strong enough to blunt Zhukov's drive. If he could manage that, he might prevent the Russians from encircling Von Manteuffel's army. That would give Heinrici the time he needed to withdraw Von Manteuffel's forces step by step to the Elbe. There was nothing left to do now but try to save his men; the complete collapse of the Reich was clearly inevitable within days. Heinrici kept a map on which he had drawn five north-to-south retreat lines, running from the Oder back to the west. The first was called "Wotan," the next, "Uecker"; the remainder were numbered. The lines were fifteen to twenty miles apart. Von Manteuffel was now on the Wotan line. The question was how long he could last there.

On the morning of the twenty-fifth, Heinrici visited Von Manteuffel. They walked in the little garden behind Von Manteuffel's headquarters, and the Third Panzer commander said quietly, "I cannot hold any longer." His face was set. "Without panzers, without anti-tank guns and with inexperienced troops already out on their feet, how can anybody expect me to hold any longer?"

"How long *can* you hold?"

Von Manteuffel shook his head.

"Maybe another day."

Through the smoke of the fires and shell bursts, the leaflets came fluttering down from the plane that flew back and forth over the ravaged city. In Wilmersdorf Charlotte Richter picked one of them up. It read: "Persevere! General Wenck and General Steiner are coming to the aid of Berlin."

Now it was essential to find out what Steiner was up to. Heinrici found him at the headquarters of the 25th Panzer Grenadier Division at Nassenheide. With Steiner was Jodl. They had already discussed how Steiner's attack should be made. Now everyone went over it once again. Then Steiner began to talk about the condition of his troops. "Have any of you seen them?" he asked.

Jodl said: "They're in first-rate condition. Their morale is very good."

Steiner looked at Jodl in amazement.

Heinrici asked quietly, "Steiner, why aren't you attacking? Why are you postponing again?"

"It's very simple," said Steiner. "I just don't have the troops. I don't have the slightest chance of succeeding."

"What do you have?" asked Heinrici patiently.

Steiner explained that his total forces consisted of six battalions, including some from an SS police division, plus the 5th Panzer Division and the 3rd Navy Division. "The Navy men I can forget about," said Steiner. "I bet they're great on ships, but they've never been trained for this kind of fighting. I have hardly any artillery, very few panzers and only a few anti-aircraft guns." He paused. "I'll tell you what I have: a completely mixed-up heap that will never reach Spandau from Germendorf."

"Well, Steiner," said Heinrici coldly, "you have to attack for your Führer." Steiner glared at him. "He's your Führer, too!" he yelled.

It was clear to Heinrici, as he and Jodl left, that Steiner had no intention whatever of attacking.

A few hours later the phone rang at the Vistula headquarters in Birkenhain. Heinrici picked it up. It was Von Manteuffel, and he sounded desperate. "I must have your permission to withdraw from Stettin and Schwedt. I cannot hold any longer. If we don't pull out now we'll be encircled."

For just a moment, Heinrici remembered the order issued by Hitler in January to his senior generals. They were "personally responsible to Hitler" and could not withdraw troops or give up positions without notifying Hitler in advance so that he could make the decision. Now Heinrici said: "Retreat. Did you hear me? I said, Retreat. And listen, Manteuffel. Give up the Stettin fortress at the same time."

In his sheepskin coat and his World War I leggings, he stood by his desk thinking over what he had done. He had been in the army exactly forty years and he knew now that even if he was not shot his career was over. Then he called Colonel Eismann and his Chief of Staff. "Inform the OKW," he said, "that I have ordered the Third Army to retreat." He thought for a moment. Then he said, "By the time they get the message it will be too late for them to countermand it."

He looked at Von Trotha, the earnest Hitlerite, and at his old friend Eismann, and explained exactly what his policy was going to be from now on: never again would he leave troops exposed unnecessarily; he would sooner retreat than throw men's lives away needlessly. "What's your opinion?" he asked them. Eismann promptly suggested that the order should be given "to retreat behind the Uecker line, remain at the Mecklenburg lakes and wait for capitulation." Von Trotha jumped at the word. "It is against the honor of a soldier to even *think* of capitulation, to even use the *word* capitulation," Von Trotha spluttered. "It's not up to us; it's up to the OKW to give the orders."

Heinrici said quietly: "I refuse to carry out these suicidal orders any longer. It is my responsibility on behalf of my troops to refuse these orders, and I intend to do so. It is also my responsibility to account for my actions to the German people." Then he added, "And above all, Trotha, to God.

"Good night, gentlemen."

It took Keitel just forty-eight hours to learn that Heinrici had ordered Von Manteuffel to retreat. He saw the withdrawal for himself. Driving through the Third Panzer's area he was amazed to see troops pulling back everywhere. Furious, he ordered both Heinrici and Von Manteuffel to meet him for a conference at a crossroads near Fürstenberg.

When Von Manteuffel's Chief of Staff, General Burkhart Müller-Hillebrand, learned of the arrangement he looked startled, then concerned. Why at a crossroads? Why out in the open? He hurried out to find his staff officers.

At the crossroads, when Heinrici and Von Manteuffel got out of their cars they saw that Keitel had already arrived with his entourage. Hitler's Chief of Staff was a picture of barely contained fury, his face grim, his marshal's baton pounding again and again into the palm of his gloved hand. Von Manteuffel greeted him. Heinrici saluted. Keitel immediately began to yell. "Why did you give the order to move back? You were told to stay on the Oder! Hitler ordered you to hold! He ordered you not to move!" He pointed at Heinrici. "Yet you! You ordered the retreat!"

Heinrici said nothing. When the outburst had ended, according to Von Manteuffel, "Heinrici very quietly explained the situation and his arguments were completely logical." Heinrici said: "I tell you, Marshal Keitel, that I cannot hold the Oder with the troops I have. I do not intend to sacrifice their lives. What's more, we'll have to retreat even farther back."

Von Manteuffel then broke in. He tried to explain the tactical situation that had led to the withdrawal. "I regret to tell you," he concluded, "that General Heinrici is right. I will have to withdraw even farther unless I get reinforcements. I'm here to find out whether I get them or not."

Keitel exploded. "There are no reserves left!" he shouted. "This is the Führer's order!" He hit his gloved palm with his baton. "You will hold your positions where they are!" He hit his palm again. "You will turn your army around here and now!"

"Marshal Keitel," said Heinrici, "as long as I am in command I will not issue that order to Von Manteuffel."

Von Manteuffel said: "Marshal Keitel, the Third Panzer Army listens to General Hasso von Manteuffel."

At this point Keitel lost control completely. "He went into such a tantrum," recalls Von Manteuffel, "that neither Heinrici nor myself could understand what he was saying." Finally he yelled, "You will have to take the responsibility of this action before history!"

Von Manteuffel suddenly lost his temper. "The Von Manteuffels have worked for Prussia for two hundred years and have always taken the responsibility for their actions. I, Hasso von Manteuffel, gladly accept this responsibility."

Keitel wheeled on Heinrici. "You are the one!" he said. "You!"

Heinrici turned and, pointing to the road where Von Manteuffel's troops were retreating, replied: "I can only say, Marshal Keitel, that if you want these men sent back to be shot and killed, why don't you do it?"

Keitel, it appeared to Von Manteuffel, "seemed to take a threatening step toward Heinrici." Then he rapped out: "Colonel General Heinrici, as of this moment you are relieved as commander of the Army Group Vistula. You will return to your headquarters and await your successor."

With that, Keitel stalked away, climbed into his car and drove off.

At that moment General Müller-Hillebrand and his staff came out of the woods. Each man had a machine pistol. "We thought there was going to be a little trouble," he explained.

Von Manteuffel still thought there might be. He offered to guard Heinrici "until the end," but Heinrici declined. He saluted the officers and got into his car. After forty years in the army, in the very last hours of the war he had been dismissed in disgrace. He turned up the collar of his old sheepskin coat and told the driver to return to headquarters.

477

The Russians swarmed in everywhere. District after district fell as the city's slender defense forces were beaten back. In some places, meagerly armed Home Guardsmen simply turned and ran. Hitler Youths, Home Guards, police and fire units fought side by side, but under different commanders. They fought to hold the same objective, but their orders were often contradictory. Many men, in fact, had no idea who their officers were. The new Berlin Commandant, General Weidling, had spread the few remaining veterans of his battered 56th Panzers through the defense areas to bolster the Volkssturm and Hitler Youths, but it was of little use.

Zehlendorf fell almost instantly. Hitler Youths and Home Guardsmen trying to make a stand before the town hall were annihilated; the mayor hung out a white flag and then committed suicide. In Weissensee, which had been a predominately Communist district before the rise of Hitler, many neighborhoods capitulated immediately, and red flags appeared—many showing tattletale areas where black swastikas had been hastily removed. Pankow held out for two days, Wedding for three. Small pockets of Germans fought tenaciously to the end, but there was no consistent defense anywhere.

Street barricades were smashed like matchwood. Russian tanks, moving fast, blew up buildings rather than send soldiers in after snipers. The Red Army was wasting no time. Some obstacles, like tramcars and rock-filled wagons, were demolished by guns firing at point-blank range. Where more sturdy defenses were encountered, the Russians went around them. In Wilmersdorf and Schöneberg, Soviet troops encountering resistance entered houses on either side of the blocked streets and blasted their way from cellar to cellar with bazookas. Then they emerged behind the Germans and wiped them out.

Phalanxes of artillery razed the central districts yard by yard.

As fast as areas were captured, the Russians rushed in the great formations of guns and Stalin Organs used on the Oder and the Neisse. On the Tempelhof and Gatow airports, guns were lined up barrel to barrel. It was the same in the Grünewald, in the Tegel forest, in the parks and open spaces—even in apartment house gardens. Lines of Stalin Organs crowded main thoroughfares, pouring out a continuous stream of phosphorous shells that set whole areas ablaze. "There were so many fires that there was no night," Home Guardsman Edmund Heckscher remembers. "You could have read a newspaper if you had one." Dr. Wilhelm Nolte, a chemist pressed into the Fire Protection Service,* saw Soviet artillery-spotting planes directing barrages onto his workers as they tried to put out the fires. Hermann Hellriegel, recently drawn into the Volkssturm, was lifted off his feet by a shell blast and thrown into a nearby crater. To Hellriegel's horror, he landed on top of three dead soldiers. The 58-year-old Home Guardsman, a former traveling salesman, scrambled out of the hole and sprinted for his home.

As the Russians drove deeper into the city, uniforms and arm bands lay discarded in the streets as Home Guardsmen began to disappear. Some units were deliberately disbanded by their commanders. In the Reichssportfeld's Olympic Stadium, Volkssturm battalion leader Karl Ritter von Halt called together the survivors of a bitter fight and told them to go home. Half the men were useless anyway; they had been issued Italian ammunition for their German rifles. "Letting them return home was about all there was left to do," Von Halt said. "It was either that, or throw stones at the Russians."

Soldiers all over the city began to desert. Sergeant Helmut Volk saw no reason to give his life for the Führer. An accountant

---

* Some of the fire engines that had left on the twenty-second returned to the city on the order of Major General Walter Golbach, head of the Fire Department. According to post-war reports, the fire engines were ordered out of Berlin by Goebbels to keep them from falling into Russian hands. Golbach, on hearing that he was to be arrested for rescinding Goebbels' order, tried to commit suicide and failed. Bleeding from a face wound, he was taken out by SS men and executed.

for the *Abwehr,* the German intelligence service, Volk had suddenly been given a rifle and put on guard duty in the Grünewald. When he heard that his unit had been ordered to the Reichskanzlei area, Volk set off instead for his home on the Uhlandstrasse. His family was not too happy to see him; his uniform endangered them all. Volk quickly took it off, changed into civilian clothes and hid the uniform in the cellar. He was just in time; the Russians overran the area within the hour.

In the command post near the Frey Bridge, Private Willi Thamm had heard something that made him decide to stay with his unit to the end. A lieutenant came in to report to Thamm's captain and, over a cup of coffee and a glass of schnapps, remarked: "Just think! The infantrymen everywhere want to desert. Today three went absent without leave on me." Thamm's captain looked at him. "What did you do?" he asked. The lieutenant sipped his coffee and said, "I shot them."

Marauding gangs of SS men, roving the city in search of deserters, were taking justice into their own hands. They were halting nearly everyone in uniform and checking identities and units. Any man suspected of bolting his company was summarily shot, or was hanged from a tree or lamp post as an example to others. Sixteen-year-old Aribert Schulz, a member of the Hitler Youth, reporting to his headquarters in a disused cinema at Spittelmarkt, saw a lanky red-haired SS trooper with a rifle marching a man into the street. Schulz asked what was happening and was told that the man was a Wehrmacht sergeant who had been found wearing civilian clothes. With Schulz following along behind, the SS man marched the sergeant down Leipzigerstrasse. Suddenly he gave the Wehrmacht soldier a violent shove. As the sergeant struggled to keep his balance the SS man shot him in the back.

That night Schulz saw the red-haired SS man again. Along with other boys in his unit, Schulz was standing watch by a barricade when he saw a Soviet T-34 tank coming along Kurstrasse. The tank was slowly turning its turret when it got a direct hit and blew up. The only survivor was immediately captured. In the Russian's pockets the boys found photographs of key Berlin landmarks. At headquarters the Red Army tanker was interrogated and then turned over to a man with a rifle. It was the same SS man. Again he walked his prisoner outside, but this time he patted the Russian fraternally and motioned for him to go. The Russian grinned and started to leave, and the SS man shot him, too, in the back. It dawned on young Schulz that the lanky marksman was the headquarters' official executioner.

Everywhere now, Berlin's defenders were being forced into the ruins of the central districts. To slow down the Russians, 120 of the city's 248 bridges were blown. So little dynamite was left throughout General Weidling's command that aviation bombs had to be used instead. Fanatics destroyed additional installations, often without checking into the consequences. SS men blew up a four-mile tunnel running under an arm of the river Spree and the Landwehr Canal. The tunnel happened to be a railway link, and thousands of civilians were sheltering there. As water began to flood into the area, there was a mad scramble along the tracks toward higher ground. The tunnel was not only jammed with standees; four hospital trains of wounded were also there. As Elfriede Wassermann and her husband Erich, who had come down from the Anhalter bunker, tried to push through, Elfriede heard the wounded in the trains screaming, "Get us out! Get us out! We'll drown!" Nobody stopped. The water was almost up to Elfriede's waist. Erich, hobbling along on his crutches, was even worse off. Fighting and yelling, people pushed and trampled one another as they tried to get to safety. Elfriede was almost in despair, but Erich kept yelling, "Keep going! Keep going! We're almost there. We'll make it." They did. How many others made it Elfriede never knew.

By April 28 the Russians had closed in on the center of the city. The ring grew tighter and tighter. Desperate battles were being fought along the edges of Charlottenburg, Mitte and Friedrichshain. There was a narrow route still open toward Spandau. Weidling's few experienced troops were trying to hold that lane open for a last-minute breakout. Casualties were enormous. The streets were littered with dead. Because of the shelling people were unable to get out of the shelters to help friends and relatives who lay wounded nearby; many had been caught when they went to stand in line for water at Berlin's old-fashioned street pumps. Soldiers were not much better off. Walking wounded who could make it to dressing stations were lucky. Those unable to walk often lay where they fell and bled to death.

Home Guardsman Kurt Bohg, who had lost most of one heel, crawled and hobbled for miles. At last he could go no farther. He lay in a street yelling for help. But the few people who dared risk the shelling to leave their shelters were too busy trying to save their own lives.

Bohg, lying in a gutter, saw a Lutheran nun running from doorway to doorway. "Sister, Sister," he called. "Can you help me?" The nun stopped. "Can you crawl as far as the congregation house next to the church?" she asked. "It's just five minutes from here. I'll help you when I get there." Somehow he made it. All the doors were open. He crawled into the hallway, then into an anteroom and finally collapsed. When he came to he was lying almost in a spreading pool of blood. Slowly he raised his eyes to see where it was coming from. He looked across the room which led out onto a garden. The door was open; wedged in it, crumpled and looking at him with soft eyes, was a black and white Holstein cow. The animal was bleeding copiously from the mouth. Man and beast stared at each other in dumb compassion.

As the Russians isolated the city's center, Weidling's forces were compressed more and more. Supplies ran out. In response to his desperate appeals for air drops, he received six tons of supplies and exactly sixteen panzer rocket-shells.

Incredibly, amid the inferno of the battle, a plane suddenly swept in and landed on the East-West Axis—the broad highway running from the river Havel on the west to the Unter den Linden on the east. It was a small Fieseler Storch, and in it were General Ritter von Greim and a well-known aviatrix named Hanna Reitsch. The plane had been blasted by anti-aircraft fire, and gasoline was pouring from its wing tanks. Von Greim, who was at the controls, had been wounded in the foot just before touching down. Hanna had grabbed the stick and throttle and made a perfect landing. The two fliers had been summoned to the Reichskanzlei by Hitler; when they arrived he promptly made Von Greim a field marshal, replacing the "traitorous" Goering as head of the now nonexistent Luftwaffe.

The Führerbunker was already being shelled, but it was comparatively safe for the time being. One other island of security remained in the center of the city. Rising up from the zoological gardens were the twin flak towers. The 132-foot-high G Tower was jammed with people: nobody knew exactly how many. Dr. Walter Hagedorn, the Luftwaffe physician, estimated that there were as many as thirty thousand—plus troops. There were people sitting or standing on the stairways, landings, on every floor. There was no room to move. Red Cross workers like 19-year-old Ursula Stalla did all they could to alleviate the sufferings of the civilians. She would never forget the sickening combination of odors—"perspiration, smelly clothes, babies' diapers, all mixed with the smell of disinfectants from the hospital." After days in the bunker many people were approaching insanity. Some had committed suicide. Two old ladies sitting side by side on the first-floor landing had taken poison at some time, but no one could tell when: because of the jam of people around them they had sat bolt upright in death, apparently for days, before they were noticed.

Dr. Hagedorn had been operating on casualties in his small hospital almost incessantly for five days. His problem was to bury the dead. Men simply could not get out because of the shelling. "In between lulls," he later recalled, "we tried to take out the bodies and the amputated limbs for burial, but it was almost impossible." At this moment, with shells smashing the bunker's impenetrable walls from all sides and shrapnel spraying the steel shutters over the windows, Hagedorn had five hundred dead and fifteen hundred wounded, plus an unknown number of half-demented people. There were also suicides everywhere, but because of the crush they could not even be counted. Still, the doc-

483

tor remembered, there were people in the bunker saying, "We can stick it out until either Wenck or the Americans get here."

Below the tower lay the vast wasteland of the zoo. The slaughter among the animals had been horrible. Birds flew in all directions every time a shell landed. The lions had been shot. Rosa the hippo had been killed in her pool by a shell. Schwarz the bird-keeper was in despair; somehow the Abu Markub, the rare stork which had been in his bathroom, had escaped. And now Director Lutz Heck had been ordered by the flak tower commander to destroy the baboon; the animal's cage had been damaged and there was some danger that the beast might escape.

Heck, rifle in hand, made his way to the monkey cages. The baboon, an old friend, was sitting hunched by the bars of the cage. Heck raised the rifle and put the muzzle close to the animal's head. The baboon gently pushed it aside. Heck, appalled, again raised the rifle. Again the baboon pushed the muzzle to one side. Heck, sickened and shaken, tried once more. The baboon looked at him dumbly. Then Heck pulled the trigger.

While the battle continued, another savage onslaught was going on. It was grim and personal. The hordes of Russian troops coming up behind the disciplined front-line veterans now demanded the rights due the conquerors: the women of the conquered.

Ursula Köster was sleeping in a Zehlendorf cellar with her parents, her 6-year-old twin daughters, Ingrid and Gisela, and her 7-month-old boy Bernd, when four Russian soldiers beat in the door with their rifle butts. They searched the shelter; finding an empty suitcase, they dumped jars of canned fruits, fountain pens, pencils, watches and Ursula's wallet into it. One Russian found a bottle of French perfume. He opened it, sniffed, and poured the contents of the bottle on his clothes. A second Russian shoved Ursula's parents and the children at gunpoint into a smaller room of the cellar. Then, one after another, all four assaulted her.

Around six the following morning the battered Ursula was nursing her baby when two other soldiers came into the cellar. With the baby in her arms, she tried to dodge past and out the doorway. She was too weak. One of the soldiers took the baby from her and put him in his carriage. The second man looked at her and grinned. Both were filthy; their clothes were gritty, and they carried knives in their boots and wore fur caps. One man's shirttail was hanging out of his pants. Each of them raped her. When they had gone, Ursula grabbed all the blankets she could find, picked up her baby, collected her little girls, and ran into a garden housing complex across the street. There she found a bathtub which had been thrown or blasted out of one of the houses. Turning it upside down, Ursula crawled in with her children.

In Hermsdorf, 18-year-old Juliane Bochnik dived under the sofa at the back of the cellar when she heard the Russians approaching. She heard her father, a linguist who spoke Russian, protesting at the intrusion. The soldiers were demanding to know where Juliane was, and her father was shouting, "I'll report you to the Commissar!" At gunpoint her father was taken out into the street. Juliane lay very still, hoping the Russians would go away. She had blackened her face and blond hair in order to make herself look older; still, she was not taking any chances. She stayed under the sofa.

In the adjoining cellar were two old people. Suddenly Juliane heard one of them shouting in a terrified voice. "She's there! There! Under the sofa." Juliane, dragged from her hiding place, stood quaking with fear. There was some talk among the Russians, then all but one left. "He was a young officer," she later related, "and, as far as I could tell in the light of his flashlight, rather neat-looking and clean-cut." He made motions whose meaning was unmistakable. She shrank back; he advanced. Smiling, he "gently but forcefully" began to remove Juliane's clothes. She struggled. "It was not easy for him," Juliane remembers. "He had a flashlight in one hand and, with typical Russian mistrust, he was keeping an eye to the rear to guard against a surprise attack."

Gradually, in spite of her efforts, he disrobed Juliane. She tried to plead, but she couldn't speak Russian. At last she began crying

485

and fell to her knees, begging to be left alone. The young Russian just looked at her. Juliane stopped crying, got hold of herself and tried another tack; she began talking firmly and politely. "I told him that this was all wrong," she recalls. "I said people don't act this way." The Russian began to look annoyed. Then, with nearly all her clothes removed, the girl broke down again. "I simply don't love you!" she cried. "There's no point to this! I simply don't love you!" Suddenly the Russian said, "Ahhh," in a disgusted voice and dashed out of the cellar.

The next morning Juliane and another girl fled to a convent run by the Dominican nuns; they were hidden there under the eaves of the roof for the next four weeks. Juliane later learned that her friend Rosie Hoffman and Rosie's mother, who had sworn to kill themselves if the Russians came, had both been raped. They had taken poison.*

Gerd Buchwald, a teacher, saw that Soviet troops were running wild in his district of Reinickendorf. His apartment was completely ransacked by women soldiers of the Red Army who seemed "to be drawn like a magnet by my wife's clothes. They took what they wanted and left." He burned what remained, and took his pistol apart and hid it in the garden. That evening a group of Russian men appeared. They were all drunk. *"Frau! Frau!"* they shouted at Buchwald. He greeted them with a friendly smile. "I had a two-day growth of beard and unkempt hair, so maybe my story worked because I looked older. I drew myself up, spread my hands and said, *'Frau kaput.'"* Apparently they understood: his wife was dead. While Buchwald stretched on his sofa they looked around, took a pair of his suspenders and then disappeared. After they had left Buchwald bolted the door. Moving the sofa, he helped his wife Elsa from the three- by three-foot hole he had dug in the concrete floor. She spent every night there for the next few weeks.

Dr. Gerhard Jacobi, pastor of the Kaiser Wilhelm Church, hid his wife successfully too. Although in his cellar many women were taken out and raped, he succeeded in hiding his wife by the adroit

* They both lived. Prompt action by a doctor saved their lives.

use of a blanket. He slept on the outside of a narrow chaise longue, his wife lying sideways on the inside. Her feet were at his head. Covered completely by a heavy blanket she was almost invisible.

In Wilmersdorf, Ilse Antz, her younger sister Anneliese, and her mother, who had initially formed favorable impressions of the Red Army, were not bothered for some time. Then one night just before dawn Anneliese was dragged out of the bed she shared with her mother. She was carried screaming upstairs to an apartment, and there she was brutally assaulted by a Soviet officer. When the Russian was finished he stroked her hair and said, "Good German." He asked her not to tell anyone that a Russian officer had raped her. The next day a soldier appeared with a parcel of food addressed to her.

Shortly thereafter another trooper forced his attentions on Ilse. He entered with a pistol in each hand. "I sat up in bed wondering which one he was going to kill me with, the left or right," she remembers. In the cold of the cellar, Ilse was wearing several sweaters and ski pants. He pounced on her and began ripping her sweaters off. Then he suddenly said, puzzled, "Are you a German *soldier?*" Ilse says, "I was not surprised. I was so thin from hunger I hardly looked like a woman." But the Russian quickly discovered his error. She was raped. As the Red Army man left, he said: "That's what the Germans did in Russia." After a time he returned —and, to her amazement, stayed by the side of her bed and protected her for the remainder of the night against other lusting Red soldiers.

After that, the Antz family experienced repeated savagery. At one point they were taken out and placed against a wall to be shot. At another, Ilse was raped again. They began to think about suicide. "Had we had poison, I for one would certainly have taken my life," Ilse recalls.

As the Russians raped and plundered, suicides took place everywhere. In the Pankow district alone, 215 suicides were recorded within three weeks, most of them women. Fathers Josef Michalke and Alfons Matzker, Jesuits in Charlottenburg's St. Canisius Church, realized just how far women had been driven by the Russian ferocity when they saw a mother and two children taken from the Havel River. The woman had tied two shopping bags filled full of bricks to her arms and, grasping a baby under each arm, had jumped in.

One of Father Michalke's parishioners, Hannelore von Cmuda, a 17-year-old girl, was repeatedly raped by a mob of drunken Red Army men; when they were finished they shot the girl three times. Critically injured, but not dead, she was brought around to the parish house in a baby carriage, the only available transportation. Father Michalke was not there at that moment, and the girl had disappeared when he returned. For the next twenty-four hours he searched for Hannelore; finally he found her in St. Hildegard's Hospital. He administered the last sacraments and sat by her bedside during all the next night, telling her not to worry. Hannelore survived. (A year later, she and her mother were killed by a truck.)

Margarete Promeist was in charge of an air raid shelter. "For two days and two nights," she recalls, "wave after wave of Russians came into my shelter plundering and raping. Women were killed if they refused. Some were shot and killed anyway. In one room alone I found the bodies of six or seven women, all lying in the position in which they were raped, their heads battered in." Margarete herself was assaulted, despite her protestations to the young man that "I am much too old for you." She saw three Russians grab a nurse and hold her while a fourth raped her.

Hitler Youth Klaus Küster, now in civilian clothes, was engaged in conversation by two Soviet officers sitting in a jeep. One of them spoke German, and he was so talkative that Küster screwed up his courage and asked an undiplomatic question. "Is it true," asked Küster, "that Russian soldiers rape and plunder as the newspapers say?" The officer expansively offered him a pack of cigarettes and said, "I give you my word of honor as an officer that the Soviet soldier will not lay a hand on anyone. All that was written in those papers are lies."

The next day Küster saw three Russians grab a woman on General-Barby-Strasse and drag her into a hallway. One soldier gestured Küster back with a machine pistol, a second held the screaming woman and the third raped her. Then Küster saw the rapist coming out of the doorway. He was very drunk and tears were streaming down his face. He shouted, *"Ja bolshoi swinja."* Küster asked one of the Russians what the phrase meant. The man laughed and said in German: "It means, 'I am a big pig.'"

In a shelter in Kreuzberg where Margareta Probst was staying, a fanatical Nazi named Möller had holed up in a locked room. The Russians learned where he was and tried to break down the door. Möller called out: "Give me a moment. I'll shoot myself." Again the Russians tried to force the door. Möller called out: "Wait! The gun has jammed." Then there was a shot.

During the next few hours the shelter was overrun with Russians looking for girls. Margareta, like many another woman, had tried to make herself as unattractive as possible. She had hidden her long blond hair under a cap, donned dark glasses, smeared her face with iodine and put a large adhesive plaster on her cheek. She was not molested. But plenty of others were. "The girls were simply rounded up and taken to the apartments upstairs," she recalls. "We could hear their screams all night—the sound even penetrated down to the cellars." Later an 80-year-old woman told Margareta that two soldiers had stuffed butter into her mouth to muffle her screams while a number of others assaulted her in turn.

Dora Janssen and the widow of her husband's batman, who earlier had thought they had got off easy, did not do so well now. In their shelter the widow, Inge, was brutally assaulted by a soldier who claimed that his mother had been taken to Berlin by force after German troops attacked Russia, and had never been seen since. Dora was spared; she said she had tuberculosis, and found that the Russians seemed thoroughly afraid of that. But Inge was raped a second time, and injured so badly that she was unable to walk. Dora ran out to the street, found a man who looked like an officer and told him what had happened. He looked at Dora coolly and said, "The Germans were worse than this in Russia. This is simply revenge."

Elena Majewski, 17, and Vera Ungnad, 19, also saw both the

good and the bad sides of the Russians. When the looting and raping began in the Tiergarten area, a young Russian soldier actually slept outside their cellar door to make sure that his fellow countrymen did not come in. The day after he left, seven or eight Red Army men entered the girls' house and demanded that they attend a party the Russians were giving next door. The girls had no alternative but to accept; in any case, they saw no real reason to be afraid at first. The place where the party was being held turned out to be a bedroom and there were about thirty soldiers in the room, but everything seemed innocuous enough. Beds had been shoved against the wall to make room for a long table on which silver candelabra, linens and glassware had been placed. A young blond officer was playing English records on a phonograph. He smiled at the girls and said, "Eat and drink your fill." Elena sat down at the table, but Vera suddenly wanted to leave. It was somehow clear that this was not the innocent party it had appeared to be.

She tried to walk out. One soldier after another prevented her, grinning. Then one Russian told her, "With thirty soldiers you *kaput;* with me you not *kaput.*" Now there was no doubt in Vera's mind about the reason for the party. But she agreed to go with the single soldier: one man *was* better than thirty, if only because it was easier to escape from one. She knew every cranny of the neighborhood; if she could get away they would never find her. But the soldier was taking no chances. He grabbed her by the hair and dragged her, twisting, screaming and clawing, toward an empty room. Somewhere along the way she tore loose and managed to trip him. Then, kicking off her high-heeled shoes for greater speed, she ran barefoot through the backyards over splintered glass and rubble until she came to a ruin in the Putlitzstrasse. There she frantically dug a hole in the dirt, pulled a discarded water pail over her head and resolved to stay there until she died.

Elena was still at the party. She was uneasy, but she was also hungry. On the table were mounds of caviar, loaves of white bread, chocolate and chunks of beef which the Russians were eating raw. They were also downing water glasses filled with vodka, and getting progressively drunker. Finally Elena saw her chance. She quietly rose from the table and walked out; to her delight no one followed her. But in the next room a fierce-looking soldier with a handlebar moustache grabbed her and dragged her into a small anteroom. He threw her down and ripped open her one-piece coveralls. She fainted. Much later, she came to her senses, pushed the drunk and sleeping man off her and painfully crawled out of the house. Like Vera, Elena hid. In a nearby house she found refuge behind a large cook stove.

Young Rudolf Reschke, the boy who had beheaded the Hitler doll, was on hand to save his mother from molestation. A Russian who tried to drag Frau Reschke off found himself involved in a tug-of-war with Rudolf and his sister Christa. The more the soldier pulled at their mother's arm, the harder Rudolf and Christa hung onto her skirts, screaming, and crying, "Mummy! Mummy!" The Russian gave up.

Some women saved themselves from rape simply by fighting back so fiercely that the Soviet soldiers stopped trying and looked elsewhere. Jolenta Koch was tricked into entering an empty house by a Russian who led her to believe someone in it was wounded. Inside was another Red Army man who grabbed her and tried to throw her onto a bed. She put up such resistance that both men were glad to see her go.

One of her neighbors, a woman named Schulz, was not so lucky. Mrs. Schulz was raped at gunpoint before the eyes of her helpless husband and 15-year-old son; as soon as the Russians had left, the half-crazed husband shot his wife, his son and himself to death.

At Haus Dahlem, Mother Superior Cunegundes heard that one mother of three small children had been dragged from her family and raped through an entire night. In the morning the woman was released; she rushed back to her youngsters—only to find that her own mother and brother had hanged all three children and then themselves. The woman thereupon slashed her wrists and died.

The nuns at Haus Dahlem were now working steadily around

the clock. They had been overwhelmed by refugees, and by Russian bestiality. One Russian, attempting to rape the home's Ukrainian cook, Lena, was so infuriated when Mother Superior Cunegundes intervened that he pulled out his pistol and fired at her. Fortunately, he was too drunk to shoot straight. Other soldiers entered the maternity wards and, despite all the nuns could do, repeatedly raped pregnant women and those who had recently given birth. "Their screaming," related one nun, "went on day and night." In the neighborhood, Mother Superior Cunegundes said, rape victims included women of seventy and little girls of ten and twelve.

She was helpless to prevent the attacks. But she called together the nuns and the other women in the building and reiterated Father Happich's words to them. "There is also something else," she continued, "and that is the help of Our Blessed Lord. Despite everything, He keeps St. Michael here. Do not be afraid." There was no other solace she could give them.

In Wilmersdorf, Allied spy Carl Wiberg and his chief, Hennings Jessen-Schmidt, who had successfully identified themselves to the Russians, were actually talking to a Russian colonel outside Wiberg's house when another Red Army officer tried to rape Wiberg's fiancée Inge in the basement. Hearing her screaming, Wiberg rushed inside; neighbors shouted that the man had taken the girl into another room and locked the door. Wiberg and the Russian colonel smashed the door open. Inge's clothes were torn; the officer's were undone. The colonel grabbed the other officer and, yelling, "*Amerikanski! Amerikanski!*" marched him outside, pistol-whipping him unmercifully. Then he stood the officer against a wall to shoot him. Wiberg rushed between the two men and begged the colonel to save the man's life. "You just can't shoot a man like this," he said. The colonel finally relented, and the officer was led off under arrest.

Certainly the most ironic sexual assault of this entire period of rape and plunder occurred in the village of Prieros, just beyond the southern outskirts of the city. The village had been bypassed by Koniev's advancing troops, and for some time it was not occupied. Finally the soldiers arrived. Among the Germans they found were two women living in a wooden packing case. Else Kloptsch and her friend Hildegard Radusch, "the man of the house," had almost starved to death waiting for this moment. Hildegard had dedicated her whole life to furthering Marxism: the arrival of the Russians meant the realization of a dream. When the Soviet troops entered the village one of their first acts was the brutal rape of Communist Hildegard Radusch.°

The Russians had gone wild. In the International Red Cross warehouses in Babelsberg near Potsdam, where British prisoners of war worked, drunken and trigger-happy Red Army soldiers destroyed thousands of parcels containing drugs, medical supplies and various dietary foods for sick soldiers. "They came in," recalls Corporal John Aherne, "went into one of the cellars, saw the huge pile of parcels and just tommy-gunned the lot. Liquids of all sorts poured out of the shattered parcels. It was unbelievable."

Next to the warehouses were the big UFA film studios. Alexander Korab, a foreign student in Berlin, watched as hundreds of intoxicated soldiers who had broken into the costume department appeared in the streets wearing "all sorts of fantastic costumes,

---

° The Russians do not deny the rapes that occurred during the fall of Berlin, although they tend to be very defensive about them. Soviet historians admit that the troops got out of control, but many of them attribute the worst of the atrocities to vengeance-minded ex-prisoners of war who were released during the Soviet advance to the Oder. In regard to the rapes, the author was told by editor Pavel Troyanoskii of the army newspaper *Red Star:* "We were naturally not one hundred per cent gentlemen; we had seen too much." Another *Red Star* editor said: "War is war, and what we did was nothing in comparison with what the Germans did in Russia." Milovan Djilas, who was head of the Yugoslav Military Mission to Moscow during the war, says in his book *Conversations with Stalin* that he complained to the Soviet dictator about atrocities committed by Red Army troops in Yugoslavia. Stalin replied: "Can't you understand it if a soldier who has crossed thousands of kilometers through blood and fire has fun with a woman or takes a trifle?"

from Spanish doublets with white ruff collars to Napoleonic uniforms and hats, to crinoline skirts. They began to dance in the streets to the accompaniment of accordions, and they fired their guns in the air—all while the battle was still raging."

Thousands of Red Army troops appeared never to have been in a big city before. They unscrewed light bulbs, and carefully packed them to take home, under the impression that they contained light and could be made to work anywhere. Water faucets were yanked out of walls for the same reason. Bathroom plumbing was a mystery to many; they sometimes used toilets to wash and peel potatoes, but they could find no use at all for bathtubs. Thousands of them were simply thrown out of windows. Since the soldiers didn't know what bathrooms were for, and couldn't find outhouses, they left excrement and urine everywhere. Some Russians made an effort: Gerd Buchwald discovered that "about a dozen of my wife's canning jars were filled with urine, the glass covers neatly screwed back into place."

In the Schering chemical plant in Charlottenburg, Dr. Georg Henneberg was horror-stricken to find that the Russians had broken into his test laboratories and were playing catch with laboratory eggs that had been infected with typhus bacteria. The frantic Henneberg finally found a Russian colonel who ordered the soldiers out of the building and locked it up.

Amidst all the senseless plundering and brutality the battle still raged. At the center of the fighting, almost forgotten by the hard-pressed defenders and the harassed people, were the Führerbunker and its occupants.

Life in the bunker had taken on an aimless, dreamlike quality. "Those who remained," Gertrud Junge, Hitler's secretary, later related, "continually expected some sort of decision, but nothing happened. Maps were spread out on tables, all doors were open, nobody could sleep any more, nobody knew the date or time. Hitler could not bear to be alone; he kept walking up and down through the small rooms and talking with everybody who remained. He spoke of his imminent death and of the end which was coming.

"In the meantime, the Goebbels family had moved into the bunker, and the Goebbels children were playing and singing songs for 'Uncle Adolf.'"

No one seemed to have any doubt now that Hitler intended to commit suicide; he talked about it often. Everyone also appeared fully aware that Magda and Joseph Goebbels planned to take their lives—and those of their six children, Helga, Holde, Hilde, Heide, Hedda and Helmuth. The only ones who did not seem to know were the children themselves. They told Erwin Jakubek, a waiter in the bunker, that they were going on a long flight out of Berlin. Helga, the eldest, said: "We are going to get an injection to prevent air sickness."

Frau Goebbels, who had an inflamed tooth, sent for Dr. Helmut Kunz, a dentist working in the big hospital bunker under the Chancellery. He extracted the molar, and afterward she said: "The children must not fall into the hands of the Russians alive. If worse comes to worst and we cannot get out, you will have to help me."

Eva Braun, hearing of the job Kunz had done on Magda's teeth, suggested that maybe he could help her with some tooth problems, too. Then, suddenly remembering, she said to him: "Oh, but I've forgotten. What's the sense? In a few hours it will be all over!"

Eva intended to use poison. She displayed a cyanide capsule and said, "It's so simple—you just bite into this and it's all over." Dr. Ludwig Stumpfegger, one of Hitler's doctors who happened to be present, said, "But how do you know it will work? How do you know there is poison in it?" That startled everybody, and one of the capsules was immediately tried out on Hitler's dog Blondi. Stumpfegger, said Kunz, broke a capsule in the dog's mouth with a pair of tongs; the animal died instantly.

The final blow for Hitler was unwittingly delivered on the afternoon of April 29 by a man sitting at a typewriter some eight thousand miles away, in the city of San Francisco. The man was Paul Scott Rankine, a Reuters correspondent who was in the city to cover the founding conference of the United Nations organization. That day he heard from the head of the British Information Services, Jack Winocour—who, in turn, had it straight from British Foreign Secretary Anthony Eden—that Himmler had made an offer of surrender to the Western Allies. Rankine sent out the story, and within minutes it was being broadcast all over the world.

It was this story that gave Hitler his first inkling of Himmler's perfidy. The news reached him during the early evening, while he was holding a conference with Weidling, Krebs, Burgdorf, Goebbels and the latter's assistant Werner Naumann. According to Weidling's account, "Naumann was called to the phone and a few moments later returned. He told us that in a broadcast from Radio Stockholm, it had been reported that Reichsführer SS Himmler had begun negotiations with the Anglo-American High Command."

Hitler tottered to his feet, his face ashen. He "looked at Dr. Goebbels for a long time," said Weidling, "then he mumbled something in a low voice which no one could understand." He seemed stupefied. "I saw Hitler later," Gertrud Junge said. "He was pale, hollow-eyed and looked as if he had lost everything." He had. "We will certainly have to shed tears this evening," Eva Braun told Gertrud and another of Hitler's secretaries.

Himmler's liaison officer at the Führerbunker, SS Gruppenführer Hermann Fegelein, who was married to Eva Braun's sister, was immediately suspected of complicity in Himmler's treason. Fegelein had disappeared from the bunker a few days before; a search had been made, and he had been found at home wearing civilian clothes and preparing to leave Berlin. He had been returned to the bunker and kept under arrest. Now Hitler concluded that Fegelein's planned departure from Berlin was tied in with Himmler's defection. According to SS Colonel Otto Günsche, "Fegelein was court-martialed and shot during the night of the twenty-eighth–twenty-ninth. His sister-in-law refused to intercede on his behalf."

It apparently was clear to Hitler now that the end was near. By dawn he had dictated his personal and political testament, leaving the reins of government in the hands of Admiral Karl Doenitz as President and Joseph Goebbels as Reichschancellor. He also married Eva Braun. "After the ceremony," recalls Gertrud Junge, "Hitler and his new bride sat for an hour with the Goebbels, Generals Krebs and Burgdorf, Dr. Naumann and Luftwaffe Colonel Nicolaus von Below." Gertrud Junge stayed with the group for only fifteen minutes, just long enough to "express her best wishes to the newlyweds." She says that "Hitler talked about the end of National Socialism, which he now thought could not be resurrected easily, and said, 'Death for me only means freedom from worries and a very difficult life. I have been deceived by my best friends and I have experienced treason.'"

That same day Hitler got more bad news: Mussolini and his mistress had been captured by partisans, executed and hung up by the heels. That night Hitler bade farewell to everyone in the bunker. The following day, with Russian tanks barely half a mile away, he decided that the moment had come. He lunched with his two secretaries and his vegetarian cook; waiter Erwin Jakubek remembered that the last meal was "spaghetti with a light sauce." Hitler made more farewells after lunch; to Gertrud Junge he said: "Now it has gone so far, it is finished. Good-bye." Eva Braun embraced the secretary and said: "Give my greetings to Munich and take my fur coat as a memory—I always liked well-dressed people." Then they disappeared into their quarters.

Colonel Otto Günsche took up his stand outside the door of the anteroom leading to Hitler's suite. "It was the most difficult thing I have ever had to do," he later recalled. "It was about three-thirty or three-forty. I tried to do away with my feelings. I knew that he had to commit suicide. There was no other way out."

As he waited, there was a brief anticlimax. A distraught Magda Goebbels suddenly came rushing up to him demanding to see the Führer. Günsche, unable to dissuade her, knocked on Hitler's door. "The Führer was standing in the study. Eva was not in the room, but there was a tap running in the bathroom so I assume she was there. He was very annoyed at me for intruding. I asked him if he wanted to see Frau Goebbels. 'I don't want to speak to her any more,' he said. I left.

"Five minutes later I heard a shot.

"Bormann went in first. Then I followed the valet Linge. Hitler was sitting in a chair. Eva was lying on the couch. She had taken off her shoes and placed them neatly together at one end of the couch. Hitler's face was covered with blood. There were two guns. One was a Walther PPK. It was Hitler's. The other was a smaller pistol he always carried in his pocket. Eva wore a blue dress with white collar and cuffs. Her eyes were wide open. There was a strong stench of cyanide. The smell was so strong that I thought my clothes would smell for days—but this may have been my imagination.

"Bormann didn't say anything, but I immediately went into the conference room where Goebbels, Burgdorf and others that I cannot now remember were sitting. I said, 'The Führer is dead.' "

A short while later, both bodies were wrapped in blankets and placed in a shallow depression outside the bunker entrance, near an abandoned cement mixer. Gasoline was poured over them and set ablaze. Erich Kempka, Hitler's chauffeur, found that even after the bodies had been set on fire "we were imprisoned by the very presence of Hitler again." The bunker's air intakes picked up the smell of the burning bodies and sucked it into the rooms. "We could not get away from it," recalled Kempka. "It smelled like burning bacon."

By nightfall the new Chancellor, Joseph Goebbels, had made his first major decision since assuming office: he had decided to try to negotiate the capitulation of the city—on his own terms. A radio message was sent out on the Soviet frequency, asking for a meeting. Soon afterward the Russians responded; they agreed to accept emissaries, and specified a place where German officers might pass through their lines.

Shortly before midnight, Lieutenant General Hans Krebs and Weidling's Chief of Staff, Theodor von Dufving (who had just been made a full colonel), crossed through the ruins, accompanied by an interpreter and two soldiers, and entered the Soviet lines. They were met by soldiers who asked to see their credentials and tried to remove their pistols. Krebs, who spoke excellent Russian, said stiffly: "A courageous opponent is allowed to keep his weapons during negotiations." The Russians, abashed, permitted them to retain their sidearms.

They were taken by car to an apartment house in Tempelhof, and were shown into a small dining room. Its furnishings still showed traces of civilian occupancy—a long table, a large wardrobe against one wall, some chairs, and on another wall a lithograph of Leonardo da Vinci's "The Last Supper." There were also several field telephones in the room. To Krebs and Von Dufving the place seemed filled with senior officers. There were no greetings and the Russians did not introduce themselves. Krebs had no way of knowing, therefore, that the man sitting opposite him was the renowned Colonel General Vasili Ivanovich Chuikov, defender of Stalingrad and commander of the Eighth Guards Army. Nor could he know that the other Russian "officers" consisted of two war correspondents, Chuikov's aide (who was also his brother-in-law) and two interpreters.* The fact was that Chuikov had been caught by surprise by the sudden request for talks and had not been able to assemble his full staff.

Krebs first asked for a private meeting with the "chief Soviet negotiator." Chuikov, taking a long Russian cigarette from the box

* With the two correspondents when Chuikov summoned them to the meeting was a visiting Soviet composer, Matvei Isaakovich Blanter, sent by Stalin to write a symphony commemorating the Berlin victory. The correspondents asked the General what to do with the composer, and Chuikov said, "Bring him along." But when Blanter arrived he was wearing civilian clothes, and it was clear that he could not be passed off as a Red Army officer. He was hastily shoved into a clothes closet adjoining the meeting room. He stayed there for most of the ensuing conference. Just before the visitors left he fainted from lack of air and fell into the room, to the utter astonishment of the Germans.

in front of him and lighting it, airily waved at the men sitting around him and said, "This is my staff—this is my war council."

Krebs continued to object, but he finally gave in. "It is my mission," he said, "to deliver a message which is extraordinarily important and of a confidential nature. I want you to know that you are the first foreigner to learn that on April 30 Hitler committed suicide."

That was indeed news to Chuikov, but without batting an eye, he said, "We know that."

Krebs was astounded. "How could you know?" he asked. "Hitler only committed suicide a few hours ago." Hitler had married Eva Braun on the twenty-ninth; she too had committed suicide and their bodies had been burned and buried. It had happened, he explained, in the Führerbunker. Once again, Chuikov hid his surprise. Neither he nor anyone else in the Soviet command had had any knowledge of such a place, nor had they ever heard of Eva Braun.

They then got down to hard negotiating. Krebs told Chuikov that Hitler had left a will behind in which he named his successors, and he passed a copy of the will across to the Russian. The problem, he said, was that there could not be a complete surrender because Doenitz, the new President, was not in Berlin. The first step, Krebs suggested, would be a cease-fire or a partial surrender—after which perhaps the Doenitz government might negotiate directly with the Russians. This attempt to split the Allies was flatly rejected by Chuikov after a hasty phone call to Zhukov. (The decision was later confirmed by Moscow.)

The negotiations went on all night. By dawn all that Krebs had gained from the Russians was a single demand: an immediate unconditional surrender of the city, plus the personal surrender of all the occupants of the bunker.

While Krebs remained to argue with Chuikov, Von Dufving made a hazardous journey back through the lines, during which he was shot at by SS troops and pulled to safety by a Russian lieutenant colonel. He finally reached the Führerbunker and there he told

Goebbels that the Russians were insisting on an unconditional capitulation. Goebbels became agitated. "To that I shall never, never agree," he cried.

With both sides adamant, the talks were broken off. In the bunker there was panic. It seemed now that every Soviet gun in the district had zeroed in on the Reichskanzlei; Von Dufving later speculated that this was the direct result of Krebs's disclosure of the bunker's location. For those in the besieged Führerbunker there were now only two alternatives: suicide or a breakout. Immediately everyone began to make plans. They would leave in small groups through the complex of tunnels and bunkers that lay beneath the Reichskanzlei building and grounds. From there they would follow the subway system to the Friedrichstrasse Station, where they hoped to join up with a battle group that would lead them to the north. "Once we broke through the Russian cordon on the north side of the Spree," Werner Naumann, Goebbels' assistant, later recalled, "we were sure we could turn safely in any direction."

Some chose the other alternative.

For the Goebbels family the choice was suicide. Werner Naumann had tried for weeks to dissuade Magda Goebbels, but she remained firm. Now the time had come. At about eight-thirty on May 1, Naumann was talking with Goebbels and his wife when suddenly Magda "got up and went into the children's rooms. After a short while she returned, white and shaken." Almost immediately, Goebbels began making his good-byes. "He said a few personal words to me—nothing political or about the future, just good-bye," Naumann later said. As Goebbels left the bunker he asked his adjutant, Guenther Schwägermann, to burn his and his family's bodies after death. Then, as Naumann watched, Joseph and Magda Goebbels went slowly up the stairs and into the garden. Goebbels was wearing his cap and gloves. Magda was "shaking so badly she could hardly walk up the stairs." No one ever saw them alive again.

The children were dead, too, and at the hand of a most improbable killer. "Only one person," said Naumann, "went into the children's rooms in the last moments before Joseph and Magda took their own lives—and that was Magda herself."

Some of those who broke out did not fare much better. A number were killed. Others fell into the hands of the Russians within hours; Hitler's bodyguard Otto Günsche was to spend twelve years as a Soviet prisoner. Some quickly became casualties—like pilot Hans Baur who, carrying a small painting of Frederick the Great given to him by Hitler, lost a leg from a shell burst and woke up in a Russian hospital without the painting. Others such as Martin Bormann mysteriously disappeared. A few actually got away—or, what was almost as good, fell into the hands of the Anglo-Americans.

Three stayed in the bunker and committed suicide: Hitler's adjutant, General Burgdorf; the OKH's Chief of Staff, General Hans Krebs, and SS Captain Franz Schedle of the bunker guards.

And now, with all other authority gone, the full responsibility for the safety of the city, its defenders and its people fell on one man—General Karl Weidling. By now Berlin was a flaming holocaust. Its troops had been pushed back into the very heart of the city. There were tanks along the Unter den Linden and the Wilhelmstrasse. There was fighting all through the Tiergarten area and in the zoo. Russian artillery was bombarding the city from the East-West Axis. Troops were in the subway stations at Alexanderplatz and Friedrichstrasse, and a fierce battle was taking place within the Reichstag. Weidling could see nothing to do but surrender. Still, he felt that he should put it up to his men. He called a meeting of his commanders and explained the situation. "I informed them," Weidling said, "of the events of the last twenty-four hours and my plans. At the end I left it to every one of them to choose another way out, but they had no other solution. However, those who wanted to try breaking out could do so if they desired."

A little before one o'clock on the morning of May 2 the Red Army's 79th Guards Rifle Division picked up a radio message. "Hello, hello," said the voice. "This is the 56th Panzer Corps. We

ask for a cease-fire. At twelve-fifty hours Berlin time we are sending truce negotiators to the Potsdam Bridge. Recognition sign—a
white flag. Awaiting reply."

The Russians replied: "Understand you. Understand you. Am
transmitting your request to Chief of Staff."

On receipt of the message, General Chuikov immediately ordered a cease-fire. At twelve-fifty on May 2, Colonel von Dufving,
Weidling's Chief of Staff, and two other officers arrived at the
Potsdam Bridge under the white flag. They were taken to Chuikov's headquarters. Soon afterward Weidling followed. Later that
day powerful loudspeakers all over the city announced the end of
hostilities. "Each hour of the conflict," General Weidling's order
read, "increases the frightful sufferings of the civilian population
of Berlin and of our wounded. . . . I command the immediate
cessation of fighting." Although sporadic firing would continue for
days, the battle for Berlin was officially over. People who ventured
into the Platz der Republik that afternoon saw the red flag fluttering over the Reichstag. It had been raised even as the fighting was
going on at exactly 1:45 P.M. on the thirtieth of April.

Although the Russians knew that the Führerbunker lay beneath
the Reichskanzlei, it took them several hours to find it. People
were grabbed off the streets and asked to direct the searchers to
the place. Gerhard Menzel, a photographer, was one who was
asked. He had never heard of the bunker. Still, he went with one
group of soldiers to the wrecked Reichskanzlei. In the labyrinth
of cellars and passageways Russian engineers led the way with
mine detectors. As soon as a room or corridor was cleared, other
soldiers collected papers, files and maps. Menzel was suddenly
given a pair of binoculars the Russians had found and told to
leave. They had arrived at the Führerbunker itself.

The first bodies they found were those of Generals Burgdorf and
Krebs. The two officers were in the corridor lounge, sitting before

a long table littered with glasses and bottles. Both men had shot themselves, but they were identified by papers found in their uniforms.

Major Boris Polevoi, in one of the first search teams to enter, made a quick inspection of the entire bunker. In a small room with Pullman-type beds fastened to the walls, he found the Goebbels family. The bodies of Joseph and Magda were lying on the floor. "Both bodies had been burned," Polevoi said, "and only Joseph Goebbels' face was recognizable." The Russians later had trouble figuring out how the parents' bodies came to be there. Presumably someone had brought them back into the bunker after their partial cremation, but the Russians never learned who. The children were also there. "To see the children was horrid," Major Polevoi said. "The only one who seemed disturbed was the eldest, Helga. She was bruised. All were dead, but the rest were lying there peacefully."

Soviet doctors immediately examined the youngsters. There were burn marks around their mouths, leading the doctors to believe that the children had been given a sleeping potion and had then been poisoned while they slept by cyanide tablets which had been crushed between their teeth. From Helga's bruises, the doctors speculated that she had awakened during the poisoning, had struggled, and had had to be held down. As the bodies were carried up to the Reichskanzlei Court of Honor to be photographed and tagged for identification purposes, Polevoi took a last look around the death room. Lying on the floor were the children's toothbrushes and a squashed tube of toothpaste.

A special team of experts found Hitler's body almost immediately, buried under a thin layer of earth. A Russian historian, General B. S. Telpuchovskii, felt sure that it was the Führer. "The body was badly charred," he said, "but the head was intact, though the back was shattered by a bullet. The teeth had been dislodged and were lying alongside the head."

Then some doubts began to arise. Other bodies were found in the same area and some of them, too, had been burned. "We found the body of a man in uniform whose features resembled Hitler's," said Telpuchovskii, "but his socks were darned. We decided that this could not be Hitler because we hardly thought that the Führer of the Reich would wear darned socks. There was also the body of a man who was freshly killed but not burned."

The matter of the two doubles was further confused when the first body was placed alongside the second, and guards and other German personnel were asked to identify them. They either could not or would not. A few days later Colonel General Vasili Soko-lovskii ordered a dental check to be made of each body. Fritz Echtmann and Käthe Heusermann, the dental technicians who had worked in the offices of Hitler's dentist, Blaschke, were turned up. Echtmann was taken to Finow, near Eberswalde, about twenty-five miles northeast of Berlin. He was asked to draw a sketch of Hitler's teeth. When he had finished, his interrogators disappeared into another room with the sketch. A short while later they were back. "It fits," Echtmann was told. Then the Russians showed the technician Hitler's entire lower jaw and dental bridges.

Käthe Heusermann was picked up on May 7; she immediately identified the jaw and bridges. The work she and Blaschke had performed some months ago was easily recognizable. Käthe was given a bag of food and driven back to Berlin. Two days later she was picked up again and this time taken to the town of Erkner. In a clearing was a row of open graves, the bodies visible in them. "Identify them," the Russian with her said. Käthe immediately recognized the bodies of Joseph Goebbels and his children. "The girls were all still wearing flannel nightgowns of a printed material with a design of small red roses and blue flowers intertwined," she said. There was no sign of Magda Goebbels.

Apparently as a consequence of her identification of Hitler's teeth, Käthe Heusermann spent the next eleven years in a Soviet prison, most of the time in solitary confinement.

What happened to the remains of Hitler's body? The Russians claim to have cremated it just outside Berlin, but they will not say where. They say that they never found Eva Braun's body, that

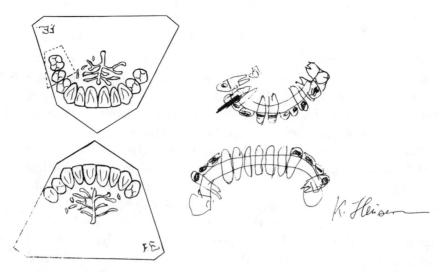

These two sketches, drawn especially for the author in 1963, were made and signed by Käthe Heusermann (right) and Fritz Echtmann, showing how they identified Hitler's teeth for the Russians. Note the position of the hanging bridge in the upper jaw, marked with a dotted rectangle in Echtmann's sketch.

it must have been consumed completely by fire, and that any normally identifiable portions must have been destroyed or scattered in the furious bombardment of the government buildings.*

On the morning of April 30, as Gotthard Heinrici walked down the corridor of his headquarters before departing for good, a young captain had stepped up to him. "General," he said, "you don't know me. I have been working in the Operations Department. Like everyone else, I know that you have been relieved and ordered to report to Plön."

Heinrici said nothing.

"I beg of you," said the young captain, "do not hurry getting there."

"What are you talking about?" asked Heinrici.

---

* It is the author's belief that the Russians were not interested in Eva Braun and made no real effort to identify her body. The first confirmation by the Soviets that Hitler was dead was made to the author and to Professor John Erickson by Marshal Vasili Sokolovskii on April 17, 1963, almost eighteen years after the event.

"Years ago," said the captain, "I used to walk behind the regimental band in Schwäbisch Gmünd on Sundays during church parade. You were a major then, sir. I later became well acquainted with the man who was then your adjutant."

Heinrici said, "Yes—Rommel."

"Well, sir," the captain continued, "I hope you will forgive me for saying that I would not like the same fate to overtake you that befell Field Marshal Rommel."

"What do you mean?" Heinrici asked, looking at him sharply. "Rommel was killed in action."

The captain replied: "No sir, he was not. He was forced to commit suicide." Heinrici stared at him. "How do you happen to know this?" he snapped.

"I was Rommel's aide," the officer told him. "My name is Hellmuth Lang. I beg of you, drive as slowly as you can to Plön. That way the war will probably be over by the time you get there."

Heinrici hesitated. Then he shook Lang's hand. "Thank you," he said stiffly. "Thank you very much."

Heinrici walked on down the corridor and out of the building. Drawn up there were the members of his small staff. Someone gave an order and every man came to the salute. Heinrici walked over to each of them. "I want to thank you all," he said. Captain Heinrich von Bila, the General's aide, opened the car door. Heinrici got in. Von Bila climbed in beside the driver. "Plön," he said.

Heinrici leaned over and tapped the chauffeur on the shoulder. "We're in no great hurry," he said.

Late the next night Heinrici reached the barracks at Plön. As he entered his room a radio was playing. There was a sudden interruption. After a low roll of drums it was announced that the Führer was dead. The time was 10 P.M., May 1.

❖   ❖   ❖

Warrant Officer Dixie Deans sat beside his German guard, Charlie Gumbach, listening to the news. It was the best news

Dixie had heard for a long time. ". . . In the battle against Bolshevism, the Führer fought to the last breath before his death," the announcer solemnly stated. Deans looked around him. He and Gumbach were somewhere east of Lauenburg, sheltering in the cellar of a house just back of the German lines. The whole family was present and the wife was in tears at the news. Deans restrained his own delight. Though the Führer might be dead, the war was not yet over. The German lines were just ahead and Dixie had to get through them. It would not be easy; the firing was heavy.

Everyone settled down in the uncomfortable quarters for the night. Sleep came easily to Deans. He had been cycling for days, trying to get through to the British lines. Now with a bit of luck he might just make it—if he could persuade the next lot of Jerries to let him by. It was the last thing Deans remembered before he fell asleep.

Hours later he awoke with a jolt. There was a tommy gun sticking in his ribs. A voice said, "Okay, chum; on your feet." Dixie looked up into the face of a tough-looking British 6th Airborne paratrooper. The area had been taken during the night, while they slept. Deans leaped up, overjoyed, and explained who he was. He and Charlie were marched back to company headquarters, then passed along first to division headquarters and then to corps. Finally they were seen by Lieutenant General Evelyn H. Barker, 8th Corps commander.

Deans quickly explained the situation. "There are 12,000 R.A.F. POWs marching toward the lines," he said urgently. "Our planes are shooting them up!" He showed General Barker where he had left the men. The General looked startled; hastily he reached for the phone—and canceled another air strike scheduled for the same area. "Everything will be all right now," said General Barker, looking relieved. "We should overrun the area within the next forty-eight hours; you'd better get some rest."

"No, sir," Deans said. "I promised Colonel Ostmann that I would return."

Barker looked at him in amazement. "Isn't that a bit silly?" he asked. "After all, we will be there in a matter of hours."

But Deans was insistent. "Well," said the General, "I'll give you a car with a Red Cross flag that may get you through. And tell those Jerries that you meet that they might just as well pack it in now."

Deans saluted. As he passed through the Chief of Staff's office he looked about him. "Where's my German guard, Charlie Gumbach?" he asked. Somebody said, "He's on his way to the POW camp." Deans was annoyed. "I'm not leaving here without him," he growled. "I gave my word of honor." Charlie was quickly returned, and they set off in a captured Mercedes with a Red Cross flag across the hood.

Two days later Dixie Deans marched his men into the British lines, his bagpipers leading the way. Men stood watching as the thin, tired R.A.F. men, heads high, tramped into the British area. Colonel Ostmann and his guards were now taken into custody. Deans and some of his men marched with them to the British POW compound. The two groups faced each other and came to attention. Ostmann stepped forward, and he and Deans saluted. "Good-bye, Colonel Ostmann," said Deans. "Good-bye, Mr. Deans," said Ostmann. "I hope we meet again." Then Deans repeated "Ten-*shun!*" and Ostmann and his guards marched into the British POW compound. As he passed, Charlie Gumbach waved.

❀ ❀ ❀

The firing was murderous. It came from every side. Busse was everywhere, yelling at his men. "On your feet! Keep moving! Only a few more miles to go! Wenck is waiting!" Busse was so tired that he did not know what hour or even what day it was. The Ninth had been fighting toward Wenck for what seemed like weeks. There was almost no ammunition left, and there was virtually no artillery, only some mortars. There were few machine guns and almost nothing to fire in them. Everywhere Busse looked he saw men collapsing, unable to move. It took all his strength and that of his officers to keep them going. Complicating matters were the thousands of refugees who had joined the columns. Food was short. There was not even enough for his own men.

Wenck could not be more than a few miles away, but Russian resistance was still stiff. Busse called up his last remaining tank. He had been holding it for this moment. He told Lieutenant General Wolf Hagemann to lead the way out. Hagemann leaped in and told the driver to gun the motor. The tank thrashed forward. They rumbled across a ditch and some rough ground. Suddenly Hagemann saw the Russian troops breaking in front of them. He looked around for something to fire. There was no ammunition for the machine guns, but he grabbed up a shotgun and began pumping shells at the fleeing Russians.

Then he heard fire coming from the other direction—from in back of the Russians. It was Wenck's men. The link-up came so suddenly that nobody really remembered afterward how it ended. Exhausted men just fell into each other's arms. Wenck and Busse had joined.

"The men of the Ninth were so tired, so worn out, in such terrible shape, that it was unbelievable," Wenck remembered. As he stood watching, one man in the midst of the columns broke away and came toward him. Wenck saw a haggard, begrimed, unshaven soldier. Not until the man was almost up to him did Wenck recognize General Theodor Busse. Wordlessly they shook hands, and then Wenck said, "Thank God you're here."

On May 7 the two armies were back on the Elbe and more than 100,000 crossed to the west to be taken by the Americans. Of Busse's original 200,000 men, only 40,000 survived.

The last message from Trans-Ocean, the semi-official German news agency, was in French. It said, *"Sauve qui peut"*—Let those who are able save themselves. Berliners took the suggestion. There were tanks, troops, baby carriages, automobiles, horse-drawn wagons, personnel carriers, self-propelled guns, men on horseback and thousands of people afoot funneling out of Berlin across the bridges leading to Spandau. The vast exodus had been going on for hours. The surrender might have been signed but shooting was still going on, and all the refugees wanted to do was escape. Occasionally the columns of fleeing Germans were shelled: apparently Russian artillery to the north and south had not yet received the cease-fire.

Young Brigitte Weber set out from Berlin in her father-in-law's chauffeur-driven car; she was wrapped in her fur coat and she had a basket of heirloom silver at her feet. Then the car got jammed in the Spandau columns, and it took ten and a half hours to travel just a few miles. She finally had to abandon the car and, like thousands of others, trudge west on foot.

The 16-year-old Aribert Schulz was astonished to find himself once again in the presence of the official SS executioner. Schulz was lying next to the red-haired man in a first-aid shelter: the lanky SS gunman had taken a full burst of fire across the stomach; he screamed for sixteen hours before he died.

Again and again, as the great throngs of people filled the roads leading toward the bridges, shells landed among them. Hildegard Panzer, traveling with Captain Kurt Ache, who was helping her with her two children—Wolfgang, nine, and Helga, five—lost the little boy and girl in the crush. She never saw them again. In all, an estimated twenty thousand people were killed and wounded in the mad exodus.

And then at last the shells stopped falling, and the refugees left the sound of gunfire behind. They walked a little farther, to be sure, then they dropped to the ground. Men, women and children slept where they fell—in fields, in ditches, in empty houses, in abandoned vehicles, on the shoulders of the roads, in the roads themselves. They were safe now. The last battle had ended.

"Abu! Abu!" Heinrich Schwarz walked through the terrible devastation of the zoo. There was nothing left now, he thought. The
zoo would never be the same again. Dead animals and rubble
were everywhere. He walked toward the pool. "Abu! Abu!" he
called.

There was a fluttering. At the edge of the empty pool was
the rare Abu Markub stork, standing on one leg and looking at
Schwarz. He walked through the pool and picked up the bird.
"It's all over, Abu," said Schwarz. "It's all over." He carried the
bird away in his arms.

On May 4, Ilse Antz slowly stepped from her Wilmersdorf cellar
for the first time in daylight since April 24. The streets were
strangely quiet. "At first, unaccustomed to the brightness, I saw
nothing but black circles before my eyes. But then I looked
around. The sun was shining, and spring had come. The trees
were blooming; the air was soft. Even in this tortured and dying
town nature was bringing back life. Up to now nothing had
touched me; all emotions were dead. But as I looked over at the
park, where spring had come, I could not control myself any
longer. For the first time since it had all started, I cried."

THE FALL OF THE CITY

The Russians fight their way into Berlin. At the top, Russian *Katushkas*—rocket launchers—firing in the city. *At bottom,* Russian troops shelter behind a Soviet propaganda sign that reads, "Forward, fighters of Stalingrad! Victory is near!" In the background is the German Victory Monument.

The Zoo Bunker. One of the twin flak towers in the zoo, it was the last stronghold to capitulate in Berlin. *Top,* before the fighting; *bottom,* after. *Above at left,* is Walter Hagedorn, a Luftwaffe doctor, who surrendered the bunker to the Russians. *Right* is Gerda Niedieck, teletype operator, who handled Hitler's last message: "Where is Wenck? Where is Steiner?"

Top left, General Krebs outside Chuikov's HQ on the morning of May 1. This unique photograph from the Soviet Defense Archives appears here for the first time. *Right,* the same house twenty years later, discovered by the author following directions given him by Chuikov in Moscow. The house at 2 Schullenburg Ring, Tempelhof, is still owned by the same person, a Mrs. Goebels. "The room was dominated by a lithograph of Leonardo da Vinci's 'Last Supper,'" recalls Chuikov. It's still there, but the table, *above,* on which the surrender was signed is now in the library of the nearby Judas Thaddeus Catholic Church.

A NOTE ON CASUALTIES

✤

Even twenty years later no one knows with any certainty what the civilian losses were during the battle of Berlin. Even yet, bodies are being unearthed from ruins, in gardens, in parks where they were hurriedly interred during the battle, and from mass graves. However, based on statistical studies, probably close to 100,000 civilians died as a result of the battle. At least 20,000 succumbed to heart attacks, some 6,000 committed suicide, the remainder were either killed outright from shelling or street fighting or died later from wounds. The number of people who fled Berlin in the last days and died elsewhere in Germany has also never been accurately estimated. If at least 52,000 were killed from bombing alone, and if the estimates above are accepted, the figure rises to more than 150,000. This does not include wounded.

How many were raped? Again no one knows. I have had estimates from doctors running from 20,000 to 100,000. Abortions were unofficially permitted, but for obvious reasons no one is willing to even guess at the number.

As for German military casualties, like those of the civilians, no one really knows. Complicating the problem is the fact that they are included in Germany's total war casualty figure; thus it is impossible to say how many fell in Berlin alone. The Russians are quite definite about their losses. Soviet Defense authorities say that they had "in excess of 100,000 killed" in the battle from the Oder to the final capture of Berlin. To me that figure seems high, but it may have been deliberately inflated to dramatize the victory. On the other hand Marshal Koniev told me that his forces alone suffered "in the entire battle from the Oder to Berlin and with my southern flank going toward the Elbe . . . 150,000 killed." Thus it would seem that Zhukov's and Koniev's combined forces lost at least 100,000 killed in the taking of Berlin. Curiously, General Omar N. Bradley, commander of the U. S. 12th Army Group, had warned Eisenhower that if he tried to take the capital he might suffer 100,000 casualties, but Bradley was talking about a total of killed, wounded and missing.

THE
SOLDIERS AND CIVILIANS
OF
"THE LAST BATTLE"

✠

What They Do Today

The following is a list of all those who were involved in "The Last Battle" and who contributed information to this book. First, the men of the Allied Armies; then the German military who opposed them, and finally the Berliners who lived in the city or its environs during March and April, 1945. At the request of the Bonn government, the addresses of German military personnel and civilians have been omitted. Occupations may have changed since this book went to press, and where an asterisk follows a name it indicates that the contributor has died since these lists were compiled. All ranks given are as of 1945.

AMERICAN

Eisenhower, Dwight David, Gen., Supreme Comdr., [SHAEF] *Gen. of the Army, Comdr.-in-Chief;* President of the United States (1952-1960), *Gettysburg, Pa.*

Bradley, Omar Nelson, Gen. [12th Army Group] *Gen. of the Army; Chairman, Bulova Watch Co., New York, N. Y.*

Abbes, Henry Charles, Capt. [30th Inf. Div.] *Project architect, Queens Village, N. Y.*

Adams, Charles M., Col. [69th Inf. Div.] *Col. (retired),* U.S. Army, *La Mesa, Calif.*

Adryan, Chester P., 1st Lt. [83rd Inf. Div.] *Special agent,* The Northwestern Mutual Life Insurance Co., *Bellefontaine, Ohio*

Allmand, James R., 1st Lt. [82nd Airborne Div.] *Occupation unknown, Hermosillo, Son., Mexico*

Anderson, Gerald J., Pfc. [30th Inf. Div.] *Motor vehicle examiner,* State of New Jersey, *Glen Rock, N. J.*

Anderson, Glen H., Col. [5th Armored Div.] *Motel owner, Daytona Beach, Fla.*

Anderson, Peter, Sgt. [30th Inf. Div.] *Superintendent,* Executive Mansion, *Albany, N. Y.*

Angeleri, Carl J., T/4 [30th Inf. Div.] *Real estate broker, Forest Hills, N. Y.*

Aralle, William, T/Sgt. [30th Inf. Div.] *Revenue officer,* Internal Revenue Service, *West Orange, N. J.*

Ayers, Kenneth Lee, 1st Lt. [84th Inf. Div.] *Maj. (retired), U.S. Army, Tallahassee, Fla.*

Baker, Clyde, Pfc. [30th Inf. Div.] *Postal employee, Piedmont, Ala.*

Bargy, James H., S/Sgt. [30th Inf. Div.] *M/Sgt. N.Y. Guard; Truck driver, Rensselaer, N. Y.*

Barnard, Robert Howard, 1st Lt. [Ninth Air Force] *Businessman, Tucumcari, N. M.*

Barrett, Charles Joseph, Brig. Gen. [84th Inf. Div.] *Col., U.S. Military Academy, West Point, N. Y.*

Batchelder, Clifton Brooks, Lt. Col. [2nd Armored Div.] *Executive, United States Check Book Co., Omaha, Neb.*

Berry, John Thomas, Maj. [82nd Airborne Div.] *Col., 101st Airborne Div., Fort Campbell, Ky.*

Berryman, Flur Woodrow, T/4 [5th Armored Div.] *Carpenter, Town Creek, Ala.*

Bestebreurtje, Arie D., Capt. [82nd Airborne Div.] *Minister, Louisville, Ky.*

Bethke, Clarence E., Capt. [84th Inf. Div.] *Occupation unknown, Tucson, Ariz.*

Biddle, William Shepard, Col. [83rd Inf. Div.] *Maj. Gen. (retired), U.S. Army; Comdt., Pennsylvania Military College, Chester, Pa.*

Billingsley, Charles, Col. [82nd Airborne Div.] *Maj. Gen., U.S. Army; Deputy Commanding General, Combat Development Command, Fort Belvoir, Va.*

Blair, William M., Jr., 1st Lt. [84th Inf. Div.] *Asst. treasurer, Colonial Bank and Trust Co., Waterbury, Conn.*

Blake, Peter, 2nd Lt. [5th Armored Div.] *Architect and author, New York, N. Y.*

Bloser, Donald Paul, Capt. [30th Inf. Div.] *Doctor of medicine, Enola, Pa.*

Bolling, Alexander R., Maj. Gen. [84th Inf. Div.] *

Bommer, Jack L., T/5 [82nd Airborne Div.] *Occupation unknown, Columbus, Ohio*

Bond, Ridgely B., Jr., Lt. Col. [84th Inf. Div.] *Brig. Gen., U.S. Army, Catonsville, Md.*

Booth, J. Edwin, Sgt. [POW, Luckenwalde Camp] *Postal clerk, Fremont, Neb.*

Bovee, Elmer William, Pfc. [30th Inf. Div.] *Owner, Bovee's Delivery Service, Addison, N. Y.*

Boyd, Elmo Hubbard, Capt. [83rd Inf. Div.] *Manufacturer's representative, Charlotte, S. C.*

Brockley, Harold R., T/4 [82nd Airborne Div.] *Post office clerk, Connersville, Ind.*

Brooks, Dwight Marion, 1st Lt. [69th Inf. Div.] *Lt. Col., U.S. Army, Fort Belvoir, Va.*

Brunow, Marcel, F. J., Lt. Col. [2nd Armored Div.] *Col. (retired), U.S. Army, Belfast, Me.*

Bunch, Doyle R., Capt. [83rd Inf. Div.] *School principal, Amarillo Public Schools, Amarillo, Tex.*

Burnette, Eugene Gale, T/Sgt. [30th Inf. Div.] *Sfc. USAIG, Furman University, Greenville, S. C.*

Burns, Stanley E., Capt. [84th Inf. Div.] *District manager, Hemingway Transport Co., Philadelphia, Pa.*

Burton, Edward J., Pfc. [82nd Airborne Div.] *Trucker, Carmichael, Calif.*

Byrn, Delmont K., Capt. [30th Inf. Div.] *Professor of Education, University of Michigan, Ann Arbor, Mich.*

Carbin, John Patrick, Jr., Maj. [30th Inf. Div.] *Lt. Col., U.S. Army, Trenton, N. J.*

Carnes, Norman D., Lt. Col. [84th Inf. Div.] *Col. (retired), U.S. Army, Denver, Colo.*

Caroscio, William J., 1st Lt. [5th Armored Div.] *Policeman, Elmira, N. Y.*

Carrall, Charles B., Capt. [30th Inf. Div.] *Priest, Hawthorne, N. Y.*

Cason, Claude Edwin, Capt. [5th Armored Div.] *Lt. Col. (retired), U.S. Army, Huntsville, Ala.*

Clark, Curtis Mason, Maj. [2nd Armored Div.] *Counsel, Norton Co., Worcester, Mass.*

Cleary, Francis J., S/Sgt. [82nd Airborne Div.] *Production manager, W. S. Rockwell Co., Fairfield, Conn.*

Closs, Maldwyn M., S/Sgt. [5th Armored Div.] *Postal clerk, Wymore, Neb.*

Coates, Edwin Morton, Lt. Col. [5th Armored Div.] *Test planner, U.S.A.F., Lancaster, Calif.*

Collier, John Howell, Brig. Gen. [2nd Armored Div.] *Lt. Gen. (retired), U.S. Army, San Antonio, Tex.*

Conran, Richard John, Lt. Col. [69th Inf. Div.] *Col., ARADCOM, Oklahoma City, Okla.*

Conte, Angelo James, Maj. [84th Inf. Div.] *Lt. Col. (retired), U.S.A.R., Levittown, N. J.*

Cook, Julian Aaron, Lt. Col. [82nd Airborne Div.] *Col., CINCLANT, Norfolk, Va.*

Cook, Tim O., Lt. Col. [83rd Inf. Div.] *Banking executive, Lamesa, Tex.*

Copp, Franklin Harold, 1st Lt. [5th Armored Div.] *Lt. Col., U.S.A.R., Falls Church, Va.*

Cosgrove, Warner G., Jr., Maj. [XIII Corps] *Partner, Shields & Co., New York, N. Y.*

Costello, James Patrick, Capt. [30th Inf. Div.] *Sgt., N.Y.C. Police, Bayside, N. Y.*

Cota, Norman D., Maj. Gen. [28th Inf. Div.] *Maj. Gen. (retired), U.S. Army, Bryn Mawr, Pa.*

Crabill, Edwin B., Col. [83rd Inf. Div.] *Col. (retired), U.S. Army, Riviera Beach, Fla.*

Craig, Bertie Edward, Lt. Col. [84th Inf. Div.] *Col. (retired), U.S. Army, Tacoma, Wash.*

Crosby, Thomas Dillard, S/Sgt. [30th Inf. Div.] *Sgt., USATC, APO, New York, N. Y.*

Cseak, Daniel T., Pfc. [30th Inf. Div.] *Bakery manager, Canton, Ohio*

Cullom, Henry Martin, Jr., Capt. [84th Inf. Div.] *Executive,* Valley Tire & Supply Co., *South Pittsburg, Tenn.*

Currey, Francis S., T/Sgt. [30th Inf. Div.] *Office worker,* Veterans' Administration Hospital, *Albany, N. Y.*

Daniels, Donald C., 1st Lt. [5th Armored Div.] *Occupation unknown, Kansas City, Mo.*

Darrigo, Joseph Robert, 1st Lt. [84th Inf. Div.] *Laborer, Darien, Conn.*

Davis, William Holt, Capt. [84th Inf. Div.] *Lt. Col., Georgia Military Academy, East Point, Ga.*

Deane, John R., Maj. Gen. [Chief, Military Mission, Moscow] *Maj. Gen. (retired), U.S. Army, San Francisco, Calif.*

Deere, Benny, Pfc. [30th Inf. Div.] *Occupation unknown, Gloversville, Ala.*

DeVault, Charles Cooper, Lt. Col. [5th Armored Div.] *Realtor, Marion, Va.*

Devenney, John J., Capt. [83rd Inf. Div.] *Civilian executive officer, Dept. of the Army, Springfield, Pa.*

DiBattista, Dominic, Pfc. [82nd Airborne Div.] *Contractor, Garwood, N. J.*

Dickenson, Glenn Gilmer, Lt. Col. [5th Armored Div.] *Col. (retired), U.S. Army; Lawyer, Augusta, Ga.*

Dilione, Charles, Pvt. [30th Inf. Div.] *Truck driver, Sea Bright, N. J.*

Dingley, Nelson III, Col. [U.S. Group Control Council] *Brig. Gen. (retired), U.S. Army, Vero Beach, Fla.*

Disney, Paul A., Col. [2nd Armored Div.] *Maj. Gen. (retired), U.S. Army, Arlington, Va.*

Doughtie, George Roberts, Capt. [84th Inf. Div.] *Executive,* Atlantic Sheet Metal Corp., *Atlanta, Ga.*

Ellis, Otto, Col. [30th Inf. Div.] *Retired, Bradenton, Fla.*

Faris, John L., Capt. [30th Inf. Div.] *Asst. manager, department store, Rock Hill, S. C.*

Farrand, Edward Gilbert, Col. [5th Armored Div.] *Maj. Gen. (retired), U.S. Army; President,* St. John's Military Academy, *Delafield, Wis.*

Fellman, Malcolm Aaron, 1st Lt. [30th Inf. Div.] *Commodity department,* Bache & Co., *New York, N. Y.*

Ficarra, Louis James, Cpl. [30th Inf. Div.] *Calender operator—leadman, Garfield, N. J.*

Fleischmann, Lawrence, Capt. [30th Inf. Div.] *Occupation unknown, Buffalo, N. Y.*

Flowers, Melvin Lamar, 1st Lt. [Ninth Air Force] *Maj. (retired), U.S.A.F., Huntsville, Ala.*

Fonderico, Vincent, Cpl. [30th Inf. Div.] *Inspector,* City Water Dept., *Rosedale, N. Y.*

Francies, Merritt Duane, 1st Lt. [5th Armored Div.] *Company pilot, Keokuk, Iowa*

Franco, Robert, Capt. [82nd Airborne Div.] *Surgeon, Richland, Wash.*

Frankland, Walter L., Lt. Col. [30th Inf. Div.] *Owner, automotive parts store, Jackson, Tenn.*

Fransosi, Arthur Arnold, T/4 [82nd Airborne Div.] *Postal clerk, Cranston, R. I.*

Galvin, Wayne W., Pvt. [82nd Airborne Div.] *Painter, Las Vegas, Nev.*

Gavin, Charles G., Capt. [30th Inf. Div.] *County extension agent, La Grande, Ore.*

Gavin, James M., Maj. Gen. [82nd Airborne Div.] *Lt. Gen. (retired), U.S. Army, Board Chairman,* Arthur D. Little Co., *Boston, Mass.*

Gazdayka, Mike, Sgt. [5th Armored Div.] *Employee,* San Francisco Examiner Dealer, *Camarillo, Calif.*

Geppert, Leo Joseph, Maj. [84th Inf. Div.] *Col., M.C.,* Brooke General Hospital, *Fort Sam Houston, Tex.*

Gillem, Alvan Cullom, Jr., Maj. Gen. [XIII Corps] *Lt. Gen. (retired), U.S. Army, Atlanta, Ga.*

Gomes, Lloyd H., Lt. Col. [84th Inf. Div.] *Col., U.S. Army, Washington, D. C.*

Grose, Thomas Warren, Capt. [5th Armored Div.] *Superintendent,* The Chesapeake and Ohio Railway, *Saginaw, Mich.*

Hadley, Arthur T., 1st Lt. [2nd Armored Div.] *Author, New York, N. Y.*

Hall, Stewart L., Lt. Col. [30th Inf. Div.] *Asst. vice president,* Occidental Life, *Los Angeles, Calif.*

Halladay, Daniel Whitney, Capt. [83rd Inf. Div.] *Dean of Students,* University of Alabama, *Fayetteville, Ala.*

Handberg, William Francis, Pfc. [30th Inf. Div.] *Commercial artist, Minneapolis, Minn.*

Handy, Thomas T., Maj. Gen. *Retired, U.S. Assistant Chief of Staff, Operations Division, Washington, D. C.*

Hardin, William B., M/Sgt. [30th Inf. Div.] *M/Sgt., U.S. Army, Akron, Ohio*

Hasslinger, Harry Ekas, Lt. Col. [XIII Corps] *Col., U.S. Army,* Veterans' Administration, *College Park, Md.*

Heilbrunn, Martin M., Cpl. [30th Inf. Div.] *Alteration manager,* Stern's, *New York, N. Y.*

Hennessy, Francis Xavier, Cpl. [30th Inf. Div.] *Lawyer, Bronx, N. Y.*

Hess, Neal A., Maj. [Ninth Air Force] *Lt. Col., U.S.A.F., Carswell Air Force Base, Tex.*

Higgins, Daniel E., 1st Lt. [5th Armored Div.] *Public relations executive,* American Cyanamid Co., *Linden, N. J.*

Higgins, Gerald J., Brig. Gen. [101st Airborne Div.] *Maj. Gen. (retired), U.S. Army; Manager, Foreign Operations,* Research Analysis Corp., *Washington, D. C.*

Hill, Edward Mitchell, Capt. [30th Inf. Div.] *Lt. Col., U.S. Army, Arlington, Va.*

Hill, John G., Col. [V Corps] *Brig. Gen. (retired), U.S. Army, Arlington, Va.*

Hillenmeyer, Walter W., Maj. [V Corps] *Partner,* Hillenmeyer Nurseries, *Lexington, Ky.*

Himes, Donald S., Lt. Col. [84th Inf. Div.] *Col., U.S. Army, New York, N. Y.*

Himmelstein, Harold, Pfc. [30th Inf. Div.] *Office worker,* Internal Revenue Service, *New York, N. Y.*

Hinds, Charles F., T/4 [2nd Armored Div.] *State archivist,* Commonwealth of Kentucky, *Frankfort, Ky.*

Hinds, Sidney R., Brig. Gen. [2nd Armored Div.] *Brig. Gen. (retired), U.S. Army; Inspector,* Defense Supply Agency, *Falls Church, Va.*

Hobbs, Leland S., Maj. Gen. [30th Inf. Div.] *Maj. Gen. (retired), U.S. Army, Washington, D. C.*

Hoffman, Morton D., Sgt. [30th Inf. Div.] *President,* Eastern States Electrical Contractors, *New York, N. Y.*

Hollingsworth, James F., Maj. [2nd Armored Div.] *Col., U.S. Army; Acting Deputy Asst. Secretary of Defense, Washington, D. C.*

Holt, Harold Norman, Col. [Ninth Air Force] *Col., U.S.A.F., Maxwell Air Force Base, Ala.*

Hopermann, Richard K., 1st Lt. [30th Inf. Div.] *Research chemist, Oakland, N. J.*

Howley, Frank Leo, Col. [U.S. Military Govt.] *Vice president,* New York University, *New York, N. Y.*

Hoy, Charles E., Col. [84th Inf. Div.] *Maj. Gen. (retired), U.S. Army, Winter Park, Fla.*

Hubbard, Allen, Jr., Capt. [30th Inf. Div.] *Lawyer,* Hughes, Hubbard, Blair & Reed, *New York, N. Y.*

Hubbard, Harry J., Lt. Col. [84th Inf. Div.] *Occupation unknown, Marfa, Tex.*

Huebner, Clarence Ralph, Maj. Gen. [V Corps] *Lt. Gen. (retired), U.S. Army, Washington, D. C.*

Huebschen, Herbert E., S/Sgt. [82nd Airborne Div.] *Agent,* Internal Revenue Service, *Beloit, Wis.*

Hughes, Shelly G., Lt. Col. [83rd Inf. Div.] *President,* Differential Steel Car Co., *Findlay, Ohio*

Hull, John Edwin, Gen. [C/S Operations—Pentagon] *Gen. (retired), U.S. Army, Washington, D. C.*

Hundley, Daniel H., Col. [Ninth Army] *Col. (retired), U.S. Army, Associate professor,* Washington University, *St. Louis, Mo.*

Hunt, Emerson Snow, 1st Lt. [102nd Inf. Div.] *Maj. (retired), U.S.A.R., Wilton, Conn.*

Husing, Christian O., S/Sgt. [30th Inf. Div.] *Owner, service station, Rockport, Mo.*

Ingraham, Gordon D., Lt. Col. [69th Inf. Div.] *Col. (retired), U.S. Army, Oakland, Calif.*

Irby, Willie B., Capt. [30th Inf. Div.] *Dairy farmer and soil conservationist,* U.S.D.A. *Blackstone, Va.*

Jacobs, Marvin Leroy, Lt. Col. [20th Inf. Div.] *Professor,* Memphis State University, *Memphis, Tenn.*

James, Robert Foote, Maj. [5th Armored Div.] *Auto dealer, Lebanon, Pa.*

James, Rowland, Pfc. [30th Inf. Div.] *Manager, Product control,* Pepsi-Cola Co., *Bay Shore, N. Y.*

Johnson, Briard Poland, Lt. Col. [2nd Armored Div.] *Maj. Gen., U.S. Army, Fort Monroe, Va.*

Johnson, Clarence J., Capt. [30th Inf. Div.] *Maj., U.S.A.R.; Public school teacher, Phoenix, Ariz.*

Johnson, Donald R., 1st Lt. [83rd Inf. Div.] *Sales supervisor, service station, Mauston, Wis.*

Jones, James Elmo, S/Sgt. [82nd Airborne Div.] *President*, Industrial Plastics, Inc. *Greensboro, N. C.*

Jones, Richard Harris, Lt. Col. [5th Armored Div.] *Asst. superintendent, Houston schools, Houston, Tex.*

Jordan, Wilhelm Oscar, Sgt. [30th Inf. Div.] *Laborer*, L and M Co., *Horsham, Pa.*

Kaczowka, Henry Rudolph, Maj. [30th Inf. Div.] *Occupation unknown, Wynnewood, Pa.*

Kaiser, Maurice Evans, Lt. Col. [XIII Corps] *Col., U.S. Army, Pentagon, Washington, D. C.*

Kehm, Harold David, Col. [Ninth Army] *Col. (retired), U.S. Army, Bethesda, Md.*

Kelly, Thomas J., Cpl. [7th Armored Div.] *Congressional Medal of Honor winner; Attorney*, U.S. Civil Service Commission, *Brooklyn, N. Y.*

Kinnard, Harold, W.O., Col. [101st Airborne Div.] *Maj. Gen., U.S. Army, 11th Air Assault Div., Fort Benning, Ga.*

Klebba, Joe H., T/Sgt. [30th Inf. Div.] *Rancher, Sheridan, Wyo.*

Kohler, Haley Eustis, Maj. [83rd Inf. Div.] *Lt. Col., (retired), U.S. Army, Owner, dry cleaning business, Lake Charles, La.*

Kolb, Roland L., Lt. Col. [84th Inf. Div.] *Col., U.S. Army, Pentagon, Washington, D. C.*

Komosa, Adam Anthony, Capt. [82nd Airborne Div.] *Lt. Col. (retired), U.S. Army, Bloomington, Ind.*

Korf, Arthur F., Capt. [84th Inf. Div.] *President*, Korf's Sixth Ave., Inc., *Kenosha, Wis.*

Korolevich, Alexander, Pfc. [30th Inf. Div.] *Employee*, Ford Motor Co., *Waldwick, N. J.*

Kotary, William Edward, 1st Lt. [82nd Airborne Div.] *Agency dept., insurance company, Wayne, Pa.*

Kotzebue, Albert, 1st Lt. [69th Inf. Div.] *Lt. Col., U.S. Army, Madison, Wis.*

Kremer, Herbert H., Sgt. [5th Armored Div.] *Civilian employee*, U.S. Coast Guard, *Jefferson City, Mo.*

Kuhlman, Martin Luther, Lt. Col. [83rd Inf. Div.] *Office manager*, Signode Steel Strapping Co., *Chicago, Ill.*

Lacey, Richard Hamilton, Pfc. [30th Inf. Div.] *Pasteurizer*, Wendt Dairy, *Niagara Falls, N. Y.*

Ladin, Samuel S., W.O. [30th Inf. Div.] *Employee*, Guardian Maintenance, *Long Island City, N. Y.*

Landis, John Ross, Pfc. [30th Inf. Div.] *Carpenter, Woodbury, N. J.*

Lawrence, Dale C., Capt. [84th Inf. Div.] *Representative*, Mosaic Tile Co., *Spokane, Wash.*

Leary, Edward J., Lt. Col. [69th Inf. Div.] *Col. (retired), U.S.A.R. Trenton, N. J.*

Leet, George Arnold, Capt. [26th Inf. Div.] *Attorney*, National Labor Relations Board, *Washington, D. C.*

Levy, Harold Joseph, Sgt. [2nd Armored Div.] *Mail carrier, Mamaroneck, N. Y.*

Lord, William T., Pfc. [30th Inf. Div.] *Production manager*, T. N. Palmer & Co., Inc., *New York, N. Y.*

Loveland, Glenn E., S/Sgt. [82nd Airborne Div.] *Employee*, Board of Education, *Shelby, Ohio*

Ludlow, Lee Eugene, T/5 [5th Armored Div.] *Occupation unknown, La Porte, Ind.*

Macaluso, Joseph Anthony, Capt. [83rd Inf. Div.] *Building contractor, New Orleans, La.*

MacFarlane, Paul William, 1st Lt. [83rd Inf. Div.] *Executive*, Dreamland Mfg. Co., *St. Petersburg, Fla.*

MacKinnin, Elwyn L., Pfc. [5th Armored Div.] *Treasurer, contracting company, Orange, Mass.*

Macon, Robert Chauncey, Maj. Gen. [83rd Inf. Div.] *Maj. Gen. (retired), U.S. Army, California, Md.*

MacVean, James Linden, Sgt. [30th Inf. Div.] *M/Sgt. (retired), U.S. Army, LeRoy, N. Y.*

Maggio, Vincent, Cpl. [30th Inf. Div.] *Mail carrier, Huntington, N. Y.*

Manni, Serge A., Pfc. [30th Inf. Div.] *Vice president,* Duro Test International, *River Edge, N. J.*

Martin, William S., 1st Lt. [5th Armored Div.] *Metal shop owner, Golden, Colo.*

McAuliffe, Anthony, Maj. Gen. [101st Airborne Div.] *Lt. Gen. (retired), U.S. Army, Washington, D. C.*

McCloud, June Raymond, S/Sgt. [5th Armored Div.] *Patrolman, city police, Marlinton, W. Va.*

McConnell, Frederick McSwain, 1st Lt. [84th Inf. Div.] *Lt. Col., U.S. Army, Instructor Group, Clemson, S. C.*

McCown, Hal D., Lt. Col. [30th Inf. Div.] *Col., U.S. Army, Washington, D. C.*

McKenna, Richard W., Maj. [5th Armored Div.] *Executive,* Ferry-Morse Seed Co., *Mountain View, Calif.*

McNees, Norman Edwin, 1st Lt. [5th Armored Div.] *Salesman,* George M. Bell & Son, *El Centro, Calif.*

McNeil, Grady, 1st Sgt. [30th Inf. Div.] *Mailer,* N.Y. Journal-American, *New York, N. Y.*

Mennow, Robert E., S/Sgt. [5th Armored Div.] *Stationery engraver, Pittsburgh, Pa.*

Merriam, Wheeler G., Lt. Col. [2nd Armored Div.] *Brig. Gen., U.S. Army, Washington, D. C.*

Millener, George Alvin, Col. [Ninth Army] *Col. (retired), U.S. Army, Knoxville, Tenn.*

Miller, William Scott, Jr., 1st Lt. [84th Inf. Div.] *Lawyer, Little Rock, Ark.*

Millett, John E., Jr., 1st Lt. [5th Armored Div.] *Occupation unknown, Minneola, Kan.*

Mirra, Adolph Raymond, Pfc. [30th Inf. Div.] *Asst. cashier,* National Bank of Westchester, *White Plains, N. Y.*

Mittleman, Herbert H., T/5 [30th Inf. Div.] *Prefabrication dealer,* Scholz Homes, Inc., *Yonkers, N. Y.*

Moore, James E., Maj. Gen. [Ninth Army] *Gen. (retired), U.S. Army, Washington, D. C.*

Morava, John Hall, Lt. Col. [84th Inf. Div.] *President,* U.S. Steel Supply, *Chicago, Ill.*

Mundt, Herman A., Jr., Capt. [83rd Inf. Div.] *Lt. Col., U.S.A.R.; Executive,* Humble Oil & Refining Co., *Durango, Colo.*

Naples, Joseph, T/5 [30th Inf. Div.] *Plant manager,* Plastic Molding Powders, *Kearny, N. J.*

Neblett, Lloyd George, Lt. Col. [Ninth Air Force] *Occupation unknown, Tulsa, Okla.*

Neilson, Henry, Col. [83rd Inf. Div.] *Col., U.S. Army, Fort Sam Houston, Tex.*

Nelson, Clarence A., 1st Lt. [5th Armored Div.] *Paint store owners, Fremont, Neb.*

Nicodemus, Robert E., 1st Lt. [5th Armored Div.] *Lt. Col., U.S. Army, Falls Church, Va.*

Norton, John, Col. [82nd Airborne Div.] *Maj. Gen., U.S. Army, Asst. Comdt., Infantry School, Fort Benning, Ga.*

Norton, Thomas Edward, Capt. [84th Inf. Div.] *Accountant, Boise, Idaho*

Nugent, Richard Emmel, Brig. Gen. [XXIX Tactical Air Command] *Dept. of Defense, Merritt Island, Fla.*

Oliver, Lunsford, Maj. Gen. [5th Armored Div.] *Retired, Williamsburg, Mass.*

Ordway, Godwin, Col. [12th Army Group] *Col. (retired), U.S. Army, Chevy Chase, Md.*

Ornstein, Richard Paul, T/5 [30th Inf. Div.] *Employee,* Savoy Knitting Mills Corp., *New York, N. Y.*

Parker, Braxton Creig, 1st Lt. [84th Inf. Div.] *Capt. (retired), U.S. Army; Civil Servant, Colorado Springs, Colo.*

Parks, Floyd L., Maj. Gen. [SHAEF] *

Pattullo, Alexander Ross, T/Sgt. [82nd Airborne Div.] *Manager of stockholder records,* The Standard Oil Co., *Cleveland, Ohio*

Pearcy, Marvin E., Capt. [2nd Armored Div.] *Maintenance planner,* Rayonier, Inc., *Hoquiam, Wash.*

Petcoff, George, 1st Sgt. [30th Inf. Div.] *Supervisor,* International Paper Co., *New York, N. Y.*

Peters, Abraham, Pfc. [30th Inf. Div.] *Vice president-treasurer,* Allied Office Supplies, Inc., *Jersey City, N. J.*

Peters, Alcee Lafayette, Jr., Maj. [84th Inf. Div.] *Lt. Col., U.S. Army, Washington, D. C.*

Peters, Earl William, Maj. [Ninth Air Force] *Lt. Col., U.S.A.F., McClellan Air Force Base, Calif.*

Philipsborn, Martin Maximilian, Jr., Maj. [5th Armored Div.] *Vice president,* Harrison Wholesale Co., *Chicago, Ill.*

Plantin, Tore Elias, Pfc. [30th Inf. Div.] *Cost estimator, Bethpage, N. Y.*

Pockler, Morris, Pfc. [30th Inf. Div.] *Occupation unknown, Brooklyn, N. Y.*

Poindexter, Clifford T., Cpl. [5th Armored Div.] *Occupation unknown, Fayetteville, Ark.*

Polowsky, Joseph, Pvt. [69th Inf. Div.] *Insurance salesman, Chicago, Ill.*

Pratt, Bernard S., Pvt. [30th Inf. Div.] *Occupation unknown, Lake Luzerne, N. Y.*

Prendergast, R. O., 1st Lt. [82nd Airborne Div.] *Maj., 42d Div. National Guard, New York, N. Y.*

Presnell, William G., 1st Sgt. [30th Inf. Div.] *Superintendent, garment production, Asheboro, N. C.*

Puetzer, Warren James, 1st Lt. [84th Inf. Div.] *Co-owner, tire service company, Corvallis, Ore.*

Pugliese, Michael R., S/Sgt. [30th Inf. Div.] *Self-employed, Stamford, Conn.*

Ramsey, Curtis Lee, 1st Lt. [5th Armored Div.] *Superintendent, textile mill, Laurinburg, N. C.*

Ransom, Paul Lewis, Brig. Gen. [Fifth Army] *Maj. Gen. (retired), U.S. Army, Hampton, Va.*

Rattray, Bruce C., Pfc. [30th Inf. Div.] *Occupation unknown, Long Island City, N. Y.*

Reilly, Edward P., Sgt. [82nd Airborne Div.] *Sales engineer,* Borg Warner Corp., *Houston, Tex.*

Reinhardt, Emil F., Maj. Gen. [69th Inf. Div.] *Maj. Gen. (retired), U.S Army, San Antonio, Tex.*

Rennolds, William Gregory, Jr., Maj. [83rd Inf. Div.] *Director of personnel,* Southern States Cooperative, *Richmond, Va.*

Ressegieu, Fred E., [5th Armored Div.] *Executive,* Bechtel Corp., *San Francisco, Calif.*

Ridgway, Matthew B., Maj. Gen. [XVIII Corps] *Gen. (retired), U.S. Army, Pittsburgh, Pa.*

Robinson, Frank Edward, 1st Sgt. [30th Inf. Div.] *Occupation unknown, Ooltewah, Tenn.*

Robinson, Howard Vernon, Jr., T/5 [2nd Armored Div.] *Self-employed, Deland, Fla.*

Rock, Julius, Maj. [30th Inf. Div.] *Doctor of medicine, Rochester, N. Y.*

Rose, Ben Lacy, Capt. [83rd Inf. Div.] *Professor,* Union Theological Seminary, *Richmond, Va.*

Ross, Winfred A., Lt. Col. [84th Inf. Div.] *Col. (retired), U.S. Army, Sun Prairie, Wis.*

Rubenstein, Charles, Pfc. [30th Inf. Div.] *Realtor, New York, N. Y.*

Sadallah, Elias A., Capt. [2nd Armored Div.] *Vice president,* Manufacturers Hanover Trust Co., *Brooklyn, N. Y.*

St. Cyr, Stede-Strephon, Sgt. [POW, Stalag 7-B] *Photographer, Toledo, Ohio*

Schmidmeister, John, Pfc. [30th Inf. Div.] *Employee,* S. Blickman Co., Inc., *West New York, N. J.*

Schommer, Francis Christian, Capt. [83rd Inf. Div.] *Wholesale toy dealer, Sheboygan, Wis.*

Schultz, Arthur B., Pvt. [82nd Airborne Div.] *Private investigator, San Diego, Calif.*

Scott, Richard H., 1st Lt. [102nd Inf. Div.] *Occupation unknown, Anchorage, Alaska*

Serilla, William Dan, Sgt. [82nd Airborne Div.] *Sky diver, Royal Oak, Mich.*

Sharpe, Granville Attaway, Lt. Col. [83rd Inf. Div.] *Col., U.S. Army,* Institute of Advanced Studies, *Carlisle Barracks, Pa.*

Shiverski, Stanley A., S/Sgt. [5th Armored Div.] *Set-up, A.M.C., Racine, Wis.*

Shonak, James Dmitrius, Capt. [83rd Inf. Div.] *Insurance executive,* John Hancock Mutual Life Insurance Co., *Boston, Mass.*

Simpson, William H., Lt. Gen. [Ninth Army] *Gen. (retired), U.S. Army, San Antonio, Tex.*

Sloan, George B., Col. [XIX Corps] *Col. (retired), U.S. Army; Senior analyst, production planning,* MacDonald Aircraft Co., *St. Louis, Mo.*

Smith, Davis Maitland, Capt. [84th Inf. Div.] *Maj., U.S. Army, Bowling Green, Va.*

Smith, Walter Bedell, Lt. Gen. [SHAEF] °

Smurthwaite, Richard J., Pfc. [82nd Airborne Div.] *Manager of product evaluation, Missile Space Div.,* General Electric Co., *Philadelphia, Pa.*

Solomon, Harold, 1st Lt. [30th Inf. Div.] *Sheet metal worker, Howard Beach, N. Y.*

Solow, Saul, 1st Lt. [30th Inf. Div.] *Lt. Col., U.S.A.R.; General manager,* Famous Coat Front Pad Co., Inc., *New York, N. Y.*

Sowers, Kenneth, Lt. Col. [84th Inf. Div.] *Col., Chaplain, U.S. Army, Washington, D. C.*

Stanford, Leslie E., Capt. [30th Inf. Div.] *Lt. Col., U.S. Army, APO San Francisco, Calif.*

Starling, Jack W., Capt. [30th Inf. Div.] *Advertising executive,* The McCarty Co., *Seattle, Wash.*

Staub, Paul, Pfc. [69th Inf. Div.] *Salesman,* Bond's, *Levittown, N. Y.*

Stephens, Richard W., Col. [30th Inf. Div.] *Maj. Gen. (retired), U.S. Army, Sun City, Fla.*

Stephens, Thomas LeRoy, T/5 [30th Inf. Div.] *Service station proprietor, Franklin, N. J.*

Stevens, Earle M., Lt. Col. [30th Inf. Div.] *General plant supervisor, Convent Station, N. J.*

Stewart, Carlton E., Lt. Col. [30th Inf. Div.] *Carpenter and builder, West Newton, Mass.*

Stewart, Carroll Richard, Pfc. [30th Inf. Div.] *Public school custodian, Canastota, N. Y.*

Stewart, Terrell Eugene, Cpl. [82nd Airborne Div.] *Linotype operator, Columbus, Ga.*

Stockwell, Richard C., 2nd Lt. [2nd Armored Div.] *City planning director, Concord, Calif.*

Stollak, Jack, T/4 [30th Inf. Div.] *Postal clerk, Bayside, N. Y.*

Sutherland, John M., Jr., T/5 [76th Inf. Div.] *Insurance salesman, Worcester, Mass.*

Talarico, George F., Pvt. [30th Inf. Div.] *Production supervisor,* Givaudan Corp., *Nutley, N. J.*

Tell, Bernard L., Cpl. [30th Inf. Div.] *Doctor of medicine, Pompton Plains, N. J.*

Toole, John B., T/5 [30th Inf. Div.] *Cost accountant,* General Electric Co., *Hudson Falls, N. Y.*

Torino, Albert M., T/5 [30th Inf. Div.] *Foreman,* Presidential Construction Co., *New Haven, Conn.*

Truman, Louis Watson, Col. [84th Inf. Div.] *Lt. Gen., U.S. Army, Fort Monroe, Va.*

Tucker, R. H., Col. [82nd Airborne Div.] *Maj. Gen. (retired), U.S. Army; Comdt. of Cadets, The Citadel, Charleston, S. C.*

Tullbane, John E., 1st Lt. [30th Inf. Div.] *Field director,* The American National Red Cross, *APO New York, N. Y.*

Valsangiacomo, Oreste V., Capt. [84th Inf. Div.] *Occupation unknown, Barre, Vt.*

Vinson, David B., 1st Lt. [U.S.A.F.] *Director,* Texas Academy for the Advancement of Life Sciences, *Houston, Tex.*

Vukcevic, Michael N., Pfc. [82nd Airborne Div.] *Machine repairman, Perry, Ohio*

Walson, Thomas Betts, 1st Lt. [5th Armored Div.] *Manager,* Merrill, Lynch, Pierce, Fenner & Smith, *Nashville, Tenn.*

Washburn, Israel Brent, Lt. Col. [5th Armored Div.] *Col. (retired), U.S. Army, McLean, Va.*

Weber, Stanley Roger, S/Sgt. [30th Inf. Div.] *Carpenter, New York, N. Y.*

Weinstein, Alvin, Pfc. [30th Inf. Div.] *Employee,* A.I.C. Construction Corp., *Fort Tilden, N. Y.*

Wellems, Edward N., Lt. Col. [82nd Airborne Div.] *Col., U.S. Army, Springfield, Va.*

West, Gustavus Wilcox, Col. [2nd Armored Div.] *Retired, Georgetown, Colo.*

Whitaker, R. B., 1st Lt. [5th Armored Div.] *Retailer, office equipment and supplies, Leavenworth, Kan.*

White, Isaac Davis, Maj. Gen. [2nd Armored Div.] *Gen. (retired), U.S. Army, Honolulu, Hawaii*

White, Myron A., Cpl. [82nd Airborne Div.] *Farmer, Grinnell, Iowa*

Wienecke, Robert H., Col. [82nd Airborne Div.] *Maj. Gen., U.S. Army, Washington, D. C.*

Williams, Walter E., Jr., 2nd Lt. [5th Armored Div.] *Postal employee, Brownsville, Tex.*

Williams, Warren R., Jr., Lt. Col. [82nd Airborne Div.] *Hdqrs. to staff, USSTRICOM, MacDill AFB, Fla.*

Williamson, Ellis W., Lt. Col. [30th Inf. Div.] *Maj. Gen., U.S. Army, Washington, D. C.*

Wiselogle, Candler R., 1st Lt. [83rd Inf. Div.] *Lt. Col., U.S.A.R., APO San Francisco, Calif.*

Wolski, Edwin Stephen, S/Sgt. [30th Inf. Div.] *SM/Sgt., U.S.A.F., Homestead, Fla.*

Woltz, William Edward, T/4 [30th Inf. Div.] *M/Sgt., U.S.A.R.; Retired shipping checker, Palisades Park, N. J.*

Wood, George B., Maj. [82nd Airborne Div.] *Rector,* Trinity Episcopal Church, *Fort Wayne, Ind.*

Wright, Nathaniel A., T/4 [84th Inf. Div.] *M/Sgt., U.S. Army, Georgia Military Academy, East Point, Ga.*

Zimmerman, Hugo, 1st Lt. [Ninth Air Force] *Col., U.S.A.F., U.S.A.F. Academy, Colo.*

BRITISH

Montgomery, Bernard Law, Field Marshal [21st Army Group] *Viscount Montgomery of Alamein, K.G. (retired), Hampshire*

Aherne, John, Cpl., King's Own Yorks (Light Infantry) [Stalag 3A, Luckenwalde] *Occupation unknown, Birmingham*

Back, Philip, F. O. [R.A.F.] *Managing director, plastics company, Berkhamsted, Hertfordshire*

Barber, Colin Muir, Maj. Gen. [12th Corps, 15th Scottish] *Lt. Gen. Sir Colin Muir Barber, C.B. (1945), D.S.O. (1940); Ripon, Yorkshire*

Barker, Evelyn Hugh, Lt. Gen. [8th Corps] *Gen. Sir Evelyn Hugh Barker, K.C.B. (1950), K.B.E. (1945), D.S.O. (1918), M.C. (Retired), Bromham, Bedfordshire*

Barnes, Frank, Lt. [7th Armored Div.] *Owner, petrol station and garage, London*

Belchem, Ronald F. K., Brig. [Chief, Operations, 21st Army Group] *Maj. Gen. C.B. (1946), C.B.E. (1944), D.S.O. (1943); London manager, B.S.A. Co., London*

Bennett, Harold Edmonde Isherwood, W.O., R.A.F. [Stalag 357, Fallingbostel] *Fl/Lt., R.A.F., Duxford, Cambridgeshire*

Binning, John Sydney, Capt. [6th Airborne Div.] *Doctor of medicine, Senior medical officer, British Railways, Eastern Region, London*

Bols, Hon. Eric Louis, Maj. Gen. [6th Airborne Div.] *Gen. Bols, C.B. (1945), D.S.O. (1944), and bar (1945); Executive, British engineering firm, Brighton, Sussex*

Bowden, William Kenneth Hope, Fl/Sgt., R.A.F. [Stalag 357, Fallingbostel] *Advertising executive, Upton Grey, nr. Basingstoke, Hampshire*

Broom, Ivor Gordon, Wing Comdr. [R.A.F.] *Group Captain, R.A.F., Brüggen, Germany*

Chandler, Charles Frederick, Sapper [6th Airborne Div.] *District foreman, gas board, Hays End, Middlesex*

Chapman, Edward, Fl/Lt., R.A.F. [Stalag 3A, Luckenwalde] *Employee, wine shippers, London*

Chown, Clement Murray, Sgt. Pilot, R.A.F. [Stalag 357, Fallingbostel] *Commercial airline pilot, Port-of-Spain, Trinidad*

Cole, Eric V., Sgt. Maj. [7th Armored Div.] *Engineer, Newcastle-on-Tyne*

Collins, John Brenton, Padre, Capt., 67 Medium Regt. Royal Artillery [Stalag 3A, Luckenwalde] *Vicar, Church of England, Edenbridge, Kent*

Counsell, John, Col. [SHAEF] *Director, Windsor Theatre, Windsor*

Cox, W. Frederick, Guardsman, Irish Guards [Stalag 3A, Luckenwalde] *Poultryman, North Reading, Berkshire*

Craig, Gordon D., Sqdn. Leader, R.A.F. [Stalag 3A, Luckenwalde] *Solicitor, Corbridge, Northumberland*

Davey, Robert, Lt. [7th Armored Div.] *Innkeeper, Torquay, Devonshire*

Davies, Graham, Pvt. [6th Airborne Div.] *Steelworker, Port Talbot, Glamorganshire, South Wales*

Davison, Wilfred, Capt. [6th Airborne Div.] *Timber company director, Peterfield, Hampshire*

531

Day, Harry Melville Arbuthnot, Group Capt., R.A.F. [Stalag 357, Fallingbostel, later Sachsenhausen] *Retired, London*

Deans, James Alexander Graham, W.O., R.A.F. [Stalag 357, Fallingbostel] *Administrative officer, London School of Economics and Political Science, Ashtead, Surrey*

Dempsey, Sir Miles Christopher, Gen. [Second Army] *Gen. Sir Miles Dempsey, G.B.E. (1956), K.C.B. (1944), D.S.O. (1940), M.C. (1918); Company chairman, Yattendon, Berkshire*

Finnie, John, C.Q.M.S. [5th Inf. Div.] *Postal official, London*

Foster, Joseph, Fl/Sgt. [R.A.F.] *Building foreman, Stoke-on-Trent, Staffordshire*

Friston, Leslie West, Pvt. [30th Corps] *Lorry driver, Chesham, Buckinghamshire*

Galbraith, Alexander Reynell, Fl/Lt. [R.A.F.] *Personnel manager, Crawley, Sussex*

Gallienne, William Albert George, Sqdn. Leader [R.A.F.] *Publican, Chigwell, Essex*

Guingand, Sir Francis W. de, Maj. Gen. [21st Army Group] *Maj. Gen. Sir Francis de Guingand, K.B.E. (1944), C.B. (1943), D.S.O. (1942); Company chairman, Johannesburg, South Africa*

Haley, A., Pvt. [5th Inf. Div.] *Packer, shoe warehouse, Ryton-on-Tyne, Durham*

Heape, John Stewart Hardman, W.O., R.A.F. [Stalag 357, Fallingbostel] *Sales manager, petrol pump manufacturer, Cholsey, Buckinghamshire*

Hennell, Charles, Sgt. Maj. [7th Armored Div.] *Police inspector, Cheshire County Police, Wilmslow, Cheshire*

Hensman, Michael Graham, Lt. [6th Airborne Div.] *Sales manager, I.C.I., Bowdon, Cheshire*

Horrocks, Sir Brian, Lt. Gen. [Comdr., 30th Brit. Corps], *Gen. Sir Brian Horrocks, K.C.B., K.B.E., D.S.O. (retired), London*

Hughes, Hugh L. Glyn, Brig. [Second Army] *Brig. Hughes, C.B.E. (1945), D.S.O. (1916), M.C., M.R.C.S.; Doctor of medicine, Director, South-east London General Practitioner Center, London*

Hughes, Thomas Rhys, Pvt. [6th Airborne Div.] *Journalist, Haywards Heath, Sussex*

Jinks, William James, Fl/Lt. [R.A.F.] *Company executive, weighing machine manufacturers, Sutton Coldfield, Warwickshire*

Jones, Gilbert Peter, Sgt. [R.A.F.] *Prison officer, Newport, Isle of Wight*

Kee, Robert, Fl/Lt., R.A.F. [Stalag 3A, Luckenwalde] *Author, television producer, London*

Kimber, Peter C., Fl/Sgt., R.A.F. [Stalag 3A, Luckenwalde] *Chief clerk, Bushey, Hertfordshire*

Lyne, Louis Owen, Maj. Gen. [7th Armored Div.] *Gen. Lyne, C.B. (1945), D.S.O. (1943); Company chairman, Kersey, Suffolk*

Mack, Kenneth Charles, W.O. [R.A.F.] *Clerk, British Railways, Norfolk*

Mainwaring, John Cecil, Pvt. [5th Inf. Div.] *Hospital porter, Hillsboro, Sheffield*

Mann, Alfred Ernest, Cpl., Royal West Kent Regt. [Stalag 20A, Thorn] *Clerk, General Post Office, nr. Dartford, Kent*

McCowen, J. L., Lt. Col. [Econ. Div., Control Commission] *Southern sales manager, Guinness, Richmansworth, Hertfordshire*

McWhinnie, Hugh, Sgt. [6th Airborne Div.] *Chargehand, paper mill, Canterbury, Kent*

Mitford, Edward Cecil, Brig. [8th Corps] *Brig. Mitford (retired), Hdqrs. Eastern Command, London*

Mogg, Ronald, W.O., R.A.F. [Stalag 357, Fallingbostel] *Press officer, Shell Mex & B.P. Ltd., London*

Moore, Walter, Pvt. [6th Airborne Div.] *Textile fitter, Keighley, Yorkshire*

Morgan, Sir Frederick E., Lt. Gen. [SHAEF] *Gen. Sir Frederick Morgan, retired, Northwood, Middlesex*

Mower, Edwin Arthur, Cpl., Royal Berkshire Regt. (now part of Wessex Brigade) [Stalag 357, Fallingbostel] *Clerk, Colchester, Essex*

Murray, Robert, Pvt. [7th Armored Div.] *Chargehand, wholesale chemist, Nelson, Lancashire*

Murtagh, Patrick Francis, Trooper, 3rd Royal Tank Regt. [Stalag 3A, Luckenwalde] *Watch and clock repairer, nr. Salisbury, Wiltshire*

Newman, John, Trooper, Royal Tank Corps [Stalag 344, Lamsdorff] *Cab hirer, Edinburgh*

Park, Thomas M., Capt., Royal Army Medical Corps [Stalag 357, Fallingbostel] *Doctor of medicine, Carnwath, Lanark*

Perrin, Roy Doublas, F.O. [R.A.F.] *Insurance mechanisation unit controller, South Croydon, Surrey*

Rabone, Joseph Patrick, Lt. [6th Airborne Div.] *Driver, M.C.D., Kingstanding, Birmingham*

Roberts, Kenneth, Pvt. [5th Inf. Div.] *Assistant inspector, General Post Office, London*

Rodley, Ernest Edward, Wing Comdr. [R.A.F.] *Commercial pilot, BOAC, London*

Rogers, Philip George, Maj. [6th Airborne Div.] *Foreign office, Orpington, Kent*

Rosdol, Sandy, Capt. [12th Corps, 15th Scottish Div.] *Foreign Office, South Ascot, Berkshire*

Ross, Donald G., Fl/Lt. [R.A.F.] *Tobacco manufacturer, Yverdon, Switzerland*

Rycroft, Robert Arthur, Cpl. [6th Airborne Div.] *Advertising controller, Thos. Cook & Son, Ltd., Meadvale, Redhill*

Rymer, James, Pvt. [7th Armored Div.] *Motor mechanic, Pickering, Yorkshire*

Shearer, John L., Capt. [6th Airborne Div.] *Manager, National Assistance Board, Hamilton, Lanark*

Spurling, John Michael Kane, Brig. [7th Armored Div.] *Maj. Gen. Spurling, C.B. (1957), C.B.E. (1953), D.S.O. (1944); Lecturer, Military History and Tactics, London and Southampton Universities, Fifehead Neville, Dorsetshire*

Strong, Kenneth William Dobson, Maj. Gen. [SHAEF] *Maj. Gen. Sir Kenneth Strong, C.B. (1945), O.B.E. (1942); Director-General of Intelligence, Ministry of Defense, London*

Suster, Ilya, Sgt. [7th Armored Div.] *Director, import company, London*

Sweeney, Michael Francis, Sgt. Maj., Irish Guards [Stalag 3A, Luckenwalde] *Salesman, nr. Oundle, Northamptonshire*

Thwaite, Alan, Sapper [7th Armored Div.] *Cinema projectionist, Morecambe, Lancashire*

Towell, Albert Cyril, Lance/Cpl. [7th Armored Div.] *Packer, electronics factory, Highcliffe-on-Sea, Hampshire*

Urquhart, John, Lance/Cpl. [6th Airborne Div.] *Industrial machine operator, Baillieston, Glasgow*

Ward, Leonard M., Lance/Bombardier, Driver [12th Corps] *Hospital administrative assistant, Hornsey*

Ward, Tom, P.O. [R.A.F.] *Structural engineer, Lancaster*

Whiteley, John Francis Martin, Maj. Gen. [SHAEF] *Gen. Sir John Whiteley, G.B.E. (1956), K.C.B. (1950), M.C. retired, nr. Salisbury, Wiltshire*

Williams, Edgar T., Brig. [Chief, Intelligence, 21st Army Group] *C.B. (1946), C.B.E. (1944), D.S.O. (1943); Fellow of Balliol, Oxford, Warden of Rhodes House, Oxford*

Wilson, Geoffrey Kenneth, Fl/Sgt., R.A.F. [Stalag 357, Fallingbostel] *Psychology Lecturer, Teachers' Training College, Leigh-on-Sea, Essex*

RUSSIAN

Koniev, Ivan Stepanovich, Marshal of the Soviet Union [Comdr., 1st Ukrainian Front] *Marshal, Inspector Gen., Soviet Armed Forces*

Rokossovskii, Konstantin K., Marshal of the Soviet Union [Comdr., 2nd Belorussian Front] *Marshal, Inspector Gen., Soviet Armed Forces; Member, Supreme Soviet*

Anikhovskii, Josef Josefevich, Capt. [Operations Staff, 6th Guards Rifle Div.]
Boltin, E. A., Maj. Gen. [Editor-in-Chief, Official Soviet War History] *Major General*
Chuikov, Vasili Ivanovich, Col. Gen. [Comdr., 8th Guards Army] *Marshal of the Soviet Union; Member, Supreme Soviet; Member, Supreme Military Council; Supreme Comdr., Soviet Land Forces*
Dolmatovskii, Eugene, Lt. Col. [War correspondent, Pravda] *Writer, poet and lyricist*
Golbov, Sergei Ivanovich, Capt. [War correspondent, 47th Army] †
Ignatov, Aleksei Andrianovich, Maj. [61st Army]
Ivanov, Georgi Vasilievich, Maj. Gen. [Comdr., 6th Guards Rifle Div.] *Major General (retired)*
Kharina, Irina Mikhailova, Guerilla agent [POW, Auschwitz] *Housewife*
Kilchevskii, Georgi Vladimirovich, 1st Lt. [Engineer, 6th Guards Rifle Div.] *Engineer*
Kjung, Nikolai, Pvt. [POW, Buchenwald]
Kurkov, Mikhail Ivanovich, Radio operator [Anti-tank Regt.]
Lazaris, Aronovich, Maj. [6th Guards Rifle Div.] *Writer*
Levchenko, Irena Nikolayevna, 1st Lt. [8th Mechanized Corps] *Lt. Col. of Armored Forces (retired), Housewife*
Litvinko, Andrei Fedosovich, Maj. [4th Guards Tank Army]
Malinovskii, Mikhail, Lt. [Regimental Political Commissar, 16th Air Force] †
Mikayoff, Igor, Lt. [Regimental Intelligence Officer, 5th Shock Army]
Novikov, Nikolai Georgievich, Sgt. [Reconnaissance, 6th Guards Rifle Div.]
Olshanskii, Alexander, Pvt. [58th Rifle Div.] *Major*
Ostrovskii, Vysoka, Col. [War correspondent, Red Star] *Author and journalist*
Parotikin, I. V., Col. [Soviet Dept. of Defense]
Pavlenkov, N. G., Maj. Gen. [Soviet Dept. of Defense] *Historian*
Platonov, S. P., Lt. Gen. [Soviet Dept. of Defense] *Historian and Chief of Archives*
Polevoi, Boris, Col. [War correspondent, Pravda, and Regimental Political Commissar] *Novelist, magazine editor*
Rogovtsev, Vasilii Petrovish, Sgt. [Rifle Co., 1st Belorussian Front]
Rozanov, Vladimir Pavlovich, 1st Lt. [Reconnaissance, 3rd Shock Army, 4th Artillery Corps]
Samchuk, John Amkeevich, Col. [Chief of Staff, 32nd Corps]
Samsonov, Konstantin Yakovlevich, Lt. [Battalion Comdr., 171st Rifle Div.] *Colonel*
Samusev, Ivan Semonovich, Sgt. [Artillery, 3rd Shock Army]
Slobyudenyuk, Grigorii Afanasyevich, Sgt. Maj., Hero of the Soviet Union [1st Ukrainian Front]
Sokolovskii, V. D., Gen. [Chief, Operations Staff, 1st Ukrainian Front to 14 April, 1945; Deputy Comdr., 1st Belorussian Front from 15 April, 1945] *Marshal of the Soviet Union; Inspector Gen., Soviet Armed Forces*
Svishchev, Nikolai Alexandrovich, Sgt. [Gun crew comdr., 1st Belorussian Front]
Telpuchovskii, Boris S., Maj. Gen. [Official historian, Zhukov's Hdqrs.]
Tilevich, Mark, Sgt. [POW, Sachsenhausen]
Troyanoskii, Pavel, Lt. Col. [War correspondent, Red Star] *Author and journalist*
Yushchuk, Ivan Ivanovich, Maj. Gen. [Comdr., 11th Tank Corps] *General of Tank Troops (retired)*

† Interviewed outside the U.S.S.R.

GERMAN

Heinrici, Gotthard, Col. Gen. [Army Group Vistula] *Colonel General (retired)*

Ache, Kurt, Capt. [Berlin Defense Unit—Zoo Flak Tower] *Private means*
Annuschek, Karl Heinz, Capt. [1st Flak Div.] *Company director*
Arnold, Hans-Werner, 1st Lt. [Luftwaffe, 9th Parachute Div.] *Civil servant*
Bensch, Willy, M/Sgt. [SS Div. Nordland] *Factory worker*
Bila, Heinrich von, Capt. [Army Group Vistula] *Seed company sales manager*
Bombach, Walter, M/Sgt. [Berlin Defense Unit] *Caretaker*
Bonath, Herbert, Pvt. [Hitler Youth] *Clerical officer, West German Army*
Böttcher, Friedrich, Lt. Col. [18th Panzer Grenadier Div.] Ministry of Defense
Bruschke, Waldemar, Co. Comdr. [Volkssturm] *Salesman*
Burghart, Roman, Cpl. [SS Div. Nordland] *Office worker*
Busse, Theodor, Gen. [Ninth Army] *Civil defense director*
Clauss, Paul, Cpl. [SS Div. Nordland] *Businessman*
Cords, Helmuth, Capt., Wehrmacht [Lehrterstrasse Prison] *Research director, Calif.*
Dethleffsen, Erich, Gen. [OKH] *Economics consultant*
Draeger, Willi, District Lt. [Berlin Fire Dept.] *Retired*
Drost, Günter, Lt. [Berlin Defense Unit] *Pharmacist*
Ducke, Josef, Lt. [18th Panzer Grenadier Div.] *Bank clerk*
Dufving, Theodor von, Col. [56th Panzer Corps] West German Defense Dept.
Eismann, Hans Georg, Col. [Army Group Vistula] *Retired*
Feldheim, Willy [Hitler Youth] *Importer*
Fritz, Albert, Lt. [Panzer Div. Müncheberg] *Accountant*
Gareis, Martin, Gen. [3rd Panzer Army] *Retired*
Gold, Walter, Sgt. [Berlin Defense Unit] *Retired*
Gröll, Artur, Cpl. [Volkssturm] *Shoemaker (retired)*
Gross, Ernst, Sgt. [SS Div. Nordland] *Electrician*
Günsche, Otto, SS Col. [Führer's Adjutant] *Company director*
Haaf, Oskar, Co. Comdr. [Volkssturm] *Radio program director*
Haas, Fritz, Cpl. [SS Div. Nordland] *Wine salesman*
Hagedorn, Walter, Capt. [Luftwaffe—Zoo Flak Tower] *Doctor of medicine*
Hagemann, Wolf, Lt. Gen. [Ninth Army] *Retired*
Halt, Karl Ritter von, Battalion Comdr. [Volkssturm] *
Hartmann, Rudolf, Pvt. [Volkssturm] *Company manager*
Heckscher, Edmund, Sgt. [Volkssturm] *
Hein, Heinrich, SS Col. [Asst. to Bormann] *Retired*
Hellriegel, Hermann, Pvt. [Volkssturm] *Traveling salesman*
Henseler, Hans, SS 2nd Lt. [SS Div. Nordland] *Independent wholesaler*
Hirsch, Alfred, Lt. [9th Parachute Div.] *Railway station luncheonette manager*
Hock, Manfred, Sgt. [Berlin Defense Unit] *Retired*
Höhne, Heinz, Fire Capt. [Berlin Fire Dept.] *Official, Fire dept.*
Illum, Gunnar, SS 2nd Lt. [SS Div. Nordland] *Taxi owner*
Jansen, Hans, Lt. [9th Parachute Div.] *Shoe store manager*
Jung, Albert, Pvt. [SS Div. Nordland] *Clerk*
Kempka, Erich, SS Col. [Führer's chauffeur] *Mechanic*
Kirchner, Heinz, Lt. [1st Flak Div.] *Church councillor*
Koder, Hans, Pvt. [SS Div. Nordland] *Office worker*
Kratschmar, Heinz, Cadet [German Navy] *Engineer*
Krüger, Heinz, Comdr. [Berlin Defense Unit] *Retired*
Krüger, Ulrich, Hitler Youth [Berlin Defense Unit] *Teacher*
Krukenberg, Gustav, SS Maj. Gen. [SS Div. Charlemagne and SS Div. Nordland]
   Retired

Kühn, Alfred, Pvt. [Berlin Defense Unit] *Retired*
Kunz, Helmut, SS Col. [SS Medical Office, Berlin] *Dentist*
Lambracht, Erich, Lt. [Berlin Defense Unit] *Retired clerk*
Lampe, Albrecht, 1st Lt. [Berlin Commandant HQ] *Doctor of philosophy*, Director of the Berlin Municipal Archives
Lang, Hellmuth, Capt. [Army Group Vistula] *Store owner*
Lohmann, Hanns-Heinrich, SS Lt. Col. [SS Div. Nederland] *Insurance company executive*
Manteuffel, Hasso von, Gen. [3rd Panzer Army] *Retired*
Meissner, Max, Capt. [Ninth Army] *Salesman*
Müller-Hillebrand, Burkhart, Maj. Gen. [3rd Panzer Army] *Lt. Gen. NATO, Paris*
Niedieck, Gerda Castrup [Women's Army—Zoo Flak Tower] *Radio programming coordinator*
Nolte, Wilhelm, Fire Col. [Berlin Fire Dept.] *Industry official*
Oppeln-Bronikowski, Hermann von, Maj. Gen. [20th Panzer Div.] *General (retired); estate manager*
Patzer, Heinz, Sgt. [Berlin Defense Unit] *Photo engraver*
Pemsel, Max, Lt. Gen. [6th Mountain Div.] *General (retired)*
Pfoser, Alfons, 1st Lt. [SS, Battle Group Todte] °
Pienkny, Günther [Hitler Youth] *Brewery employee*
Pluskat, Werner, Maj. [Artillery Comdr., Magdeburg] *Engineer*
Refior, Hans, Col. [Berlin Commandant HQ] *Director, industrial combine*
Reichhelm, Günther, Col. [Twelfth Army] *Company director*
Rein, Hans, Lt. [9th Parachute Div.] *Judge*, Administrative Court
Reitsch, Hanna, Fl/Capt. [Luftwaffe] *Aviation consultant*
Reuss, Franz, Maj. Gen. [Luftwaffe] *Business executive*
Reymann, Hellmuth, Maj. Gen. [Berlin Commandant] *Retired*
Römling, Horst, Hitler Youth [Berlin Defense Unit] *Secondhand dealer*
Rose, Heinz, Maj. [Volkssturm] *Retired*
Schack, Friedrich August, Gen. [32nd Army Corps] *Retired*
Scherka, Erich, Cpl. [1st Flak Div.] *House painter*
Schirmer, Bruno, Police Lt. [Berlin Police Dept.] *Police official*
Scholles, Hans-Peter, Sgt. [SS Div. Nordland] *Wine merchant*
Schuhmacher, Manuel, Lt. [Ninth Army] *Art photographer*
Schulz, Aribert [Hitler Youth] *Typesetter*
Schumann, Werner, Capt. [Zoo Flak Tower] *Doctor of medicine*
Sixt, Friedrich, Lt. Gen. [101st Corps] *Retired*
Speidel, Hans, Maj. Gen. [Potsdam Military Prison] Lt. Gen., NATO
Steiner, Felix Martin, SS Gen. [Group Steiner] *Retired*
Strauss, Erwin, District Lt. [Berlin Fire Dept.] *Retired*
Strenka, Gustav, Police Supt. [Berlin Police Dept.] *Retired*
Thamm, Willi, Pvt. [Berlin Defense Unit] *Master house painter*
Timm, Walter, SS Lt. [SS Div. Nordland] *Market researcher*
Ulisch, Walter, Lt. [Berlin Defense Unit] *Executive, health insurance office*
Usberg, Otto, Sgt. [26th Panzers, 1st Army Corps] *Businessman*
Verleih, Max, Regt. Supply Officer [Berlin Defense Unit] *Minister (retired)*
Volk, Helmut, Sgt. [OKH] *Employee*, Berlin Senate
Voss, Peter, 1st Lt. [3rd Army Corps] *Bank clerk*
Wedell, Günter, 1st Lt. [Berlin Defense Unit] *Doctor of medicine*
Wenck, Walther, Gen. [Twelfth Army] *Company director*
Werner, Franz, Paymaster [Berlin Defense Unit] *Retired clerk*
Wetzki, Hans Joachim [Hitler Youth] *Senatorial assistant*
Winge, Hans-Joachim, Pvt. [SS Div. Nordland] *Purchasing director*
Wöhlermann, Hans Oscar, Col. [56th Panzer Corps] *Retired*

Wrede, Fritz, Cpl. [Wehrmacht] *Retired*
Wurach, Kurt, Maj. [Ninth Army] *Veterinarian*
Zabeltitz, Leonhardt von, Capt. [1st Flak Div.] *Estate owner*

BERLINERS

Antz, Ilse [Wilmersdorf] *Director, children's home*
Apitzsch, Bertha [Schöneberg] *Nurse (retired)*
Batty, Marie [Pankow] *Housewife, London*
Baumgart, Johanna [Zehlendorf] *Housewife*
Bayer, Anne-Lise [Wilmersdorf] *Housewife*
Bethge, Eberhard [Lehrterstrasse Prison] *Minister*
Blank, Georg [Köpenick] *Retired*
Bochnik, Juliane [Reinickendorf] *Actress*
Boese, Helena [Wilmersdorf] *Teacher*
Bohg, Kurt [Lichtenberg] *Assistant director, trade school*
Bollensen, Lydia [Wilmersdorf] *Dress designer*
Bombach, Marianne Lorenz [Wilmersdorf] *Housewife*
Borgmann, Ruby [Charlottenburg] *Housewife*
Buchwald, Gerd [Reinickendorf] *Director,* Board of Education
Burmester, Charlotte [Schöneberg] *Telephone supervisor*
Sister Caspario [Wilmersdorf] Mission Sisters of the Holy Sacred Heart
Cords, Jutta Sorge [Lehrterstrasse Prison] *Housewife, Calif.*
Curth, Franz [Lichtenberg] *Window washer*
Dehn, Madeline von [Mitte] *Professor of zoology*
Diekermann, Ruth Piepho [Wilmersdorf] *Actress*
Dietrich, Willi [Mitte] *Baker*
Dohndorf, Emmy [Tempelhof] *Retired*
Durand-Wever, Anne-Marie [Schöneberg] *Doctor of medicine*
Eberhard, Elisabeth [Zehlendorf] *Housewife*
Echtmann, Fritz [Charlottenburg] *Dentist*
Fenzel, Klaus [Tempelhof] *Archaeology student*
Florie, Manfred [Reinickendorf] *Typesetter*
Friedrichs, Paul [Potsdam] *Catholic priest*
Frölich, Hans [Charlottenburg] *Police commissioner*
Geisler, Erika Wendt [Friedrichshain] *Housewife, Conn.*
Goertz, Eugen [Charlottenburg] *Director, insurance company*
Golz, Kurt [Tempelhof] *Baker*
Haller, Annemarie Hückel [Tiergarten] *Graphologist*
Happich, Bernhard [Zehlendorf] *Priest*
Harndt, Ewald [Fangschleuse] *Dentist*
Heck, Lutz [Tiergarten] *Zoologist*
Heim, Wilhelm [Tiergarten] *Doctor of medicine*
Heinrich, Erich [Treptow] *Hospital administrator (retired)*
Heinroth, Katherina [Tiergarten] *Zoologist*
Hellberg, Irmgard [Steglitz] *Housewife*
Henneberg, Amalia [Charlottenburg] *Doctor of medicine*
Henneberg, Georg [Charlottenburg] *Vice president,* West German Health Office
Hennig, Margarethe [Charlottenburg] *Housewife*
Hensel, Alex [Friedrichshain] *Municipal employee*
Hentschel, Frieda [Steglitz] *Housewife*
Heusermann, Käthe Reiss [Charlottenburg] *Dental technician*
Heydekampf, Hildegard von [Wilmersdorf] *Housewife*

537

Hofmann, Margarete [Spandau] *Housewife*
Hohenau, Ilona [Tempelhof] *Musician*
Höhn, Karl [Neukölln] *Baker*
Holz, Hans [Kreuzberg] *Retired*
Horltiz, Albert [Charlottenburg] *Mayor (retired)*
Hunsdörfer, B. [Wedding] *Doctor of medicine*
Jacobi, Gerhard [Charlottenburg] *Bishop of Oldenburg*
Jakubek, Erwin [Mitte] *Restaurant owner*
Janssen, Dora Grabo [Neukölln] *Housewife*
Jentgen, Lotte [Zehlendorf] *Chemist*
Jodl, Luise [Zehlendorf] *Housewife*
Johst, Elisabeth Schwarz [Tiergarten] *Zoologist*
Kay, Rose von Winkel [Spandau] *Housewife, Yorkshire, England*
Kelm, Alexander [Wilmersdorf] *Engineer (retired)*
Ketzler, Gertrud [Charlottenburg] *Editorial secretary*
Klotz, Jurgen-Erich [Tempelhof] *Book dealer*
Klunge, Helga Ruske [Kreuzberg] *Housewife*
Koch, Jolenta [Tempelhof] *Housewife*
Köckler, Maria [Charlottenburg] *Political society chairman*
Kolb, Ingeborg [Spandau] *Researcher*
König, Ilse [Schöneberg] *Medical laboratory technician*
Korab, Alexander [Babelsberg] *Newspaper correspondent*
Kosney, Herbert [Lehrterstrasse Prison] *Mechanic*
Kosney, Kurt [Lehrterstrasse Prison] *Mechanic*
Köster, Ursula [Zehlendorf] *Housewife*
Kraemer, Franz [Wilmersdorf] *Jeweler*
Kraft, Fritz [Wedding] *Retired city councillor*
Krüger, Albert [Steglitz] *Police officer*
Küster, Klaus [Reinickendorf] *Musician*
Lamprecht, Günther [Wilmersdorf] *Doctor of medicine*
Langen, Paula [Mitte] *Retired*
Leckscheidt, Arthur [Kreuzberg] *Minister*
Lévy, Hanni Weissenberg [Schöneberg] *Housewife*
Lietzmann, Sabina [Wilmersdorf] *Journalist*
Lilge, Irmgard Rosin [Wedding] *Stenographer*
Lipschitz, Eleanore Krüger [Lichtenberg] *Doctor of political economy*
Mahlke, Walter [Wilmersdorf] *Retired printer*
Maigatter, Elfriede Eisenbach [Kreuzberg] *Housewife*
Majewski, Elena Wysocki [Tiergarten] *Housewife*
Matzker, Alfons [Charlottenburg] *Catholic priest*
Menzel, Gerhard [Charlottenburg] *Photographer*
Meyer, Herbert [Neukölln] *Telephone supervisor*
Michalke, Josef [Charlottenburg] *Catholic priest*
Miede, Hans [Charlottenburg] *Chemist*
Milbrand, Elisabeth [Schöneberg] *Telephone supervisor*
Müller, Werner [Reinickendorf] *Policeman*
Naumann, Werner [Mitte] *Company director*
Nestriepke, Siegfried [Wilmersdorf] *Retired*
Neumann, Edith [Kreuzberg] *Housewife*
Neumann, Kurt [Wedding] *Police commissioner*
Panzer, Hildegard [Wilmersdorf] *Radio network employee*
Penns, Wilhelm [Köpenick] *Section manager*
Perseke, Erich [Neukölln] *Retired*
Pfeuti, Emma Müller [Zehlendorf] *Housewife*

Piotrowski, Walter [Wedding] *Butcher*
Poganowska, Richard [Zehlendorf] *Dairy farm worker*
Probst, Margareta [Kreuzberg] *Homeopathic therapist*
Promeist, Margarete [Tiergarten] *Housewife*
Radusch, Hildegard [Prieros] *Civil servant (retired)*
Rau, Dorothea [Tiergarten] *Housewife*
Ravené, Liese-Lotte [Tempelhof] *Municipal employee*
Reineke, Ella [Tiergarten] *Administrative assistant*
Reisner, Käthe [Zehlendorf] *Housewife*
Reschke, Rudolf [Zehlendorf] *Advertising copywriter*
Richter, Charlotte [Wilmersdorf] *Retired*
Richter, Helene [Neukölln] *Retired*
Riedel, Gustav [Tiergarten] *Zoologist (retired)*
Rocholl, Edit [Zehlendorf] *Foreign Office employee*
Römling, Horst [Prenzlauer Berg] *Secondhand dealer*
Rosensaft, Josef [Belsen Concentration Camp] *Realtor, New York*
Rosenthal, Hans [Lichtenberg] *Radio and television entertainer*
Rosetz, Günther [Neukölln] *Retired*
Rühmann, Heinz [Zehlendorf] *Actor*
Ryneck, Erich [Pankow] *Retired*
Saenger, Erna [Zehlendorf] *Housewife*
Saenger, Ingeborg [Zehlendorf] *Social worker*
Sauerbruch, Margot [Mitte] *Doctor of medicine*
Schadrack, Else [Pankow] *Administration employee*
Schewe, Ida [Kreuzberg] *Retired*
Schirach, Henriette Hoffmann von [Munich] *Housewife*
Schmidt, Paul [Schöneberg] *Minister*
Schneidenbach, Hilde [Schöneberg] *Secretary*
Schoele, Gertrud Radeke [Neukölln] *Administration employee*
Schroeder, Helena [Schöneberg] *Telephone supervisor*
Schröter, Georg [Tempelhof] *Writer*
Schultze, Erna [Friedrichshain] *Secretary*
Schultze, Robert [Köpenick] *Economist*
Schulz, Wilhelm [Steglitz] *Deputy police commissioner*
Schwarz, Heinrich [Tiergarten] *Retired*
Schwarz, Margarete [Charlottenburg] *Certified accountant*
Schwerdtfeger, Albert [Lehrterstrasse Prison] *Retired*
Schwinski, Werner [Pankow] *Textile representative*
Sobek, Johannes "Hanne" [Mitte] *Sports store owner*
Stalla, Ursula Möhrke [Tiergarten] *Clerical worker*
Stammer, Gertrud [Charlottenburg] *Office worker (retired)*
Sternfeld, Leo [Tempelhof] *Cinema owner*
Thiemann, Camilla [Schöneberg] *Housewife, London*
Tietze, Albrecht [Wedding] *Doctor of medicine*
Ulrich, Gertrud [Steglitz] *Housewife*
Ungnad, Vera Wysocki [Tiergarten] *Technical designer*
Van Hoeven, Pia [Schöneberg] *Actress*
Vogel, Erich [Zehlendorf] *Bottling plant foreman*
Vollert, Else [Wilmersdorf] *Retired*
Wagner, Herta Alwes [Schöneberg] *Housewife*
Walbrecht, Gerda Carl [Tiergarten] *Housewife*
Wassermann, Elfriede Haubenreisser [Kreuzberg] *Housewife*
Weber, Brigitte [Charlottenburg] *Housewife*
Wehmeyer, Dorothea [Charlottenburg] *Stenographer*

Weigand-Schott, Inge [Charlottenburg] *Actress*
Weinsziehr, Stefanie [Wilmersdorf] *Manager, yard goods company*
Wellmann, Ruth [Charlottenburg] *Housewife*
Weltlinger, Margarete [Pankow] *Housewife*
Weltlinger, Siegmund [Pankow] *Stockbroker*
Wendt, Walter [Tiergarten] *Retired*
Winckler, Charlotte [Wilmersdorf] *Housewife*
Wohlgemuth, Albert [Wedding] *Police commissioner*
Youngday, Brigid Jungmittag [Prenzlauer Berg] *Housewife, London*
Zacharias, Fritz [Charlottenburg] *Police commissioner*
Zarzycki, Bruno [Neuenhagen-Hoppegarten] *Businessman*

FRENCH

Bourdeau, André [POW, Marienfelde camp] *Railway worker, Lisieux*
Boutin, Jean [Forced laborer, Spandau] *Machinist, Paris*
Delaunay, Jacques [Forced laborer, Tempelhof] *Architect, Evreaux*
Demoulin, Clovis [POW, Klinker camp] *Teacher, Boulogne-sur-Mer*
De Puniet de Parry, Sophie [Forced laborer, Treptow] *Writer, French West Indies*
Douin, Jean [Forced laborer, Pankow] *Engineer, Paris*
Gasquet, Marc [Forced laborer, Marienfelde camp] *Draftsman, Paris*
Gouge, Robert-Albert [Forced laborer, Pankow] *Salesman, Paris*
Hambert, Philippe [Forced laborer, Zehlendorf] *Architect, Paris*
Legathière, Raymond [POW, Düppel camp] *Perfume shop manager, Paris*
Savary, Jacques [Forced laborer, Spandau] *Engineer, Vincennes*

DANISH
Jeppesen, Axel B. [Embassy Chaplain, Zehlendorf] *Minister, Viborg*

DUTCH

Stoffels, E. Jan [Dutch correspondent, Mitte] *Journalist, Amsterdam*

SWEDISH

Myrgren, Erik [Swedish church official, Wilmersdorf] *Minister, Stockholm*
Sandeberg, Edward [Swedish correspondent, Zehlendorf] *Journalist, Stockholm*
Westlèn, Erik [Swedish church official, Wilmersdorf] *Retired, Stockholm*
Wiberg, Carl Johann [Allied agent, Wilmersdorf] *Manufacturer*

BIBLIOGRAPHY

❖

Adlon, Hedda, *Hotel Adlon*. New York: Horizon Press, 1960.
Anderson, Hartvig, *The Dark City*. London: The Cresset Press, Ltd., 1954.
Andreas-Friedrich, Ruth, *Berlin Underground*. New York: Henry Holt, 1947
Baldwin, Hanson W., *Great Mistakes of the War*. New York: Harper & Bros., 1949.
Belsen. Irgun Sheerit Hapleita Me'haezor Habriti. Israel: 1957.
Bennett, D. C. T., Air Vice-Marshal , *Pathfinder*. London: Frederick Muller, Ltd., 1958.
Bentwich, Norman, *They Found Refuge*. London: The Cresset Press, Ltd., 1956.
Berlin: Figures, Headings and Charts. Berlin: Press and Information Office, 1962.
Bernadotte, Count Folke, *The Curtain Falls*. New York: Alfred A. Knopf, 1945.
Bird, Will R., *No Retreating Footsteps*. Nova Scotia: Kentville Publishing Co.
Bishop, Edward, *The Wooden Horse*. London: Max Parrish & Co., Ltd., 1959.
Blake, George, *Mountain and Flood—the History of the 52nd (Lowland) Division, 1939-46*. Glasgow: Jackson, Son & Co., 1950.
Blond, Georges, *The Death of Hitler's Germany*. New York: Macmillan, 1954.
Boldt, Gerhard, *Die letzen Tage der Reichskanzlei*. Hamburg: Rowohlt, 1947.
Bradley, Gen. Omar N., *A Soldier's Story*. New York: Henry Holt, 1951.
Brereton, Lt. Gen. Lewis H., *The Brereton Diaries*. New York: William Morrow, 1946.
Bryant, Sir Arthur, *Triumph in the West, The War Diaries of Field Marshal Viscount Alanbrooke*. London: Collins, 1959.
Bullock, Alan, *Hitler: A Study in Tyranny*. London: Odhams Press, Ltd., 1952.
Butcher, Capt. Harry C., *My Three Years with Eisenhower*. New York: Simon and Schuster, 1946.
By Air to Battle. Official Account of the British Airborne Divisions. London: H. M. Stationery Office, 1945.
Byford-Jones, Lt. Col. W., *Berlin Twilight*. London: Hutchinson & Co., 1947.
Cartier, Raymond, *Hitler et ses généraux*. Paris: Librairie Arthème Fayard, 1962.
Churchill, Peter, *Spirit in the Cage*. London: Hodder & Stoughton, 1954.
Churchill, Winston S., *The Second World War* (Vols. 1-6). London: Cassell & Co., Ltd., 1955.
Clark, Alan, *Barbarossa: The Russian-German Conflict, 1941-45*. New York: William Morrow, 1965.
Clay, Gen. Lucius, *Decision in Germany*. New York: Doubleday, 1950.
Cooper, John P., Jr., *The History of the 110th Field Artillery*. Baltimore: War Records Div., Maryland Historical Society, 1953.
Cooper, R. W., *The Nuremberg Trial*. London: Penguin Books, Ltd., 1947.
Counsell, John, *Counsell's Opinion*. London: Barrie & Rockliff, 1963.
Craig, Gordon A., *The Politics of the Prussian Army: 1640-1945*. New York: Oxford University Press, 1956.
Crankshaw, Edward, *Gestapo*. New York: The Viking Press, 1956.
Crawley, Aidan, M.P., *Escape from Germany*. London: Collins, 1956.
Cumberlege, G. (editor), *BBC War Report, 6th June, 1944—5th May, 1945*. Oxford: Oxford University Press, 1946.

D'Arcy-Dawson, John, *European Victory*. London: Macdonald & Co., Ltd., 1946.

David, Paul, *The Last Days of the Swiss Embassy in Berlin*. Zurich: Thomas, 1948.

Dawson, Forrest W., *Saga of the All American* (82nd Airborne Div.). Privately printed.

Deane, John R., *The Strange Alliance*. New York: The Viking Press, 1947.

Dempsey, Sir Miles, *Operations of the 2nd Army in Europe*. London: War Office, 1947.

Djilas, Milovan, *Conversations with Stalin*. London: Rupert Hart-Davis, 1962.

Doenitz, Admiral Karl, *Memoirs*. Cleveland: World Publishing Co., 1958.

Donnison, F. S. V., *History of the Second World War—Civil Affairs and Military Government, North-West Europe, 1944-46*. London: H. M. Stationery Office, 1961.

Duroselle, Jean-Baptiste, *From Wilson to Roosevelt*. Cambridge: Harvard University Press, 1963.

Ehrman, John, *History of the Second World War—Grand Strategy* (Vols. V and VI). London: H. M. Stationery Office, 1956.

Eisenhower, Gen. Dwight D., *Crusade in Europe*. New York: Doubleday, 1948.

Erickson, John, *The Soviet High Command, 1918-1941*. London: Macmillan & Co., Ltd., 1962.

Essame, Maj. Gen. H. *The 43rd Wessex Division at War* (*1944-45*). London: Wm. Clowes & Sons, Ltd., 1952.

Falls, Cyril, *The Second World War*. London: Methuen & Co., Ltd., 1948.

Farago, Ladislas, *Patton: Ordeal and Triumph*. New York: Ivan Obolensky, Inc., 1963.

Feis, Herbert, *Between War and Peace*. Princeton: Princeton University Press, 1960.

Feis, Herbert, *Churchill, Roosevelt, Stalin*. Princeton: Princeton University Press, 1957.

Fittkan, Msgr. Gerhard A., "Darkness over East Prussia" in *A Treasury of Catholic Reading*. New York: Farrar, Straus & Cudahy, 1957.

Flower, Desmond, and Reeves, James (editors), *The War, 1939-45*. London: Cassell & Co., Ltd., 1960.

Folttmann, Josef, and Muller-Wittne, Hans, *Opfergang der Generale*. Berlin: Bernard & Graefe.

Foreign Relations of the United States, the Conferences at Malta and Yalta, 1945. U.S. Government Printing Office, 1955.

Freiden & Richardson (editors), *The Fatal Decisions*. London: Michael Joseph, Ltd., 1956.

Fuller, Maj. Gen. J. F. C., *The Conduct of War, 1789-1961*. London: Eyre & Spottiswoode, 1962.

Gallagher, Matthew P., *The Soviet History of World War II*. New York: Frederick A. Praeger, Inc., 1963.

Gallagher, Richard F., *Nuremberg: The Third Reich on Trial*. New York: The Hearst Corp., 1961.

Gaulle, Charles de, *The War Memoirs of* (Vols. 1-3). New York: Simon and Schuster, 1955.

Gavin, Lt. Gen. James M., *Airborne Warfare*. Washington: Infantry Journal Press, 1947.

Gavin, Lt. Gen. James M., *War and Peace in the Space Age*. New York: Harper & Bros., 1958.

Genoud, François (editor), *Le testament politique de Hitler*. Paris: Librairie Arthème Fayard, 1959.

Germany Reports. Germany: The Press and Information Office of the Federal German Government, 1955.

Gilbert, Felix (editor), *Hitler Directs His War*. New York: Oxford University Press, 1950.
Gilbert, G. M., *Nuremberg Diary*. New York: Farrar, Straus & Cudahy, 1947.
Gill, R., and Groves, J., *Club Route in Europe*. Hanover: British Army of the Rhine, 1945.
Gisevius, Hans Bernd, *To the Bitter End*. London: Jonathan Cape, 1948.
Goerlitz, Walter, *History of the German General Staff*. New York: Frederick A. Praeger, 1953.
Guderian, Gen. Heinz, *Panzer Leader*. New York: E. P. Dutton & Co., 1952.
Guingand, Maj. Gen. Sir Francis de, *Generals at War*. London: Hodder & Stoughton, 1964.
Guingand, Maj. Gen. Sir Francis de, *Operation Victory*. London: Hodder & Stoughton, 1947.
Hagemann, Otto, *Berlin the Capital*. Berlin: Arnai, 1956.
Harriman, Averell, *Our Wartime Relations with the Soviet Union*. Statement submitted to a Joint Senate Committee, 1951.
Harriman, Averell, *Peace with Russia?* New York: Simon and Schuster, 1959.
Hausser, Paul, *Waffen SS im Einsatz*. Gottingen: Plesse, 1953.
Hechler, Ken, *The Bridge at Remagen*. New York: Ballantine Books, 1957.
History of the 4th Armoured Brigade, The. Privately published.
Hollister, Paul, and Strunsky, Robert (editors). Columbia Broadcasting System War Correspondents' Reports: Edward R. Murrow, Quentin Reynolds, William Shirer, Winston Burdett, Charles Collingwood, Joseph C. Harsch, Eric Sevareid, Bill Downs, Howard K. Smith, Larry Lesueur, Quincy Howe, Richard C. Hottelet, Maj. George Fielding Eliot, George Hicks. *From D-Day through Victory in Europe*. New York: CBS, 1945.
Horrocks, Lt. Gen. Sir Brian, *A Full Life*. London: Collins, 1960.
Howley, Brig. Gen. Frank, *Berlin Command*. New York: G. P. Putnam's Sons, 1950.
Inkeles, Alex, *Public Opinion in Soviet Russia*. Cambridge: Harvard University Press, 1950.
Irving, David, *The Destruction of Dresden*. London: William Kimber, 1963.
Ismay, Gen. Lord, *The Memoirs of*. New York: The Viking Press, 1960.
Jackson, Lt. Col. G. S., *Operations of Eighth Corps*. London: St. Clements Press, 1948.
Joslen, Lt. Col. H. F., *Orders of Battle, Second World War, 1939-45*. London: H. M. Stationery Office, 1960.
Kesselring, Field Marshal, *Memoirs*. London: William Kimber, 1953.
Kindler, Helmut, *Berlin*. Germany: Kindler, 1958.
Kronika, Jacob, *Der Untergang Berlins*. Flensburg: Christian Wolf, 1946.
Leahy, William D., *I Was There*. London: Gollancz, 1950.
Lederry, Col. E., *Germany's Defeat in the East—1941-45*. London: War Office, 1955.
Leonhard, Wolfgang, *Child of the Revolution*. London: Collins, 1957.
Liddell Hart, B. H.,*The German Generals Talk*. New York: William Morrow, 1948.
Liddell Hart, B. H. (editor), *The Red Army*. New York: Harcourt, Brace, 1948.
Liddell Hart, B. H.,*The Tanks*. London: Cassell & Co., Ltd., 1959.
Life (editors of), *Life's Picture History of World War II*. New York: Time, Inc., 1950.
Lippmann, Walter, *U.S. War Aims*. Boston: Little, Brown, 1944.
McMillan, Richard, *Miracle Before Berlin*. London: Jarrolds Publishers, Ltd., 1946.
Mander, John, *Berlin: Hostage for the West*. Baltimore: Penguin Books, 1962.
Marshall, S. L. A., *Men Against Fire*. New York: William Morrow, 1947.
Martin, H. G., *History of the 15th Scottish Division 1939-45*. London: William Blackwood & Sons, Ltd., 1948.

Matloff, Maurice, *Strategic Planning for Coalition Warfare, 1943-44.* Washington, D.C.: Office of the Chief of Military History, Dept. of the Army, 1954.

Members of the 224th Parachute Field Ambulance, *Over the Rhine, A Parachute Field Ambulance in Germany.* London: Canopy Press, 1946.

Mission Accomplished. The Story of the Fighting Corps, A Summary of Military Operations of the XVIII Corps (Airborne) in the European Theatre of Operations, 1944-45. Schwerin, Germany: XVIII Corps.

Montgomery, Field Marshal Sir Bernard, *An Approach to Sanity—A Study of East-West Relations.* Lecture to the Royal United Service Institution. London: 1945.

Montgomery, Field Marshal Sir Bernard, *The Memoirs of Field-Marshal The Viscount Montgomery of Alamein, K.G.* London: Collins, 1958.

Montgomery, Field Marshal Sir Bernard, *Normandy to the Baltic.* Privately published by Printing & Stationery Service, British Army of the Rhine, 1946.

Moorehead, Alan, *Eclipse.* New York: Coward-McCann, 1945.

Moorehead, Alan, *Montgomery.* London: Hamish Hamilton, 1946.

Morgan, Gen. Sir Frederick, *Overture to Overlord.* London: Hodder & Stoughton, 1950.

Morgan, Gen. Sir Frederick, *Peace and War—A Soldier's Life.* London: Hodder & Stoughton, 1961.

Morison, Samuel Eliot, *The Invasion of France and Germany, 1944-45.* Boston: Little, Brown, 1959.

Mosely, Philip E., *The Kremlin and World Politics.* New York: Vintage Books, Random House, 1960.

Mosley, Leonard, *Report from Germany.* London: Gollancz, 1945.

Murphy, Robert, *Diplomat among Warriors.* New York: Doubleday, 1964.

Musmanno, Michael A., *Ten Days to Die.* New York: Doubleday, 1950.

Nobécourt, Jacques, *Le dernier coup de Dès de Hitler: la bataille des Ardennes.* Paris: Robert Laffont, 1964.

North, John, *North-West Europe, 1944-45.* London: H. M. Stationery Office, 1953.

Oldfield, Col. Barney, *Never a Shot in Anger.* New York: Duell, Sloan and Pearce, 1956.

Parker, Col. T. W., Jr., and Col. Thompson, *Conquer, The Story of the Ninth Army.* Washington, D.C.: Infantry Journal Press, 1947.

Paths of Armor. History of the 5th U.S. Armored Division. Atlanta: Albert Love Enterprises, 1945.

Patton, Gen. George S., Jr., *War As I Knew It.* Boston: Houghton Mifflin, 1947.

Phillips, R. (editor), *The Belsen Trial.* London: William Hodge & Co., Ltd., 1949.

Poelchau, Harald, *Die letzten Stunden.* Berlin: Volk und Welt, 1949.

Pogue, Forrest C., "The Decision to Halt on the Elbe, 1945" in *Command Decisions.* Greenfield, Kent (editor). London: Methuen & Co., Ltd., 1960.

Pogue, Forrest C., *The Supreme Command.* Washington, D.C.: Office of the Chief of Military History, Dept. of the Army, 1954.

Radcliffe, Maj. G. L. Y., *History of the 2nd Battalion. The King's Shropshire Light Infantry in the Campaign NW Europe, 1944-45.* London: Basil Blackwell & Mott, Ltd., 1957.

Ridgway, Gen. Matthew B., *Soldier: Memoirs.* New York: Harper & Bros., 1956.

Riess, Curt, *The Berlin Story.* London: Frederick Muller, Ltd., 1953.

Rollins, Alfred B., Jr. (editor), *Franklin D. Roosevelt and the Age of Action.* New York: Dell Publishing Co., 1960.

Roosevelt, Elliott, *As He Saw It.* New York: Duell, Sloan & Pearce, 1946.

Roosevelt, Franklin D., *Nothing to Fear, The Selected Addresses of Franklin D. Roosevelt, 1932-45.* Boston: Houghton Mifflin, 1946.

Royce, Hans (editor), *Germans against Hitler.* Bonn: Berto, 1952.

Rumpf, Hans, *The Bombing of Germany.* London: Frederick Muller, Ltd., 1963.

Russell, Lord, of Liverpool, *The Scourge of the Swastika.* London: Cassell & Co., Ltd., 1954.

Russell, William, *Berlin Embassy.* New York: E. P. Dutton, 1941.

Salmond, J. B., *The History of the 51st Highland Division, 1939-1945.* Edinburgh and London: William Blackwood & Sons, Ltd., 1953.

Saunders, Hilary St. George, *The Fight Is Won. Official History Royal Air Force, 1939-1945* (Vol. III). London: H. M. Stationery Office, 1954.

Saunders, Hilary St. George, *The Red Beret.* London: Michael Joseph, Ltd., 1950.

Schoenberner, Gerhard, *Der gelbe Stern.* Hamburg: Rutten & Loening, 1960.

Scholz, Arno, *Outpost Berlin.* Berlin: Arani, 1955.

Shabad, Theodore, *Geography of the U.S.S.R.* New York: Columbia University Press, 1951.

Sherwood, Robert E., *The White House Papers of Harry L. Hopkins* (Vols. I and II). London: Eyre & Spottiswoode, 1948.

Shirer, William L., *Berlin Diary.* New York: Alfred A. Knopf, 1943.

Shirer, William L., *End of a Berlin Diary.* New York: Alfred A. Knopf, 1947.

Shirer, William L., *The Rise and Fall of the Third Reich.* New York: Simon and Schuster, 1960.

Short History of the 7th Armoured Division, June 1943-July 1945, A. Privately published.

Shulman, Milton, *Defeat in the West.* London: Secker and Warburg, 1947.

Smith, Jean Edward, *The Defense of Berlin.* Baltimore: The Johns Hopkins Press, 1963.

Smith, Gen. Walter Bedell (with Stewart Beach), *Eisenhower's Six Great Decisions.* New York: Longmans Green, 1956.

Snyder, Louis L., *The War. A Concise History, 1939-1945.* London: Robert Hale, Ltd., 1960.

Stacey, Col. C. P., *The Canadian Army: 1939-45.* Ottawa: Kings Printers, 1948.

Stein, Harold (editor), *American Civil-Military Decisions.* University of Alabama Press, 1963.

Steiner, Felix, *Die Freiwillingen.* Gottingen: Plesse, 1958.

Stettinius, Edward R., *Roosevelt and the Russians: The Yalta Conference.* New York: Doubleday, 1949.

Stimson, Henry L., and Bundy, McGeorge, *On Active Service in Peace and War.* New York: Harper & Bros., 1948.

Strang, Lord, *Home and Abroad.* London: Andre Deutsch, 1956.

Studnitz, Hans-Georg von. *While Berlin Burns.* London: Weidenfeld and Nicolson, 1964.

Tassigny, de Lattre de, Marshal. *Histoire de la première armée française.* Paris: Plon, 1949.

Taurus Pursuant: A History of the 11th Armoured Division. Privately published.

Taylor, Telford, *Sword and Swastika.* New York: Simon and Schuster, 1952.

Thorwald, Juergen, *Flight in the Winter.* London: Hutchinson & Co., 1953.

Tidy, Maj. Gen. Sir Henry Letheby (editor), *Inter-Allied Conferences on War Medicine, 1942-45, Convened by the Royal Society of Medicine.* London: Staples Press Ltd., 1947.

Toland, John, *Battle.* New York: Random House, 1959.

Trevor-Roper, H. R., *The Last Days of Hitler.* London: Macmillan & Co., Ltd., 1947.

Trial of German Major War Criminals, The (Vols. 1-26). London: H. M. Stationery Office, 1948.

Tully, Andrew, *Berlin: Story of a Battle.* New York: Simon and Schuster, 1963.

The 12th Yorkshire Parachute Battalion in Germany, 24th March—16 May, 1945. Privately published.

United States Division Histories:
   XIII Corps—One Hundred and Eighty Days; 117th Inf., 1st Btn., 30th Div.—Curlew; 83rd Inf. Div.—Thunderbolt; 84th Inf. Div., The Battle for Germany by Lt. Theodore Draper; *113th Cavalry Group—Mechanized "Red Horse"; 119th Infantry; 30th Artillery Div.; 331st Infantry—We Saw It Through* by Sgt. Jack M. Straus; *329th Infantry—Buckshot; XIXth Corps; 102nd Division; 34th Tank Btn., 5th Armored Div.; 30th Inf. Div.; 120th Inf. Regt.; Fire Mission—The Story of the 71st Armored F.A. Btn. in the ETO; History of the 67th Armored Regt. 1945; History of the 117th Infantry, 1944-45.* Washington, D.C.: Dept. of Defense.

Verney, Maj. Gen. G. L., *The Desert Rats, The History of the 7th Armoured Division.* London: Hutchinson & Co., 1954.

Verney, Maj. Gen. G. L., *The Guards Armoured Division.* London: Hutchinson & Co., 1955.

Victory Division in Europe, The. A History of the 5th U.S. Armored Division. Gotha, Germany: privately printed, 1945.

Wallace, Sir Donald MacKenzie, *Russia on the Eve of War and Revolution.* New York: Random House, 1961.

Warlimont, Walter, *Inside Hitler's Headquarters, 1939-45.* New York: Frederick A. Praeger, 1964.

Webster, Sir Charles, and Frankland, Noble, *The Strategic Air Offensive against Germany, 1939-45* (Vols. 1-4). London: H. M. Stationery Office, 1961.

Wellard, James, *General George S. Patton, Jr.: Man under Mars.* New York: Dodd, Mead, 1946.

Werth, Alexander, *Russia at War, 1941-45.* New York: E. P. Dutton & Co., 1964.

Wheeler-Bennett, J., *Nemesis of Power—The German Army in Politics 1918-45.* London: Macmillan & Co., Ltd., 1953.

White, D. F., *The Growth of the Red Army.* Princeton: Princeton University Press, 1944.

White, W. L., *Report on the Germans.* New York: Harcourt, Brace, 1947.

Wilmot, Chester, *The Struggle for Europe.* London: Collins, 1957.

Windsor, Philip, *City on Leave.* London: Chatto & Windus, 1963.

Woodward, Llewellyn. *British Foreign Policy in World War II.* London: H. M. Stationery Office, 1962.

Younger, Carlton, *No Flight from the Cage.* London: Frederick Muller, Ltd., 1956.

RUSSIAN BOOKS, OFFICIAL PAPERS AND DOCUMENTS

Andronikov, N. G., and others (collective authorship), *Bronetankovye i mekhanizirovannye voiska Sovetskoi Armii* (Tank and mechanized forces of the Soviet Army). Moscow: Ministry of Defense of the U.S.S.R., 1958.

Batov, Gen. P. I., *V pokhodakh i boyakh* (Campaigns and battles). In the series *Voennye Memuary.* Moscow: Ministry of Defense of the U.S.S.R., 1962; *History of the 65th Army.* Moscow: Military Publishing House, Ministry of Defense of the U.S.S.R., 1959.

Boltin, Gen. E. A., and others (collective authorship), *Istoriya Velikoi Otechestvennoi Voiny Sovetskovo Soyuza, 1941-1945* (History of the Great Patriotic War of the Soviet Union, 1941-1945). Vols. 1-6. Moscow: Dept. of History, Institute of Marxism-Leninism, and Ministry of Defense of the U.S.S.R., 1960-64.

Chuikov, Col. Gen. V. I., and Gen. Krebs, *Stenographic record of conversations between Berlin: 30 April—1 May, 1945.* Document. Moscow: Soviet private archives, individual possession; "Shturm Berlina" in *Literaturnaya Rossiya* ("The Storming of Berlin" in *Literary Russia*). Moscow: March 27, 1964; *The Beginning of the Road*. London: MacGibbon & Kee, 1963.

Correspondence 1941-45: Winston Churchill; Franklin Roosevelt; Josef V. Stalin; Clement Atlee (Vols. 1-2). Moscow: Foreign Languages Publishing House, 1957.

Ehrenburg, Ilya, *We Come As Judges*. London: *Soviet War News*, 1945; "Lyudi, gody, zhizn" in *Novyi Mir* ("People, Years, and Life" in *New World*). Moscow: 1962-63.

Gladkii, Lt. Col., 8 Guards Army, *Interrogations Report of. Opisanie peregovorv s nachalnikom Generalnovo shtaba Sukhoputnykh Voisk Germanskoi Armii generalom pekhoty Gansom Krebsom i komanduyushym oboronoi goroda Berlin generalom artillerii Veidlingom o kapitylyatsii nemetskikh voisk v Berline* (Record of conversations with the Chief of the General Staff of the Land Forces of the German Army, General of Infantry Hans Krebs, and the Commander of the Defense of the City of Berlin, General of Artillery Weidling, on the capitulation of German Forces in Berlin). Document. Moscow: Ministry of Defense Archives.

Gvardeiskaya tankovaya (History of the 2nd Guards Tank Army). Collective authorship. Moscow: Ministry of Defense of the U.S.S.R., 1963.

Kochetkov, Col. D., *S zakrytymi lyukami* in the series *Voennye Memuary* (With Closed Hatches). Moscow: Ministry of Defense of the U.S.S.R., 1962.

Krivoshein, Gen. S. M., *Ratnaya byl'* (This Was War). Moscow: Military Publishing House, Ministry of Defense of the U.S.S.R., 1959.

Neustroyev, Lt. Col. S. A., *Put' k Reikhstagu* (The Road to the Reichstag) in series, *Voennye Memuary*. Moscow: Military Publishing House, Ministry of Defense of the U.S.S.R., 1948; "Shturm Reikhstagu" (The Storming of the Reichstag) in *Voenno-istoricheskii Zhurnal*, 1960.

Platonov, Lt. Gen. S. P. (editor), *Vtoraya mirovaya voina 1939-1945 gg. Voenno-istoricheskii ocherk* (The Second World War, 1939-1945, Military-historical outline). Moscow: Military Publishing House, Ministry of Defense of the U.S.S.R., 1958.

Popiel, Lt. Gen. N., "Vperedi—Berlin!" (Forward—Berlin!) in *Zvezda* (Star). Personal memoir. Moscow: Military Publishing House, Ministry of Defense of the U.S.S.R., 1958.

Poplawski, Gen. S. G. (editor), *Boevye deistviya Narodnovo Voiska Pol'skovo, 1943-1945 gg* (Combat operations of the Polish National Army, 1943-45). Moscow: Ministry of Defense of the U.S.S.R., 1961.

Samchuk, I. A., *13-ya Gvardeiskaya* (13th Poltava Rifle Division). Moscow: Ministry of Defense of the U.S.S.R., 1962.

Shturm Berlina (The Storming of Berlin). Collective authorship (Soviet participant accounts). Moscow: Ministry of Defense of the U.S.S.R., 1948.

Simonov, K., *Front Ocherki i rasskazy 1941-1945* (The Front. Sketches and stories, 1941-1945). Moscow: Ministry of Defense of the U.S.S.R., 1960.

Smakotin, M. P., *Ot Dona do Berlina* (From the Don to Berlin). Combat history of the 153rd Rifle Division, later 57th Guards Rifle Division. Moscow: Ministry of Defense of the U.S.S.R., 1962.

Solomatin, Col. Gen. M. D., of Tank Troops, *Krasnogradtsy* (1st Krasnograd Mechanized Corps). Moscow: Ministry of Defense of the U.S.S.R., 1963.

Soviet War News (Vols. 1-8, 1941-1945). London: Soviet Embassy Press.

Stavka Directives: 2-23 April, 1945. Document. Moscow: Ministry of Defense of the U.S.S.R.

Sychev, Gen. K. V., and Malakbov, Col. M. M., *The Rifle Corps Offensive*. Moscow: Ministry of Defense of the U.S.S.R., 1958.

Telpukhovskii, Boris Sejonovitsch, *The Soviet History of the Great National War, 1941-45.* Moscow: Military Publishing House, Ministry of Defense of the U.S.S.R., 1959.

Troyanovskii, Lt. Col. P., *Poslednie dni Berlina* (The Last Days of Berlin). Moscow: Ministry of Defense of the U.S.S.R., 1945.

Vyshevskii, V., *Dnevniki voennykh let* (Diary of the War Years). Vol. 4. Moscow: Publishing House for Artistic Literature, 1958; *Sobranie sochinenii* (Collected Works). Moscow: Publishing House for Artistic Literature, 1958.

Weidling, Gen., Interrogation of. By representative of the Soviet commander, Maj. Gen. Trusov. Document. Moscow: Ministry of Defense Archives, May, 1945.

What We Saw in Germany with the Red Army to Berlin. Thirteen Soviet war correspondents. London: Soviet Embassy Press, 1945.

Yedenskii, P. I., *The Berlin Operation of the 3rd Shock Army.* Moscow: Military Publishing House, Ministry of Defense of the U.S.S.R., 1961.

Yuschuk, Maj. Gen. I. I., of Tank Troops, *Tank Operations and the Storming of Berlin.* Moscow: Military Publishing House, Ministry of Defense of the U.S.S.R., 1962.

Zhilin, Col. P. A., *Vazhneishie operatsii Velikoi Otechestvennoi Voiny 1941-1945 gg* (The Most Important Operations of the Great Patriotic War 1941-1945). Moscow: Ministry of Defense of the U.S.S.R., 1956.

Not listed above are battle orders, maps, intelligence estimates, extracts from certain interrogation reports and other voluminous documentation supplied to the author by the Soviet government and its various agencies.

GERMAN MANUSCRIPTS, MILITARY STUDIES AND CAPTURED DOCUMENTS

Adjutantur der Wehrmacht beim Führer, *Beurteilung der Feindlage vor deutscher Ostfront im grossen—Stand 5.1.45* (Estimate of Soviet intentions). Document. German Military Archives.

Arndt, Lt. Gen. Karl, *39th Panzer Corps, 22 April—7 May, 1945.* Office of the Chief of Military History (hereafter referred to as OCMH), Dept. of Army, U.S.A., MS B-221.

Blumentritt, Gen. Guenther, *The Last Battles of the AOK Blumentritt, 10 April—5 May, 1945.* OCMH, MS B-361; *Battles Fought by the 1st Parachute Army, 29 March—9 April, 1945.* OCMH, MS B-354.

Busse, Gen. Theodor, *The Last Battle of the 9th German Army* (Vol. 5). German Military Research Studies, *Military Science Review*, April, 1955.

Edelsheim, Gen. Freiherr von, *Capitulation Negotiations between the 12th German Army and the Ninth U.S. Army, 4 May, 1945.* OCMH, MS B-220.

Eismann, Col. Hans Georg, *Eismann Papers: Diary, Narrative and Personal Notes by the Chief of Operations, Army Group Vistula, 14 January—7 May, 1945.* Also, letters, battle sketches and other military studies prepared for Col. Gen. Heinrici. German sources.

End of Army Group Weichsel (Vistula) and Twelfth Army, The, 27 April—7 May, 1945, and Ninth Army's Last Attack and Surrender, 21 April—7 May, 1945. Research studies by Magna E. Bauer, 1956. Foreign Studies Branch, OCMH.

Estor, Col. Fritz, *The 11th Army, 1-23 April, 1945.* OCMH, MS B-581.

Feindkrafteberechnungen (FHO): Feb. 19—Apr. 15, 1945 (Estimates of enemy strength). Document. German Military Archives.

FHO: "Wesentliche Merkmale des Feindbildes" for April 23-28 1945 (Enemy order of battle; telegrams). Document. German Military Archives.

Fighting Qualities of the Russian Soldier, The (German estimates of). *Vol. II, No. 8.* OCMH, MS D-036.

Gareis, Gen. Martin, *Personal Papers and Diary of the Commander of the 46th Panzer Corps, 1945.* German sources.

Gehlen, Gen. Reinhard, *Gedanken zur Feindbeurteilung 2.2.45* (Estimate of Soviet intentions). Document. German Military Archives; *Vermutliche Weiterführung der sowj. russ.—Operationen . . . (Fremde Heere Ost): Stand: 2.2.45.* Document. German Military Archives.

Gen. StdH/Abt. FHO (Chef): "Befehle Op.-Abt." (Operational Orders: 7 March—25 April, 1945). Document. German Military Archives.

Heeresarzt/OKH: (German casualties, July 1943—April 1945 for German Army central military medical authorities). Document. German Military Archives.

Heinrici, Col. Gen. Gotthard, *Account by the Commander of the Army Group Vistula of the Last Battle of the Reich, 1945.* Translated by Susanne Linden; *Heinrici Papers and Diary.* Translated by Professor John Erickson, 1964; *Heinrici: Army Group Vistula War Diary, March-April, 1945.* Translated by Dr. Julius Wildstosser, 1963; *Heinrici Telephone Log,* as recorded in *Army Group Vistula War Diary* by Lt. Col. Hellmuth von Wienskowski, 20-29 April, 1945. Translated by Helga Kramer, 1963; *Papers, monographs, maps, battle sketches,* provided by Col. Gen. Heinrici for the author's use. Translated by Ursula Naccache.

Hengl, Gen. Georg Ritter von, *The Alpine Redoubt.* OCMH, MS B-461.

Hofer, Gauleiter Franz, *The National Redoubt.* OCMH, MS B-458, B-457.

Jodl, Col. Gen. Alfred, *Diary Extracts; Operation Eclipse Notes and Affidavit; Nuremberg Notes; Private Papers.* All translated by Frau Luise Jodl for the author's use.

Koller, Gen. Karl, *The Collapse Viewed from Within* (The diary notes of General Koller, German Chief of Air Staff, 14 April—9 May, 1945). British Air Ministry Archives.

Kriegstagebuch: OKH/Gen. Stab. des Heeres: Operationsabteilung. 4 April—15 April, 1945; 16 April—24 April, 1945. Document. German Military Archives.

Krukenberg, SS Maj. Gen. Gustav, *Battle Days in Berlin* (by the Commander of the SS Nordland Division). Personal manuscript prepared especially for the author.

Lageberichte Ost: 1-21 April, 1945; 23-28 April, 1945; 29 April, 1945. Document. German Military Archives.

Last Russian Offensive, The, 1945 (27th Corps Sector). OCMH, MS D-281.

Letztes Kriegstagebuch O.d.M. (Doenitz) (Bormann's telegram, signals on devolution of power re: Hitler's death). Documents. German Military Archives.

Notizen nach Führervortrag (to 31 March, 1945; for the Eastern Front). Document. German Military Archives.

Operation Eclipse. Captured and annotated copy from files of Organisationsabteilung, Generalstab des Heeres. Translated by John Flint.

Organization of the Volkssturm from Organisationsabteilung, Generalstab des Heeres. Document. German Military Archives.

Politische Angelegenheiten (The German White Book). German Military Archives.

Raus, Col. Gen. Erhard, *The Pomeranian Battle and the Command in the East. Discussions with Reichsführer SS Himmler and Report to the Führer.* OCMH, MS D-189.

Refior, Col. Hans, *Diary of the Chief of Staff of the Berlin Defense Area, 18 March —5 May, 1945.* German sources.

Reichhelm, Col. Günther, *Battles of the 12th Army, 13 April—7 May, 1945* (By the

Chief of Staff). OCMH, MS B-606; *Personal papers, maps, diary*. Given to the author.

Reitsch, Fl/Capt. Hanna. Accounts extracted from U.S. and British interrogation and summarized in the *Nuremberg Papers;* Personal narrative in the U.S.A.F. psychological evaluation and study, *Air Medical Intelligence Report of Flugkapitan Hanna Reitsch, 1945.*

Remagen Bridgehead, The, 11-21 March, 1945. OCMH, MS A-965.

Rendulic, Col. Gen. Lothar, *Army Group A, South, 7 April—7 May, 1945: Report of the Commander.* OCMH, MS B-328.

Reymann, Gen. Hellmuth, *Personal Account of the Battle for Berlin by the Commander of the Berlin Defense Area, 6 March—24 April, 1945.* German sources.

Schramm, Professor Percy E., *Wehrmacht Losses, World War II. German War Potential at the Beginning of 1945.* OCMH, MS B-716.

Schultz, Maj. Joachim, *OKW War Diary Extracts, 20 April—19 May, 1945.* Translated by Giselle Fort. German sources.

Weidling, Lt. Gen. Helmut, *The Final Battle in Berlin, 23 April—2 May, 1945* (By the last commander of the Berlin Defense Area). Translated from the Soviet Defense Dept. *Military Historical Journal* by Wilhelm Arenz. *Military Science Review,* Jan., Feb. and March, 1962.

Wenck, Gen. Walther, *12th Army: Report of the Commander.* OCMH, MS B-394; *Personal Journal and Maps.* Given to the author.

Willemer, Col. Wilhelm, *The German Defense of Berlin.* With contributions by: Col. Gen. Gotthard Heinrici, Col. Hans Georg Eismann—Army Group Vistula; Maj. Gen. Erich Dethleffsen, Maj. Gen. Thilo von Trotha, Col. Bogislaw von Bonin, Col. Karl W. Thilo—Army High Command; Col. Hans Oscar Wöhlermann, Artillery Commander—56th Panzer Corps; Col. Gerhard Roos, Chief of Staff—Inspectorate of Fortifications; Col. Ulrich de Maizieres, Operations Branch—Army General Staff; Maj. Gen. Laegeler—Replacement Army; Lt. Gen. Helmut Friebe, Lt. Col. Mitzkus —Deputy Headquarters, Third Corps; Lt. Gen. Hellmuth Reymann, Commander—Berlin Defense Area; Lt. Col. Edgar Platho, Artillery Commander—Berlin Defense Area; Lt. Col. Karl Stamm, Maj. Pritsch— Wehrmacht Area Headquarters; Col. Gerhardt Trost—Luftwaffe; M/Sgt. Schmidt—Ordnance; Col. Erich Duensing, Police Commander—Berlin; Dr. Hans Fritsche, Chief, Radio Dept.—Propaganda Ministry; and Col. Guenther Hartung. Introduction by Col. Gen. Franz Halder, former Chief of the German General Staff. OCMH, MS P-136.

Wöhlermann, Col. Hans Oscar, *An Account of the Final Defense Eastward and in Berlin, April—May, 1945* (By the Artillery Commander of the 56th Panzer Corps and later Artillery Commander of the Berlin Defense Area). German sources.

SELECTED ARTICLES

Aichinger, Gerhard, "Wenck and Busse at the End of April, 1945." *Tagespiegel,* January, 1957.

Andreas-Friedrich, Ruth, "Observation Post Berlin." *Die Zeit,* July, 1962.

Arzet, Robert, "The Last Ten Days." *Tagespiegel,* March, 1946.

Bailey, George, "The Russian at Reims." *The Reporter,* May 20, 1965.

Baldwin, Hanson, "Victory in Europe." *Foreign Affairs,* July, 1945.

"Battle for Berlin, The." *Revue de la défense nationale,* January—June, 1953.

Bolte, Charles G., "Breakthrough in the East." *The Nation,* January, 1945.

Cartier, Raymond, "The Day Hitler Died." *Paris-Match*, July, 1962.
Chatterton-Hill, Dr. G., "The Last Days in Berlin." *Contemporary Review*, May, June, 1946.
Codman, Lt. Col. Charles R., "For the Record: Buchenwald." *Atlantic Monthly*, July, 1945.
Creel, George, "The President's Health." *Collier's*, March, 1945.
"Dead Heart of Berlin." From a Special Correspondent, *The Times* of London, June, 1945.
Ehrenburg, Ilya, "On to 'Tamed Berlin.'" *New York Times Magazine*, August, 1944.
Erickson, John, "The Soviet Union at War (1941-45): An Essay on Sources and Studies." *Soviet Studies* (Vol. XIV, No. 3). Oxford: Basil Blackwell, 1963.
Flynn, John T., "Why Eisenhower's Armies Did Not Take Berlin." *Reader's Digest*, August, 1948.
Franklin, William M., "Zonal Boundaries and Access to Berlin." *World Politics*, Vol. XVI, No. 1, October, 1963.
Freidin, Seymour, and Fleischer, Jack, "The Last Days of Berlin" (two articles). *Collier's*, August, 1945.
Geilinger, Dr. Eduard, "The Siege of Berlin" (A Swiss correspondent's account). *Neue Zürcher Zeitung*, June, 1945.
Jacobi, Oscar, "Berlin Inferno." *New York Times Magazine*, January, 1944; "Berlin Today." *New York Times Magazine*, September, 1944.
Kuhn, Irene Corbally, "Patton: 'The Russians Really Took Us for Suckers.'" *Human Events*, November, 1962.
Lauterbach, Richard, "Zhukov." *Life*, February, 1945.
"Letters from Berlin." *Catholic World*, November, 1945.
Mitchell, Donald W., "Allied Pincers Close on Germany." *Current History*, March, 1945.
Morris, Joe Alex, "Germany Waits to Be Saved." *Collier's*, September, 1945.
Mosely, Philip E., "Dismemberment of Germany." *Foreign Affairs*, April, 1950; "The Occupation of Germany." *Foreign Affairs*, July, 1950.
Olson, Sidney, "Defeated Land." *Life*, May, 1945.
Paret, Peter, "An Aftermath of the Plot Against Hitler: the Lehrterstrasse Prison in Berlin, 1944-45." *Journal of the Institute of Historical Research* (Vol. 32, No. 85). University of London. The Athlone Press, 1959.
Powell, Robert, "Berlin Today." *Fortnightly*, October, 1945.
Prinz, Gunther, "When the Guns Fell Silent." *Berliner Morgenpost*, May, 1945.
Rosinski, Herbert, "The Red Flood." *U.S. Army Combat Forces Journal*, July, 1953.
Sayre, Joel, "Letter from Berlin." *The New Yorker*, August, 1945; "That Was Berlin" (five articles). *The New Yorker*, September, October, 1948.
Singh, Brig. Thakul Sheodatt, "The Battle of Berlin." *Journal of the U.S. Institute of India*, 1949-50.
Sondern, Frederic, "Adolf Hitler's Last Days." *Reader's Digest*, June, 1951.
Thompson, John H., "Meeting on the Elbe." *Chicago Daily Tribune*, April, 1945.
Warner, Albert, "Our Secret Deal over Germany." *The Saturday Evening Post*, August, 1952.

ACKNOWLEDGMENTS

⁂

The information for this book came principally from the participants themselves—the men of the Allied armies, the German troops they fought, and the Berliners who survived the battle. In all, over two thousand people contributed to the book. Over a three-year period beginning in 1962, some seven hundred men and women provided written accounts as well as interviews. They gave me memorabilia ranging from diaries to maps, and from personal accounts to cherished scrapbooks. The names of these people appear in the list of Soldiers and Civilians.

Their information was fitted into a military skeleton developed from American, British, Russian and German sources. Unit after-action reports, war diaries, division histories, intelligence summaries and interrogation reports were obtained, along with personal interviews from key military and governmental figures of the period, many of whom turned over to me their own files, documents and notes. The total accumulation of research filled ten filing cabinets and contained such disparate information as the amount of fuel in Berlin gasometers before the battle and the fact that Marshal Rokossovskii wore a wrist watch with a built-in compass.

An enormous number of people helped on the project. It could not have begun at all without Lila and DeWitt Wallace of the *Reader's Digest*, who placed at my disposal the vast research resources of their organization and who underwrote many of the costs. I would like to pay tribute to my friend Hobart Lewis, President and Executive Editor of the *Digest*, who was unstinting in his efforts to make the book possible. I also want to thank those men and women in the *Digest's* bureaus in the United States and Europe who collected research and interviewed scores of participants. It would be unfair to single out any particular individuals. I would like instead to name them in alphabetical order by bureau. *Berlin:* John Flint, Helgard Kramer, Suzanne Linden, Ruth Wellman; *London:* Heather Chapman, Joan Isaacs; *New York:* Gertrude Arundel, Nina Georges-Picot; *Paris:* Ursula Naccache, John D. Panitza (Chief European Correspondent); *Stuttgart:* Arno Alexi; *Washington:* Bruce Lee, Julia Morgan.

Thanks must be given to the U. S. Department of Defense for permission to research in the historical archives. In particular, I want to acknowledge the help of Brigadier General Hal C. Pattison, head of the Office of the Chief of Military History and his associates: Magda Bauer, Detmar Fincke, Charles von Luttichau, Israel Wice, Hannah Zeidlik and Dr. Earl Ziemke—all of whom gave time and assistance to me and my associates. My thanks also to the director of the World War II Records Division, Sherrod East, who permitted a day-by-day record investigation for months. Others in the Records Division were equally kind: Wilbur J. Nigh, Chief of the Reference Branch, and his associates, Lois Aldridge, Morton Apperson, Joseph Avery, Richard Bauer, Nora Hinshaw, Thomas Hohmann, Hildred Livingston, V. Caroline Moore, Frances Rubright and Hazel Ward. Working closely with this group was Dr. Julius Wildstosser who had the painstaking job of examining miles of microfilm and translating thousands of German documents for me and my *Reader's Digest* associates.

I owe special debts of gratitude to former President Dwight D. Eisenhower; Field Marshal Bernard Law Montgomery, Viscount Montgomery of Alamein; General Omar N. Bradley; Lieutenant General Sir Frederick Morgan; General Walter Bedell Smith; General William H. Simpson; Lieutenant General James M. Gavin; Lord Ismay; Lieutenant General Sir Brian Horrocks; Lord Strang; Ambassador W. Averell Harriman; Ambassador Foy D. Kohler; Ambassador David Bruce; Ambassador Charles Bohlen; Earl Attlee; Mrs. Anna Rosenberg Hoffman; Major General Sir Francis de Guingand; Sir Miles Dempsey; Lieutenant General Evelyn Barker; Major General Louis Lyne; Major General R. F. Belchem and Professor Philip E. Mosely. These individuals and many other American and British officers and diplomats helped me to understand the military and political background of the period and to unravel the reasons why the Anglo-American forces did not continue their advance on Berlin.

I am grateful to the Russian government for their courtesy in allowing me to see hitherto unrevealed documents, orders, interrogation reports and other papers from their defense files. We did not see eye to eye on many matters and my methods were not always as diplomatic as they might have been. I found, however, that a blunt and candid approach to the Soviet military was returned by them. On the matter of the rapes in Berlin, for example, it was suggested to me by certain members of the U. S. State Department and the British Foreign Office that it might be undiplomatic to raise the question. President John F. Kennedy disagreed with that view. His words to me before I left for the Soviet Union were to the effect that the Russians probably would not mind in the least, because at heart they were horse traders. He felt I should speak bluntly and "lay it on the table." I did, and the Soviet authorities responded in kind. There were some awkward moments, however. Although I had been invited by the Khrushchev government to conduct my research, the border police at Moscow airport tried to take from me the very papers that the Soviet Defense Department had given me! The Red Army officers, Marshals Koniev, Rokossovskii, Sokolovskii and Chuikov, were kindness personified, generous with their time and their information, as were the other Soviet military men I interviewed. That this liaison could be established was in large part due to my associate on that trip, Professor John Erickson of the University of Manchester, whose linguistic abilities and expert knowledge of Russian affairs proved invaluable.

In Germany, Dr. Graf Schweintz of the Press and Information Department of the Bonn government opened many a door. General A. Heusinger of the NATO command in Washington wrote scores of letters of introduction. Colonel Theodor von Dufving, the former Chief of Staff of the last Berlin Commandant, General Karl Weidling, spent days going over the last battle with me. General Walther Wenck, General Theodor Busse, General Martin Gareis, General Erich Dethleffsen, Lieutenant General Hellmuth Reymann,

General Hasso von Manteuffel, General Max Pemsel, Lieutenant General Friedrich Sixt, SS General Felix Steiner, General Burkhart Müller-Hillebrand, SS Major General Gustav Krukenberg, Colonel Hans Refior, Colonel Hans Oscar Wöhlermann and Frau Luise Jodl—all helped in every way possible to reconstruct the battle and those last days in Berlin.

There were many others who aided in one way or another: Leon J. Barat, Deputy Advisor for the Institute for the Study of the U.S.S.R. in Munich; Rolf Menzel, then Editor-in-Chief, Radio Berlin; Lieutenant Colonel Meyer-Welcker of the German military archives institute; Frank E. W. Drexler, editor of the Berlin paper *Der Abend;* Robert Lochner, head of RIAS in Berlin; Raymond Cartier of *Paris Match;* Dr. Jurgen Rohwer of the Library of Modern History in Munich; Dr. Albrecht Lampe of the Berlin Municipal Archives; Karl Röder of WAST, the German veterans organization; Carl Johann Wiberg; Marcel Simonneau of the Amicale Nationale des Anciens P.G. des Stalags; Dr. Dieter Strauss of Siegbert Mohn Verlag, the publishers. To these and many others, my most sincere thanks.

I have saved to the last my thanks to Colonel General Gotthard Heinrici for the German side of the story. Over a period of three months we shared countless interviews and conversations. He fought each phase of the battle again. He allowed me to use his personal notes, documents and war diaries. Even though he was plagued by illness, he always gave generously of his time. Without him, I do not think this book could have been written. In some twenty years as a writer, I have rarely encountered a man of such dignity and honor—nor one with such memory for detail.

How do I thank those who stood by me during the writing? My darling wife who collated, indexed, edited, rewrote—and at the same time looked after our family during the long years of researching and writing; my good friend and severest critic Jerry Korn, whose sharp editing pencil moves so brilliantly across paper (he will not get a chance at this page); my invaluable secretaries, "Horty" Vantresca and Barbara Sawyer, who typed and retyped, filed, answered phones and backstopped all the rest of us; Suzanne and Charlie Gleaves, who were just there when I needed them; Peter Schwed and Michael Korda of Simon and Schuster, who, togther with Helen Barrow (production manager), Frank Metz (art director), Eve Metz (designer), and Sophie Sorkin (copy chief), had to put up with my impossible demands; Raphael Palacios, whose meticulous maps and sense of humor are more than any author can hope to have; Dave Parsons of Pan American Airways, who moved trunkloads of research all over Europe without losing a single item; my friends Billy Collins and Robert Laffont—my publishers in England and France—who waited so long for this book that they almost called it "Watch on the Ryan"; my lawyer, Paul Gitlin, whose help, guidance and temperature-taking were extraordinary; my representatives Marie Schebeko (in France) and Elaine Greene (in England), who have helped by work, courage, support and belief—to them all, my deepest thanks.

—C.R.

INDEX

❖

555

Intelligence agents *(continued)*
 Wiberg, 23, 59, 136-38, 366-67, 400-1, 492
 Internal Affairs Ministry building, 302
 International Red Cross warehouses, 493
 Invalidenstrasse, 441, 442
 Invasion, *see* Operation Overlord
Iowa, U.S.S., 140, 141, 145-49
Ismay, General Sir Hastings, 139, 161, 232
Italian Army, 376
Italy, 156, 235, 446
Ivanov, Major General Georgi Vasilievich, 356
"Ivy Division" (4th Infantry Division), 128
Izvestia (newspaper), 429

J
Jacobi, Dr. Gerhard, 486-87
Jakubek, Erwin, 495, 497
Janssen, Dora, 418-19, 460, 489
Jehovah's Witnesses, 431-2
Jessen-Schmidt, Hennings, 137-38, 366-67,
 401, 492
Jesuits, 25, 487
Jewish Community Bureau, 41
Jews, 28, 327
 remaining in Berlin, 40-44, 262-63, 461-64
Jodl, Colonel General Alfred, 78, 83, 116, 173,
 226-27, 261, 268, 339, 376, 401-4,
 435-36, 467, 474
 Eclipse maps and, 96-104, 436n
 Hitler's remark on suicide to, 405
 marriage of, 107
Jodl, Luise, 97-101, 103n, 107, 401-2, 405n
Johnson, Lieutenant Colonel Briard P., 284
Johnson, Colonel Walter M., 292
Junge, Gertrud, 494-97
Jungmittag, Biddy, 36

K
Kaether, Colonel, 428
Kaganovich, Lazar M., 248
Kaiser-Wilhelm Memorial Church, 14, 165,
 486
Karinhall, 300-1, 397, 426
 evacuated, 401-3
Karlsbad, 76
Karlshorst, 42, 447
Karstadt's department store, 417, 450-52
Katukov, Colonel General Mikhail Yefimo-
 vich, 193-94, 302, 348, 361-62, 367-68
 First Guards Tank Army of, 302, 361,
 367-68, 390-91, 428
Katushkas, 345, 348-49, 420, 479, 513
"KCB" pill, 32
Keitel, Field Marshal Wilhelm, 78, 226-28,
 260, 261, 403
 attempts to persuade Hitler to leave Berlin,
 435-36

Keitel, Field Marshal *(continued)*
 determination of, 467-68
 dismisses Heinrici, 476-77
 visits Wenck, 436, 443-45
Kelm, Alexander, 453
Kempka, SS Colonel, Erich, 337, 498
Kennan, George F., 157, 183
Kesselring, Field Marshal Albert, 277, 297,
 404
Ketzler, Gertrud, 33, 166
Khudyakov, Marshal Sergei V., 79n
Kiel, 124, 329
King, Captain Charles, 134
King, Admiral Ernest J., 140, 147
Kinnard, Colonel Harold, 125
Kinzel, General Eberhard, 92-93, 221-22, 225,
 229-30, 427
Kloptsch, Else "Eddy," 37-38, 60, 493
Klosterdorf, 386
Klotz, Jurgen-Erich, 409
Kluge, Field Marshal Günther von, 66, 75
Knight, Captain Jack A., 307-8
Knoblauch, Eva, 437
Koch, Ilse, 327
Koch, Jolenta, 491
Köckler, Maria, 35
Koenig, Lieutenant General Joseph, 177
Kohler, Major Haley E., 285
Kolb, Ingeborg, 20-21, 58
Kolb, Robert, 20-21, 58
Kolb, Lieutenant Colonel Roland L., 289
Kolberg, 66, 269
Kolberg (film), 373
Koller, General Karl, 261, 405, 426-27, 436,
 468
Koniev, Marshal Ivan Stepanovich, 21, 38,
 184, 194, 248n, 449, 472
 background of, 245-46
 called to Moscow, 243-51
 drives for Berlin, 391-93, 396, 412, 434
 fears unilateral surrender, 354-55
 Neisse offensive of, 353-57, 368, 385
 plans attack on Berlin, 250-51, 254
König, Ilse, 408
Königin-Luise Strasse, 18, 166
Königsberg, 378
Köpenick, 166, 358, 372
Korab, Alexander, 493
Korolevich, Pfc Alexander, 332
Kosney, Corporal Herbert, 46-48, 61, 262,
 431-32, 440-42
Kosney, Kurt, 47-48, 61, 262, 431-32
Köster, Ursula, 484-85
Köthenerstrasse, 171
Kotzebue, Lieutenant Albert, 470-71
Kraft, Fritz, 408
Kramer, Staff Sergeant Wilfred, 324
Krampnitz, 436
Krebs, Lieutenant General Hans, 80, 225,
 276-77, 385, 403, 404, 413-15, 426-28,
 434, 438-39, 448, 472, 496, 497, 515